SERENA JOSEPH-HARRIS

THE TWILIGHT OF AMERICA'S OMNIPRESENCE:

CHINA'S AGGRANDIZEMENT IN A NEW ERA OF MULTIPOLARITY

FORTIS

AN ADDUCENT NON-FICTION IMPRINT
JACKSONVILLE, FLORIDA
WWW.ADDUCENT.CO

THE TWILIGHT OF AMERICA'S OMNIPRESENCE:

CHINA'S AGGRANDIZEMENT IN A NEW ERA OF MULTIPOLARITY

By Serena Joseph-Harris

Developmental Editor - Joel A. Harris

Cover Design - Joel A. Harris

ISBN 978-1-937592-33-2

First Edition - 2015

A Sirius International (Caribbean) Defense Contractors Ltd. Series

http://sirius-defense-joseph.com

Published by Fortis (a Non-Fiction imprint from Adducent)

Jacksonville, Florida

www.Adducent.co

Published in the United States of America

ABOUT THE AUTHOR

A former High Commissioner of the Republic of Trinidad and Tobago to the United Kingdom of Great Britain and Northern Ireland, Serena Joseph-Harris has contributed inter-governmentally in an array of leadership and advisory capacities including national security council advisor, strategic intelligence director, governmental expert on drug control, the combating of money laundering, terrorist financing and the illicit trafficking of small arms and light weapons. Ms. Joseph-Harris is widely acknowledged in international, regional and bi-regional policy and expert group forums in the United Nations specifically in relation to disarmament affairs; the Organization of American States Inter-American Drug Abuse Control Commission where she served as Chair of the Governmental Experts Group of the Multilateral Evaluation Mechanism; and the European Union Latin America Caribbean Coordination and Cooperation Mechanism on Drugs where as Co-President representing Latin American and Caribbean interests she worked alongside the German and British Co-Presidencies in succession. She has consistently promoted dialogue, forged consensus and advanced clear-minded solutions to the welter of issues confronting governments in both hemispheres.

Ms. Joseph-Harris is a sought after policy analyst and strategist. Her pertinent and well-timed publications include books, white papers and monographs themed along the lines of non-conventional and emerging threats. Recent works include "*Treatise on Western Hemispheric Security Issues*" Volumes II and III, "*Fifth Republic or Fourth Reich?*" and "*The Alpha Barrier of North-South Dialogue.*"

As a keynote speaker and guest lecturer she has taken the podium at the Institute for National Strategic Studies (INSS) Washington D.C; the William J. Perry Center for Hemispheric Defense Studies Washington D.C; the Royal United Services Institute for Defense and Security Studies (RUSI), Whitehall, London; and the Royal Military College (RMC) Kingston, Ontario, sharing and exchanging ideas with teaching faculty, diplomatic professionals, research fellows, policy makers, defense planners, and intelligence analysts.

Ms. Joseph-Harris is a member of the Friends of the Inter-American Democratic Charter, a group of former presidents, prime ministers and cabinet ministers, who seek to increase the visibility and understanding of the Inter-American Democratic Charter and to more effectively prevent democratic tensions from erupting into crises. Members consult with one another and informally advise the Organization of American States (OAS) about challenges to democratic development in the Americas and engage in a variety of activities including private assessment visits to countries experiencing difficulties with democratic governance to draw attention to the potential contributions of the Democratic Charter.

CONTENTS

"Politics is ideological and, like other mythic constructs, a political ideology can be a rather ungainly concoction of fact and values, assumptions and illusions. It often gains credence only after frequent repetition and ritualistic affirmation. But while people may come to believe profoundly in a particular political position, ardent belief alone cannot true that position with reality."

Professor William E. Rees

To Anthony and Joel

ACKNOWLEDGEMENTS

This book is a solemn tribute to the men and women of the Americas who have dedicated their lives to the security and peace of the hemisphere. Unwavering allegiance and commitment to democracy, liberty, and justice by which we are inextricably bound inspired this project. To those that I had the privilege of working alongside and who fell in line of duty, I salute you.

The present volume is a brew emanating from career and personal life experiences. For this reason, I am deeply indebted to institutions and persons that have contributed in various ways major, minor or at times inadvertently and unknowingly to my professional life, especially this book.

I wish to express gratitude to serving and former members of the security community in the Greater Caribbean for the privilege and honor of serving alongside you and learning so much from you. The experience provided me much food for thought that is demonstrable in the project's scope. I particularly wish to thank Allison my former staff assistant who, during my tour as High Commissioner in London, spurred my inclination to pen ideas for a worldwide readership.

My heartfelt appreciation is extended to personnel from the Drug Enforcement Administration (DEA), the Federal Bureau of Investigation (FBI), the Central Intelligence Agency (CIA), the Institute for National Strategic Studies (INSS), and the Royal Military Academy in Kingston, Canada. I am particularly grateful to Colonel John Cope (Ret.) of the National Defense University (NDU), Washington D.C. whose passion, tenacity, and commitment to the hemispheric defense policy is legendary. His generous referrals within the NDU fraternity were an asset to this and related endeavors.

Candyce Kelshall, research fellow in Security and Intelligence Studies at the University of Buckingham England was a gem in her instrumentality in ushering me through a discrete line-up of professionals in London's diplomatic and intelligence circles. Her "must see" list was groomed to perfection. These associations proved to be extremely constructive in discharging me of the insight, and at times impiety, demanded of this project. For her part, I am very thankful.

To even the casual reader it will be apparent that my intellectual debts are legion. Working alongside my younger son Joel whose role was simultaneously that of supporter and critic was the most fulfilling part of this project. Integrating scholarship with a wealth of ground level experiences was one of my biggest challenges. In this regard, he pushed me beyond my perceived limits with his excruciating penchant for perfection and appetite for savvy, all in deference to our deeply appreciated readership. His forthrightness and tenacity fortified this endeavor all the way through to its completion.

Others who helped substantially through their loyal and generous support include Melissa and Darrell to whom I am profoundly grateful. The extraordinary patience, reliability and efficiency of my publisher, Dennis, and his support staff, in particular Karen, who conscientiously stuck with me throughout this project, is deeply appreciated.

I owe everything to my family's loving support, warmth, and loyalty without which *The Twilight of America's Omnipresence* would not have been penned.

FOREWORD

By R. Evan Ellis[1]

The re-emergence of China as a principal actor on the world stage is one of, if not the, defining attribute of the strategic landscape of the twenty-first century. Yet while there is widespread acknowledgement of the importance of China's rise, its meaning and implications are subject to divergent interpretations that expose fundamental differences in perspective and philosophy about the international system.

For the multitude of contemporary popular and scholarly works written about the rise of China, an implicit or explicit theme is almost always the question of *power.* Some, such as Martin Jacques' *When China Rules the World* make this proposition explicit: whether or not by design, the expansion of China's economic, military, and other capabilities alters both its relative standing vis-à-vis other actors in the global system, such as the United States, as well as the system itself.

The myriad of ways in which the literature examines and debates the rise of China, in conjunction with its impact on the United States only reinforces the centrality of the question of *power* in understanding the concept.

The debate between the (usually Chinese) scholars who assert the "peaceful" nature of China's development, versus those (often in the U.S.) who imagine a hidden intent by the P.R.C. to dominate the global order, implicitly concur in asserting, or taking as a point of departure, that the expansion of China's capabilities is transforming global institutions and the position of other actors.

In a similar fashion, those who debate the continuity of P.R.C. growth in the face of challenges such as the "middle income trap," difficulties in the China's health care system, education, pollution, an aging workforce, or discontented minority groups, each begin from the premise that the reason that their analysis is relevant is that the continuation of China on its current trajectory would fundamentally transform the international system.

In addition to highlighting the issue of power and the transformative impact of China's "rise" on the U.S. and the international system, such analyses also highlight the different normative perspectives of those who examine the phenomenon. On

---

[1] Dr. R. Evan Ellis is Research Professor with the Strategic Studies Institute of the U.S. Army War College. The views expressed are strictly his own.

1

one hand, authors writing from a Western perspective may fret about the implications of such developments on U.S. security, or the U.S. led liberal economic order underpinning the geopolitical status quo. Some, in the third world, adopt a more celebratory attitude toward the rise of China and the associated "demise" of the U.S. Some hope to find in the rise of China the emergence of a new order which facilitates their development and frees them from the hegemony of the existing capitalist system.

Among Chinese scholars, a key question is whether the United States, as the anointed leader of the existing order, will "allow" Chinese power to surpass that of the United States without attempting to "block" its rise.

Yet each of these normatively different perspectives echoes the same presumption - that the continuation of the current trend implies a China whose power and place in the international system, in some way displaces that of the United States.

In the classic literature on international relations, scholars have sometimes measured power within the international system in terms of a nation's objective characteristics, such as the size of its economy, its military, or its technology base. Power has also been discussed in terms of the ability of nations, or other actors in the international system, to exert influence through cultural affinities, international institutions and regimes. Yet whether power is conceived in traditional "hard" or "soft" terms, the literature on the rise of China highlights the degree to which power is understood in relative and relational terms. However much the Chinese economy may grow and diversify, and however much its military and technology base may expand, the ultimate measure, or affirmation of Chinese power is the displacement, in some sense, of the United States and the prevailing international system.

There is no inherent geographic, economic or historic reason why the United States is the referent for the rise of Chinese "power," except for the fact that it is widely seen to be the dominant actor in the current international system. Thus since the U.S. is perceived to be "number one," China's rise is understood with respect to how it displaces the U.S.

At the core of the present book by Serena Joseph-Harris, *The Twilight of America's Omnipresence* is the complex concept of power, and the linkage between the rise of the P.R.C. and a corresponding loss of position by the United States, the dominant actor in a previous global order, now fading.

Reflecting the enormity and multifaceted nature of the subject which it takes on, the present work does not develop and argue a single idea so much as it weaves a rich intellectual tapestry as it considers the topic from a multiplicity of perspectives.

Reflecting the author's experience as both a scholar and a practitioner, the book links the economic and security dimensions of China's rise and its impact on the U.S. to the philosophical realm. In the process, we are led on a journey that Ms. Joseph-Harris is uniquely qualified to take us on... It is neither a U.S., nor a Chinese, nor a "neutral" perspective, but one which blends the multiple, disparate points of view of this exceptional author, who is at once, an intellectual, a security professional, a successful afro-Caribbean businesswoman, neither disposed to fully accept the "win-win" Chinese development narrative, nor to fully identify with, and bereave the loss of the U.S.-led capitalist order. Indeed, the very title of the book, which speaks of "omnipresence," directs the readers' gaze to a world order of infinite and self-determining frontiers as part of the grand stage of U.S. and P.R.C. rivalry. The reader is reminded of the sense of place from which Ms. Joseph-Harris observes the rise of China... her small island nation of Trinidad and Tobago, from which China and the U.S. are not mere powers, but past and potential possessors of global "omnipresence."

This distinctive work has a way of unexpectedly turning conventional attitudes and presumptions on their side to reveal new insight through new perspective. As she takes on Chinese engagement in the Americas, for example, Ms. Joseph-Harris provocatively shows that such activities not only follow the logic of Chinese strategic and economic imperatives, but also highlight the decline of the U.S. "empire" globally, which until now, was primarily circumscribed by territorial and geopolitical demarcations.

The author highlights the seeming contradiction that exists in U.S. culture that is, at once, pragmatically business oriented, yet prone to frame the world in a struggle between good and evil. Then she goes on to show how China as a "civilization state," with its dramatic rise and successes, challenges the uniqueness of American exceptionalism, upon which the very U.S. self-concept is based.

The book is a massive work, with over 650 pages divided into five sections containing 19 chapters, each of which could stand alone. In the end, it takes the reader on a journey which, more than providing answers, exposes us to the complexity and multidimensionality of this important phenomenon which is not only transforming China and the position of the U.S. in the world, but also places such as Ms. Joseph-Harris' Trinidad and Tobago which are caught up in the transformation as participants, and not just as observers of great power maneuvering.

Like all good journeys, it is only partly about a destination, and is as much about providing experiences whose contemplation transforms us, the travelers... It is a journey worth taking...

R. Evan Ellis

Carlisle, Pennsylvania

June, 2015

PROLOGUE

his enquiry is historically rooted in the confluence of events that precipitated the demise of old Europe and the simultaneous rise of America to superpower status over a fifty-year period following the end of the Second World War. This section seeks to address the shortsightedness of presentism—the tendency to narrowly focus on matters of current concerns—which have a long historical development, creating the perception that the past, present and future are mutually exclusive.

China's current challenge to American hegemony necessarily entails a succession of events prior to and during the Second World War when the world stood at America's feet. Like a resolute lioness closing in on a frantic herd of zebras, America lunged for the kill, wrenching from imperial Europe its very essence as the latter squirmed, struggled and agonizingly succumbed to the last vestiges of 500 years of sustained world dominance. Thereafter, the die was cast for ascent to superpower status, with the collapse of Europe precipitated by World War II, and the surreptitious involvement of America's armed forces in concert with a tightly-knit consortium of clandestine entities that worked assiduously in devising and consolidating what is commonly known today as the Western Alliance.

Following the Second World War, Britain and France could no longer persist in imperial consolidation. The French were particularly hard-hit. Efforts at overreach in Indo-China (Vietnam, Laos, and Cambodia) and thereafter in Algeria in either guerilla or conventional warfare proved inadequate and by 1954 the French had abandoned Indo-China entirely. The period was also one of changing responsibilities in imperial relationships. In the case of Britain, although the Labor government had granted Independence to India in 1940, Britain harbored the hope that India would cooperate militarily with her against the Soviet Union, in compensation for the loss of the Indian army from which the former previously drew considerable land force strength. Furthermore, the British Commonwealth, which comprised independent parts of the former Empire, was perceived as a buffer by means of which Britain could continue to project and maintain its influence.

Beginnings of the Western Alliance:
The Stay-Behind Army in Europe

Firstly, the book briefly recounts the North Atlantic Treaty Organization's secret stay-behind armies established on the heels of World War II in all countries of Western Europe. The purpose of these underground cells was to be in a prime state of readiness to launch an offensive against an anticipated Communist war that would someday challenge Europe. It was the collusive assessments of Great Britain and the United States that contributed to what would be regarded in closed circles as a shadow war. In 1940, former British Prime Minister Winston Churchill had set up the secret "stay-behind" army Special Operations Executive (SOE) to set Europe ablaze by aiding resistance movements and carrying out subversive activities in enemy-held territory. By 1944, London and Washington had accentuated their concerns on the importance of keeping Western Europe immune from the specter of Communism. It was the view of the Anglo-Americans that the establishment and securing of these secret networks with the knowledge and concurrence of respective host governments was a sure way of proactively circumventing the Communist take-over of Europe. Following World War II, in accordance with this thinking a network of similarly-styled detachments was set up in short order throughout the continent, drawing upon the experiences and strategies of the original SOE officers.

It would also be recalled that in 1940 with Britain's situation becoming increasingly desperate, Prime Minister Churchill had dispatched Lord Lothian, his ambassador to the U.S. to negotiate with President Roosevelt over ways and means that intelligence could be shared between the two countries. In exchange for secret details of Britain's latest developments in radar, Churchill asked the Americans for "certain technical information." These tentative exchanges laid the groundwork for an intricate and enduring intelligence sharing relationship which would be concretized by the end of World War II. When the war ended the U.S. and the U.K. together with Canada, Australia and New Zealand would sign a secret pact that signaled an alliance among the key nations of the English-speaking world that would more commonly be referred to as the Five Eyes.

With the accouchement of the Cold War, the fight against an internal enemy had already become an integral aspect of European politics, supported by the West along lines similar to the Anti-Nazi resistance of 1939-1945. Unsurprisingly, the North Atlantic Treaty Organization (NATO) pact signed in 1949 mirrored the philosophy behind this scheme of stealth. Thereafter, covert entities composed of highly trained militia would become a defining feature of the Western Alliance. The special relationship shared between America, as a teeming mistress and her trusted friend, confidante, and comrade in arms, Great Britain was thus sealed. Having conceptualized the NATO precisely to fight this anticipated war, the West was nonetheless continuously challenged by the strength of the Soviet Union as the Soviet bloc consistently amassed greater and greater numbers of troops, tanks, planes, guns, and other equipment.

In Italy, the stratagem of installing stay-behind units would see the creation of the Gladio, a covert organization amply stocked with a network of communications, arms, explosives, and related war-faring devices. Right-wing extremists, fearful of a takeover by Italian Communists, became increasingly linked with Gladio armies and conducted a trail of massacres and atrocities, which they blamed on the Communists. After years of continuing travail in the course of which the Italian society was racked by a trail of violence and intimidation labeled "the strategy of tension," which was in effect an attempt to destabilize in order to stabilize, on August 03, 1990 the Italian Prime Minister, standing in for the Parliamentary Commission, finally admitted to a shocked audience for the first time in Italy's post-war history, that a NATO-linked secret security apparatus had in fact existed in the country. He then committed to presenting a Report on the matter to the Parliament. By 2000, the findings of a Parliamentary-constituted Commission that was subsequently set up concluded that "these massacres, those bombs, these military actions had been organized, promoted or supported by men inside Italian state institutions linked to the structures of United States intelligence..."

Regarding the U.K. involvement, in November 1990, British Conservative Party member Rupert Allason, editor of Intelligence Quarterly Magazine under the pen name Nigel West, confirmed to the Associated Press, "We (the British) are heavily involved ... and still are in these networks' and 'have certainly helped finance and run with the Americans several networks ... and through the MI6 together with the CIA, were directly involved." Allason also stated that after 1949, the Command and Control Structure coordinated the stay-behind armies for Special Forces of NATO, within which Britain's Special Air Service Special Forces had pledged a strategic role.[1]

Official attribution of these dealings would be forthcoming five years later when the London-based Imperial War Museum disclosed for the first time the MI6 involvement in Gladio operations. In one of the windows dedicated to the MI6 was the following inscription: "Among MI6 preparations for a Third World War was the creation of stay-behind parties ready to operate behind enemy lines in the event of a Soviet advance into Western Europe."

Similarly, the ELAS of Greece was created along with the Seferberlik Taktik Kuburu (STK) of Turkey. The latter was reputed for its extreme violence, its express mission being to integrate Turkey solidly into the Western alliance. In Germany, on the orders of the Pentagon, the U.S. Counter Intelligence Corps

(CIC) with right-wing extremist support, hunted down Nazis and recruited them into the German stay-behind network. A calculated geopolitical maneuver of this sort led up to a secret protocol signed many years later between the United States and Germany in May 1955, which precluded criminal prosecution of right-wing extremists on the part of the West German government.

In the case of Norway, two central figures were directly involved in the setting up of a similar organization—the ROCAMBOLE—with assistance from the CIA, the first Vilhelm Evang, Director of the Norwegian Secret Service and the second, Jens Christian Hague, the country's first post-World War Defense Minister. In the Netherlands, the equivalent organization, G III C, was administered by the country's military secret service the GS III. Belgium's secret stay-behind army had two branches code named SDR A8 and STC respectively. The former was a civilian corps operating within the civilian secret service; whereas the second comprised military personnel trained for combat, sabotage operations, parachute jumping, and maritime missions.

Regarding France, nowhere in Western Europe, possibly with the exception of Italy, was the Communist Party so widely supported. As a consequence, the U.S. and British Special Forces devised Plan Bleu to forestall the French Communist Party from coming to power. Plan Bleu agents were heavily funded by representatives of industry such as Peugeot and Renault. OPC—a branch of the CIA under Frank Wisner—was instrumental in the establishment of similar outfits in Stockholm and supported the training of other arms in neutral Sweden as well as in Finland and other NATO members, Norway and Denmark.

Thus, an effective front line was drawn across Europe and extended from as far off as Szczecin at the Baltic Sea to Trieste on the Adriatic Sea, and it was along this line (coined "the Iron Curtain" by Winston Churchill) that military power of either side was delineated and strategically dispersed. The network was very tightly administered. The Supreme Headquarters of Allied Powers Europe (SHAPE), a direct organ of NATO's apparatus, coordinated the actions of Gladio based on the accounts of former Gladio Secretary General, Manfred Werner. Werner averred to the fact that the NATO Office of Security coordinated, monitored, and implemented NATO security policy. Moreover, the Director of Security also served as Chairman of NATO's Security Committee in which the Heads of Security of NATO members would meet regularly to discuss matters relating to espionage, terrorism, subversion, and deliberate on how communism could affect Western Europe and the Alliance.

II

America's Historic Apprehension of Domination
of Another World Power

A second and equally critical element that sets the stage for the book's theme is the deep-seated and historic apprehension of America over the possible emergence of a rival power with aspirations for world hegemony. A secret 1954 Report prepared for the White House by a Commission headed by former U.S. President Herbert Hoover states in part:

> *"It is now clear that we are facing an implacable enemy whose avowed objective is world domination. There are no rules in such a game. Hitherto accepted norms of human conduct do not apply... If the United States is to survive, longstanding American concepts of fair play must be reconsidered... We must learn to subvert, sabotage, and destroy our enemies by more clever, more sophisticated, more effective methods that they used against us.*[2]*"*

From all indications, as this enquiry will demonstrate, this uniquely American cast of mind however flawed or substantiated, persists. Side by side with this disposition was America's palpable contempt for the perceived incapacity of other societies in the international system to fend for themselves in the face of the emerging ideological menace. More recently, such demeanor manifests itself in the contemporary war against terrorism. In the Pentagon's estimation, citizens of Europe were somehow unable to perceive the real and present danger of Communism; as a result Europeans needed, or more explicitly deserved to be manipulated. The apprehension festered continually within the bowels of the Pentagon and would be transposed on the European society, as America actively orchestrated and fueled the mania of anti-Communist sentiment and rhetoric that swept across the continent in the ensuing decades.

Having set ablaze the irreconcilable ideological divide, America cast its eyes on the spoils of war. The Peenemunde Aero-Dynamics Institute had already developed two high-speed wind tunnels to test guide missiles and projectiles. Both operated at more than twice the maximum speed of any wind tunnel developed in America (Reference: - S.M. Hastings[3] "The NS WC/WOL Wind Tunnels" NSWC Pamphlet, August 1979, ONH). The Carl Zeiss factory in Juna was similarly stripped of its premier scientists and infrastructure, but not before the Russians kidnapped several glass technicians and scientists, a fact that was purposely concealed by the Americans since they had engaged in the same acts in contravention of international law[4]

The initial scramble for scientists and their technology was a mere harbinger of the ultimate bonanza that lay ahead. All in all, a total of 1,160 research and scientific personnel would subsequently be mustered in en masse by the US under Operation Paperclip, along with hundreds of the brightest minds from Germany. At the time of Germany's surrender in May 1945, Army Ordnance, Combined Intelligence Objectives Sub-Committee (CIOS), and other scientific teams had thoroughly assessed every primary technical scientific target in that country. In fact, it was reported that jealous industry rivalries erupted even between American teams and among the four allied nations that were competing fiercely over the spoils of war. That competition, particularly from the standpoint of the Soviets, heightened with Germany's partition into four occupied zones.

Looking back then to the past course of events, the meteoric ascendancy of the United States as the first and only superpower is beholden to successes riddled with compulsion and unscrupulous pillage. Thus, as allied troops advanced inland from the beaches of Normandy, teams of scientific investigators from various U.S. agencies trailed their wake in search of whatever research installations that would yield up Hitler's scientific achievements and brain trust. These teams were saturated with U.S. army and navy personnel, Army Air Force teams, and Office for Strategic Services (OSS) intelligence agents attached to special military units called T-forces. At their peak, some of the contingents would number as a many as 10,000 scattered from afar off as the United Kingdom, where their command group the Combined Intelligence Objectives Sub-Committee (CIOS) was headquartered, as well as in other parts of France, Belgium, Holland, Luxembourg, and Germany.

While Hitler's bomb project may have lagged behind the Americans, this was by no means the case for chemical warfare. The Germans had reportedly already eclipsed the Americans in this sphere of experimentation, having invented three new nerve gases—tabun, sarin and soman—which were far more deadly than the mustard gas used by the Allies at that time. Additionally, the Germans were conducting chemical warfare experiments on both animals and humans. At Raubkamner, for example, the Americans encountered a main laboratory and nine annexes containing no less than four thousand photographs of humans, ostensibly political prisoners that were detained in concentration camps. Closer investigations would disclose that in some instances, lethal liquids had been applied directly to the skins of experimental subjects.[5]

The policy of the U.S. at that time was jaded with ambiguity, incongruities, flawed thinking, and moral hazard. This was evident across the entire ambit of government, but more pertinent to the military and intelligence enclaves since even as one arm of the military was working untiringly to bring Nazi criminals back as blameworthy "war criminals," other camps were surreptitiously using any means necessary to protect Nazi scientists and facilitate them with safe haven in America. Ultimately, the methods and mindset the Germans brought with them not only resulted in breaches of national security within the U.S. government, but also led to the horror of having U.S. soldiers used as research guinea pigs later on, a situation that proved reprehensibly indistinguishable to the modus operandi of the Nazis. This was but one aspect of the downside of America's dizzying soar to world dominance following the war. Further to this and by a perverse twist of fate, a jilted Russia, America's one-time World War II collaborator, became the new enemy as the axis shifted rather inelegantly, heralding the dawn of the Cold War.

The rise to world dominance on America's part was therefore by no means a seamless soar as the inside story so lividly discloses. To the contrary, a polarity of interests mired the best efforts of hard-working men and women within the highest levels of government and this was recognizable long before World War II had ended. The rationale behind the grafting of German scientists en masse was to gather as much evidence as possible that earned them a decided advantage ahead of the U.S. and the allied forces. However, a further objective lurked within the military — to ensure the Department of Defense maintained a clear technological lead ahead of the rest of the world, once the war had ended. On that account, a major aspect of the campaign was directed towards preventing scores of German scientists from eluding capture and escaping to other countries, primarily Latin America, to continue their wartime research and by extension, maintain their scientific lead and possibly share it with other competing powers. Germany at all costs had to be stripped bare once and for all of all her scientific capability to raise another war. Consequentially, certain segments of the armed forces collaborated and abetted with government agencies that were similarly engaged in exploiting legal or institutional lacunas in the U.S. system, in order to access Germany's brain trust.

Among the more important retrievable assets for the American high command was Wernher von Braun, Prussian physicist and rocketeer and principal collaborator in the building of the A-4 rocket (which would become known as the V-2), who surrendered to the American high command in June 1945. Von Braun had headed the Black List, the code name ascribed to German scientists and engineers targeted for immediate interrogation by U.S. military experts, although evidence suggests that British intelligence officials and scientists were actually the first to interview him in depth in order to gain information they suspected would have been denied them by U.S. officials. The transfer of Von Braun and his supporting specialists to America was authorized by the U.S. Secretary of State on June, 20, 1945 and facilitated by the U.S. Joint Intelligence Objectives Agency.

The latter created false employment histories for the members of that team thereby expunging their Nazi Party memberships.

Von Braun and his former Peenemunde staff would be instrumental in the refurbishing, assembly and launch of a number of V-2s that were shipped from Germany to New Mexico in the development of the Redstone Rocket Arsenal which represented the first live ballistic nuclear tests conducted in the United States; the subsequent development of Jupiter C which successfully launched the West's first satellite, the Explorer I, on January 31, 1958; to be followed by the development of concepts for human presence in space, manned space missions as large-scale undertakings, and by no means least the lunar orbit rendezvous initiative that decisively ushered America's entry into the space race. Some of his former German colleagues were occupied with parallel rocket designs and projects, more specifically, the Sputnik program being pursued in Russia.

The Rules of the Game

It was common knowledge that U.S. Immigration laws debarred members of axis powers from entering the country. The Joint Chiefs of Staffs' overt policy requiring that the Commanding General in the European theater "exclude from further research activity any persons who held key positions in German war research" reinforced this posture. Thus, upon capture, ardent Nazis and German investors were supposed to be replaced by persons who were less politically suspect since JCS policies, officially at least, favored the prosecution of Nazi war criminals and vigorously promoted the de-Nazification of Germany.

Ultimately, the lead up to the war against Japan proved to be the deciding factor in circumventing written codes that were, until then, frustrating the advancement of agendas that were manifestly tangential to official U.S. orientations. This turning point would come with the commissioning of Project Overcast (the forerunner of the Paperclip Project), which was approved by the JCS. The objective of this special project was "to assist in shortening the Japanese war" and it was limited to the exploitation of "a few chosen rare minds" of German nationality, whose skills could not be fully exploited in Europe. The original intent was that once these teams of handpicked German scientists were brought to America and their exploitation was successfully concluded, they would be repatriated to Germany. The grand design was made possible by a series of maneuvers that included but were not limited to invoking the Ninth Proviso of U.S. Immigration law, which gave the Attorney General the authority to admit into America cases with military implications or those affecting national security, in tandem with the CIA Act of 1949. The latter provision permitted the facilitation of cases of special interest, specifically the entry into the U.S. of a quota of 100 individuals a year, "without regard to their inadmissibility under Immigration or any other laws." The Joint Intelligence Objectives Agency (JIOA) Governing Committee approved their selection and thereafter passed the names to the Attorney General for approval in a contrivance that ultimately achieved the sought after fait accompli.

Three military intelligence agencies formed the power base behind the campaign - the Joint Intelligence Committee (JIC), the Joint Intelligence Objectives Agency (JIAO), and the Exploitation Branch under Army Intelligence (G-2) in the War Department General Staff (WDGS). JIC was the de facto intelligence arm of the JCS and provided advice to the JCS and the State Department on policy and procedure regarding the German scientist project. JIOA, on the other hand, assumed direct responsibility for running the program, which was subsequently disbanded in 1962. The WDGS, in the meantime, was responsible for the implementation of each phase of the project and more specifically, preventing escape and evasion that could potentially embarrass the government. The German specialists, including the most eminent rocket technicians of the day, operated out of discretely dispersed military bases.

It is also to the credit of extraordinary functionaries within the defense and covert circles that America was able to harvest the brilliance of the ilk of Herbert Wagner, chief missile design engineer for the German Henschel Aircraft Company, and more importantly, the de facto creator of the HS-293, the first German guided missile used in combat during World War II. Along with his two assistants, Wagner was the first of his clique to touch U.S. soil after the war, arriving on May 19, 1945 in a military transport plane.[6] As recently as April 26 1985, some of the members of the original German rocket team posed for a group shot in front of the Saturn V Rocket at the Alabama Space and Rocket Museum in Huntsville, Alabama. Captured in an exclusive Linda Hunt photo were:

- Eberhard Rees
- Konrad Dannenberg
- Weiner Sieber
- Hannes Liebsten
- Karl Heimburg
- O Ho Hirschler
- Hannes Luehrsen
- Walter Haeussermann
- Helmut Horn
- Eric Neubert
- Weiner Voss

- Bernard Tessman
- Guenther Haukohl
- Ernst Lange
- Dieter Grau
- Wilhelm Angele
- Theodor Vowe
- Herbert Bergeler
- Willie Kuberg
- Walter Jacobi
- Helmut Zoike
- Robert Paetz

Amidst the ephemeral dramas punctuating the history of our time, debates continue to be ignited over how the national interest of a country should be defined, and the even more contentious issue - whether the violation of a country's laws could be justified on the merit of an overarching and often politically jaded philosophy. With the passage of time many of these operations, despite their rather clouded context, took on a life of their own. Paperclip for example, morphed into Project 63, and thereafter to Project National Interest. During that period, no plot or person was considered too unsavory to be brought into the fold.

The international landscape is now a drastically altered one. Nationalism competes fiercely with the desirability of creating a viable and consensual international order with new institutions serving as the foci for multilateral diplomacy. Critics of American power canvass strongly in favor of multi-polarity. Of even greater irony is the fact that nations that are among the more vocal in railing against what they perceive as U.S. bellicosity and resort to the use of force, are themselves not necessarily unsusceptible to similar behavior.

III

A third element of significance that underpins this project is the striking chain of historical analogues that can be drawn between the events of World War II, the circumstances propelling America's current expansion into war theaters, and hostilities in North Africa, the Middle East, Central Asia extending to the Pacific rim, and the resurgence of Africa to central prominence on the world stage. In her Farewell Speech as outgoing U.S. Secretary of State delivered to the Council on Foreign Relations on January 31, 2013, Hillary Clinton averred to the fact that energy diplomacy is now pivotal to U.S. foreign policy and the U.S. was maintaining its national security and economic preeminence worldwide[7] by adopting "smart power" initiatives.

Readers would recall that Germany entered the battle for oil as an imperial great power at the beginning of the twentieth century. During that era, the German empire and major banks under its aegis, chiefly the Deutsche Bank, had gained considerable leverage over the Turkish Petroleum Company formed in 1912, and by extension, over potential oil deposits in the Ottoman Empire. Thus, Hitler's strategic ambitions during the last months of 1941 and the first of 1942 rapidly morphed into the formulation of a campaign that focused on securing supplies of oil reserves. Logically, economic considerations were as important to the formulation of a new strategy as the depleted state of his eastern armies and air fleets which were severely weakened from five months of offensive fighting, followed by two months of intensely defensive engagements. Fearful of heavy cutbacks on Rumanian oilfields and intent on the acquisition of new sources that would prove essential if he were to wage a prolonged war against the growing list of nations that he opposed, Hitler ramped up a major two-pronged campaign. Firstly, he would launch offensives in the Crimea to protect Rumanian oil centers from Soviet air attacks and secondly, he would make a powerful thrust into the Don River and immediately thereafter to the Caucasus to deliver that oil-rich region into German hands.

In order to fully comprehend Hitler's insistence on the capture of the region around Baku specifically, which sits atop one of the world's richest oilfields and the wider Caucasus, bounded by the Black Sea on the west and the Caspian Sea on the east, the reader must appreciate that 80 percent of Soviet oil (24,000,000 tons in 1942) came from the Baku reserves. Moreover, German economists had come to realize during the first year of Nazi rule that the nation's heavy dependence on overseas imports of crude oil would be a serious problem in the event of a war. At that time, Germany was importing a staggering 85 percent of the roughly 3 - 7 million tons it consumed per year, primarily from the United States, Venezuela, and Iran. The remainder came from domestic crude production and its nascent synthetic oil industry.

Albert Edward Gunther, British Petroleum geologist commissioned by the British government to report on the condition of oilfields in Germany in 1945, noted:

> *"...Hitler's obsession with the Caucasus lay in the knowledge that the Continent of Europe is not endowed with oilfields sufficient for modern war. German spoils from the countries she occupied enabled her for a while to dominate the continent, but not to win long drawn out battles in the plains of Russia, in the deserts of Africa, on the high seas and in the air over the whole periphery of Europe. Only by victory over Russia could the Nazis hope to secure the economic wealth on which, in the long run, that tyranny rested.*[8,9]

Joel Hayward provides a statistically supported detail on the German dilemma tallying that in 1938, the last full year of peace, only about 7,500,000 tons of oil consumed in Germany was produced domestically by oil refineries recently built, with the bulk of the other 5 million tons coming from the United States, Venezuela and Iran; that a smaller but nonetheless significant amount of 450,000 tons came from Rumania; and that it was on account of that state of affairs that when Germany's imports of oil finally ceased in September 1939 with the imposition of the Anglo - French naval blockade, the Reich was dealt a devastating blow. Against this setting, today, the Liquefied Natural Gas for NATO Act introduced by U.S.

Senator Lugar is appreciably one in a string of expediently devised preemptive measures being taken by the U.S. government, to relieve US-NATO allies' vulnerability to an over-reliance on Russian and Iranian gas supplies. [9]

In a meticulously worded memorandum dispatched to his commissioner of foreign exchange, Herman Goring, Hitler had mapped what he considered the economic and military priorities of the Reich. This was based upon the central tenets of Mein Kamp and on his own vulnerability assessment. The short-term goal would be mobilizing the economy to attain political and economic self-sufficiency. This necessitated the production of raw materials essential for modern warfare at the fastest pace combined with initiatives that would mitigate the dire oil situation. This was not to be. Had the stratagem been successful, the German army would have been adequately outfitted for war within four years, and the economy endowed with a capacity for all-out overseas offensives within a similar time frame. Accordingly, unlike the rapid campaigns that typified 1939 and the early months of 1941, the massive offensive launched in June of 1941 to overpower the Soviet Union depleted the Reich's oil reserves and reserve stocks signaling the ominous downswing of its eastern front exploit by late October of that year.

These parallelisms lend salience to Zbigniew Brzezinski's prognostication:

> *"...how America "manages" Eurasia is critical. Eurasia is the globe's largest continent and is geopolitically axial. A power that dominates Eurasia would control two of the world's three most advanced and economically productive regions. A mere glance at the map also suggests that control over Eurasia would almost automatically entail Africa's subordination.* [10]*"*

Africa's Resurgence to Global High-Profile

Africa presents itself at the heart of the Sino-American contest. Internal, regional and global conflicts have intersected on the Great Continent in complex patterns which have evolved with the passage of time and shaped the march of history, so that although the match between America and China would appear as the overriding factor, this perception recedes in the broader context of waves of European confrontations of the past that manifest themselves in the present, and inevitably, do not fit squarely into a bipolar framework. Demonstrative of this, the climatic periods of Anglo-European interventions germane to present day events can be traced to four identifiable time frames beginning with the first decade of the twentieth century.

During the initial phase Britain, France, Germany, Belgium, Italy, Portugal and Spain all established regimes in Africa with the singular ambition of emasculating its resources, wealth, people and their cultures. The second significant twentieth century phase occurred during the decolonization period (1956-1975) and was succeeded decades later by an era characterized by state collapse (1991-2001). Subsequently, the global war on terror touched off (2001 to date) and continues to metamorphose. Arguably, the most consequential of these interventions is the ongoing escalation of military engagements, whereby external interests are aggravating long-standing hostilities, and for the most part, stoking much larger conflagrations with devastating ramifications for hordes of indigenous peoples. This military campaign, which is shepherded by the United States, is metastasizing with alarming velocity into regions as afar off as Central and Southern Asia and making its way to the South China Sea, placing Africa at the fulcrum of an end day global tussle.

Of consequence is the consolidation of strategic alignments synchronous with emergent multi-polarity. Former colonial powers have all regrouped to maintain their distinct interests; and Russia - reminiscent of its dominance in a bipolar world prior to the collapse of the Soviet Union when it led a coherent bloc that included most of Eastern Europe - is reasserting itself through realignments with emerging blocs, such as the BRICS. Most notable of all, much of Eastern Europe now falls under NATO's officialdom. China, in the meantime, is jostling with the Soviets in a manner reminiscent of the sixties when Moscow maintained distinct interests alongside Cuba, Yugoslavia and in many parts of Africa that served as proxies to westward communist expansion.

In order to better comprehend China's resolve to re-assert itself at this point in time and maintain a foothold in Africa, it is critical that the reader appreciate from the outset which powers dominated multilateral world trade prior Europe's five hundred year triumph spanning the fifteenth to nineteenth centuries, what commodities were being traded by these players, the expansiveness of intraregional and intercontinental commercial networks they commandeered and beyond everything, the dynamic and resilience of the dominant monetary systems in the world during the operative era. Contrary to the doubts and denials of Euro-centrists, between 1500 and 1899 and even throughout the preceding millennium, there was in place a global economy with a worldwide reserve of labor and multilateral trade whose primary routes entered, exited, and transited Afro-Eurasia and which altogether governed world trade. The preeminent role enjoyed by Africa, China and India in the world economy was spawned by their access to primary products and combined absolute and relative productivity in manufactures. This commercial network traversed the Ottoman Empire, which occupied crucial geographic and economic crossroads and derived wealth from substantial local and regional production, commercialization and division of labor from an array of sectors, including private, public, and sub-public enterprises. Among the primary commodities traded between Africa and the Middle and far East were gold, silver, porcelain, salt, ivory, cotton, derived textiles from cotton and silk, and horses, metals such as steel and copper, and leather products.

Analogous to the present state of intercontinental global trade, there was competition between alternative products from different regions, between products grown under different climatic conditions, as well as among product substitutes. This well-defined political and economic complex was the key factor that motivated Europeans to seek greater access to Africa and Asia in relationships that were irrefutably symbiotic.

Intraregional trade within Africa itself was complemented by maritime dominance which was spawned by three integral factors - the first was the sheer size and scale of the continent; the second, which is consequential to the first, was its geostrategic interface with all premier oceanic routes; and the third was the seamanship of indigenous mariners who maintained firm control over regional commerce. Simultaneously, as vectors of highly valued commodities, the Atlantic and Indian Oceans and Mediterranean Sea complemented the preponderance of overland caravan routes where desert and oceanic commercial systems converged and digressed. The phenomenal network facilitated burgeoning flows of money and dry and dietary goods and was sustained by viable internal monetary systems underpinned by instrumentations for tax and duty collections.

What's more, China maintained a centrality in the world silver market via its East Asian tributary system and a balance of trade surplus with all its trading partners. The Chinese were net importers of silver out of America which arrived via Europe, West Asia, India, and South-East Asia in Manillan galleons, as well as from Japan. Other regions of the world such as Japan and Europe relied largely on the continuing infusions of silver into their monetary systems to offset their trade deficits. Simultaneously, Western and Southern Europe, which was in a state of perpetual deficit, was relegated to being a major importer of both silver and gold bullion to cover recurrent trade imbalances. At the height of the colonization era, Europe's fiscal imbalances were substantially mediated by the unfair advantage derived from an ominous trans-Atlantic slave trade piloted and promoted by imperial powers in tandem with the opportunity costs of "free" labor imposed by European powers on the indigenous peoples of the Americas, where gold and silver mining burgeoned.

North Africa has historically been central to the trade of the entire Mediterranean region. Beyond Egypt, the Phoenicians had dominated North Africa, with Carthage being the most important city controlling trade. Egypt, and later the Roman city of Alexandria, came to be the primary hub of the

Mediterranean trade for several centuries, and certainly well into the nineteenth century, it persisted as one of the most developed parts of the world. Similarly, the Sudan traded extensively with Chad and Libya, and further afield with China, India, and the Arabian Peninsula. The Axximite Kingdoms of Ethiopia and Eritrea had established a powerful navy and trade links that were maintained during the first millennium, extending outwards to the Byzantine Empire and India.

Alongside this, the Swahili Kingdoms and major city-states, strewn across 2,500 miles from Somalia to Mozambique, formed the bases of other trade empires today known as Kenya, and Tanzania, each of which controlled trading posts to the Middle and Far East and flourished due to their premiership in the Indian Ocean trade. Carbon steel that had been produced in pre-heating draft furnaces in the area of Lake Victoria was, until the nineteenth century, technologically superior to what Europe had been churning out.[11] These attainments are a mere microcosm of the Afro-Eurasian exchange that was at once pivotal to regional and inter-continental trade and economics.

Africa held a unique pride of place in relation to the supply of gold to the world market, with the bulk leaving its shores many centuries before 1500. Even afterwards and despite the Minas Gerais-Brazil gold boom that spanned 1680 to the mid-eighteenth century, supplies continued to flow from West Africa, from Nubia via Egypt to Constantinople-Istanbul, and from Ethiopia to Egypt reaching peak production in the sixteenth century.

Hitherto, although European peoples benefitted considerably from global expeditions for the period 1500 to 1800, by no means did they dominate world affairs until early modern times. Prior to that, and certainly before the nineteenth century, most of the Western Hemisphere and Africa lay well beyond Europe's reach. However, aided by their accumulated geographic knowledge, once the Europeans embarked upon exploration and arrived at their destinations they capitalized on commercial opportunities. Most prominent among these were the English, Dutch and Portuguese who organized expeditions with the backing of the state and private merchants that funded powerful joint stock companies.

In Africa, the Portuguese were among the first European arrivals to have established fortified coastal trading posts and ultimately succeeded, albeit in spite of truculent internal resistance, in wresting established routes from the control of African merchant ships through a combination of brute force and subterfuges, the latter involving proselytization to Islam or Christianity as the case may be.

Ipso facto, it was the influence of Islam that facilitated the meteoric rise of the Arabs as a military force when their armies marched into Egypt in 639 AD ending 600 years of Roman occupation.[12] The die was then cast for the never-ending global jihad that rages on today. After this inceptive conquest the Arabs bored their way beyond Egypt's borders to the west where they overran Byzantine-ruled Libya, pressed into Tunisia and Algeria and thereafter penetrated Morocco where they still persist as the dominant force. This accounts for the contemporary demographic make-up of Northern Africa - Egypt, Sudan, Libya, Algeria, Tunisia, Morocco, and as far eastward as Zanzibar, where Arabs are overwhelmingly represented.

In contrast, China successfully staved off attempts by Europe to set up trade centers along its peripheral parts, in place of which it elected for a path of self-defined insulation. This stance was met with bloody reprisals from powerful British interests that were ably backed both by the government and the crown, leading to the infamous chain of opium wars that rocked the very foundations of Middle Kingdom and resulted in internal collapse, thereafter falling prey to Japanese colonization. If truth be told, the unfurled conspiracy to legalize the sale of opium and turn an entire nation into drug addicts of the worst breed, thereby eviscerating its social fabric in the interest of enriching the few while pursuing expansionist ambitions, has resulted in a legacy of unceasing repercussions. The humiliation that was incurred and from which China has since bounced back filters in its current dealings with other world powers, particularly those with a concomitant and deeply entrenched imperial past like the United States and the cast of other major players comprising the present day Western Alliance.

In addition to this, by the eighteenth century migratory hordes of Russian forces had extended their presence into the Caspian Sea region by absorbing much of the Caucasus, a vibrant multi-ethnic region that embraces the present day states of Georgia, Armenia and Azerbaijan, in a thrust that has permanently altered the demographic complexion of that region. It is in this context that the Western Alliance, specifically an expanding NATO configuration, is perceived by China as well as Russia to be no more than a maligned encroachment in the region and the geopolitics at play is reciprocal as shall be explained.

In a post-Soviet world there are political reasons for an aggressive U.S presence in the Caspian region. Richard Morningstar, a former U.S. Ambassador for Caspian Basin energy diplomacy affirmed that the fundamental objective of U.S. policy in the Caspian Sea is to install pipelines that must be commercially viable and serve the goal of "...establishing a political and economic framework" for America. In this connection, BP has wittingly routed the web of pipelines comprising the East-West energy corridor, which was created to transfer gas resources of the Middle East, the Caspian, Siberia, the Russian and Scandinavian Arctic, North Africa and the Gulf of Guinea to converge at the heart of the E.U., through countries sympathetic to U.S. policy. This was most evident with the signing of the intergovernmental treaty between Azerbaijan, Georgia and Turkey.

Conversely, ideas favoring installations through more obvious and economically viable routes such as the Baku-Novoossiyk that traverses Russia; linking Sangachal to the Iranian pipeline system to transport Azeri crude to the terminals of the Persian Gulf; or even placing lines across Central Asia onward to China were all scotched by BP in capitulation to U.S. interests. A similar train of thought would undoubtedly apply in the co-opting of African countries earmarked for the "Southern Corridor." Henceforth, China would inevitably find itself at odds with the U.S. in this new scheme that entails a Trans-Sahara pipeline that would run for 4,300 kilometers northwards from the coastal Niger Delta, across the entire Sahara to Hassi R'Mel in Algeria, and connect with existing lines in the Mediterranean to countries in southern Europe such as Italy and Spain.

Mega-intercontinental trade projects that are underway are therefore a reflection of the geopolitical landscape that has seen the transformation of a bipolar world to one of multi-polarity and power center realignments. This amplifies the relevance of the Trans-Pacific Partnership, which is an expanded version of the 2005 Trans-Pacific Strategic Economic Partnership Agreement. Both settlements address emergent trade issues and propose free trade among Australia, Brunei, Chile, Canada, Japan, Malaysia, Mexico, New Zealand, Peru, Singapore, the United States, South Korea and Vietnam. In a similar vein, the Trans-Atlantic Trade and Investment Partnership between the European Union and the United States; the Regional Comprehensive Economic Partnership embracing ten ASEAN members, in addition to Australia, China, Japan, New Zealand and the Republic of Korea; free trade concordats between China, Japan and the Republic of Korea, not to mention the more recent pacts between the European Union and Japan, are blueprints of emerging power centers that would have implications for American and Chinese long-term aspirations.

On this account, the world system today is best appreciated in terms of the imperial ambitions of greater and lesser powers, concentrations of influence that affect decision-making, blind allegiance to ideology, protectionism for the benefit of the rich and the accompanying social consequences. Against this setting, twenty-first century expansionism and force projection by the U.S. into the Asia Pacific, the Middle East and North Africa, catalyzed by proxy confederations such as NATO in parallel with China's widening circuit of diplomatic moves and partnerships on all continents, have introduced new levers in the realms of economic and energy diplomacy, bearing semblance to conditions that went hand in hand with World War II.

The global war on terror and the struggle for absolute control over oil and other vital strategic reserves now subordinate all other concerns and are key stimulants behind the imperial frame of mind. Added to this, seven out of the ten fastest growing economies in the world are located in Africa and this is by no means unlooked for. Furthermore, the formalization of trade pacts, as described, is a vindication of the extent to which self-efficacy among Western nations and pro-West allies is being ramped up and fortified. Stratagems such as these are meant to secure the concluding "encirclement" of Asia by America in spheres well beyond force projection. This grand scale design is intended to curtail China's assertion as a regional hegemony and thwart consortiums within its wider international embrace that could potentially place U.S. puissance at risk on an imposing world stage.

The Twilight of America's Omnipresence juxtaposes the twists and turns of twenty-first century power interplays shaping world affairs, defense policy, force projection, economic interests as well as present and future diplomacy against the metanarrative of Empire.

INTRODUCTION

*T*hat China is a growing world power is undeniable. It is currently the most populous country in the world with an estimated 1.35 billion people,[1] one-fifth of the world's population, compared to the 318.5 million[2] in the United States. Goldman Sachs predicts that by 2050 the three largest economies in the world will be China followed closely by America and India. In April 2011 the International Monetary Fund forecasted that China would have outstripped the United States as the world's leading economy by 2016.

China is presently the largest trading partner of the United States, Japan, Australia, and India and has accumulated the most prodigious holding of foreign currency in the world, totaling $2.65 billion of which $1.5 billion is in U.S. dollar holdings. Given this pace of growth the country would have accrued the world's largest consumer market by the end of this decade. In Latin America, China offers a welcome diversification of markets and is also a competitor for manufactured goods. The primary challenge for the U.S. goes beyond the commercial; the region provides 30% of U.S. oil imports.

The present text is a direct response to China's strategic progression into the Americas. The strategic advancements deployed by the People's Republic of China within the Inter-American community on multiple fronts are presenting critical and far-reaching challenges to America's political, economic and military interests. The hypothesis rests on an orthodox and enduring viewpoint propagated among occidental scholars who perceive China's propensity to eclipse the United States as imminent. On the contrary, this notion of China's imminent mastery over the global system will be shown to be without foundation..

Amidst the corral of opinions filtering into the global discourse is the notion that China has already risen to Great Power status and is now attempting to unbalance U.S. predominance. This case was made in the testimony of Peter T.R. Brookes, Senior Fellow for National Security Affairs and Director of Asian Studies Center of the Heritage Foundation before the Sub-Committee on the Western Hemisphere, Committee on International Relations, United States House of Representatives on April 06, 2005. Other illustrious thinkers, such as General Colin Powell as featured in the article "China Becoming Economic Power" in United Daily News dated June 14, 2005, acknowledged China's military enlargement, was not lured as to her capability to surpass the U.S. militarily, but saw her integration into the international system as one of overall strategic importance. In the article "China Shifts Center of Gravity" dated June 13, 2005 former U.S. Secretary of State Henry Kissinger expressed the view that U.S.-China cooperation was invaluable to the promotion of world peace.

We join this debate at a crucial stage. One of the more recent voices to have entered the argumentations is Richard D. Fisher Jr. His discourse, "China's Military Modernization," [3] offers a comprehensive and well-timed illumination on China's dramatic military build-up. Fisher contends that China is building a military capability that far exceeds its regional defense needs and is on a trajectory to compete with the U.S. and achieve Asian dominance. Similar dominance, he argues, will be extended into strategic priority areas.

I concede with Fisher's standpoint to the extent that it carries "interpretation and opinion but no answers", a remark made by Arthur Waldron, Lauder Professor of International Relations University of Pennsylvania, in the Foreword of Fisher's title. Indeed, the relative importance accorded by China to the developing world and more specifically, to strategic partner states, is unmistakable; however, in building a case I shall demonstrate that the body of contemporary sentiments fly in the face of American omnipresence. There remains no choice but to pull the rug from under the feet of these and other contenders and define this concept of omnipresence which accordingly tilts the scale of the argument decidedly in America's favor.

Professor William E Rees, respected Canadian educator and subscriber to the Journal of Higher Education, argues that policy in the sense of action is often propelled more by myth than science and is based on political expediency and what would appease public sentiment. He goes further noting that "politics is among those domains of human activity least beholden to sound academic research" and that by extension, this status quo may well be at odds with an understanding of policy issues among academics. Rees' viewpoint is embodied in the dictum of Henry Kissinger author of <u>On China</u>,[4] who asserts, "It is not a matter of what is true that counts, but a matter of what is perceived to be true."

Chris Hedges, author of <u>Empire of Illusion</u>[5] and Pulitzer Prize winner takes no prisoners in alluding to Kissinger's injunction. "Those who succeed in politics" he muses, "are those who create the most convincing of fantasies." James E. Cote and Anton L. Alular divulge the same principle in these terms: "Politics is ideological and, like other mythical constructs can be a rather ungainly concoction of fact and values, assumptions and illusions. It often gains credence only after frequent repetition and ritualistic affirmation. But while people may come to believe profoundly in a particular political position, ardent belief alone cannot true that position with reality." This chorus of acknowledgement for society's illusion upsurge and the false consistency that is lent to the chaos of existence is reason enough to concern us with what is in fact the reality.

Omnipresence denotes ubiquity, being everywhere at all times. Omnipresence spells pervasiveness, as distinct from a fixed presence in time and space: an exertion and assertion of self that frustrates obvious reach. The term refers to an overarching posture that imposes on its objects the imperative to yield, to relent. It is an imposition of will, tangible and at once virtual. It prevails and is inescapable as it defies all possible domains of power. It is a disposition on the part of the world to assimilate America. This undoubtedly distinguishes America historically from other global powers, from other contenders for world hegemony and from pretenders to ultimate dominion. This speaks of superpower, the arbitrary projection of power outwards.

Empire - a concept more at home in the contemporary lexicon contemplative of ultimate power under a new logic and structure of rule is too Lilliputian a term to befit the otherwise sophisticated description of America's dominant stature amidst the coliseum of world powers. For all practical purposes, the term "empire" conveys supreme power that is exerted over a vast number of territories beyond the demarcated jurisdiction of a particular authority. From this perspective, empire entails domination over land, sea, air and their various constituent parts. In light of the exponential changes taking place in the 21st Century, the traditional concept of empire is now defunct because it never anticipated human sway at the sub-atomic and genetic levels; influence on the collective human mind; a global information grid with a capacity to facilitate the connection of traditional forms of information with all source intelligence; let alone expansionism extending to the virtual domain and the far reaches of inner and outer space. Thus, empire is already that of the past, while omnipresence emerges as a phenomenon germane to the present and the future.

China's invigorated diplomacy has successfully masked domestic existential undercurrents of social discontent, institutional fragility, and political repression that have pitted the "Middle Kingdom" towards destabilization. These presage its ultimate collapse and the absence of critical vigor in Beijing renders such an outcome the more likely. Much of the quagmire surrounding China's tangle of interrelated histories is attributable not only to challenges presented by external rivals but also to internal turmoil that appears to reach breaking point.

The present text assesses the impact of these developments on the wider world stage while admitting to concurrent domestic challenges.

America in all likelihood will endure as the world's dominant power politically, militarily and culturally. In contrast the country's economic preeminence will fade away in gradual progression as the center of the global economic system reorients towards Africa and East Asia.

What the Chinese presence in the Americas does, however, is confirm that the preoccupation of the United States with its Middle East agenda throughout the 2000s was propitious to other interests. Against this backdrop of opportunistic fervor China adjudged the 2001 to 2008 draw - down of U.S. presence in Latin America and the Caribbean, as one of strategic opportunity.

In fact, a former Secretary of Defense William Perry, went on record in a 2005 address in Hong Kong, wondering aloud whether People's Liberation Army (PLA) generals would seek to persuade the top leaders of the Chinese Communist Party to seize the opportunity to take action against Taiwan because "the U.S. is pinned down in Iraq and will not be able to come to the defense of Taiwan."

How then will China fare as a new player and as a growing world power in the face of mature and time-tested alliances that characterize the Americas?

Historically, power shifts within Latin America and the Caribbean have evolved around anti-hegemonic blocs or alliances pulled together by complementary grievances. Prevalent amidst these distinctions is the unwritten concession that the United States is the region's undisputed dominant player. This pattern of state conduct is recognized from the standpoint that countries will promote their interests and maintain their security by joining forces and collaborating with strategically compatible partners. The dynamic has energized the emergence of many of the region's existing coalitions and intergovernmental political entities.

Power, greater or lesser, evolves around coalitions of interest. Under the balance of power thesis, when states observe the emergence of a coalition their natural inclination is to collaborate among themselves and, fearing the possibility that they may become victims of a new and emerging condominium, will proceed to form a counter-alliance. We see this pattern even in distant regions of the world where, for example, the military buildup of China, produced ramifications in the form of an active procurement agenda among other regional players in the Asian peninsula such as Japan, Taiwan and India.

Alliances so formed tend to be undergirded by ideological affinities that invariably give rise to frictions within regional systems. Affected countries may thereby find themselves pressed into rival camps, at times unwittingly. However, amidst this setting, if a common source or threat were to present itself coalitions may likely intersect in a countervailing, agglomerated response. Existing political divisions within any given camp may further aggravate the scenario.

In The Market and Masses of Latin America[6] Andy Baker, policy analyst and researcher on mass political behavior calls attention to the period of the Latin American "move to the left," noting that during and after the region's "lost half decade" most Latin American countries – Argentina, Bolivia, Brazil, Chile, Ecuador, Guatemala, Nicaragua, Paraguay, Peru, Uruguay and Venezuela- either elected presidents from leftist parties or chose ones that openly criticized the Washington Consensus. This "move to the left" has, in the 2008 estimation of Edward Schumacher-Matos, Harvard University Visiting Professor in Latin American Studies, been confined and may well have reached its limits.

Atypical fluidity and constant tilting of the balance are some of the criteria that define the present status quo of the Inter-American system. We observe how changes in power concentrations correlate with alliance formations, and in the context of our debate, with the political and economic motivations and priorities of the United States, as the overarching aficionado in Inter-American matters.

Firstly, certain members of the constituent Inter-American system are regarded as secondary players, as distinct from the first-tier league occupied by Mexico, Brazil, Colombia, Argentina and, perhaps Chile. Secondly, China has assumed a self-defining role on the wider global stage, as it makes common cause with belligerent states such as North Korea and Iran. In the early 2000s, for example, China signed a series of crucial bilateral compacts with the Islamic Republic of Iran. Among these was a Framework Agreement of the Cooperation of the Oil Sector, discharged on April 20, 2002. Furthermore, Iran has been supplying China with more than 15% of its oil imports; reciprocally, there are scores of large-scale projects in Tehran funded by the Chinese government.

These developments challenge the notion of America's unique claim to exceptionalism since China continues along a largely self-defining course in the global and regional spheres. In answer to this, however, there are counter-weights to China's aggressive diplomacy that the U.S. has effectively deployed.

In the context of China's presence in the Americas, will it be perceived as an arbiter and balance or as a competitor? Alternatively will its presence take a toll on already existing tensions? In the exercise of diplomatic engagements are there likely to be strains between Beijing and the United States that would spur the former into taking sides that involve the cooptation of local actors? Several possibilities can be mapped in consideration of the range of options that exists.

One consideration will be whether the pursuit of external trade partnerships by Latin American and Caribbean nations that are intent on veering away from overreliance on the U.S. will necessarily rebalance the scales in China's favor. Caribbean Community (CARICOM) trade with China is undisputedly on the increase. However, statistics reveal a healthy and increasing balance of trade surplus in China's favor. From an intraregional perspective, Dr. Annita Montoute of the University of the West Indies Institute of International Relations, posits that China's role in contributing to trade and economic development in the region through developmental assistance and investment, is a threefold one: it may serve as a voice for southern countries; it can assume the part of an intermediary between the Caribbean and developed societies in multilateral affairs; and it presents to the Caribbean an alternative model to time-honored aid and development assistance programs promoted by the U.S. and the E.U. What's more, while the top ten commodities exported by China to CARICOM consist of manufactured goods CARICOM's top ten exports to China are, in contrast, largely raw materials. Moreover, the Chinese market is not being fully exploited by CARICOM entrepreneurs, and Chinese businesses may well be competing against local enterprises committed to the promotion of self-sufficiency through craftsmanship and farming. In Montoute's estimation should the trend go unchecked, it would ultimately work to the detriment of CARICOM.

Another point of note is that Commonwealth membership endows Caribbean members with a unique and undervalued political cohesion that is demonstrably stronger and more enduring than what obtains in other intergovernmental bodies such as the Organization of American States (OAS) and the Association of Caribbean States (ACS). This anomaly is attributable to the common history and tradition.

Based upon Commonwealth precepts, members are at liberty to exercise the prerogative to associate with other political groupings of choice. Nonetheless, this voluntary association of sovereign states, many of which are former British colonies in combination with the United Kingdom overseas territories, remains inextricably bound to a common system of shared language, culture, law, education, democratic traditions and goals. This defining feature is of particular strategic value to the U.S. as Britain's closest ally.

Commonwealth members embrace international cooperation as an essential tool of statecraft in removing the causes of war, promoting tolerance, combating injustice and securing development of peoples of the world. Members are similarly committed to multilateralism in interstate affairs, in recognition of its primacy to the advancement of peace and progress. Further to this, Commonwealth countries resoundingly concur on the rejection of coercion as an instrument of policy to the extent that this principle is firmly etched in their respective norms and constitutional traditions. This ethic contrasts with the Chinese tradition. All in all, these canons resonate in the array of multilateral compacts that guide and govern state-to-state conduct in Inter-American affairs.

Despite these distinctions, and for all their collective creativity and intellect, Western scholars have sustained a partiality in their outlook on the Latin America-Caribbean grouping, and by extension on consequential assessments undertaken on long-range trends and possible shocks, which inform U.S. policy regarding its strategic rear. An in depth and coherent body of research including corresponding strategic assessments specific to this geopolitical area is rather parched, a fact that has contributed to the token attribution accorded to the region by contemporary thinkers. Professor Evan Ellis of the William J. Perry Center for Hemispheric Defense Studies has sought to provide a corrective to this void insofar as it relates to Sino engagement in the Americas.

Edward Schumacher-Matos, Robert F. Kennedy Visiting Professor in Latin American Studies at Harvard University and one of the principal collaborators behind the Department of Defense 2007-2008 Trends and Shocks Project, having adduced six key strategic trends, the dangers they pose to America and their defense relevance, acknowledged the predicament in these terms: "Latin American policy today has no direction. Negatives dominate it. The right has forced American policies into one set of negatives. Anti-Castro, anti-Chavez, anti-immigrant, anti-Kyoto, anti-everything that smells of social generosity or moving to the left are part of that set." Conceding to this ostensibly Westphalia predisposition, he recommends that the U.S. should henceforth reengage the region with "a positive inspiring agenda."

Significantly, one of the conclusions of the Trends and Shocks Project to which Schumacher was undisputedly committed was Beijing's negligible political and military influence in the region that would not pose a security threat to Washington for some time. Secondly, the biggest danger of China's influence would more likely be an overreaction on the part of the United States to a perceived threat that is "more idea than reality." This analysis is corroborated in a 2007-2008 remonstration put out by Susan Shirk, a former Deputy Assistant U.S. Secretary of State responsible for China who argues that, "our overreactions, which are read by the Chinese public and its leaders as an expression of our hostile intentions towards China, could turn China from an economic rival into an all-out enemy." Thirdly, the Project found that China's influence in the region would only increase, given its competitive bid for natural resources. However, a notable shift in perception has since occurred and it is reflected in Professor Evan Ellis's strategic assessments.

Consistent with this logic, nonetheless, China is resolved to pursuing a multi-tiered strategic, political, and economic agenda. Already, it has secured an impressive chain of bilateral and multilateral trade accords. Effectively applying soft power to cultivate goodwill and friendships, the Chinese have made notable progress in the procurement of raw materials and energy by increasing the country's equity stakes in resource exploitation, and formalized institutional engagements through regional intergovernmental institutions. Also significant is Beijing's arms sales dealings with Latin American countries hand in hand with an impressive and steady force build-up at home, in accordance with its ambitious military modernization program.

All these developments emphasize a shift from a foreign policy that was largely ideologically driven during the 1960s and 1970s to a more proactive and pragmatic approach that demonstrates a preoccupation with regional and global multilateralism, confidence building among its immediate neighbors in the Asian peninsula, cultivating soft power, the promotion of multi-polarity, and in general, avoiding the political meshes, such as unwavering doctrinaire stances, to which other major powers, like the United States, were historically prone.

Simultaneously, Beijing's relations with other parts of the developing world underwent apposite changes despite retaining important elements of continuity. Thus, the "new security concept" which was ushered in as part of the Five Principles of Peaceful Co-existence while effectively discharging traditional balance of power politics, fostered the concept of national sovereignty and embraced a more liberal view regarding democracy in international affairs. This paradigm, formally inaugurated through the auspices of the Bandung Conference, would thereafter have a direct impact on China's relationship with developing countries and support for the national liberation of members, was superseded by stark economic realities: – Beijing's inability to sustain foreign aid to states in sub-Saharan Africa and communist guerillas in Thailand. This diminished revolutionary posture would be a key factor in successfully broaching relations with regimes in Latin America and the Caribbean during the 1980s and 1990s.

Despite a decisively new diplomacy, the nature and extent of China's influence in the Americas is a rapidly evolving phenomenon.

The U.S. has been pursuing a constructive and conciliatory approach and this tone was reflected in the informal summit between leaders hosted by President Obama in June 2013. President Obama's assertion several years previously resonates in this caucus:

"...the (U.S.-China) relationship has not been without disagreement and difficulty. But the notion that we must be adversaries is not predestined..."

The forgoing statement's optimistic intonation, masks critical issues at stake in the global arena. A case in point is whether China is disposed to adapting to its new role as a viable democratic partner alongside the United States. Like Russia, China has resisted changing its imperial ethos to a more nationalistic position. This state of affairs is undeniably connected to China's enduring civilization, its history as a continental player and checkered past as a regional power. Unlike other Asian countries like Japan, South Korea and Taiwan China was never a vassal of America. Neither can it be said in simplistic terms that it is a typical nation state undergoing a phase of monumental transformation.

My disquisition will demonstrate that the present mindset of Chinese decision-makers is reflective of the country's key institutions of power, at the heart of which is the Chinese Communist Party (CCP). The extent to which the Party has continued to maintain an unwavering hold on the past through its policies of repression, despite the rhetoric being propagated around the world by an ostensibly new democratic elite, will be illustrated. Left unchecked, this internal contradiction has the potential of stoking instability and large-scale social unrest.

Contending Theoretical Approaches

The Challenge to Realism

One of the more expounding features of this inquiry is the phenomenon of competing conceptual models among various actors in world politics, their roles and relationships in international relations, specifically subnational actors designated as intergovernmental bodies like the World Bank Group; transnational corporations such as IBM; inter-regional and inter-continental alliances exemplified in the North Atlantic Treaty Organization as well as the rich diversity of hybrid entities that allow for both governmental and non-governmental representation.

At the most general level, an actor in world politics has been defined as "any entity which plays an identifiable role in international relations" (Evans and Newnham, 1990:6). The notion was subsequently honed by Oran Young (1972:140), who understood an actor in world politics to mean:

Any organized entity that is composed at least indirectly of, human beings, is not wholly subordinate to any other actor in the world system in effective terms, and participates in power relationships with other actors.

Based on the principles of sovereignty and international law all states are juridically equal. But one of the truisms of world politics is that nothing is distributed equally on the face of the globe whether people, their talents, climate, geographical features, technology, the quality of air or other distinctions such as resources, opportunity and capability. Consequently nation states, through their respective rulers and proxies, have historically sought to exert power and influence over others through an array of channels, the more commonplace being elected officials, influencers and latterly, through transterritorial and interconnected actors embodying the interests of very powerful nations.

It is against this backdrop that the authors of Realism have traditionally drawn on history's lessons to explain certain themes regarding the behaviors of men, considered the movers and shakers of world politics and have applied these recurrent themes to a world view so to speak or school of thought that promotes the basic need of human survival. Thus, Thucydides' depiction of the Melian dialogue contrasted the individual's desire to see righteousness rule in international relations with the reality that justice was defined by the powerful. The Melians had appealed to the Athenians' democratic sense of justice and argued their right to neutrality. The Athenians, in turn, educated the Melians on the state of nature whereby "right , as the world goes, is only in question between equals in power...[and] of the gods, we believe, and of men we know, that by a necessary law of nature they rule wherever they can." In a similar form of logic, Niccolo Machiavelli's suggested path for what he perceived as successful rule included not just relations among City-States but relations within such states. Oft-times linked to Realism, as a former soldier and political consultant to one of the leading City-States in 16 th Century Italy, this name became synonymous with the politics of underhanded, immoral, self-serving actions. This is a common misperception, perhaps a parody - the underlying rationale for Machiavelli's advice to the Duke of Urbino was not to facilitate the principalities from being led by "ungrateful, fickle, hypocrites and dissemblers, evaders of dangers and lovers of gain," but rather to fearlessly and uncompromisingly promote the effective rule of these states in a world bereft of morality while engendering popular support, since in the former's view, it was "much safer to be feared than loved."

Since World War II, Realism, also known as power politics, has dominated the world of international relations. The meaning and importance of theory, however, are only made clear by examining the prevalent misconceptions of it. So that although Realism has provided for a large number of scholars and foreign policy makers the basic assumptions for the analysis of world politics (Smith , 1989:5) as a distinctive paradigm, it continues to be strongly and very credibly challenged.

The key to understanding political Realism lies in the concept of power. Morgenthau (1949:13) contends that "international politics, like all politics, is a struggle for power, to increase power, or to demonstrate power." It has been assumed that as states have the necessary resources to exercise power, they are consequently the most important actors. And since Realists see the state as constituting the most significant actor in terms of interstate relations (Grieco, 1998) the state, acting through its government, is seen as a unitary rational actor which pursues, above all, national interests and competes in this matter with other nation states in an environment characterized by anarchy (Russet and Starr, 1989:28). According to realists, actors in world politics are defined on the basis of three criteria: sovereignty, recognition of statehood and the control of territory and population.

The challenge to Realism emerged in earnest during the mid-1970s from various scholarly developments (Banks, 1985:16) with the emergence of multinational corporations, international organizations and transnational organized groups. The unlooked for development led many scholars to question state-centrism because the theory assumes that states are the only important actors in world politics. Robert Kohane and Joseph Nye were among the first scholars to call for a revision of this state-centric paradigm because it failed to recognize the importance of non-state actors. In their 1971 essay collection, "Transnational Relations and World Politics," the authors identify the specific phenomenon of transnational interaction as "the movement of tangible or intangible items across state boundaries when at least one actor is not an agent of government" (Kohane and Nye, 1971: 722-24).

In order to test the importance of the growing influence of non-state actors, a series of empirical studies was undertaken during the 1970s. One such work, Kjell Skjelbaek's essay "The Growth of International Non-governmental Organization in the Twentieth Century," found that the number of international nongovernmental organizations had grown from 1,012 in 1954 to 1,899 in 1968 while their numbers increased from 4.7% per year in 1954-1968 to 6.2% per year in 1962-1968. Another empirical study carried out by Richard Mansbach et al, "The Web of World Politics: Non-State Actors in the Global System(1976)," relied on the Non-State Actor project using events data in three key regions – Western Europe, the Middle East and Latin America from 1948 to 1972 - in order to investigate the empirical emergence and behavior of non-state actors(Mansbach et al., 1976:14-15).Their findings indicated that half of the interactions of the regions involved nation states as actors and targets simultaneously and that 11 percent involved non-state actors exclusively. A subsequent study, the 1981 explorative work, "In Search of Theory: A New Paradigm for Global Politics," yielded equally invaluable findings which would further challenge the theoretical landscape. Having ranked by order the number of actors that appeared in their data according to frequency of behavior, and having thoroughly investigated the order by percentage of conflict they initiated, the analysis found that non-state actors are not only present but were in fact significant actors in world politics; and furthermore, that nine of the ten most conflict-prone actors were non-state actors while only eight of the 26 governments in the study were involved in any conflict at all. The conclusion was that the neglect of actor variation and diversity within the realist paradigm leads to marked distortions that make the paradigm less than complete.

The relevance of all of this to the present discourse is clear - politics within the state is fundamentally about the hierarchical organization of power; while international politics operates in the context of "anarchy" or the dispersion of power among a diversity of sub-national actors.

Emerging Powers in Global Governance

The second main body of theoretical challenges that frames this inquiry relates to the rigorous debates associated with emerging powers in global governance. This theme has set the stage for a fundamental rethinking of world politics in an era of waning dominance of U.S. power as a force for remaking the world in its own image vis-à-vis China's dramatic rise. The consensus opinion is that the relative decline of the U.S. is probably irreversible and the transition to multipolarity is well in train.

While China's rise is irrefutable, its meaning continues to be hotly contested. Central to the contentions is whether the rise represents a challenge to or a further consolidation of neoliberal hegemony on a global scale. This is based on the assumption that China is a competitor whose development aspirations have been radically constrained by a new form of global constitutionalism and American monetary power so as to conform to neoliberalism. Deploying a structurationist approach and an eclectic/regulatory analysis of the People' Republic of China, Gerard Strange argues in his essay "China's Post -Listian Rise: Beyond Radical Globalization Theory and the Political Economy of Neoliberal Hegemony," that China has in fact challenged neoliberalism by projecting its growing power through constitutionalized global governance. In point of fact, and certainly in the estimation of this book, declining American power provides an opportunity for

34

China to consolidate its long-term strategy of consensual development. So that by dint of paradox, global economic governance is in effect increasingly central to the unraveling of neoliberal hegemony.

This opens another salient point in the inquiry - what is the net result or the likely possibilities of the deconcentration of power in the evolutionary transition from unipolarity to multipolarity? The notion of "twilight" confers the idea of amorphous transitioning... it bodes the dawning of something new and seemingly undefinable. How do we define tomorrow in terms of its most probable pattern and in the face of ever-present and ever-changing cycles and self-defining frontiers?

In his essay, "Emerging Powers in an Age of Disorder," Randall Schweller offers a pathway between two extremities - the one offering a pessimistic outlook and the other adopting a more optimistic stance. Pessimists view unfolding multipolarity as a permeation of world politics by insecurity, rivalry, arms races, nationalism and fierce competition for scarce resources, themes all vigorously pursued in this book. This school of thought is rooted in historical power shifts such as those that provoked the rise of Napoleonic France and the unification of Germany. The augury of a great power-conflict end game between the U.S. and China in their perspective therefore represents a repetition of repeated cycles of global war that were responsible for the dismemberment of the old world order; accordingly beyond this time-cycle metaphor of history the pessimists predict that the future will resemble the past.

In contradistinction optimists, who are essentially neoliberal institutionalists or structural neoliberals, see multipolarity as an opportunity for great powers, both old and new, to find ways to jointly manage the global architecture while preserving the central features of the neoliberal order. This would entail a form of statecraft that embraces multilateralism, restraint, accommodation, reciprocity and cooperation all working in concert to co-manage a stable yet evolving world order. Optimists prognosticate that beyond multipolarity lies a new age of liberal peace, prosperity and progress.

Schweller develops his thesis on a middle ground, arguing that the prediction of great power conflict is overly pessimistic whereas the expectation of great power concert is too hopeful. In their stead, he introduces the notion of "entropy" as a metaphor of historical movement. This present age of entropy, according to his thesis, signals a realm of unknowable complexity typified by the flattening and chaotic nature of the world hand in hand with the rise of unbounded power, similar to useless energy. He sees world politics as succumbing to "the unstemmable tide of increasing entropy" and "subsumed by forces of randomness and enervation" and identifies three models of the concept of entropy. The models are at one in terms of the inevitability of power diffusion but are nonetheless at odds on the likely consequences of deconcentrated power. These are distinguished below:

- Great power Conflict: Emerging Powers as Spoilers
- Great -power Concert: Emerging Powers as Supporters
- Time's Entropy – Emerging Powers as Conflicted States

The differences between the three distinct models are based on the interests and roles of the respective emerging powers. How does China fare in this script?

In the first of three scenarios depicted in Schweller's schema, the great power conflict model, a gap emerges over time between the actual distribution of power in the international system and the distribution of prestige or reputation for power, throwing the system into disequilibrium in light of a declining hegemon that finds itself being forced to grant one concession after another to its challenger. The latter on the other hand is imbued with insatiable revisionism and its demands for prestige often go hand in hand with additional international responsibilities and obligations. In the case of the U.S., America was able to pay the price of its global responsibilities when the baton of global leadership was passed from Great Britain following World War II, as previously described. Assuming global responsibilities however would appear to lie beyond the PRC's grasp for many reasons which are imparted in the ensuing chapters of this book.

Schweller's second model envisages an emerging great power assuming the role of supporter of the declining hegemon and the status quo. This is a view that is widely propagated among liberals who believe that the transition to multipolarity will unfold smoothly because the world is primed for peace. They see new powers becoming seamlessly integrated into international institutions, much akin to China's transition to World Trade Organization membership. What is not accounted for in this postulation is that rising non-Western powers, like China and Russia, do not always share the U.S. and indeed Western view on global governance. A second and very pertinent consideration is that assuming increased international commitments in addition to the promotion of revisionist claims entails substantial trade-offs, for an emerging power, as Beijing has repeatedly stumbled upon. This implies, inter alia, building internal capacity by redressing internal domestic imbalances such as the rapid urbanization of the population, dangerous socio-economic dislocations and related phenomena all of which are examined in the current text. These issues have percussive internal implications for PRC homeland policies. So that while under this model a declining hegemon may be predisposed, as America now is, towards encouraging rising powers to accept more of the responsibilities of global challenges, a classic example being the issue of climate change, the emerging player may, as China has done, display a degree of reluctance in assuming its share of that global burden rather than recognize it as an opportunity to co-manage. The stance is manifestly based on the latter's residual interests at home.

China is a Conflicted State with Multiple Ideological Strands

In the third interplay, emerging powers can be construed as conflicted states with multiple identities, singly or jointly assuming the roles of "spoilers," "shirkers" and "aggressors" depending on the issue and the targeted audience. Here is where China has demonstrably and alternatively embraced each of these roles based on *real politic*. Schweller contends that in the case of China, the root of this disposition and the conduct of the state is enmeshed in multiple ideological strands harbored within the PRC, each of which characterizes a distinct genre of constituents. Moreover, the choice of state conduct is underpinned by no purposeful attempt at political reform that would otherwise mediate these fundamental distinctions.

The first ideological strand is *"conservative pragmatism"* which is the dominant posture of the ruling elite that guides policy and political action. The second speaks to *a nationalism* fueled by the media and catalyzed by growing tensions with the West over its human rights track record. The third, which has come to be regarded as *"the new left,"* is being promulgated among a minor ideological force championed by camps of neo-Marxist and neo-Maoist academics. The fourth is liberalism, which to date remains a largely marginalized ideology, and is expected to pose a serious long-term threat to the Chinese Communist Party regime. Liberalism incidentally is currently the most coherent and programmatic of all of the competing ideologies in China.

Other emerging powers which are also contenders for primacy, albeit in a regionalized capacity, as cases in point India, Brazil and Russia of the BRICS, have competing visions and adopted independent stances on many major issues. Brazil has consistently spurned attempts to urge for stronger sanctions against Iran's nuclear program. Alongside India as a leading democracy and economic engine in the global south, Brazil has consistently demonstrated its ability to flex its muscles politically speaking, vindicating its standing as a spoiler, one of the three great power models proposed by Schweller. On the other hand, India's liberal outlook places it in the other category as a likely junior partner rather than competitor of the U.S. notwithstanding the prevalence of strong Hindu nationalist sentiments and the country's long-standing ambitions to attain a credible second-strike nuclear capability.

37

Power transition theory is a didactic theory about a rising state that is on the verge of overtaking a stronger but declining one. The more systemic versions of the theory are referred to as hegemonic-war cycle theory or preponderance war theory. However, neither considers alliances in power and international politics.

Lastly, the emergence of the modern caliphate with aspirations to set up alternative political systems is compelling analysts to study anew the implications of emerging powers through a different pair of lenses. The phenomenon poses a direct threat to the Westphalian system by at once eroding and supplanting traditional geopolitical parameters. Its current manifestation, the Islamic State of Iraq and the Levant (ISIL) has coerced nations, even great powers like the U.S. and China along with their sworn backers, to alter the way they relate to each other by adopting non-traditional solutions commensurate with fifth generation warfare (5GW)... consumed in a vortex of violence, fighting for the unplanned, confronting the unknown by any available means, and unable to deal with the unexpected.

Prussian military theorist, Carl von Clausewitz, argues that military power must be focused on the center of gravity of the enemy force in order to destabilize and break it. Fourth generation force warriors, who are highly disaggregated such as guerillas, terrorists, and organized rioters apply force to an enemy without giving him a point at which to carry out a decisive counterstrike with two goals in view – to survive and to impose such a level of violence on the enemy as to create a psychological sense of insecurity, impotence and hopelessness. Fifth generation warfare (5GW) is what occurs when the world's disenchanted determine to (mis)direct their collective estrangement towards a single object which in their estimation epitomizes what they hate; what they distrust; what they do not understand or what they lack. For the moment, the ire appears to be coalescing around the global jihad that is rooted in al-Qaeda; and the target is the United States, the world's sole superpower. On this account, the ultimate challenge to U.S. international premiership is more likely to emanate from a concert of interests and not necessarily any single peer state.

PLAN OF THE BOOK

The Layout

The book comprises 19 chapters and is presented in five parts. Part I is a five-chapter examination of the elements of state power and the relative capacities developed by the U.S. and China to attain these elements in furtherance of their unconcealed ambitions. Part II consists of chapters six and seven, which survey the more recent aspects of China's economic transformation, commencing in the late 1970s. The causes and consequences of the country's persistent institutional weaknesses and the political commitment and capacity of the government to avert a possible collapse of internal institutions are hashed out.

Part III, comprising chapters eight to 12, is dedicated to America's global projection, made possible by its institutional capacities on all fronts, and in the exponential scientific and technological advancements being attained in the sphere of defense. The world of inner space and the craft of stealth endow America with a unique advantage over its principal challenger and effectively recast ongoing argumentations in support of China's prowess and looming dominance.

Parts IV and V uncover corporatism as a cultural phenomenon and as an emerging monolith in global governance evidenced in the uncontested power now being wielded by business and banking enclaves. The experience is common to the U.S. and China. The challenge to state capacity posed by corporate interests is compounded by non-conventional threats as both powers square off over vital reserves primarily energy, water, land, rare earth minerals and oil.

Chapter Contents

Chapter One affirms America's resolve to maintain prowess in all decisive domains of power - militarily, economically, technologically and culturally and bears witness to its "soft power" overtures as it assumes a more assertive role in many spheres. Drawing from a reserve of open source data, including Reports to Congress, the enquiry takes account of the extent to which the U.S. is institutionally configured to project itself abroad through the convergence of its defense and foreign policy agendas; these are uniquely interwoven into historical idealism that transcends party politics. It is these enunciated ideals that define the elements of domination.

Chapter Two outlines the universal constituents of global power status and adopts these as yardsticks in tracking China's progression to that ranking. The enquiry notes that unlike the U.S. whose meteoric rise to the status of superpower spanned a 70 year period following World War I, China is designated as a developing country that has chalked up an impressive record of fast-paced and sustained economic growth, which escalated as recently as the 1970s. Martin Jacques, author of <u>When China Rules the World,</u> is careful to note that one of the great legacies of the era of European domination is the notion of nation state to which China sought to define itself but that China is nonetheless, only latterly and still only partially, a nation state for the most part. On this basis he opts for the designation "civilization state." That being said, China's development process remains devoid of democratic norms and strongly buttressed by a peasantry that displays a tremendous capacity to adapt and innovate. Existing tensions among China's neighbors in East, South and Central Asia – countries that make up its first offensive line – are taken into consideration. Herein China's vulnerability emerges in this context despite its verifiable standing as an Asia-Pacific power. The reaction of the Chinese Communist Party to unfolding tensions in intraregional affairs is twofold. While asserting itself through retorts and open hostilities within the Asia-Pacific community, it cultivates strategic allies in an expanding westward radius of economic, political, cultural, and military alliances.

In **Chapter Three**, the global matrix of defense spending patterns is examined and that of the U.S. and China are reviewed and contrasted with the spending patterns of significant other players. A breakdown of figures discloses disproportionately high spending levels on military expansion by the Chinese government. In juxtaposing the U.S. Quadrennial Defense Review 2010 against the 2008 and succeeding Chinese White Papers, a keenly contested "race" is discernible. This conclusion is arrived at on the basis of a steady and unprecedented escalation of procurement and the increasing sophistication of acquired assets. In addition to this, China's bid to "catch up," and if possible, maintain par with the U.S. has catapulted it into reciprocal military access in the Americas. This is one of the regions of the world where the U.S. has historically relied on cooperative security arrangements, bolstered by basing footprints. In this vein, it is argued that America's global military projection, by virtue of her Basing Footprints, Unified Command Plan, and Ballistic Missile coordinating and cooperative capacities attest incontrovertibly to the formidability of its outward projection. This defense architecture, which facilitates institutions, installations, political/military coalitions and strategic partnerships spans all continents and lend credence to the material drawbacks with which any rival must contend.

In reinforcing this argument, **Chapter Four** gives an appraisal of the Inter-American security architecture and its impressive legacy of institutional coordination and interoperability while noting that despite the fact that political and ideological divergences skew the regional dialogue from time to time, the "good neighbor" policy which is a distinctly U.S.-inspired aphorism, defines and shapes hemispheric affairs.

Chapter Five juxtaposes America's strategic projection in Latin America with current campaigns in Eurasia. The latter constitutes one of the more formidable challenges that America must confront in a post-Cold War era. A central point is the Obama administration's policy of expansionism which involves difficult choices, arguably even contradictions, among these the option to exercise overwhelming military power as displayed under the Bush administration following 9/11 vis-à-vis the deployment of soft power initiatives; upholding the principle of national sovereignty while enforcing regime change; and the overreach of military power to further strengthen its hegemon which clashes with a desire to showcase its universal appeal.

Part II consists of two chapters. **Chapter Six** offers a glimpse into the current institutional imbroglio confronting the Chinese government and introduces a cross-section of perspectives. Through the lenses of one school of analysts who bemoan the absence of a blueprint for China's transition and take issue with the "experimental approach to planning and implementation" adopted by Deng Xiaoping, the discourse draws attention to alternative developmental models that potentially make way for a more open and democratized process.

Chapter Seven tracks China's economic transition to world player, lauds some of the quantum leaps made and identifies some of the counterweights that constrain the government's set goals. Among them institutionalized corruption; the absence of a democratization agenda; the insufficiency of representative forums to address and diffuse growing pockets of citizen dissent; political repression; massive urban drift and weak financial institutions whose character inspires policies and practices that ignore dire consequences. Given China's sheer magnitude, when such challenges are taken in tandem with the incapacity of the government to respond on multiple fronts to any medium to large-scale crisis, the vulnerability of the state becomes apparent.

Part III unveils the extent of America's omnipresence as an entrenched feature of the present global order. **Chapter Eight** examines the universality of American power and influence. It describes how this feature is systematically and spontaneously diffused through a range of state and non-state actors and institutions.

Chapter Nine expands on this theme by exploring tools of persuasion, their overall psychological effects on the wider public, and how they are employed through a panoply of non-state actors for the purpose of shaping ideas, influencing tastes and opinions and mustering mass support. The role of propaganda and social engineering to induce consent and to mobilize the public into a compliant collective are placed in perspective. The media is recognized as an integral aspect of the propaganda industry and a potential threat to the much clichéd democratic process that is being ingeniously engineered by the state and corporate apparatus to filter ideas and ideologies into the wider global sphere, and ultimately to shape global opinion.

Chapter Ten acknowledges present advancements and forecasts future revolutionary trends that would characterize technology and its applications in inner space. This has decisively placed the U.S. ahead of the rest of the world. In simplest terms, intelligence derived from human origins (in the human brain) and from technological origins will be ultimately projected into matter and energy by reorganizing these properties, thereby unleashing maximum levels of computation. This epoch-making brain-machine interface is already emerging in combat theaters around the world and will extend exponentially to other domains of human existence. Ultimately, there will be no distinction between human and machine, between virtual and physical. The ongoing revolution neuters the present fixation with scale and proportionality.

Chapter Eleven distinguishes cyberspace as a new and controversially mired center of gravity in the contemporary information contest sweeping across all continents, while noting that the evolution of the United States to the sole superpower of the 21st Century has been enabled to a large extent, politically and militarily, by cyberspace. The Chapter acknowledges the unprecedented spate of cyber attacks worldwide; the significant number of actors and communities that have a role in cyberspace, and the sharply divergent policy approaches adopted by U.S. and Chinese administrations to the global information system.

Chapter Twelve demonstrates how a range of statecraft tools consistently employed by America offsets China's preoccupation with size, numerals, scalability and proportionality in its calculations made to match supremacy. These attributes include having a long-term vision and strategy that is matched with a panacea to time and time again successfully co-opt allies and marshal support among partner nations. These criteria give the U.S. irrefutable advantage over China despite the latter's aggressive conduct in East Asia and the South China Sea.

Part IV examines the impact of the global economic downturn by examining its underpinnings, which are deeply tied to western financial systems. It identifies systemic cogs within the global complex that are impacting on the evolving balance of power. Forces are undoubtedly at work producing fresh centers of power and associated political and economic alignments. Either way, the U.S. and China emerge as the primary global players, economically and politically, with the European Union providing a fulcrum.

Chapter Thirteen anatomizes the global economic crisis and the extent to which it has exposed all nations to systemic risks. It recognizes that the heart of the problem is the fractional reserve banking system whereby money is being lent out in excess of what banks actually hold on their balance sheets. This financial wizardry which entails the creation of money out of thin air, virtually from a computer screen, charging interest on it, and underwriting it with a complex and almost indecipherable grid of financial instruments, is mirrored in Hans Schicht's Paper, <u>The Death of Banking and Financial Politics.</u> Therein, the author admonishes:

> *"Any permission given to the banker to issue monetary paper or forms of credit additional to the original basket is an authorization to steal, and should therefore be stamped unconstitutional. The fact that the banker is allowed to extend credit several times his own capital base and that the banking cartels, the Central Banks, are licensed to issue fresh paper money in exchange for treasury paper, have provided them with free lunch for eternity."*

Schicht states bluntly

> *"For over one hundred and 50 years, robbery has been going on, increasing hyperbolically and building to an ultimate crisis. Year after year the banker's slice of the world asset basket has been growing and growing. The banker has become the almighty.... Everybody, people, enterprise, state, and foreign countries all have become slaves chained to the banker's credit doors."*

Commiserating with this logic, the discussion traces what is substantially a system of expropriation of the like unprecedented in world history. Within the last decade the trend has galloped away, fueled by a core of bankers and financiers that have surreptitiously subjugated not only people and businesses, but also entire governments. As a consequence, all states are now at risk and the issue is to a lesser degree one of how best to maintain or wrest global leadership, and more one of how best to exert leverage, power, and influence transnational interests. Neither the U.S. nor China is immune to the dynamic. In point of fact, in the case of the U.S. the enormity and global range of its banking and financial institutions renders it more risk-prone than other countries in the world.

Chapter Fourteen maps historical contours in world hegemony and major shifts in the balance of power. As the global system careens towards increasing multipolarity, the trend is compounded by the multifaceted nature of U.S. policy, which is dispersed across multiple and often competing fronts and aimed at:

- Staving off Chinese ascendancy by seeking domination in the West Pacific. To this end the American strategy is to 'manage' Asia's maritime edge in an arc that extends from the Persian Gulf and Indian Ocean to the South China Sea and North-West Pacific. The action plan demands the preservation of air and maritime superiority
- Promoting a broader Middle East agenda central to which is supporting the security of the state of Israel. This is fraught with its own machinations that entail the judicious sequencing of military operations in an offensive campaign that targets seven countries for regime change, beginning with Iraq, to be followed by Syria, Lebanon, Libya, Iran, Somalia, and the Sudan
- Containing the ambitions of emerging powers in the Asian global south. This policy has been affirmed by Deputy Secretary of State William Burns who stated "Asia's rise has been so dramatic that it is not just remaking Asia's cities and economies – it is redrawing the geostrategic map. For instance, half of the world's merchant fleet tonnage now passes through the South China Sea."
- Contracting America's overseas interests and commitments in the face of altered domestic circumstances - a weakened domestic economy and an insurmountable national debt

Finally, the discussion takes note of emerging fissures in China's economic plans and projections. Illustrative of this, during the first quarter of 2012, the PRC was reeling under systemic tensions emanating from political and economic instability in the Persian Gulf, North Africa and, Eurasia. As a result of these developments, Beijing authorities were less optimistic about China's short and medium-term economic outlook in stark contrast to the unmitigated fervor that typified the two preceding decades.

This turnaround was reflected in Premier Wen's "Annual Report to the People's National Congress" in March 2012. He advised of the government's intent to decrease targeted economic growth to 7.5% in 2012, down from the 8% that it had previously set as the projected minimum growth target. It will be recalled that at its peak the economy had grown at an annual pace of 14.2% and as recently as 2010, held an encouraging 10.4 %. The present 7.5% growth was therefore the slowest pace registered by the country in 22 years. This prompted an attempt by the government to steer the economy towards slower and more sustainable economic expansion by pushing for a minimum average annual growth of 7% through to 2015. Beijing is hopeful that this will be attained with lessened emphasis on exports and a focus on investments in extensive domestic construction and infrastructural projects, as the country reacts to weakened demand for exports to Europe, and corresponding slumps in foreign investment from Europe and the U.S.

Section V spotlights historical parallelisms between the political and economic conditions that existed prior to and during World War II, the present welter of global financial issues, and the tendency of U.S. and Sino administrations to put into practice centrally controlled economic management in order to stave off a looming free fall.

Chapter Fifteen draws immediacy to the import of corporatism in both societies and the power wielded by interconnected and centralized monetary systems, in tandem with the banking sector, and a determinate body of opinion shapers who are backed by heavily funded think tanks and the mainstream media. This institutional leviathan constitutes "the real government" as opposed to the highly visible elected officials that daily mount the steps on Capitol Hill.

This generation of decision-makers embraces a brand of economic policy that promotes centralized planning through monetary and fiscal control. Monetarist policies performed by central banks have resulted in the debasement of the U.S. dollar further compounded by an array of retaliatory tactics deployed by the Chinese in the form of non-kinetic attacks against the U.S. and non-conventional resource-based, currency, cyber and trade wars, to name a few. Not surprisingly the existing global economic system is more fragile than ever and is becoming increasingly unstable in the absence of meaningful reform.

Chapter Sixteen scrutinizes the disproportional reliance of the U.S. on China for rare earth minerals and America's attempts to reverse the imbalance. On the one hand China is intent on controlling its 97 percent of commercially retrievable reserves and this state of affairs is aggravating already existing political, economic and diplomatic tensions among its Asia Pacific neighbors and European trade partners that continue to haggle over the practicality of pledges made under the Copenhagen Accord of December 2009. At the heart of the Accord were the imperative to reduce greenhouse emissions and the employment of strategies to limit the maximum global average temperature to 2 degrees Celsius above pre-industrial levels.

Although the Copenhagen Climate Control Conference was historical insofar that it significantly advanced the infrastructure that was required for effective global climate change cooperation, failure to arrive at a universally binding agreement has resulted in the existence of a largely unenforceable field of political intents that the

Chinese are currently exploiting to the detriment of the U.S and many of its allies. While remonstrating China's posture, the chapter challenges the U.S. to throw its gauntlet into the ring by recommitting to the reduction of greenhouse emissions and by taking cognizance of domestic research findings that underscore the deleterious effects of non-orthodox approaches to drilling and the harnessing of alternative energies.

There are other issues at play. In what now appears to be a no-win contest the limits placed by the U.N. on greenhouse emissions are now deemed insufficient to alleviate a looming crisis because they fail to account for carbon sources of fossil fuel held in reserve in the stock exchange. A horizon scan of global conservation issues for 2014 undertaken by William Sutherland et al discloses that at the end of the day governments may be forced to choose between advancing the global agenda for climate change and risking a financial crisis or alternatively risking a financial crisis in favor of climate change. The anomaly has arisen because of the discrepancy between the current stock market valuation of the fossil fuel industry which is based on known and projected fuel reserves and the commitments made by governments following the Copenhagen Conference. Placed in context it has been suggested that carbon purchased from 2013 to 2050 should not exceed 600-900 Gt Co2 for the probability of a > 20% emission rate. In actual fact the carbon embedded in the known global coal, oil, and natural gas reserves amounts to 2860 Gt CO2. Parallel to this, reliable reserves held by companies listed in stock exchanges around the world already amount to 762 Gt CO2. Irrespective of the looming climate catastrophe the industry invests over $650 billion annually in exploring new fossil energy sources and in new extraction methods. America, Britain and Australia to name a few have taken the lead in the crazed shale boom with confidence and totally unfazed. The reserves presently held in stock in the 200 largest such companies in the world are valued at U.S. $4 billion. Unless fossil fuels are burnt, the market value of these stocks held would plummet green house emissions. The prevailing dilemma is fraught with disputes., which no single nation can take on alone. For sure the business community, governments and civil society at all levels must put aside their differences to work towards concrete solutions in addressing climate change.

Chapter Seventeen takes stock of the diversity of players and the complexity of conflicts prevalent in Africa today. The Great Continent not only lies at the heart of the Sino-American contest but it also serves as a fulcrum for America's expanded military advancements across Asia all the way downwards to the South China Sea, as part of a concluding encirclement of the Chinese. Whereas the competition between the U.S. and China may appear to be the dominant factor, the chapter underscores the significance of waves of European confrontations of the past, and how they are impacting on the present amidst prevailing hostilities among regional powers, now complemented by Russia and China.

The analysis delves into the motivations behind China's vigorous re-assertion at this particular historic juncture, and employs as a first line of references, the circumstances that catapulted Europe's meteoric rise between 1400-1800 and its current downswing. Concomitant with all of this are refractory confrontations that are being propelled by ideological divergences, ethnic clashes, political divide, intensified militarization and an all-out, ominous lunge among European powers and Asian giants for the world's most prolific reserves of energy supplies, arable land, water, and vital mineral reserves.

The role of diplomacy as the quintessential art of statecraft is enmeshed not only in the business of public affairs, but also in the personal choices of elected leaders. This is the underpinning theme in **Chapter Eighteen**, which advocates the need for innovation in current diplomatic systems, given the increasingly heterogeneous make-up of global political actors, political coalitions and re-alignments, and the complexity of global issues. To what extent are these changes amenable to U.S. and at once China's interests, is explored.

Finally, **Chapter Nineteen** spells out the determinants of an ultimate resolution shedding light on the primeval element amidst the ongoing U.S. - China dichotomy. Culture emerges as the germ, driving force and postlude of the dramatic end game.

CHAPTER ONE

THE AMERICAN POLITICAL IDENTITY

The question is how America will lead in the 21ˢᵗ Century, not if it will.

Hillary Rodham Clinton,
July 15, 2009

*A*merica – a child of the Enlightenment – was born out of revolt and ire against absolute monarchy, colonialism and imperial Britannia. It has enlarged this revolutionary impulse to the paradoxical opposition against universal repression and constraint. The enlargement fueled by the Calvinist Protestant Ethic, the bonanza of capitalism in addition to technological innovation necessitates the mobilization of every state institution, functionary and resource at its disposal on the homefront and beyond culminating in America's intangible global projection.

In 2009, the incoming Obama administration was making calls for the adoption of "a whole-of-government approach" to the US foreign policy agenda and simultaneously strengthening its civilian- led tools of diplomacy promoted by the State Department. Chairman of the Joint Chiefs of Staff, Admiral Mike Mullen and Secretary of Defense Robert Gates were canvassing for the promotion of the role of civilian authorities to circumvent what they perceived as the continuing militarization of US foreign policy. They recognized that the role and missions of civilian agencies were by no means synonymous with that of the military, but rather complementary to them.

This observation was taken aboard the 2010 Quadrennial Defense Review which ultimately reflected the revised thinking:

> *"Years of war have proven how important it is for America's civilian agencies to possess the resources and authorities needed to operate alongside the US Armed Forces during complex contingencies at home and abroad. This alludes to the need for a clearly defined civilian mission.*[3]*"*

The merits of this approach were endorsed by a cross-section of academia, policy analysts and defense planners, including Professor Gordon Adams of the International Relations School of International Service and American University

Fellow, Henry L. Stimson Center (2009). An even higher level of synthesis was forthcoming several years before from then Secretary of State Condoleezza Rice; her appraisal struck a sharp cord on the role of civilian institutions of the twenty - first century by placing emphasis on governance, development and international responsibility. Her perspective was that the overarching role of the civil authority was to:

> *"....advance freedom for the benefit of the American people and the international community by helping to build and sustain a more democratic, secure and prosperous world composed of well governed states respond to the needs of their people, reduce widespread power and act responsibly with the international system..."*

In a crucial break from the Bush tradition, the current regime committed then to a "new era of engagement" based on common interests, shared values and mutual respect. These maxims would be invoked against the setting of a strategic framework designed:

- To reverse the spread of nuclear weapons, prevent their use and build a world free of their threats
- To isolate and defeat terrorists and counter violent extremists while reaching out to Muslims around the world
- To encourage and facilitate the efforts of all parties to pursue and achieve a comprehensive peace in the Middle East
- To seek global economic recovery and growth by strengthening America's domestic economy, advancing a robust domestic agenda, expanding trade that is free and fair and hosting investment that creates decent jobs
- To combat climate change, increase energy security and lay the foundation for a prosperous, clean energy future
- To support and encourage democratic governments that promote rights and deliver results for their people
- To articulate a path forward regarding involvement with inner and outer Europe, and emerging nations from the dismantled Soviet bloc.

This is an unrivalled and overpowering remit with a definitively global dimension manifesting intent, on the part of the U.S. government, to project its goals and ideals as the overarching framework of the wider global agendum. A front burner item on the administration's early agenda was the restoration of America's seriously impaired international image. To this end a dual approach was adopted – firstly, came the delivery of a series of high-profiled public speeches at strategically determined venues worldwide, including Prague, Cairo, Tokyo and Istanbul. The President himself took the podium. This was followed in close order by a succession of tactically administered deployments of Hillary Clinton, Secretary of State throughout 2009-2010. Her mission was unambiguous and indeterminate - to secure the government's resolve by reinforcing, promoting and executing America's foreign policy agenda, as envisioned and articulated by the President.

The administration formally promulgated that liberty, democracy, justice and opportunity would continue to serve as maxims of the American tradition and precepts for stated goals. These, it asserts, will be executed through "soft power" as it assumes a heightened role in development aid and in the integration of civilian and military action in conflict-ridden areas of the world.

America must plan for a future security environment that is larger than China and towards this end its strategy must be proportionately configured and calibrated. The strategy is premised on the fact that over the next 20 years the confluence of trends with rapid social, cultural, technological and geopolitical change will create greater uncertainty and this long-term trend will be compounded by:

- The unprecedented speed and scale of change; and
- The unpredictable and complex interactions among the trends themselves
- The interaction of trends and the nature of the shocks that they might generate

The resolution to the prevailing watershed is the development of an institutional agility and flexibility and the promotion of cooperation with interdepartmental, non-governmental and international partners. This admits to the importance of building a capacity that would enable America through the prolific dispersal of its "whole-of-government" institutional apparatus to influence trends and mitigate shocks in order to protect its own interests. Central to all of this is the Department of Defense whose responsibility it is to plan for a future security environment by acting to reduce risk and developing the capacity to hedge against it.

INSTITUTIONAL MOBILIZATION
Quadrennial Diplomacy and Defense Review

In a notable departure from the customary appropriations-based practice, whereby the U.S. Department of State maps its missions on a year to year basis, the 2010 Quadrennial Diplomacy and Defense Review offered instead a longer term projection of its intent, missions and capacities and identified shortfalls in resourcing. This lends to the robustness of state institutions charged with the execution of the foreign policy program.[4] The Review was also considered as a precursor to institutional reforms and corrective measures that would be adopted by the Department of State to deliver on the government's overseas programs. The document addressed:

- The range of current and ensuing global threats, challenges and opportunities that would have to be tackled in ensuing decades
- The current status of the U.S. approaches to diplomacy and development with emphasis on the relationship between diplomacy and development in existing policies and structures
- A clear statement of overarching foreign policy and development objectives specific to the U.S. policy priorities as well as expected results with an emphasis on the achievable and not merely the desirable
- A set of recommendations on performance measures to assess the outcomes, and where feasible, the impact of executing the program

The Quadrennial Review thus set the tone for an assertive and sustained response to pledges made by the President during his election campaign and immediately upon assuming office. This included undertakings made during the Fifth Summit of the Americas April 17-19, 2009 to Heads of State and Government of the Organization of American States and to other international communities such as Afghanistan, Pakistan and Iraq. A significant feature of this text was America's heightened role in delivering development aid, a primary pillar of the country's foreign policy agenda. Thus, diplomacy and defense would complement each other, at best reinforcing and producing a multiplier effect so as to maximize impact.

The State Department's commitment to furnishing the expertise and resources necessary for delivery of its foreign policy agenda was registered in the following terms:

> *"To advance U.S. interests what is required is talented diplomats to foster partnerships and negotiate needs, a top-notch military, experts in development to steer crucial investments and the material conditions of people's lives from strengthening health and education to improving agriculture and access to food and water; exports to promote transformational change, support good governance; fair and open access to global markets; facilitate the building of strong political and economic institutions and a thriving civil society."*

Alongside these Departmental schemes, the Department of Defense has been examining strategic trends, their relevance, how these may overlap to produce strategic "shocks" and how the U.S. might prepare for such events to mitigate risks and capitalize on opportunities. In formulating this appraisal, the 2008 National Defense Strategy recognized that "increasingly the Department of Defense will have to plan for a future security environment shaped by the interaction of powerful strategic trends."

It was in furtherance of this goal that a further initiative referred to as the "Trends and Shocks Project" was conceived and integrated into the wider defense posture.[5] The Project expressly mapped how key long-term global trends may overlap to produce strategic shocks and how the U.S. might prepare itself for a range of eventualities to mitigate risks and capitalize on opportunities.

Further to this, the project prognosticated that taking into account the key thematic areas (conflict, demographics, economy, environment, culture, identity, governance and science and technology) and the confluence of these trends, the only recognizable authority endowed with the capacity to deliver was the Department of Defense. Table 1.1. Accordingly, this level of military offensive leg to the strategic planning process enables the U.S. to secure "high ground" in terms of global dominance and simultaneously catapults it ahead to influence the global agenda and shape and mobilize opinion in the wider sphere.

America is the only power whose military establishment is configured to respond to the rivalries and competitions that were unleashed on the world following World War II, culminating with the prevailing global Jihad.

All ensuing conflicts, despite their diverse sources, have a common, definable and yet elusive character – they tend to be spurred by regional and local tensions, spawned by ethnic, religious or other forms of communal hostility and do not conform to international norms governing hostilities and war. Because they do not match the character of state-to-state conflict and are often among communities, they are self-defining and transnational in nature carrying with them unique and durable geopolitical complexities that interact with each other.

TABLE - 1-1
SHAPING THE FUTURE: KEY TRENDS

Categories	Examples
Conflict	• Increasing lethality and scope of irregular changes and agile non-state threats • Military operations in new domains: outer space • Rise in new military competitors: Asia petrodollar states • Increasing nuclear proliferation
Demographics	• Youth bulge: 87 percent of people ages 10-19 live in developing states • Global aging: the ranks of those over the age of 60 are growing by about 2% every year – 60 percent faster than the overall population. Primarily affects Europe and Japan. • Urbanization: By 2025, nearly 60% of global population will live in cities. • Migration between and within states to economic opportunity and away from conflict
Economy	• Continued economic growth and trade facilitated by globalization and rise of Asia • Growing gap between rich and poor within and between countries • Increasing regional and global integration of economies • Increasing Asian influence in international markets
Environment	• Growing overall resource consumption (food, water, energy, minerals, timber) • Resource scarcity and disruptions to distribution(water, energy) • Disruptive climate change leading to rise in sea level, changing climatic zones and environmental stress
Culture, Identity and Governance	• State remains dominant unit in international system • Strong but challenged U.S. leadership in international arenas (global commons) • Increasing influence of the individual, group, private sector and non-governmental organizations on the international system • Strong national and sub-national bonds sustained and reinforced through Internet communication and remittances

	• Increasing tension between individual rights and group rights
Science and Technology	• Technology Information, miniaturization/nano, bio, power, robotics • Increased proliferation of technologies and knowledge

SOURCE: Reproduced from US Dept. of Defense [Fighting Chance edited by Neyla Arnas - Table I-I]

In this vein, Philip Cerney identified four specific factors as the germ of these "durable disorders", namely:

- Competing institutional and overlapping jurisdictions of state, non-government and private interest groups
- More fluid territorial boundaries both within and across states
- Growing alienation between entities in the global system responsible for innovation and communications on one hand and disfavored, fragmented hinterlands on the other
- Increased inequalities within and isolation of permanent underclass and marginalized groups[6]

Another important backdrop of contemporary conflict in terms of long-term trends is the particularity of evolving technologies. Michael Moodie, member of the National Intelligence Council's Long Range Analysis Unit and the Global Futures Forum, estimates that despite the fact that technological innovation does not automatically translate to new military capabilities and that organizational, bureaucratic and social factors may retard progress, there are technologies in the making that would significantly influence the conflict environment. These include biotechnology, nanotechnology, directed energy weapons, advanced information systems and cheaper and more reliable space lift items.[7] Many of these effectively shift the current geographic conflict into the virtual realm thereby betraying its transnational character.

How are these "disorderly spaces", which remain beyond the boundaries of any single state, which set their own rules, define their own game plans and rules of engagement, intimidate elected governments, stoke instability between and among regions to the extent that they assume global and unlimited dimensions, monitored and commandeered?

This is a collective global responsibility, requiring a new logic and structure of rule, a single logic of rule, a juridical conceptualization and a supranational ordering. Michael Hart and Antonio Negri reckon that such an ordering had

54

found its place in the United Nations, but not as we know it today.[8] They suggest that Kelsenian hypothesis constituted the germ of the idea, envisioning "a real base of effectiveness for a transcendental schema of the validity of right situated above the non-state." They note that to date the theoretical responses to the constitutionalization of a supranational world power are grossly inadequate and that furthermore, the entire life of the U.N, from its inception to the end of the Cold War has displayed nothing more than "a long history of ideas, compromises and limited experiences more or less towards the construction of a supranational ordering."

Their quarrel with the ineffectiveness of the U.N to discharge its powers beyond the creation and monitoring of politically and/or legally binding authorities, goes to the very essence of what supranationality demands. In their view, the transition being witnessed today from traditional international law as defined by contracts and treaties to the definition of a new sovereign supranational world power, however incomplete though necessary, will push the world to the very heart of what constitutes supranational sovereignty. This constitution must embrace direction under a single conductor, "given the force to conduct where necessary 'just wars' at the borders against the barbarians and internally against the rebellious."

This new paradigm encompasses both system and hierarchy. It comprises the centralized construction of norms (which will inevitably incorporate a universal ethical foundation) and the production of a legitimacy that is worldwide. Currently, all conflicts, crises and dissensions are accelerating this process of integration and by the same measure, the need for a centralized supranational global authority. Process and need are thus the primary catalysts propelling the political evolution - this signals the twilight of modern sovereignty.

Whereas the aim of modern governments takes them to finite dimensions thereby limiting their capacities as to what they can and cannot do, the notion of supranationality and the movement towards its unbounded space and time will, in its nascent stages which we are now witnessing, erode the capacity of existing international institutions, even the very efficient ones. The question then arises as to whether the global agenda is adequately positioned to bridle this transition.

In America's estimation, her interests are the world's interests. In her statement before the Senate Foreign Relations Committee on January 13 2009, former Secretary of State Hillary Clinton asserted that "America cannot solve the most pressing problems on our own and the world cannot solve them without America." This enquiry argues that interests of the rest of the world are, however, not necessarily America's; and herein is the paradox of universality and the dialectic of omnipresence.

The projection of America on the world scene requires expansive government from within. In Machiavelli, expansive government is pushed forward by the dialectic of the social and political forces of the Republic; only where the social classes and their political expressions are posed in an open and continuous play of counter-power are freedom and expansion linked together. In contrast, the notion of supranationality is about a new imperial terrain with alternative political organizations of global flows and exchanges and any attempt to subvert or contest may well be met with enormous powers of repression. Accordingly, democracy is beyond call of reckoning amidst a supranational monolithic architecture; and the nation state, which has been the guarantor of the present international order, is the present element that is constraining the emerging supranational edifice.

Are we presently witnessing an apocalypse – the glimmer of inevitability as the door gives way to piercing rays of light illuminating the present and unmasking the forces that are already at work in resolving this global dilemma?

Like the government, capital harbors a constant need for expansion. Every limit appears as a barrier to be transcended. In other words, one of the central arguments of the Marxist tradition is that there is an intrinsic relation between capital and expansion and that capitalist expansion inevitably takes the form of political imperialism. The logic lies in what Marx saw as the constant operation of capital through a reconfiguration of boundaries, overflowing its borders and internalizing new spaces. Herein lies the potency behind America's expansionism and omnipresence - international corporatism.

Benjamin R Barber, Whitman Professor of Political Science at Rutgers University notes in his title <u>Jihad vs. McWorld</u> that today corporations have become more central players in global affairs than nations, spotlighting that they abjure the very idea of nations or other parochialism that limits them in time and space [9] In his estimation, their customers are typically "a universal tribe of consumers defined by needs and wants that are ubiquitous." Summing up the argument, he concludes that there is no activity more intrinsically globalizing than trade, no ideology less interested in nations than capitalism, and no challenge to frontiers more audacious than the market.

The political status of corporate economic power in America is integral to the respective ideologies professed by the republican and democratic parties. This concept of corporate economic power, which chapter 15 expands on, and its place on the power trajectory was identified by Sheldon S. Wolin as one of five preconditions for superpower status, all of which were satisfied during the Bush administration.[10] The others were: the power of the state itself, the integration of modern science and postmodern technologies, a military addicted to technological innovation, and religious fundamentalism. This array of powers, in Wolin's view, constantly superseded previous limits and was totalizing in the sense of infinity. The status quo was aggravated further by the imbalance, as he perceived it, between the constitutionally limited powers of government on the one hand, and the relatively unconstrained power of corporate capitalism, on the other. This anomaly was undoubtedly the result of government's reliance on corporate capital to provide major funding for the other two powers.

A further distinction can be drawn between economic power and political power. Political power, which is the power of government, is not necessarily a reflection of citizen power; in point of fact it may well be far removed from the power of the citizenry. Citizen power is all about freedom that can be exercised in order to express what people want, how they wish to be governed, the methods of worship that they chose to adopt and practice and the type of education they prefer for their children. Economic mobilization of the citizenry, on contrast, results in a de-emphasis of political mobilization, so that economic considerations supersede the political. From Wolin's standpoint, the venerated status now being accorded the economy implies that the three elements freedom and democracy as facets of political mobilization are no longer on equal footing with free enterprise which lies at the heart of economic mobilization. In this context freedom and democracy will be subordinated by free enterprise, in a relationship that obscures the political incorporation with a phenomenon that is branded by the author as economic incorporation.

The outcome of economic corporatism is manifold. Firstly, economic structures that define free enterprise are inherently autocratic, elitist, and primed for expansion and by extension, the internationalization of capital and the burgeoning of American-owned transnational corporations. Secondly, when priorities of the economy trump the political, unequal rewards ensue accentuating wealth and power disparities. Thirdly once the open market system becomes dominated by large corporations as is the case in America, the market becomes a corruptible melting pot for power concentrations. The movers and shakers behind these relationships determine prices, wages, patterns of consumption, the fate of neighborhoods, cities and states and ultimately, entire nations and geopolitical spaces. By this means, power becomes effectively internationalized. It is omnipresent.

Through the internationalization of capital the U.S. has accrued for its exclusive benefit internationally dispersed linkages that are monumental in scale and global outreach and realized by the fundamental principles of the Bretton Woods system, adopted in 1944. These were:

- America's economic hegemony in a post-World War world;
- Agreement for monetary stabilization between the U.S. and other dominant capitalist countries (Europe followed by Japan) over the traditional territories of European imperialisms, previously dominated by the British pound and the French franc; and finally
- The dictating of a quasi-imperialist relationship of the U.S. over all subordinate non-socialist countries

Bretton Woods would hitherto cede control over the global capitalist economy to a series of governmental and international organizations including the International Monetary Fund, the World Bank and last but not least, the U.S. Federal Reserve. To date, this invention continues to serve as a force multiplier for U.S. power and influence and a major pillar for sustaining American global supremacy by giving rise to an international order that not only replicates but institutionalizes abroad many of the features of the American system. This trait is not necessarily behooved to the Chinese.

Thus far, our focus on American identity has captured aspects the American narrative, as understood, interpreted and told by a wide cross-section contemporary occidental scholars and analysts. Reciprocally, how China perceives America and to what extent this perception influences and informs its foreign policy disposition is equally crucial to an appreciation of Chinese motivation and the identity or the defining character that spurs this motivation.

In 2009, a mixed team of academics (Peter Hays Gries, Qingmin, H. Michael Crowson, and Huajian Cai) collaborated in a survey in the U.S. and China respectively with the objective of exploring the structure and consequences of Chinese national identity.[11] They examined the concepts of "patriotism" and "nationalism" and the impact of these concepts on China's foreign policy stance towards the U.S. The survey entailed (a) assessing the nature of Chinese patriotism and nationalism (b) determining how patriotism and nationalism differed between America and China and (c) gauging what impact these had on Chinese foreign policy attitudes.

The conclusions of the study were rather profound in terms of their corroboration of historical biases that cloud some of the motivations behind state conduct. The key findings were that:

- Firstly, patriotism and nationalism in China are empirically distinct. This is not the case in the U.S.
- Secondly, nationalist historical beliefs are integral to the structure of Chinese national identity. Historical beliefs co-varied with patriotism and nationalism, suggesting that histories of the national past and national identities of the present are mutually constituted. Nationalist historical beliefs furthermore powerfully predicted perceptions of U.S. threats, which then powerfully affected U.S. policy preferences.
- Thirdly, the "U.S. threat" as perceived by China has distinct military and humiliation dimensions. The perceived humiliation threat had a stronger impact on China's U.S. policy preferences than military threat
- Fourthly, nationalism rather than patriotism has an impact on foreign policy preferences. Variations in Chinese nationalism, whether between individuals or across time, appear to be related to variations in both threat perception and foreign policy preferences and may warrant further research

These findings, which are supported empirically, corroborate the scholarship of Fitzgerald, Callahan, Gries and Barne, who argue that the "Century of Humiliation" is central to Chinese nationalism today. The results are also consistent with earlier research surveys that demonstrated that in China beliefs about the past affect perceptions of mutual threat.

The outcome of such appraisals underscores the importance of reconciling histories to the type of confidence building that is so necessary and central in the present climate, to China's future relations with the U.S. and for that matter, its neighbors in the Asian peninsula, such as Japan and Korea. Indeed, the policies of Mao towards peripheral societies in previous decades were a direct consequence of the rivalries and ambitions of other Asian powers, and more particularly, Japan's aggressions.

In this chapter we undertook a succinct overview of the U.S. political cast of mind, which I consider an important precursor to any concerted enquiry evolving around America's status as the world's only superpower. We have seen how America is ideologically driven to assume the realms of global dominance and how her ideals are profusely manifested in policy, strategy and application across government. We also recognize that her domestic institutions at various levels are specifically buttressed to facilitate worldwide projection and were exposed to brief

59

insights into the importance of corporatism, in terms of its political influence and international reach. Each of these themes will be segmented and exhaustively analyzed in subsequent chapters.

We then balanced our enquiry with an epigrammatic but necessary reference to elements of the Chinese identity and how the uniquely Chinese character informs the country's perception of the U.S. as a possible threat. The research study cited invoked historical points of reference that were relevant to the present Chinese disposition; however, a more comprehensive analysis lies beyond the scope of the present text.

Chapter Two examines the elements of state power and reckons on their impact on the U.S. and China as either boldly asserts itself on the world stage.

CHAPTER TWO

POWER COMPONENTS

"Instead of seeing China through the prism of a conventional nation-state, we should think of it as a continental system containing many semi-autonomous provinces with distinct political, economic and social systems."

Martin Jacques

here exists a functional relationship between the political, economic and military power of a nation and the elements of this power are derived from two distinguishable sets of properties. The first set of properties consists of relatively permanent traits such geography, natural resources and raw materials; the second set is distinguished by aspects of a more mutable nature such as a country's population, leadership, industrial, and military capacities.[1]

Properties of the latter group are shaped by a plethora of cultural and ideological indices, including the qualities of individual and collective intellect that set one nation apart from another. This theory is rooted in anthropological perspectives governing cultural patterns. With this in mind, as we discuss China, it will become increasingly apparent that the Confucian philosophy, which is deeply etched in the country's past, is very much alive in the ethic that pervades its primary institutions.

Confucianism is founded upon the principles of harmony — everything occupying a unique space and fulfilling a designated role. One of the basic tenets of Confucianism is that people owe their obligations to rulers within a social hierarchy. Another is that each person holds a unique station with attendant duties and responsibilities. This principle applies equally to persons at the upper rungs in society as it does to the lowliest of peasants, all strewn along an expansive social continuum. Confucianism, however, has undergone many reforms in its history and can be regarded as a synthetic tradition; certain core values have nonetheless been retained such as the primacy of family life and extended networks of clans, the nodal role of the state, the resolution of conflict through mediation rather than litigation, and the importance of values and morality as essential regulators of human behavior.

It is to the credit of American big business that China's integration into the world economy has been negotiated. An extension to this was China's capacity to assume many of the indicators of a world power. Having achieved this China is now challenging the U.S. its principal sponsor.[2] The 1980s -1990s marked this irony. Firstly, the 1972 accord between the U.S. and China presaged the establishment of formal diplomatic relations between the two countries that ultimately occurred in 1979. Secondly, the U.S. provided crucial support for China's admission to the International Monetary Fund and the World Bank in1986. Thirdly, in 1982 China was awarded observer status to GATT. A fourth and very critical point was that from the 1980s and onward, the U.S. had become the paramount market for Chinese exports. Finally, with the collapse of the Soviet Union in the 1990s China's gaze towards the U.S. as an economic and political ally became even more accentuated.

In this chapter we focus on those elements considered to be inextricably linked to China's ascent to great power status, namely its ability to feed itself, its access to critical natural resources, military capability, the quality of military leadership and the robustness of its industrial base. These constitute primary determinants of a country's domestic stability and its capacity to project itself as an international state actor.

ELEMENTS OF NATIONAL POWER

Food Supply

Self-sufficiency in food, the most elemental of natural resources exerts significant influence on a nation's power. A nation that is self-sufficient in food supply has a decisive advantage over countries that are heavily reliant on food imports. Conversely, deficiencies in homegrown food are a potential source of weakness to a country socially, economically, and politically. Despite these conclusions, the status quo of a country in this area can be altered by artificially- induced developments triggered by a range of measures such as modulations in consumption patterns, the levels and scale of agricultural output, and in localized conceptions about agricultural techniques. These are public policy tools that are at the disposal of any government.

The hallmark of self-induced change occurred in China during the "Grassroots Socialism" era. Promoted in 1958, this chapter of its history was marked by the launch of a policy referred to as The Great Leap Forward, inspired by Mao Zedong. In rolling out this policy, People's Communes were established across China's vast expanse of rural areas while peasants were made to engage in single commodity production of steel to the detriment of agricultural production.[3] Notwithstanding the avowed determination of the government to exceed in agricultural yields, there was a dramatic decline in the output of most goods, a fact that precipitated the "Great Chinese Famine" and subsequently, the reneging by the Mao regime of its palpably calamitous policy.[4]

In one of the first econometric studies undertaken to assess the relative importance of the causes of the Great Famine, Justin Lin and Dennis Yang argue that a combination of factors had contributed to the deaths of over 30 million burgesses during the famine of 1959-1961.[5] The primary reason attributed was the agglomeration of institutional changes, natural calamities and policy blunders. Later studies have unearthed the fact that during the years of the famine, output had actually dropped by 15% in 1959 and had fallen even further to 70% in 1961-1962. The famine was exacerbated further by the implementation of certain rural/urban and institution-based policies governing the distribution of grain that was produced. Yet another variable was the ill-advised adoption of revolutionary agricultural techniques, specifically "close planting" and "deep-ploughing." A Russian pseudo-scientist—Trofin Lysenko—whose ideas were highly regarded by the Mao regime advocated such techniques.

The late 1990s saw a reversal of practice with the change in Chinese leadership and the onset of policies of pragmatism and economic openness introduced by Deng Xiaoping. During that period, the government introduced countervailing measures including targeting reductions in capital investment heavy industry, increasing prices paid by the state to farmers and arranging a series of bonuses to raise workers' incomes. The communal labor system was dismantled and instead, fields were leased out to farm families on terms that allowed greater autonomy in their choice of cultivated crops.[6] These measures resulted in an increase in crop yields and general productivity levels. Additionally, the rural population, of its own volition, diversified into light industry and trade on terms that were not necessarily fatal to overall per capita food output.

The future of food supply is being re-defined by scarcity where a world of 9 billion people is confronted with political upheaval, scarce resources, and soil mismanagement.[7] Wang Tao, a leading Chinese desert scholar has reported that each year some 1,400 square miles of land in northern China is degenerating into desert as a result of soil erosion. Wang's observation is corroborated by satellite imagery disclosing two major desert bowls on the earth's surface, one stretching across northern and western China and western Mongolia; the other across Central Africa.

Given the fact that the world would need to increase its food supply by 70% in the year 2050, China's current dependency on food import, when taken with parallel factors such as desert encroachment and massive urban drift of the peasant population into the cities in search of employment, are principal factors that will compel the government to move speedily to mitigate the potential of future famine.

Raw Materials

No less vital to China's survival is accessibility of raw materials, particularly in light of its military modernization program. The absolute and relative importance that raw materials hold for a nation's power is correlated with the technology of warfare being practiced at the relevant time in its history. This relevance has been heightened with the mechanization of warfare.

Fundamental changes in technology and industrial production for military advancement purposes have assigned new values to basic metals such as coal, iron, copper, lead, manganese, sulphur, zinc, aluminum and nickel. An established illustration of this is the release of the uranium atom and the harnessing of its energy for application in nuclear warfare. This unparalleled accomplishment has led to a modification of the actual and potential hierarchy of nations in terms of their relative state power. On this note, China's place along the trajectory of nuclear states (now ranking tenth), has undoubtedly reinforced her status as a rising power.

Today about 63% of the world's uranium is produced in Kazakhstan, Canada, and Australia and an increasing proportion of this numerical (now 36%) is produced by means of in situ leaching. Table 2-1 shows Production in mines by tons for the five-year period 2005-2009.

At the end of 2009, 57% of uranium produced worldwide was by means of conventional underground and open pit methods; 36% was by means of in situ leach (ISL) and in 7% instances uranium was derived as a by-product. In terms of plant capabilities, conventional mines are typically equipped with mills that facilitate the crushing of the iron ore, which is thereafter grounded and leached with sulfuric acid to dissolve the iron oxides.

TABLE - 2-1
PRODUCTION OF URANIUM (IN MINES)
BY COUNTRY 2005-2009

Country	2005	2006	2007	2008	2009
1.Kazakstan	4,357	5,279	6,637	8,521	14,020
2.Canada	11,628	9,862	9,476	9,000	10,173
3.Australia	9,516	7,593	8,611	8,430	7,982
4.Namibia	3,147	3,067	2,879	4,366	4,626
5.Russia	3,431	3,262	3,413	3,521	3,564
6. Niger	3,093	3,434	3,153	3,032	3,243
7.Uzbekistan	2,300	2,260	2,320	2,338	2,429
8.USA	1,039	1,672	1,654	1,430	1,453
9.Ukraine	800	800	846	800	840
10.China	750	750	712	769	750
11.South Africa	674	534	539	655	563
12.Brazil	110	190	299	330	345
13.India	230	177	270	271	290
14.Czech Republic	408	359	306	263	258
15.Malawi	-	-	-	-	104
16.Romania	90	90	77	77	75
17.Pakistan	45	45	45	45	50
18. France	7	5	4	5	8
19. Germany	94	65	41	0	0
Total World Tons, U3 O8	41,719	39,444	41,282	43,853	50,772
	49,199	46,516	48,683	51,716	59,875
Percentage of World Demand	65%	63%	64%	68%	76%

SOURCE: WNA Market Report Data (Retrieved November, 2010)

At the mill of a conventional mine or treatment plant of an ISL operation, the uranium is separated by iron exchange prior to being dried and packed, usually as U3 O8. Some mills and ISL operations use carbonate leaching instead of sulfuric acid, depending on the ore body. Where uranium is recovered as a byproduct, the treatment process is likely to be even more complex, demanding expanded infrastructural capacity.

Three facts assume a new prominence on the basis of our power calculus, namely:

- That in 2009 no more than ten countries globally enjoyed controlling interests in marketing 89% of the world's uranium mine production.

- China now ranks among the top 10 countries in the world thus assuming a prominence in power calculations on the basis of uranium production from mines.
- At the end of World War II, the United States and the Soviet Union, the primary adversaries (and having each attained the status of great powers), had attained near self-sufficiency in the very war materials that serviced their industrial capacity for waging war.

Regarding supply and demand of copper, by the mid-2000s China had become the world's largest copper consumer outstripping U.S. demand, absorbing 6% of available global production and consuming roughly one-third of the global output of steel, 40% of cement and 12% of energy consumption.

Oil

As was the case with the emergence of uranium in the world market, the importance of oil has created a shift in the relative power of politically leading nations. The historic oil embargo imposed by oil producing countries in 1973-1974, followed by sudden and prohibitive price increases per barrel of this commodity, brought into focus the power wielded by oil producing states around the world.

Having considered the long-term implications of this trend for U.S. vital interests, the 2006 Annual Threat Assessment of the National Security Agency (NSA) flagged jurisdictions deemed to be direct national and international concern on the criterion of state conduct, namely

- Russia's assertiveness towards the Ukraine and Georgia
- Iran's nuclear brinkmanship; and
- A "populist petro-diplomacy" being flaunted by Venezuela's president, Hugo Chavez

The Agency then sounded a cautionary note in presaging foreign policy tensions apt to stoke global agitation by Chinese (and Indian) firms, intent on "inking" new oilfield development deals abroad and purchasing stakes in foreign oil and gas interests.

Within 36 months of promulgation of the Assessment, the 2010 buy-out of the Aramco subsidiary based in the Dutch Antilles by the Chinese legitimized its concerns. Not only will this development have the potential to increase oil investment and overall global supplies, but simultaneously, it will more readily enable countries such as Iran, Syria, and the Sudan which already pose a significant national security threat to the U.S.

In the context of the wider international societal implications of this stir, formerly powerless states are now able to exert decisive leverage over countries that otherwise possess all the implements of state power at their disposal, with the exception of oil. The latter grouping has hastened to initiate a raft of expedients to barricade themselves from the vicissitudes of international oil supply manipulation. Among the cornucopia of counter- measures resorted to are: restrictions on domestic use; stockpiling of reserves; and executing programs designed to develop alternative sources of energy. These now constitute the current "game changes" underway in the global energy security impasse.

Russia now sits atop one-fifth of the world's natural gas reserves, supplies Western Europe with a quarter of its needs and delivers the bulk of oil through pipelines crisscrossing the Ukraine and Belarus. Its sights are set on energy markets further east and pipeline projects with China. Apart from that Eurasia accounts for three-quarters of the world's known gas resources, as we speak.

Jeremy Black in his book, "Great Powers" predicts the emergence of a "resource war" that is likely to have precipitous international consequences. He foresees that "surrogate struggles will be mounted via client and allied movements and Cold War methods would consequently be revived in order to stage the resource war." These events, as he sees it, will have implications on the balance of power since "in the absence of an ideological dimension among a number of major powers competing for raw materials, shifting alignments will be created."

Black further identifies the U.S. and China as principal contenders in the ensuing foray with India, Japan, Russia and the European Union occupying a designated second tier of countries.

The Chinese position on this is based on convenient pragmatism—that the Americans, Europeans, the Japanese and "other friends of the West" have already claimed the lion's share of the world's energy supplies. As a latecomer to the international energy market, as Susan Shirk observes, Beijing is now cornered, thus compelled to proceed along a path of bilateral trade relationships with countries like Sudan, Burma, Venezuela and Iran – countries in which U.S. sanctions forbid American companies from doing business[8] These engagements incontrovertibly run counter to the U.S. foreign policy agenda whereby urgent steps are being taken to isolate these very countries, by political and economic means. As case in point to bolster this concern, close bilateral ties with Burma will furnish China with leverage to exploit the use of naval facilities on several Burmese offshore islands in the Indian Ocean and exert itself in Southeast Asia and the Strait of Malacca.

China ranks among the top 20 oil producing countries in the world but is a non-exporter of that product. Oil dependency has therefore become a basis for Beijing to energize the country's diversification drive as local oil companies actively stake out the globe to acquire equity oil that is reckoned to be secure.

The Organization of Petroleum Exporting Countries (OPEC) Monthly Oil Market Report (October, 2010) advised that almost all of the anticipated growth in oil demand throughout 2010 was attributed to the non-OECD region and that China's "overheating economy" had pushed the country's oil demand up by more than 5.6%. This was equivalent to almost half of the total world oil demand growth. The rest of the non-OECD regions were simultaneously pulling for more oil usage in 2010, exceeding 0.5mb/d.

In noting China's economic indicators, which were exceeding expectations pushing the GDP to 9.5% growth hand in hand with oil usage, the country's oil demand growth was forecast at 0.4mb/d in 2010, averaging 8.7mb/d. Table-2-2.

The enquiry notes China's conspicuous oil outreach in the Americas, particularly with Venezuela, which is also an acknowledged major U.S. supplier. Also pertinent is the fact that the overheating of the Chinese economy and corresponding escalation in demand for oil has been cited by OPEC as one of three continuing challenges to the global economic recovery; the others being the sovereign debt situation in the Euro-zone, persistent high unemployment and a depressed housing market in the U.S.

The issue here then becomes not one of whether China is a friend or a foe in relation to the U.S. but rather, what kind of strategic challenge does it pose to U.S. claims amidst competing and yet complementary stakes in economic provinces.

TABLE - 2-2
WORLD OIL DEMAND FORECAST FOR 2011, mb/d

	2010	1Q11	2Q11	3Q11	4Q11	2011	%
North America	23.68	23.89	23.83	23.85	24.01	23.89	0.91
Western Europe	14.21	14.07	13.97	14.17	14.19	14.10	-0.79
OECD Pacific	7.66	8.10	7.27	7.19	7.92	7.62	-0.58
TOTAL OECD	45.55	46.06	45.06	45.20	46.12	45.61	0.13
Other Asia	10.04	10.13	10.33	10.13	10.34	10.23	1.91
Latin America	6.05	5.92	6.17	6.34	6.28	6.18	2.04
Middle East	7.26	7.40	7.33	7.67	7.44	7.46	2.69
Africa	3.27	3.34	3.31	3.21	3.35	3.30	1.11
TOTAL DCs	26.62	26.79	27.14	27.34	27.41	27.17	2.05
FSU	4.03	4.02	3.80	4.21	4.26	4.07	1.06
Other Europe	0.68	0.67	0.61	0.64	0.68	0.65	-4.22
China	8.71	8.65	9.22	9.49	9.17	9.13	4.90
TOTAL "OTHER REGIONS"	13.42	13.35	13.63	14.33	14.11	13.86	3.28
TOTAL WORLD	85.59	86.20	85.83	86.87	87.64	86.64	1.22
Previous Estimate	85.51	86.11	85.69	86.74	87.67	86.56	1.22
Revision	0.08	0.08	0.15	0.13	-0.03	0.08	0.00

SOURCE: Organization of the Petroleum Exporting Countries, Monthly Oil Market Report, October, 2011

Industrial Capacity

The possession of a robust industrial base is another factor that lends itself to state power. This hallmark sets countries apart, distinguishing between those countries with potential national power from others with actual national power. A country's industrial base is reliant upon the quality of its productive capacity, levels of managerial organization, technological capabilities, and propensity towards inventiveness and sense of business acumen. These factors all feature prominently in the calculus of China's rise.

According to the U.S. Department of Commerce, China's industrial production had grown by 22.9% in 2006 alone. A related study undertaken by Duke University, which can be regarded as a barometer for future industrial

69

potential, disclosed that in the year 2004 China conferred 351,000 four year degrees in engineering, compared to 134,000 in the United States.

As a global power, China's dominance in the South-East Asian region is bolstered by a modern military that is preeminent in all its aspects.

In contrasting China with the United States and the Soviet Union, which were at once peer rivals and world powers, this enquiry notes that during the Cold War the U.S. and the Soviet Union were able to draw upon their strength from an industrial base that was endowed with vast amounts of coal and iron as well as a robust infrastructure of industrial plants. The latter could deliver on the basis of the transformation of raw materials into industrial products. Industrial capacity continues as a similarly accentuated feature today in countries possessing vital resources such as capital, expertise and raw materials. Potentially, China is configured for this quantum leap forward.

It is noteworthy that the most expansive industrial base in China, in the Northeast, has survived the persistent influence of the planned economic system of the past and in the process lost its lead place in the country's contemporary reform and opening up. Long-term policy support for this and other regions will spur a much-needed momentum for the wide- scale revitalization of non-coastal areas. These areas could then serve as part of China's expanding industrial foundation.

Military Preparedness

Paramount to national power is a country's military preparedness. Following the founding of the People's Republic of China in 1949, a new era of constructive political and economic relationships was inaugurated. China's domestic needs have compelled a look beyond its immediate and more familiar peripheries for additional markets, new investment destinations and natural resources, and complementary to this to create a military establishment commensurate with its international status.

Fifteen years ago, Zbigniew Brzezinski declared that America maintained a technologically peerless military establishment, was the only nation with effective global reach, and stood undisputedly supreme in all four decisive domains of global power—militarily, economically, technologically and culturally. Militarily, the U.S. was maintaining a clear lead in major innovations in warfare technologies. These were particularly conspicuous in the following confrontations: the submarine which was used in the first World War by Germany against British shipping; the tank which was employed in concentrated numbers at the closing of

World War I; strategic and tactical coordination of the air force with land and naval forces following World War II; and more recently, the possession of nuclear weapons and unmanned craft capable of discriminating and inflicting mass destruction.

In all these areas America clearly outstripped the rest of the world.

Brzezinski's conviction was reformulated in the 2006 Quadrennial Review, which remitted China's status as "the greatest potential to compete militarily with the United States." By 2011, the commentary would be a clichéd concern warranting clear-minded re-examination in an openly competitive global theater in which the Chinese brand of military diplomacy was being enacted within the Americas.

The Introduction of this book alluded to the alteration of China's Cold War ideological goals from an insurgent revolutionary agenda of hostility towards the capitalist world to a retreat from that path. China is now vying for first world economic status around the table of eminent global players; the reforms put in train in 1978 by Deng Xiaoping displaced the Stalinist-styled central planning with a modern market economy. Another diplomatic tool being applied is its soft power approach.

Opponents in Beijing, however, have advanced competing viewpoints on some of the existing policies, and are fiercely advocating for a dramatic military buildup. The Politburo Standing Committee, for example, has been a particularly active agitator for this cause. Possessed of self-ascribed temerity and political clout, the Committee has remonstrated that China's pacific initiatives should run parallel to an equally aggressive and offensive war-faring impulse, an assertion that is likely to have prompted the recently revised government position favoring military expansion.

China's Military Policy

The 2008 Biennial White Paper is among the most updated, wide-ranging, authentic, and publicly accessible authorities on Chinese military policy and strategy. The sequel in 2011 was based on many of the earlier predictions. Both editions offer an official roll out of the military and strategic intentions of the government to protect its territory and people while working alongside the international community in constructing a peaceful, prosperous and harmonious world.

71

The Strategy is described as one of "active defense," connoting that China will only engage after an enemy has attacked and will not seek hegemony or engage in military expansion at any time, irrespective of how developed she becomes. There has been a demonstrated shift in policy between what obtains now and a decade or so earlier, that of preparing for the likelihood of a large-scale nuclear war. In contrast to this posture, the Chinese are advertising their engagement in what is described as "peacetime construction."

A new importance has been placed on deterrence in crisis and wars, the significance of bilateral, multilateral and regional engagements as tools of deterrence and the promotion of a leaner and more modernized military configuration. This revised configuration will facilitate a wider continuum of activities and responses ranging from emergency rescue, disaster relief, construction and national development.

The modernized military will thus reflect features that are specific to these grand designs, namely:

- "Informationalization": a coordinated network-centered enhancement program that pervades all capability areas and will ultimately prove to be a major performance measuring criterion
- "Leapfrog Development": whereby a commitment has been made to develop equipment that is not only technologically advanced but permits a reduction in the size of the armed forces, to be replaced by reforms and upgraded within the national defense reserves
- "Enhanced investment" in large-scale air defense
- "Force Protection planning," by which the army will migrate to a position of trans-regional mobility. Individual army units will thereby be diminished in scale (made smaller and lighter), with increased emphasis on aviation

The "force protection planning" component of modernization is illustrative of decisive shifts in force configuration. Further modifications will take the following form:

- Development of capabilities for long distance maneuvers, rapid assaults and special operations
- In terms of seaborne capabilities, the navy's equipment will be upgraded and improved to fight in distant waters
- Regarding aerial capabilities, the Air Force will be transitioning from territorial air defense to offensive and defensive operations; accordingly, there will be enhanced capabilities in reconnaissance and early warning, air strikes, missile defense and strategic projection.

Nuclear Capability

The country's current arsenal is configured to provide a range of deterrents by means of standard nuclear long-range missiles, ballistic missiles tipped with conventional rather than nuclear weapons, counter space attack capabilities and non-kinetic means of damaging critical nodes at a distance. No significant investments have been recorded in new nuclear capabilities. Rather, indications are that the Chinese artillery force (its main provider of nuclear weapons) would maintain the status quo with the issue of conventional and nuclear weapons upon request from the Military Command.

Strategic Rollout

Of cardinal importance is the fact that China has the most active land-based ballistic and cruise missile program in the world. She is currently developing and testing several new classes and variants of offensive missiles, forming additional missile units, qualitatively upgrading certain missile systems and developing methods to counter ballistic missile defenses.

In the sphere of aerial assets the PLA is acquiring a fleet of highly accurate cruise missiles which includes: domestically produced ground-launched DH-10 land attack cruise missiles; domestically produced ground and ship launched YJ-62 anti-ship cruise missiles outfitted on the domestically produced LUYANG 11-class guided missile destroyers (DDGs); Russian SS-N-22/SUNBURN supersonic ASCM outfitted on China's OVREMENNYY-class DDGs acquired from Russia; and Russian SS-N-27B/SIZZLER supersonic ASCM outfitted on China's Russian built KILO-class diesel electric submarine.

By the end of 2009, the PLA had already deployed between 1050 and 1150 CSS-6 and CSS-7 short-range ballistic missiles to units opposite Taiwan. Variants of these are being introduced to improve upon ranges, accuracies and payloads. The PLA is also developing anti-ship ballistic missiles (ASBM) based on a variant of the CSS-5 medium-range ballistic missile. This missile has a range in excess of 1500km and is armed with a maneuverable warhead. When integrated with appropriate command and control systems, it delivers on a capability to attack ships, including aircraft carriers such as U.S. carrier battle groups in the Western Pacific Ocean.

Dr. Andrew Erickson, China expert at the U.S. Naval War College observed that, "China does not want to start a war but rather seems to wield its military might to win without fighting by deterring actions that it views as detrimental to its core national interests; one such interest is to deter Taiwan from declaring independence." For this reason China is currently focusing on a regional anti-access or area denial strategy.

Nuclear forces are also being modernized with the addition of more serviceable delivery systems, as for example the road mobile, solid propellant DF-31 and DF-31A intercontinental range ballistic missiles (ICBN). The latter has a range in excess of 11,200km and can reach most locations within the continental U.S. There is speculation that a new road mobile is being assembled with the capability of carrying multiple independently targeted re-entering vehicles (MIRV).

In addition to bolstering domestic nuclear capabilities China has been actively enabling countries that it deems to be of strategic advantage. In mapping such maneuvers, Fisher discerns a hierarchy of state actors which he profiles as "terrorist linked to either a Sunni Muslim terrorist faction, (possibly linked to Osama bin Laden), or a radical terrorist Shiite faction with ties to Hezbollah or Iran," all occupying a first tier.

Pakistan, Iran and North Korea have been designated as "first-tier strategic partner states," on the basis of their readiness and ability to share and transfer ballistic missile technology to other belligerent partners. Pakistan had been tagged for transfer technology to North Korea and Iran. Similarly, Iran had been tracked in the transfer of cruise missile technology to Hezbollah while North Korea has shared ballistic missile technology with Pakistan, Iran and Syria. Saudi Arabia, Syria, Egypt, Bangladesh, Turkey and Brazil, in Fisher's calculations, warranted "second tier" classification.

Abdul Qadeer Khan, founder of Pakistan's nuclear program, having admitted to selling nuclear equipment and technology to Libya, Iran, and North Korea spent some five years under house arrest in Pakistan. He was finally released in 2009. His dealings were in fact state-sanctioned. In the mid-1990s, there were no less than 13 high-level government-led missions from Pakistan to North Korea, comprising scientists and military officers. The objective of these sojourns was to assist North Korea in designing and equipping its nuclear facilities in exchange for North Korean assistance in Pakistan's missile technology long-term scheme. The upshot of these exchanges was the interception of a cargo ship containing aluminum tubing in the Suez Canal in April 2003, following Germany's calculations that its contents were bound for North Korea. The specifications of the tubing suggested that they may have included P-1 centrifuge components intended for use as outer casings for G-2 (P-2) centrifuges, of which A.Q. Khan had written extensively, a fact that was subsequently confirmed by Pakistani President, Pervez Musharraf, in August 2005.

China's mission is evidently to serve as a catalyst for secondary proliferation among states. Chapter 3 of Fisher's <u>China's Military Modernization</u> provides a didactic and insightful account of sales, transfers by consignment, and technical assistance among strategic partner countries.

Blue Water Navy

Regarding naval prowess, the PLA boasts of being the largest force of principal combatants, submarines and amphibious warfare ships in Asia. Its naval assets include 75 principal combatants, in excess of 60 submarines, 55 medium and large amphibious ships and approximately 85 missile–equipped patrol craft.

A new military base has been installed in Hainan Island; its capacity can accommodate both attack and ballistic missile submarines and advanced surface combatants. This base provides direct access to international sea lanes and permits the stealthy deployment of submarines into the South China Sea. Additionally, the country's first aircraft carrier scheduled to commence sea trials late in 2011, placed China among a select global bracket of countries invested with similar types of naval assets. Table 2-3.

China's current force of nuclear attack submarines is being expanded and may be complemented by a further five advanced type 095 SSNs to the present inventory. 13 SONG-class (Type 039) diesel electric attack submarines are on the current inventory and 15 additional hulls are under construction for this class. Together the SONG SS, YUAN SS and SHAN SSN will be capable of launching the new CH-SS-NX-13 ASCM, once the completion and testing of the missile has occurred.

TABLE - 2-3
Aircraft Carriers per Country, 2011 01 June

Country	No. Aircraft Carriers
1. United States	11
2. Italy	2
3. Spain	1
4. Russia	1
5. India	1
6. Brazil	1
7. Thailand	1
8. France	1
9. United Kingdom	1

SOURCE: Jane's Fighting Ships
[Aircraft 50 and over Speed 29-30 Knots]

A range of airborne early warning and control aircraft are being developed, including: the KJ- 200 based on the Y-8 transport for AEWC, intelligence collection and maritime surveillance; the KJ 2000, based on a modified IL-76 transport and airframe; 2 LUYANG 11-class (Type 052C) DDGs fitted with indigenous HHQ-9 long-range surface to air missiles (SAM); 2 dUZ HOU-class (Type 051c) DDGs equipped with Russian SA-N-20 long-range SAM and 4 JI^ NGKAI11- class (Type 054A) guided missile frigates(FFG) to be fitted with medium-range HHQ-sixteen vertically launched naval SAM. 60 of the new HOUBEI-class (Type 022) catamaran fuel missile patrol boats each of which can carry a weight of up to eight YJ-83 ASCMs have already been deployed.

Driving this impressive inventory is a strategy on China's part that is informed and influenced by a tradition of strategic literature which peddles the vigorous embrace of war as "an essential art that demands preparation and consideration" as mirrored in Sun Tzu (596-544 BC) The Art of War and complementary writings subscribing to subterfuge that incorporate "the employment of deception, infiltration, bribes and sex to undermine enemies."

Military Leadership

Focusing on the civilian-military relationship in China, Chua Li Chen, Director of Research of the John L. Thornton China Center, noted that there has been a pervading concern on the part of the Chinese government over the power and influence of the military despite the absence of any serious challenge from the latter. Notwithstanding this concern the intent of the government is to strengthen the capability of the military and attain this through appropriate increases in defense budgeting. Chen's perception is supported by several factors chief of which are the ineffectiveness of civilian leadership, heightened social tensions, and public dissent alongside the PRC's clichéd "great power" aspirations in a fiercely competitive world environment.

Against the setting of domestic and overseas tensions, the role of the Central Military Commission (CMC) is pivotal to our debate. When the Commission was established in 1982, the intent of the government was to strengthen civilian control over the military by underscoring the role of the People's Liberation Army as the recognized defender of the state itself. Domestic policy, in contrast, would be the preserve of the civilian administration. It was also envisioned that the Commission would provide another layer of supervision, distinct from "party supervision," with Commission members being elected by the Central Committee of the Communist Party.

To date, the Central Military Commission retains responsibility for directing China's 2.25 million strong armed forces, comprising active and reserve components of the PLA, the Chinese People's Armed Police Force and the militia. The active components of the PLA consist of the standing army, which is essentially responsible for defense, control and social order and a second body of troops, the reservists which are incorporated in times of war, or when called upon, to assist in the maintenance of social order. The latter arrangement is in effect a cooptation.

The Chinese military leadership carries tremendous weight in domestic politics. This was expected to have played out, politically speaking, at the Eighteenth Party Congress scheduled for 2012. A large-scale turnover of top appointees was envisaged, a development no doubt critical to how China configures itself to traverse an unchartered path in its contested new world role from 2012 and beyond.

The military elite constitute a major sub-group in the Chinese Communist Party. Of the 371 members of the Committee attending the Seventeenth Congress, sixty-five or 18% is appointees of the Central Committee. Based on the current attrition chart, the following changes were imminent:

- Seven out of ten current members of the CMC were expected to retire in 2012
- The next layer of newcomers to replace these seven, were occupying all the top positions in the military, namely: directorships of General Staff, the

> Political Department, Logistics and Armaments as well as commanderships of the three major services – air, navy and artillery.

- Two of the three youngest leaders most likely to assume command positions held PhDs in engineering and accumulated extensive work experience in aerospace and missile technology – a guarantee to C 4-1 command, control and intelligence infrastructure.
- The congress was disposed to install current commanders of the seven military regions into top important directorship posts

Amidst this build-up are compelling domestic issues that include:

- Rising political tensions
- Economic disparities
- Public health crises
- Surges in ethnic conflicts
- High levels of official corruption
- Environmental degradation
- Workers' strikes
- High-profiled social injustices

This scale of popular disaffection imperils stability and registers against the present and future leadership.

Another on-the-horizon challenge was the prevalence of major fault-lines within the upper echelons of the military with the onset of the scheduled elections, specifically within the Central Military Commission. The two major contenders for top leadership positions, General Xu Qiliang and General Wang Wanquan, exploited factional ties within the Party apparatus to maximize political advantage.

In contradistinction, the U.S. military is historically accomplished having prevailed in a series of recent ongoing conflicts and succeeded in multiple contingencies. To date, World War II was by far its largest military commitment. The scenario comprised combat operations occurring in multiple theaters of operation from Europe to North Africa to the Pacific. The threat in that instance sprung from within the Axis imperialist powers of Germany, Italy and France desirous of expanding their respective empires and spheres of influence. This capability to simultaneously deploy military forces to the two major theaters is (according to Richard J. Kilroy Jr. of the Virginia Military Institute) attributable to two predominant yet often overlooked criteria that have worked to America's advantage, namely:

"...the providence of history, geography and politics that provided safe borders to its north and south... the lack of an internal threat that would have required a large home stationing of combat-ready forces committed to the internal defense of the nation..."

Divergently, neither of these criteria is favorable to China.

The Asian peninsula is replete with perennial tension. This state of affairs heightens the likelihood of regionally based counter-Sino ferment. On the other hand, the Inter-American system has accrued institutional attenuations, primarily designed to promote and foster a "good neighbor policy."

Within the community, for example, the obligation among states for mutual assistance and common defense is the linchpin of their common defense policy. These canons are etched in a landmark mutual defense pact, the Inter-American Treaty for Reciprocal Assistance, which came into force on December 03, 1948. The central tenet of this accord is that an attack against any one country within the Americas is deemed as an attack against all. The catalyst for this compact was a realization on the part of the U.S. that the Axis powers of Europe had been making overtures to Latin American governments for military cooperation. It was against the backdrop of these entreaties that an Agreement was drawn up to confront the prospects and scope for international aggression and obligate nations to re-assure each other of their respective intentions. The policy thereby engendered remains of enduring and historical value today.

The CCP-led government is by no means satisfied with a world order in which the United States is the dominant power. This is a conviction put forward by Richard Fisher in his analysis of the country's global posture, primary of which is its checkered engagement in offensive wars, in raking through all attempts for regional hegemony. These overly assertive gestures, in Fisher's view, had imposed situations of extreme risk and sacrifice on its own population highlighting the intent and determination of the authorities in Beijing. In carefully building his case Fisher cites the Korean War when China lost 250,000 troops; Den Xiaoping's 1979 war against Vietnam in which China again incurred staggering losses amounting to 20,000 lives; and in 1989 under Hu Jintao, Vice President when a total of 170,000 troops were deployed from Chengdu military region to suppress political protests in Tibet.

Fisher concludes that notwithstanding China's growing dependence on global goodwill for vital commercial and resource access, recent experience points to a predisposition to seize upon opportunities to alter power relationships and power balance. Such conduct, in his estimation, presages calculated acts of aggression.

Should this conviction hold the Chinese can be expected to resort to decisive use of military force on the basis of a range of factors one of which is its militarily endowments.

In contrast to China the U.S. legacy of strategic partnerships regionally and extra-regionally, in particular the relationship it enjoys with allies is rooted in deep and time-tested ideological traditions and common values. In tactical terms, an ally of the U.S. stands with the country through multiple conflicts. From a strategic standpoint, such states will assist and support U.S. intelligence and defense capabilities, and make possible accessibility of ports and training facilities for use by U.S. armed forces. In the sphere of defense, America's allies will actively and proactively contribute to the securing of the approaches to the homeland and other borders, and assist in saving the lives of U.S. citizens both on and off the battlefield. Finally, in terms of economic relations, through trade, technological innovation and job creation, an ally would be expected to contribute to strengthening the U.S. economy through reciprocal trade and commercial pacts.

Chapter Three examines the preemptive posture adopted by the U.S. against the setting of irregular conflicts and emerging threats within and beyond the Americas. We then scope the status quo of military to military contacts initially between the US and China, and thereafter between China and members of the Latin America Caribbean community. Our conclusion will be that despite China's burgeoning military expansion at home, the impact of its contacts in Latin America is relative. This finding is reinforced by the primacy attached by Latin American governments to trade and economic diversification, areas that find favor with the Chinese wider long-term policy agenda for the region as distinct from military mobilization.

CHAPTER THREE

A NEW GAME OF BALANCE

"It is a matter of intelligence. We enhance our understanding of China's strategic doctrine and can reduce the potential for miscalculations and access between the People's Liberation Army and the United States and other Western forces."

Congressman De Lay
Congressional Record-House June 09, 1999

*T*he precondition for being a hegemonic power including the ability or otherwise to preside over a formal or informal empire is economic strength. In Paul Kennedy's encomium to modern global politics, <u>The Rise and Fall of Great Powers</u>, the author affirms that although the United States is at present still in a class of its own economically, and perhaps even militarily, there were two great tests that ultimately challenge the longevity of every major power, that America will eventually also have to confront. The first was whether in the military and strategic realms it could preserve a reasonable balance between its perceived defense requirements and the means it possesses to maintain these commitments. The second was whether it could preserve the technological and economic bases of its power from relative erosion in the face of ever-shifting patterns of global production.[1]

Kennedy expands on his argument by noting that America is inheritor of a vast array of strategic commitments which had been made decades earlier when its political, economic, and military capacities to influence world affairs were more assured. Against this setting, Martin Jacques notes that already America is beginning to face the classic problems of imperial overreach.[2] This implies that decision-makers in Washington must contemplate the fact that the sum total of U.S. global interests and obligations today exceeds the ability for the U.S. to singlehandedly project itself to defend them.

A classic case in point is the U.S. role in NATO. In the 2000s, it was estimated that the total cost of America's involvement in the war in Iraq was $3 trillion and following this, we saw America's deployments strewn across an even wider global radius and growing steadily longer in duration and more frequent. Having overplayed its hand in Iraq, the U.S. entered Afghanistan in the form of a fresh surge backed by NATO forces, and by April 2011 was caught up in the Libyan conundrum in North Africa. In this most recent foray, NATO forces, particularly Britain, France and Germany have played an ostensibly leading role. Notwithstanding this, the U.S. is historically the largest contributor to the total cost of maintaining the NATO campaign as the alliance widens its spread across Europe and the Middle East.

NATO members contribute in many ways to the alliance, the chief of which is the deployment of their own armed forces funded by national budgets. Certain commonly conducted activities are paid out of three NATO-run budgets, namely the civil budget, the military budget, and the security investment budget. The countries' share of common funds is based on per capita gross national income and other considerations.

Within NATO there are three budgets that come under direct funding arrangements: the civil budget, the military budget, and the NATO Security Investment Program. According to Congressional Research Service Report RL 30150 dated April 22, 2010, the U.S. contribution to NATO's military budget provided for through the Department of the Army's Operation and Maintenance Account (Support for Other Nations) was 25%. This translated into $408,051 million in 2009 FY and $430,381 million for 2010 FY, respectively. The sum of $462,488 was requested by the Obama administration in 2011.[3]

Chapter Three begins with a survey of the global matrix of defense spending patterns, while spotlighting the three main powers – the United States, Great Britain and China. Secondly, the Chapter notes that with the ebb and inflows of historical military exchanges between the U.S. and China, an understanding of "the other's intention" is a prudent barometer to utilize in building confidence between the two powers. Of interest to the U.S. therefore, would be China's present military exchanges with its Latin American and Caribbean partners as part of its prodigious diplomatic portfolio. Having examined the country's White Paper governing its diplomatic agenda for Caribbean and Latin American societies, the conclusion is that trade promotion, the securing of natural resources for domestic use, and the severing of diplomatic ties with Taiwan are the raison d'etre behind Chinese activism within Latin America and the Caribbean. These bilateral partnerships being cultivated by China, however, fail to eclipse the long-standing trade links that already exist with the U.S. as the main trading partner of Caribbean and Latin American states. Thirdly, and finally, the Chapter juxtaposes the extent of U.S. military and intelligence footprints across the European geopolitical bloc, a status quo that has endured since the end of World War II and the establishment of NATO as the political and ideological embryo of the Western Alliance, as we know it today. We establish how the European liaison, buttressed by the "special relationship" between the U.S. and the British, has contributed to the robustness and viability of the Western Alliance, as a vital U.S. strategic leg. This undoubtedly places China at a decided strategic disadvantage.

U.S. Defense Spending

For the 2010 fiscal year, the base budget of the U.S. Department of Defense was $53.8 billion, increasing to $66.8 billion when the cost of overseas contingency operations was subsumed into the initial figure.⁴ This budget component represents federal expenditure committed to the Department of Defense to meet America's defense related expenditures. The allocations cover the cost of salaries, training and health care of uniformed and civilian personnel, the maintenance of arms, equipment and facilities, operations, and the development and purchase of new equipment. The approved allocation covers the entire cost of upkeep for the Army, Navy, Air Force, and Marine Corps.

A noteworthy aspect of defense budgeting is that the costs of the missions in Iraq and Afghanistan had been met through supplementary funding bills outside of the Federal Budget and were accordingly not reflected in the Department of Defense's official breakdown of expenditure. Additionally, the "black budget" military spending to which the Pentagon is given access is also not officially registered under Federal spending. From 2010 and thereafter, the wars in Iraq and Afghanistan were categorized as Overseas Contingency Operations and formally subsumed in the official budget. Table 3-1

TABLE - 3-1

FEDERALLY BUDGETED MILITARY EXPENDITURE
OF US DEPARTMENT OF DEFENSE, FISCAL YEAR 2010
BY TITLE

COMPONENTS	FUNDING	CHANGE 2009-2010
Operations and Maintenance	$283.3 billion	+4.2%
Military Personnel	$154.2 billion	+5.0%
Procurement	$140.1 billion	-1.8%
Research, Development, Testing and Evaluation	$79.1 billion	+1.3%
Military Construction	$23.9 billion	+19.0%
Family Housing	$3.1 billion	-20.2%
TOTAL SPENDING	$685.1 billion	+3.0%

BY SERVICE

SERVICE	2010 BUDGET REQUEST	% OF TOTAL	NOTES
Army	$243.9 billion	31.8%	
Navy	$149.9 billion	23.4%	Excluding Marine Corps
Marine Corps	$290.9 billion	4.0%	Total Navy Budget
Air Force	$170.6 billion	22.0%	
Intelligence	$50.0 billion	7.0%	Estimate given due to classification
Defense Wide	$118.7 billion	15.5%	

PROGRAMS SPENDING IN EXCESS OF $1.5 BILLION

PROGRAM	2011 BUDGET	CHANGE 2010-2011
1. F35 Joint Strike fighter	$11.4 billion	
2. Ballistic Missile Defense	$9.9 billion	
3. Virginia Class submarine	$5.4 billion	
4. Brigade Combat Team Modernization	$3.2 billion	
5. DDG 51 Aegis-class Destroyer	$3.0 billion	
6. P-8A Poseidon	$2.9 billion	
7. V-22 Osprey	$2.8 billion	
8. Carrier Replacement Program	$2.7 billion	
9. F/A-18E/F Hornet	$2.0 billion	
10. Predator and Reaper Unmanned Aerial System	$1.9 billion	
11. Littoral Combat Ship	$1.8 billion	
12. CVN Refueling and Complex Overhaul	$1.7 billion	
13. Chemical Demilitarization	$1.6 billion	
14. RQ-4 Global Hawk	$1.5 billion	
15. Space-based Infrared System	$1.5 billion	

Military-related expenditure that is unaccounted for in the budget would include:

- Nuclear weapons research, maintenance, clean-up and production - these are met under the allocations for the Department of Energy

- Payment of pensions to retirees of the military and their widows and families – these costs are the responsibility of the Department of the Treasury
- Defense spending that is not "military in nature", paid for by the Department of Homeland Security
- Counter-terrorism spending by the FBI
- Intelligence gathering spending by NASA.

Historic Spending Levels

The Department of Defense projected costs for the 2011 fiscal year amount to $1.003-$1.223 trillion, with the largest allocation $721.3 billion going to the operations and personnel and the second largest $66.2 billion going to Veterans Affairs. For the 2010 fiscal year, the budget accounted for almost 19% of United States federal budgeted expenditures, 28% of estimated tax revenues and 4.7% of the Gross Domestic Product (GDP). The 2010 budget, estimated at $664 billion is reportedly higher, remuneratively, than any other point in American history, yet 1.1%-1.4% lower as a percentage of the GDP, than the amount spent on defense during the peak of the Cold War military spending in the late 1980s.

The 2009 U.S. military budget accounted for 40% of global "arms spending" and was over six times that of the military budget of China, using the nominal US dollar rate. The United Kingdom, America's closest ally, which serves as a vital military base to the U.S. and which has historically been a reliable "intelligence partner" is the second highest spender (in cash terms) on defense in the world behind the United States. Like the U.S. the additional net costs incurred in operations in Iraq and Afghanistan is not sourced from Britain's Defense Budget, but rather from a separate vote under the Treasury Reserve.

Since 2001, the United Kingdom's Treasury Reserve has been providing an additional 9.5 billion pounds to the Defense Budget to cover operational costs for engagements in the Middle East by means of a process specifically designed to facilitate flows of money to ground commanders with the required expediency.[5] Expenditure for defense in the U.K represented 5.8% of total government expenditure in 2006-2007, when one strips away at specific elements like the cost of pensions. Table 3-2.

TABLE - 3-2
DEFENSE BUDGET FOR THE UNITED KINGDOM OF GREAT BRITAIN AND NORTHERN IRELAND

ITEMS Million Pounds	2007-2008	2008-2009	2009-2010	2010-2011
Resource Budget	32,618	33,602	35,165	36,702
Capital budget	7,404	7,871	8,187	8,871
Total Dept. Expenditure Limit	32,579	34,057	35,365	36,890
Of Which near Cash	29,411	30,763	31,921	33,628

China, which is officially a world nuclear state, boasts the world's largest standing army comprising 2.25 million men, and carries the world's second largest defense budget.

China's military expenditure is released annually as a single overall figure and a component of the country's annual government budget. The published figure for 2010 was $77.95 billion. This is reflective of an increase of 7.5% over the published figure for 2009, comprising 1.4% of the GDP, compared to 4.7% in the case of the U.S. defense budget. In contrast, the defense budget for Britain and France, as a percentage of their respective national budgets is approximately 2%. See Table 3-3.

TABLE - 3-3
LIST OF COUNTRIES BY MILITARY EXPENDITURE, 2009

RANK	COUNTRY	MILITARY EXPENDITURE 2009	% of GDP, 2008
1.	United States	663,255,000,000	4.3%
2.	China	98,800,000,000	2.0%
3.	United Kingdom	69,271,000,000	2.5%
4.	France	67,316,000,000	2.3%
5.	Russian Federation	61,000,000,000	3.5%
6.	Germany	48,022,000,000	1.3%
7.	Japan	46,859,000,000	0.9%
8.	Saudi Arabia	39,257,000,000	8.2%
9.	Italy	37,427,000,000	1.7%
10.	India	36,600,000,000	2.6%
11.	South Korea	27,130,000,000	2.8%
12.	Brazil	27,124,000,000	1.5%
13.	Canada	20,564,000,000	1.5%
14.	Australia	20,109,000,000	1.8%
15.	Spain	19,409,000,000	1.2%

SOURCE: Stockholm International Peace Research Institute

The Chinese military budget finances employee salaries, training, the maintenance of equipment and facilities, support for new and ongoing operations, the development and procurement of weapons, equipment, and vehicles.

The 7.5% increase in its 2010 financial allocations was the lowest in several years that followed a string of double-digit figures in military spending on advanced hardware and technology. Given its powerful trajectory of expansion in substantive terms, this decrease has done little to assuage concerns among its neighbors, particularly in view of the fact that defense spending on "research and development" remains highly classified.

Chinese military spending had doubled between 1997 and 2003 and continued growing at an annual rate, not exceeding 10 percent until 2005. A comparison with other countries in terms of absolute expenditure between 2004-2007 ranks China as second to the United States, among the world's top 15 countries in the area of defense spending. Table 3-4.

TABLE – 3-4
ABSOLUTE DEFENSE SPENDING BY UNITED STATES, UNITED KINGDOM, JAPAN, PEOPLE'S REPUBLIC OF CHINA, RUSSIA, AND REPUBLIC OF TAIWAN

COUNTRY/REGION	OFFICIAL BUDGET	DIA	SIPRI	
United States	419.3 billion	475.3 billion	475.3 billion	419.3 billion
United Kingdom	58.6 billion	47.4 billion	47.4 billion	
Japan	45.8 billion	45.8 billion	42.4 billion	
People's Republic of China	29.9 billion	90-130 billion	30.7 billion	63.06 billion
Russia	14.5 billion	70.0 billion	19.4 billion	70.0 billion
Republic of China (Taiwan)	7.6 billion		7.7 billion	

U.S. Defense Policy and Strategy

The 2010 Quadrennial Defense Review scripts the underpinning philosophy, doctrine, and strategic priorities and may be viewed as the counterpart of the Chinese Biennial White Paper. The high point of the Review is the identification of the key missions of the military:

- To defend the U.S. and support civil authorities at home
- To succeed in counter insurgency, stability and counter-terrorism operations
- To build security capacity of partner states
- To deter and defeat aggression in anti-access and area denial
- To prevent the proliferation of weapons of mass destruction and counter weapons of mass destruction
- To operate efficiently in cyberspace

The Review noted the complex security landscape stemming from current conflicts with which America was confronted and identified a modified strategic approach to rebalance existing military capabilities while also reforming processes and institutions. A notable component of the modified approach to the Department's overall mission was the abandonment of the (former) planning construct for the shaping and sizing of the force based on the two major regional conflicts in the Middle East specifically Iraq and Afghanistan. The force structure would be adapted to facilitate a wider continuum of operations ranging from homeland defense, defense support to civil authorities in responding to disasters, deterrence, and preparedness for current and future types of wars.[6]

The release of the Nuclear Posture Review, 2010 followed the Quadrennial in close succession. The former provides a conventional rollout of the U.S. nuclear policy, strategy, and capabilities as well as force posture for the ensuing five to ten year period. The last such report was promulgated under the Bush administration on December, 31, 2001 in the aftermath of 9/11 wherein the core assets and capabilities identified comprised offensive strike systems, defenses both active and passive, and a revitalized defense and infrastructure that would provide new capabilities in a timely fashion to meet emerging threats.

The intent of the 2001 Review was manifestly:

- Shifting defense planning from a threat-based approach to a capabilities-based approach so that in the course of the decade 2001-2011 there would be in place a credible deterrent to the lowest level of nuclear weapons consistent with U.S. and allied security

- Migrating from the Cold War triad of intercontinental ballistic missiles (ICBM), submarine-launched ballistic missiles (SLBM) and long-range nuclear-armed bombers (ICBMs; SLBMs) to be integrated into non-nuclear strategic capabilities in order to strengthen the credibility of offensive deterrence

- Introducing a defensive deterrence infrastructure, since following the Cold War, the U.S. infrastructure in that area had contracted and atrophied— the application of exquisite intelligence on the intentions and capabilities of adversaries and force adjustments would ensure greater precision of strikes and defenses

In differentiation, the 2010 Nuclear Posture contains significant alterations in outlook. In a notable departure to its predecessor it reduces the role and number of weapons in America's nuclear arsenal, declassifies nuclear stockpile details, rules out the development of further cutting edge weapons by the U.S. and prohibits the use of nuclear weapons against non-nuclear states[7]

As of September 2010, there were 5,113 warheads in U.S. stockpiles accounted for and an additional 8,748 that were reportedly dismantled between fiscal years 1994-2009. Imbedded in the current Nuclear Posture Review is the intent of the present administration to accentuate transparency in its nuclear policy and strategy and promote a wider non-proliferation agenda. In furtherance of this agenda, a crucial Pact was signed between the United States and Russia in 2010 to replace the START 1 Agreement, which expired in December 2009. As signatories, the U.S. and Russia are now obligated to cap fielded strategic nuclear weapons to 1,550 warheads while the number of deployed and non-deployed delivery vehicles should not exceed 800.[8]

Thus, the systematic stripping away by the U.S. of Chinese attempts to leverage and gain advantage militarily, whether in Asia or in the Americas, is multi-pronged in approach. Firstly, when viewed from a broader and long-term perspective, this type of maneuver serves to advance the medium to long- term designs of the U.S. to stem, and ultimately neutralize, the nuclear arms race. Secondly, it curtails whatever advantages China could potentially accrue in covert maneuvers with its recently groomed "strategic partners." Consequentially, parallel countermeasures on the part of the U.S. in relation to state actors in Asia with a history of strained relations with China, specifically India and Taiwan, are relevant to the debate on hand. We shall therefore examine some of these more closely.

Sino-India

The Sino-India relationship has a somewhat checkered history, influenced by the rise and waning of tensions and predictably, the United States has been exploiting these frictions to its best advantage. China's employment of military force in 1950 to subjugate Tibet, prolonged territorial disputes over "the McMahon line" drawn up by the British in 1914 followed by the 1964 nuclear test are part of a wider body of rather thorny constituents that persists in the countries' respective bilateral ties until today.[9] Indeed, the 1964 tests had an impact on Indian strategic thought, spurring a strong argument by India to match the Chinese by developing a domestic nuclear capability. India performed its first nuclear test in 1974 with the avowed intent of peaceful deterrence, as distinct from possible deployment of an offensive first strike.

Today, India possesses short and intermediate range ballistic missiles, nuclear-capable aircraft, surface ships and submarines under development as possible delivery systems and platforms. In terms of its arsenal, estimates suggest that there are approximately between 40 and 90 nuclear weapons. India has ambitions of possessing a nuclear triad when the lead ship of her nuclear powered submarines Arihant Class formally joins the Navy in 2012. India has thus facilitated the U.S. with a viable counterweight to China, an advantage that has long materialized with a bilateral accord on civil nuclear cooperation, signed in 2005.

This particular agreement was at best non-conformist and involved a series of complex aspects that were novel and fraught with caveats:

- A civil-military nuclear Separation Plan in India
- An India /IAEN Inspections Agreement
- An exemption grant from India's Nuclear Suppliers Group
- An export control cartel, formed after the country's first nuclear test in 1974
- The passage by U.S. Congress into law of the U.S.-India Nuclear Cooperation Approval
- The passage by U.S. Congress of a Non-proliferation Enhancement Act on October 08, 2008.

Apart from the discernible political and economic advantages to the United States, the civil nuclear cooperation agreement package presents an opportunity for easing the overall global demand for crude oil and natural gas over the medium to long-term. As a nuclear power India thus provides a feasible counterweight to China's potential emergence as a regional hegemony.

Sino-Taiwan

Consistent with a notoriously checkered relationship defined by distrust, the dramatic demobilizing of one of its own satellites by the Chinese was a clarion call of its intention and indeed wherewithal, to challenge American advantage, even in the space domain.[10]

In the context of China's overall military modernization, senior commanders in Beijing have drawn reference to the Taiwanese issue as the central rationale for hefty defense spending and an overtly ambitious military strategic program. They hasten to cite the threat posed to China by Taiwanese separatist movements and the possibility that such movements may well escalate into open and lethal conflict, capable of seriously impairing China's interests, politically and economically. They have asserted that the principal means by which any great or emerging power such as China endeavors to either maintain or re-establish the power balance at its disposal is through the instrumentality of its armaments. Thus, the announced sale of arms to Taiwan by the U.S. in January 2010 automatically pitted the U.S. and China against each other and re-ignited historical tensions. China retorted by suspending all military exchanges with the U.S. and by imposing sanctions on all companies identified as parties to the transaction.[11]

The immediate fall-out was patent: firstly, the incident presented a further rupture to U.S.-China relations and one that prompted an aggressive retreat on China's part; this would be redressed one year later with the visit to China of the US Secretary of Defense Robert Gates to be followed in close order by a state visit to Washington by the Chinese Premier. Secondly, the incident placed an effective restraint on Beijing's strategic calculus regarding Taiwan's unremitting affirmation of self- government. Thirdly, it brought to the fore and at once reinforced the diplomatic status quo between China and Taiwan, which the U.S. is prepared to secure even militarily.

Reciprocally, Taiwanese defenses in the sphere of air and naval capabilities exist primarily to counter a range of perceived threats that may emanate from its opponent. In addition to the US-donated Osprey mine-hunting ships, Black hawk helicopters, missiles, machine guns, ammunition, night vision gear, radar equipment, and information technology, Taiwan's defenses include:

- An air and defense infrastructure, the bulk of these being early warning air and defense assets strategically positioned on the western side of the island nearest the Taiwan Strait
- Surface to air missiles - layered surface to air missile coverage protects the nation's major population centers, key national installations, military facilities and domestic infrastructure
- Area air defense surface to air missiles - Taiwan's area air defense systems include the long-range U.S.-produced Patriot PAC-2 Modified Air Defense System (MADS), the long-range Taiwan produced Tien Kung-1(TK1) and Tien Kung 11(TK11) and medium-range U.S.-produced Improved Homing All The Way Killer (1-HAWK). This network provides protection to key installations and in relation to the outer islands provides coverage along key air avenues of approach from the mainland
- Short-range tactical SAMs, which augment the area air defense SAMs and include shoulder-fired man-portable air defense systems (MANPADS); the units can also be stationed at airfields and other military installations to augment longer range systems. Other assets include the Avenger System (short-range Stinger missiles fired from launchers on wheeled vehicles), Antelopes (infrared air to air missiles, also vehicle-mounted) and Chaparral units for tactical air defense.
- Combat aircraft, namely 146-F-16 AB; 126 F-CK-1A/B; 56 MIRAGE 2000 and 60 E5E/F on inventory.

South and East China Sea Claims

ASEAN members (Brunei, Malaysia, and Vietnam) have had long- running disagreements with China over parts of the South Sea. In the East China Sea, China has discriminately invoked the principle of "natural prolongation" upon which she bases her claim to the entire continental shelf extremity from the mainland to Okinawa Trough. In contrast, she vehemently repudiates application of the same principle by Vietnam and Malaysia, choosing instead to pass an enactment at home outlawing any map that does not depict her claims, that are etched in the form of a" U-shaped Line." The line in effect demarcates those areas over which China intends to exercise sovereignty.

The "U-shaped Line" now potentially extends to all countries in the world that exercise rights in the South China Sea consistent with the U.N. Convention on the

Law of the Sea. The instrument has been signed and ratified by 160 countries. China's U-shaped Line lies beyond the 12 nautical line limit for sovereignty, beyond the likely limits for the Exclusive Economic Zone (EEZ) and beyond the equidistant line between the Spratlys, Paracels and opposite coasts.

According to the U.N Convention, a coastal state only has sovereignty in the belt of territorial sea up to 12 miles (22 Kms) adjacent to its baseline. Other states have no rights but for "innocent passage." Beyond the 12 mile boundary the coastal state has specific rights, such as exclusive economic rights applicable in the exclusive economic zone area and exclusive rights to exploit the seabed and subsoil in the extended continental shelf. On the basis of the Chinese claim the implication is that the Paracels, Spratlys and Scarbour Shoals can potentially be subjected to any state's sovereignty. Should a state proceed to claim sovereignty, it can in fact impose full jurisdiction over waters where international law should otherwise be paramount. On the same principle, any claims to the exclusive economic zone will be tantamount to encroachment either on maritime zones of other states or high seas where columns of water and parts of the seabed belong to the international community.[12] Of significance in this impasse is the fact that international law and state practice never accord to an island an EEZ boundary that lies beyond an equidistant line between itself and the opposite coasts belonging to larger islands and continental land-masses. In the context of China's claims, the "U-shaped Line" not only goes beyond the 12 nautical mile zone but also beyond any imaginable equidistant.

At the end of the day, China and Japan remain bitterly engrossed in competing claims of sovereignty over the South Sea Islands and amidst the ongoing feud, the following other claims await resolution -

- Paracels, which should be resolved bilaterally between China and Vietnam
- Scarbough Shoals, which should also be resolved on a bilateral basis between China and the Philippines; and
- Spratlys, which should be settled on the basis of a multilateral accord among the states of Brunei, China, Malaysia and the Philippines.

China's pre-occupation with the security of her borders and her claims in the South China Sea are incongruous with any ambitions that she may entertain to gain a foothold in other geopolitical blocs. Geography is a primary constraint. So too is the lack of trust and congeniality that would otherwise have secured her regional pre-eminence politically in Asia.

U.S. - China Military to Military Exchanges In the West

From the perspective of the U.S. government, reciprocal military access serves as an important cornerstone in building and preserving peaceful relationships with other nation states and provides a pathway for transparency and confidence building. In demurral to this ideal is the role of espionage in state-to-state engagements.

China's remarkable string of successes in penetrating the U.S. government, particularly in the area of military technology is a vindication of its strategic positioning politically and militarily and it is on this merit that military to military exchanges between the two countries continue to be mired with distrust and acrimony. We observed this status quo crystallizing in the Congressional debate from as far back as June 1999 in which the U.S. administration adopted decisive measures, often hard-lined, to limit military to military exchanges between its armed forces and China's People's Liberation Army. A controversial Bill was sponsored that sought the outright abandonment of such exchanges on grounds that military contacts of the past were exploited by the Chinese to isolate the vulnerabilities of the U.S. and position the PLA advantageously for future conflicts. The sponsors noted that access to U.S. military bases, even on a reciprocal basis, yielded opportunities for serious security breaches, citing the US Army Training Center and the Navy Fighter Weapons School, as specific targets that had been seriously compromised. These observations were subsequently legitimated in disclosures that emerged from the Cox Report and Rumsfeld Commission.

One of the decisive outcomes of the legislative enactment was the placement of acute restraints on the powers of Secretary of Defense in relation to future exchanges and contacts. Beyond this, additional curtailments were included in specific clauses of the Bill, as reproduced below:

(a) LIMITATION – The Secretary of Defense may not authorize any military - to -military exchange or contact described in sub-section (1) to be conducted by the armed forces with representatives of the People's Liberation Army of the People's Republic of China

(b) COVERED EXCHANGES AND CONTACTS – sub-section (a) applies to any military to military exchange or contact that includes any of the following:

(1) Force projection operations

(2) Nuclear operations

(3) Field operations

(4) Logistics

(5) Chemical and biological defense and other capabilities related to weapons of mass destruction

(6) Surveillance and reconnaissance operations

(7) Joint war-fighting experiments and other activities related to warfare

(8) Military space operations

(9) Other war-fighting capabilities of the Armed Force Arms sales or military–related technology transfers

(11) Release of classified or restricted information

(12) Access to the Department of Defense Laboratory

(c) Subsection (a) does not apply to any search or rescue exercise or any humanitarian exercise

The Bill was further shored up by imposition of mandatory requirements on the Secretary of Defense to (1) report annually to the Committee on the Armed Forces of the Senate and the Committee on the Armed Forces of the House of Representatives respectively on a summary of specific topics and questions asked by Chinese participants in the course of military contacts and (2) offer an assessment of how military to military contacts with the PLA "fit into the larger security relationship between the United States and the People's Republic of China."

The more specific concerns that had spurred these highly debated embargoes were:

- China's incremental migration from a traditional land-based people's army in favor of a comprehensive strategic and nuclear strike capability by land, sea and air

- Its clandestine efforts to acquire the most secret and sensitive of United States military technologies, including the know-how to replicate the W88 warhead, then regarded as "the most dangerous security breach in 50 years"; and

- Presentiments, which were subsequently confirmed, that the Chinese had assisted the North Korean missile program, in addition to their known and suspected sales of missile and nuclear technologies to "terrorist states".

Fisher traces the oscillation of Sino-U.S. military exchanges, noting that the first real opening in contacts took place during the latter stages of the Carter administration, when anti-Soviet entente was sealed with the commencement of intelligence co-operation. This cooperation was thereafter expanded to include the commissioning of CIA listening posts in Northern China directed at the Soviet Union. Beyond these schemes, exchanges fluctuated under the later stages of the administration of George H.W. Bush and the subsequent Bush administration.[13]

On the other hand tensions mounted under the Clinton administration, as demonstrated in China's reaction to U.S.-Taiwanese exchanges during that period in the form of military exercises around Taiwan in 1995 and 1996, respectively. The mid-2000s was a relatively lukewarm period in relations with at least two missions of note – firstly, the viewing by Admiral Mike Mullen in 2007 of PLA Navy maneuvers involving a Type 039 Song-class submarine; secondly, a tour of the Second Artillery Office Building and a Lulu class destroyer by the U.S. House Armed Services Committee.

Military Exchanges in Latin America

While the Chinese are not necessarily building a significant presence militarily in Latin America, the human and commercial infrastructure that they are investing in the region have the potential to exert notable leverage for the possible disruption and distraction of US interests, should relations between the two powers deteriorate significantly. This was the conclusion of a 2007 Study "The Military Strategic Dimensions of Chinese Initiatives in Latin America" undertaken by the Center for Hemispheric Policy, University of Miami. The Study also noted that whereas economic motivations had in fact dominated expanding Chinese engagements in the Caribbean and South America, a caveat to Chinese outreach was the diplomatic recognition of Taiwan as part of the People's Republic of China.

Beijing's military contacts with Latin American countries must therefore be assessed within the wider context of "forging stronger political mutual trust and close cooperation in economics, trade, science and technology, culture, education, mutual support, and close cooperation in international affairs", a principle iterated in the Chinese 2008 White Paper on Latin America and the Caribbean, and cemented in the more recent 2010 edition. The title in question is suggestively mute on military affairs but its release was, nonetheless, strategically timed to coincide with two major events of regional and geopolitical significance, namely:

- The G20 Summit hosted by the former US President George H. W. Bush on November 08 of the same year. On that occasion Chinese premier, Hu Jintao seized the opportunity to assuage fermenting concerns over growing Latin America-Sino military exchanges, simultaneously advising that their respective countries shared a common interest in combating terrorism and other non-traditional security issues
- The 16th Asia-Pacific Economic Leaders' Summit (APEC) in Lima, Peru on November 22-23. This visit to Latin America was tactically timed amidst burgeoning bilateral trade negotiations, which attained $102.6 billion in 2007, exceeding China's originally projected benchmark of $100 billion by 2010.

Sino-Latin American bargaining, ostensibly to disrupt the legacy of U.S. preeminence, therefore warrants more exhaustive points of reference for the purposes of our enquiry and for a more insightful appraisal of U.S. leveraging in the region. This places an imperative for historical context and a survey of intraregional politics.

Noteworthy is the fact that those diplomatic, political, economic and other relations between China and many Latin American societies in the 1980s and 1990s transpired at a time when right-wing military regimes were defining the regional political landscape. Their political models were less aligned to China's ideologically than those of the elected civilian governments that succeeded in the 2000s. It was not until Latin America's recessionary "lost half decade" set in between 1998-2008 that voters in many Latin American countries – Argentina, Bolivia, Brazil, Chile, Ecuador, Guatemala, Nicaragua, Paraguay, Peru, Uruguay, and Venezuela – elected leftist presidents who were overtly critical of the tenets of the Washington consensus. We can conclude definitively that the incipient stages of Sino-Latin American relations contravened the typical blend of ideological affinity and instead found root in mutual trade and commercial concerns.

A second and equally significant argument is that among the principal proponents for Sino-Latin America relations was the Latin American business sector which favored the free market policies that were being allowed full rein by the right –wing administrations. The "new Left" that succeeded however was confronted by a dilemma of "mass outrage over post privatization price increases" and, once elected to office, morally hampered in ability to resurrect protectionist barriers against imports and foreign investors; such measures would no doubt have stoked inflationary pressures. Left wing Governments therefore studiously veered away from any large-scale reform reversals, shifting instead, to the wisdom of affordability and the quality of goods and services. Trade relations with China therefore answered to concerns that were germane to Latin American communities.

A fourth criterion that consolidated Sino-Latin America trade ties was Cuba's status as an adversary-in-common between the Latin American Right and the Chinese. A fifth and equally significant factor was equally politically disposed, continuing concerns of the U.S. regarding the human rights track records of the Chinese and Latin Americans. The U.S. policy posture, taken in combination with China's non-doctrinaire stance in its dealings with Latin American countries, constituted a fortuitous amalgam that served as an enabling factor and collective rebuff that fueled future bilateral and multilateral ties.

Finally, it should be noted that the military concerns of many Latin American countries hinge around specific domestic threats, which have endured for several generations, the most conspicuous being-

- The activities of the Revolutionary Armed Forces of Colombia (Fuerzas Armadas Revolucionarias de Colombia-Ejercito del Pueblo), a Marxist-Leninist revolutionary guerilla organization which to date remains the largest and oldest insurgency on the continent; and

- The Shining Path (Sendero Luminoso), a Marxist guerilla organization in Peru.

Unlike the United States, Beijing has conspicuously opted to avoid any entanglement in the localized antagonisms of its partners, consistent with the tenets spelled out in its 2008 White Paper, and its 2010 successor.

<hr/>

Chinese Policy and Strategy

The themes of "transformation", "development", "peace" and "multi-polarity" resonate in the chapeau of the Chinese White Papers (2007; 2010) on Latin America and the Caribbean. The former articulates in part that:

> *"...As the largest developing country in the world, China is committed to the path of peaceful development and the win-win strategy of opening up. It is ready to carry out friendly cooperation with*

98

all countries on the basis of the Five Principles of Peaceful Co-existence and build a harmonious world of durable peace and Common prosperity..."

The document goes beyond this, spelling out in clear terms how China, as the largest developing country in the world is prepared to sustain "steady and all-round growth" in its relation with the Caribbean particularly, while recognizing the region not only as an important part of the developing world but a major force in the international arena. On this premise the Chinese determined to strengthen dialogue and communication; seek to develop partnerships in economic cooperation and trade; intensify exchanges to promote development and progress of human civilization and uphold its "One China" policy, a position supportive of the ultimate re-unification of its Republic.

The Chinese Overall Plan

Regarding the Caribbean community, China has projected a comprehensive cooperation agenda in many spheres of national life – politically, economically, culturally/socially and, in general, along the lines of peace, security and judicial affairs.

Politically, the PRC contemplates a momentum of close exchanges with Caribbean governments, their parliaments, political parties and governmental agencies. Through these contacts Beijing would forge ahead with dialogue and consultations in divers fields, including economy and trade, science and technology, and culture and education. In the economic province, the Chinese have stated their intent to work alongside Caribbean counterparts on the basis of mutual benefit to be secured through:

- Investing in manufacturing, agriculture, forestry, fishing, energy, mineral resources, infrastructure and the service sector
- Setting up of consultative and professional exchanges between Chinese monetary and financial regulatory authorities and financial institutions with Caribbean counterparts
- Promoting exchanges and cooperation in agricultural science and technology, intensifying agricultural trade and creating information exchange mechanisms
- Facilitating infrastructural construction in the areas of transport, information and communications, water conservation and hydropower

- Deepening mutual benefit cooperation in resources and energy within bilateral cooperation frameworks
- Promoting cooperation of tourism through exchange visits
- Rendering economic and technical assistance devoid of political conditionality; promoting multilateral cooperation to bring about more equitable trading regimes and providing forums for a greater role of decision-making for developing countries
- Promoting forward exchanges in the form of trade and related missions in the business sector

China's Diplomacy Anchored in Trade Interests

These advancements will be augmented by cultural and sports exchanges, consular cooperation, and joint ventures with goals set on environmental protection, climate change, disaster relief and reduction and strengthening of capacities for poverty alleviation projects.

Through its self-styled campaign to promote "Peace, Security and Judicial Affairs" Beijing has specifically undertaken to actively carry out military exchanges and defense dialogue and cooperation with Caribbean countries through mutual visits by defense and military officials of both sides that would incorporate training, peacekeeping, and practical cooperation in the non-traditional security field, such as the combating of terrorism.

Reciprocal military access between China and Latin American countries therefore lies within the larger framework of an ostentatious diplomatic portfolio that is anchored the rationality of expanded trade links. The miscellany of programs represented within China's diplomatic portfolio, the accelerated pace of military exchanges and arms sales discernible in the 2000s would appear to supersede any perceived intent on China's part to decisively establish its imprint militarily in the region. [14]

Notwithstanding this, Chinese regional investments, in terms of human and commercial infrastructure, provide both a foundation and a rationale for unremitting influence in regional affairs. A further point of note is that its impressive cyber capabilities discharges the need for that country's established physical presence as a precursor to the lethal attack against the interests or defenses of any country deemed an adversary or against which there is a nurtured animosity. In this regard, the U.S. is mindful that its adversaries also have access to cutting edge developments and although they may not seek to challenge the U.S.

directly, they may attempt to do so through asymmetric means. Chapter Eleven expands on this theme.

All in all, understanding and interpreting the relative political and economic motivations in Beijing's partnerships is by no means a straightforward process since invariably one works in tandem with the other.

These observations mirror the position taken by Gabriel Marcella, editor of "Americas Quarterly - Fall 2009" in his appraisal of R. Evan Ellis's article "China in Latin America: The Whats and Wherefores." Marcella asserts that although a foundation has been laid by China in Latin America for further military cooperation, it is unlikely to displace the United States as the preeminent source of equipment and doctrine in the Latin American military. Secondly, as he sees it, China has linked trade incentives and aid to Central American and Caribbean countries in furtherance of its campaign to ultimately neuter the diplomatic recognition of Taiwan.

In Marcella's thinking, it is in pursuance of purely "rational interests" that China has employed a range of foreign policy tools "from diplomatic, cultural and military to economic with a heavy emphasis on trade and investment." Having cogently argued his case, he discredits any notion that "Chinese activities are a zero sum exercise where the result is a potential political loss for the United States."

This perspective bears merit and is corroborated in the body of "strategic partnerships" (znanlue huoban guanxi) that has emerged in the last two decades between China and South American nations. Brazil, Venezuela, Mexico, Chile, Bolivia and Argentina typify this trend. They are all committed to shared interests in the sphere of democracy in international affairs and multi-polarity – these, incidentally are the ostensible markers in international circles of an unwritten code of collective soft balancing against U.S. hegemony.

In addition, Chung-Chian Teng, professor in the Department of Diplomacy at National Chengchi University and author of Latin American Studies; Political Communication and Skills of Negotiation and Governments and Politics (all in Chinese) re-affirms China's growing economic power through the provision of trade and investment opportunities in Central and South America, and in making his case, cites the line-up of recent projects:

- Its 10 year investment plan with Argentina in which China pledged to invest more than $19 billion, inclusive of an $8 billion investment to expand the country's railway system

- Its "strategic alliance" with Chile in which China is now Chile's largest purchaser of copper; substantial loans to Chile from China's National Development Bank; and the establishment of a joint venture company between the Chinese Minmetals Group and the Corporacion Nacional del Cobre de Chile

- Its comprehensive Cooperation Agreement between Brazil's Petrobras and China's Sinopec. Under this strategic relationship there will be cooperation in oil exploration, production, refining, marketing, pipes and technology; and the construction of a 1,225 mile natural gas line at a cost of $1.3 billion

- The operation of three major oilfields in Venezuela by CNPC-Orimulsion, Caracoles and Intercampo.

Other major achievements scored were the conferring by China of "full market economy" status on Argentina, Brazil and Chile; the elevation of China's partnership agreements with Argentina from "full range cooperative" to "strategic" and in respect of Peru, promotion to "full range cooperative." An adjunct to these elevations is the designation of Brazil, Argentina, Chile, Mexico, Peru, Venezuela and several Caribbean nations as "Chinese group travelers' destinations."[15]

Sino-Chile

Of all the Latin American countries, Chile was the first to have established diplomatic relations with China from as far back as December 15, 1970. Following this offices of Military Attaches were opened in either country. President Hu Jintao's 2004 visit to Chile was a historical marker, with respective governments courting consensus on the establishment and development of a comprehensive cooperative partnership which would embrace military-to-military exchanges between the Chilean Navy (Armada de Chile), the Chilean Air Force (Fuerza Aerea de Chile) the Carabneros Corps and China's People's Liberation Army. Thus, the first set of escalated exchange visits, including naval exchanges and visits by the Chinese to the Chilean Groundforce Warfare Academy and Campaign Tactics Training Center materialized during the 1990s-2000s, a period that may well be regarded as the crucible of current Chile-China relations. These exchanges would be eclipsed with the historic docking of the Chilean Navy's training vessel in Shanghai in 2001, and subsequently in Hong Kong in 2002. Tables 3-5(a) and 3-5(b).

TABLE - 3-5 (a)
VISITS OF CHINESE MILITARY EXECUTIVES TO CHILE 1990s-2000s

DESIGNATION/NAME	YEAR
Air Force Commander Wang Hai	1991
Defense Minister Chi Haotian	1994
Navy Commander Zhang Lianzhong	1996
Central Military Commission Vice-Chairman Zhang Wan-man	1997
Air Force Commander Liu Zhunyao	1998
Executive Deputy Chief of General Staff Guo Boxing	2000
Chief of Staff of Armed Police Force Chen Chuankuo	2001
Navy Commander Shi Yunsheng	2002
Chief of Air Force General staff He Weirong	2002
Director of Commission of Science, Technology and Industry for National Defense Li Zhibing	2002

SOURCE: Developed by Writer

TABLE - 3-5 (b)
RECIPROCAL VISITS PAID TO CHINA BY CHILEAN MILITARY EXECUTIVES
1990s -2000s

DESIGNATION/NAME	YEAR
Chilean Air Force Commander Fernando Mathei Aubel	1993
Commander- in -Chief of the Army Pinochet	1993,1997
Commander of armed Police Rodolfo Stange	1993
Defense Minister Edmundo Perres Yoma	1994
Navy Commander Jorge Martinez Busch	1996
Air Force Commander Fernando Rojas Vender	1998
Director of armed Police bureau Fuergatt	1999
Army Commander Yisuleta	2000
Air Force Commander Rios	2001
Vice Minister of Defense and President of the Chilean Space Agency Nelsen Heresy; Director General of Armed Police Bureau Alberto Cienfuegos	2002

SOURCE: Adaptation by Writer

Sino-Brazil

Brazil is arguably China's most important trading partner in Latin America, supplying 45% of its soybean imports and other agricultural products as well as iron ore and petroleum. Edward Schumacher-Matos (2008) observes that despite

103

Brazil's "economic muscle" as a rapidly developing economy, her exports, nonetheless, with the exception of bio-fuels, do not feature "fruits of the technological revolution" that lie at the core of future economic power.

China and Brazil have strengthened defense and military ties and launched jointly developed satellites, with the former country funding 70% of the costs. Through ongoing cooperation, Brazil has now positioned itself to acquire Chinese rocket technology in exchange for advanced optical technology. Chinese rocket technologies will ensure not only the advancement of a discrete missile program embarked upon by the Brazilian government but also self-reliance on its space program. The dual use of technology in these fields facilitates civil cooperation in downstream areas, thereby bestowing credibility to the parent project. In the area of arms manufacture, Brazil's major aviation and arms manufacturing company and the China Aviation Industry Cooperation II have jointly developed a medium transport turbo-jet aircraft, a 30-50 foot aircraft with a flying range of 3000 kilometers and a further 90 units are scheduled for procurement.

Most of the senior officers in Brazil's army now attend the Flagship One Year Course offered by the National Defense University of the People's Liberation Army, in addition to a shorter one month program for Caribbean and Latin American officers. On the other hand, fewer Chinese officers have been able to benefit from reciprocal training opportunities due to language constraints.

Sino-Bolivia

In the case of Bolivia, Chinese military aviation companies have made decisive inroads in arms sales. Together with Peru and Paraguay, the Bolivian military took delivery of M60 aircraft on payment terms including a $35 million line of credit. The Bolivian Air Force is currently contemplating transitioning from its "A" aircraft to the J-7 fighter jet, a Chinese equivalent of the Russian MIG-21. This determination has since culminated in a commitment to purchase six light military K8 aircraft worth $58 million for deployment in counter narcotics operations. As recently as August 2010, the Chinese defense minister and his Bolivian counterpart officially recommitted to military exchanges and the promotion of military ties.

Sino-Argentina

The Argentine military is a well-organized force, comprising the Argentine Army (Ejerceto Argentino); the Navy of the Argentine Republic (Armada Republica);

and the Argentine Air Force (Feurza Aerea Argentina) but has been seriously constrained by prolonged economic hardship. Officers occupying the upper echelons of the military have been training at Beijing's National Defense University in strategic disciplines. Additionally, Chinese fighter jets have been on display at exhibitions hosted by the Argentine government, betraying a level of interest in such hardware by the host government.

Argentina has a nuclear industry with potential for new partnerships with China. In furtherance of this, China plans to construct 42 new nuclear reactors over a twenty-year period to meet domestic power generation needs. Additionally, a new 300 megawatt 4th generation nuclear reactor is jointly engaging the attention of China and Argentina's Comision Nacional del Energia Atomica (CONEA). The development and fueling of an SAC-C surveillance satellite laser ranging facility at San Juan University in Argentina is also being pursued through joint cooperation between the two countries. Further opportunities for reciprocal support exist by virtue of Argentina's space launch and observations facilities at the southernmost latitudes. This is of strategic value to China's future prospects in observing or potentially launching satellites into near polar orbits.

Despite the flurry of trade, defense and related partnerships, the United States endures as the established and main trading partner for OAS members. Mexico is by far the biggest importer and exporter in Latin America and is fully integrated through the North American Free Trade Area (NAFTA) Agreement with its northern partners - the United States and Canada. Close to 86% of Mexico's exports and 50% of its imports are traded with its northern allies. In November 2010, Mexican exports were valued at $2.8 billion – consisting primarily of manufactured goods, oil and oil products, silver, fruits, vegetables, coffee, and cotton.

A survey of Venezuela's trade portfolio will disclose that the Bolivarian Republic is another U.S. key trade partner (49% exports; 24% imports), with the petroleum sector accounting for over 80% of all export earnings. In addition to oil Venezuela also exports steel, aluminum, transport equipment, textiles, apparel, beverages, and foodstuffs.

Sino-CARICOM Relations

The overall picture is that trade partnership preferences and export/import volumes are decisively skewed in favor of the U.S., a trend conspicuously mirrored among Anglophone Caribbean countries that were former British colonies. This grouping comprises signatories of a regime of intergovernmental political and economic pacts through shared membership of the CARICOM, the predominantly Anglophone intergovernmental body in the Caribbean Basin. Table 3-6.

TABLE - 3-6
TRADE PORTFOLIO OF CARIBBEAN
COMMUNITY MEMBER COUNTRIES 2010

COUNTRY	EXPORTS	IMPORTS	*PRIMARY DESTINATIONS FOR EXPORTS	*PRIMARY SOURCE COUNTRIES FOR IMPORTS
1.Antigua & Barbuda	Manufactured goods	Food, consumer and capital goods	USA, UK, CARICOM, Canada	USA
2.Bahamas	Machinery, vehicles, chemicals, refined petroleum, crawfish, fish, rum	Machinery, vehicles, manufactured goods, food, fuels, chemicals	USA, Germany, Spain, France	USA, South Korea, Japan
3.Barbados	Chemicals, sugar, manufactured goods incl. electrical components, rum	Consumer goods, food, beverages, machinery, construction materials, fuels	CARICOM, USA UK	USA, Trinidad & Tobago CARICOM
4.Belize	Citrus concentrate, fish products, sugar, bananas	Machinery, transport, equipment, manufactured goods, fuels, food, chemicals	USA (52%), UK, European countries	USA (40%), Mexico
5.Dominica	Manufactured goods, bananas, agricultural produce	Food, consumer goods, fuel, transport equipment, machinery,	Japan, UK, Jamaica, USA	Japan, USA, China, Trinidad & Tobago

106

chemicals

COUNTRY	EXPORTS	IMPORTS	*PRIMARY DESTINATIONS FOR EXPORTS	*PRIMARY SOURCE COUNTRIES FOR IMPORTS
6.Grenada	Manufactured goods, nutmeg, mace, cocoa	Capital goods, chemicals, fuels	USA, Germany, Netherlands, St Lucia	UK (13%), USA (20%), Trinidad & Tobago
7.Guyana	Gold, sugar, prawns, rice, bauxite, timber	Manufactured goods, consumer goods, fuels	USA, Canada UK, Netherlands Antilles	USA, Netherlands Antilles, Trinidad & Tobago
8. Jamaica	Alumina, bauxite, sugar, bananas, clothing	Raw materials, fuels, consumer goods, food, capital goods	USA (29%), Canada, UK	USA (44%)
9.Trinidad & Tobago	Petroleum and petroleum products. liquefied natural gas, methanol, ammonia, urea, steel products	Mineral products, lubricants, machinery, manufactured goods, food	US 44%; Spain 6.1%; Jamaica 5.1%	US 27.8% Russia 11.5% Brazil 7.8%
10.St Kitts & Nevis			USA, UK, Canada	USA, Italy, Trinidad & Tobago
11.Suriname	Alumina, gold, crude oil, lumber, shrimp, fish	Capital equipment, petroleum, cotton, foodstuffs, consumer goods	Canada 38.6%, US 12%, Belgium 11.6%, UAE 9.5%, Netherlands 6.1%, Norway 5,5%	US 26.6&, Netherlands 16%, T&T 15.1%, China 8.4%, Brazil 4.7%
12.St Lucia	Bananas		UK, USA	Brazil, USA

13. St. Vincent & the Grenadines	Bananas, eddoes, dasheen, arrowroot, starch, tennis racquets		France, Italy, Greece, USA	France, Singapore, Trinidad & Tobago, USA
14. Haiti	Apparel, manufacture, oil	Food, manufactured goods, machinery, raw material	US 90%; Canada 4%; France 1.5%	US 51%; Dominican Republic 19%; China 11%

*Countries listed in descending order by export/import volume
SOURCE: Adapted from - The Commonwealth Book Year 2010

Historically, the Caribbean has maintained trade and economic relations with the U.S, Canada and the European Union. More recently there has been increased diversification with the expansion of trade with players from the emerging BRIC economies, among these, China.

China is presently the third largest investor in the Caribbean with the U.S. and European Union occupying the two top spots. China's share of foreign investment in the region is currently 9% with a trade value of US $156 billion. In September 2011 on the occasion of the Caribbean China Economic and Trade Cooperation Summit, hosted in Port of Spain by the government of Trinidad and Tobago and attended by Chinese Vice Premier Wang Qishan, the PRC pledged the sum of US $1 billion to CARICOM members in the form of loans and preferential joint payments towards economic development. The gesture paved the way for recipient CARICOM countries to continue to benefit from extensive infrastructural development as well as training opportunities for Caribbean professionals at universities in China.

An important factor in the deepening of trade relations between China and Caribbean countries is what this engagement, however providential it may prove, augurs for the future of regional integration among the members of this bloc. More explicitly speaking, since 2008 no less than six CARICOM countries have received loans from the International Monetary Fund (IMF). These were Belize, Dominica, Grenada, St. Kitts and Nevis, and St. Vincent and the Grenadines. The loans were negotiated primarily under the Rapid Access Component of the IMF's Exogenous Shocks Facility (ESF) and carried minimal conditionality. However, a possible change in gear that can arise due to the confluence of factors would include: the issue of coherence between the conditions attached to the loans by donors such as the IMF; bilateral partnerships in which countries may be bonded under other regimes; the consolidation of policies under the requirements of the Caribbean

Single Market and Economy (CSME), the economic union to which countries are politically and legally bound, and the emergence of China as a third force in terms of trade relations.

This is one of several very interesting pointers raised by Annita Montoute in her Study "Emerging Players in the Caribbean" (June 2011) produced for the European Center for Development Policy Management. Montoute's project probes the history of how the region became weaned of preferential trade treatment from the European Union - an aspect of the geopolitical past to which this writer averred in Fifth Republic or Fourth Reich (2010), - and concluded that the Caribbean effectually represents part of a more all-encompassing Chinese strategy to:

- Control global trading routes since the region falls within the sphere of U.S. Influence.
- Infiltrate fuel markets as in the case of liquid nitrogen gas produced and exported by Trinidad and Tobago as well as bauxite from Jamaica.
- Consolidate food supply, hence the procurement of sugar cane cultivation lands in Jamaica, hitherto referred to in the Chapter.
- Secure its access to large reserves of natural gas, bauxite, and fish stock.
- Exploit vast areas of fertile land as obtains in Guyana. Belize and Suriname.
- Gain a foothold on access to the U.S. market, illustrated by heightened trade and investment activity in the Bahamas.
- Isolate Taiwan in furtherance of its One China policy. Currently, there are 23 nations in the world that have maintained diplomatic relations with Taiwan and CARICOM members are well represented within this grouping, namely Belize, St. Lucia, St. Kitts and Nevis and St. Vincent and the Grenadines.

The Caribbean Basin is undoubtedly home to a greatly expanded and intensified economic presence of China, a status quo that is intensely anatomized by scholars such as R. Evan Ellis of the William J. Perry Center for Hemispheric Defense Studies of the National Defense University Washington D.C. and Ambassador Richard Bernal of the Inter-American Development Bank. Indeed, CARICOM Member States have come to regard the new era of trade relations with the People's Republic of China as a fortification of their collective mission to incorporate well-endowed players in their quest for economic, social and cultural development, long-term trade, the acquisition of development assistance and technical cooperation. This forage for widened horizons extends beyond China to emerging regional blocs such as the more recently constituted Community of Latin

American and Caribbean States (CELAC) as well as Brazil, Russia, South Africa, and India of the BRICS membership.

Established on August 01, 1973, by the Treaty of Chaguaramas CARICOM's primary goals are to attain improved overall standards of living for its people; full employment of labor and other factors of production; accelerated and coordinated economic development and convergence; expansion of trade and economic relations with third states; enhanced levels of international competitiveness; greater levels of success in economic leverage, and effectiveness of Member States in dealing with all other States and entities of any description; enhanced coordination of Member States' foreign and economic policies; enhanced cooperation in terms of efficient operation of common services and activities for the benefit of its people and intensified activities in areas such as health, education, transportation and telecommunication.

Economic and trade integration, as envisaged from the outset would enable the free movement of goods, services and labor within the region and initially, at least, protect the regional space as a first step towards full integration into the wider global economy. It was also envisaged that the CSME-promoted single market and economy would surmount the limitations of scale and scope imposed on Member States by sheer virtue of size.

Despite very visible areas of functional cooperation within the Community, exemplified in several time-honored institutions such as CARICOM Secretariat based in Guyana, the Caribbean Development Bank, the more recently inaugurated regional security architecture the centerpiece of which is the Implementation Agency for Crime and Security, and the Caribbean Court of Justice headquartered in Port of Spain, Trinidad, many of the core objectives of this well-conceived intra-regional multilateral pact, remain unfulfilled. A more widened discourse on the issue, however, escapes the scope of this enquiry.

Nonetheless this central fact, compounded by other considerations, such as the susceptibility of the region to transnational crime and severe fiscal deficits currently experienced among many Member States, has by no means served as a deterrent to the entry of new players into the region, in search of economic partnership opportunities.

The Inter-American Development Bank's continued surveillance on CSME trade performance concedes that between 1990-1998 intraregional exports had increased from US $590 to US $999 million while in sharp distinction extra-regional markets had simultaneously declined from US $3.6 billion to US $3.3 billion. All in all, intra-regional trade comprises a vast and disproportionate segment (14.5%) of CARICOM's total trade, a concern that has been registered by Professor Norman Girvan, one of the region's most longstanding and respected scholar.

According to the International Trade Center's Trade Map Database, the principal exports from CARICOM to China are: aluminum oxide (14%), lumber tropical hardwood (145%), bitumen and asphalt (77%), ferrous waste, scrap of iron or steel (N/A), non-coniferous logs (-2.9%), poles, piles, conifers not sawn (29%), electric conductors for voltage>= 1,000 (8%), and copper-zinc base alloys, iron wrought (128%). Thus, as much as 98% of the region's wrought copper-zinc alloys find a market in China but despite this the region does not appear to be reciprocating, proportionately at least, by exploiting opportunities within the Chinese market through the sale/ export of indigenous coffee, rum, pipe fittings, iron and steel, contact lenses, dried fish, rock lobster, frozen shrimp, prawns, mollusks, and waste scrap of alloy steel.

Conversely, the Chinese have been remarkably agile and proactive - importing cargo vessels and other vessels for transporting goods and persons (21%), tankers (N/A), floating docks (N/A), footwear outer soles rubber or plastic (12%), new pneumatic rubber tires for buses and lorries,(16%), t-shirts, single vests etc. (16%), preservatives fresh or chilled garlic(12%), and pneumatic tires for motor cars, station wagons and racing cars (86%).

As an economic bloc, the region is presently hampered by barriers to integration due to setbacks such as excessive documentation for trade transactions; disparities in the administration of customs laws; dissimilar tax regimes; "arbitrary" import taxes; misaligned investment regimes; the non-existence of workable codes in free zones, and the absence of a regime on government procurement. More recently, a hiatus has been placed on advancement towards the introduction of a single currency through a common currency monetary union, a development that was scheduled to occur in 2015 alongside the process of regional capital market development. A prerequisite of this is the existence of open markets, factor mobility, a system of fiscal transfers or alternatively, a form of policy coordination within Community membership.

Simultaneous with these concerns, Chinese investment and trade have progressively burgeoned with the deepening and expansion of relations with CARICOM Governments in many spheres of activity, some of which are expanded on below:

- Major Construction Projects: This array of heavily invested projects includes the construction of an airport in Nassau, capital of the Bahamas, the construction of a terminal at the Vere Bird International Airport in Antigua; investment into deep sea port and major highway development in Suriname at an estimated US $6 million.

- Financial Activity: Illustrative of this is the volume of finance being funneled through the region as Chinese construction companies secure lucrative contracts for the construction of major highways, ports, and resorts funded by loans from Chinese investments banks such as the China Development Bank and the Export-Import Bank.
- Purchase of Interests: The buy-over of interests particularly in relation to primary products has been another notable trend. Examples of this occurred in the purchase (by the Chinese) of 70% of the interests in Omai bauxite mine in Guyana in 2007; investments in hotel resorts on Grenada in 2011 as well as in the Bahamas; and the purchase of an ethanol refinery as well as sugar cane fields in Jamaica in 2010.
- Tax Shelters: There is evidence of increased activity in the prohibitively large flows of funds emanating out of China to countries within the Caribbean notable for tax incentives promoted by their respective governments and for the proliferation of offshore financial centers - a trend that extends to countries outside of the CARICOM bloc.

Having surveyed the trading patterns between China and the Caribbean States within the last decade, Montoute arrives at some inexorable conclusions in terms of the long-term implications for Caribbean countries that are politically drawn to China, and the demonstrated confidence that CARICOM is displaying towards China as a preferred partner for aid and development assistance:

- A huge deficit exists between CARICOM and China, which is increasing to the extent that it is becoming unsustainable. This state of affairs can only be offset if Caribbean countries boost their exports to China against the current wave of infrastructural projects.

- Trade relations between CARICOM and China tend to be bilateral and this status quo could potentially lead to countries competing against each other for Chinese aid, thereby eroding the spirit of regional integration.

- The pattern of trade is skewed towards the importation of manufactured goods from China and the exportation of raw materials. There is no transfer of technology and where demands for labor arise this works to the advantage of Chinese nationals who are brought in under the terms of government-to-government project agreements.

All in all Caribbean countries are being drawn away from the United States and the European Union as preferred trading partners largely because of the Chinese policy of non-interference in the domestic affairs of host societies and the fact that the PRC is not driven by ideological considerations and specific underpinning tenets of the Inter-American charter such as "democracy," "human rights" and "good governance."

Concerns over Exorbitant Money Flows in Region's Financial Systems

Many drivers of insecurity have dominated Caribbean societies over the years the most important being their exploitation as a primary transit zone for the illicit trafficking of drugs and firearms and the associated funneling of illicit proceeds derived from trans-border crime. The United Nations Office on Drugs and Crime (UNODC) in its Transnational Organized Crime Threat Assessment, 2010 deemed drugs "the highest value commodities trafficked internationally." According to the assessment, which meticulously traces illegal flows of profits internationally, drugs now represent a long-term source of income for organized crime groups operating out of the region with linkages in North America, West Africa and Europe.

Like any legitimate commercial activity, market forces drive transnational crime. The Financial Action Task Force (FATF) had estimated that in the late 1980s, roughly U.S. $424 billion (0.8%) in the United States or 0.5% of the global GDP would have been available for laundering money. Based on 2009 data, this would have amounted to U.S. $1.2 trillion. The IMF figures stated that money laundering amounted to an estimated 2% to 5% of the global GDP – approximately U.S. $0.6 to U.S. $1.5 trillion in the late 1990s. A more recent study in the developing world was undertaken by William Baker, founder of Global Finance Integrity, based on its study of 12 categories of transnational crime, including illicit drugs and firearms trafficking. That study arrived at an estimated U.S. $650 billion in criminal proceeds per annum, the largest sources being derived from illicit drugs (50 %), followed by counterfeit (39 %), human trafficking (5 %) and illicit trade in other sectors.

Caribbean Basin tax shelters, and specifically those countries falling within the cusp of primary drug transshipment, are firmly in the radar of the U.S. International Narcotics Drug Control Report 2012. The Bahamas, the British Virgin Islands, the Cayman Islands, and the Dominican Republic have been registered as nations "of primary concern" to the United States government. Antigua and Barbuda, Barbados, Grenada, Trinidad and Tobago, St. Kitts and

113

Nevis, St. Lucia, St. Vincent and the Grenadines and Suriname are all deemed to be jurisdictions "of concern" while Dominica and Barbuda remain "under monitor."

The significance of this notification lies in the fact that despite having adhered (albeit at an uneven pace) to the global regime of the FATF recommendations, these are identified venues within the region that are considered risks to U.S. interests and/or that of the wider global community. Alongside this phenomenon, Caribbean Basin countries, as illustrated in the preceding sections, have been recipients from both Chinese firms and the People's Republic of China, of a preponderance of lucrative contracts and foreign direct investments (FDIs) and this unprecedented level of commercial and trade activity exceeds usual parameters - a state of affairs that maintains the interest of academia at the William J. Perry Center for Hemispheric Defense Studies of the National Defense University.

U.S. Grand Strategy for Global Military Outreach

Against the setting of the global economic downturn in 2008-2009, and from the standpoint of the U.S. grand strategy and its economic foundation, the question to be posed is whether its array of military liabilities could continue to carry the U.S. as the premier global power. Paul Kennedy argues that in seeking to resolve this debate, historical precedents are not convincingly encouraging. He observes that it has been a common dilemma that in previous "number one" countries, when their relative economic strength began to ebb, overseas challenges to their dominant status compelled such countries to commit an increasing amount of resources to the military sector. This chapter has already charged the U.S. and other industrialized countries of such courses of action by highlighting apportionments to defense spending[16]

Despite this, the gap between American interests and capabilities abroad remains acute and its forces are now at full stretch. With recent incursions into Libya by NATO forces in March 2011 and the confirmed official involvement of the U.S. in the protection of civilians pursuant to the relevant U.N. Resolution, whether and for how long America is able to maintain its decisive geopolitical edge is a hydra-headed issue defined not only on the basis of economics, but also on an array of other strengths that it retains, including its long-held allegiances and diplomatic capital. Notwithstanding its formidable portfolio as the de facto arbiter in many a major global conflict, America continues to be shored up by "an impregnable array of wealthy, powerful, and democratic allies across the globe." Additionally, its technological resources and the dexterity, foresight, and resolution with which its foreign policy is discharged undergird its irrefutable supremacy as an international player. This was one aspect of our focus in Chapter One.

Indeed, the role assumed by Britain, Canada, France, Norway, Denmark and Germany in the ongoing Libyan conflict is parabolic of future trends in terms of reliance on allied support, and interoperability amidst an increasingly demanding program of engagements, and their consequential logistical juggling acts. It is similarly reminiscent of the front line in Europe at the height of the Cold War, which Winston Churchill referred to as "The Iron Curtain." This consisted of the deployments along a line extending from Szczecin in the Baltic Sea to Trieste in the Adriatic Sea, created by western European powers to curtail a possible Russian military occupation of Western Europe. The enterprise, commonly referred to as "stay-behind armies," was a device of the CIA of the U.S. and the Secret Intelligence Service (SIS or MI6) of the United Kingdom. Other major actors included security services in a number of European countries.

Taking these factors into account, there is every indication that the U.S. despite the obvious challenges of imperial overreach will maintain its present status as the linchpin of the western alliance system, and taking into account current political nuances within the European Union. This section will accordingly turn to the impact and relevance of the U.S. Basing Footprint internationally and the degree to which its forces are still able to conduct prompt, sustained, and synchronized operations with combinations of forces tailored to specific situations. For this to occur, the requisite access and freedom to operate in all domains – land, sea, air, space, and information, is an imperative. Finally, we will explore the strategic rationale for "stay-behind armies," which remain dispersed throughout the Europe of today and consider the arguments as to their future role being advanced from a juridical and political standpoint.

Full Spectrum Dominance

At first sight it is obvious that the U.S. national security program is uniquely aligned with the international security environment and stands ready to respond across the full range of potential military operations. Transportation, communications, and technology continue to evolve and foster expanded economic ties and awareness of international events. The blueprint that has been formulated for the future, to be followed by the military, is enunciated in Joint Vision 2020 (released in March 30, 2000), and evolves around the concept of Full Spectrum Dominance.

The concept spells out the ability of the U.S. forces, operating alone or with allies, to defeat any adversary and control any situation, across a range of military operations. Joint Vision 2020 anticipates a range of conflicts from nuclear war, to major theater wars, and smaller scale contingencies. Thus, the spiraling debacle of unrest currently engulfing the Northern African nations, and the wider radius of enduring hostilities in Afghanistan and the Gaza, along with continuing skirmishes in the further removed parts of Asia and Africa, fall within the scope of conundrums and scenarios envisioned in the document. Furthermore, while spectrum dominance is the ultimate goal, attaining it necessitates investment in the full capacities of the total force, namely: domination maneuver, precision engagement, focused logistics, and full dimensional protection. Building these capabilities to their fullest level demands that the military must be "fully joint" by 2020 – intellectually, operationally, organizationally, doctrinally, and technically.

Important markers in the Joint Vision 2020 are its expansion of the concept of interoperability in the international security environment, its intent to develop a global information grid, a resolution to minimize "sources of friction," and development of the capacity for information superiority. These criteria will push to the very limits the universality of U.S. global outreach and the inherent elasticity of its institutional and other proficiencies. We will examine each in turn.

Firstly, experiences with the NATO alliance in the 1970s and 1980s made it imperative that in order for forces to operate as seamlessly as possible and attain highest levels of efficiency, joint doctrine and information sharing needed to become a reality, administratively, operationally, and technically. The notion of interoperability was therefore expanded to address this new paradigm. As an addendum to this point, as recently as March 2011, Admiral Giamaolo Di Paola, Chairman of NATO Military Committee and Senior Military Advisor to the Secretary General of the Alliance, reflected in a feature address at the Royal United Services Institute (RUSI) in London, on the widely held view that NATO remains the most capable political-military alliance in the world. Noting that its new security challenges are enshrined in the Strategic Concept that is intended to shape the transformation of forces, structures, and procedures in the next ten years, he pressed home the need for NATO to commence interaction with emerging powers and international organizations. This rationale presages the evolution of the western alliance beyond the Atlantic Community, a move that will escalate the enlargement and stabilization of America's orbit of influence throughout and beyond the Eastern Hemisphere.

The second marker pertains to the global information grid. This concept is the desideratum so to speak to decision superiority in the environment. Such a facility will furnish the U.S. military with a network-centric environment thereby enabling it to integrate various forms of information operations with sophisticated all source intelligence, surveillance, and reconnaissance in a "fully synchronized information campaign." The grid, as initially proposed in the Joint Vision, will serve as "the globally connected, end to end set of information capabilities, associated processes, and people to manage and provide information on demand to war-fighters, policy makers, and support personnel."

Thirdly, in terms of information superiority, this potential will be developed to permit the collection, processing, dissemination, and uninterrupted flow of information while exploiting and denying the adversary the ability to do the same. Moreover, this can be discharged in a non-combatant situation or in a scenario figuring no clearly defined adversary, when friendly forces have the information they require to achieve operational objectives.

A fourth marker of significance is the concern expressed over minimizing "sources of friction" while conceding that such criteria can never be completely eliminated by virtue of their close interconnection with the human condition. The identified sources of friction are:

- The effects of danger and exertion
- Uncertainty and chance
- Unpredictable actions of other actors – to this end our earlier discussion in Chapter One, regarding the agglomeration of events that may culminate in a global "shock" will by extension constitute a source of friction
- Frailties of machine and information. Cognizance must be taken of exponential changes in the sphere of technological evolution; these changes will precipitate a greatly diminished potentiality for such occurrences. This discussion is expanded on in Chapter Ten.

Human frailties. Chapter Ten provides engaging insights into some of the far-reaching trends being phased into the military and aimed at minimizing human casualty by incrementally exporting battle theaters into cyberspace.

America's Basing Footprint

The strategies and military doctrines discussed thus far are the main pillars promoted by the U.S. to maintain its strategic superiority and exert its omnipresence. Preserving the desirable strategic situation that it now enjoys, however, requires a globally preeminent military for both today and the future. Among the more distinguished and authoritative works on America's scheme to preserve global leadership and maintain its preeminence globally, was the "Report of the Project for the New American Century" (September 2000), which was co-chaired by Donald Kagon and Gary Schmitt. Although very ma years have transpired since the initial promulgation of the document, its tenets and proposals retain their original relevance and validity.

The Recommendations of the New American Century were intended to leverage America to maintain and expand on its global presence in all domains, and advocated the taking of steps to:

- Maintain nuclear strategic priority, basing its nuclear deterrent upon a global nuclear net assessment that weighs the full range of current and emerging threats
- Reposition U.S. forces to respond to Twenty-first Century strategic realities by shifting permanently based forces to South-East Europe and South-East Asia, and correspondingly changing naval deployment patterns to reflect growing U.S. strategic concerns in East Asia
- Modernize current U.S. strategic forces selectively; and
- Develop and deploy global missile defenses to defend America's homeland as well as its allies for U.S. projection around the world
- Control the new "International Commons" of space and cyberspace and pave the way for creating a new military service, U.S. Space Forces, with the mission of space control.
- Exploit the "Revolution in Military Affairs" in order to ensure long-term superiority of U.S. conventional forces. To this end, a two-stage transformation process was proposed aimed at (1) maximizing the value of current weapons systems through the application of advanced technologies and (2) producing more profound improvements in military capabilities between single services and joint service experimentation efforts; and
- Increase defense spending

The Report was premised on the notion that the U.S. is the globally recognized interlocutor of world peace while alluding to "potentially powerful states" that were taking issue of the current status quo and were eager to change it if the opportunity presented itself. It affirmed that any breach in the status quo occasioned by global players that were so inclined would "endanger the relatively peaceful, prosperous, and free condition" enjoyed by the world. The acknowledged deterring factor in this dynamic was the global presence of American military power. This imperative to mold the international security order with American principles and interests is etched in a number of other authorized briefs that either support or feed directly into current defense policy and doctrine, including the historic "Defense Policy Guidance" drafted in the early months of 1992.

The constitutive elements of the Project for the New American Century are being pursued and are presently at uneven phases of maturity, but nonetheless well advanced. One of the more conspicuous indicators of American international outreach, for example, is its Basing Footprints around the world, which provide the critical framework for pursuing the elements of the Project. [17]

The strategic benefit of these U.S. bases is threefold:

- They afford the U.S. a forward position with which to project its military power
- They guarantee American access to markets and strategic commodities like energy - the global economy is literally lubricated today by the safe flow of energy supplies and any interruption of that supply will have seriously destabilizing consequences. This renders the Middle East a high priority area
- They serve as a symbol of American global power

This prodigious spread of military resources is unparalleled and specifically aimed at maintaining a global "Pax Americana" which translates into a U.S.-sponsored version of international peace. Impressively, at the height of the War in Iraq, there were no less than 737 military bases assigned across every key region in the world, commandeered by 1,840,062 military personnel, and supported by an additional 473,306 Defense Department civil service employees and 203,328 local hires. These overseas bases are invested with an aggregation of infrastructure, including barracks, hangars, hospitals and other buildings, constituting a portfolio that exceeds 539,000 facilities, located on more than 5,570 sites or approximately 29 million acres. Table 3-7.

TABLE - 3-7
NO. SITES BY MILITARY SERVICE/WHS 2009

Area	Army	Navy	Air Force	Marine Corps	WHS	Total
United States	2004	1011	1590	123	14	4742
Territories	29	72	19	1	0	121
Overseas	293	136	261	26	0	716
Total	2326	1219	1870	150	14	5579

SOURCE: Base Structure Report 2009

TABLE - 3-8
U.S. BASING FOOTPRINT BEYOND THE HOMELAND AND THE AMERICAS 2011 (UNCLASSIFIED)

Area	Base Location	Personnel
Africa	Camp Lemonia Djibouti Camp Similia, Kenya Manda Bay, Kenya FOLs in Ethiopia and Ghana	1000
Europe	BaumholderAnsbach/Kaiserslautautern, Germany Wiesbaden, Germany Ramstein, Germany Vianza, Italy Dae Molin Air Base, Italy Naval Station Rota, Spain USAF Bases, United Kingdom Incirlik Air Base, Turkey Benelux, Belgium LOCs Bulgaria, Romania	8400 2,500 2,500 2,600 1,200 800 9367 1,514 2000
Central Asia	Manas Air Base, Kyrgyzstan Afghanistan (10-15 bases)	1,000 59,000(pre-surge) 89,000(post-surge)
East Asia	South Korea Mainland, Japan Kadena Air Base, Okinawa Marine Corps Air Station, Okinawa Troops on Location, Philippines	28,000 4,000(includes civilians) 18,000(includes civilians)
Middle East	Bases in Iraq Troops in Saudi Arabia Troops in Egypt	171,000 (227) (225)

SOURCE: Developed by Author

American bases in Europe are intimately tied to the reality of NATO and the Cold War. According to Zbigniew Brzezinski, America's central geostrategic goal in Europe is "to consolidate the U.S. bridgehead on the Eurasian continent so that an enlarging Europe can be a more reliable springboard for projecting into Eurasia the international democratic and cooperative order." Moreover, in the context of American-European relations, European nations are highly dependent on the U.S. for security protection and therefore any expansion in the scope of Europe will automatically be an expansion in the scope of direct U.S. influence. Originally, European installations were commissioned to serve as defenses against the now defunct Soviet Union. Consequentially strategic concerns over Kosovo and neighboring Eastern Europe and NATO's continuing mission will factor into decisions concerning the retention of sizeable permanent bases in Europe.

Brzezinski believes "the enlargement of NATO and the E.U. would serve to invigorate Europe's own waning sense of larger vocation, while consolidating, to the benefit of both Europe and America, the democratic gains won through the successful termination of the Cold War." Along this logic, with Europe's commitment now made and the widening of NATO, Europe has now become expanded and is geopolitically part of the Euro-Atlantic space.

In the case of Central Asia, three primary considerations will determine continued U.S. force presence, namely:

- The geopolitics surrounding the Russia-China-United States triangular relationship
- The critical importance of the region to the war in Afghanistan. In 2005 the Karshi Air Base in Khanabad was closed and following this, an unsuccessful attempt was made to decommission Manas which was a critical point for transiting of troops
- Energy considerations

The priority and indeed greatest challenge for America will be to enlist strategically compatible partners in the region.

Regarding the Middle East, the Pentagon is fully committed to a permanent troop presence. Defense executives are of the view that a permanent presence would serve as a deterrent to inter-state conflict and also facilitate safe access to and shipment of sizeable military resources. Another crucial point is the need to assuage localized sectarian concerns. To this end, the Department is likely to canvass for the continued presence of troops beyond the formal withdrawal to serve as a buffer against Shiite domination of Iraqi Sunnis and Kurds. According to the American Forces Press Service (July 11 2011), Defense Secretary Leon E. Panetta raised three points with Iraqi President Jalal Talabani and Prime Minister Nouri al-Maliki, while "neither pressuring nor pleading" to underscore the imperative for continued troop presence:

- The urgent need for the Iraqi government to appoint defense and interior ministers
- The rising number of attacks by extremist elements backed by Iran and provided with Iranian weapons – these pose a threat both to U.S. troops and Iraqis; and

- The fulfillment of the next stages of the 2008 Security Partnership which require U.S. troops to be out of Iraq by December 31 2011

With 100,000 American combat forces on the ground in Afghanistan, the Obama administration had been banking on the commencement of a drawdown from July 2011 onwards, with forces due out by 2014. Ultimately these projections would be subject to advice provided by the Pentagon and Congressional assent.

East Asia also retains a sizeable contingent of U.S. Cold War military bases. There have been reductions in troop levels in South Korea and similar reductions in Japan. With China now the preponderant military and economic power in the region, an important factor will be its choice of regional strategic partners. Currently, the PRC is gravitating towards Pakistan, North Korea and Russia's Far East. Any escalated force presence in the region will pay close heed to alliances that are favorable to the Chinese.

Unified Command Plan

A Unified Command Plan braces the Basing Footprints. It is a schema defining the dispersal of missions, responsibilities, and geographic areas of responsibility and military assets and comprises six geographic combatant commands and four functional combatant commands. The former are responsible for planning and conducting military support for stability, security, transition, and reconstruction operations, humanitarian assistance, and disaster relief.

The specific geographic combatant commands are: Africa Command, Central Command, European Command, Southern Command, Pacific Command, and Northern Command, while Transportation Command, Strategic Command, Special Operations Command, and Joint forces Command constitute the functional commands.

The Joint Chiefs of Staff (J5) is the designated forum for conducting reviews of the Unified Command Plan and this is done on a biennial basis. Some major modifications were made in 2009 and subsequently in 2011, the latter having been signed off by the President in the week ending April 08 2011. The major amendments to the 2009 Plan were intended to:

- Give added emphasis to specific geographic areas in order to "head off" problems before they reached crisis proportions; and

- Prevent the creation of "ungoverned spaces" that would eventually become troublesome and could potentially be used as terror havens

In 2011, J5 agreed to:

- Shift AOR boundaries in the Arctic region to leverage long-standing relationships and improve unity of effort by giving U.S. Northern Command responsibility to advocate for Arctic capabilities
- Codify the presidential approval to de-establish the U.S. Joint Forces Command
- Expand the U.S. Strategic Command's responsibility for combating weapons of mass destruction and developing a Global Missile Defense Concept of operations
- Give U.S. Transportation Command responsibility for planning global distribution operations
- Reconfigure the maritime boundary of U.S. Africa Command to include all of Cape Verde's Exclusive Economic Zone; simultaneously altering the maritime boundary between U.S. Africa Command and U.S. Southern Command so that the South Sea Islands now fall under the purview of Southern Command.
- Re-name U.S. Special Operations Command Psychological Operations to Military Information Support Operations, replace the word "transformation" with develop and shape.
- Delineate what functions of Joint Forces Command will remain un-adapted.

The language of the more recent revisions signed off by the President wasdic suggestive of the decommissioning of Joint Forces Command some time later in 2011 and strengthening the role of Strategic Command in combating Weapons of Mass Destruction (WMD).

U.S. Global Missile Defense Missile Defense Agency (MDA)

The global dispersal of military assets also extends to missile capabilities. The U.S. has advanced its capacity to build and consolidate relationships with allies and international partners in this sphere of activities. Personnel from U.S. Strategic Command, U.S. Northern Command, U.S. Pacific Command, U.S. Forces Japan, U.S. European Command and others all operate aspects of the missile defense systems. Additionally, there is in place a number of bilateral and multilateral cooperative programs with partner nations including the United Kingdom, Japan, Australia, Israel, Denmark, Germany, Netherlands, Czech Republic, Poland, and Italy. The Missile Defense Agency is also an active participant in NATO-led activities in order to maximize opportunities to develop a more integrated NATO ballistic defense missile capability.[18]

The forgoing configurations are integral to America's global projection against the setting of a strategic mission plan, the core intent of the MDA being:

- To expand missile defense capabilities
- To increase the number of its international missile defense framework partners and combatant commanders
- To develop an MDA workforce with the capability of executing its international strategy, and furthering opportunities for international cooperation, personnel exchanges, training and internships

Table 3-9 on the overleaf provides a non-random open source selection of cooperative projects and programs being pursued by the Missile Defense Agency.

Command, Control, Battle Management, and Communications

The expansiveness of U.S. ballistic missile defense systems is borne out in the C2BMC system. This facility links, integrates, and synchronizes individual missile defense elements, systems, and operations, creating an optimized layered missile defense capability that enables response to threats of all ranges in all phases of flight. C2BMC is in effect the force multiplier that integrates global and regional networks and synchronizes missile defense systems and operations to maximize performance. It is the vital operational network that enables the President of the United States as Commander of the Armed Forces, the Secretary of Defense, and combatant commanders to dynamically manage designated networked sensors and weapons systems, to achieve their global and regional mission objectives.

Space Tracking and Surveillance

The MDA also operates a Space Tracking and Surveillance System, a two-satellite constellation, which serves as the experimental space layer of the Ballistic Missile Defense System (BMDS). Using sensors that can detect visible and infrared light, the STSS satellite constellation is part of a collection of land, sea, air, and space-based sensors. Moreover, a future space-borne sensor of the BMDS has been specially assembled to track ballistic missiles shortly after launch especially throughout their mid-course flight. This apparatus, referred to as the Precision Tracking Space System (PTSS), will provide sensor data to the BMSD Battle Manager, which will in turn send tracking data to deployed Aegis cruisers/destroyers and their onboard intercept of enemy ballistic missiles, thereby increasing the missile raid handling capacity of the BMDS.

TABLE – 3-9
U.S. Partnerships in Missile Defense Agency
Sponsored Cooperation Projects and Programs

Country	Project	Status
1. Italy	MEADS Partner	Research and development
2. Japan	Forward-based X-Bard Radar Siting, 21" Missile Development	Research and development
3. Czech Republic	RDT & E Cooperation; Possible Infrastructure Assets for European Defense	Research and development
4. United Kingdom	Flyingdales UEWR; Joint Project Arrangements for Cooperative Projects	Research and development
5. Kingdom of Denmark	Upgraded Early warning Radar	Research and development
6. Commonwealth of Australia	Advanced technology Cooperation	Research and development
7. The Netherlands	PAC – 3; Maritime BMD Cooperation	FDMDP
8. Republic of Poland	Potential RDT & E Cooperation; Future Vote in European Missile Defense	
9. Russian Federation	Strategic cooperation; transparency Dialogue	
10. State of Israel	Arrow Deployed; Arrow System Improvement Program; Development of Short-range BMD; Upper Tier Program	
11. Federal Republic of Germany	MEADS Partner; Laser Cross Link technology	
12. Kingdom of Bahrain	Missile Defense discussions	
13. NATO Membership	Completed tasking to explore architects to supplement European site	
14. Kingdom of Saudi Arabia	Requested BMD requirements analysis	
15. French Republic	Cooperative project potential	
16. Republic of India	Discussions on RDT & E	
17. United Arab	Request for THAAD	

Emirates	
18. Republic of Korea	Missile Defense discussions
19. Ukraine	Conducting missile defense project RDT & E; agreement being drafted
20. Qatar	Expressed interest in missile defense
21. Kuwait	Expressed interest in missile defense
22. Romania	Missile defense discussions

SOURCE: http://www.mda.mil/system/international_cooperation.html

This elaborate amalgamation of systems comprising a Unified Command Plan, Basing Footprints, and Space Command missions position the U.S. for telluric and outer space domination (the latter falling under Strategic Command), in respect of which there is no peer rival.

Within the homeland, the main challenges confronting the government have historically been inefficiencies in the defense procurement process particularly in the field of competitive bidding; evolving defense policy; the sheer variety of military contingencies that place varying demands on armed forces and weaponry; the nuanced decision-making apparatus between the Defense and the State Departments and the attending role of the National Security Council. To this must be added the more recent impact of the economic recession on America's industrial complex amidst other sector declines and the accompanying increase in protectionist policies. Any analysis of these very important institutional domestic components, although very helpful to this discourse, lies beyond the scope of the present text.

Communication lines between the respective government departments were strengthened in the course of the first four-year term of the Obama administration by the Bureau of Political and Military Affairs, which was headed by Assistant Secretary Andrew Shapiro in 2011. Apart from providing the office of the Assistant Secretary with a global perspective on political-military issues, the Bureau renders support by negotiating Basing Agreements, reviewing military exercises, facilitating overseas operations, and assigning embedded Foreign Policy Advisors to military service branch chiefs and combatant commanders worldwide. Other responsibilities of note include the promotion of regional stability and strengthening relations with friends and allies through security assistance programs.

The "Stay-Behind Armies" of Western Europe

Much of the resilience of the Western Alliance is to be found in legacy items. These include the operations of "stay-behind armies," which were integral to the NATO pact signed among the allies in 1949 following the World War II.[20] This special project entailed the creation of forces, referred to as the Gladio that would remain quiescent until war brought them into play. The rationale for this deployment was the expectation among Western powers of an impending war with the Soviet Union (later, the Soviet Bloc), which consistently had greater numbers of troops, tanks, planes, guns, and other equipment than Western nations.

In 1940, British Prime Minister Winston Churchill created the secret stay-behind-army SOE to set Europe ablaze by assisting resistance movements and carrying out subversive operations in enemy-held territory. After WW II the successor "stay behind secret units" referred to as the Gladio, was set up and incorporated the experiences and strategies of former SOE officers.

Administratively, the NATO Office of Security coordinated the activities of the Gladio. The former was an arm of SHAPE based in Brussels.[21] This Office has been an integral part of NATO since its inauguration in 1949. According to a former Secretary General of Gladio, Manfred Worner, the Director of Security coordinated, monitored, and implemented NATO security policy, simultaneously serving as Chairman of NATO's Security Committee, in which the Heads of Security Services of member countries met regularly to discuss matters of espionage, terrorism, subversion, and other threats, including at that time communism in Western Europe. In 1953 a Special Committee was set up under General Raymond Calster, Chief of the Belgium Military Secret Service, with the objective of coordinating the Special Forces Section of Gladio. This particular sphere of operations fell under the exclusive directorship of British or American officers.[22]

The Creation of a "Special Relationship"

The "stay-behind armies" were mobilized and fostered by the British and American intelligence agencies, with the British assisting financially in the operations, while closely collaborating with their CIA and the MI6 counterparts.[23] Following WW II, the "stay behind" network of secret militias was coordinated by the Command and Control structure for Special Forces of NATO within which the British Special Air Service (SAS) played a strategic role. Their techniques of recruitment involved establishing distinct networks for spying on occupiers, for sabotage, and subverting enemy occupation. Training was provided by the intelligence services of Britain and the U.S. and initial or chief agents were thereafter permitted to recruit additional sub-agents.

These units were strategically dispersed throughout Europe, even among nations that committed to neutrality during the war. In Belgium the network was referred to as Absalom. In the Netherlands, the network, labeled G III C, was administered by the Dutch military secret service. In this jurisdiction, the enterprise consisted of two branches, namely the SDR A8 (a military arm whose members were specially trained in combat, sabotage, parachuting, and maritime operations) and a civilian arm, the members of which were tasked in discrete communications, operational mobilization and intelligence gathering. France was a particularly important jurisdiction to the Americans and the British since nowhere in Western Europe, except perhaps in Italy, was the communist influence as strong after the war as it was among the French. Thus, on the initiative of the U.S. and British Special Forces (SAS), a secret network, the Plan Bleu was established. Many of its agents received strong support and financial backing to fund their anti-Communist campaigns, from wealthy industrialists, such as the Peugeot and Renault syndicates.

Although Turkey was officially neutral during the war, a top U.S. priority was to integrate that county solidly behind the Western anti-Communist defense system. Accordingly, the STK, was established. Regarding Germany, on the orders of the Pentagon, the U.S. CIC tracked down Nazis, brought them to trial at Nuremburg, and recruited selected right-wing extremists (including Klaus Barbie, a former Gestapo officer), in the setting up of the German "stay behind network," labeled the BDJ-TD. As a caveat for future cover, German Chancellor Adenauer signed a secret protocol with the U.S. upon West Germany's entry into NATO in May 1955, in which it was agreed that German authorities would refrain from active pursuit of known right-wing extremist elements. The Norwegian version of the "stay behind" secret entities was designated the "RACOMBOLE" Operation, and was similarly trained, funded and outfitted with the tacit approval of the state and support from the U.S., British military and intelligence agencies.

The current debate surrounding the concept of secret service armed forces is fueled by the extent to which the activities of these networks were misdirected in the past, to their continued usage as footprints of the Western Alliance, and their value to the U.S. in the new dispensation of the War on Terrorism which has succeeded the Cold War.

Lacking in a Soviet invasion in Western Europe, many cells of this secret network took on the task, nominally on NATO's behalf, of preventing a "shift to the left" in the political balance of host countries throughout Europe. This pattern became discernible in Italy, Portugal, Belgium, the Netherlands, Denmark, Norway, Germany, Greece and Turkey.[24] Through a trail of massacres, extreme acts of violence, and naked terror, these networks collaborated with right-wing extremists in an attempt to induce conservative reactionary tendencies, and force the masses to reject "the Left" and turn to the state for security. The modus operandi of the discredited arms of Gladio jolts concerns regarding the mass manipulation of entire communities and societies and its wider implications for transparency, accountability and democracy.[25]

At the end of the day, the American-led campaign of democratization and the role of legacy entities supportive of this cause should mirror the very ideals to which the Secretary of State alluded in Chapter One. This would guarantee that the outward expansion of the U.S. proceeds with agility and popular support, and not be consistently jaded with latent antagonisms that find root in a questionable past.

Economic Realities

China is America's most important great power competitor and the US-China relationship is the most important great power relationship of the 21st Century. Ni Feng, journalist in "China Today" observes that, "the economic ties between China and the U.S. are interlocked in a framework of mutual benefit, a framework that will be further strengthened as the importance of the two parties to each other is more mutual in nature." [26] Despite this assertion, Feng is of the view that the current climate favors ultra-caution in the area of bilateral trade and cooperation as a result of what he perceives as an "unequal interdependence" that is favorable to the U.S. from a strategic standpoint.

He theorizes that, "so far China is still in a passive position when disputes arise and is the minor player in an unequal interdependence." This passive status, in his view, affords the U.S. the ability to maintain its power superiority, take disputes in stride, and initiate actions as the mood strikes it. With this type of leverage the U.S. can play the trade imbalance and the exchange rate issues to its advantage to influence bilateral trade policies and even the Chinese economic decision-making.

Robert S Ross, Professor of Political Science at Boston College foresees neither a friendly nor primarily cooperative relationship between Washington and Beijing, but rather one of continuing competitors, based on the strategic outlook. He surmises that, "...the issue for the U.S. is not whether rising China is a friend or foe. Rather, it is what kind of strategic challenge China will pose to U.S. interests and what the implications will be for U.S. security, the U.S.-China relationship, and regional and global stability."

In the realm of econometrics, U.S. - China trade volume reached $300 billion in 2010 while China's trade surplus stood at $250 billion, a differential that is being used as a point of reference to substantiate U.S. trade protectionist sentiment. On the other hand, as the fastest growing economy in the world, China is not necessarily disposed to a trade surplus. In acknowledging the differential, the U.S. maintains that continuing trade imbalance between the two countries is attributable to China's competitive advantage due to its lower currency value and has repeatedly proposed currency appreciation as a remedy for the current deficit. It is a fact that a country's currency becomes more valuable when it is enlarging economically as a power.[27]

Moreover, since 2005, the RMB exchange rate against the U.S. dollar has increased by a mere 5%. In 2010 the figure was 3.5% for that year only. On this basis, it has been reckoned that the RMB should be able to sustain appreciation in the near future. China, in the meantime, is under extreme pressure to realize profits at home while simultaneously attempting to mitigate its critical unemployment level. The ongoing state of affairs had restrained the Chinese from any move towards appreciating the RMB, particularly in the wake of the appreciation of the Japanese yen. Such a strategy was employed in 2005 when China instituted a gradually controlled appreciation in response to the upgrading of its industrial structure to cater for increased levels of exports.

Lastly and by no means less important, the U.S. administration is according top priority status to ongoing interchange with the Chinese on economic and strategic associations through the China-U.S. Strategic and Economic Dialogue. The unique merger of economic and strategic forums was facilitated by President Obama, upon assuming his first term in office and is presently the venue of highest stature on which the two countries confabulate on matters covering most fields and with the broadest scope.[28] Given the stature of the U.S. and China as the world's largest and second largest economies respectively, the anticipated Dialogue is being regarded as "the weather vane for the international community."[29]

Chinese Ministry of Defense

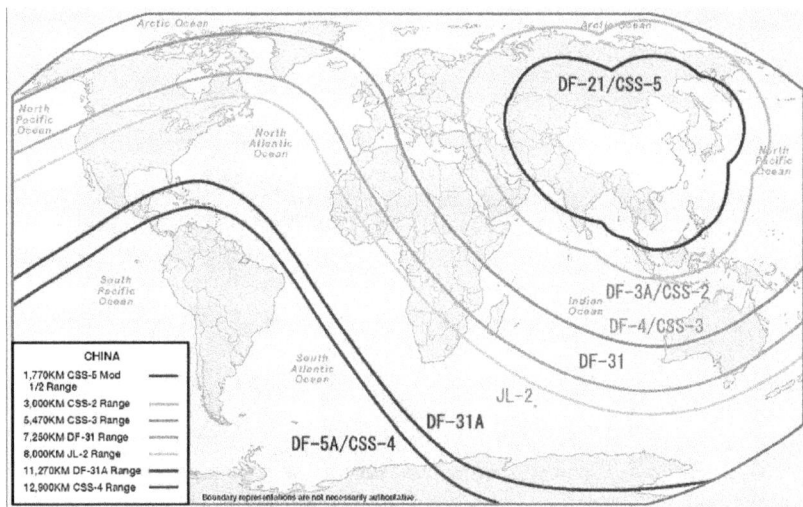

Chinese Weapon Ballistic Range

Boeing P-8A Poseidon: Ocean patrol and antisubmarine aircraft outfitted with state-of-the-art sensory equipment and destined to replace PC-3 Orion Model.

CVN-78 Aircraft Carrier: Touted as the most expensive piece of military equipment ever assembled, the aircraft carrier will be nearly three football fields long, weigh more than 100,000 tons, and have the capacity to support 75 aircraft. It will replace the USS Enterprise.

The Trident is the latest and most advanced version of the U.S Navy's ballistic missiles, is equipped with a thermonuclear warhead and is carried by most Ohio-Class submarines.

CHAPTER FOUR

INSTITUTIONAL CONFIGURATIONS IN THE INTER-AMERICAN FRAMEWORK

"The steady growth of Chinese geopolitical reach including facilities in the mid-Pacific, Cuba, and the Bahamas, in the Caribbean, and now in Panama, offer warning signs against the once unquestioned U.S. strategic control of the Western Hemisphere.....the Monroe doctrine is relevant here and I for one would not hesitate to employ it as a political guard against external encroachments in Latin America."

John T. Tierney
Institute of World Politics,
Washington

Cooperative security seeks to reduce rather than confront the prospects and scope of international aggression through the preventative association of participating states to protect their security. Within given geopolitical regions, such as Central and South America and the Caribbean, such code of state conduct imposes on participating countries an obligation to assure each other of their respective intentions by:

- Fostering transparency
- Strengthening multinational institutions designed to maintain peace and resolve conflict
- Promoting confidence building through ongoing military contact; and
- Supplying peace keeping forces upon request from international bodies

This established practice stands in strident contrast to deterrence as a more conventional approach to repelling the hostile actions, whether real or perceived, of another country. As a variant to the cooperative approach, deterrence compels the need to repel an attack from beyond a nation's borders. Such course of action tends to culminate in more lethal outcomes that may range from moderate casualties to the large-scale destruction of critical infrastructure.

The Inter-American system is the oldest regional society in the world. Simon Bolivar first put the notion of a hemispheric union in 1826. He proposed the creation of a League of American Republics with a common military, a mutual defense pact, and a supra-national parliamentary assembly. Several decades later, the topic of the pursuit of regional solidarity and cooperation would again come to the forefront at the Fifth International Conference of American States held in Washington from November 1889 to April 1890.

Upon the formation of the OAS on May 05, 1948 there were 21 members. The later expansion of the organization saw the addition of the newly independent members.

Within the Americas, the concept of cooperative security emerged during the 1930s in response to surreptitious overtures that were being made by the axis powers to increase their political and economic leverage in the Americas. Today the system is conserved by an assemblage of national and supranational institutions and organs united under the logic of rule and having to contend with radically heterogeneous global forces beyond the hemisphere. The system consists of various institutions, of which the OAS and its General Secretariat are familiar examples, treaties, agreements, conventions, and other diplomatic instruments, and embraces the countries identified by these institutions and instruments as member States.[1] It is bolstered as well by equally significant informal concessions, which guide the conduct of respective states, in ways that are not necessarily registered in the body of the OAS Charter and affiliated instruments. The most compelling example of this is relations between the U.S. and other OAS members. Each country's political, economic, and cultural interests, its ideological tenets, as well as its capacity if at all to leverage with the United States sway these interactions.

Indeed, the power differential between the U.S. and other OAS members is even less amenable to measurement than the wealth disparity and this very widely acknowledged asymmetry translates into the uneven and at times discordant nature of national interests. In essence, this has proven to be the essential catalyst and central reason for the existence of the Inter-American system. In fact, ever since its inauguration in 1889, members of the Latin American community have maintained a decisively subordinate position to the U.S.[2] State-to-state differentials are the more pronounced when members of CARICOM are subsumed in the geopolitical line-up.

Historically, the period 1933-1947 immediately following the coming into force of the Rio Treaty as the beacon for Pan American solidarity was a relatively harmonious one, which heralded what would in future years be more popularly regarded as "the good neighbor policy." The express intent of this collective political stance was to reduce rather than confront the potential for international aggression.[3]

In the years following World War II (1947-1967), however, the dynamic was altered. Despite the fact that member States consistently re-affirmed their common commitment to the policy of non-intervention, their interests became increasingly divergent. The tenuous status quo would be considerably aggravated by the military intervention of the U.S. in the Dominican Republic in 1965.[4] During the late 1960s, a period of strong nationalist sentiment swept through the British colonies, aggravating the region's mercurial social and political mood. Simultaneously, as the East-West rivalries intensified with increased military contacts between the Soviet Union and Cuba, North Korea, Vietnam, Czechoslovakia and other communist countries, there were corresponding security concerns filtering into the region's political agenda regarding Soviet encroachment.[5] (U.S. Department of State 1984; U.S. Department of Defense 1984; Adkin 1989; Payne 1991)

Using Cuba as a proxy, Moscow's strategy, which proceeded well into the 1980s, was primarily to:

- Split the allegiances of former British colonies
- Use revolution in the eastern Caribbean to spur unrestrained illegal migration into the United States
- Induce Caribbean participation in the drug trade to corrupt existing democratic institutions
- Gather information and intelligence through a range of measures as for example increased reconnaissance flights including TU 95s based in Cuba
- Create naval bases to escalate the range and mobility of Soviet surface ships
- Amass a preponderance of assets at bases throughout the Caribbean, including tanks, frigates MIGs and medium SS-4 missiles

It was against this checkered Cold War political tradition that the Inter-American system sprung. Its supporting pillars were shaped, however, by two fundamental edicts, both of which emanated during and immediately following the critical World War II period, namely:

- Resolution VIII also referred to as the Act of Chapultepec, which contained a provision mandating the drafting and adoption of a collective security treaty and the creation of a hemispheric defense system based on reciprocal assistance in the event of aggression against an American State by a non-American State. This mandate culminated in the Inter-American Treaty for Reciprocal Assistance, more commonly referred to as the Rio Pact

- Resolution IX, which compelled the reorganization and strengthening of the hemispheric defense system and charged the Governing Board of the Pan American Union to prepare a relevant draft charter for the Ninth International Conference of American States. This draft was the precursor to the current OAS Charter.

The objects of the Organization, propounded by the founding nations, are contained in Article 4. Therein members resolutely committed to:

- Strengthening the peace and security of the continent
- Preventing possible causes of difficulties and to insure the pacific settlement of disputes that may arise among the Member States
- Providing for common action on the part of those States in the event of aggression
- Seeking the solution of political, juridical, and economic problems that may arise among them
- Promoting by cooperative action economic, social and cultural development

The first section of this Chapter describes the basic architecture of the Inter-American system, identifies contemporary regional security points at issue, and muses on the ramifications of a possible "Chinese threat" against the backdrop a lock-down of the Panama Canal. The latter has consistently harried U.S. defense planners and policy makers since the late 1990s. The Chapter then examines the most crucial institutional linkages within the Inter-American defense community and concludes that the hemispheric history of multilateralism - articulated in the Rio Pact, interoperability, and joint training buttressed as it now is by a discernible chain of intergovernmental, bilateral, and multilateral agreements committing signatories to cooperative security and shared responsibility - have significantly diminished the likelihood of a viable challenge to U.S. military and defense hegemony in the Americas.

We expand on this idea in Chapter Five by comparing the status quo in the Americas with that in the Middle Eastern Hemisphere. The ensuing chapter demonstrates that an elaborate scheme of "base footprints" is now chaperoned by a multi-track system of mediation, which was initiated and administered by the U.S. Department of State following the events of 9/11. This system promotes conflict resolution through the agency of business, private citizenry, the media, religion, activism, research, training and education, and philanthropy. It is illustrative of a policy of soft power, permeates all levels of society, while incorporating citizens with a diversity of skills into the mediation process. Thus, the full range of conflicts and hostilities that exists at national, local, and sectarian

137

levels is presently being tackled by non-military means. A classic exemplification of the application of this policy of soft power is the Middle East Partnership Initiative (MEPI), which is funded and marshaled by the U.S. Department of State. For the purposes of this Chapter, however, we confine ourselves to the Inter-American experience.

The Inter-American Security Campaign: Post-World War II North America, Latin America, the Caribbean

Prior to World War II, the United States and Canada had formed a bilateral security relationship in 1940 through the Ogdensburg Declaration with the establishment of the Permanent Joint Board of Defense (PJBD). Through the Board, U.S. and Canadian senior military officers chaired consultative forums offering advice to both the President of the United States and the Canadian Prime Minister respectively, regarding the "defense of the northern half of the Northern Hemisphere."

Following the war, both countries became parties to a series of multilateral and bilateral agreements aimed at cementing common defense concerns. The most comprehensive of these was, of course, the 1949 North Atlantic Treaty Organization (NATO), which effectively cemented their security relationship in the context of the post-World War II threat of Soviet Communism. Security cooperation was expanded further with the formalization of the North American Air Defense Command Formation (NORAD), which catered for the territorial defense of the Northern Hemisphere from ballistic missiles and other air-borne threats to both nations.[6]

The U.S. response to threats in the southern geographic approaches was through its institutionalization of perimeter defenses supported by a unified command plan described in Chapter Three. Core security concerns that occupied the attention of the U.S. government were the internecine inter-state conflicts among Latin American nations, Soviet aggression during the years of the Cold War, and more recently, the drug wars being waged by cartels whose activities attained unprecedented scale during the 1980s, and have persisted to this very day.

Some aspects of this earlier history are more thoroughly illustrated and penned in the works of Latin American scholars the ilk of Jorge Dominguez, himself admitting that "historically to be sure, organized international non-state military forces had been the scourge of Central America and the Caribbean." Beyond the Cold War era, the demobilization of armed forces (wherein many former soldiers and members of defunct guerilla movements had reorganized themselves and regrouped) had become an exigent political concern among many Latin American governments, since these groups continued to pose serious and unrelenting challenges to internal domestic stability. Unevenly dispersed groups of armed combatants were evolving at an exponential pace and proceeding to serve as instruments of criminal organizations seeking enrichment. Equally significant is the prolific expository work on contemporary Caribbean security issues, inclusive of the drug trade and its impact on regional societies, as well as trends towards militarization, churned out by Ivelaw Griffith.[7]

In addition to these contemporary challenges, it was becoming increasingly apparent that democracy of itself did not necessarily deliver on its promise of peace in the region. To the contrary, Latin America was virtually being racked by the very process of democratization in countries such as Chile, Argentina and Brazil, all of which transitioned from rule by military regime to that of democratically elected civilian presidents during the 1980s to 1990s. Citing the experiences of Venezuela/ Colombia; Belize/Guatemala (1991); Chile/Peru (1992) and Chile/Argentina (1991), Dominguez builds a cogent case that in spite of the ushering in of democratic governments in these jurisdictions during the 1980s and 1990s, and the settlement of long-standing territorial disputes among neighbors, the likelihood of détente among affected states was becoming increasingly more elusive.

Based on his own observations, Dominguez hypothesizes that inter-state security issues in Latin America displayed a tendency to exhibit what he pegs a 'status quo bias,' that is to say, states find it inexorably difficult to alter the status quo whether this translates into either making peace or breaking peace. He expands the argument by establishing that the most successful designs for peacemaking in Latin America actually occurred under the totalitarian rule of military governments. This pattern was particularly conspicuous among Southern Cone jurisdictions where, as cases in point, settlements were struck in the Beagle Dispute involving Argentina as well as in the Ecuador/Peru conflict case in Central America. The latter dispute had remained unresolved throughout 1991-1995.

His rare illation is betrayed in the findings of other contemporary scholars, such as Mares and Desch. The latter assert that the spread of democracy across Latin America appears to exhibit 'an indeterminate relationship' with the maintenance of peace in the region. Beyond this, they suggest that in order to make the consolidation of democracy compatible with peace in the region, there should be a marriage between domestic and international leadership to foster the process. This prescription, in their view, would not only secure the basis for civilian supremacy over the armed forces within individual countries, but also resolve extant disputes and ensure more effective governance of Inter-American security institutions.

Caribbean societies have been similarly overwhelmed by divers security issues, the latest being their exploitation as a primary transit zone for the illicit trafficking of drugs, firearms, and the funneling of illegal proceeds derived from trans-border crime. UNODC, in its 2010 Transnational Organized Crime Threat Assessment, deemed drugs 'the highest value illicit commodities trafficked internationally.' [8] According to the assessment, having inked the most prodigious flow of illegal profits internationally, drugs now represent a long-term source of income for organized crime groups operating out of the region with linkages in North America, West Africa, the United Kingdom and Europe. Established trafficking routes typically follow market forces from the less developed countries in the south, Colombia, Peru, Bolivia, to the more developed vicinities in the north such as the United States, the United Kingdom, Canada and Europe. Moreover, 38% of the global demand for cocaine now originates in North America and together Colombia, Peru and Bolivia presently account for the bulk of global supplies, rendering the Caribbean corridor a transshipment zone of regional and international concern. These trends and patterns are corroborated in the UNODC Annual World Drug Reports of 2009 and 2010 respectively.

In terms of their commercial significance, the Caribbean archipelagic chain stretches along a generally southeasterly direction from Florida to the northern tier of South America, facilitating relatively narrow passages through which commerce is allowed to navigate. The Strait of Florida between Key West and Havana is one of the wider passages, 90 miles across, and comparatively smaller than the straits between Cuba and Haiti, and the tiny islands of the Lesser Antilles and between Venezuela and Grenada.

From a geo-commercial standpoint, 44% of all tonnage entering the United States transits the Caribbean Basin. Additionally, many minerals of strategic and commercial importance to the U.S. originate within South America and ply the Caribbean Basin along chartered routes as for example copper from Peru and Chile; tin from Bolivia along with manganese and chromium for steel production, and nickel and cobalt; bauxite (of which aluminum is a principal derivative) from Jamaica and natural gas from Trinidad and Tobago.[9]

U.S. interests, thus extend persuasively beyond the homeland borders. In the course of preserving these interests the U.S. asserts itself over other nations whose capacities are manifestly subordinate to its own, in the role of assumed leadership, invariably interpreted as dominance. Traditionally, the U.S. defense security policy has been to maintain regional dominance or at a very minimum exclude clearly hostile and powerful foreign rivals. The policy was bluntly violated on several occasions in the not long past, in an era when Cuba had become a Soviet forward base, and subsequently in the 1960s - 1980s, when Grenada fell to a left - wing military coup and the Nicaraguan government had succumbed to revolutionary forces.[10]

Against this historical background, China's presence has re-ignited long-held concerns which resurged in 2010, concomitant with what was more widely referred to as "the Aramco deal." The maneuver was one more in a close succession of impressive markers pin-pointing China's long-term plans and strategic thought in securing oil supplies in Latin America and the Caribbean. Based in St. Eustacius, one of the five islands that make up the Netherlands Antilles grouping, Aramco, a subsidiary of Strata Terminals, boasts of prodigious storage capacity of 11.3 million barrels as well as shipment facilities, and was formally owned and operated by New Star Energy of San Antonio, Texas. Prior to 2010 and following a 22 year low in U.S. demand, the terminals had served as a hub for tankers conveying oil from South America and the Middle East to the United States.

The initiative has also been viewed as one that is contemplative of the economic gains that will inevitably cascade from China's access to deeper and wider shipping channels, enhanced overhead clearance, and diminished navigation time. Collectively, these would accrue in 2012 when major refurbishing work on the Panama Canal is scheduled for completion, further underscoring well-timed and calculated steps by the Chinese to capitalize on an unprecedented opportunity.

The regional rejoinder to this advancement was reminiscent of the prevailing political mood several decades ago when the Torrijos-Carter Treaties were signed on September 07, 1977 by the U.S. and Panamanian governments, effectively abrogating the exclusive rights and privileges enjoyed by the U.S. in relation to the usage and control of the Panama Canal and its contiguous zones. Under the preceding 1903 Hay–Brunau Varilla Treaty, the U.S. was authorized to build the Canal, operate it for perpetuity, and govern the ten-mile wide and forty-mile contiguous area around the Canal, designated 'the Panama Zone.'[11] Until 1999, the complex therefore represented a strategically important asset to the U.S. and its allies. Firstly, as an important international trading route, the Canal was an invaluable commercial and economic asset. Secondly, the contiguous zones of the Canal served as appended settlements to a number of U.S. military facilities, among which was the Howard Air Force Base, former headquarters of U.S. Southern Command (SOUTHCOM).

Having relinquished these rights and privileges, concerns harbored by analysts and defense planners morphed into the necessity of preserving freedom of navigation and maintaining unimpeded lawful commerce based on the principles of customary international law. This lingering unease, however well substantiated, was heightened by other concerns that at strategic level, China's predisposition to hostile actions by virtue of its potential control over the Canal and its contiguous sea lanes, constituted a potential threat to U.S. security interests and that America's logistical planning at tactical level was correspondingly placed at risk.

The issue that yet persists in the present scheme of things is two-fold: does China have the capacity and political will to prohibit America's ability to act effectively and could China acting on its own behalf, or acting on behalf of any other hostile power(s) with which it might seek to ally, take Taiwan in furtherance of its long-term strategic ambitions. Other conjectures are a hostile Iran, moving in the Persian Gulf or North Korea and advancing across the 38th parallel. Along this logic, a stockpile of possible scenarios has been tossed-up among analysts, spurred no doubt by the logistical practicalities as well as by an increasingly intolerant political climate at home, towards America's apparent diminished preeminence regionally.

Joining in the early stages of the debate was Retired Admiral Tom Moorer, a former Chairman of the Joint Chiefs of Staff, Chief of Naval Operations, Commander-in-Chief Pacific Fleet, Supreme Allied Commander Atlantic, and Commander-in-Chief of the Atlantic Fleet.[12]His specific concerns, dating as far back as 1999, were amplified by the leasing of port authority facilities by the Panamanian government to Hutchinson Balboa, a Hong Kong-based holding Group. He conjured that:

- In the event of a military confrontation necessitating the immediate use of the Canal to support forward deployed U.S. forces, control of ports at either end of the Canal by an "unfriendly power" would place the U.S. at a strategic disadvantage
- The forward deployed forces in the Eastern Mediterranean (NATO) or the Persian Gulf require the same assurances for logistical resupply from the Pacific to the Atlantic through the Canal; control by a 'hostile power' of the approaches and anchorages would interdict timely transit and require "taking the Canal by force"
- In situations of immediate threat, violations of the Panama Treaty cannot readily be resolved by a legal right even arbitration, the resolution of which may be unforeseeable during the operative period of a conflict

In sum, a disproportional Chinese presence, or as the case may be, leverage, would patently compromise the efficiencies of logistical planning by U.S. armed forces to support the entire forward deployed military capacity of the United States to imminent threats, where the time to transit from sources of supply to deployed forces was critical, given the constraints confronting the U.S. if its choke points were hampered by the presence or control of "unfriendly forces."[12] This chapter suggests that the wherewithal exists within the Latin America /Caribbean system to mitigate this and related conceivable menaces.

Concept of Collective Security

The collective security framework of the Americas is marshaled by the U.S. government through the Department of Defense, underpinned and strengthened by those of other supporting nations regarded as friends or allies of the U.S. The mechanism is specifically designed to provide certainty of collective action among governments and frustrate aggression in threatening scenarios. On the topic of collective security, Inis L. Claude (Jr) notes:

> *"...If the hope which it encourages should prove illusory, it stands convicted of contributing to the downfall of states whose security it purported to safeguard. If it merely warns off aggressors that they may encounter concerted resistance, it fails to achieve full effectiveness in its basic function, that of discouraging resort to violence, and if its warning should be revealed as a bluff, it stimulates the contempt for international order which it is intended to eradicate..."*

In Claude's view, the most basic absolute in the theory of collective security is the requirement of certainty. This Chapter makes a case that the Organization of American States, the premier intergovernmental body on regional affairs is institutionally configured through its array of organs and departments and appropriately supported in juridical terms, through the OAS Charter and other supporting instruments to discharge the regional collective security mandate.

In conceding to the role and respective doctrines of the region's dominant military establishments, the Chapter determines how these elements contribute to the synchronization of a collective security framework that is relevant to new and emerging threats in the Americas. We conclude that the legacy of intergovernmental cooperation in the political, economic, and social spheres, the commitment of governments to peace and security, reinforced by confidence building expeditions, as for example through training and joint exercises, have had the effect of neutralizing potential shifts in the balance of power matrix that could be triggered by an unfriendly rival.

Collective Security Architecture in the Americas
The Inter-American Defense Board (IADB)

A primary institutional pillar undergirding the cooperative security framework of the hemisphere is the Inter-American Defense Board, which was founded in 1942 at the height of the Second World War with the objective of contributing to the defense of the region. The Board and its supporting organs are constituted by serving military officers. In 1962, the Inter-American Defense College was established to complement the role of the Board. The College curriculum mirrors the strategic, social, politico-economic and military affairs and related contentions that are pertinent to the Americas. Its student body is comprised largely of commissioned ranks at the level of colonels or its equivalent. Relevant Chiefs of Staff convene on a periodic or "as the need arises" basis to share experiences and convoke on common concerns, while leveraging and drawing upon the experiences of more formalized and affiliated forums such as:

- The Conference of American Armies
- The Inter-American Naval Conference
- The System of Cooperation of American Air Forces
- The Joint U.S. Mexican Defense Commission
- Regularly shared routine military exercises for the air forces and navies, as for example, Operation UNITAS and PANAMAX.

The OAS

The premier intergovernmental institution representing countries within the Americas is the OAS. The General Assembly was designated the overarching body of the institution after certain fundamental amendments were made to the Charter. This occurred following major revision of the Protocol of Buenos Aires, which was formally adopted on February 27, 1967. The Charter, in its present form, charges that the General Assembly convene once annually in Regular Session. Under special circumstances and with the approval of two-thirds of the Member States and the Permanent Council, Special Sessions may be convened.

Customarily, member states take turns at hosting General Assembly Meetings and are represented on these occasions by their chosen delegates. Each state has one vote and a simple majority makes decisions. Within the period 1971-2010, three Regular meetings were hosted by Member States of CARICOM and 11 by the United States.

The Permanent Council comprises several committees, chief of which are:

- The General Committee.
- The Committee on Judicial and Political Affairs
- The Committee on Management and Civil Society Participation in OAS Activities
- "Special Committees" so designated and constituted to tackle special interests that are regarded as significant concerns, as for example drugs, firearms, and human trafficking

New and emerging security threats within the region are addressed on two specific forums, namely, the Committee on Hemispheric Security and the Special Committee on Trans-national Organized Crime. Given the importance of the phenomena within the Americas, Chairmanship of the latter Committee has been evenly shared among Members throughout the 2000s. Table 4-1.

TABLE - 4-1
CHAIRMANSHIP OF SPECIAL COMMITTEE ON TRANSNATIONAL
ORGANIZED CRIME IN OAS 2001-2011

COUNTRY	YEAR
1. Bolivia	2000-2001
2.Panama	2001-2002
3.Mexico	2002-2003
4.Paraguay	2003-2004
5.Nicaragua	2004-2005
6.Chile	2005-2006
7.Costa Rica	2006-2007
8.St.Kitts and Nevis	2007-2008
9.Mexico	2008-2009
10.Canada	2009-2010
11.Guatemala	2010-2011

SOURCE: Adopted by Author

Of crucial importance to the Permanent Council is a fiat that it should serve as a consultative organ under Article 83 of the OAS Charter as well as under the provisions of the Inter-American Treaty for Reciprocal Assistance, the Rio Treaty. Thus, in situations of imminent threat the Permanent Council can be summoned for necessary dialogue, discussion, and determination on conflicts and contentions among or between Member States.

Military Doctrine and Legacy of Key Players:
U.S. China, Latin America, Caribbean

Military doctrine guides the philosophy and objectives of how a country's military establishment is configured and deployed. It consists of concepts, principles, tactics, techniques, practices, and procedures that are necessary and integral to the efficient organizing, training, equipping and employing of tactical and surface units. These elements in turn derive legitimacy from constitution, laws and regulations. Doctrine invariably reflects opinions and authoritative pronouncements of the upper echelons of the military and civilian leaders concerning what is and is not militarily possible and necessary. It is markedly influenced by a range of variables including military technology, national geography, and the capabilities of adversaries especially the capability of one's own organization. Together, these constitute the central tenets of military practice.

The strategic doctrine of the U.S. military, formulated under the Quadrennial Review prior to 9/11 registers a suite of requirements. 1-4 -2-1. 1 pertains to the defense of the U.S. homeland; 4 refers to the deterring of hostilities in four key regions of the world; 2 denotes having the strength to win swiftly in two near simultaneous conflicts in those regions, and 1 is representative of the ability to win decisively in at least one of those conflicts. Complementary to this, the defense doctrine extends to unconventional warfare – this refers to a broad spectrum of military and paramilitary operations, normally of extended duration, predominantly conducted through, with, or by indigenous or surrogate forces, which are organized, trained, equipped, supported, and directed in varying degrees by an external force. This is a form of insurgency, which exploits grievances and is ultimately intended to undermine and overthrow a government believed to be oppressive by the UW force. In this given scenario, the conflict is likely to go beyond guerilla warfare and invariably it will include subversion, sabotage, intelligence activities, and unconventional associated recovery. Although U.S. doctrine assumes within the given context that there will be a "government in exile" with which the plan can be developed and corroborated, this is not always the case.

This doctrine, which is of equal significance in today's reality of irregular and unconventional war, can be traced to the 1960s when President John F. Kennedy formally registered the first public endorsement to national liberation movements involving the cooptation of Special Forces, as a means of countering Soviet expansion. The Libyan foray of March/April 2011 is one of the more contemporary illustrations of the application of this doctrine.

Indications are that as of June 30 2011, the Libyan Interim National Council, although in situ but strongly backed by external contingents as well as coalition forces, were positioned to assume the realms of legitimate power, with the imminent deposing of the Gadhafi regime. The Council was claiming its legitimacy on the basis of the decisions of local councils set up by rebels in Libya on February 17 2011. The identities of Council members in Al Buntan, Al Gubbah, and Benghazi were publicized but those members in the cities of Ajabiya, Zintan, Misratah, Nabut, and Ghatt remained undisclosed for security reasons. The Council had committed to honoring international and regional agreements signed by the foundering regime and were calling on countries to recognize it on the basis of international legitimacy. Moreover, having pledged to secure peace in the liberated cities, it stressed that heads of envoys and Libyan representatives in the United Nations, the Arab League, and all international and regional organizations that "joined" in the revolution would be thereby deemed as its legitimate representatives in these places.

In vindicating this mode of war on the occasion of an address to the U.S. Military Academy, President Kennedy affirmed the following:

> *"...We need to be prepared to fight a different war. This is another type of war, new in its intensity ancient in its origin, war by guerilla, subversives, insurgents, assassins; war by ambush instead of combat, by infiltration instead of aggression, seeking victory by eroding and exhausting the enemy instead of engaging him..."*

This ability to create and support resistance forces expands on the range of options available to national command and fills a niche intermediate between diplomacy and all-out warfare. The U.S. doctrine of special operations emphasizes that commanders cannot dominate a politico-military environment in the same way in which a conventional force can exert "battlefield dominance." Special Forces, which are discriminatingly endowed with an intelligence mission and capacity, invariably prepare the battle space for other more orthodox units and fall within the scope of the respective Regional Unified Combat Command, to which they are subordinate.

"Posse Comitatus" and Alternative Role of Military

The U.S. defense/foreign policy nexus has continued to evolve in response to new and emerging threats resulting in the revising and re-shaping of military doctrine at home and abroad. This is of particular relevance in the face of "drug wars" that have racked the Americas for decades and are presently spiraling out of control in Mexico.

In 1989 the Congress conferred authority on the Department of Defense to assume a lead role in the detection and monitoring of drugs entering the United States. This edict represented a major departure from the provisions of the Posse Comitatus Act of 1878, which stressed the importance of distinctions between the role of civilians and that of the military. Thus, within the confines of U.S. borders the detection and eradication of drugs would remain the domain of law enforcement, while outside U.S. borders the defense posture was officially to deter drugs from compromising the approaches to the homeland.

Thus construed, the Posse Comitatus concept has been rendered non-applicable to those roles fostered by the U.S. military with their foreign counterparts through engagement, training and joint exercises. "Alternate roles" have been correspondingly assumed by Caribbean and Latin American armed forces operating collaboratively with the U.S. The Shiprider Agreements to which many Caribbean countries have signed on, whereby joint forces commit to cooperation and interoperability with the U.S. military by sharing assets to interdict drugs, are clear illustrations of the applicability of this doctrine.

The British defense doctrine by which the military practices of former colonies continue to be guided, in contrast, assumes a two-tiered approach consisting of a Defense Context and a Military Doctrine. The Defense Context spells out the distinctions between defense policy and military strategy, while highlighting the importance of addressing security issues through a comprehensive rather than an exclusively military approach. The Military Doctrine on the other hand describes the likely employment of the British Armed forces in pursuit of defined policy goals, the components of fighting power (conceptual, physical and moral) and, the British approach to the conduct of military operations, specifically mission plan, maneuvers approach, and a war-fighting ethos requiring the acceptance of risks.

Armed forces of the Caribbean Commonwealth Community continue to be guided by rules and regulations rooted in the British constitution and system, despite prolonged exposure to North American experiences based on an extended and formalized history of joint training and interoperability.

Traditional views surrounding the role of the military in Latin America have been altered and revised over time. At the extreme end of the continuum, one school of thought is that the armed forces in Latin America perform no useful functions and that their repeated interventions in politics and the unremitting demands that they have placed on state treasuries have contributed to the manifest failure of the region's governments to steer political and economic development. This is one of the thoughts put forward by Lyle N. McAlister in his brief entitled "Changing Concepts of the Role of the Military in Latin America." Indeed, this hypothesis has been invoked from time to time to advance arguments favoring either the abolition or drastic reduction of Latin American military establishments.

The alternative scholarship tabled by thinkers such as Dominguez (1998) repudiates this viewpoint. Among his well-researched findings is that when confronted with external threats, the Latin American military has displayed a predilection to "shy away from war and consolidate peace." He also points out that historically, rapprochement has been employed as a typical mode of entente among Latin America's military forces, and was a practice that could be traced from as far back as the 1880s when distributions of military capabilities and other types of resources tended to be stable. Thus, from a historical standpoint, the fundamental role of Latin America's military would appear to have been that of defending the homeland.

Another equally poignant perspective held by Dominguez is that the Latin American military establishments had become so preoccupied in the discharge of their core function in protecting the homeland in twentieth century experience, that the primary threats in many of these nations had actually originated from within their domestically-focused armed forces. In his assessment, this ongoing proclivity had prompted many affected Governments into a range of responses in an attempt to neuter potential threats from being spawned within the military, the most innocuous of which was the posting of contingents on overseas missions.

Caribbean countries, which were former British colonies, share different histories and contrasting civilization inheritances to those of their Latin American counterparts. Early nineteenth century industrialization in England precipitated two crucial developments in the region, namely the emergence of new social structures and the creation of a newly founded industrial bourgeoisie. The emporium responded to this transformation by augmenting its power and control over the colonies through the institutionalization of regular police forces whose responsibility it was to exercise continuing restraint over the communities in which they were established. By socially embedding itself within the community through the police, the state could readily respond to popular disturbances and dissension with a degree of flexibility appropriate to the challenge.

In the post-World War II period, however, the call for a West Indies Federation would trigger a wave of constitutional re-organization among those colonies that were desirous of obtaining their independence from Britain. It was against this setting that the Caribbean "standing army" rose to prominence. In "Quest for Security in the Caribbean: Problems and Promises in Subordinate States," Ivelaw Griffith identifies the primary factors that led to early militarization in the region, namely:

- The fact that responsibility for the security of the former colonies had passed from Britain to the newly formed independent states
- The number and size of their units
- The economic feasibility of commissioning equipping and maintaining them
- The extent to which the political agenda of host governments would be advanced by their continuation
- The ideological ideals of governments
- The clear and present risks of internal and external security

An extraneous but nonetheless relevant and material factor was the U.S. policy regarding the size of national armed forces. The official disposition of the Pentagon at the height of Soviet incursions in the region was to emphatically oppose the commissioning of large offensively oriented armies in Caribbean nations and institute a long-term plan "for avoiding future Cubas." Such a plan would invariably include a long-term economic vision accompanied by military measures to foster conditions that allow economic growth. Chief among U.S.-driven security measures would therefore be the open support of "pro-West regimes."

West Indian "standing armies" were thus modeled after the British Imperial Army from which returning troops were repatriated after World War II. Following the war, some of these localized regiments were disbanded. However, many years later when it was established that one of the constitutional prerequisites for independence was the commissioning of a national defense force, the disbanded units were re-commissioned. Having re-established an indigenous armed force, its role and structure were legislated to discharge the following missions (1) perform certain ceremonials (2) provide internal security; and (3) provide a token show of force in the event of external aggression. External threats during the 1960s were primarily attributed to territorial/border disputes. However, in the contemporary setting, forces are now configured to deal with multi-dimensional threats requiring extensive maritime interdiction exercises and border control missions.

Illustrative of these socio-political dynamics was the case of British Guiana. In the early 1960s British Guiana was assailed by social and political conflicts as well as unresolved border disputes with Venezuela and Suriname. This spurred the formation of a local "defense force", in actuality an amalgam of the British Guiana Special Service Unit (an elite arm of the Police Service) and three of the original seven companies that comprised the British Guiana Regiment that was partially disbanded in 1947 after the war. However, as a result of the regime's Marxist affiliations with the Soviet Union during the 1960s to 1980s, the reduction in the size of its armed forces was a caveat for normalization of relations with the United States. A similar caveat had in fact been extended to the Nicaraguan government regarding resumption of aid extended by the U.S.

The overarching protocol governing intraregional military to military cooperation in the Anglophone Caribbean is the Agreement Concerning Cooperation in Suppressing Illicit Maritime and Air Traffic in Narcotic Drugs and Psychotropic Substances in the Caribbean Area, 2003. The Article 4 provisions address:

- Prevention, interdiction, and investigation of illicit trafficking in narcotic drugs, psychotropic substances, arms and ammunition and persons
- Combating terrorism and other threats to national security
- Prevention of smuggling
- Threats to security as a result of natural and other disasters
- Immigration and pollution control
- Protection of off-shore installations
- Prevention of piracy, hijacking, and other serious crimes

Localized standing armies comprising regular and reserve elements were originally commissioned in Antigua and Barbuda, the Bahamas, Barbados, Belize, Dominica, Guyana, Jamaica, St. Kitts and Nevis and Trinidad and Tobago. The Dominican Defense Force was subsequently abolished in 1981. In other countries, aerial and naval units subsequently complemented the core guard force. A significant aspect of sub-regional cooperative security arrangements is that in direct response to no less than two failed coups on the instigation of the military in Dominica (1979-1981) and following the installation of a Marxist government in Grenada (1979-1981) - each event marking a clear break from unbroken democratic tradition - a Regional Security System (RSS) was established by treaty among the armed forces of the Organization of Eastern Caribbean States (OECS).

Table 4.2 shows Military Expenditure as a Percentage of the Gross Domestic Product of CARICOM countries currently furnished with military forces.

Chinese Military Orientation

Chinese literature discloses the use of all means of power to obtain objectives – everything is a potential weapon. Deception and guile lie at the heart of Chinese military philosophy, which embraces the employment of every aspect of subtlety against the foe. Additionally, the Chinese have placed emphasis on building a force that is capable of attacking the enemy's infrastructure and relying on new technologies to shape the battlefield. For this reason the threat of outright cyber war has become a real and present threat to both eastern and western hemispheres and this theme is duly expounded on in Chapter Eleven.

TABLE – 4-2
MILITARY EXPENDITURE OF CARICOM MEMBER STATES AS A
PERCENTAGE OF GROSS DOMESTIC PRODUCT 2009

CARICOM MEMBER STATE	MILITARY EXPENDITURE AS % OF GROSS DOMESTIC PRODUCT
1.Antigua and Barbuda Royal Antigua and Barbuda Defense Force	0.5 %
2.The Bahamas Royal Bahamian Defense Force (Land Force, Navy, Air Wing)	0.7 %
3.Barbados Royal Barbados Defense Force (Land - based Troop Command and Coast Guard)	0.8 %
4.Belize Belize Defense Force (Army, Air Wing, Volunteer Guard)	1.4 %
5.Guyana Guyana Defense Force (Army, Coast guard, Air Wing)	1.8 %
6.Jamaica Jamaica Defense Force (Ground Forces, Coast Guard, Air Wing)	0.92 %
7.Trinidad and Tobago Trinidad and Tobago Defense Force (Army, Coast Guard, Air Guard)	.3 %
8.Suriname National Army (Army, Naval Wing, Air Wing)	0.6 %

SOURCE: Adapted from Central Intelligence Agency website

Fisher's list of "disturbing choices" made by China is a vindication of a historical path being pursued that is counterproductive to U.S. interests. These include:

- Preparation for war against Taiwan amidst growing nationalist outrage

- Pursuit of political-military hegemony in Asia despite its ostensible push for multilateralism within the peninsula
- Proliferation of nuclear weapon and missile technology in Pakistan, North Korea and Iran
- Resisting efforts by the U.S. and its allies to isolate North Korea and Iran regarding the mobilization of nuclear weapons programs by both countries
- Pursuing active military entente with Russia and
- Undertaking a program of global cyber espionage and surveillance in key capitals around the world.

The People's Liberation Army continues to be held up as a model of ideological commitment and maintains a tight relationship with the Chinese Communist Party. Positions adopted by China's military regarding Japan, Taiwan and the United States, according to Susan L. Shirk's "China Fragile Superpower," tend to be more hawkish than those being promoted by the country's civilian officials. Members of the PLA, for example, are indoctrinated with the notion that "Taiwan presents the last unfulfilled mission of the PLA to liberate the whole country." In essence, China's PLA espouses two primary principles: the "one China" principle that Taiwan must accept and equally significant, the principle of opposition to American hegemony.

Notwithstanding the clear advantage held militarily by the U.S. intransigent concerns over China's medium to long-term intentions may be partially informed by the likelihood of an ominous arms build-up that could challenge U.S. primacy, such as obtained in the concluding years of the Cold War. It will be recalled that in the late 1980s, even while the Soviets were claiming to be disarming under Gorbachev's glasnost /perestroika policy, the USSR had in fact undergone its most massive arms build-up in almost 72 years in power. In 1985, for example, the Soviets enjoyed a 5-1 conventional lead in arms and manpower over the U.S. and at least a 5-1 strategic nuclear lead. See Table 4.3. The U.S. Government publication "Soviet Military Power 1988," reported that the value of the Soviet military procurement budget was greater than that of the U.S. and this advantage allowed the Soviets to deploy significantly more weapons to its forces in the field. The successful conclusion of the SMART disarmament Treaty by the Obama administration, referred to in Chapter Two, has effectively diminished U.S. and Russian arsenals of strategic warheads, revived on the ground inspections, and introduced new procedures to allow both countries to inspect each other's arsenals to verify compliance.

Principles Guiding Military Alliances in the Americas

Alliances that evolved within the Americas following World War II were based on the principle of containment whereby geopolitical groupings would provide a protective shield and buffer against westward Soviet as well as Chinese expansionism. Overall, these pursuits were enshrined in an agglomeration of defense pacts that were globally dispersed - the South-East Asia Treaty Organization (SEATO), the Central Treaty Organization (CENTO) and the North Atlantic Treaty Organization (NATO). These accords effectively legitimized the U.S. base footprint, which is elaborated on in the previous Chapter and continue to shape many of today's intergovernmental security agreements. Within the narrower hemispheric context, politico-military alliances and national interests have influenced the distribution of U.S.-controlled forward operating locations in the region, some of which are mirrored in numerous bilateral Defense Cooperation Agreements.

TABLE – 4-3
MAJOR WEAPONS SYSTEMS PRODUCTION FOR U.S. AND USSR (1985-1988)

Weapon	USSR	US	Ratio
Intercontinental Ballistic Missiles	450	56	8.0 : 1
Sub-Launched Ballistic Missiles	375	107	3.5 : 1
Sub-Launched Cruise Missiles	4,400	2,250	1.9 : 1
Short-Range Ballistic Missiles	2,150	0	2150 : 1
Surface to air Missiles	63,000	9,800	6.4 : 1
Tanks	13,300	3,475	3.8 : 1
Other Armored fighting Vehicles	18,100	4,175	4.3 : 1
Towed Field Artillery	4,400	1,075	4.1 : 1
Self-Propelled Artillery	4,100	475	8.6 : 1
Multiple Rocket Launchers	1,900	225	8.4 : 1
Self-Propelled AA Artillery	500	26	19.2 : 1
Submarines	34	15	2.3 : 1
Surface Warships	34	21	1.6 : 1
Bombers	190	103	1.8 : 1
Fighters/Fighter Bombers	2,750	1,850	1.4 : 1
Anti-Sub Aircraft	20	26	.8 : 1
Helicopters	1,850	1,500	1.2 : 1

SOURCE: "Soviet Military Power 1988" – U.S. Government

Strategically Dispersed U.S. Military Bases in the Americas

Within the Americas, the decommissioning and relocation of bases formerly held in Panama under the 1903 Hay-Branau Varilla Accord resulted in significant changes. One such change was the stationing of Forward Operating Locations (FOLs) throughout the southern hemisphere. These sites serve primarily as military bases for the mobilizing of counternarcotic surveillance flights and also ensure an unbroken overseas U.S. military presence in host countries. In addition to the stationing of FOLs, Counter Drug Radar sites have been deployed across Colombia and Peru, venues of the world's largest sources of coca production. Tables 4-4 and 4-5.

TABLE – 4-4
NON-RANDOM SAMPLE OF STRATEGICALLY-SITED FORWARD
OPERATING LOCATIONS (FOLs) OF US WITHIN CENTRAL AMERICA AND
NORTHERN CARIBBEAN

COUNTRY LOCATION	MISSION
1.Guantanamo Bay, Cuba	Permanent overseas US presence. Provides support for contingency operations in Caribbean; counter narcotic operations and houses certain migrants; detention facility for captured parties with suspected Al Qaeda and Taliban links.
2.Soto Cano, Honduras	Non-permanent presence. Military exercises; civic assistance projects disaster relief; support for counter- narcotics operations; part of Joint task Force (JTF) Bravo's mission.
3.Manta, Ecuador	Non-permanent presence on leased facility. U.S. Navy P3 maritime patrol aircraft assist in counter drug detection and monitoring missions under Cooperative Security Agreement.
4.Aruba	Leased facility comprises both permanently assigned staff and temporarily deployed personnel to assist in counter drug detection and monitoring missions under Cooperative Security Agreement.
5.Cuacao, Netherlands Antilles	Non-permanent presence. U.S. presence is host to F16s, Navy P3s, E-2 airborne early warning planes, E-3 EWASs and other military aircraft along with temporarily deployed military personnel and operators.
6.Comalopa, El Salvador	Non-permanent presence. Facility hosts Four P3s or similarly-sized aircraft focusing on maritime drug trafficking in Pacific under Cooperative Security Agreement.

SOURCE: Adopted by Author

TABLE – 4-5
STATIONING OF US-CONTROLLED COUNTER- DRUG RADAR SITES IN
COLOMBIA AND PERU, SOUTH AMERICA

DISTRICT	LOCATION
1. Latica, Colombia	South- eastern Colombia
2. Miranda, Colombia	Venezuela's borderline
3. Roochacha, Colombia	North-east on Caribbean coast
4. San Andres, Colombia	East of Nicaragua along Caribbean Sea
5. San Jose del Guaviare, Colombia	Southern /Central Colombia
6. Tres Esquinas, Colombia	South-west near Ecuadorean border
7. Iquitos, Peru	Amazon river near Colombian border
8. Pucallpa, Peru	On the Ucayali river near Brazil
9. Andoes, Peru	Northern Peru between Colombia and Ecuador

SOURCE: Developed by Author

Mutual Cooperation in Defense and Military Affairs

Two primary streams of activity in which the U.S. has decisively maintained an imprint in regional defense and military affairs are:

- Training
- Joint military exercises

The enquiry at hand will demonstrate how this commitment is being discharged and ferret out some of the key issues that have put state-to-state relationships to the test from time to time. The section focuses on the extent to which the International Military Education and Training Program (IMET) has, as an instrument of America's national security and public policy and a key component of the U.S. security assistance agenda, served to enrich Inter-American solidarity. We undertake a comparative analysis of U.S. expenditure on the IMET program in the Americas with other regions of the world, thereby showing the extent to which the program is expediently linked to America's strategic priorities.

Politically speaking, any alternative to the existing partnerships between the U.S. and its allies in the Americas derived from a rich history of institutional networking and military to military contacts would have to display a countervailing preponderance of benefits to host countries, to bring about any meaningful changes in allegiance or viable power shifts.

156

U.S. Sponsored Security Assistance Training

Caribbean and Latin American countries have historically benefitted from a range of U.S.-funded security assistance programs extended to countries designated as "friendly" by the U.S. government. The cost of these programs is borne by the U.S. taxpayer and is accordingly meticulously weighted in terms of material or exchange value to the government's political and strategic interests. The assistance packages typically comprise a training component, which is complemented by joint exercises as well as military to military exchanges. In 2010 the government committed $108,000 to IMET funding, disbursed by region as displayed in Table 4-6.

TABLE – 4-6
U.S.-SPONSORED INTERNATIONAL MILITARY ASSISTANCE PROGRAM BY
REGION FOR FISCAL YEAR 2010

ITEM BY REGION	APPROVED BUDGETARY ALLOCATION
1.Africa	$15,232
2.East Asia and the Pacific	$8,930
3.Europe and Eurasia	$30,205
4.Near East	$18,593
5.South and Central Asia	$13,480
6.Western Hemisphere	$16,455
GLOBAL	
E -IMET Schools	$5,105
General Costs	-
No Year /Carry Forward	-
TOTAL GLOBAL	$5,105

SOURCE: Developed by Author

IMET is one feature of a comprehensive assistance package officially referred to as the Security Assistance Training Program. The other elements of this program are Foreign Military Sales, the Professional Military Exchange (PME) and the Unit Exchange. IMET, in particular, is a grant program established by Congress as an element of the government's Arms Export Control Act of 1976. Grants disbursed under IMET enable foreign governments that are financially incapable of paying for training under the Foreign Assistance Act.

Serving military personnel within the Americas enlist for courses from a vast compendium of offerings made available on an annual basis from among approximately 150 U.S. based military schools. There are three main categories of program offerings: the Professional Military Education which provides leadership training; a technical component which equips participants with the skills required to operate specific weapons systems or fulfill the demands of a specific military specialty and the E-IMET menu. Through IMET, the U.S. government has perfected the art of cultivating institutionally induced friendships within the Latin American and Caribbean military communities while promoting and enhancing these contacts throughout the hemisphere.

The original intent of Congress in inaugurating this "assistance" program is articulated in Section 2347(b) of the Foreign Assistance Act, which mandates the implementing authorities to:

- Encourage effective and mutually beneficial relations and understanding between the United States and foreign countries in furtherance of the goals of international peace and security
- Improve the ability of participating foreign countries to utilize their resources, including defense articles and defense services obtained by them from the United States with maximum effectiveness, thereby contributing to greater self-reliance by such countries
- Increase the awareness of nationals of foreign countries participating in such activities of basic issues involving internationally recognized human rights. To this end, the International Military Education and Training Accountability Act (S 647) – introduced on March 29, 2001 seeks to increase transparency by requiring that the State and Defense Departments, respectively, be more forthcoming about "the human rights records" of IMET alumni

These objectives display patent congruities with the designs and aspirations of the Department of Defense, the primary implementing organ of the IMET Program, namely - to establish rapport, understanding and communication links with host countries; to foster the attainment of self- sufficiency in host countries in the area of training and to furnish countries with the requisite skills to operate and maintain U.S.- origin equipment.

Complementary to IMET is the Foreign Military Financing Scheme (FMF), another component of U.S. aid programs. Funding for FMF is dispensed and administered by the Department of State which supports DOD costs for the purchase of U.S.-manufactured defense equipment, strengthening military relationships, promoting professionalism between the U.S. and military forces in "friendly countries," improving foreign military capabilities of countries that control the land approaches to the U.S. and the Caribbean as the U.S. "third border," and providing equipment and training in peacekeeping operations, as obtains in countries such as Haiti.

Non-Monetary Advantages of IMET

IMET' s track record as an instrument of influence by means of which the U.S. government " shapes the doctrine, operating procedures, values, choice of weaponry of foreign militaries and occasionally the policies of recipient governments," is well established. Table 4.7 displays Budgetary Allocations on Account for the IMET programs as of June 2010 in respect of the Western Hemisphere.

TABLE – 4-7

INTERNATIONAL MILITARY EDUCATION AND TRAINING ACCOUNT
SUMMARY (CURRENT AS OF JUNE 2010) WESTERN HEMISPHERE

COUNTRIES/ ACCOUNTS	2006 Actual	2007 Actual	2008 Actual	2009 Actual	2010 Actual	2011 Request
1.Argentina	1082	1205	904	915	900	900
2.Bahamas	399	239	186	137	200	200
3.Belize	294	310	216	267	200	200
4.Bolivia	-	57	179	225	380	390
5.Brazil	-	28	174	252	610	650
6.Chile	646	662	550	525	900	960
7.Colombia	1673	1646	1421	1400	1695	1695
8.Costa Rica	-	80	172	364	380	400
10.Dominican Republic	1328	1048	946	722	850	900
11.Ecuador	-	43	178	304	380	400
12.El Salvador	1782	1824	1619	1574	1750	1800
13.Guatemala	488	467	491	254	800	825
14.Guyana	312	358	268	283	300	325
15.Haiti	213	215	182	235	220	220
16.Honduras	1218	1404	936	329	700	700
17.Jamaica	908	806	750	823	750	800
18.Mexico	8	57	357	834	1050	1100
19.Nicaragua	740	631	483	409	900	950
20.Panam	894	677	162	253	750	800
21.Paraguay	-	44	191	348	400	425
22.Peru	-	44	169	398	650	725
23.Suriname	196	139	150	153	260	280
24.Trinidad and Tobago	-	40	100	95	170	180
24.Uruguay	-	45	238	427	450	480
25.Eastern Caribbean (OECS)	695	703	587	661	810	850
26.Total Western Hemisphere	12,876	12,771	11,609	12,207	16,455	17,155
27.Total	86,744	85,877	85,877	93,000	108,000	110,000

SOURCE: US Department of State – Bureau of Political-Military Affairs

Before and After 9/11: An Overview

During the Fiscal Year 2000, the U.S. distributed almost $50 million in military training funds through IMET, with $9.8 million or 18% allocated to the Western Hemisphere. A total of 2,684 soldiers from Latin American countries benefitted. Following the events of 9/11, funding soared. In 2006, for example, overall IMET funding worldwide surged to $86.7 million, reflecting a 75% overall increase. Funding for military training in Latin American countries increased correspondingly in 2006 to $13.6 million. During that year 3,221 soldiers pursued training programs ranging from counter- intelligence to helicopter repair. Colombia was a principal beneficiary with 90% increased IMET funding. A 200% increase was awarded to El Salvador and Nicaragua respectively and a 400% increase went to Panama.[13]

Apart from IMET assisted programs the U.S. pursued arms sales programs through Foreign Military Sales (FMS) and Direct Commercial Sales (DCS). The top 15 recipients of such sales in Latin America took delivery of more than $3.6 billion in military hardware and weaponry between 2000-2003, with Brazil topping the list followed by Argentina, Mexico and Venezuela.

Despite the patent advantages of training and military exchanges, there have been instances when U.S. policy has resulted in the withdrawal of program benefits, as a result of overriding domestic interests. Using the International Criminal Court (ICC) impasse of the 2000s we will demonstrate how China was able to gain some strategic advantages in the region militarily when countries were excised from the IMET facility and how this strategic loss was recouped by the current administration under soft power initiatives. This proves to some extent that as the oldest regional society in the world, the Inter-American system is endowed with a reserve of political and diplomatic capital that is unmatched globally.

Country Eligibility for Military Assistance Training

Amidst what may be regarded as a teeming portfolio in the realm of military assistance rendered to friends and allies there have been occasions when fidelity to the U.S. as a sponsor of first choice has waned and played itself out to the advantage of rivals. Such retraction came to a head in the 2000s with the entry into force of the Statute of Rome in July 2002 bringing into being the ICC. This event coincided with a period when the U.S. was virtually "pinned down" in Iraq and China's momentum of diplomatic investments in Latin America was proceeding apace and to all indications, went uncontested.

Although the Rome Statute (under which the world's first permanent court was set up to prosecute individuals accused of war crimes and human rights abuses) had mobilized popular international support among human rights groups and most democratic nations, the U.S. declined to be a party to it. Its concerns rested on ICC's possible assertion of jurisdiction over U.S. soldiers who could be charged with "war crimes" arising (from the standpoint of the U.S.) from the legitimate use of force, or U.S. civilians who could be charged for conduct related to carrying out U.S. foreign policy initiatives.

Under the Bush administration, America reacted to the ensuing international impasse by seeking bilateral immunity accords with signatories to the ICC that would effectively exempt U.S. citizens from prosecution by the world court. This course of action was further insured with the shepherding by the U.S. government of the American Service Members Protection Act, incorporated as Title 11 of HR 4775 of the FY 2002 Supplemental Appropriations Act (PC 107-206). The provision bluntly prohibited military assistance to those countries that declined to sign the Section 98 bilateral Agreements with the U.S. Furthermore, Section 574 of the FY 2005 Foreign Operations Appropriations (Division D of P.L 108-447) extended the relevant provisions of the law to include Economic Support Funds.

The sequestering of ICC signatories created a rippling effect in the mid-2000s, a fact that was compounded by searing dissonance over the issue among various government bodies in Washington. On the one hand, the Department of Defense called for the delinking of military training programs from ASPA; on the other the Bureau of Political-Military Affairs of the Department of State, an antipode in temperament and outlook to the military, maintained unwavering support for retention of the sanctions[14]

The upshot of this policy was that Caribbean nations deferred to the United Kingdom and Canada for military training and support to the extent that national budgetary limitations in these jurisdictions would permit. Latin American countries, on the other hand, made overtures to the Chinese for alternatives to their customary reliance on the U.S. Additionally, key projects earmarked for funding by the U.S. such as democracy promotion ventures within Latin America, were temporarily stymied.

The Obama administration committed to "a new era of engagement" with Inter-American partners in 2009 and consistent with this resolve forged the Caribbean Basin Security Initiative (CBSI), the La Merida and Plan Colombia campaigns, which were conceptualized under the preceding administration.[15]

161

Ultimately, the capacity of the U.S. to muster strategic advantage through military aid is sustained by a foreign policy agenda committed to -

- Inducing particular policy selections of recipient governments, including voting patterns within the U.N and other intergovernmental bodies
- Imposing preconditions regarding state conduct (as illustrated in events surrounding the signing of the "Section 98 Bilateral Agreements"). These caveats, once elicited, would work towards America's long-term political interests and goals
- Influencing preferences on political issues that would prove to be strategically advantageous to the homeland. It should be noted that Trinidad and Tobago was one of a mere seven nations that had strenuously opposed the U.S-led invasion of Grenada, having voted against U.N Resolution 38/7 on grounds that such course of action constituted "a flagrant violation of international law and of the independence, sovereignty and territorial integrity of that State"
- Spurring political objectives of host nations by strengthening democratic institutions, promoting multi-party democracy and protecting justice systems from collapse. This has been the focus of engagement with Latin American countries since the 1980s

Interoperability through PANAMAX Exercises

China's demand for primary products (petroleum, iron ore, coal, grain) and its growth in the global consumer product container trade have been the main drivers of world trade increases. Alongside this, it should be noted that of the bulk US cargo imports, more than 90%, arrive by ship (DOT 2009). Therefore, the U.S. and its Inter-American partners as well as China have a stake in unfettered trade flows at key choke points such as the Panama Canal. The following are noteworthy logistics, in the wider framework of competitive transportation systems supporting the U.S. and the trade interests of many of her Atlantic-based allies:

- Firstly, in the mid-2000s the Maritime trans-Pacific route containership services between Asia and the U.S. west coast, was the preferred route accounting for 75% of Asian imports with an average navigation time of 12.3 days plus 6 days from the west to the east coast
- Secondly, the Asia-Pacific Canal (U.S. East Coast route) accounted for 19% of Asian imports to the U.S. with an average navigation time of 21.6 days; and

- Thirdly, the Asia-Suez canal handled 6% of Asian imports to the U.S. with an navigation time averaging 21.1 days (SCT 2009)

Competitive transportation systems are critical for economic growth and unremitting increases in global trade have placed strains not only on the U.S. logistics system, but also on the entire world transportation network. Understanding trade flows and international trade lanes is critical to optimizing systems investments and developing corrective and pro-active measures to guarantee the safe passage of commercial and other traffic. As alluded to earlier, the Panama Canal is one of the most strategically and economically crucial pieces of infrastructure in the world, rivaled in importance, and by far less so, only by the Suez Canal, the Cape of Good Hope and Cape Horn (ACP 2006).

PANAMAX Exercises

In 2003 the U.S. instituted "PANAMAX," a joint multinational exercise, initially restricted to three countries - the United States, Panama and Chile.[16] The overarching goal of this campaign was to develop, test command, and control forces at sea, board, search and seize, execute entry port control planning, and engage in open water diving and riverine patrols. The mission plan was ultimately aimed at attaining the overall security and defense of the Panama Canal and surrounding regions so as to secure vital U.S. interests.

According to the 2011 Army Posture Statement, the role of the U.S. Army in these exercises is "to provide forces and Title 10 support to combatant commanders." In this context, the Army's highest priority is to support ongoing combat operations and to recognize the long-term strategic importance of building the capacity of partner country armies and developing appropriate levels of interoperability with them. On this merit, the U.S. army is committed to providing forces to meet combatant commander exercise requirements as force availability allows and to conduct multinational exercises when feasible.[17]

This acknowledges that the strategic environment is one of "persistent conflict." The rationale therefore amidst strained demands for resources is that the demand for U.S. forces will decrease as partner nation's security forces become more capable and their respective governments feel confident employing them against threats thereby reducing reliance on U.S. forces.[18]

PANAMAX, co-sponsored by U.S. Southern Command, is specially designed to execute stability operations within the framework of U.N Security Council

Resolutions, provide interoperability training for participating multinational staff, and build participating national capability to plan and execute complex multinational operations. Twenty countries from within the Americas including Canada have been co-opted into the mission and participate in annual drills and friendly exchanges. One such iteration occurred August 16-27 2010 and included a contingent of no less than 2000 civilian and military personnel from 18 nations engaged in simulated exercises near Panama and the U.S.

Typically, PANAMAX is shepherded by a multinational task force. In 2011, however, several modifications were made in deference to the changing security environment in the Americas. These included the following:

- Colombia assumed leadership for the land component of the exercise. Notably this nation had recently become a signatory of the U.S. State Department's Proliferation Security Initiative, which aims to stop the trafficking of WMD. Accordingly, the 2011 exercise was designed to include two proliferation security events

- There was added emphasis on cybercrime operations. This development comes against the backdrop of the close bilateral ties being forged with these and other Latin American countries by China and the prevailing defense doctrine of the Chinese as it makes common cause with countries ideologically opposed to the U.S. This is elaborated further in Chapter Eleven

In the succeeding Chapter we examine the issue of how U.S. expansionism eastward of the Atlantic community is being maintained. The exercise of primacy in this region entails an acute awareness of the role of political geography in international affairs.

Brzezinski believes that what is required in Eurasia is a combination of three imperatives, namely:

- Preventing collusion and maintaining security dependence among "vassals."
- Keeping "tributaries" pliant and protected; and
- Preventing adversaries from forming hostile coalitions

Chapter Five discusses how the U.S. is proceeding with this strategy and adapting its statecraft to reshape global affairs by maintaining its omnipresence through a policy of expansionism. The backdrop to this strategy was the 2003 invasion of Iraq – an engagement, which resulted in the squandering by the U.S. of its soft power as its deployments became steadily longer and armed forces came under huge strain. The period also saw the commencement of a huge current account deficit, which accounted for 6.5% of the country's GDP at the height of the occupation in 2006.[4] Chapter Five surveys the change in gear in terms of revised policy approaches of the Obama administration in the course of its first term as it introduced soft power, while sustaining its ongoing commitments for transition management and military superiority.

CHAPTER FIVE

AMERICA'S POLICY OF EXPANSIONISM IN EURASIA

"America's global primacy is directly dependent on how long and how effectively its preponderance on the Eurasian continent is sustained."

Zbigniew Brzezinski

ifteen years ago Brzezinski forecasted that the current dominant American global system, within which the threat of war was then "off the table", is likely to be a stable one only in those parts of the world in which American primacy, guided by a long-term geo-strategy, rests on compatible and congenial sociopolitical systems, linked together by American-dominated multilateral frameworks. Simultaneous with this, he noted that should China as a major power continue to grow economically and militarily, but having failed to democratize, there was likely to be an emerging situation of intensifying conflicts with its neighbors, as now obtains.[1]

This chapter addresses how U.S. expansionism east of the Atlantic is being promoted. Nominally, Eurasia constitutes:

- The largest continent in the world
- Home to the world's most populous societies including the majority of the world's Islamic population
- The crucible for Islamic fundamentalism
- Endowed with some of the world's most politically assertive countries, largest economies, and prolific spenders on military weaponry
- Locale to a high concentration of nuclear powers

On the basis of these and other distinctions, the progressive expansion of democracy into Eurasia and throughout newly formed states that were members of the erstwhile ideological bloc of the Soviet Union, is indispensable to America's continued global reach.

166

Shifts in U.S. Policy: Hard to Soft Power

Within the preceding decade, important shifts in American foreign policy occurred that would exact a severe toll on its engagements in Eurasia. Martin Jacques, in expounding on some of these changes noted, "...the Bush presidency's foreign policy marked an important shift compared with that of previous administrations; the war on terror had become the new imperative." This change in course drastically altered America's relations with Western Europe by according reduced significance to the region. To reinforce this point he explains that following the invasion of Iraq, the U.S. proceeded to preside over the shaping of global affairs and rapidly found itself beleaguered in Iraq and enjoying less global support than at any time since 1945.

In Jacques estimation:

> *"Failing to comprehend the significance of deeper economic trends, as well as misreading the situation in Iraq, the Bush administration overestimated American power and thereby overplayed its hand, with the consequence that its policies had exactly the opposite effect to that which had been intended: instead of enhancing the U.S.'s position in the world, Bush's foreign policy seriously weakened it. The neoconservative position represented a catastrophic misreading of history."*

He also discerned that the principle of national sovereignty was severely denigrated during that era and instead, regime change was affirmed. Needless to say this instance of real politic worked to upset America's universal popularity.[2]

Acknowledging this as the status quo of the Bush administration, Joseph S Nye Jr. affirms that "...the United States was correct in altering its national security strategy to focus on terrorism and weapons of mass destruction after September 11, 2001." Despite this ostensible endorsement of policy approach, he argues that whatever its justification, "...the means that the Bush administration chose focused too heavily on hard power and did not take enough account of soft power." The latter was the very device successfully being adopted by terrorists to gain general support and elicit recruits[3]

Essentially, this was the framework inherited by the present Obama administration, which has proceeded to maintain America's global projection. America's global primacy, as Brzezinski cogently argues is dependent on how long and how effectively her preponderance in the Eurasian continent is sustained. Hard power, as deployed by the U.S. rests on inducements or threats. Nye observes that a country may obtain what it wants in world politics on the merit of admiration from other countries of its values and comprehension of its agenda. This is distinct from inducement to change instigated by threat or use of military force.

Soft power, on the other hand, may be exercised on the basis of the ability to shape the preferences of others by deploying those assets that produce attraction. This attraction could be to shared values and to the justness and duty of contributing to the achievement of those values. One source of soft power is popular culture and this theme is elaborated on in Chapters Eight and Nine of Section 3. Another source of soft power stems from government policy and this is best appreciated when one considers the impact of American foreign policy abroad. Nye demonstrates that the 2003 Iraq War provided an epitome of how the actions of administrations can potentially engender international unpopularity. A significant point he discusses is that the values forged at home by a government, such as democracy, affect the preferences of state and non-state actors abroad.

In Chapter One we surveyed the strength of U.S. idealism as a vehicle for promoting its international agenda. A notable observation made by Joseph Nye was the issue of how the use of force could severely jeopardize a country's economic objectives, and by extension the economic interests of other nations, given the interconnectedness of the global economy. While the use of force could jeopardize the economic goals of the U.S. combining such a policy with the exercise of soft power would favor American goals and interests since war-related risks are a deterrent to investors who control flows of capital in a globalized world.

A closely appended issue is the need to preserve friendships even in the face of open hostilities and nowhere is this more demonstrable than in the issue surrounding over-flight rights. Since the global projection of military force will routinely require access and overhead flight rights from other countries, soft balancing can potentially have real effects on hard power because support for America in such scenarios becomes a critical issue. Nye notes U.S. soft power losses can be traced to the country's foreign policy and remonstrates, "...Bush went to war having failed to win a broader military coalition or U.N authorization." The consequences emanating from that decision proved inimical to America's popularity abroad and resulted in rise in anti-American sentiment and a spurt in terrorist recruitment.

The lesson coming out of this is that the practice of hard and soft power should be judiciously weighed and discriminatingly administered so as to defray any likelihood of operating at cross-purposes with the overarching policy goals of the government.

Multi-track Diplomacy via MEPI

The centerpiece of the U.S. policy in the Middle East is the Middle East Partnership Initiative (MEPI), which was inaugurated in 2002 following the events of 9/11 and is presently being administered by the U.S. Department of State.[4] Two regional offices were set up in the summer of 2004 and now serve as the hub for the propagation of democratic idealism under the ambit of community level mediation, more commonly referred to as "peacekeeping." The first outfit, Tuni's Regional Office, covers the countries of North Africa - Algeria, Egypt, Libya, and Morocco as well as Lebanon, Israel, Jordan, and West Bank-Gaza. The second unit was the Abu Dhabi Regional office, which services the nations of Bahrain, Kuwait, Oman, Qatar, Saudi Arabia, United Arab Emirates, and Yemen. In terms of delivery and impact, the more successful programs delivered under MEPI thus far have focused on advocacy, activism, human rights, and education - areas with a high concentration of women and youth as special interest groups.

The MEPI Regional Office in Abu Dhabi has been particularly agile in its outreach. It has been instrumental in the funding of a website, TAKALM that is run by a team of journalists and bloggers advocating for human rights and freedom of speech and was the principal product of a Workshop that was hosted in Beirut in December 2009 attended by participants from Bahrain, United Arab Emirates, Kuwait, Lebanon, Jordan, Egypt, Morocco, Palestine, Tunisia and Sudan. Sponsorship came from a special BMENA Civil Society grant.

The power of individual agency is vindicated by the overwhelming involvement of women and youth as target groups and members of non-governmental organizations. The latter now claim to act as the "global conscience" and have collectively developed new norms, by discriminatingly pressing governments and business leaders to change policies and indirectly, by altering public perceptions of what governments and the corporate sector should be doing. Not only has the number of types of these groups increased globally; so has their range of transnational contacts. Among the more prominent and widely known organized lobbies are: Amnesty International, the International Red Cross, Greenpeace, and Doctors without Borders. These and others have become established global players that have been able to call the attention of governments and the mainstream media to issues and mobilize mass support.

MEPI's inauguration is firstly an exoneration of the incapacity of pure government mediation to come to grips with the complexities of modern conflict. Secondly, it is recognition of this fact by the U.S. government. Thirdly, it is in effect the type of U.S.- dominated multilateral architecture advocated by Brzezinski, and one that effectively excludes any external or intervening authority such as the United Nations. The program can accordingly be tailored to meet the specific goals set and targets identified by the U.S. State Department thereby addressing vital U.S. interests. In a sense MEPI is thus an ideological footprint reflective of the government's soft power approach, akin to the Basing Footprint that symbolizes hard power. The Initiative, in terms of design and mode of administration, is archetypical of multi-track diplomacy - a model of soft power that incorporates all levels of society into the mediation process along nine thematic campaign lines referred to as "tracks", namely:

- Government or "Peacemaking" through Diplomacy. This is the world of official diplomacy expressed through the formal aspects of the governmental process
- Non-governmental/Professional or "Peacemaking" through Conflict Resolution. At this level, professional and non-governmental action are set in motion to analyze, prevent, resolve, and manage international conflicts by non-state actors
- Business or "Peacemaking" through Commerce. This is the realm of business and the actual and political effects of business intervention on peace-building through the provision of economic opportunities, international friendship and understanding, informal channels of communication, and support for other peacekeeping activities
- Private Citizen or "Peacekeeping" through Personal Involvement. At this track level individual citizens become involved in peace and development activities through citizen diplomacy, exchange programs, private voluntary organizations, non-governmental organizations and special interest groups
- Research Training and Education or "Peacemaking" through learning. At this level of mediation, education and training become the agents of change and transformation by empowering the human agent
- Activism or "Peacekeeping" through Advocacy. This covers the field of peace and environment activism on such issues as disarmament, human rights, social and economic justice, advocacy of special interest groups regarding special government policies
- Religion or "Peacemaking" through Faith in Action. The seventh track examines beliefs and peace oriented actions of the spiritual and religious community and such morality based movements as pacifism, sanctuary and non-violence
- Funding or "Peacemaking" through Providing Resources. This area focuses on the funding community – foundations and philanthropists that provide the financial support for many of the activities pursued on the other tracks

- Communications and the Media or "Peacekeeping" through Information. At this level public opinion gets shaped through exposure to the media such as through print, film, videos, radio, electronic systems and the arts.

MEPI is thus configured to fuel congenial sociopolitical systems supported by a U.S. administered pro-democracy campaign as an integral part of America's grand strategy for global pre-eminence. This strategy for dominance in Eurasia, as a critical building block in ultimate attainment of American omnipresence, is undoubtedly the primary goal behind the progressive propagation of democracy across the continent that is evident today. Strategically speaking, because of America's unique relationship with a widening Europe – consolidated through NATO in a Trans-Atlantic partnership - Europe is now positioned as a "more viable springboard for projecting into Eurasia the international democratic and cooperative order."[5]

MEPI is fully endorsed by the U.S. Department of State and committed to the promotion of more participatory politics, sustainable economic growth, civil society conducive to human rights and civic activism, especially the empowerment of women and youth in the Middle East and North Africa. The program's objectives, as stated on its website, disclose:

> *"From within the near Eastern Affairs Bureau of the State Department, MEPI advances U.S. foreign policy goals by supporting citizens' efforts at economic, social, and political empowerment, expanding opportunities for women and youth, and helping communities work alongside governments in shaping their own futures. MEPI's activities underscore President Obama and Secretary Clinton's commitment to democracy and civil society, and follow the approach the President laid out in his Cairo speech: engaging with peoples as well as governments, in a spirit of mutual respect and rooted in a commitment to universal values."*

In Tunisia, for example, a MEPI Regional Office is co-located with the American Embassy. That outfit manages MEPI local projects in Algeria, Egypt, Israel, Jordan, Lebanon, Libya, Morocco, West Bank/ Gaza and Tunisia. Tunisia was catapulted to prominence in December 2010 when Mohammed Bouazizi, a local fruit vendor set himself afire and figuratively lit the fuse that inflamed political uprisings across North Africa and the Middle East. By February 2011 popular collective revolt precipitated the deposition of Tunisia's President Zine El Abidine Ben Ali from office. Inspired by the success of the Tunisia uprising, thousands of Egyptians turned to the streets and voiced their displeasure over the dire need for reform measures; and after 30 years of rule the President Hosni Mubarak was ousted. Frustrations expressed among the Egyptians and subsequently the Saudi

Arabians, the Syrians, the Algerians and Yemenis were similar. An end to restrictive laws regarding freedom of speech , the right to protest, appeals for the elimination of corruption, calls for job creation amidst persistently high levels of unemployment and the din of mass frustration and despair among the youth, and the need to suppress escalating food prices were the common and recurring themes of public protest.

The MEPI Regional Offices administered through Tunis accounted for more than $5 million in program funding in 2010. Additionally, Abu Dhabi's regional offices extend their operations to Bahrain, Kuwait, Oman, Qatar, Saudi Arabia, United Arab Emirates, and Yemen. The organization explicitly does not provide funds to foreign governments; neither does it negotiate bilateral assistance agreements. Instead, it works in partnership with civil society organizations, rather than through government-to-government assisted programs.

Thus, the detonation of collective protest that eventually swept through southwestern parts of the continent between 2010-2011 mirrors the brunt of "soft power politics" that is specifically designed and funded to catalyze the democratization of the Middle East and North Africa and incarnate the American ideal.[6] Equally significant is the fact that MEPI regional offices cover 12 of the 19 countries that thus far constitute the crucible of Middle East and North African dissent. Table - 5-1.

MEPI Administered Programs and the "Revolution" in Progress

The discernible social and political convulsions in the Middle East and North Africa have generated ongoing debate in western circles over the imminence or otherwise of an emerging democratized Islamic sub-continent. Much of the debate evolves around the extent to which fundamental changes will ensue, particularly in Tunisia and Egypt, in which the sitting governments were effectively dislodged. None of the spasms being witnessed, however, constitutes the classic model of a revolution. John Dunn author of Modern Revolutions sets out, "what revolutions are in fact is political struggles of great intensity, initiated by political crises within particular historical societies and resolved, insofar as they are resolved, by the creation of a political capacity to confront the historical problems of these societies in ways that their pre-revolutionary regimes had proven wholly incapable of doing.[7]

TABLE - 5-1
TABLE SHOWING COUNTRIES IN WHICH MIDDLE EAST PARTNERSHIP
INITIATIVE IS ACTIVE 2011

Country	MEPI Location of Operation	Start Date of Protests	Outcome
1. Tunisia	✓	18 Dec 2010	Coup d'état
2. Algeria	✓	28 Dec 2010	Major protests
3. Lebanon	✓	12 Jan 2011	Protest
4. Jordan	✓	14 Jan 2011	Protests [Prime Minister and Cabinet dismissed]
5. Mauritania		17 Jan 2011	Protests
6. Sudan		17 Jan 2011	Protests
7. Oman	✓	17 Jan 2011	Protests [Dismissal of Ministers]
8. Yemen	✓	18 Jan 2011	Sustained civil disorder [Resignation of MPs]
9. Saudi Arabia	✓	21 Jan 2011	Protests
10. Egypt	✓	25 Jan 2011	Coup d'état
11. Djibouti		28 Jan 2011	Protests
12. Morocco	✓	30 June 2011	Major protests
13. Iraq		10 Feb 2011	Major protests
14. Iran		14 Feb 2011	Major protests
15. Bahrain	✓	14 Feb 2011	Sustained civil disorders [Dismissal of Ministers]
16. Libya	✓	15 Feb 2011	Civil war ongoing
17. Kuwait	✓	18 Feb 2011	Protests [Resignation of Cabinet]
18. Western Sahara		20 Feb 2011	Protests
19. Syria		15 Mar 2011	Sustained civil disorder [Resignation of Government]

SOURCE: Collated by J. Harris, Analyst, 2011

Dunn asserts that twentieth century revolution has proved to be more overwhelmingly destructive than its historical predecessors and that the main cause for this was the increased strength of twentieth century state power and the far greater density of state involvement in the everyday lives of its subjects. Another very salient point that he puts forward is that the prowess of post-revolutionary state powers in reconstructing the societies and economies over whose destinies they preside, has proven to be appreciably limited. This is exemplified in the experiences of China, the Soviet Union, Viet Nam, Nicaragua, and Cuba in their pursuit of socialist agriculture, all of which endured "longstanding and baffling managerial problems."

Dunn credits the work of sociologist Theda Skocpol in <u>States and Social Revolutions</u> (1979), and her earlier review of the work of Barrington Moore, as a striking and helpful contribution to the debate on what constitutes the central features of a revolution. Skocpol pointed out that the transformation of a state was an indispensable aspect of any true revolution. Her work actually complemented the Marxist focus on the class struggle, by combining the history of class relations and productive organization with a realist perspective on the domestic and international predicament of state power. As she saw it, it was profoundly wrong to think of states as "facing principally down-wards, in stolid repression of their subjects, in sly complicity with local holders of social power, or in selfless and indefatigable service to the public good." In her view, it was necessary to consider the "horizontal political pressures upon state power" since every modern state was fundamentally a unit of an international system of other states, and this was a key factor in the reproduction of social and economic power within its own territorial purlieus.

At the end of the day, the politically vexing element of what constitutes a modern revolution can be reconciled in terms of whether the transformation of the state has occurred and been replaced by a new order - the latter, namely the reconstruction of a superior social order, remains altogether more contingent and elusive in the present context. Skocpol places in perspective twenty-first century struggles, noting that such struggles have seldom, if ever, been credited to issues surrounding the ownership and control of wealth, and that even within this context, they have always been framed and constrained in their course by efforts to either constrain or reconstruct the power of the state. She raises a very significant point, that is to say increasingly; these struggles engage quite directly the power of other states. Another discernible pattern that she identifies is that the institutions of a particular state do not merely express and sustain a domestic pattern of class of class power but also "defend with greater or less efficiency a range of local or territorial interests, in stolid repression of their subjects, in sly complicity with local holders of social power, or in selfish and indefatigable service to the public good."[8]

What is certain amidst the present catalytic events sweeping through the Middle East and North Africa is that a process has been set in motion to stoke fundamental change while the "local holders of social power" struggle to grapple with their immediate options. As a consequence of this unfolding dynamic collective revolutionary actions are occurring at uneven levels of organization and being amplified before a world audience, much to the credit of the information revolution. This phenomenon has rendered the internal affairs of nation states all the more pervious to universal scrutiny.

Dr. Alon Ben-Meir, Professor of International Relations and Middle East Studies at New York University and specialist in peace negotiations between Israel and the Arab States aired this position in Cross Talk: "Arablutionary" (Russia Today Channel) on May 23, 2011:

> *"I think all Arab governments with no exception in one form or another will have to introduce some kind of reform in order to meet the expectations, the hopes and the aspirations of the people. In that sense, there are revolutionary changes that the Arab world has never experienced before and these changes are going to continue for some time to come because the wave of instability or revolution is going to continue for a while and no Arab country is going to follow the same pattern. Each country is going to adopt different kinds of approaches."*

Ben-Meir belongs to the camp of scholars of Middle East Studies who perceive the significance of the current convulsions in the wider setting of their historical significance and the chances of success of the Arab Peace Initiative (API). In his mind, the API has the best possible chance of succeeding if the Arab states are committed to achieving a united front, which will in turn stoke opportunities for a regional balance of power, against the backdrop of an increasingly belligerent Iran. In other words, a collective and democratized Arab world that finds within itself an absolution in Israel's ultimate right to exist, will translate into two outcomes: truncate the ongoing cataclysm wracking North Africa and the Middle East and pave the way for the fulfillment of Palestine/Israeli peace negotiations. The question that arises is how realistic is this paradigm?

Governments are now sharing the stage with actors who can use information to enhance their soft power. To prove this point, Gaith Sager, founder and editor of Arab Crunch, chronicles that, "after the revolution in Tunisia and Egypt, as Twitter has been used as a tool to fuel the revolution, Twitter became a household name in the Arab world just like Facebook." An infographic about Digital Marketing Trends in the Middle East from socialbakers and IQPC estimated the number of Twitter users in the Arab region at about 5.5 million, an increase of 136.5% growth rate. The same report flagged approximately 15-18 million users of Facebook and 30.2 million social media users in the Middle East. Moreover, Twitter users in Saudi Arabia increased by a staggering 240% in 2010[9]

MEPI, by virtue of its manifold tiers of activity, is laying the groundwork for fully established democracies - which go beyond the mere rule of law and incorporate all other aspects of civil society such as freedom of speech, freedom of movement, plural opposition, transparency, relative equality, cross-border consensus and civic participation. Michael Munger, Professor at Duke University, alluded to the potential incongruities that would arise if the institutional framework to support a Western system style of government was devoid of the fundamental mechanisms that guaranteed freedom, justice and self-determination. In his thinking on Cross Talk (May 23, 2011),

> *"If I close my eyes and think what it is that makes the Western system of government actually work, what allows people self-determination is not the ballot box; it's an independent judiciary and the rule of law."*

His further concern was the likelihood of an unaltered status quo following a constitutional election. To this end, he observes that, "...if we urge countries to have elections before they have any kind of institutions... it will be one election and done." He proposes that the establishment of institutions that allow people self-determination and offer pragmatic resolutions to socio-political problems ought to precede constitutional elections that are actively being spurred by the United States; furthermore, while noting that many of the developmental concepts that are being introduced are alien to the Arab world, he perceives the critical role to be served by civil society in the transformation of communities.

Among MEPI's more widely promulgated programs are:

- The "Journalists and Bloggers Advocacy for Human Rights." This was launched in Beirut in December 2009 with the involvement of 30 participants from Bahrain, the United Arab Emirates, Kuwait, Lebanon, Jordan, Egypt, Morocco, Palestine, Tunisia, Yemen, and Sudan. The program was coordinated by the Yemen based non-governmental organizations (NGO) Human Rights Information and Training Center (HRITC), in cooperation with MEPI as part of a BMENA Civil Society Grant.

- The "Know Your Rights Program." The program was launched in October 2000 and its goals are to empower women in the United Arab Emirates so that they understand their rights under the law and gain an awareness of their current status. The program was jointly facilitated by the United Arab Emirates General Women's Union, a long-standing civil society partner for MEPI and the U.S. Mission. Its primary objective is to establish a National Strategy for the Advancement of Women the stated goal of which is to promote Emirate women's participation in education, media, social work, health, legislation, environment, especially politics and executive fields. The first phase of the program consisted of 12 Training Workshops and Four Task Forces – participants were oriented on the provisions of pertinent U.N instruments such as (a) the Convention on the Rights of the Child and (b) the Convention on the Elimination of All

Forms of Discrimination against Women. An important point of note is that the promotion of gender equality and empowerment of women is one of the eight Millennium Development Goals set by the United Nations in an effort to tackle key international development objectives by the year 2015.

- "Empowering Young Activists in Jordanian Civil Society." Al Vidin Jodi Research Center, a Jordan-based NGO, facilitated this program with support from a MEPI local grant. Participants were trained in techniques for active and effective involvement on their organizations and in an understanding of the role of civil society in a democratic system

- The Civic Development Foundation in Yemen. Officially endorsed by MEPI as part of its civic education project, the aim of the project is to engage high school students in Grades 10-12 in civic activities essential to a "successful democracy." Students identified and addressed issues of concern in their communities and participated in public service initiatives, volunteer opportunities, and political activities.

Education has also provided a primary medium for the promulgation of democratic thought and American ideals, as an agent of mediation and transformation, and for wielding other soft power resources. The American University is an exemplification of the diffusion of American scholarship and culture through its various campuses in the Middle East: Cairo, Kuwait, Dubai, Sarah, Beirut, Lebanon, Aleppo in Syria and Dubai in the United Arab Emirates. The attire of female students is demonstrative of western standards and outlook – bareheaded and jeans-clad.

Since its founding in 1919 by an American millionaire, the Cairo campus has been identified with the elite of Egyptian society, providing the country with many of its government and business leaders. Both sons of the recently ousted president Hama Mubarak attended the American University Cairo (AUC), as well as his wife and former first lady, after whose name the Conference Hall was designated. Following the ousting of the president in 2011, the building was re-named the Waheed Building. Beyond the illustrious make-up of its guild of graduates, the AUC has been the venue for historic speeches delivered by Presidential candidates following the events of February 11. Lisa Anderson, AUC's president states that she sees the institution playing a distinctive and potentially vital role in the "new Egypt" in "...demonstrating to other universities that campuses should be the strongholds of free speech, vigorous debate, and creative independent thinking."

Throughout the rest of Eurasia the picture is a checkered one. Of the two largest countries in Asia, India can be referred to as a Federal democracy despite its significant internal challenges while China remains outside of the democratic column. Indonesia's constitution has been re-written to circumvent a possible reversion to a Sukato-styled dictatorship, as obtained prior to 1998. Cambodia and Laos have continued to reel under the ravages of poverty and devastation that were aggravated by the Vietnam War and this has proven to be an unremitting and strained process. Burma's dictatorship persists while its principal bastion for freedom and human rights, Aung San Suu Kyi, remains (as of 2011) under house arrest, a situation imposed by the country's military regime. In the Middle Eastern countries, deep-seated systems of authoritarianism, corruption, and misogyny jilt attempts for fundamental transformation. In the Arab world, where the preponderance of national revenues is generated from their oil-base sectors, the bulk of wealth remains in the hands of closely-knit indigenous elite clans while religious extremism continues to take root and proliferate.

Despite these stark variations, the international debate is framed by a desire to conform to common universal values and by a commitment to respect and uphold the rule of law. This is a collective responsibility and one not necessarily given to any single state. The ongoing crisis in North Africa and the Middle East, in particular the Libyan conundrum, has precipitated a chain of perennial disputations regarding the right to protect civilians, the subject of humanitarian intervention, and the use of force.

Muammar Gadhafi had ruled Libya for more than 40 years by tyranny and by brutally opposing any individual or group that resisted the ideologies he sought to enforce following the 1969 revolution. He has effectively criminalized the peaceful exercise of expression and association, refused to permit independent journalism and advocacy, and authorized torture and extra judicial executions, including the mass killing of 1200 detainees in Abu Salim Prison in June 1996. Additionally, Libya has taken formal responsibility for the terrorist attacks that brought down the Pan Am Flight 303 over Lockerbie in Scotland, killing 270 people of which 189 were American citizens. High-ranking Libyan officials have claimed that Colonel Gadhafi had personally ordered the attack.

According to accounts given by GlobalSecurity.com, on February 11 2011 clashes between Libyan supporters and opponents of Colonel Gadhafi, erupted and this event precipitated attacks on belligerent Tripolians averse to the sitting regime. Warplanes and helicopters struck opponents and the onslaught was compounded by orchestrated attacks by armed African mercenaries who opened fire on protesters. By February 23, the massive evacuation of foreigners was commenced. The Turks and Chinese were the largest groups to have evacuated by air, land, and sea, with the Turkish evacuation of 25,000 constituting the largest in that country's history.

By February 27, the U.N refugee agency divulged that 100,000 persons had fled Libya into Egypt and Tunisia; and by March 13 the Libyan Human Rights League revealed that 6000 persons were killed within the first two weeks of the uprising. The U.N intervention on March 11 was on the instigation of key members of the Western Alliance – the United States, the United Kingdom, France and the United Kingdom, with Susan Rice of the U.S. delegation retorting, "...the Security Council had acted to ensure that democracy prevailed."

U.N as Legitimate Representative of World Opinion

Set side by side with these argumentations is the standing, albeit the issue, of the U.N as the legitimate representative of world opinion and summit consensus vis-à-vis the dominance and propensity to hegemony displayed by the U.S. in her own right and as one of five permanent members of the Security Council.

These contentions are central to the triumphant execution of the U.S. long-term strategy for global expansion through democratization and were equally relevant to the intent and purport of U.N Security Council Resolution 1972 (2011). The Resolution in effect:

- Condemned the gross and systematic violation of human rights, including arbitrary detentions, enforced disappearances, torture and summary executions.
- Condemned acts of violence and intimidation committed by the Libyan authorities against journalists, media professionals, and associated personnel.
- Considered that the widespread and systematic attacks currently taking place in the Libyan Arab Jamahiriya against the civilian population may amount to crimes against humanity.
- Authorized members that had notified the Security Council to "take all necessary measures, notwithstanding paragraph 9 of Resolution 1979 (2011) to protect civilians and civilian populated areas under threat of

attack in the Libyan Arab Jamahiriya, including Benghazi, while excluding a foreign occupation force of any form on any part of Libyan territory."

The primary issue, relevant to the debate at hand, is to what extent is the U.S. restrained in its exercise of hard power, and the overall pursuit of global hegemony, having regard to prevailing international consensus on these issues, based on a chain of well-established precedents and opinions emanating from the U.N. In addressing these issues we shall consider the body of politically binding positions adopted at Summit levels and the status of the U.N as the overarching authority to give effect to collective and legitimate global opinion and associated decisions.[10]

Summit Consensus Regarding the Right to Protect

A crucial facet of U.S. omnipresence in the global landscape is the issue of unilateral intervention and reserving its right of freedom of action, as demonstrated in the Invasion of Iraq in 2003. Either of these prerogatives is integral to the notion of expansion through progressive democratization of Eurasia. This continues to be a hotly debated topic that appears to have found resolution in Summit Consensus, based on the Corfu Channel Case. In that matter, the International Court of Justice held that the alleged right of intervention is a manifestation of the policy of force because it gives rise to a series of abuses and can lead to perverting the administration of justice. This opinion was adopted at the South Summit of 133 States April 2000, when parties "rejected the so-called right of humanitarian intervention which has no basis in the United Nations Charter or in the general principles of international law."

A further endorsement of what has come to be known as "the Corfu principle" was forthcoming at the High-Level U.N Panel on Threats Challenges and Change. On that occasion, the Non-Aligned Movement concluded that, "Article 51 needs neither extension nor restriction of its long understood scope," adding that, "for those impatient with such a response, the answer must be that in a world of perceived or potential threats, the risk of the global order and the norm of non-intervention on which it continues to be based is simply too great for the legality of unilateral preventive action, as distinct from collectively endorsed action, to be accepted. Allowing one to act is to allow all – which is of course unthinkable." The Corfu principle was again re-affirmed at the United Nations World Summit in 2005.

Further to these endorsements, The International Commission on Intervention and State Sovereignty on Responsibility to Protect (2001), sought to extend the Corfu principle to embrace a situation in which "the Security Council rejects a proposal or fails to deal with it in a reasonable time." The Report of the Commission authorized that in those given circumstances "action within an area of jurisdiction by regional or sub-regional organizations under Chapter VIII of the Charter, subject to their seeking authorization for the Security Council be barred." Emanating from this edict, two considerations are noteworthy, namely:

- The Constitutive Act of the African Union asserts the right of the Union to intervene in the affairs of a member state "in respect of grave circumstances" and
- In contrast, the Charter of the OAS bars intervention "for any reason whatever" in the internal or external affairs of any other state.' The purport of the instrument was manifestly to deter intervention from the "colossus of the North," although arguably this was never attained.

International consensus has thus placed a compelling onus on the U.S. to exercise soft power in order to "win hearts and minds" and advance the policies and long - term vision of successive administrations. As a consequence the global projection of American military force whether through humanitarian grounds or otherwise must include "soft balancing." Furthermore, the effectiveness of U.S. policies will ultimately depend on the cooperation of host countries; and the degree of cooperation that foreign governments are willing to muster will in turn be invariably affected by attraction or repulsion, in relation to what America stands for, and how she markets her agenda abroad.

Another related bone of contention is the decision-making process in the U.N Security Council and the fact that the five permanent members of the Council are not perceived as equals in terms of their operative authority. Noam Chomsky interpreted the issue on the basis of two limbs, observing that:

- The Consensus of the World Summit adheres to the Corfu principle and its descendants only if we assume that the Security Council is a neutral arbiter. It plainly is not. Five permanent Members control the Council and they are not equal in operative authority. One indication is the record of vetoes – the most extreme form of violation of a Security Council Resolution...The U.S. is by far in the lead in vetoes"; and
- There have been a few principles in international affairs that apply quite generally. One is the maxim of Thucydides that the strong do as they wish, while the weak suffer, as they must. A corollary is what Ian Browne calls

"the hegemonial approach to law-making: the voice of the powerful sets precedents."

The universal remedy proposed by Chomsky to this nagging dilemma is the elimination of the veto power so that the U.N can follow the will of the majority.[8]

This book advocates closing "the absence of consensus gap" by maximizing soft power resources. In notable distinction to America China, like most Asian countries, lags in soft power resources and is outpaced by Japan in this sphere. While Chinese culture does provide a measurable degree of soft power, its domestic politics and value system place restraints on how it is exercised.

The American presence in Eurasia will continue to be jaded by turbulence and sporadic violence and amidst all of this, the outflow of support and goodwill among Asian nations would be critical to the success of U.S. expansion. This enquiry acknowledges that the Obama administration has been making identifiable adjustments to the style and mode of its foreign policy. America can conceivably retain primacy in this region by drawing upon a flush and enduring legacy of Basing Footprints acquired during the Cold War, rallying an expanded NATO to its cause, managing and containing China and Russia on Asia's further removed eastern perimeter, and stoking the currents of transition presently sweeping across the Middle East and Africa. On the other hand, despite its regional command as Asia's economic power, China will continue to be dogged by the inherently precipitous contradictions spawned by an open market economy and a closed government. Chapters Six and Seven unravel some of the PRC's more contentious and unresolved internal struggles.

PART II

"Thereafter the political doctrinaire dominated and crippled the technician in a struggle that cried aloud for technical competence."

H G Wells
The Shape of Things to Come

OVERVIEW

*I*n 1978 Deng Xiaoping inaugurated an ambitious economic reform program in China. This enterprise was as revolutionary as it was experimental and pursued with a clear intent of rescuing China from the extreme ravages and political dislocation brought about during the period of the Mao Zedong-inspired Cultural Revolution. Xiaoping's initiative was also intended to secure the political legitimacy of the Chinese Communist Party and cement its continued hold on China as it strove to disentangle itself from an ignominious political past.

The Chinese government refers to the current economic system as "market socialism", "state capitalism" or a "market-oriented mixed economy under one-party rule." The current system is the product of a series of major reforms set in train since the 1970s.

Not surprisingly, the take-off to the reforms entailed dismantling cultural and institutional bulwarks that epitomized the Mao legacy. This included the overhauling of land use and settlement policies, essentially this meant – awarding long-term leases to peasants and providing them with inducements for the self-marketing of their produce.

Central to Deng Xiaoping's vision was the transformation of China from a centralized/ planned economy into a socialist market regime that would respond to the dictates of the open free market model that was evolving and spreading in the wider international arena. At the inception of this transition every effort was made to preserve the state's public shareholding in business, banking and industry and perpetuate the socialist system, so that the Communist Party could endure.

Having embarked in this direction, financial sector reform accelerated in the 1990s, following the Asian financial crisis of that period and continued through China's subsequent admission to the World Trade Organization (WTO) in 2001. To all indications the legacy of totalitarianism that followed banking practices, the administration of agricultural enterprise, manufacturing, social services was being systemically revamped. Foreign investment was closely monitored, cautiously administered and strategically determined by the government. By this means pragmatism had become a central feature of the economic planning process.

The goal set by the government in the 1980s to double the nation's Gross Domestic Product between 1980 and 1990 was achieved by 1995. The government has since resolved to raise the per capita GNP to the average of all developed countries by 2050.

Deng Xiaoping thus adhered to some of the core principles of the Maoist regime while remaining open to new ideas about organizing production. His one disadvantage, it is suggested, was the absence of a blueprint. As a consequence of this, as China proceeded along a genuine process of economic transition, reforms tended to be gradual and evolutionary, and not clearly foreseen or designed in advance since neither a process nor an ultimate objective was conceptualized beforehand (Lin 1989).

Retrospectively, one may argue that the reform process was marked by substantial ex-post coherence and significant resilience. In sum, the process was "woven together by many strands and the actions of millions of individuals pursuing their own interests."

The central hypothesis of Part II is that the execution of reform programs that were volitionally underpinned by socialist principles has led China to a current state of bureaucratic brinkmanship, penultimate to an internal political collapse. We will demonstrate that there can be no resolution to the pursuit of unbridled market capitalism that proceeds hand in hand with the retention of political despotism, as now prevails. The Chinese experiment has therefore led to serious institutional incongruities and overall instability. This state of affairs is evident in the banking, industrial and service sectors.

The status quo is compounded by what Guy Sorman identifies in his <u>Empire of Lies</u> as "yardsticks to progress." Sorman's yardsticks, we shall argue, are actually contributing to a thinning of the Communist Party's legitimacy, and proving to be the government's Achilles heel. These are:

- The degree of endemic corruption among bureaucrats
- Social polarity between the rich and poor; and
- The intensity of grassroots opposition to officials

To these can be added the country's human rights track record, simmering nationalist sentiments and environmental and public health issues.

Tens of millions of workers have been rendered redundant with the dissolution of large state-owned enterprises which were previously responsible for their social needs, including welfare, education and health. Currently these sectors have fallen prey to severe public under-investment.

Chinese economic success and military prowess are therefore shrouded in a mire of social ferment and deep public resentment at home and this is presenting authorities in Beijing with serious challenges. So potent is this domestic menace that the government has devised a raft of carefully calibrated strategies to ensure the Communist Party's survival.

Firstly, senior government officials display a higher level of tolerance towards demonstrations by publicly sympathizing with dissenters and their grievances. Secondly, concerted attempts are being made to co-opt key members of interest groups such as college students and the social and political elite. Thirdly, individual freedoms have been improved through diminished censorship in areas such as entertainment. Fourthly, the government has ensured its ability to pre-empt any serious political threat by strengthening its coercive powers. A fifth aspect of the government's survival kit is maintaining the support and allegiance of the People's Liberation Army through various tools of patronage.

Chapter Six lays the groundwork for Section 11 by providing a theoretical basis formulated by Bromley and Rao (2006).They decipher the weaknesses of the reform process, pursued by Deng Xiaoping by:-

- Identifying three stylized institutional tiers or building blocks upon which all economic, business and industrial institutions are built
- Acknowledging the existence of the society's legal foundations which undergird human actions against the backdrop of institutions
- Explaining how the process of transformation ought to proceed within the framework of these building blocks – this is referred to as "mediation" phase and it facilitates human and systems interaction as well as feedback loops.

Our conclusion will be that ultimately, it is the workers, bosses and "others" at the third tier (ground) level that are directly involved in the production process and are intimately engaged in the "games-theoretical" interactions, the sum total of which give rise to actual or real productivity. A further conclusion will be that it is at this level of the transformation process that critical endogamous institutional changes, necessary for successful or real transformation, occur. The phenomenon is compounded by the prevalence of systemic corruption.

Mao Yushi, an independent Chinese intellectual, has taken issue with the much clichéd success story of China. While he readily alludes to the country's economic gains – a phenomenon that is amply substantiated by an annual growth rate of 9 to 10 percent - he is quick to draw attention to the "countless instances of manipulated figures" resorted to by the government through its official statisticians.

With the application of his own revised statistics he makes a case that China's current growth is not sustainable due to "natural bottlenecks" as well as institutional flaws. Scarcity of energy, raw materials and water in his view, account for the former and is augmented by widespread damage to the environment, soil depletion, pollution and resultant epidemics and social crises spurred by mass internal migration patterns.

In Mao's estimation, "economic development in China is not a miracle but an illusion."

Chapter Seven provides a synopsis of how of globalization has impacted on China's domestic and foreign policy. We observe China's response by initially aligning itself with the responsibilities attached to membership of global organizations such as the World Trade Organization. Our examination of the economic transformation process and its effect on identified sectors unearths institutional tensions that have emerged and impacted negatively on major programs being pursued by the government. These dysfunctions are mirrored in the banking, business, and social sectors and are amplified by case study analysis.

Focusing on the social services sector, we assess how the policy of de-collectivization was administered within the health care system through a decidedly top-down approach. This template exemplifies the more large-scale challenges whereby weak systems and corruption have fueled unemployment, environmental degradation, and urban drift. These are precursors to ominous institutional collapse in the absence of political resolve to alter the status quo.

CHAPTER SIX

CHINA'S SHIFT FROM CENTRALIZED PLANNING TO FREE MARKET ENTERPRISE

hina's economic transformation that proceeded concurrently with the era of globalization has presented a formidable task for analysis and deciphering among scholars. Any such attempt appropriately ought to be initiated with the application of stylized facts concerning reality, rather than orthodox principles or fundamental theorems of economic theory. The primary challenge with orthodoxy-inspired assertions is that they do not fare well with observable realities. Martin Weizman's "Economic Transition: can theory help?"(European Economic Review, 1993, Vol 37, pp. 549-555) does not provide a general answer to the question but raises a proposition – that vaguely defined property rights have a distinctive competitive advantage under certain structural and institutional conditions. Compatible with this outlook, Lo and Zhang, in a paper entitled "Making Sense of China's Economic Transformation," premised their study on the notion that any explanation of the strengths and limitations of the dynamics of the Chinese economic transformation would need to draw on a range of relevant and alternative theories, rather than seek to adopt a template.[1] Their study thus provides an analytical account of an explanation and interpretation of the dynamics and developmental implications of the country's economic transformation by drawing upon the following:

- The Marxist Theory of Capitalist Accumulation
- The Post-Keynesian Theory of Demand Determination; and
- The Schumpeterian Theory of Innovation

The post-1978 reform era in China was particularly significant for many reasons. Firstly, the late seventies signaled the eruption of capitalist globalization attributing its worldwide importance. Secondly, during the first half of this period, China's economic growth was driven primarily by improvements in "allocative efficiency" as well as "productive efficiency." Thereafter, from the 1990s until the present time, economic growth has been increasingly based on improvement in returns derived from a growth path characterized by "capital deepening." During both periods the growth path and the institutional frameworks that emerged in China appeared to have contradicted the principles of the free market economy - the mainstream doctrine of globalization. Finally, simultaneous with all of these developments were three successive catastrophes besetting the non-Western world namely (a) the "lost decades of development" in most parts of the developing world in the 1980s and 1990s (b) the systemic crisis in countries that were formerly a part of the Soviet bloc between the mid-1980s and the end of the century; and (3) the financial and economic crisis that devastated most parts of East Asia in the closing years of the century.

Moreover, while the growth of per capita real GDP for all low and middle income economies in the rest of the world was an average annual rate of a mere 4.5%, China's per capita income had climbed at an average of 8.8% per annum in the 1980s and 9.3%per annum in the 1990s. This performance was impressively sustained throughout the first seven years of the 21st. century. Both orthodox establishments and left wing scholarship have found these continuing feats impressive and paradoxical.[2]

From the orthodox market perspective, China's model has deviated from the associated doctrines of the Washington Consensus and it was for that reason that the authorities of the USA, the European Union, and Japan had refused to grant their recognition to China as a "market economy."[3] The orthodox establishment, that is to say, the transition doctrine of the Washington Consensus (IMF 2004), has been consistently outspoken in rejecting the Chinese paradox of economic transformation and there is a recurring claim that given a longer time-span, the economic collapse of a scale comparable to the East Asian crisis, as a consequence of China's deviation from established universal doctrines, is inevitable. According to Dr. Lo, what the orthodox establishment regards as particularly objectionable amidst China's reformed economic institutional concerns is the country's widespread violation of the principles of individualistic property rights along with governmental intervention in economic affairs (the state-business relationship); soft budget constraints (the finance-industry relationship); and rigid employment and compensation symptoms (the worker-enterprise relationship).

Left wing critical scholarship, on the other hand, recognizes that China is on a capitalist transformation course through neo-liberalization. Indeed, writers in this camp hold that capitalism can never deliver development on a world-significant scale and reject the notion that China's growth performance is tantamount to real development. Rather, they interpret this pace of growth as "a super exploitation of Chinese labor" as well as an "undercutting of the working class."[4]

Paul Kennedy offers a historical perspective, surmising that the indications of reform and self-improvement in China during the period of Deng Xiaoping's leadership were not only remarkable but suggestive of the "etatiste pace" of change typical of France in the Colbert era, the early stages of Frederic the Great' s reign, or Japan in the post- Meiji decades. He notes that between 1980-1987, China was straining to develop its power with a measure of pragmatism, by balancing the

189

desire to encourage enterprise and initiative with an equal determination to direct events, so that the country's national goals could be achieved "as swiftly and smoothly as possible."[5] Moreover, the longer term war-fighting power plans, the drag of the agricultural sector on the economy, the country's drive towards industrialization, along with its profligate and extravagant consumption of energy, compounded by the scramble for foreign trade and investment – altogether placed China on a projection (along with all the changeable factors upon which it rested), that could not be calculated with any measure of exactitude.[6]

In Kennedy's judgment, given these vicissitudes, the Chinese strategy would have ineluctably involved "a sophisticated balancing act, requiring careful judgments as to the speed at which these transformations can safely occur, the amount of resources to be allocated to long-term as opposed to short-term needs, the coordination of the state's internal and external requirements, and – last but not least in a country which still has a "modified" Marxist system – the ways by which ideology and practice can be reconciled." In acknowledging the challenges that were confronting the Chinese during the early reform period (1980-1987), Kennedy's overall summation was that the country's record was thus far impressive, but nonetheless contingent on many things among which was "keeping a tight hold on military expenditures."

Despite China's steadfast commitment to economic growth, the government remained equally resolved not to become too reliant on imported foodstuffs, foreign capital, manufactures, or markets of any one country. In deference to this point, we will note in subsequent Chapters the specific measures adopted by the government to drastically reduce its dependency on foreign technology by systematically weaning the system of imported patented products and providing inducements to entrepreneurs for innovation.

Jonathan Pollack described the Chinese strategy as a shrewd and brazen application of political, economic, and military resources but by the same token, indeterminate. He saw China's as a singular international position, which spelled of uncertainty in much the same mold as Kennedy did. Indeed, Deng Xiaoping's methods attracted critique from several camps.[7] Among its detractors was an innocuous but potent scholastic team (David Bromley and Yang Yao), who proposed an institutional model, which in their view is archetypical of the type of structural and process architecture, that should have been applied by Deng from the inception and thereafter, as his economic and social reforms ran their course[8]

David Bromley and Yang Yao pinpointed three stylized institutional tiers which would serve as buttresses for development prescriptions necessitating major economic and social reforms and corresponding institutional adjustments. Further to this, the Bromley and Yao construct rests on three premises, namely:

- That economic policy reform is necessarily the "essence of experimentation and a recursive process of learning what works"
- That a policy prescription is in actuality a prediction because it predicts an outcome
- That the very act of prescribing invites observation, monitoring, assessment, feedback and modification of the prescription

The first and uppermost institutional tier, relevant to the Bromley and Yao model, consists of a core of persons who exercise ultimate oversight over a country's founding Charter which is embodied the Constitutional Rules of society. In the Chinese context, the Central Committee and the National People's Congress would occupy the first tier. At the second level are the institutional rules of the economy, exercised by business and pertaining to matters such as labor and output/product. At the third (ground) level are working rules of going concerns that directly affect people.

The analogy is applied to the structural framework of the economic sector and how it operates. At the first tier of this framework is the stock of natural capital, such as mineral deposits, soil and territorial water. These are referred to as "factor endowments." At the middle level lies society's stock of man-made capital, comprising factories, and machinery and transportation assets. The third level functions as the repository for human capital, which is the relevant "factor endowment" related to that level.

"Factor endowments" at each of the three tiers are regarded as nominal in terms of their value, because they have not as yet been mediated by the institutional architecture of the economy. "Mediation" is the concept that is admitted into the model in order to explain the transformation that occurs at any of the three tiers as a result of the allocation of nominal endowments to real or deployable endowments.

An illustration of the dynamic of mediation is where, for example in the third tier, the potential labor force, is evaluated as "X", but this is a tentative figure, contingent to the availability of persons who may be otherwise deployed, such as those on sick or maternity leave. Having factored this into the construct through mediation, the real or deployable endowment at the third tier translates into the actual labor force.

Underpinning the entire construct will be a constellation of institutions that provide the legal foundations of the entire system in the spheres of labor, capital and production, to name a few.

A further distinction has been made between "imposed institutional arrangements" which are the conscious and purposeful instruments of national and provincial economic policy and "individual institutional arrangements". The former fall under the control of institutions which are tasked with parametizing behavior in the course of economic activity; the latter occur after the fact and mushroom in response to the new rules of the economy and are placed within parameters set by imposed arrangements.

Consequently, imposed institutions serve to liberate behavior by mandating new structures with which going concerns will experiment and interact. As a result of this interaction, endogamous changes will ultimately emerge in the form of specific behavioral patterns that allow change to take form.

This model, when transposed on the constitutional and political architecture in China, provides a facsimile of the decision-making process that in actuality drives the economic reform program, and pinpoints the "locus for purposeful guidance concerning desired general directions for the Chinese economy."

As the designated change agent positioned at the highest levels of government, Deng Xiaoping possessed the general knowledge of the structure of the factors of production and the consumption programs. On the other hand, his knowledge of more specific production activities was limited. His central challenge therefore was to stoke those engine rooms in the system that would send the correct signals to second and third - tier levels of business activity. A further challenge presented itself, once the transformation process was rolled out - that of inducing responses and feedback in the production periods that immediately followed an experiment. The Bromley and Yao prognosis is applied to explain the complex institutional challenges that are now evident, based on the distinctions that have been drawn in applying this methodology.

Another important facet of the Bromley and Yao construct is the juxtaposition they present between the "experimental model" applied to reform (designated the "Social Planner" approach as adopted by Deng Xiaoping), and the strategy that is typically adopted in transitioning to the Western-styled free market economy - the latter they consciously brand as the "Washington doctor" approach, simulative of the Washington Consensus.

The former (the experimental model), they claim, consists of managing specific aspects of the economy by picking winners and calling for specific output targets, after having tried to manage or control the economic process. One may argue that this modus operandi is reminiscent of China's extended history in its application of centralized planning. The Washington Consensus approach, in contrast, issues prescriptions and strives to get institutional pre-conditions right.

Against this backdrop, when difficulties come into view, as they are wont to, the inclination of the "Social Planner" is to:

- Decide which sector warrants immediate attention
- Determine whether, with this uncertainty, a refinement in one sector would have imperfectly known implications on another; and
- Adjudge, if this is at all possible, whether there is an empirical basis for pronouncing on what changes are required institutionally

Placed in this context, the quest for institutional adjustment is likely to be a misguided one in the absence of any blueprint or criterion as to what is better or right. This was essentially the nature of the dilemma with which Deng Xiaoping was confronted as the reforms rolled out. Furthermore, the absence of efficient feedback mechanisms among the three identified institutional tiers, taken in tandem with unprecedented and unanticipated surges in the pace of growth of certain sectors, further heightened the challenges precipitated by the reform.

The fallout that emanated from the elimination of agricultural tax in 2008 is a classic illustration of this anomaly and the relevance of "individual institutional arrangements." The tax withdrawal was instigated at provincial level with the expectation that an unwarranted onus would have been removed from 10 million rural residents, thereby narrowing the large and growing income gap between rural incomes and those of the east-west urban areas. However, the measure gave rise to an induced response that was unanticipated by the local arms of government. Prior to the tax withdrawal, local government bodies had benefitted substantially from tax revenues, which were applied to underwrite the cost of public utilities such as roads, health care, and education. In response to the tax break, local government bodies instituted a municipal-styled tax regime. This consisted of the aggressive levying of family planning councils for violation of rules relating to the stipulated quota of children per family - a move that spurred widespread rural unrest.

Central to the Bromley and Yao model is the premise that pragmatism lies at the heart of economic policy because policy reform is necessarily "the essence of experimentation and a recursive process of learning what works." Thus a policy prescription is, in actuality, a prediction because it necessitates forecasting a desired outcome. The Bromley team recognized that the act of prescribing invites a consequential responsibility to follow up by observing, monitoring, assessing, eliciting feedback, and should the need arise, modifying the prescription. What Deng attempted in 1978 was adhere to some of the core principles of the Maoist regime while simultaneously remaining amenable to new ideas about organizing production. This approach was, however, devoid of any formula or yardstick upon which predictability could be gauged.

Absence of Blueprint

The inclination of thinkers to readily juxtapose the reform process undertaken by developing countries such as China, with the often pilloried and debated Washington Consensus, is therefore easily appreciated. The Consensus may be regarded as the antithesis of experimentation. As Bromley and Yao perceive it, in the application of the Washington Consensus approach to reform, deductive convictions are advanced as "universal truths" and this explains why its results have been hotly contested (Easterly 2001; Rodrik 2003; Stiglitz 2002). Advisedly, its institutional changes necessitated by its execution, which are regarded as a caveat to successful implementation, should preferably be understood as a form of purposeful experimentation, requiring avenues for feedback and accompanied by a desire to attempt new plausible arrangements should the need arise. For these reasons, the Consensus, which was originally intended to serve as the lowest common denominator of policy advice being dished out to Latin American societies by Washington-based institutions, has continued to attract ubiquitous disagreement among a full body of respected sceptics.[9]

For the record its original tenets were:

- Fiscal discipline
- A redirection of public expenditure priorities towards fields offering both high economic returns and the potential to improve income distribution, such as primary health care, primary education and infrastructure
- Tax reform to lower marginal rates and a broader tax base
- Interest rates and liberalization
- A competitive market exchange rate
- Trade liberalization
- Liberalization of inflows of foreign investment
- Privatization
- Deregulation to abolish barriers to entry and exit

- Secure property rights

Moses Naim, editor of "Foreign Policy," attributes the ongoing universal discordance to the fact that at the time of conception, the Consensus was devised to fill an "ideological vacuum", having coincided with the collapse of the Soviet Union and the accompanying disenchantment with socialist ideas and central planning that pervaded "many developing countries outside the Soviet bloc." In his view, given this history the model once adopted, became "an ill-suited and temporary substitute for the all." It was not surprising therefore that very often an incomplete version of the blueprint was being adopted – a situation that invariably held out calamitous consequences for many countries. The Mexican crash of 1994 is illustrative of this trend.

China therefore had to define and redefine her own methodology and barometer for success, albeit mindful of the experiences of other developing countries, including others with a history of central planning that sought to transition to open free market enterprise.

The "Blackhole" of Economic Reforms – Public Institutions

Naim maintains that in most countries public institutions absorb efforts and investment that yield obscenely low returns to society and that their personnel practices distort labor markets, reduce the countries' overall productivity, impair international competitiveness and are easy prey to vested interests that steer the implementation of policy away from the public good. Added to this, these entities are familiarly the locale for endemic corruption, which impairs and discredits reform initiatives. The monitoring and revamping of state institutions thus becomes an administrative imperative, particularly in light of their central importance to the workability of government-led reform. This type of institutional marshaling requires long-term commitment and the capacity to tackle difficult challenges that lack pre-ordained solutions, particularly where the policies in question are being politically driven.

Lo and Zheng provide an alternative interpretation of the Chinese institutional quagmire. They observe that a mix of "market-conforming elements" and "market-supplanting elements" has constituted the country's reformed economic institutions. In addition to this, the country's developmental achievements have been largely ascribable to the conforming elements while its accumulated problems appear to have been ascribable to the supplanting elements. Moreover, the problems so derived have tended to outweigh the country's achievements.

This predicament is by no means unique to China. Institutional malfunction, as an integral component of Latin America's economic liberalization undertaking in the 1990s, needed to be tackled, once it was recognized that state institutions were buckling to the many levels of reform. In like manner, the authorities in Beijing must respond to the essential exigencies of practical application on the basis of their own perceptive deciphering of reality. In "Competition, Deregulation, and Modernization in Latin America" Naim notes as a point of interest that economic reforms in Latin America since the 1970s had initially focused on economic stabilization, and subsequently on liberalization and deregulation. It was not until the final phases of the reform process that the necessary legal, regulatory, and statutory institutions complementary to modern global capitalism, were recruited.[10]

Biglaiser and Brown reinforce the indispensability of institutional reform as a component of the economic liberalization process through their application of the scientific approach[11] Their research note, "The Determinants of Economic Liberalization in Latin America," takes account of the fact that previous work on political institutions and their impact on economic reform, provides a number of testable hypotheses that are rarely examined within a multivariate framework They note, among other things, that a range of criteria has factored into the contingent of setbacks that affect the depth and speed of economic reform. With the application of time-series cross-sectional data, their research provides a multivariate test of the impact that institutions have in the different components of structural reform. These findings suggest that specific institutional arrangements are important for the attainment of specific kinds of economic reform. Despite these results, politicians are by no means deterred by institutional and ideological hurdles that emerge in the course of enacting the relevant reforms.

Chile, similar to China, is widely regarded as a leader in the worldwide trend towards liberalization of markets that challenged the 1970s. In the former case, the transition compelled the introduction of a coherent set of reforms that touched on almost every aspect of economic life. Significantly, one of the novel aspects of these changes was the creation of a wide network of interwoven institutions explicitly designed to minimize the discretionary power of government authorities. These outfits were created by statute law or constitutional amendment, thereby rendering them relatively inflexible to alteration. (Corbo et al 1996).[12]

Tables 6-1 and 6-2 featured at the end of this Chapter, demonstrate the key systemic drawbacks diagnosed by Moses Naim that accompanied major reforms throughout Latin America. Represented as a matrix, the indices show the correlation between various institutional tensions that arose and their systemic origin. This writer is of the view that many of China's current institutional challenges could well be arrested by adopting "mediation" (referenced in the

Bromley and Yao model) as part of a wider panoply of government-led interventions. The importance and urgency of this intervention is exacerbated by other criteria - the country's population size and fluctuations in its labor force.

Two significant demographic features that are directly connected to the forgoing model will be examined in the subsequent section. When the reform process was formally launched in 1978, China's population was 963 million. This figure is expected to increase by 2020 to 1.4 billion. China is presently obligated to feed 1 billion people on 250 million acres of arable land, compared to the U.S. 400 million acres of crops for 230 million people.[6] Additionally, whereas in the early 1970s, 70% of the labor force was employed in agriculture, the move towards an industrialized base and the relocation of large multinational corporations to China to take advantage of much cheap labor, gave rise to massive urban drift away from agricultural production in the rural areas. A further point of note in relation to the labor force is that in 1978 the country had 118 million non-agricultural workers, compared to 369 million in 2002 and peaking to 533 million by 2020.[13]

The scale effect of population growth and mass migration shifts is that China would find it increasingly difficult to feed its population, and as we recognized in Chapter Two, this potential of a country is a primary index of state power and state projection. A second point of note is a decidedly human-security/ economic factor, namely, the multiplier effect that these developments would exert on urbanization and state-supported services such as health and education, public utilities, and unemployment levels. In the subsequent Chapter, we will scrutinize more closely the economic transformation process, its repercussions on some of the state-controlled institutions, and its continuing impact on the country's growing internal instabilities.

TABLE - 6-1
TWO STAGES OF ECONOMIC LIBERALIZATION

	Stage I	Stage II
Priorities	• Reduce inflation	• Improve social conditions
	• Restore growth	• Increase international competitiveness
		• Maintain macro-economic stability
Reform Strategy	• Change macro-economic rules	• Create and rehabilitate institutions
	• Reduce size and scope of state	• Boost competitiveness by the private sector

197

	• Dismantle the institutions of protectionism and statism	• Reform production, financing and delivery of health care, education and other public services
Typical Instruments	• Drastic budget cuts and tax reform	
	• Price liberalization	
	• Trade and foreign investment liberalization	
	• Private sector deregulation	
	• Creation of "social emergency funds" by-passing social ministries	
	• "Easier" privatizations	
Principal actors	• Presidency	• President
	• Economic Cabinet	• Congress
	• Central Banks World Bank & International Monetary Fund	• Public bureaucracy
	• Private Financial Groups and foreign portfolio investment	• Judiciary
		• Unions
		• Political Parties
		• Media
		• State & Local Governments
		• Private Sector
Public Impact of reforms	• Immediate	• Medium and Long-term
		• Low public visibility
	• High Visibility	
Administrative complexity	• Moderate to low	• Very high
Nature of Political Costs	• "Temporary corrections" widely distributed among population	• Permanent elimination of special advantages for specific groups
Main Governmental Challenge	• Macro-economic management by insulated technocratic elites	• Institutional development highly dependent on middle-level public sector management

SOURCE: Moses Naim: Latin America's Road to the Market – From Macro Economic Shocks to Institutional Therapy (San Francisco 1994)

TABLE – 6-2
SOURCES OF INSTITUTIONAL MALFUNCTION

TYPES OF MALFUNCTION	SOURCE OF MALFUNCTION	CHARACTERISTICS
Resource-related	▪ Chronic congestion (over-demand and under-funding)	▪ Typical for new initiatives; limits access to those with sufficient influence
	▪ Inadequate input	▪ Insufficient educated workforce
	▪ Concentration of funding on personnel costs	▪ Insufficient resources for resolving key organizational issues; precludes flexibility and innovation
Politically driven	▪ Capture by special interests	▪ An external related group exercises influence over directives and ideology
	▪ Corruption	▪ Distorts objectives
	▪ Politicization	▪ Recommendations and remuneration heavily influenced by political patronage
	▪ Volatility	▪ Institutional priorities fluctuate due to shift in other priorities or political turnover
Organizational	▪ Goal ambiguity	▪ Lack of clarity manifested in overly ambitious objectives
	▪ Monopoly/Monopsony control	▪ Only one body provides service and workers
	▪ Degree of government involvement	▪ A hands-on approach by government, especially in terms of the economy or monetary policy

SOURCE: Moses Naim: Latin America's Road to the Market From Macro Economic Shocks to Institutional Therapy; (ICEG 1994)

CHAPTER SEVEN

CHALLENGES FROM WITHIN

"Of all China's problems, the one that trumps everything is the need for stability. We have to jump on anything that might bring instability.....and we can't care what foreigners say....we will use severe measures to stamp out the first signs of turmoil as soon as they appear..".

Deng Xiaoping

lobalization has been the clichéd motivation for many third world countries that resolved to transition to free open market economies. Convinced that trade liberalization would lead to export-led job creation, higher standards of living, and a progressive redistribution of wealth, China was no exception. In the Chinese experience a seemingly limitless supply of rural labor provided a comparative advantage, which ought to have aided the process. Or so it was thought. Liberalization was nonetheless fraught with inherent challenges of its own, much of which impacted on the state-controlled apparatus, which was compelled to adapt to variations in business practices. This chapter examines some of the vicissitudes besetting China's health sector reform to illustrate this concern. The banking sector has also been struck with institutional challenges, both politically and systemically.

Economic Reform and Economic Globalization

Beijing's decision-makers were of the view that economic reform was necessary for many reasons but nonetheless harbored their own concerns. One was the disintegration of the Soviet Union in 1999. Drawing upon that experience, Beijing recognized the need to avoid making moves that could potentially prove to be politically destabilizing. A second reason for the country's reform was the brutally competitive environment that was being thrown out by its Asian neighbors, Japan, South Korea and Taiwan, and the enormous flows of foreign capital being devoured by these economies. A third and more important reason was China's imminent admission to the WTO, which occurred in 2001.[1]

200

It should be noted that unlike the Soviet transition to marketization that followed the collapse of communism, the Communist Party of China (CPC) retained political power and the language and symbols of socialism. The larger state-owned enterprises that persist today and the banking system are cases in point. Similarly, the degree of state planning that endures among the dominant state-controlled segments of the economy is a throwback of the country's ignominious history of central planning.

As a consequence of these factors, the influence of the CCP pervades all tiers of China's economic system, its extent being determined by:

- The country's decision-making hierarchy whereby decisions are made by the state regarding the use of economic inputs, who makes them, and how they are executed.
- The coordinating mechanism whereby centralized planning is perpetuated by CPC members.
- The productive property rights which pertain to issues of ownership, whether property is held publicly, privately or in common by all of society.
- The incentive system whereby mechanisms for inducing economic agents to engage in economic activity, are put into effect.

The forgoing are examples of key institutional and social dynamics with which external forces must now wrestle. The early stages of economic take-off during the seventies saw mass migration of China's rural work force from land to industry.[2] During this period the wage levels of unskilled labor remained extremely depressed. With the onset of the eighties and increases in investment, economic activity shifted to the cities and to industrial complexes that began mushrooming in the coastal provinces. Today, the situation is a decidedly altered one with multinational corporations dominating China's exports and many indigenous Chinese firms investing abroad and establishing overseas subsidiaries.

Chronology of Transformation in Banking Sector

During the 1990s, high levels of mismanagement and corruption had gripped Chinese state-controlled enterprises. The banking sector was the paradigm of such malaise after decades of continuous state-imposed curtailments of its operations. When the People's Republic of China was founded in1949 three major shifts occurred, namely banks that were owned and operated by the outgoing regime were taken over by the PBC; private banks were turned into banks that were jointly owned by private shareholders and the state; and most foreign banks opted to leave the county. After 1982, the government gave permission for foreign banks to host operational branches in China, with the primary expedient being to attract foreign investment. Further concessions were extended in 1985 when foreign banks were allowed to operate branches in China, but with limited operational scope within the country's designated four Free Economic Zones.

Having gained accession into the World Trade Organization in 2001, China introduced regulatory permission for foreign investors to hold minority stakes in local banks. Prior to this, the purchase of stock in local commercial banks was prohibited and each equity investment was pursued on a case-by-case basis. Since an important proviso of WTO membership was commitment of China to the complete liberalization of the country's banking sector within the five-year transition period from then onwards, the entry of powerful European and American Banks into the Chinese market took its natural course. Furthermore, of significant import was the fact that U.S. support for China's accession to the WTO was premised not only on achieving economic benefits for the United States, a goal that has had mixed results, but also on achieving political and civil change in China.[3]

Since the mid-2000s, the options exercised by foreign investors in China have evolved from small-scale commercial banks to large-scale ones, including listed banks, nation-wide joint stock banks, and state-owned commercial banks. Further to this, the government actively promoted a policy of encouraging Chinese banks to court partnerships that would assist in amassing capital and improving management (Han; Bing 2006). Economic diplomacy has paid off and today, Chinese banks have joined the global league of the world's largest banks. Table 7.1.

Despite this notable track record the liberalization of the banking sector has not been achieved without challenges, the primary being firstly the resolve of the CCP to maintain a socialist system amidst a marketization drive and an aggressive foreign investment portfolio. The upshot of this was that the banking sector continued to be administered politically by top Communist Party members and was therefore straddled by external control. A second challenge was the application of outmoded tools such as lending caps and reserved ratios by domestic regulators. A third was the surge in bank lending to absolute levels notwithstanding the recent global slump and weaker overseas demand for Chinese products.[4] The unabashed high level of opacity in lending policies despite improved public reporting, was a further setback which triggered two additional areas of concern among regulators, namely loans backed by local municipal guarantees and loans transferred off banks' balance sheets to trust companies and a range of other entities. The fifth factor that has seriously impacted on the success of liberalization was the unrelenting spate of capitalizations. As an illustration of this in 2010, at least $89 billion had to be raised to fill the financial "craters" in the system created by large-scale loan defaults.

In January-May 2010, four of the five largest state-owned banks in China were providing prohibitive levels of credit support to small and medium –sized enterprises (SMEs).[4] The amount of outstanding loans totaled roughly $878 billion. Within this time period, loan portfolios increased as follows:

- 61% of ICBC's credit extension went to SMEs, an increase of 325.4 billion yuan; and SME loans accounted for 49% of total loans
- ABC increased its SMG loans by over 240 billion yuan, accounting for over 50% of total loan increases
- SME loans in BOC increased by 44% reaching 1.1 trillion yuan involving over 34,000 clients

TABLE – 7-1
WORLD'S BIGGEST BANKS BY MARKET CAPITALIZATION JULY 2010

	50 100 150 200 250
Industrial and Commercial Bank of China	* * * *
China Construction Bank	* * * *
HSBS	* * * *
JP Morgan Chase	* * * *
Bank of America	* * * *
Wells Fargo	* * * *
Bank of China	
Agricultural Bank of China	* * * *
CitiGroup	* * * *
Santander	* * * *

SOURCE: Bloomberg Company Prospectus (Adaptation)

Elements of Economic Globalization

Three principal strands of globalization are simultaneously at work in China: the economic, the political and the ideological. Of these, the economic is pre-eminent (Gill 2003).[6]Economic globalization encompasses three components: the internationalization of production, the freeing of world trade and the globalization of financial institutions, primary among which are transnational corporations.

The primary vehicle for internationalized production in China today is the collective occupation of transnational corporations. In tangible terms, at one level production units operate outside the country in which the corporation is headquartered; at the second level a division of labor is instituted, so as to minimize the cost of assembly of products.

Until 2005, the private sector in China was contributing to roughly 70% of the country's Gross Domestic Product while the economic reform process, which commenced in 1978, was moving along in two phases: the first which persisted throughout the seventies and eighties involved the de-collectivization of agriculture; the second, which occurred between the 1980s and 1990s, placed specific focus on privatization measures, on the contracting out of state-owned industry, the lifting of price controls and protectionist policies, and on Regulations. The banking and petroleum sectors, in particular, were consciously preserved as state-controlled enclaves. These and other policy priorities were specifically geared towards aligning China with international commercial trends.

The second constituent of economic globalization entailed the freeing up of world trade and the reduction of protectionism. This was consistent with the international market trends of the 1990s when global free trade had become integral to international economic and financial systems, and was premised on the notion that free trade will ultimately contribute to more efficient economic production, distribution, and exchange.

China was admitted as a member of the World Trade Organization in 2001. By that time the country was fully committed to the liberalization of its regime in order to better integrate into the world economy. The key obligations of a WTO member were/are:-

- Provision of non-discriminatory treatment to all WTO members; all foreign individuals and enterprises including those not invested or registered in China would be accorded the right of trade on terms no less favorable than that accorded to Chinese owned companies

- Elimination of dual pricing practices as well as differences in treatment accorded to goods produced for sale in comparison to those produced for export
- Deferring on the use of price controls for purposes of affording protection to domestic industries or service providers
- Revision of existing domestic laws and enactment of new legislation in compliance with the WTO Agreement
- The right of all enterprises to import and export goods and trade them throughout the customs territory with limited exceptions, within three tiers of accession to the WTO Agreement
- Absence of export subsidies on agricultural products

By 2000, China had become the seventh leading exporter and eighth largest importer of merchandise trade, with exports: $225.1 billion (3.9% share); and imports: $225.1 billion (3.4% share). In the area of commercial services the country was the twelfth leading exporter and tenth largest importer: exports $29.7 billion (2.1% share; imports: 34.8% (2.5% share). By 2010 China ranked second among the top ten U.S. trading partners, second only to Canada and Mexico in imports. In April 2011, the IMF forecasted that China would have surpassed the U.S. as the world's economic power by 2015. Table 7.2 refers. These quantum leaps in trade volumes and investment are consistent with projections common among occidental scholars within the past decade.

The third element of economic globalization pertains to the globalization of financial transactions. Such transactions tend to exert a dual effect. Firstly, financial markets are now more relevant as determinants of currency values, which are calculated on the basis of comparisons with other currencies rather than on the basis of gold bullion in holdings, notwithstanding a reversion among certain jurisdictions to the latter in more recent years with the faltering of the U.S. dollar. A second point of note is with the onset of electronic money flows, capital could now be more easily directed into speculative activity rather than production.

One of the outcomes of this paradigm is that capital flows can now move more independently of national governments and by extension national economies, and significantly so, more closely at the behest of international markets.

The surge in capital flows, as part of the wider global agglomeration of economic activity, triggered an escalation of business and commerce in the late 1990s and early 2000s. Within this period China was accredited as:

- One of the world's largest trading nations

- Recipient of more direct foreign investment than any other country in the world
- Largest borrower from the World Bank
- Largest recipient of official development assistance in the form of interest concessionary loans from industrialized countries
- One of two "transition economies" with ready access to the international capital and equity market[7]

Chriss Street is one among a growing stream of proponents who represent that China's growth has been largely empowered by currency manipulation accompanied by the exponential growth of risky bank lending.[5] Noting this central thesis, as iterated in <u>Death by China: A Global Call to Action</u>, Street regards currency manipulation as "the secret weapon of the China economic model," and the exponential growth of risky bank lending as yet another lethal weapon [8] He observes that within the last two years as Asian economies and foreign exchange resources expanded dramatically, the *yuan* gained 4.6% versus the dollar. This modest rise compares with currency gains of 31% of the Indonesian *rupia*, 22% for the South Korean *won*, and 21% for the Singapore dollar. This strategy makes China's exports more attractive. This theme is expanded on in Part IV in the context of the spate of currency wars unleashed against the U.S. dollar and intense argumentations being mounted that favor the replacement of the dollar as the leading reserve currency.

In Street's estimation, the additional issue of risky bank lending is in effect a default policy triggered by the fact that the Chinese government does not provide adequate social welfare programs and restricts citizens' investment options to bank accounts. To date, approximately 40% of Chinese household income is deposited in state-owned banks each month. The banks "leverage" these deposits by ten times and loans by 75% of the huge sums of cash at low interest rates to state-owned enterprises and the remaining 25% are appropriated to real estate enterprises.

TABLE - 7-2

TOP U.S. TRADING PARTNERS TOTAL TRADE,
EXPORTS, IMPORTS. SEPTEMBER, 2010

TOTAL TRADE (GOODS)

RANK	COUNTRY	EXPORTS	IMPORTS	TOTAL	%TOTAL TRADE
	Total all Countries	107.8	166.4	274.2	100%

	Total 15 Countries	75.5	122.4	197.8	72.2%
1	Canada	21.9	2.30	449	16.4%
2	China	7.2	35.0	42.2	15.4%
3	Mexico	14.0	19.8	33.8	12.3%
4	Japan	5.0	10.0	15.0	5.5%
5	Fed. Republic of Germany	4.1	6.8	10.9	4.0%
6	United Kingdom	3.9	4.0	7.9	2.9%
7	Korea, South	3.0	4.3	7.3	2.7%
8	France	2.3	3.5	5.7	2.1%
9	Taiwan	2.4	3.3	5.7	2.1%
10	Brazil	3.0	1.7	4.7	1.7%
11	Netherlands	3.1	1.5	4.6	1.7%
12	Singapore	2.3	1.7	4.0	1.5%
13	India	1.4	2.4	3.9	1.4%
14	Venezuela	0.9	2.8	3.8	1.4%
15	Saudi Arabia	0.9	2.7	3.6	1.3%

EXPORT (GOODS)

COUNTRY	EXPORTS (SEPTEMBER)	% TOTAL EXPORTS
Total, All Countries	107.8	100 %
Total Top 15 Countries	79.0	73.3 %
1. Canada	21.9	20.3%
2. Mexico	14.0	13.0%
3. China	7.2	6.7%
4. Japan	5.0	4.6%
5. Federal Republic of Germany	4.1	3.8%
6. United Kingdom	3.9	3.7%
7. Netherlands	3.1	2.9%
8. Korea, South	3.0	2.8%
9. Brazil	3.0	2.8%
10. Hong Kong	2.7	2.5%
11. Taiwan	2.4	2.2%
12. Singapore	2.3	2.2%
13. France	2.3	2.1%
14. Belgium	2.1	2.0%
15. Australia	2.0	1.8%

IMPORT (GOODS)

COUNTRY	IMPORTS (SEPTEMBER)	% TOTAL IMPORTS
Total All Countries	166.4	100%
Total, Top 15 Countries	125.5	75.5%
1. China	35.0	21%
2. Canada	23.0	13.8%
3. Mexico	19.8	11.9%
4. Japan	10.0	6.0%
5. Federal Republic of Germany	6.8	4.1%
6. Korea, South	4.3	2.6%
7. United Kingdom	4.0	2.4%
8. France	3.5	2.1%
9. Taiwan	3.3	2.0%
10. Ireland	2.9	1.7%
11. Venezuela	2.8	1.7%
12. Nigeria	2.8	1.7%
13. Saudi Arabia	2.7	1.6%
14. India	2.4	1.5%
15. Russia	2.3	1.4%

SOURCE: Foreign Trade Division, U.S. Census Bureau, Washington D.C (Modified November 10, 2010 at 8.40 a.m.) U.S. Department of Commerce

Cost to China of Investing in Volatile Countries

Another aspect of questionability in the realm of economic performance lies in the country's line-up of preferred allies. In Chapter Two note was made that the quest to secure energy sources has taken Beijing along a path of mutual attachments that are inconsistent with Western Hemisphere non-proliferation policy. Furthermore, in order to reinforce its position, the Chinese government was one among five that abstained from voting in favor of U.N Resolution 1973(2001) at the 6498th Security Council Meeting on March 17 2011. The offshoot to China's posture and the significance of its alignments in exercising its prerogative to abstain emerged soon after the "NO FLY" policy adopted under the U.N Resolution took full effect. The Chinese government remonstrated that air strikes in Libya were directly responsible for the demobilization of scores of state-owned companies and businesses operating out of Libya. At the onset of the NATO-led raids, 75 Chinese companies held operations in Libya, contracting 50 large-scale projects with an aggregate contract value of $18.8 billion. Of these, 13 are state-owned enterprises, most of which were engaged in the construction and telecommunication sectors.

208

These companies subsequently suspended operations in Libya and at least 25 have reported looting and attacks on their properties, resulting in direct losses of $1.5 billion.

Economically speaking, investments in volatile countries deemed by Beijing to be "strategic partners" are typically encumbered by a range of risks that place Chinese investments in serious jeopardy. Conjecturally, this may have been one in a range of criteria that figured in the rationale to institute the "No fly" policy, a position which from its very inception, was met with strong resistance from the Chinese government. The course of action undoubtedly highlights another very salient factor in terms of who or what are the constituents of "...the West" and the potential of these elements, acting in concert, to undermine and seriously impair China's interests, including its investments in overseas territories[9]

Political Globalization and Multilateral Diplomacy

One of the more discernible outcomes of "political globalization" is that traditional boundaries of statehood are being systematically eroded in the interest of broader international exigencies.[7] The phenomenon has impacted on the decision-making powers of governments, on occasions voluntarily and in others involuntarily. Gradually, political prerogatives are being stripped away and subordinated to bloc interests. This phenomenon was set in train from as early as the Cold War period when the Soviet bloc structure apparatus operated in parallel with Western alliance systems.

The more recent execution of this process has seen a flourishing of international agreements by regime in the form of treaties, conventions and normative principles that are adopted to shape the behavior of states in a broad spectrum of areas such as human rights, weapons control, financial regulatory provisions, environmental protection, and gender-related issues. These themes all feature towards attempts at universality and harmonization. Further attempts at global harmonization and standardization and the institution of supranational governance structures will continue to place corresponding restraints on the capacity of the state as a primary actor. (Gill, 2008).

China's membership of the United Nations Security Council has served, thus far, as an effective counterweight to fermenting opposition in the international sphere. Moreover, multilateralism has been the cornerstone to Beijing's approach to international relations.

209

Among the more striking Chinese accomplishments in consensus and confidence building is the exercise of political sophistication through engagements within regional groupings exemplified within the under-listed geopolitical blocs:

- Asia, through the ASIAN Plus 3 grouping, launched in 1997 and the 2000 FTA with ASEAN
- The Middle East, in the context of the Sino-Arab Cooperation Forum established in 2004 and the Free Trade Agreement with the Gulf Cooperation Council
- Africa, under the China-Africa Cooperation, inaugurated in 2000
- Latin America, by virtue of the PRC's acquisition of Permanent Observer Status in the Organization of America States in 2004 and thereafter the Inter-American Development Bank
- The Caribbean, under the auspices of the China-Caribbean Economic Corporation meeting which held its inaugural convocation in February 2005

Reforms in the Health Care System – Impact of De-collectivization

The economic reforms of the 1980s resulted in phenomenal changes in China's health care system among which was the introduction of a de-collectivization policy that was integral to the reform process. The modified system effectively did away with the collective welfare system that was installed by the Mao regime following the 1949 revolution. Under the former system, a substantial part of the rural population (no less than 45%) was covered under the cooperative medical scheme.

The newly introduced three-tiered scheme within China's health sector facilitated national, provincial and local level networking among industrial and state-enterprise hospitals. China's Ministry of Public Health was the designated public entity with ultimate responsibility for the delivery of the health policy of the Communist Party. This policy was premised on the employment of preventative medicine and led to a degree of improvement in methods of administration. During its sentience, the average life expectancy in China rose from 32 years in 1950 to 69 in 1985.

In terms of its operational effectiveness, the three-tiered approach ensured that at the first (ground) level, teams of paramedical personnel, designated "bare-foot doctors" functioned out of village medical centers, which serviced the needs of the rural population. At the second tier was a system of "township health centers" which were de facto outpatient clinics staffed by assistant doctors, each with a capacity to service 200,000 to 600,000 patients.

One of the principal merits of this system was that it appreciably stemmed a considerable number of epidemic diseases to which China had become severely prone. For example, cholera, plague, typhoid and scarlet fever were near to fully eliminated in the 1970s but following the initial phases of the reform in the 1980s there was a conspicuous resurgence of diseases such as hookworm, dysentery, tuberculosis, hepatitis and malaria.

These types of institutionally-attributed dysfunctionalities leading to program failure were analogous to the phenomena identified by Moses Naim in his prognosis of Latin America's major reform in the 1980s. Specific categories of institutional malfunction were typical in this phase of economic transitioning: those that were issue-related; those that were politically motivated and those that owed their genesis to organizational indispositions. [10]

Issue-related dilemmas, as explained, arose where persons with sufficient influence were not easily accessible or where there was an insufficiently educated work force or where resources needed to resolve key organizational issues were insufficiently deployed. In the present context, at political level, there were situations when directives and ideologies emanating from the inner workings of the decision-making process in Beijing trumped more practical concerns of program implementers operating at provincial and local levels. One likely reason for this was fluctuations or shifts in institutional priorities and budgeting, a phenomenon identified in the Bromley and Yao model as "imposed institutional arrangements." These are actions that are influenced and parametized at the level of the CCP, which had been directing focus away from non-productive investments. Finally, at organizational level, conservative interests superseded many ambitious objectives. This phenomenon is discriminatingly connected with the mushrooming and spread of corruption, often among political loyalists.

Edward Fokuoh Ampratwum of the University of Cambridge affirms that in many transition countries, the shift from command economies to free market economies has created massive opportunities for the "appropriation of rents", that is to say, excessive profits, and this has often been accompanied by a change from a well-organized system of corruption to a more chaotic and deleterious one. [11] In acknowledging this dilemma, the World Bank contends that the principal way to reduce corruption is to encourage deeper and more thorough economic liberalization and deregulation of borrowers and equally important, reforming and strengthening public institutions (Riley 2004). Indeed, this latter point corroborates the salience of Naim's conclusions.

Some of the identified drawbacks specific to China's health reform scheme were:

- Lack of financial resources
- Relaxation of certain sanitation and anti-epidemic programs
- Breakdown of the brigade system
- Lack of affectation on the part of government to the ominous signs of neglect
- Increased costs of medical treatment
- Limited funds or continued education of the "bare-foot doctors"
- Collapse of cooperative medical programs
- Dysfunctions between professionals trained in Western medicine and those trained in the practice of traditional Chinese medicine - the former had been gaining acceptance but nonetheless there had been a failure to synthesize the two schools

Closely associated with the issue of institutional malfunctioning is the predilection of the Chinese Communist Party to nurturing the culture of mismanagement and corruption in an attempt to maintain the status quo. The mismanagement of the country's AIDS epidemic is archetypical in terms of bringing to the fore the extent of deep-rooted systemic dysfunction that persists within the state apparatus compounded by collusion among the authorities to mask pertinent issues.

This reality is confirmed in a Study commissioned in 1996 by the Department of Epidemic Research, Shanghai Hygiene Anti-Epidemic Center, the objective of which was to establish "the socio-economic factors of vulnerability to AIDS pandemic in the future and to develop strategies for the prevention and control of the disease." The study concluded that China, holding one-sixth of the world's population, could potentially contribute to rising infection rates, unless urgent proactive steps were taken by the government to stem its spread.[12] Taking proactive steps, however, would necessitate an acknowledgement of the crisis by the government, a course of action to which CCP was averse.

Policy and Response of Chinese Communist Party

When HIV surfaced in China in the 1980s it was largely associated with practices deemed by Chinese authorities to be of "Western origin." They labeled the phenomenon "proof of capitalistic dissolution" and were by no means forthcoming in the admission a serious health threat. Indeed, the experience in the province of Henan epitomizes the classic matrix of institutional malfunction, corruption and political expediency that is uniquely Chinese. A point of note is that whereas in developed countries MSM accounts for 70% of HIV infections, and in sub-Saharan Africa heterosexual contact is a major transmission route, China's problem is unique in that it is associated with drug use.

The initial response of the government was prompted by the infection of four hemophiliacs with the virus in 8s by imported factor VIII. Thereafter, the use of imported blood products was prohibited and in its place a "for profit blood collection" system was initiated. Under this system peasants would be paid $5 per blood donation.

This indiscriminate practice opened the door for a new route of transmission since donors contributed several pints per day in a situation that was aggravated further by the reckless management of specimens by health personnel - the plasma would be removed from the specimens and the blood returned to donors. Illogically, the blood of multiple donors was commonly mixed prior to being returned to the donors with no tests for AIDS being conducted.

The extent of the Chinese AIDS epidemic and its contentious nexus with blood collection units was unearthed by prominent physician, Goa Yaojie in 2005. Until 1994, according to Dr. Yaojie, AIDS was officially a "state secret" in China. The epidemic that erupted in Henan owed its origin to the selling of blood, which had become a main source of income for scores of impoverished burgesses. Several AIDS victims reportedly used these funds to pay fines imposed by the family planning departments for exceeding an officially prescribed quota of two children per family unit. Rather than have their property confiscated by the state for having a third child, couples bribed the tax collectors operating the family planning centers. Thus, the AIDS pandemic was directly linked to systemic corruption and sustained by a rigid state policy that kept it afloat as a lucrative business. Approximately one million new cases of AIDS come to the attention of Chinese hospitals each year.

Based on Dr. Yaojie's account, national authorities reacted to the odium by:

- Barring all entry to villages in Henan province, thereby quarantining no less than 37 villages
- Disseminating new maps of Henan, that excluded the names and locations of affected villages, so that nationally in terms of official geo-mapping , these villages did not exist

- Disseminating official concerns that information on Henan would adversely affect trade with that province
- Discouraging migration out of Henan to other provinces[18]

The state fostered policy is recounted by Guy Sorman, reputed French public intellectual, in the following terms:

> *...Apart from the horror (of Henan) the story is so illustrative of the Party's methods. Any wrongdoing is necessarily foreign; if exposed it has to be stoutly denied, wild grass must be weeded out. But under no circumstance should one lose face in front of Westerners who hold the key to economic development...*[14]

China's reform process has undoubtedly been fraught with impediments, but as we have seen in Chapters six and seven, much of this is attributed the role of the CCP, mismanagement, and corruption. In tracking the critical phases of the transformation process we come to grips with the steady escalation of challenges confronting the government.

The first major barrier was the undertaking of decentralizing the State apparatus as a precondition for the reform of the economic system. Secondly, the decision-making process had to be correspondingly decentralized. This included the de facto granting of property rights and fiscal power to different levels of local government. Next came the necessity to curtail budgetary allocations at the level of central government, for the purpose of redirecting expenditure to the centers of gravity of development, that is to say, the provinces of Shanghai, Yangzi, and Delta.

The fourth and equally major phase of the transition process was China's entry into the World Trade Organization, an exercise involving a fifteen-year roll over period. Within this timeframe, China actively canvassed for American support by establishing diplomatic ties with Washington in 1979. Following this, she entered the International Monetary Fund and World Bank in 1996 and acquired Observer status in GATT in 1982. In the meantime, her trade with the U.S. was becoming increasingly prolific and by the mid-1990s there were discernible signs of a retreat on the part of the state from the provision of goods and services such as education and health, a lowering of tariff barriers, and the adoption of an open trade regime.

The fifth major tranche of changes consisted of direct foreign investment. During this period, the center of gravity in economic development shifted from the cities to manufacturing bases, more specifically the Guangdong Province. By the year 2003, China had become the largest recipient of direct foreign investment in the world. In the meantime, her inward investments were being ploughed into subsidiaries of multinational corporations with the aim of exploiting large resources of cheap labor and making her exports more globally competitive.

Socially and politically speaking, this fast-paced development has come at a high price. The concentration of manufacturing gave rise to large-scale rural/urban shift and a de-scaling of agricultural production as peasants moved away from the land. Large-scale manufacturing also precipitated environmental degradation and pollution as well as soil depletion. Official data collection and analysis, which is by right the purview of the government, had been abandoned between the years 1960-1980, and once this enterprise was officially re-commissioned, there were incongruities in methods of collection and analysis, a situation which was compounded by state-orchestrated manipulation.

It has been argued that China's current pace of growth is unsustainable due to the fact that such pace would result in the emergence of natural bottlenecks in the form of scarcities of water, energy, and raw materials. These are all tangible manifestations of systemic issues warranting not only direct state intervention, but also fundamental alterations in the political culture, which of itself remains embedded in the country's Communist legacy.

The real and present ferment of social discontent cannot be suppressed indefinitely. An observation raised by Brzezinski bears directly on the Chinese status quo. He notes that, "experience teaches that pressures for democratization from below, either from those who have felt themselves politically suppressed (intellectuals and students) or economically exploited (the new urban labor class and the rural poor), generally tend to outpace the willingness of rulers to yield."[15] Susan L. Shirk, a former Deputy Assistant Secretary of State responsible for America's relations with China under the Clinton administration, has closely studied Chinese rulers for three decades and offers insights into their line of thinking and concerns in her book, China: A Fragile Superpower. [16]

Having assessed and highlighted the fragility of China's political institutions against the setting of intensified nationalism, mass protests, and the availability of information through the Internet, Shirk proposes paradigm shifts in state conduct, which in her view, could assist the Chinese leadership in exculpating itself from the "present dilemma", and arriving at "politically practicable" solutions. She acknowledges as this book does, that "their system reacts to crises both too slowly

215

and too impetuously" and that as an alternative to focusing on "organizational fixes" to improve crisis management, domestic counterweights should be developed to relieve internal pressures for bellicose actions.

Several of her reappraisals are noteworthy. Firstly, the types of efforts being adopted by the CCP to rebuild its legitimacy following the Tiananmen Square uprisings in the form of patriotic education campaigns and campus and media commemorations of humiliations suffered at the hands of the Japanese, should preferably be de-emphasized or discontinued. These types of overtures promoted by the CCP have, in Shirk's view, fanned the flames of assertive nationalism, which have fed into the glorification of xenophobic violence. The earlier dispensation of Chinese nationalism had deep historical roots and was largely confined to students who had formed the precursors of the Kuamingtan and Chinese Communist Party in the earlier part of the century; the current wave of nationalism is a mass phenomenon designed to compensate for China's fall from greatness which, in the view of the present leadership, is tantamount to a historical aberration. It is this type of nationalist fervor that is defining the mindset of the most populous nation in the world. In distinction to this present mood, more positive nationalism can be promoted by highlighting the country's successes. The hosting of the 2008 Olympics is a case in point of the positive type of forum that can be exploited by the Chinese to promote nationalist sentiment.

Another of Shirk's propositions is that the interest groups that have highest stakes in China's globalized economy, such as private businesses, deserve to be allowed a voice on the country's foreign policy and even be admitted as CCP Members. Such a move would redress the present disconnect between the economic reform measures that are in progress and the political system which remains in large part highly centralized and unreformed.

The decontrolling of the media is also strongly advocated. Chapter Nine expounds on the potential of the media as an instrument of propaganda and state control. In this regard, the present text notes that China's commercialized newspapers, magazines, television, and Internet news sites are directly orchestrated, monitored, and controlled by the CCP Propaganda Ministry and that media content is disproportionately biased in favor of passionate nationalism. Moreover, earlier in this section we assessed the impact of state-driven suppression of information on the efficiencies of the state apparatus and on the overall quality of service delivery in the health sector. A more liberalized media would undoubtedly free the public domain to more accurate information on public opinion, liberate the market place of ideas that are now either suppressed or latent, and assist the Chinese collective leadership in consolidating its legitimacy at home.

PART III

OVERVIEW

*S*heldon S. Wolin, winner of 2008 Lannan Notable Book Award for his publication, Democracy Incorporated: Managed Democracy and the Specter of Inverted Totalitarianism, portrays America as a country in which citizens are politically submissive and where elites are intent on keeping them that way. He posits that at best, the nation has become a "managed democracy," where the public is shepherded and not sovereign. At the other end of the continuum, he sees America as a place where corporate power no longer answers to state controls but makes clear that despite the fact that America is neither morally nor politically comparable to totalitarian states like Nazi Germany, unchecked economic power risks verging on economic power and assumes its own unnerving pathologies.

This troubling diagnosis complements Naomi Wolf's ground-breaking prognostication in The End of America: Letter of Warning to a Young Patriot. Wolf purports that following the events of 9/11, a classical "fascist shift" occurred in America whereby a series of tipping points were set in train by the government resulting in stunning alterations of the American democratic tradition. This, she explains, is discernible in the form of ten classic steps typically resorted to by the government of every known dictatorship that has metastasized during the twentieth century beginning with Italy under Mussolini in the 1920s; Germany under Hitler in the 1930s; Russia under Stalin in the 1930s; East Germany in the 1950s; Czechoslovakia in the 1960s; China under Mao Ze Dong throughout the 1950s but less potent towards the dawning of the new millennium; followed by Thailand and Burma in the 2000s.

Every known despot in her view, whether left or right, follows a predictive blueprint that is currently visible in the storm clouds gathering over present day America. She perceives in her apparently estranged homeland, a recreation of how dictatorships have set about systematically demobilizing the practices and institutions that define the democratic process. In her thinking, addressing this perennial predisposition to tyranny fell to the founders of the unique American experiment, who incorporated appropriate checks and balances in the course of drafting the country's constitution and laws more than two hundred years ago and advisedly so. Focusing on the expedients that are presently under way and pushing America into becoming what she discerns as a "closed society," Wolf identifies the following specific courses of conduct on the instigation of the state:

- The invoking of a terrifying internal or external threat

- The creation of secret prisons outside the rule of law that deny prisoners due process; the legalization of torture against individuals, particularly marginalized groups; the creation of military tribunals to facilitate special types of trial
- The establishment of a paramilitary force that can be readily summoned to terrorize ordinary citizens. The "black shirts" of Italy and the "brown shirts" of Germany are analogous cases in point
- The institution of a complex surveillance apparatus that targets ordinary citizens
- Imposition of restrictions on the press, supported by draconian legislation that expands on the definition of such concepts as espionage
- Subversion of the rule of law to facilitate the operations of agents provocateurs and thereby provide an excuse for state-instigated crack downs

Part III reveals the true "America." The text aligns itself with some of the observations made by Susan Shirk, a former U.S. envoy to the Asia /Pacific, regarding America's reputed preeminence, vis-à-vis the "near panic in some quarters of American society," as she describes it, in relation to China's revival as a world economic power. Shirk notes, for example, that China's challenge could well have a salutary effect to the extent that it stimulates America to improve upon its own weaknesses, specifically in the area of its "ballooning government deficits."

Shirk is a prolific writer and respected and long-standing expert on Chinese affairs. In China Fragile Super Power, having called attention to the chain of precedents in which America was successful in outstripping the inclinations of other powers that attempted to challenge her lead, she spurs America to "touch the tape," calling to mind the space race of the 1950s, which was fueled by early Soviet ambitions and the Japanese meteoric rise to manufacturing and investment in the 1980s. Such feats provided catalysts in America's quest for global preeminence. By the same token, America is cautioned against an overreaction to China, as its perceived economic rival. Such responses, in her estimation, risk being interpreted by the Chinese as retaliatory.

Part III demonstrates the extent of American cultural and political dominance through the agencies of intergovernmental participation, mass communication, and soft diplomacy. It examines the role of corporatism, its internationalization, and the unique place of propaganda (Chapter Nine) in the state and corporate apparatus and its part in the inducement of mass compliance. This point is extended to the unprecedented role now being played by celebrities (Chapter Eight) in propagating American ideas, values, and policies.

Chapter Ten and Chapter Eleven probe revolutionary breakthroughs in information technology, the use of cyberspace as a war-fighting domain and potentials held out in conquering inner and outer space. The potency of stealth as a tool of dominance becomes manifestly clearer and diminishes the relevance of scalability as a yardstick in the determination of preeminence, as expanded on in Chapter Twelve. All of these are decidedly unrivalled aspects of American power, which autograph omnipresence.

CHAPTER EIGHT

DEFINING AMERICA

"Cultural domination has been an underappreciated facet of American global power... Its attraction may be derived from the hedonistic quality of lifestyle it projects, but its global appeal is undeniable."

Zbigniew Brzezinski

*A*merica is everywhere and everything. America is the landscape. It is the world. It is the universe. It is in outer space. It is in inner space. It is in the skies and on the seven seas. It is on the highways, on the billboards, in restaurants, in books and magazines, in the movies. It is echoing across the skylines of every major capital in the world.

China's conduct is merely a nod to America's universal reach. China is saluting America, not eclipsing it. As much as it would wish to overshadow American power and assume strategic high ground, America is beyond puissance. The replacement of Google's search service by the Chinese government with its own technology on March 28, 2011 goes beyond exacting a major dent in the U.S. giant's presence. Rather, it was a remonstration to American omnipresence.[1]

In like manner, the crackdown by the Chinese government during the first quarter of 2011 upon the public release of maps containing sensitive or confidential information and on businesses offering mapping services and related online facilities, is a vindication of the government's commitment to curtailing attempts that could compromise or assail its vital interests. Currently, there are no less than 42,000 websites in China offering maps. This online service opens the floodgates to increases in information leakages that could prove harmful to the country's vital interests.[2]

America's dominance as a global power exceeds material productive forces, such as military assets, technological gadgetry, the free market, capitalization, transnational corporations and the boardrooms of big business. The nation's stature goes beyond membership of major political, economic and military alliances in the world to an international webwork of friends, allies and vassals. Also affiliations and syndicates embedded in the global intelligence architecture spanning every nook and cranny of both hemispheres are not to be forgotten.

As is the custom of the World Bank – a United Nations international financial institution[3] – an American citizen is elected the head, though till recently some effort has been made to diversify the monotony of the leadership. Jim Yong Kim, a Korean American physician and anthropologist, is currently the President having been elected on April 16, 2012. A European Union representative – Christine Lagarde - heads the IMF, notwithstanding American leadership of this entity. Be that as it may, the largest member of the Fund is the United States, with a current quota of SDR 42.1 billion (about $65 billion). Measured against America's ranking, China comes in behind at third place[3]

America is the center of gravity around which global power relationships have evolved following World War II and will continue to evolve. Politically speaking, it is the driving force of the United Nations, OAS, NATO, the Asia Pacific Economic Forum (APEF), NAFTA, WTO; in sum the linchpin of the western alliance. Even in the face of apparent non-congeniality the U.S. holds sway in every sub-continent and region in the eastern and western hemispheres.

Moreover institutions by virtue of their core beliefs, ideals, maxims, and essence do not simply perish but evolve, consolidate and endure. Rosemary Foot examined the role of the U.S. in international financial institutions with specific reference to the World Bank and the IMF, She detailed the role of the U.S. through formal power structures but also in terms of influence.[3] The country functions as both formal means such as U.S. financial contributions, and informal practices that have developed over time. Foot argues that notwithstanding the weight of U.S. influence, it would be inaccurate to consider the World Bank and the IMF as mere instruments of U.S. power. America's credibility rests in part on their ability to "create some political distance between themselves and their most powerful state patron." Over and above that, the separation of powers between the Executive branch and Congress constrains temptations of absolute rule.

Other considerations that factor into the U.S. vis-à-vis "rest of the world" power dynamic are:

- U.S. domestic political conditions – the separation of powers and authority between the Executive and Congress may either enhance or constrain influence
- Interlocutors in host governments may or may not share the same technological mindset or ideological predisposition of the U.S. and international institutions

America maintains a unique reserve of diplomatic capital that is difficult to rival. Its tools of statecraft are of distinctive reach and guile. America is the ultimate collaborator, the classic colluder, the unabashed interlocutor, and the indomitable abettor, Samuel Huntington, Eaton professor of the Science of Government at Harvard notes that the U.S. must maintain its "initial primacy" for the benefit of the world because alone among nations its national identity is defined by a set of universal, political, and economic values, specifically liberty, democracy, equality, private property, and markets. China does not value these said principles, which are engendered in American politics.

America resounds an omnipresent voice on every issue that is of global significance ranging from human rights, democracy, nonproliferation, the environment, energy, trade, commerce, banking, the arms trade, drugs, terrorism, including issues of migration, health care and gender affairs. Its unmistakable sway and ranking among friends, allies and rivals alike transcends geography. America continues to shape the international rules of engagement and the global agenda. China's locus is albeit far less-defined, though by no means underestimated.

For all its ascribed "inverted totalitarianism", fixation on pre-emptive wars, unrestrained militarism, contempt for former allies and hatred of terrorists, obsession with "the savage other," whatever label one cares to affix, whatever accolade one dares to confer, America can still to evoke a universal fervor that heralds "we are the world."

The Ultra-Rich Givers

American icons are among the ultra-rich givers of the world. The philanthropic efforts of the likes of Bill Gates and William Barron Hilton are legendary and generate quintessential rippling effects. Hilton pledged $1.7 billion to the funding of his family's humanitarian foundation. Other notable donors include Jon Huntsman who endowed the Huntsman Cancer Institution with $700,000,000 towards finding a cure for cancer.

It is to the credit of the William Gates Foundation, established in 1994, that public access computers with internet connection became integral to the American library system. During its nascent stages the Foundation was re-named the Gates Learning Foundation to reflect the expanded focus that was being placed on minority students preparing for college.

Between 1994-2010, $24,470,000,000 in grants went towards the funding of local and overseas programs, with the lion's share of $14,350,000,000 apportioned to global health. The grants were applied to advance science and technology thereby saving lives in poor countries and making possible vital interventions such as the provision of vaccines, drugs and diagnostics in areas in which they were most needed. Equally impressive is the line-up of prominent, time-tested syndicate interests that have come forward and partnered with the Foundation, among which are the International AIDS Vaccine Institute, the World Health Organization's Special Program for Research and Training in Tropical Diseases and Global Health Progress. The Gates Foundation is currently an uncontested leader in global public health issues.[4]

Philanthropy is an acknowledged hallmark of American culture from its inception – an observation made by Alexis de Tocqueville in the 1800s – the landscape for philanthropy in China is markedly different. Unlike China, which accumulated a considerable amount of wealth within the last decade, America's history of wealth accumulation and philanthropic involvement dates back to entrepreneurs like John D. Rockefeller Sr. and Andrew Carnegie. This history is reinforced by the fact that America offers its citizens and corporations tax incentives for contributing to charities, a facility that is non-existent in China. This provides an inducement for generosity among the wealthy, whose incomes would otherwise go towards the payment of hefty taxes. According to 2013 estimates roughly 72% of the total amount given to charitable organizations in the U.S. came from private individuals ($335.17 billion); 5.7% from foundations ($48.96 billion); and 5% from corporations ($17.88 billion). In contrast, 80% of donations in China emanate from the corporate sector.

Chinese openhandedness was demonstrated overwhelmingly immediately following the devastating earthquake that hit south- western China in 2008, a calamity that resulted in untold physical and environmental damage and mortality. Immediately following the disaster, the country was inundated with individual donations for that year accounting for 54% of 15.7 billion Yuan which was three times higher than the previous year. Another factor, which brings its influence to bear in generous giving, is of course the country's increasingly privately held wealth. There is no denying that China is today one of the world's fastest growing producers of billionaires. According to the 2013 Forbes list, 122 billionaires are based in mainland China, second behind the U.S. while Hong Kong had 29 and Taiwan 26. China's Rich List put out by the Hurun Report, the leading authority on China's high net worth individuals, exceeded these figures in its estimates noting that the number of billionaires is upward of 300. Further to this, the widening wealth disparity persuaded the new elite to reciprocate by providing generous donations to the social sector initiatives. The promotion of higher education and caring for the elderly population are popular enterprises to which benefactors readily pledge.

Forbes 2014 Top 100 China Charity List spotlights the scale of magnanimity among Chinese donors. In 2014, the 100 names appearing on the list contributed an estimated 4.6 billion yuan (US $713.73 million), a drop of 4.6 billion yuan over the preceding year. Twelve persons donated in excess of 100 million yuan (US $16 million) each, with a notable segment of the benefactors representative of the real estate sector. Wang Jialin, chairman of Dalian Wanda Group, one of China's largest real estate developers, topped the list with a total of 438 million yuan (US $700 million) while earning the title of the richest person on the Chinese mainland.

In 2010 Jack Ma designated China's richest man, was featured in the Forbes 48 Heroes of Philanthropy listing. Jialin's plans include helping farmers increase their crop yields and introducing educational reforms. He has spearheaded a $5 million Alibaba donation to launch Grameen China and provide microcredit loans in Mongolia and in the Sichoan earthquake zone. Other names cited in the 2010 list were:

- Chen Feng, who owns a privately held group anchored in Hainan airlines and who donated $1.6 million to the United Nations World Food program to feed girls attending schools on Ghana and to provide support for youth and disabled people
- Dang Yanboa, president of NINGXIA Baofeng Energy Group who pledged $186 million to help university bound students in his native Ningxia region in northwestern China. This sum will cover financial aid for 10,000 students through 2010. Over the last seven years Yanhao has provided assistance to more than 100,000 poor students in Ningxia and was named China's No. 2 donor by the Beijing Normal University's philanthropy research institute
- Fan Jianchuoa, a real estate developer and private collector of the Fan Jianchuan Group, has spent $160 million to build a still growing 32 building museum complex in Sichuan province over the last eight years. He has dedicated eight buildings to memorabilia from the Sino-Japanese war era and $25 million to the 8 million relics from the Cultural Revolution
- Ren Yuanlin, chairman of Yangzijiang Shipbuilding who in December 2014, gave $41 million to his foundation to support projects aimed at increasing respect for the elderly, workers and public service. Yuanlin has donated a 28% stake of his company to the foundation which was originally set up in June 2012.

One aspect of Chinese altruism which cannot be overlooked is the impact of Western sway. Zhang Xin, co-founder and chief executive officer of SOHO, the largest prime office real estate developer in China shared the impact of her experience as a foreign student in Britain many years ago:

> *"For many Chinese of my generation, out first point of contact with western philanthropy was the financial aid we received when we studied abroad. Very few of us had money – most only had raw ambition. We were "PhDs:" poor, hungry and deterred. Financial aid has formed our lives"*

But even more compelling than this revelation is the impact of American influence on wealthy Chinese - a fourth driver of entrepreneurial generosity. This was underscored by the personal involvement of Bill Gates and Warren Buffett in wooing Chinese philanthropists for the Giving Pledge project in which they are encouraging the world's richest people to commit most of their wealth to charity. The effort received a considerable boost in 2010 when the duo visited China for the purpose of winning over high net worth Chinese to philanthropic pursuits. There are indications that the mission has yielded success. A mere four years hence, Zhang Xin's assertion underscores this point:

> *"I believe that the year 2014 is a turning point in Chinese philanthropy. This tradition is finally getting the impetus it needs to flourish because of an emerging group of Chinese entrepreneurs who are socially conscious, globally engaged and hoping to make a positive and lasting impact on China and the world..."*

Xin's company pledged $100 million in financial aid scholarships for Chinese undergraduate students attending leading international universities. The company's first gifting remit of $15 million was given to Harvard University and the second of $10 million went to Yale. Eileen Heisman, current Chief Executive Officer of the National Philanthropy Trust was even more commendatory in noting that, "The underlying philosophy of philanthropy is compassion and there is definitely a strong sense of compassion among the people in China."

But how does China match the only superpower on the basis of charitable donations? Firstly, according to the Charities Aid Foundation, the PRC was ranked 133 among 135 countries for donating money and last for volunteering. In 2010 using Gallop surveys of 195,000 people in 153 nations, the poll found that China and India, the world's fastest growing economies, ranked 134 and 147, respectively making them among the least altruistic countries in the world. In contrast the U.S. has consistently ranked in the first ten countries and in 2014 the U.S. and Myanmar shared first place. The Charities Aid Foundation further noted that there appeared to be a positive correlation between the presence of the (Theravaala) Buddhist community in Myanmar - a country populated with 500,000 monks - and their beliefs and key paths to merit, underscoring that each country's distinctive culture resonates in the predilection of its people.

Many celebrities, both American and non-American, are formally affiliated with the United Nations. The former Secretary General, Kofi Annan acknowledged the praxis, simultaneously noting that celebrities, unlike career diplomats, are able to capture the public spotlight through their entertainment value, and engage in a convincing way with young people under unorthodox but impact-loaded guises. Moreover, in Annan's estimation, their songs, music and dance acquitted them as effective promoters of goodwill and worthy causes. On this basis celebrities were inducted into the goodwill ambassadors program.

Andrew F Cooper in <u>Celebrity Diplomacy</u> assessed the role played by celebrities who have propelled themselves, and by extension America, onto the global stage, and their flamboyant circumvention of truncated protocols and etiquette to raise exorbitant sums of money for international causes.[5] In his view, unofficial public diplomacy is now epitomized in celebrity diplomacy.

Cooper, by the same token, makes a rather unsettling observation. He highlights his perception of a "gap between the renown accorded to western celebrities, as opposed to persons of similar status originating from the global South". Among the more popular American celebrities, many of yore, to the present that come to mind are: Jane Fonda, Jimmy Carter, Bill Clinton, Angelina Jolie, Oprah Winfrey, Elizabeth Taylor, Michael Jackson, Michael Douglas and Ted Turner[8] In contradistinction to the visibility enjoyed by these celebrities, similar recognition is not accorded to non-western figures from South Asia and Africa, whose equivalent regional fame has catapulted them to global celebrity prominence. Cooper attributes the glaring anomaly to what he dubs "a built in Anglo-sphere bias" that smacks of cultural imperialism.[6]

Cooper pursues a more didactic outlook, initially at least, in unraveling the phenomenon, mesmerizing that "a universal ethos is presented that is very much at odds with the parochial attitudes of the tight restrictions of sovereignty." He finally emerges from the debate in chapter six of his book, sub-titled <u>Uneasily Moving Celebrity Diplomacy beyond the Anglo-sphere</u>, with a resolution that is as self-evident as the notion of omnipresence, conceding that:

> ".the actors at the core of the enterprise are not just a small group located in the north-western quadrant of the globe. They belong to a narrow sub-set of extremely high-profile individuals fame is a projection of the cultural

power of the Anglo-sphere whether based in Hollywood or the metropolitan axes of the music industry."

He describes the United States and the United Kingdom as "the two central hubs" from which celebrity diplomats emerge thereby constituting a web of domination, and concludes that "ownership of this project is narrowly constructed, with trespassing by outsiders carefully controlled." Having identified the intrinsic dynamics of this web, Cooper unabashedly compares the grooming and projection of these celebrities to the globalization processes which like celebrities, assumes a typically top-down approach and radiates out of the Anglo-sphere culture.

The American celebrity is in effect an incarnation of the American way. That way, as distinct from an ideal, is defined in how, why, where and what is push for. Celebrities push for recognition and support by becoming plugged into transnational policy-making. They raise public awareness about global governance, underdevelopment, poverty, socio-economic inequalities, conflicts, global equity and other global irregularity issues. Bono and Bob Geldof have made African debt relief a staple feature of the G8 agenda and notables like Bill and Melinda Gates administer a foundation on a much larger budget than the World Health Organization[8]

Unlike the exclusive world of mainstream diplomacy, the style of celebrities is defined by activism on the world stage. They operate through a matrix of complex relationships that gives them leverage; they can openly engage top tier world leaders; they have mass appeal; they are seized of individual capacity to raise money and are able to channel and shape media attention while effectively deploying their natural talents, be it song, dance, sport, music or drama. An archetypical illustration is Michael Jackson and the self-defining space that he once, and arguably continues to occupy, in the global arena with an unmatched legacy.

With nothing other than genius and charisma Jackson transcended cultures, societies and communities across the world. He possessed the unique capacity to rival the office of the president in terms of the world figures that he once-upon-a-time rubbed shoulders with, bolstered by an unrivalled universal following that spanned no less than two generations. Jackson's legendary fame as a singer and performer snowballed into unanticipated areas, even transforming enduring tradition. Cebu Provincial Detention and Rehabilitation Center in the Philippines is one such example.

Recall that aback in 2007, a pilot project was introduced at the Center with the objective of enhancing the inmate rehabilitation process by combining exercise with "their love to sing and dance." Several videos were made of the inmate's performances; the most viewed was a four minute video clip on YouTube featuring 1,500 inmates imitating the zombie dance in the music video of Jackson's "Thriller."[7] The inmates' Thriller performance made it to the pages of the international Time magazine's list of the most watchable internet videos for 2007; the interpretation of the video was ranked fifth of the "ten most popular viral videos" of the year. Competing in this list were personages of the stature of Hillary Clinton (a former U.S. Secretary of State), Will Ferrell and Chris Crocker for his "Leave Britney Alone" clip. Time magazine noted the performance of the inmates was made "in homage" to Jackson and reported that the viral video had been downloaded more than nine million times – a figure that increased to a staggering quota of 15 million by January 18 of the following year, accelerating to 23 million by June of 2009.

When taken in tandem the indispensable attributes of global reach – influence, power, visibility, and mediation - exclude the competitive disadvantages of the more formalized and rigid national structures. This new cohort of non-state actors, all American, has successfully wielded agency by re-defining the boundaries of international relations and articulating their own agenda, with some of the most important movers and shakers in world politics.

Hollywood, to that end is no novice in statecraft, let alone public relations. It goes without saying that the movie industry as far back as the beginning of the twentieth century promotes U.S. foreign policy both in a manner reflective of the existing status quo and evocative of a Universalist ideological superstructure meant to minimize cultural heterogeneity. Major film studios in partnership with an ever-expanding national security apparatus work night and day to portray America as the quintessential force of good engaging agents of evil in a postmodern world teeming with calamity, chaos, injustice and terror. Former CIA Acting General Counsel John Rizzo publicized the agency's tight-knit relationship with Hollywood stars, who unbeknownst to many, function as covers for secret intelligence operations overseas. In highlighting the usefulness of soliciting the services of studio executives, producers, directors and prominent actors Rizzo stated, "Their power and international celebrity can be valuable - it gives them entrée to people and places abroad. Heads of state want to meet and get cozy with them. Their film crews are given free rein everywhere, even in places where the U.S. government doesn't normally have it."[8]

Far removed from the sexualized image of Marilyn Monroe's skirt fluttering in mid-air or Elizabeth Taylor's memorable turn as the celluloid queen of Egypt Hollywood disseminates an American brand of values, aesthetics, ideas, customs and norms commensurate to its imperial project. America, like the great conqueror of old Thutmose III, Alexander the Great, Julius Caesar, Charlemagne, and Napoleon is driven by the illusory ambition to govern the entire known world.[9] The country seeks to define the prevailing socio-political order of the dominant Germanic culture, which is expressed through allegory, folklore, myth, or verisimilitude. It follows that motion pictures like the *Star Wars* saga, *Saving Private Ryan* (1998), *The Lord of the Rings* film series (2001-2003), *Beowulf* (2007), *Thor* (2011), and *Snow White and the Huntsman* evince moral ideals and meaning steeped in a Germanic ethos, which valorizes patriotism, war, militarism, murder and theft.[10]

Undeniably, Hollywood dominates the cinematic marketplace. In 1998 the 39 most successful movies in the world were all American illustrating a truly global impact. Benjamin Barber himself observed American films assumed a commanding presence at the Cannes Film Festival in the early nineties. So why is this the case? Contemporary American cinema displays an endless circulation of commodities whether they be merchandise, theme parks, Blu-Ray, DVD, soundtracks, prequels, and sequels, mirroring the fluctuating desires of global consumers, more so, the logic of globalization in a domineering capitalist system. For films to be marketable to a worldwide audience that cuts across the fluid boundaries of race, ethnicity and creed, studios utilize the strategy of assimilating different elements from national and independent cinemas in an apparent move to "soften" America's cultural specificity. With that motive to downplay U.S. superpower status, the process of globalization paradoxically demands openness to cultural relativism, a willingness in other words to address difference in relation to non-Western cultures within the structure of filmic text. Such an undertaking is made easier in light of America's cosmopolitan character, living up to its reputed fame as a country of immigrants. Naturally the big screen captures signifiers of difference.

The opening credits of the 2006 Spike Lee heist film *Inside Man* features an Indian song "Chaiyya Chaiyya" sung by Sukhwinder Singh that appeared in the Hindu film *Dit Se* even though the setting is modern-day New York. From the very start the audience is made aware of the fact that to be American is to be part of an open-ended project. On this basis the American identity is not an essentialist category in the modern sense, but rather, a hodge-podge of converging cultural groups. Hence people of various backgrounds – African, Arab, Cuban, Chinese, Japanese, Taiwanese, Korean, Irish, French, German, English, Jew, Russian, etc. – all hold valid claims of citizenship. Cornel West in exploring what does it mean to be American writes, "from Thomas Jefferson to Elijah Mohammed, Geronimo to Dorothy Day, Jane Adams to Nathaniel West, it holds out the possibility of self-transformation and self-reliance to New World dwellers willing to start anew and recast themselves for the purpose of deliverance and betterment."

At the heart of the matter lies the American dream, a yearning to rise above mediocrity in the socioeconomic order and the still as yet unfulfilled promises of liberty, equality and fraternity. Indeed the cultural assimilation in film has proven more strident and ineradicable than physical conquest. Film is merely a mechanism through which the American brand is sold with the acquiescence and consent of the masses negating the other crude alternative of empire building: imposition.

CHAPTER NINE

DEMOCRACY AND MASS MANIPULATION

"Democracy freedom and the rule of law may not be technically synonymous, but in the West they are intimately connected in our minds and political practice."

Bob Rae

"The most essential skill in political theater and consumer culture is artifice. Political leaders, who use the tools of mass propaganda to create a sense of faux intimacy with citizens, no longer need to have to be competent, sincere, or honest. They need only to appear to have these qualities. Most of all they need a story, a personal narrative. The reality of the narrative is irrelevant. It can be completely at odds with facts. The consistency and appeal of the story are paramount. Those who are best at deception succeed."

Chris Hedges

merica lies at the epicenter of two diametrically opposed forces. On the one hand, consumer capitalism at global level is systemically dismantling traditional social and economic barriers between nations and transforming a world traditionally segmented by diverse institutions into a streamlined and blended uniform market. This is the central tenet of economic globalization, which was discussed at length in Chapter Seven. On the other hand ethnic, religious and racial animosities are leading to an increasing level and intensity of conflict and precipitating fragmentation of regions and sub-regions of the global community. We alluded to such phenomenon in the Chapter One discourse which addressed the character of contemporary community conflicts that now occupy a "growing number of increasingly disorderly spaces." These conflicts may range in scope, intensity, motive, and duration from major power competition to community level antagonisms.

232

Benjamin Barber views the two sets of forces as paradoxically interdependent, suggestive of a continuing dialectic that would remain deeply rooted in the global landscape. In the meantime, America is engaged in promoting democracy across both hemispheres as the ultimate cornerstone of a free, fair and just society, the pillar of free enterprise, and the nucleus of the rule of law. These are aspects unique to the modern nation state atypical to Western society.

Eldon Taylor, practicing criminalist with doctoral degrees in Psychology and Metaphysics, in his groundbreaking publication Mind Programming makes a compelling case that for a democracy and an economy supporting it to work, the systematic manipulation of masses is necessary.[1] The unlikelihood that everyone in a society would share the same views compels the need to shape and muster public opinion in order to ensure the orderly running of a community. It is on this merit, Taylor argues, that the manipulation of opinion and behavior has been assumed by "certain groups of people in society" who have taken their craft to very sophisticated levels.

In chapter three of his exegesis, "Strategies for Manipulation" Taylor identified ten principles or compliance strategies, which he garnered from the teachings of Edward Bernays who is reputedly the "father of public relations." According to Taylor, the posited principles have been successfully adopted in the corporate world of business and advertising and assimilated into the state apparatus with the primary goal of manipulating public opinion and behavior.

Bernays' wider objective was to devise and apply scientifically proven strategies to "control the dumb masses." His central observation was that "democracy is administered by the intelligent minority who know how to regiment and guide the masses." This viewpoint he rigorously pursued by evolving various communication forms through the application of Freudian theories, while adopting a scientific approach labeled the engineering of consent. By introducing these orientations into corporate life, Bernays literally revolutionized the worlds of public relations, communications and marketing. His select clientele, which included Fortune 500 members, politicians, and publicists effectively deployed these tools to shape and reshape the world of advertising and sales while influencing communities at home and abroad.[2]

Propaganda is the centerpiece of this celebrated apparatus of manipulation and its inherent potency as a political tool, and potential in terms of universal application, is borne out in Bernays' pronouncement that :

> "...those who manipulate this unseen mechanism of society constitute an invisible government which is the true ruling power of our country. In almost every part of our daily lives, whether in the sphere of business or

politics, our social conduct and our ethical thinking we are dominated by a relatively small number of persons who understand the mental processes and social patterns of the masses. It is they who pull the wires that control the public mind....[3]

This chapter argues that against the backdrop of the dialectic to which Bernays alludes, America's steadfast resolve to export and promote the democratic ideal as the preferred political standard worldwide, American celebrity diplomats take on a unique role in occupying the "mind space" of people around the world. Andrew Cooper's blunt assertion that "universalism in intent must be matched by universalism in personnel" is an iteration of the logic behind this underscored role. It is therefore noteworthy that "creating opportunities for non-state actors to advance America's interests by uniting diverse partners around common concerns" is the formally enunciated policy of the present administration as represented by the U.S. Secretary of State in her landmark address to the Council on Foreign Relations in July 2009. In a very unique and unostentatious manner this writ discharges American celebrities and for that matter patriots in general to pursue soft diplomacy in America's interest and on America's behalf.

Cooper notes that traditional modes of state-centric diplomacy are confronted with serious challenges in terms of their normative claims of legitimacy as well as with the compression of time and space efficiency. He observes that opportunities have now emerged for an increasing number of non-state actors to shape the agenda on a range of issues and that such agents are able to attract attention and mobilize resources.[4]

International Alliance of Unelected Plutocrats

This section of the enquiry explores the nuances of the role of the American celebrity diplomat, the criterion for the legitimacy of such actors, issues of allegiance, and the intersection of politics and state-centric and global agendas with the personal aspirations and motivations of these notables. We argue that American celebrities are in effect an adjunct to "the establishment" and that by virtue of a robust and open-ended version of individual agency and their privileged transnational trajectory, they are effectively augmenting American omnipresence in the global arena and simultaneously and seamlessly blending with the onward rush of globalization. This book concedes to a new reality - that celebrity diplomats now constitute an international alliance of unelected plutocrats whose power is derived from their wealth, and whose actions as distinct from their decision-making capacity, enable them to transcend governments.

An initial undertaking in this section is to put to rest the hotly debated issue of whether what a celebrity diplomat delivers on the world stage is in fact public diplomacy. Should diplomacy remain the exclusive province of career diplomats? Cooper broadsides the issue by pointing to the distinctiveness of the discipline of diplomacy as a facet of government, specifically the matter of criteria for representation and how these are pegged to legitimacy. He observes that there is no basis for regarding celebrity diplomats as members of the formalized guild of diplomats. He then patronizes the dilemma even further by introducing a caveat to his argument - that if diplomacy is wedded to everyday activity along a wide continuum and a robust and open-ended version of individual agency, then the normative claims of traditional state-centric diplomacy are eroded.[4]

This enquiry challenges Cooper's position and suggests that the criterion for legitimacy, which is construed to be the diffusion of power to non-state actors by recognized intergovernmental bodies such as the U.N and activist-based organizations, is fulfilled in spheres other than individual agency and guild membership, and moreover is effectively deployed with the application of the "Taylor" principles of compliance, inherent in human nature. This acquired legitimacy among celebrity diplomats, as we shall see, is bolstered by their ability to combine the assertive individual attributes typical of western culture with an appreciation of the broad spectrum of universal and cosmopolitan values. Additional strengths are their capacity to seamlessly engage with minimal bureaucratic restraints, on multilateral forums and interface with a blend of top-notch state and non-state personages. It may also be argued in specific instances that the role of the celebrity diplomat defies the boundaries of easy categorization.

Another important and often underscored aspect of celebrity diplomacy is that it bridges the existing rift between official diplomatic culture and domestic society by the creation of viable links. This anomaly has arisen because of the very nature of the intergovernmental process, which displays a proclivity to marshal and husband information, thereby divesting official diplomats of spontaneous or recurrent interface with massive audiences.

Contemporary diplomacy calls for a recalibration of statecraft that goes beyond the mainstream apparatus of government since there are many features of the international system that dispose it to personages with a tradition of humanism. One such feature is the distinctly human dimension of global issues; another is the fact that many of these issues, as universal in scope as they may be, have a decidedly moral compass. This hybridism is more readily discernible among the celebrities themselves. This outlook is strongly supported by postmodernists, who recognize that the international system would be far more responsive to a tradition of humanism than it would be to statist approaches. The former, they argue, is more hospitable and accommodating to individual initiative.

American celebrities are American citizens and citizenship incurs allegiance to the state, and by extension, to the interests of the state. American celebrities are thus bonded legally and morally to "the establishment" and what it projects to the world as the American ideal and American interests. On this merit, American celebrities who practice diplomacy in the capacity of goodwill ambassadors can be validly regarded as appendages of the state itself irrespective of what premises their motivations, be it a sense of social responsibility, emotional instrumentalism, or a competitive spirit.

Bob Dylan's checkered history as a rock singer accentuates one common denominator, that he is an American. From political activist, to polemicist, born again evangelical Christian, hard-core Zionist, poet, and musician; all notions of subversive potentiality, including the censorship of his concert songs by Chinese Culture Ministry officials in 2011, are nullified by the fact that as a long assimilated elderly rebel, Bob remains an American legally and at heart.[5]

American celebrity diplomats are engaged in the art of selling a product and that product is "themselves." Appended to this product is a cause that is invariably politically driven and some causes may logically intersect with others. Politics is about people, their beliefs and belief systems, their ideas, concerns and interests. Politics demands a point of view on something. It demands the mobilizing of opinion and mustering of support. Causes trigger the imperative to adopt positions and positions must be processed and reincarnated in the form of proposals, which in turn may evolve into policy. Causes necessarily span a broad continuum of issues that range from universal issues such as human rights, poverty, the global diaspora pertaining to civilian refugees, famine, climate change, proliferation, pandemic and disease, war, peace, conflict resolution, energy and gender affairs to more localized debates. Are any of these devoid of some degree of political coloration? Can any of these matters be seriously addressed or resolved in the absence of national or regional-centric thought, consideration, and other forms of multilateral agency?

Such business necessitates multilateral advocacy capped with supranational intercession since no single state actor, no single state, no single region can bring about a resolution to the inherently complex and multifaceted body of dilemmas, in respect of which they are constituted. Any global stratagem that aims to confront them must therefore incorporate:

- Central planning
- Multilateralism

- Direct action
- Logistics
- Division of labor
- State cooperation
- Consensus building
- Projection

- Strategy
- Capital and other related resources
- International law
- Formal diplomacy
- Volunteerism

Additionally, in order to sustain and preserve the resolution of an issue, once it has been formally inculcated and adopted, a new order of sorts may have to be instituted to exercise the level of monitoring and social control that supersedes the types of restraints currently imposed by the typical apparatus of modern statehood.

The closest analogy to celebrity diplomats in the international sphere is perhaps NGOs, which occupy a space that can potentially challenge the capacity of the modern nation state. Indeed, the strength and quality of their business of advocacy have earned formidable niches that are unfettered by national structures; this affords NGOs an enviable, competitive advantage not beholden to full-fledged career diplomats.

Celebrities become celebrities by successfully marshaling the tenets of compliance and manipulation, the very tools that ensured their meteoric rise as entertainment icons. These are "corporatist" techniques, which have a proven success formula, having perennially shaped the world of advertising, communications, and public relations, and swayed the tastes and behavior of audiences and consumers at home and abroad. Indeed, Taylor's compliance techniques have become the cornerstones of modern corporatism, of the highly-clichéd phenomenon of "McDonaldization," and remain firmly imbedded in Bernays vision to "control the dumb masses." The fact that these techniques are continuously applied to preserve the status quo is testimony to their successful application.

Taylor's Compliance Principles

Taylor refers to the regime of techniques of manipulation deployed today as "compliance principles". He claims that they are "wired into our being" making us vulnerable to manipulation. They consist of "social beliefs, reciprocity, association, conditioning, authority, liking, scarcity, drives, justification and authority." The effective deployment of these criteria either singly or in combination influences opinions, decisions, and behavior. "Association", "authority" and "liking" are by far the most potent blend on the scale of criteria and are inextricably connected to the cult of personality and its constituents - celebrity status, allure, universal appeal, and charisma. Such attributes evoke magnetism on the world stage.

"Association" and "authority" serve as mitigating factors to what may otherwise be regarded as a lack of legitimacy. "Association" is about garnering favorable feelings about a person, product or circumstance. That sound, visuals, and music move upon our primordial nature and can be used to effectively punctuate and influence feelings and situations is a truism. Similarly, in the case of "authority," people rely on authorship and endorsement on which to base their opinions and choices relating to a product or service. "Liking" on the other hand, is based on the mechanics of rapport or the science of neurolinguistic programming and is administered in the fields of sales and techniques of interrogation, particularly among political and religious groups.

On the issue of "justification" Cooper demonstrates how readily this principle can be invoked in extenuating circumstances demanding radical action, a classic example being the events of 9/11 which are beyond cliché. An event of such significance in every sense constituted a "shock" to the American and wider global publics; hence the adopted idiolect invoked to describe "an event that punctuates the evolution of a trend, and in so doing undermines the assumption on which current policies are based." America was "under attack" and this "justified" the full and immediate mobilization of the entire breadth of the country's state apparatus, and the automatic suspension of rights and civil liberties of its citizens and visitors extending even to the sovereign rights of other nations. 9/11 ultimately and forever changed the way the world was and much of the fallout politically and socially was on the instigation and behest of the U.S. government, on the basis of "justification." The international society ceded to U.S. fear and fervor in almost unquestioning capitulation and tractability. A non-state actor, endowed with the "justification" to move millions and play to massive events, could similarly instigate this type of far-reaching action or reaction. In a far removed context, such collective response may even take the form of counter consensus or protest.

American Bono has epitomized many of core aspects of this section, not only by spanning boundaries in the area of global social issues, but also through projecting an unorthodox persona as a moral entrepreneur with a decidedly evangelical outlook. His unabashed political agenda ranges from lobbying members of the U.S. Congress on anti-apartheid to the U.S. position in relation to Central America. Internationally, he has penetrated the G8 in his "efforts to end global poverty" message and bridged ideological divides in politics at home in

America and abroad. Bono brings audiences to the government and to the United Nations.

In like manner, the high-profile advocacy of Richard Gere, in his capacity as chairman of the Board for the International Campaign for Tibet was clearly political, catapulting him in direct line of fire with the Chinese government whose efforts to politically isolate the Dalai Lama are universally known. Gere "took the fight" to the United Nations Headquarters in New York in 1999, a gesture that placed in spotlight the contentious undercurrents at work. Whatever were Gere's initial motivations, these would converge more directly with those of the U.S. government one year later when he rendered personal support to the its resolution at the United Nations Human Rights Commission in Geneva, pillorying the Chinese government for their tenuous human rights record.

More recently, the announcement by American superhero, Superman, in 2011 of the renunciation of his American citizenship represented an historic incongruity whereby politics and soft diplomacy collided. Citing reasons for such course of action, Clark Kent asserted, "I am tired of having my actions construed as instruments of U.S. policy." He postures that the world is too connected for him to limit himself with a national identity and that he has accordingly shorn himself of the political complexities of nationalism. His however, is an isolated case that stands on its own merit and in effect is an affirmation on his part of American omnipresence.[4]

Atypical of a beloved American icon that stands for "truth, justice and the American way" and who in effect personifies American idealism, Superman's newly adopted global mission threatens to disrupt patriotism, including the long-held assumption of sovereignty, in the allegorical sense. Laura Hudson, reporter from Comics Alliance concedes, "from a realistic standpoint it makes sense; it would be impossible for a nigh–omnipotent being ideologically aligned with America to intercede against injustice beyond American borders without creating enormous political fallout for the U.S. government." This change in political impetus proves revolutionary in a period when America is swamped at home with a cacophony of nationalist sentiments on the one hand, and pockets of disempowerment on the other, notably the Tea Party Movement, the 9/11 Truthers, the right-wing media, and the more recently discredited Birthers, not to mention "Occupy Wall Street" which elicited near universal appeal.

Though a fictional hero in the D.C. universe, Kent's audacious renunciation of national identity is but a microcosm of the larger and more ominous political realities defining the complex hybridity of interdependence, multilateralism, public diplomacy and international affairs as a whole. Perhaps of greater significance is the whole question of global governance in the 21ˢᵗ Century and the yet unexplored realm of global citizenship.

Similarly popularized is Al Gore's academy award winning documentary, "An Inconvenient Truth," which portrays the long-term effects of global warming and its potential for disaster, and which has had a significant impact on the international community's perspectives on the issue. The subject matter of the documentary is now officially incorporated into the national school curriculum in Australia, the United Kingdom, New Zealand, Czech Republic, Germany, the Canadian province of British Colombia, and Spain, an occurrence that has no doubt been spurred by the authority that Gore garnered in his former capacity as U.S. Vice President. The film content has been successfully diffused into a range of academic disciplines and has even inspired subsequent environmentally-oriented documentaries, one of which was created and narrated by another illustrious film personality and American, Leonardo Di Caprio.

Distinguishable throughout all this is the fact that the United States retains considerable ability to set the global agenda and thereby confer importance and legitimacy to what constitutes an issue, a problem, a crisis or an outrage. American ideas and opinions on ideas filter around the world and this capacity, irrespective of the media, constitutes a core element of global power that remains unmatched.

In notable differentiation to the U.S., which Cooper describes as being "saturated with accomplished personnel" in the celebrity diplomat milieu, Europe, Africa, and the global South enjoy a comparably low profile. The ostensible lack of representative boundaries, in Cooper's estimation, calls into further question the legitimacy of the enterprise. The present text argues that it is the very fact of the lack of equitability in representation that lends probity to the assertion of American omnipresence, by juxtaposing her global reach in the province of soft diplomacy, against the conspicuous lack of visibility of celebrity diplomats representing other continents and regions.

The outcome of this new trove of representation in the international arena is that there is now a new breed of global aristocrats, who have emerged as a world plutocracy and who are deploying their money, power, and influence to re-shape the rules. The affiliates of this cohort are anything but elected. They appear to have an ever-expanding reach that defies jurisdictional and territorial bounds. Represented in this group are entrepreneurs, entertainers, media moguls, and former politicians. The machinations and range of influence of this super-class are chronicled in titles such as:

- David Rothkoff's "Superclass: The Global Power Elite and the World They Are Making" (2009)
- Jeff Faux's "The Global Clan War: How America's Bipartisan Elite Lost Our Future and What It Will Take To Win It Back" (2006)
- Moses Naim's "Illicit: How Smugglers, Traffickers, and Copycats Are Hijacking The Global Economy" (2006); and
- Jonine Wedel's "Shadow Elite: How The World's New Power Brokers Undermine Democracy, Government, and the Free Market."

Propaganda Machinery and Effects on Global Outreach: Promote Democracy by Controlling the Masses

As we have recognized thus far, a new and self-defining plutocracy backed by the screen and the airwaves offer unmediated media to audiences all around the world. There is ongoing debate, however, in relation to two closely appended issues. The first is whether the media in America has not exceeded its proper bounds by circumventing the constraints of state and private power, even to the point of threatening the existence of democratic institutions; the other is whether the conduct of the media constitutes a direct challenge to the broader interests of the society and government. This section of the text is dedicated to analyzing and discussing each of these.

The Media as a Circumventor of State Power

A Study sponsored by Freedom House many years ago unearthed what was described as a pervading culture in the new journalism, that is to say, "an often mindless readiness to seek out conflict, to believe the worst of the government or of authority in general, and on that basis to divide up into the good and the bad." The Study, "The Tet Offensive of 1968," was widely hailed as a landmark contribution that offered definitive proof of the irresponsibility of the media as a "...notable new source of national power." Described as a classic of modern scholarship, the Study also demonstrated that in their incompetence and biased coverage reflecting the "adversary culture" of the sixties, the media in effect lost the war in Vietnam, thus harming the cause of democracy and freedom.

This assessment of the media was reinforced in more recent judicial thought emanating from the remarks of Judge Gurfein, in his delivery of a ruling that rejected attempts by the government to bar publication of the Pentagon Papers. On that occasion, having upheld the view that the media as a "tribune of the people" must be "...suffered by those in authority in order to preserve the even greater values of freedom of expression and the right of the people to know," the judge by the same token seized the opportunity to admonish the said media, describing it as "...a cantankerous press, an obstinate press, an ubiquitous press." An equally weighted summons calling for a democratized media emanated from the Executive Director of Freedom House, Leonard Sussman, who posed the question, "Must free institutions be overthrown because of the very freedom they sustain?"[5]

As previously divulged, the democratic ideal is being promoted through the instrument of propaganda, which has become the de facto substitute for new and creative ideas, ideology, and knowledge. Propaganda is deployed with the exclusive intent of shaping and influencing how people are being made to feel and thereby stoking consensus. We shall demonstrate that not only is the ingenious application of compliance techniques by the major media and its agents integral and indispensable to this process but also how the process is orchestrated and maneuvered among mutually compatible interest groups. The ultimate goal of the major media at the end of the day is to preserve the status quo, maximize profits, and sell America to the world.

It was in deference to these and related issues regarding the freedom of the press and the imperative to restore a balance between the government and media, that a 1975 Study on "Governability of Democracies" was assumed by the Trilateral Commission. The Study acknowledged that the role of the media and its agents was to serve as organs of the democratic ideal and as instruments of activism in promoting this ideal. However, in noting that that the de facto actions of the media were at times so discharged as to "...thwart or promote the policies and broader interests of the government," the Commission arrived at some inexorable conclusions, the most consequential of which were:

- The media had become a notable new source of national power
- The media constituted one aspect of an excess of democracy that resulted in the reduction of governmental authority at home and a decline in the influence of democracy abroad
- The discernible crisis in democracy resulted from efforts of previously marginalized sectors of the population to organize and press their demands. Such reaction precipitated an overload that hindered the democratic process from functioning properly

- There was therefore a consequential need for moderation in democracy. This would necessarily entail barring public interference with important matters.[6]

Noam Chomsky recapitulated the Commission's stance in concluding that the American public should ultimately be reduced to "...traditional apathy and obedience and driven from the arena of political debate and action" in the interest of preserving democracy. His overriding concern, however, went beyond the findings of the 1975 Study and resided in the fact that the perspectives of the Commission regarding the media as a potential source of national power and the catalyst of excessive democracy, was representative of the values of a relatively small but very powerful body of liberal elites specifically from the United States, Europe, and Japan and lead figures of the Carter administration.[7]

This syndicate of interests, as he saw it, traversed "special interests" (a concept of contemporary political rhetoric that refers to workers, farmers, women, youth, the elderly, and the handicapped and ethnic minorities), as well as the notable sector of corporations, financial institutions and other business elites. In his view, the category of "ethnic minorities",, which constitutes the Democratic right, had become historically aligned with "the vigorous defense of democracy worldwide," at times engaging in excesses in pursuit of the noble cause.

In elaborating on his concerns, Chomsky recounted the era of the Ronald Reagan presidency. In his recollection, during this period the Democratic opposition supported programs in furtherance of republican-sponsored activist policies all aimed at projecting U.S. power abroad. This undertaking in his mind must have entailed the purposeful mobilization of a range of instrumentalities, including "subversion," "international terrorism," and "propaganda." The garnering of public opinion at home for these and a barrage of related policies would have necessitated the engineering of support through methods involving the tactical deployment of authority, propaganda, and justification.[8]

Chomsky's theorem gained credence in 2010 in the circumstances surrounding the defrocking of a senior member of the armed forces in July of that year. The reaction of the mainstream media to the unorthodox level of access accorded to the journalist who broke the story, Rolling Stones writer, Michael Hastings, mirrored a collective vitriolic depreciation from the mainstream for a journalist who, in their estimation earned no merit to the "inner circle of trust." In their own minds such sphere of influence is not beholden to representatives of the "counter-cultural" community of publishers and their reporters.[8]

Glenn Greenwald's summary of the situation namely, the "extraordinary identification" exhibited by mainstream reporters, is illuminating in attesting to what he described as "a sense in the Washington media and the establishment press that if you have the choice to avoid embarrassing or otherwise harming somebody in power, that it is the responsibility of the reporter to protect the powerful." This standard, to which the mainstream media appeared to have unquestionably and collectively adverted, is consistent with the model of professionalism in the mind of Jenny McIntyre, a former Pentagon correspondent, who prudently proffered as a point of reference and ideal, "the U.S. military's rules of journalistic engagement."

The Military as a Standard Setter in the Public Domain

Like corporations and the mainstream media, the military-industrial establishment avails itself of a range of methods to introduce ideas and portrayals into the public domain that uphold the idealism of society, both morally and jurisprudentially. Among the mechanisms employed to discharge this unique role are the Departmental Film Unit, its associations with film producers, and the use of commercial media, and television. The Department's ultimate goal in its film industry assignations is to support film-makers in portraying America's armed forces in "an accurate or plausible manner." To this end, the establishment has formalized its role by:

- Creating a special portfolio, that of Special Assistant to the Secretary of Defense for Entertainment Media.
- Establishing Liaison offices in the Pentagon and Los Angeles. These outfits maintain a critical eye on film scripts that seek to incorporate the modes of the military into productions destined for the world audience. The unique relationship between the establishment and Hollywood is regarded as "mutually exploitative" with the Pentagon deriving the advantage of managing the image of the military in terms of depiction of messages and film portrayals, and the film makers obtaining reciprocal access to equipment/props that would otherwise lie beyond the scope of their budgetary limitations, and/or, in the case of certain weapons systems, their legal capacity.[9]

The leverage that the establishment is able to exert on film content is further reinforced by the margin of discretion the Department is allowed in the field of authorized closed-budgeting, procurement, and investment, described in Chapters Two and Four. The Department is similarly agile and resourceful in terms of human resource networking capabilities. To illustrate this point, Chris Hedges, in his Empire of Illusions chronicles that "the majority of the military analysts on television are former military officials, many employed as consultants to defense industries, a fact they rarely disclose to the public." Assuming this is in fact the case, one can all but infer that America's military establishment, which is vital to preserving the country's image and capacity as a power, winning wars, and maintaining dominance overseas is able to positively shape public opinion and sentiment on matters such as weapons systems, expansion of wars, and the causes and effects of war in a manner that is consistent with and aligned to the policies of the government. This pride of place can only be guaranteed by discretionary access to various institutions, among which is the mass media.

Hollywood and America's National Security Apparatus

Thus far, we discussed in general terms the role of Hollywood in the propagation of the American culture worldwide. In the present section we observed the role of the media as the vanguard of corporatism in America and in the spreading and filtering of ideas. We alluded to the fact the propaganda machinery extends throughout the corporate and state apparatus and that propaganda of itself is a pillar of the democratic process, serving as a conduit to stoke consensus and mobilize public opinion and support. We also noted the stabilizing influence of major media houses in relation to persons or institutions of influence that opt to assume a pariah role that may not necessarily support the best interests of the state. This became evident in the hapless circumstances surrounding the defrocking of a senior member of the armed forces and the level of containment that was appropriately canvassed as a standard to uphold, in terms of media access.

The often misunderstood convergence between the Los Angeles-based film industry and America's national security apparatus, as the consummate vanguard of the status quo is of relevance to this aspect of our enquiry. The most significant factor characterizing Hollywood is its especially concentrated corporate ownership, its level of commercialization, and by no means least, the extent of state involvement.

The vast majority of the world's movie business from production to distribution is owned by a mere six film studios, namely: Disney, Colombia/Sony Pictures Entertainment, Paramount Pictures, 20th. Century Fox, Warner Brothers, and Universal. These studios, which are collectively referred to as "the majors," are all owned by multinational parent corporations; in similar sequence, these are: Walt Disney Company, Sony, Viacom Inc., and Time Warner Inc. and (until 2009)

245

General Electric Vivendi. MGM, United Artists, Lionsgate, and DreamWorks SKG are among the smaller outfits.

The most recognizable aspect of intersection of interests in relation to the government and Hollywood is in the sphere of ownership and control of studios. As a political priority, the government's primary concern is that America's cultural heritage is not ceded to or controlled by another nation in the world. For this reason, the government to 25% limits foreign ownership and control of American film studios; moreover, further restrictions ensure that control of studio output remains in California and New York. As an inducement to the studios, the government has established a corresponding system of tax incentives and introduced a relaxed regime of rules regarding media consolidation. Reciprocity is therefore a primary pillar of the Government/Hollywood alliance.[10]

A second point of note concerns the principle of capitalization. The main tool of "the majors" is capital. Capital influences industry standards and therefore the choice of film is closely aligned to what would appeal to American audiences. The president of Paramount, David Kirkpatrick describes it in these terms, "You need a homogenized piece of entertainment... something that is not particularly edgy." In addition, product placement and merchandizing deals contribute substantively to profits. To reinforce this point, Matthew Alford's "Reel Power" notes that "studios are run by MBAs whose entire training and experience is to avoid risk." Alford mentions that since the 1990s, the majority of Fortune 500 companies have diverted parts of their business portfolio to product placement in the film industry and companies have been specifically set up to hone product placement and place products as efficiently as possible. He adds that despite the fact that Hollywood must sell the film, instant brand recognition had now become the "key", to the extent that film output is a highly derivative process.[11]

The third and most critical point is the imperative to project to the rest of the world through film the American ideal, simultaneously disseminating narratives that are familiar to American audiences. Herein lies the ingenious confluence demanded of creativity and novelty value, political savvy, and the maximizing of profits. Americans relish their country's role, one that is illustrative of "might and muscle." Recent expeditionary missions of America in Iraq and Afghanistan catapulted the global responsibility of the U.S. which has since seized upon the opportunity to commit to long-term political and military interventions. All of this has opened occasions for narratives that provide what Alford refers to as "particularly self-congratulatory endorsements of the benevolence of U.S. power."[12]

War films, as depicted by Hollywood, seduce people into a Dionysian stupor by invoking the halo of America's mythic heroism, more specifically its redemptive power to rid the world of baneful evil. America is typically represented as the archetypical force of good that is juxtaposed to an evil other. The celluloid fetishized image of war, so commonplace to contemporary films, bears an idiosyncratic semblance to a quasi-religious experience that is sacred. Thus, Hollywood has transformed war into a secularized rendering of religion.

The following are some of the "Pentagon-backed films" produced within the last two decades that are illustrative of the archetypical typeset in which the military is cast:

- Pearl Harbor 2001
- Hart's War 2002
- We Were Soldiers 2002
- The Great Raid 2005

- Black Hawk Down 2001
- Tears of the Sun
- Behind Enemy Lines 2001
- Iron Man 2008

"We Were Soldiers" was a re-enactment of the first engagement of the U.S. in Vietnam, depicted in sharp contrast to the narrative in Apocalypse I (1979), which established the "insanity and brutality of U.S. involvement in Vietnam"[13] The director of "Tears in the Sun" had a two-fold aim, namely to portray Africa's agonies as well as the heroism of the Navy Seals.[14] The film indicates that by intervening militarily, the U.S. will suffer losses but will nonetheless benefit spiritually as a benevolent force by living up to its inherently good values. This particular genre of productions possessed a proclivity to be empathetic and supportive to the U.S. troops, protect the reputation of units and platoons by showcasing their edifying attributes, upholding the moral and political motives of engagement, placing a high premium on human life, and reflecting the doctrine and ideals of the military, the breach of which would carry consequences.

In sharp distinction, films which depicted the motives of the establishment as morally ambiguous, failed to promote and/or highlight abiding American values, omitted or refused to obfuscate events that would embarrass the military, were not forthcoming about the inherent difficulties in intervening militarily and/or focused disproportionately on the banal aspects of battle-zones such as civilian deaths were spurned, and rightly so in the view of this book, by the Pentagon.

Pentagon, as a recognized part of the corporatist-state superstructure, did not countenance "Thin Red Line," due to its disparaging depictions of "cowardly callous soldiers and alcohol abuse in the battlefield." Neither did "Full Metal Jacket" and "Casualties of War" receive support because of their less than honorable portrayals of the military.[15]

Citing a handful of notoriously critical movies in the cinema such as "Redacted," "War Inc.," "The Quiet American," along with "Avatar," "The Good Shepherd," "Lord of War," "Total Recall," "Starship Troopers," "Nixon," and "Syriana," Alford notes that it is to the credit of the establishment-supported films, that the notions that "the U.S. is essentially good and that U.S. force is an effective means to solving political problems" have been consistently reinforced. To such extent it is unlikely that a few, very exceptional pictures will succeed in offsetting the positive effects of that tradition.

The Patriotic Agenda – Love America

Chomsky suggests that "to confront power is costly and difficult" and that in contrast, "conforming to a patriotic agenda imposes no such costs." Herein lies the inducement for compliance. Offering an anecdotal viewpoint of media dynamics, he describes the universality of U.S. influence in imposing itself on the worldview of issues and crises and on the inherently skewed modus operandi of U.S. media coverage. In his words "no argument is demanded for a condemnation of Iran or Libya, for state-supported terrorism; discussion of the prominent – arguably dominant - role of the United States and its clients in organizing and conducting this plague of the modern era... supporting evidence, however compelling, is dismissed as irrelevant". The media and intellectual journals, in his estimation, display an inclination towards one of two options, either to laud the government's dedication to the struggle for democracy or alternatively, to inveigh against the means employed to achieve an acknowledged meritorious goal.[16]

Reinforcing his central concern over the non-negotiable posture assumed by the major media houses regarding the "good intentions" of the government, Chomsky asserts "...any challenge to the underlying patriotic assumption is virtually unthinkable within the mainstream and, if permitted, expression would be dismissed as a variety of ideological fanaticism, an absurdity, even if backed by overwhelming evidence."

Undoubtedly, the role of the media is inextricably connected to upholding the status quo. Logically, its mission is to serve as the institution of choice and the consummate organ through whose instrumentality the perspectives and interests of the American power complex are effectively diffused.

Walter Lippmann, former Dean of U.S. journalists, and author of <u>Public Opinion</u> viewed the manufacture of consent as a revolution in the practice of democracy. Consent, in his estimation, had increasingly become a regular organ of popular government; and the engineering of consent was a natural development when "the common interests very largely elude public opinion entirely and can be managed only by a specialized class whose personal interests reach beyond the locality." Lippman further contends that, "the manufacture of consent is capable of great refinement," and adds with a touch of poignancy:

> *"It is no longer possible, for example, to believe in the original dogma of democracy; that the knowledge needed for the management of human affairs comes up spontaneously from the human heart. Where we act on that theory we expose ourselves to self-deception, and to forms of persuasion that we cannot verify. It has been demonstrated that we cannot rely upon intuition, conscience, or the accidents of casual opinion if we are to deal with the world beyond our reach."*

Similar ideas are standard across the political spectrum. Bernays incontrovertibly affirmed that democratic leaders must play their part in engineering consent to socially constructed goals through the media and to implement policy through the mechanism of the state. In his view, if the freedom to persuade happens to be in the hands of a few it should be recognized that such is the nature of a free society. Harold Laswell explained that the notion that "men are the best judges of themselves" was mere dogma; rather, it is the elites who must be ensured the means to improve their will, for the common good. Thomas Bailey observed following World War II that, "because the masses are notoriously short-sighted and generally cannot see danger until it is at their throats, our statesmen are forced to deceive them into an awareness of their own long run interests." He asserts that, "deception of the people may in fact become necessary unless we are willing to give our leaders in Washington a freer hand." [17]

At the end of the day, if democracy is to be exported abroad it must be managed at home. To put it simply, if the population cannot be controlled and propaganda fails to work, the state has no recourse but to be forced underground to clandestine operations and secret wars, proportional to the scale of popular dissidence. This underscores, beyond doubt, the societal purpose served by the information industry in all its aspects in furtherance of America's outward projection.

CHAPTER TEN

ON THE THRESHOLD OF INFINITE

"But it turns out that we are central, after all. Our ability to create models—virtual realities—in our brains, combined with our modest looking thumbs, has been sufficient to usher in another form of evolution: technology. That development enabled the persistence of the accelerating pace that started with biological evolution. It will continue until the entire universe is at our fingertips."

Ray Kurzweil

"Harnessing the basic power of the universe" fell to America. This is how the firestorm rained on Hiroshima at 8.15 am local time, was placed in triumphant context by President Harry S Truman, on August 06 1945. A tremendous roaring sound followed by a crushing blast wave, emitting unimaginable heat, and traveling through a fire-wind at a velocity of 40 mph, would forever change the course of history. Dropped from an American B29 Super Fortress, the bomb containing the equivalent of 12-15 thousand tons of TNT, ripped through an area of five miles, annihilating 60% of the island's infrastructure and claiming 140,000 lives.[1] The mind-numbing historic landmark signaled the dawn of a new era of technology and the reconfiguration of the international order, to what it is today.

There were other time portals that America would open – she seized leadership of the space race, despite a string of Russian achievements that began in the late 1950s and distinguished by the R-7 Rocket which was the first to escape the earth's gravity into solar orbit; to be followed in close order by the first photographic images of the farther side of the moon executed by Luna1, 2, and 3.[2] In accelerated response, the U.S. launched a ground-breaking trail of military space and missile projects including the establishment of a civilian space agency, the National Aeronautics and Space Administration.[3]

These indicators go well beyond a pioneering momentum and competitive edge. President Kennedy projected the mission's global significance when he declared that it "may hold the key to our future on earth." It represented "a great new American enterprise," he postured, consistent with long-range aspirations and worthy of inclusion in the 1961 Mission Statement before Congress presented by his Vice President and Chairman of the National Space Council. America's deep space enterprise portended American leadership on earth and throughout the universe. The space enterprise was one arm of an ambitious two-tiered policy that was launched in the 1960s to maintain a strategic lead ahead of the rest of the world. The second tier was the Mutually Assured Destruction (MAD) program. MAD shored in the industrial base for the production of intercontinental ballistic missiles in mass quantities to bridge the prevailing missile gap with the Soviet Union.

Forty-two years after the historic moon landing of the Apollo II mission on the Sea of Tranquility on July 20, 1969, Chinese aspirations to match the triumph are lagging. Ye Peijian, chief scientist of Deep Space Exploration at the China Academy of Space Technology alluded to China's three-phased plan for space exploration. The first phase witnessed the launch of Chang e-2; the second was a projected moon landing in 2013; and the third mission would include the collection of rock samples from the moon and return of the spacecraft to earth some time in 2017.

China is a member of the United Nations Committee on the Peaceful Uses of Outer Space and a signatory to all United Nations treaties and conventions on space. The China National Space Administration, an agency with the Commission of Science, Technology and Industry for National Defense is responsible for the country's space programs. Satellite launch centers are based in Jiuquam, Xichang, Taiyuan and Wenchang. In addition to a number of home-based space tracking sites China shares space tracking facilities with France, Brazil, Sweden and Australia.

The debarking of a man on the moon by China, to trace the footsteps of Neil Armstrong, Michael Collins, and Buzz Aldrin, is scheduled for 2030, a time lag considered generational in the context of contemporary technological evolution. Given that technological paradigm shift rates are being drastically reduced with each passing decade thereby rendering many systems prone to obsolescence before they hit ground, and having regard to the fact that interstellar travel, migration and population by humans are becoming increasingly counterproductive in the face of smarter systems, China's 2030 marker is but a pyrrhic triumph.

China's evolving prowess in outer space exploration is clearly intended to challenge rivals. Its resolve has translated into the acquisition of an upgraded suite of surveillance, communication and navigation satellites to be used in war-fighting engagements and the configuration of equipment to attack space assets held by competitors. When compared with the U.S., China had about 34 satellites in the mid-2000s, and their capacities/delivery included surveillance, electro-optical, and radar. Chapter V of Fisher's China's Military Modernization provides an illuminating appraisal of the present and medium-term satellite constellation along with the immediate responses of the relevant U.S. authorities to these advancements.

The Principle of Exponentially

In striking contrast, the consistent lead taken by America in the sphere of technology is attributed to the fact that the pace of change of human-created technology is accelerating and its powers are expanding at an exponential pace. Exponential growth is by nature a deceptive phenomenon since it begins almost imperceptibly at a slow pace and thereafter picks up and explodes with unexpected rapidity. Human progress is exponential in that it expands by repeatedly multiplying by a constant rather than linear i.e. expanding by adding a constant. Thus, as we witness the breath-taking pace of changes in our midst, we can anticipate the social repercussions that follow them, the pace of these repercussions, and the corresponding paradigm shifts they will demand of us. This will compel a need for transnational activism in all spheres of life economically, politically, socially, culturally, militarily and technologically.

Ray Kurzweil, author of Singularity is Near postulates that given the rapidity of technological advances, ultimately man will transcend the limitations of his biological body and brain. In linking the projected ascendance of artificial intelligence to the future of the evolutionary process, he predicts that ultimately the non-biological portion of our intelligence, derived from machine technology will be trillions of trillions of times more powerful than unaided human intelligence. At that critical juncture, man would transcend the limitations of his biological body and brain. The culmination of the merger of biological thinking and existence with technology would result in a world that would be human but nonetheless transcending man's biological roots.[4]

Kurzweil was one of five members of the Army Science Advisory Group (ASAG), which advises the U.S. Army, and vicariously the government, on priorities for science research on the overall technological directions that ought to be taken by the army and the rest of the armed forces.[5] He rues a common error made by prognosticators for technological progress, that is, the tendency to consider the transformation that will result from a single trend in the current dynamic as a stand alone as if nothing else would change. An example of the perspective adopted by these contenders is their treatment of the issue of life extension as a notion that would necessarily trigger overpopulation and the consequential exhaustion of limited material resources. This is far from the case.

In fact, this stance totally discards the comparable wealth creation derived from other fields such as nanotechnology and artificial intelligence. Kurzweil pulls the example whereby nanotechnology-based manufacturing devices in the 2020s will have the capability to create almost any physical product from inexpensive raw materials and information, consequentially eradicating their inherent concerns.[6]

The U.S. military in its scientific research program executed by the Defense Advanced Research Projects Agency (DARPA), the Office of Naval Research, and the Joint Forces Command Project Alpha is utilizing this brain-chest of knowledge.

Beyond any doubt, America will maintain the mantle as the only superpower, particularly in light of what Kurzweil recognizes as the law of accelerating returns that is at work. In his view, we are presently at an early stage of technological transition. The acceleration of paradigm shifts at this juncture, defined as the rate at which very fundamental technical approaches are budding, as well as the exponential growth of the capacity of information technology, are both beginning to reach a critical juncture. This is the stage at which the exponential trend is becoming easily discernible to the observer. Beyond this current stage, the trend will escalate at breath-taking pace to the extent that its progression curve will become almost vertical. With a growth rate so phenomenal, the very fabric of human history, in his view, will appear to have been ruptured.

In the first three chapters of this enquiry we discussed the elements of America's defense policy, doctrine and application in terms of the country's deterrence and offensive posture. This is necessary for present and future investments of its defense capabilities and in the interest of securing its alliances and military networks. We also alluded to the importance of U.S. allies who are willing to defend America's values and accepted principles of behavior and to the fact that America has an obligation to continue to support the stability and sovereignty of such nations.

But even more important to America is setting her sights on the infinite, her jurisdiction and authority beyond the more obvious and discernible parameters – inner space and outer space. Plans are well advanced for sweeping changes and modifications in war-fighting deployments and technologies. In terms of her defense leg, the Army Science Advisory Group of the government has devised a transformation process that envisions an armed force that is "highly responsive, network-centric, capable of swift decision, superior in all echelons, and able to provide overwhelming massed effects across any battle space." The present text will scope some of these trends and their impact on ultimate dominion.[7]

Firstly, in the context of land forces, the army is already into the deployment of Brigade Combat Teams (BCTs) of about 2,500 soldiers, unmanned robotic systems, and Future Combat System (FCS) equipment. It is envisaged that this land force configuration will be furnished with its own intelligent computational capabilities and be endowed with a common operating picture of the battlefield, which will be translated for it. Moreover each soldier will be able to receive, cull and hone information through diverse sources and by a variety of means that will include retinal displays and direct neural connection. This capability will be embodied in unmanned aerial devices (in terms of levels of miniaturization, the size of bumblebees), through a process of reverse engineering.[8]

Secondly, a new uniform material, comprising an exoskeleton, is being deployed with the ultimate goal of dramatically reducing the load of each soldier and rendering a nearly impenetrable exterior mass to protect soldiers. Additionally, "exomuscles", derived from new nanotechnology-based material will artificially increase the physical strength of combatants and form a nearly impenetrable mass around the human body. All of this will be augmented with the deployment of aerial unmanned vehicles with more sophisticated navigational capabilities and complex interaction between "right and left vision" systems.[9]

Future communications and information networks also place America in a decisive lead. Centralized communication hubs will be relegated to obsolescence. The third aspect of modernization is the self-organizing capabilities of future Combat Systems which will enable information to be gathered from each soldier and each piece of equipment on the battlefield, and in turn, provide information displays back to each human and machine participant along the information chain. Such technology will be deployed to infiltrate, disrupt, confuse, or destroy enemy communications, through electronic means as well as by means of cyber warfare, with the use of software pathogens.

As a result of these quantum leaps, the fighting force of the future would essentially be a robotic one that incorporates tactical autonomous combatants that have a level of supervised or full autonomy within defined mission bounds. These types of forces will be available along a continuum of sizes, ranging from nanobots and microbots, at the lower end of the scale to comprehensive compact configurations, with the capability to traverse the most extreme and challenging types of terrains.

These sweeping alterations address some of the concerns posed by Paul Kennedy more than two decades ago regarding the strategic rationale of the U.S. army, the air force and the navy, based on the country's expanding commitments to the NATO Alliance which admittedly brought it closer to Europe, to Israel in the Middle East, to Japan, as well as its other imperatives in addressing "aggression from unpredictable regimes."[10] Kennedy's claims are as relevant as they are instructive. He notes:

> *"as the British and French military found in their time, a nation with extensive overseas obligations will always have a more difficult "manpower problem" than a state which keeps its armed forces solely for self-defense; and a politically liberal and economically laissez-faire society—aware of the unpopularity of conscription –will have a greater problem than most..."* [11]

He elaborates on the same point while observing that " this concern about the gap between American interests and capabilities in the world will be less acute had there not been so much doubt expressed – since at least the time of the Vietnam war – about the efficiency of the system itself." This book affirms that the direction being taken by the military sector towards precision missions with fewer casualties confronts head-on and mitigates the dilemma prognosticated by Kennedy decades ago, in terms of devising solutions that would achieve maximum levels of efficiency and economies of scale.

One of the more extravagant concepts earmarked to come on stream by the 2020s is the inauguration of the Autonomous Intelligent Network and System Program comprising self-organizing swarms of robots. The concept envisions "a drone army" of unmanned autonomous robots in the water, on the ground, or in the air commandeered by humans who have decentralized command and control. The rationale for this innovation is the capacity of biological swarms to devise intelligent solutions to complex problems (as may arise in the battle theater), despite the fact that the skills needed for a resolution do not necessarily reside in any given member of the colony. It is envisioned that when problems arise within the drone, its internal programming would trigger self-generated solutions without direct human intervention.[12] Notably, from afar back as 2003, DARPA announced that a battalion of 120 military robots built by I Robot, would be fitted with swarm intelligence software to enable it to mimic the organized behavior of insects. It is envisaged that with improved technology, as systems de-scale, the principles of self-organizing swarm intelligence will play an increasingly important role.

On this merit, the variations of remote controls presently being developed and configured will drastically reduce the number of personnel being deployed and minimize on the level of casualties by moving personnel away from direct line of fire in combat. Additionally, the removal of the pilot from a vehicle dispenses with the requirements for supporting human life; by extension vehicular designs could be of considerably diminished size.

Irregular war-fare being fought out in the inhospitable locales such as Afghanistan, Pakistan, and more recently Libya, compels the introduction of a fourth paradigm - a force presence with unconventional devices such as smart Weapons, Nano-Weapons, and Complex Sensor Systems. Indeed, the trend towards the deployment of unmanned aerial devices escalated after the coalition engagements in Iraq and Afghanistan. This most recent generation of weapons systems constitutes the fourth major technological paradigm.

Nanotechnology of today is primarily concerned with miniaturization, focusing on objects and technologies that are less than 100 nanometers in size. Within this framework of scalability, the chemical, physical, and electronic properties of matter have the propensity to become altered with very critical implications for the types of materials that are at the disposal of the defense community. It is surmised that the next generation of nanotechnology will considerably alter man's relationship with molecules and matter and the consequences for this paradigm will be ground-breaking in terms of the opportunities and risks that it holds out for the military.

Already research on nanosystems has produced programmable, molecular factory systems that are producing non-structured materials and devices and growing them to macroscale size. Apart from the recognizable commercial benefits, these enabling technologies will bring into being a new industrial and defense manufacturing base with the capacity to produce at short notice and in mass supply, systems of varying scale. Apart from coatings for improved armor, the technology that is being applied provides the armed forces with a competitive edge while serving a range of military functions, which include:

- Biological agent detection and identification in laboratory chips
- Decontamination of areas using nanoscale catalysts
- Reconstruction of "smart" materials in specific circumstances; although smart matter still nominally follows the laws of physics it is extraordinarily intelligent to the extent that it can harness these laws to manipulate matter and energy at will
- Reduction of infection from injuries by incorporating nanoparticles into materials
- Creation of ultra-strong materials by combining nanotubes with plastic
- Creation of self-heating materials
- Generation of self-healing plastics by incorporating microspheres and a catalyst into a plastic matrix

Education through Virtual Interaction

The "Trends and Shocks Project Report," discussed in Chapter One revealed the extent to which America was advancing in R&D nanoscale materials and applications and projected that the ability to stay ahead would be contingent to the supply of creative and technically well-educated R&D talent that was available.[13] Neil Jacobstein, Chairman and Chief Executive Officer of Teknowledge Corporation in Palo Alto and Senior Research Fellow in the Digital Vision Program at Stanford University(2006) who served as one of the Project collaborators noted that the ability of the United States to grow or import sufficient talent in the sphere of science and engineering and to keep apace with demands at home for this expertise will be a deciding factor on whether or not the present lead can be sustained. Noting that China and India were on the heels to possibly outstrip America's talent base over the next 20 years in this field on the basis of the demographic flaw, he arrived at this conclusion:

> " may be a follower of commercial investment in nanoscale material but it will have to lead with the rest of the National Nanotechnology Initiative in order for the United States to stay in the lead for molecular manufacturing capabilities. The Productive Nanosystems Technology Roadmap and associated Working Group Proceedings from Battelle, Foresight, Institute for Molecular Manufacturing, and others outline several ongoing trends and visible pathways to achieve productive nanosystems manufacturing capabilities.[13] "

Virtual learning Delivery Modes

Some of Jacobstein's concerns have been allayed in the context of exponential advancements in the field of education that will revolutionize the nature and learning delivery modes. Currently, bandwidth limitations and the dearth of three-dimensional displays limit three-dimensional interchanges in information sharing environments through routine web access. However, in the near future colleges in America will follow the lead taken by MIT and increasingly students will be able to attend virtual classes. By then, visual-auditory virtual-reality environments will be equipped with full immersion capabilities, very high resolution, and accordingly be convincingly real. This upgraded environment will provide the student with high-quality virtual laboratories where experiments could be conducted in any scientific field. Similarly, students of the arts and humanities will benefit from virtual interaction.

257

Weapons of larger size are already becoming increasingly obsolete with the use of nanotechnology and intrusive access capabilities. Complex sensor systems also known as smart dust and developed by the Defense Advanced Research Projects Agency can now be transplanted onto the territory of any overseas nation of choice to provide detailed surveillance and support classified missions in peacetime and/or in combat theater. This quantum leap represents a fifth major component in military technological advancement. The power for these devices will be derived from several sources among these nano-engineered fuel cells or through conversion of mechanical energy from their own movement, from wind, or possibly thermal currents. In terms of their capabilities, nano-weapons are the ultimate surveillance electronic contrivances. They have the capacity to function as "invisible spies" by monitoring enemy territory, identifying persons of interest through thermal and electromagnetic imaging and eventually DNA tests, identifying weapons, and executing missions to destroy designated enemy targets.[14]

Law of Accelerating Returns and the Cosmos

Given this rate of progress, consideration must be given to the implications of the law of accelerating returns to intelligence in the cosmos. Kurzweil points to an impending dilemma that is inescapable. He notes that the estimated optimal computational capacity of a one liter one kilogram computer at around 10 to the forty-second power cps is sufficient to perform the equivalent of ten thousand years of thinking, and anticipated the daunting technological requirements to achieve computational capacities within a range that will allow the more intelligent management of energy and heat. He forecasts that there will come a time when civilization will attain levels in which it will not restrict computation to one kilogram of matter and delved into some of the practical considerations that are likely to provide difficulties in reaching upper limits.

Computational Capacity to Exceed Solar System

According to the history of computation, the power of computation expands both inward and outward. On this premise, the computational capacity of our solar system, as we know it, is in the range of 10 to the seventieth power and 10 to the eightieth power cps. It is estimated that its limits will be attained by the 22nd Century. What is observable is that over the last several decades, scientists have been able to place twice as many computational elements on each integrated circuit chip about every two years. This represents inward growth towards greater densities of computation. Correspondingly, outward growth has occurred and so has the number of chips, estimated at about 8.3 per year. Kurzweil postulates that it is reasonable to expect both types of growth to continue once we approach the limits of inward growth and that upon attaining the limits of matter and energy in our solar system to support the expansion of computation, there will be left no choice for us but to continue to expand outwardly as the primary form of growth. Simply put, we will need to expand beyond the solar system and such a process must entail the attainment of the speed of light or exceeding that speed.

This standard opens the door to other issues such as how do we expand our intelligence beyond the solar system? It has been established that at the end of the last millennium, non-biological intelligence on the earth would have been many trillions of times more powerful than biological intelligence. The expansion of intelligence beyond the solar system will ultimately entail exceeding the speed of light and having to overcome the dangers of sending people or advanced organisms and equipment to other galaxies. In the case of the latter, it is posited that material-based devices should be sent instead of biological humans taking into account that the former could take root in another planetary system and replicate itself by finding the appropriate materials such as carbon. A further advantage to this maneuver is that nanobots are extremely small and could travel close to the speed of light, could gain a foothold by self-replicating, as well as obtain information through a selection of options, including:

- Pure information transmissions that involve energy only and not matter, excelling the speed of light
- Embedding the information needed into the nanobots' memory

The transmission of solar-system-sized intelligence will inevitably entail defying the speed of light. The potential to engineer around this limit has important implications for the speed with which we will be able to colonize the rest of the universe with our intelligence. It is pedagogic that on the occasion of the Apollo II Moon Mission, it was the flag of the United States that was hoisted, a gesture to which is owed a rich genealogy of historical significance; conquest, jurisdiction, and dominion. Space law is currently in its nascent stages and as it evolves persuasive authority will no doubt fall to the chain of precedents that is emerging through custom and practice by the U.S. as the conspicuous pioneer of the space enterprise. Despite the anticipated challenges that will be presented in engineering around the speed of light, there is every indication that the U.S. is well on track to circumventing this anomaly, at the very least theoretically. Kurzweil has already hypothesized two solutions.

The first option entails the use of space-time tunnels known as wormholes, which lie in dimensions beyond the commonly known ones. Kurzweil claims that adding energy and following other requirements of quantum physics and general relativity could expand the wormholes to allow objects larger than subatomic particles to travel through them. The second option is sending humans through the tunnels, but this may prove itself both risky, if not impossible. A modification to this method, conjectured by Thorne et al, consistent with general relativity and quantum mechanics involves expanding a spontaneously generated subatomic sized wormhole to a larger size by initially adding energy, and thereafter stabilizing it with the use of super conducting spheres in the two connected "wormhole mouths." Having expanded and stabilized the wormhole, one of its mouths (i.e. entrances) is transported to another location, while keeping its connection to the other entrance, which remains on earth.[15]

Equally noteworthy is the fact that engineering improvements already exist to permit links to be established anywhere in the universe. Kurzweil estimates that a three-month period would be required to establish a link between Earth and Vega because the two ends of the wormhole would maintain a space/time relationship. He hypothesizes that by traveling arbitrarily close to the speed of light, the time required to establish a link for both communications and for transportation to other locations of the universe, even those of millions of billions of light years away, could be relatively brief.[16]

The second conjecture is to change the speed of light itself. Recent theories suggest that the speed of light is mutable and that it was significantly higher during the early phases of the history of the universe. What is certain is that ultra-high levels of intelligence will in fact expand outward at the speed of light. This however may not necessarily be the limit of the speed of expansion and even assuming the speed of light may prove itself immutable, the limit of the speed of expansion would not necessarily restrict reaching other locations through wormholes. A team of physicists under John Barrow of Cambridge University commenced work on a tabletop experiment with the goal of testing the ability to engineer a change, albeit a miniscule one, in the course of altering the speed of light.[17]

Evolving Code of Universal Ethics and the Singularity Paradigm

America is undisputedly stirring on multiple fronts with a resolve to improve the human condition through advances in science and technology. Combining pragmatic optimism with rational thinking, considerable progress has been made in computational power, life extension, nanotechnology, and the like. Advances in the field of military technology represent one facet of a plethora of revolutionary changes.

Interestingly, the quantum leaps that abound have triggered an evolving framework of values and standards, a development that is now spurring the need for consilience regarding the concepts of computational power, life extension, nanotechnology and other epochal advancements. At the heart of this erudition are the recurring themes of endless extension, transcending restriction, bioethical abolitionism, "singularitarianism", and "technogaianism" which, when viewed singly or in combination, betray the need for a universal code, for the most part, a drastically overhauled value system. On whom shall this responsibility be conferred?

America stands on the threshold of the infinite. America is part of a tellurially-bound community of nations that has yielded a technology creating species that is to say, man himself, and that species has created computation. Ultimately, following the paradigms cited in this chapter, the intelligence of man would saturate the matter and energy in his vicinity and expand outwardly to almost the speed of light, possibly circumventing its limit. The zenith of technological feat will then occur when the forces of the cosmos are outmaneuvered and harnessed and thereupon usher the eon of synthesizing human intelligence with machine.

Singularity is a future period during which the pace of technological change will be so rapid and its impact so deep, that human life will be transformed irreversibly. The currents of change now visible will alter with perhaps shocking vindication for some, many of the concepts hitherto embraced and the long-held assumptions upon which they are founded. Our perspectives will be altered incontrovertibly and forever both in terms of the significance of the past and its implications for the future.

Singularity disrupts the intuitive linear view of the ever-accelerating progress of technology and its social repercussions. Its founding principle is that human progress is exponential, expanding by repeatedly multiplying, distinct from expanding by repeatedly adding a constant. In the absence of this caveat, our unexamined intuition leaves us no choice but to perceive that change occurs at the same time rate that we have most recently experienced. These premises are mirrored in postmodern philosophy.

Thus, America's avowed commitment to continuously improving the human condition through advancements in science and technology is already precipitating a pluralistic framework of values and standards. These epoch-defining advances demand conciliation of thought in the canons encompassing various philosophical debates: bio-ethical abolitionism, life extension, singularitarianism, technogaianism, freedom of information and other contested issues, all representing a newly evolving code of universal ethics. Such revolutionary worldviews presently confronting us embrace nominalism, lacerate the notion of absolute truth; thereby amputating society's moral compass. Illustrative of this, religious pluralism, which rejects claims of exclusivity to the source of truth held by many organized religions and which present hindrances to the ultimate attainment of peace and security, now constitutes a global preoccupation of ever-shifting value systems. These fundamental tenets and propositions are all wedded to postmodernism and are central to the manifesto of "extropism" penned by Dr. Max More in his groundbreaking work, The Principles of Extropy. [18]

These instigations were by no means unforeseeable. In Bzezinski's Between Two Ages: America's Role in the Technetronic Era (1970), the writer presaged that it would have been possible and even tempting to exploit for purely strategic and political purposes research on the brain and on human behavior. He noted with anticipation that "no matter how deeply disturbing the thought of using the environment to manipulate behavior for rational advantages to some, the technology permitting such use will very probably develop within the next few decades and be available primarily, and to begin with exclusively, to the most advanced countries."[19] In a similar vein, Dr. J. F. Gordon Mac Donald, a highly reputable geophysicist specializing in problems of warfare, presaged that "...accurately timed artificially excited strokes could lead to a pattern of oscillations that produce relatively high power levels over certain regions of the earth..." [20] Thus, by a masterful stroke, to the credit of science, it becomes possible to seriously impair the brain performance of entire populations in select regions in the world with the application of the relevant technology.

These ground-breaking junctures which were then contemporaneously inconceivable prompted the following appraisal from Donald M. Michael in "Some Speculations On The Social Impact of Technology"[21] –

"...whether it is used to kill, hurt, nauseate, paralyze, cause hallucination, or to terrify military personnel and civilians, the systemic use of ...(non-conventional technologies e.g. kill rays etc.)... biological and chemical warfare will require the resolution of major moral and ethical problems..."

Preparations for the Thirty-Eighth Summit of the G8 scheduled to be held on May 18-19, 2012 on the margins of the NATO Summit in the United States spotlighted these very debates in the context of the issue of crowd control, and more specifically, the deployment of Active Defense Systems to disrupt, delay and diffuse impending protests. As a gesture of goodwill and confidence building, a demonstration of the application of the device was hosted for the media under the aegis of the armed forces at Marine Corps Base in March 2012 for the purpose of promoting and clarifying its utility among the security forces.[22] Significantly, these developments may be construed as trendsetters for imminent asymmetric warfare where strategy will be a critical factor in offsetting deficiencies in scale. Strategy in war theaters employs one of three options: attrition-maneuver; blitzkrieg-lightning strike; or limited aims-fait accompli. Closely wedded to asymmetric conflict is the deployment of technology with the full range of potentialities, many of which are discussed in this chapter, but all of which place the U.S. at a decided advantage over contenders for primacy.

While conventional deterrent theory argues that the military superiority of a relative stronger power coupled with a credible retaliatory threat will prevent an attack by opponents, this "peace through strength" belief can be readily challenged since an unfazed and motivated weaker adversary may well employ military force if its key decision-makers perceive that they stand a chance of achieving limited objectives in a short-lived contretemps. This holds particular significance in the context of sharp dissensions in the Asia-Pacific region and the assertiveness brazenly displayed by China, and periodically, by North Korea. All of this confirms that strategy and long-term planning are integral to gaining advantage over one's opponents.

The present dispensation of Postmodernism discards the notion of statism and totally deconstructs any notion of synthesis or ultimate resolution. Causal views of time and history are rejected and the idea of linearity and determinism are wholly abandoned. Its ethics embrace multiple possibilities. The future can only be viewed in historical and exponential terms. It is against resolution. It is against closure. It is against product. Instead, it countenances a randomness and deferral of completion, fragmentation and multiple possibilities. Circumventing the speed of light will take us to new frontiers. This feat will permit saturating the universe with solar system scale intelligence, which is deemed by post human theorists to be man's ultimate fate, an achievement that would otherwise take billions of years.

The term singularity, as reproduced by Kurzweil, is a conceptual import "adopted by mathematicians to denote a value that transcends a finite limitation, such as the explosion of magnitude that results when dividing a constant by a number that gets closer and closer to zero." A mathematical function, however, never achieves an infinite value because division by zero is mathematically impossible to calculate. Furthermore, quantum mechanics disallows infinite values. The harnessing of such power, in terms of man's ability to see beyond the event horizon, build machines that have powers greater than their component parts by combining the self-organizing principles of the natural world with the accelerating powers of human initiated technology, and be everywhere at all times is a universal enterprise that can only conceivably rest with the undisputed superpower of today... and tomorrow.

CHAPTER ELEVEN

AT WAR IN CYBERSPACE

Innovations in technology are changing the tactics of modern conflict. There are new tools in today's arsenal of weapons. Helped by advances in electro-magnetics and modern information and communication technology, a new form of electronic warfare has been created. It is called cyberwar and is increasingly recognized by governments and the military as posing a potentially grave threat. And it is not just cyberwar that is a growing phenomenon. The internet has empowered cyberactivism, allowing people to share information and mobilize support to take direct action – both online and on the streets.

Al Jazeera World 19/02/12

regory Rattray, former Director of Cyber Security on the White House National Security Council notes that "the evolution of the United States into the sole superpower has been significantly enabled both politically and militarily by cyberspace." By the same token he observes "the growth in human activity in cyberspace has created an operating environment that permits a range of competitive activities from protest to crime, to espionage to disruptive attacks."[1] This point was underscored with the discovery of the Stuxnet virus in 2010, which pointed to nation state involvement in cyber-attacks at unprecedented level, and even prior to that, in the Ghostnet penetrations of the Dalai Lama's networks in 2009. The 2006 U.S. National Defense Strategy iterates, "successful military operations depend on the ability to protect information infrastructure and data. Increased dependence on information networks creates new vulnerabilities that adversaries may seek to exploit." These across the board industry views are echoed in many empirically supported studies, among these the Computer Response Team Coordinating Center at the Software Engineering Institute which has accurately tracked marked increases over time in U.S. vulnerabilities.[2] Reinforcing all of these findings, NSA Director Admiral Michael Rogers warned late in 2014 that he expects U.S. critical infrastructure (assets essential to the functioning of a society and an economy such as water supply systems, electric grids, and transportation systems) to be attacked, while noting that multiple foreign nations and groups already possess the ability to shut down a U.S. power grid and that several others were investing in the same capability.

This chapter posits that through the enabling power of technology an array of state and subnational actors continue to ruthlessly challenge the U.S. economically and militarily and notwithstanding this, America's political resolve, its technological edge backed by the cooperation and support of time-tested Western partnerships enable it to prevail. In contradistinction, how Beijing sees itself (a perspective that is widely promulgated in doctrinal writings embraced by the Communist party), is vastly different. From the standpoint of the PRC, cyberwar waged on its homefront among its masses is one component of a larger global theater that it shares with the U.S. and the rest of the world. The PRC is therefore continuously embattled on two fronts – domestically and globally; and its battlespace away from home is comprised primarily of nations that consider the ideology and actions of the Chinese Communist Party – which is what drives national and foreign policy - inimical to their individual and shared interests and goals.

The bases for China's engagements in the borderless theater of cyberspace, looking past international norms, can be traced in acclaimed writings such as The Art of War[3] and Unrestricted Warfare.[4] The former, widely considered the Sino magnum opus on strategy, provides insightful literature that enunciates the basic principles of effective combat such as deception and infiltration - tools that are best exploited in systems outside traditional, state-centric boundary conditions. The latter, in respect of which section V of this book provides further details, is an exposition of an opponent's contemporary weaknesses and how these can be penetrated and overwhelmed using non-conventional methods.

Richard Fisher's analysis of PRC cyber warfare capabilities and the chances of a successful attack by China on the U.S. reveals that existing Chinese capabilities that exploit inner and outer space could potentially cripple America by decommissioning its military's primary means of surveillance and communication. In support of this prognosis, he cites a line-up of high-casualty wars instigated by China and its seemingly blind quest to conquer and reclaim Taiwan - despite an ominous record of losses in previous engagements. This is reinforced, in his view, by the dubious disposition to find common cause with regimes with established terrorist linkages - a course of conduct that raises serious doubts over Chinese fidelity to the global good.[5]

Any qualms that may be harbored about China's disposition in the global arena are vindicated by the British GCHQ, which cautioned in a 2010 report:

> *"China has a capability and very wide-ranging cyber program targeting the full spectrum of government, military and government targets. The Chinese mount a large number of relatively unsophisticated attacks, often using publicly known vulnerabilities and have successfully compromised networks globally... This assessment is based on attacks that have been detected and does not preclude more sophisticated and targeted attacks from China."*

Lesser reported on are China's own vulnerabilities at home. Dr. Lennon Yoo-Chung Chang, author of <u>Cybercrime in the Greater China</u> [Rc] explains that currently the world's online population exceeds 2 billion of which 500 million reside in China, and based on his own indepth analysis, concludes that the situation in China in relation to regulatory responses is extremely severe. His observations are supported by the contents of a 2012 Report released from a Workshop hosted by the University of California, San Diego entitled "China and Cybersecurity: Political, Economic, and Strategic Dimensions"[7Th] The document provided an empirically supported assessment that corroborates Dr. Chang's findings. It established, for example, that the PRC's Internet information security was very seriously compromised - in 2011 an estimated 8.531 million computers in China were attacked on a daily basis by rogue programs. A separate sample of bank websites taken by China's Software Test Center revealed that most of the sites failed the minimum assessment criteria and moreover, that 60% of a sample size of 25,000 persons had their personal information stolen.

Inherent Dichotomies in U.S. and Chinese Philosophy

Notwithstanding its unenviable track record in international telecommunications, China by all indications is out of its depth when it comes to the management and regulation of cyber space activities at home. Some may argue that the state of institutional gridlock compounded by the political control wielded by the Communist party, has actually assisted in promoting the PRC's articulated philosophy and ambitions for the country to attain technological preeminence globally by any means, however unmerited.

Another anomaly resides in the fact that the PRC is consistently ill-disposed to multilateral approaches to resolving cyber-related issues. It is important to note that the worldwide adoption of digital networks and supporting technologies has reduced the cost of doing business and removed traditional market barriers formerly dictated by geographical and political boundaries. The internet has become the dominant driver of economic growth and innovation in the world economy. Given the nature of cyberspace and the exponential growth in the number and diversity of its users, inter-governmental cooperation is the sine qua non for its effective regulation and management. This is premised on the notion that nations enjoy some measure of comparable, if not compatible, goals and shared interests.

Based on these two fundamental distinctions – the one, a laissez-faire approach to regulation and responsible management; and the other, an antipathetic stance to multilateral efforts, ongoing tensions are being fueled. Furthermore, there are two competing visions of cyber governance that have traditionally constrained the U.S.- which supports a multi-stakeholder model that incorporates the efforts of governments, businesses, civil society and technical experts - vis-à-vis a competing group of contenders such as China and Russia that are otherwise disposed. It was on this score that during the Plenipotentiary Conference of the U.N. Inter-Telecommunications Union (ITU), the U.S. and Westerners clashed with China, Russia and their backers over proposals to transfer certain internet governance proposals to the ITU.

Against the backdrop of these disparate perspectives that inhibit the attainment of a universal consensus on cyber-related issues this chapter will demonstrate America's proactive posture to cyber security and its commitment to multilateral engagement in the interest of all. This commitment was catalyzed shortly after 9/11 when the government set up the Inter-American Committee against Terrorism (CICTE), an OAS-driven initiative administered under the Secretariat for Multidimensional Security. Central to the mandate of this body was the shoring in of the critical infrastructural architecture throughout the Americas by introducing a full armory of measures, one being cybersecurity. CICTE currently enjoys resounding support from the OAS membership and serves as a beacon for best practices in other regions of the world.

"Global Trends 2025: A Transformed World," a medium-term strategic assessment produced by the U.S. National Intelligence Council identifying key trends, the factors that drive them, where they are likely headed and how they might interact, notes that the international system that was constituted following the second World War would be almost unrecognizable by 2025. One area of this visible transformative process lies in the sphere of IT. This sector underwent the most significant transformation since the Industrial Revolution beginning in the mid-eighteenth century, and advances in technology continue to pose challenges of uncertain character and scale. There are four identifiable reasons for this, which are examined in this chapter: first, the complexity of global governance systems made possible by the distinction between physical and functional regions with the physical referring to territorial, military and economic spaces controlled primarily by states, and the functional defined by non-territorial factors such as culture and the market which are primarily the purview of non-state actors; second: the diversity of actors in parallel with the asymmetric nature of global hostilities; third: the escalation of online criminality that is successfully exploiting the diffusion of technology; fourth: the migration to "fifth generation warfare" precipitated by the evolving character of the war on terror and its nexus with transnational organized crime. The chapter concludes with an insightful overview of critical issues and ambiguities that prevail upon the need to develop norms of appropriate behavior in cyberspace, buttressed by an international legislative framework that is binding on all nations in order to address the challenges of this new frontier. Beijing is averse to the basic tenets of this proposed architecture.

The first factor that accounts for the uncertain character and scale of challenges besetting cyberspace relates to the changing nature of governance in the international system due to the weakening of state capacity compounded by simultaneous changes in the make-up of regions. Regions are now appearing on the basis of transactions and externalities. Although the state remains the dominant player on the world stage, with the steady erosion of state capacity governments now have increasingly less control over a range of critical strategic assets including flows of information, technology and financial transactions. On the other hand, non-state actors are assuming larger roles and strengthened leverage in local, regional and international affairs.

Raimo Vayrynen, of the University of Notre Dame and Helsinki Collegium for Advanced Studies, provides insights that are of significance to this debate in his essay "Regionalism : Old and New." He notes that, "*in the study of regions, the key dimensions center around the division of the world by levels of analysis and by physical-functional distinction. In international affairs, the study of regions is predicated on the notion of anarchy, which leads sovereign states to work to control specific territories and to form regional security complexes. On this basis, regions are defined by spatial clusters of states that the logic of anarchy has facilitated, positively or negatively, becoming dependent on each other. The study of functional regions does not need the assumption of anarchy since the driving force is the environment... or culture... So that whereas the physical definitions of regions is usually provided by states in an attempt to re-*

affirm their boundaries and organize themselves into territorially exclusive groups, functional conceptualizations of regions emanate from the interplay of subnational and transnational economic, environmental and functional processes that states are only partially able to control (2003)."

Noting the above in combination with recent scholarship on the topic, for example, Lake and Morgan, (1997); Mansfield and Milner (1997); Scott (1998); Solingen (1998); Baldwin et al 1999; Hettne, Innotai and Sunkel (1999); Hook and Kearns (1999); Mattli (1999); Page (2000), this inquiry argues that the theoretical foundations of regions and regionalism that preceded the end of the Cold War are currently being challenged by related scholarship on emerging norms and practices that no longer recognize traditional borders as a fait accompli, and by virtue of this, diminish the notion of great power contestation that is exclusive to China and the U.S. Part of this paradigm is the shifts to technology in tandem with the role of globally dispersed subnational actors that are not only averse to Western norms but defy all known frontiers.

The second and related consideration: the asymmetric nature of hostilities that corral diverse players with oft-times competing interests and fueled by hyper-connectivity. Nowhere is the phenomenon better exemplified than among U.S. adversaries - axis players of yore, that all recognize America's information advantage and military supremacy, which they repeatedly put to the test. As an example Iran and North Korea have appeared most willing to conduct disruptive and destructive cyber-attacks against the U.S. and other foreign targets. Their tactics have included data swipes, destruction of computer hardware, and denial-of-service. China and Russia have exhibited some of the most advanced and lethal capabilities and high-tech mavericks operating out of both countries have been linked to especially disruptive attacks that exploited the build-up of regional tensions. The phenomenon surfaced in 2007 shortly after a Soviet statue depicting World War II soldiers was publicly destroyed. This politically volatile incident triggered a trail of low-tech attacks on government websites that quickly escalated in sophistication, causing the country's largest bank to cease web operations when the attack reached its worst point - running botnets on over 85,000 computers and in the process bringing down 58 websites all at once. Subsequently, Russian-based actors launched a wave of attacks in 2008 against Georgian targets; to be followed in close succession by the Sino-Japanese escalated territorial tensions in the South China sea where cyber-attacks became par for the course. In yet another regionally based conundrum, at the height of North-South Korean face-offs, the "northerners" leveraged a string of destructive operations leading to serious compromises in the South Korean national identification systems. As well, in the course of more recent tensions surrounding the Iranian nuclear program, cyber-attacks were launched against two Saudi Arabian energy firms, ostensibly in retaliation against the U.S. for cyber operations against the Iranians.

A third pointer: as major powers rely increasingly on digital networks and as inter-state tensions become exacerbated, weak governance and regulatory systems have opened doors to an escalation of online criminality among an array of actors including terrorists, narco-traffickers, weapons proliferators, black market intelligence traders and organized criminals who, in an increasingly networked world, now have greater access to information, technology, finance, sophisticated deception-and-denial techniques, and most importantly, to each other.

The fourth variable: the chapter aligns itself with the global concerns surrounding the far-reaching usage of cyberspace by emergent violent social movements such as Hezbollah and the Islamic State which currently pose near and present threats to the U.S. along its "third border." In this vein, the global war on terror seeks to confront a new and common adversary – one that is at once hybrid, (both conventional and asymmetric), decentralized, polycentric and segmentary. Its elevated mode of warfighting, by its very nature, enables buy-in from multiple social and national groups that are operating along loosely defined agendas and ideologies. This war is one of ideas and ideology and for this reason defies state-centric responses. Unlike the first four generations of warfare, which were all focused primarily on territorial objectives and necessitated either conquering an enemy or gaining or holding territory, fifth generation warfare has no single state objective and is being effectively waged unconventionally in a borderless environment. Cyberspace provides the ideal province, and on this merit, lends greater discursiveness to the U.S.- China match.

II

The Cyber Architecture- A General Overview

In architectural mode of expression, cyberspace comprises the agglomeration of systems and networks orchestrated by rules established by software and communication protocols. As an operating environment cyberspace is defined as a "domain characterized by the use of electronics and electromagnetic spectrum to store, modify, and exchange data via networked systems and associated infrastructures"

271

The latter medium spans a wide range of activity that includes:

- The Internet and computer software applications
- Traditional circuit switched networks and protocols such as SS7, microwave networks, long-haul fiber, and satellite networks using ATM and synchronous optical network protocols to carry digital signals
- The use of analogue signals and transmissions from air traffic control radars
- Air defense systems
- Supervisory data and control systems based on proprietary algorithms and protocols for power grids that drive their use

Systems such as the global positioning systems, for timing information and telecommunications hotels which have the capacity to "switch" and "route" infrastructure interconnecting them provide supporting systems to cyberspace. In sum, the domain of cyberspace is governed both by laws of physics and rules of code that control both physical and logistical systems. Equally intricate is the population of facilitators in the cyber space community, which includes:

- Producers of software, hardware, and algorithms that make up cyberspace
- Operators of long-haul telecommunications networks, Internet service providers (ISPs), and a wide array of supporting services such as timing and domain name services
- ISPs, domain name registrars, Web hosts, cellular providers, and others who provide digital services that enable use of the Internet and other communications mediums in cyberspace
- Users ranging from global multinational corporations running extensive cyber infrastructures with top-notch cadres of expertise to individuals with little to no technical knowledge
- Governments at all levels that establish and enforce legal, regulatory, and policy frameworks for activity in cyberspace
- Nongovernmental stakeholder organizations whose activities range from establishing agreements on protocols, assignment of Internet addresses, and advocating the privacy rights of users.

International Agreements

The United States and China are primary actors in the wider global Cyber Security regime which (with the exception of the OAS pact, which is regional in reach) consists of the under-listed instruments:

- U.N. General Assembly Resolution 55/63. Combating Criminal Misuse of Information Technologies
- U.N. General Assembly Resolution 56/121. Combating Criminal Misuse of Information Technologies
- U.N. General Assembly Resolution 53/239. Creation of Global Culture of Cyber Security
- U.N. General Assembly Resolution 58/199. Creation of Global Culture of Cyber Security and Protection of Critical Infrastructure Systems
- OAS General Assembly Resolution AG/RES.2004 Fourth Plenary Session held in June 08, 2004
- U.N. Budapest Convention
- The Busan Consensus, 2014

One of the foundational instruments in the global effort to create a universally binding agreement on cybercrime is the Council of Europe's Convention on Cyber Crime which entered into force in 2004[8] In light of the fact that the Convention was open for signature by non-E.U.- members it is thus not in the strictest sense a regional instrument. It has since been ratified by the United States, a non-member of the Council. The treaty sets up guidelines for data sharing between governments in cross-border cases of bank fraud, identity theft, child pornography, phishing, and other on-line manifestations of electronic trans-border infractions. There is a clear divergence in political thought, however, regarding the introduction of an internationally binding regime. Therefore, apart from basic procedural and cooperation commitments, crucial state actors have been less than forthcoming and these, in particular, are widely suspected of sponsoring various forms of cyber-attack for political purposes.

One of the incipient and less heard of attempts at securing a global consensus was jointly sponsored within the U.S. by a consortium of interests comprising the Hoover Institution, the Consortium for Research on Information Security, and the Center for International Security and Cooperation. This syndicate convened at Stanford University in December 6-7, 1999 with the objective of exploring the need and methods for effecting international cooperation in dealing with cybercrime and terrorism. The product of their deliberations was "The Stanford Draft," [9] which took five primary elements into account, namely:

- That cybercrime was transnational and required a transnational response
- That cyber criminals exploited weaknesses in the laws and enforcement practices of states
- That the speed and technical complexity of cyber activities requires pre-arranged, agreed procedures for cooperation in investigating and responding to threats and attacks
- That a multilateral convention will ensure that States Parties adopt and enforce laws, cooperate with each other and formulate and agree on standards and practices
- That an international agency be created for use as a common forum to discuss and respond to needs for technical assistance to developing states

Despite arguments not favoring a single regime to which all nations should be obligated, there are very compelling advantages to such an approach that, in the opinion of this inquiry, ought not to be readily dismissed, namely:

- Areas not covered under existing international agreements should be appropriately placed under such an instrument. Examples considered were attacks utilizing viruses, denials of service, and other forms of destructive conduct
- Certain types of conduct deserved to be uncompromisingly criminalized
- Areas of disagreement between states should be resolved failing which lacunas would persist that would be favorable to criminal elements

Differing state opinions over the role of the internet have delayed efforts to create an internationally binding regime that addresses cybersecurity. The U.N.-led Budapest Convention, also referred to as the Convention on Cybercrime, is the most recent attempt to formulate a common body of laws but this last effort has been trumped for several reasons. Firstly, the instrument fails to come to terms with the most politically relevant and consequential issues such as the military use of cyberspace; secondly it has been signed by a mere 50 states but lacks enforcement and oversight powers and authority; lastly Russia and China which are crucial players in any such agreement, have refused to sign up, choosing instead to produce their own proposal to bring to the attention of the U.N. General Assembly, entitled "International Code of Conduct for Information Security." (A/66/359). Promulgated in 2011, the draft contained norms and suggested laws that are prima facie a mere re-iteration of earlier ideas of Western nations and placed much focus on the State authority over internet based policy. The West was not in favor of the approach perceived in the text, which seemed to lack a cooperative spirit.

UNODC has also been at the forefront of U.N.-led initiatives, focusing on online organized crime and child abuse; while the ITU has been busy drafting international standards in a number of areas including expanding the accessibility of the internet to ensure emergency telecommunication lines. There is an ITU- Study Group 17 constituted by a small body of researchers that is currently immersed in creating standards on important vulnerabilities such as smart phones, cloud computing and social media. Another commendable effort at regulation is the Tallin Manual on International Law Applicable to Cyber Warfare, the most fully framed attempt, as of now, to consider the legal aspects of cyber-attacks. This exceptional handbook is the product of three years of assiduous effort among 20 international legal scholars, which delves into the complexities of cyber conflict, the implications of cyber war on State responsibility and issues surrounding sovereignty. One of its discoveries – which in the view of this inquiry is by no means unexpected - is a recognition that cyber conflict does not always follow the lines of current legislative standards, meaning that many areas of inconsistency may have to be negotiated on a case-by-case basis.

U.S. National Cyber Security Policy and Philosophy

In noting that U.S. national policy can influence the overall use of cyber space, Gregory Rattray also observes that unlike China, the stance of the U.S. has been laissez-faire. This very feature in the view of this writer, lends to its more universal appeal. [10] U.S. national regulations and positions on international forums emphasize the economic benefits of loose control in empowering innovation and access by all users to services provided by the internet and other cyber space mediums. Such an approach, however, entails a degree of risk since it limits an understanding of the potential weaknesses of the overall system and the ability of miscreants to orchestrate coordinated activity across systems if required. Rattray advocates that the U.S. should develop methods and intellectual capital to analyze and answer such questions. Mindful that one of the primary concerns on hand will be to manage cyber space risks posed by the increasing global production, operation and ownership of key IT and communications that underpin the ability of the U.S. military and other government infrastructure operations, he encourages the development of dedicated programs (which will no doubt necessitate the appropriation of prohibitive financial resources, intellectual capital, and long-term strategies) in order to mitigate risks at all levels.

In his view such a strategy would demand:

- An understanding of "shifting opportunities and vulnerabilities embedded in the evolving foundations of cyberspace"
- Aggressively managing its equities across the range of social, economic, and military concerns
- Establishing a better protected cyber space by pursuing redundancy and diversity in undersea cable, satellite ground stations and fiber optic routing - a course of action that will minimize the incidence of chokepoints in key infrastructural hubs and physical connectivity.

In deference to these and related concerns, President Obama had directed a 60-day "comprehensive clean slate review" in 2009 during his first term in office with the objective of assessing the adequacy of U.S. policies and structures for cyber security. [11]The Report emanating from this exercise was a thorough one that addressed policy, strategy, and standards in relation to the security of and operations in cyber space, and encompassed the full range of cyber defense mechanisms including threat reduction, vulnerability reduction, deterrence, international engagement, and other tools needed for a comprehensive national response. Integral to the U.S. strategy is the promotion and defense of a free, open, and interconnected internet as a U.S. foreign policy priority.

The State Department, in contrasting its approach in February 2011 with that of certain non-Western jurisdictions, observed, "...repressive regimes are censoring search results and imposing laws that restrict online discourse and access to information."[12] Contrastingly, the Department "not only works to combat censorship, but to ensure the safety of communication and access to information in the new terrain of the 21st Century." Currently, the Net Freedom Task Force is the Department's policy-making and outreach body for Internet Freedom and has a direct reporting line to the Under Secretary for Democracy and Global Affairs and the Under Secretary for Governance, Energy, and Agricultural Affairs. Part of its remit is to engage with foreign governments when bloggers or Internet activists come under attack

This chapter acknowledges that proponents of wider national goals vis-à-vis those promoting defense-specific-priorities may not always see eye--to eye. For example, a front burner military priority is for the installation of more effective cyber defenses and coordinated responses, particularly against non-state actors that challenge political interests nationally and internationally. This may to some degree be tangential to broader and more idealistically rooted goals aimed at "fostering global markets and democratic dialogue." Perhaps a more fundamental illustration of defense-specific concerns is the designation of cyberspace by the Department as a war-fighting domain and of cyber-attacks as acts of aggression tantamount to "acts of war," warranting military retaliation. The premise is that America's defense industrial base is a vital and indispensable component of the country's critical infrastructure and on this merit, has an exceptional mandate to discharge. Underscoring this point, a recently launched initiative has been the promotion of programs that are directly aimed at "countering violent extremist and enemy ideology." To this end, the Department is employing specially-developed software that would allow appropriately authorized personnel to create multiple fake on-line identities known as "soft puppets." This extraordinary form of cultural diffusion, which calls for a high level of acumen, finesse and sensitivity - attributes no doubt behooved to the Department - entails going into "chat rooms" and other on-line fora using Arabic, Fazi and languages common to the Middle East and South Asia, with the objective of "spreading pro-American messages."

America's Multilateral Posture Exemplified within OAS

As iterated, America has adopted a multilateral approach to cyberspace infractions. The U.S. shepherded the establishment of an Inter-American institutional architecture to be administered by the Inter-American Committee against Terrorism (CICTE) - an ambitious regional campaign that effectively co-opts the full OAS membership, and is anchored in the community's legacy of multilateralism, shared responsibility, and partnership. The initiative is a product of a Resolution emanating from the Permanent Council to the General Assembly of the OAS, which entrusted to the Committee on Hemispheric Security the mandate to develop and execute a comprehensive Inter-American Strategy to Combat Threats to Cyber Security.[13]

The OAS General Assembly noted that the internet and related networks and technologies had not only become indispensable tools for OAS member states but through their agency tremendous growth in national and by extension global economies were spurred. These new technologies had made possible tremendous improvements in efficiencies, productivity, and creativity across the hemisphere. The Assembly also acknowledged that the Internet had triggered threats that endangered the entire community of users and that the destruction of data, the misappropriation of information, the manipulation of users' privacy, and the defrauding of business could stymie government functions and disrupt telecommunication services and other critical infrastructure. Such threats, in the view of the Assembly, could not be addressed by any single government or by adopting a single discipline or practice.

This concern persists and is validated in a publicly released version of "The Federal Bureau of Investigation's Ability to Address The National Security Cyber Intrusion Threat April 2011," after the fact appraisal which confirmed that for 2008 the Department of Homeland Security had reported 5,499 known intrusions on U.S. government computer systems alone, a 40% increase over 2007.

The stance of the OAS General Assembly, which mirrors a commonality and mutuality of interests among Member States and the multi-polarity of economic and security concerns, can be found in the transcript of OAS Resolution AG/RES 1939.XXXIII-O/03, on the subject matter "Development of Inter-American Strategy to Combat Threats to Cyber Security." This is in striking contrast with the Chinese posture, the primary goal of which is to excise China from the rest of the global community in pursuit of cyber preeminence. On the other hand, the cornerstone of the Inter-American Strategy, intergovernmental cooperation and co-responsibility, is mirrored in U.S. foreign policy which prefers a global outlook that thrives on shared interests and democratic idealism.

Secretary of State Hillary Clinton articulated America's stance in her address to the Senate Foreign Relations Committee in January 2009 in these words,

> *"...America cannot solve the most pressing problems on our own and the world cannot solve them without America. The best way to advance America's interests in reducing global threats and*

seizing global opportunities is to design and implement global solutions."

Accordingly, the key components of the Strategy betray an intergovernmental and multidimensional character. Provision has been made for the constitution of an Experts Group comprising representatives of OAS members whose mandate would be to promote policy and foster cooperation; the operation of Cyber Security Incident Response Teams on a 24 hour per day basis; the designation and certification of team members by participating governments; the provision of legal consultation to support government ministries and legislatures in the drafting of legislation, regulations and policies; the fostering of public/private partnerships; and the adoption of cybercrime policies and legislation at national level with the objective of protecting Internet users and preventing and deterring the criminal misuse of computers and computer networks while respecting users' privacy and individual rights.

China's Cyber Space Policy

In contrast to the Inter-American posture, the rationale behind China's Cyber Space doctrine is in reducing its dependency on "the West" for advanced technologies and instead, promoting indigenous innovation (zizhue chuangxin). With this in view, the government has targeted that its existing dependency on external technologies of 50% would be diminished to 30% within the next decade and adopted this as a priority goal in shaping its "2006 National Medium and Long-Term Plan for the Development of Science and Technology." The Plan, produced by the State Council of China and released on February 09 2006, formulates three tracks of activity, namely, industrial policy; state-directed technology; and cyber and industrial espionage.[14]

According to the State Council of China, the National Plan serves as a guide so that regions and governmental departments will organize science and technology activities and direct research and development institutions such as universities, research institutes and enterprises in a unified way, as enunciated by the central government. Its emerging priorities were the promotion of science and technology development in selected key fields and the enhancement of innovation capacity.

The development of energy, water resources, and environmental protection are being treated as prioritized programs since these would serve as the pillars of the country's socio-economic development. Innovation in information technology, new materials, and advanced manufacturing technology are deemed equally in the interest of upgrading the country's industrial base. Similarly, biotechnology would be a crucial aspect of long-term developmental economics since it would ultimately lead to a reduction in the threat of serious disease in the country and improve overall health standards. Simultaneously basic research, frontier research, and interdisciplinary research were promoted as the engine drivers of sustainable development in science and technology. In support of this rationale, the National Plan identified a breakdown of 11 fields, 68 topics, 16 special programs, and for research plans as priorities over the next fifteen- year period. To reinforce its long-term vision, China would promote reform within the science and technology management system and public research institutions to better integrate resources and effectively organize science and technology activities.

The political resolve to execute this agenda flows from the highest levels of the Chinese policy-making apparatus - at the meeting of the Political Bureau of the CPC Central Committee, regarding the "National Medium and Long-Term Science and Technology Development Plan" which was presided over by Hu Jingtao, General Secretary of the Central Committee, the following resolutions were made:

- *We must continuously achieve qualitative leaps in the development of China's productive forces by driving and relying on S&T programs and innovations with higher consciousness and on a more extensive scale, so as to facilitate faster and healthier development of China's economy and society...*
- *We must be keenly aware of the fact that the S&T development level of China as a whole still lags behind the advanced level and we must do all we can to catch up...*
- *We must make all endeavors to become a master of a group of kernel technologies in a number of important fields, take command of a batch of independent intellectual property rights and build a group of enterprises and brands with international competitiveness by sparing no efforts to reinforce the original innovations, integrated innovations, and digestion and absorption of and innovations based on introduced advanced technologies so as to provide powerful S&T supports to China's economic and social development and modernization of national defense...*[15]

In pursuit of an expedient industrial policy, the government launched a full battery of 20 medium- to long-term mega-science and engineering projects. Integral to their success is the government's aggressive approach towards state-driven procurement, encouraging the development of competing technologies among entrepreneurs, and imposing technology transfers from multinational corporations in return for market access – in sharp contrast to the laissez-faire posture of the U.S. Consistent with governmental autonomy, in 2009, Beijing imposed a requirement on companies to provide evidence that their products included indigenous innovation and were free of foreign intellectual property, as a proviso for having such products registered in official state catalogues. Thereafter in 2010, the government ordered high-tech companies to surrender encryption codes for their smart cards, Internet routers, and other technology products as a condition for their inclusion on the state catalogue. Another strategic device adopted by the establishment is its pro-activeness in standard-setting, as is the case with cell phones (TD SCDMA), WiFi (WAOI or WLAN Authentication and Privacy Infrastructure), DVDs (AVS, the audio visual coding standard), RFID (Radio Frequency Identification), and other technologies.[1T]

Traditional and non-traditional espionage is being activated as a separate track of activity. Evidence of cyber-attacks emanating from China is corroborated by the nature of sophisticated attacks against select multinational corporations, which have reported theft of proprietary information by hackers. Among the better-known affected companies are Google, NASDAQ, Du Pont, Johnson and Johnson, General Electric, and RSA. Following a trail of cyber-attacks in the late 2000s, the U.S. Secretary of Defense noted in the September 2010 issue of Foreign Affairs that "the threat to intellectual property is less dramatic to the threat to critical infrastructure; it may be the most significant cyber threat that the United States will face over the long-term."[17]

Concerning cyber-industrial espionage, many camps have wagered on the capability of China to seriously debilitate the U.S. economically or militarily in the sphere of cyber war. Some of these conjectures were examined a 2009 Report entitled "Capability of the People's Republic of China to Conduct Cyber Warfare and Computer Network Exploitation." This insightful document, originally destined for the U.S.-China Economic and Security Review Commission, was put together by a team comprising Steve Devise, Bryan Krehel, George Bakos, and Christopher Barnett of Northrop Grumman Corporation.[18] The transcript carried the following themes:

1. The strategy of the PLA for computer network operations at the campaign and strategic levels, so as to comprehend how China was integrating this capability into overall planning efforts

2. The identity of "the principal institutional and individual actors" in Chinese computer network operations and what linkages exist between civilian and military operators

3. Possible targets of computer network operators against the U.S. government and the private sector that are frequently attributed to China

4. The timeline between alleged intrusions by the Chinese into U.S. government and industry networks to provide a broader context to their activities

5. The formal IW strategy adopted by the Chinese – this is officially referred to as "Integrated Network Electronic Warfare." This mechanism consolidates the offensive mission for both the computer network attack (CAN) and IW under the PLA General Staff Department's 4th Department (Electronic Countermeasures); wherein the computer network defense (CND) and intelligence gathering responsibilities likely belong to the GSD 3rd Department (signals Intelligence);and in the Report's estimation, possibly a variety of PLA specialized IW militia units.

6. The training and equipping of the PLA – the force is being outfitted to use a variety of IW tools for intelligence gathering and to establish information dominance over its adversaries during a conflict.

7. Relationship between PLA and civilian sector – the PLA was found to be reaching across a wide swath of China's civilian sector with the objective of incorporating individuals with specialized skills from the commercial, industrial, and academic fields. The Report unearthed apparent collaboration between the PLA and more elite and sophisticated hackers.

8. The existence of an organized underground hacker community – while the hacking community operated surreptitiously and there was evidence of links with the PLA, this was not a general trend; what was discovered was the existence of "black-hat programmers," more specifically, individuals or groups who participate routinely in the penetration of U.S. networks. These operate with the use of customized tools and exploit the vulnerabilities that software vendors have not as yet discovered.

The main conclusions of the document were:

- In a conflict with the U.S. China would most likely use its computer network operation capabilities to attack select nodes on the U.S. military's Non-classified Internet Protocol (NIPRNET) and unclassified and civilian contractor logistics networks in the continental U.S. and allied countries in the Asia/Pacific region
- The ultimate goal of this form of aggression would be "to delay U.S. deployments and impact combat effectiveness of troops already in theater."
- That assuming that the "blackhat operators" are in fact responsible for some if not all of the exploitation; this would mean that the Chinese possess a "mature and operationally proficient capability."

These findings are consistent with Richard R Fisher's commentary on "How the CCP-PLA Challenges America and Its Allies."[19] He forecasts that "a variety of PLA radio frequency weapons and cyber-warfare weapons can be expected to target the Army FCFs", which represents an attempt to meld barely proven technologies to create a powerful but medium weight and rapidly deployable force, while cautioning that the U.S. army should work towards preventing its network from becoming the "Achilles heel" of its future force. He concludes that any resolution to current vulnerabilities must involve an amalgamation of the most recent breakthroughs in stronger nanomaterial-based armor, energy weapons, and more efficient hybrid engines, and cautions that singular reliance on secure broad-band networks was inadvisable.

Notwithstanding having an irrefutably robust policy and strategic architecture in place, Gregory J. Rattray firmly maintains that for the U.S. to maintain a clear lead in cybersecurity, it is imperative that the government continue to invest heavily in the training and development of an exceptionally strong team of experts, specifically dedicated to reviewing and modifying the rules and protocols governing the Cyber Environment. Another further observation he makes is that:

> *"Choices about open versus closed systems and more defensible versus more accessible cyberspace at the national level will depend on the ability to balance intelligence, military, law enforcement, commercial, and social objectives."*

This whole-of-government perspective provides a sound basis to de-conflict the "primary roles" assumed for cyber security policy currently discharged by the Department of Homeland Security which is responsible for protecting critical infrastructure and the National Security Agency, which is responsible for politically classified computers and networks. There are other bodies as well whose areas of responsibility are crucial to protecting U.S. information systems such as the Federal Bureau of Investigation, the Central Intelligence Agency and of course the Department of Defense. Each of these arms of government is responsible for developing and implementing a strategy for protecting its own computer systems while being mutually supportive of the roles of other bodies.

Noting that the ultimate responsibility for homeland cyber security appears "scattered among various departments," Kevin New of the National Defense University Press offered his own constructive views on the issue many years ago, namely - that a position of Director of Cyber Security could be created and modeled along the lines of the Director of National Intelligence.[20] Unfeigned interventions such as this are warranted by trends that paint a picture of an "at risk" American landscape. Illustrative of this, a Report titled "America's Cyber Future: Security and Prosperity in the Information Age" issued in June 2011 noted that although the U.S. GDP grew to US $2 trillion more than it would otherwise have due to the information technology revolution, such advancements could be easily eroded by the cumulative effects of cybercrime emanating from acts of espionage, theft of classified information, trade secrets, intellectual property pilferage, all of which are the drivers of military power and global competitiveness. The report then went on to issue a compelling cautionary note, "...although cyber Armageddon does not appear imminent, cyber-attacks are more than a nuisance and more than criminal activity. They constitute a serious challenge to the U.S. national security and demand greater attention from America's leaders"[21]

III

The Full Brunt of Inter-continental Linkages, Emerging Regionalisms, and Hyper-connectivity

Doctrines, policies, edicts and institutional arrangements as talked through in the earlier parts of this discourse constitute the collective embodiment of interests of the key players but do not necessarily confront some of the wider and increasingly complex global contours. Nowhere is this better exemplified than along the U.S. immediate geographic approaches - its "third border" which epitomizes the hyper-connective nature of the contemporary environment, although the trend is not uncommon in other regions of the world. And herein lies the importance of its time-tested friendships not beholden to Beijing.

As America's acknowledged "third border," Latin America and the Caribbean constitute an integral part of its traditional continental sanctuary[22] This is a locale known for escalating U.S.-Sino rivalry in the spheres of military assistance, alliance building, economic investment and aid and cultural exchanges and is fraught with plurilateral diplomacy spawned through a growing number of political unions and economic blocs with overlapping and at times ideologically distinct persuasions.[23] As paradoxical as the suggestion may seem, the status quo calls attention to the sagacity of possible future collaboration between the two contenders, in light of the staggering volume of economic losses that could be incurred, should a region-scale cyber-attack be successfully launched by an adversary.[24]

This level of hyper-connectivity is typical of other parts of the Western Hemisphere as well. The U.K., America's closest ally and official gateway to Europe and the Middle and Far East, recognizes the implications of this exposure. A 2010 GCHQ internal missive reads in part:

> "China's industrial espionage comprises the single greatest threat to U.S. technology...Various U.K. companies have also been targeted and large amounts of data have been lost."[25]

Regarding Russia, which is pursuing a self-defining course of aggression in the dual capacity as an ally of strategic convenience to Beijing and fellow member of the BRICS, GCHQ affirms:

> "Targeting of U.K. government departments is assessed to be a priority for Russia and is likely to be ongoing. Governments, industry and academic institutions across a range of sectors have been targeted. Russia is judged to pose a U.K. threat to U.K. communications in a variety of countries, and U.K. data may be at risk due to compromises of networks outside of U.K. control."[26]

Further to this, the Director of GCHQ, Britain's acknowledged National Technical Authority for Information Assurance, said in the organization's 2015 foreword of the re-presented "10 Steps to Cyber Security,"

"In GCHQ we continue to see real threats to the U.K. on a daily basis, and I'm afraid the scale and rate of these attacks shows little sign of abating." [27]

In 2014, British-based Information Security Breaches Survey found that as many as 81% of large companies in the U.K. had reported some form of security breach costing each organization an average of between 600,000 to one and a half million pounds sterling.[28] Cyber security has therefore become a "Tier One" national security priority in Britain given the damage already being wrought on the British economy through inundated attacks, in combination with similarly serious concerns being raised over the likelihood of having British classified defense data stolen by stealth through sophisticated hacking methods. In fact the odds favoring systems penetration are extremely high. In July 2014, reports surfaced that Chinese hackers had infiltrated the networks of three Israeli defense contractors obtaining information of the Iron Dome System, UAV technology, ballistic missiles and detailed schematics of the Arrow III missile interceptors.[29]

These developments vindicate post-war concerns that led to the Five Eyes concordat which was signed in 1947 between the U.S. Britain, Canada, Australia and New Zealand and maintains relevance. Intercontinental cooperation presently takes the form of cooperation initiatives among the Anglophone Commonwealth, rooted in the United Kingdom. This includes but is not exclusive to mutual access to internationally dispersed "listening stations" – wartime legacy items.[30] The efficacy of this time-tested compact is continuously reinforced by new and unconventional global threats. More lately, in the wake of the hacking of Sony Pictures computers and the U.S. military command's twitter feed (wherein comments were posted promoting Islamic State militants), the U.S. and U.K. took the unprecedented decision of running "war games" and "cyber-attacks" on each other as part of a series of re-invigorated joint defense exercises, in this instance targeting online criminality. The proposed "war games" are scheduled to commence in 2015 and will include The Bank of England and commercial banks targeting the City of London and Wall Street. It is anticipated that subsequent exercises will test critical national infrastructure; and in yet another unprecedented joint endeavor, agents from both nations will be cooperating in cyber-cells involving the MI5 and the Federal Bureau of Investigation.[31]

America's "Third Border" Vulnerabilities

The threat picture on America's third border is strongly influenced by the following:

- The nexus between transnational crime and violent extremism in the Americas, which is officially acknowledged
- China's rapid ascendance as a global player in the telecommunications field and unanimous endorsement among Latin American and Caribbean governments as a preferred trading partner
- The Americas' emergence at the crest of an historic transformation of the world's energy systems

The (2015) "Report on Cybersecurity and Critical Infrastructure in the Americas"[32] confirmed the spiraling level of cyber-attacks in the hemisphere and their heightened sophistication. The report also reveals that the critical infrastructure sector emerges "as an especially vulnerable attack vector due to aging facilities and the presence of "bolt-on-half measures and Band-Aids" in lieu of comprehensive security systems"[31]

An important point of note in the estimation of this book is that the internet was not initially designed with security in mind and was never intended to go public but now serves a user population that is growing exponentially, while providing a critical range of functionalities, all essential to the preservation of life and maintaining the conduct of day-to-day global affairs in banking, travel, trade, communications and commerce, to name a few. Added to this, the Western internet infrastructure alone currently has approximately 60 T bps bandwidth. Consider that the 2014 attack on Spamhaus reached 400 Gbps and that the perpetrators would later attack the London Internet Exchange (LINX), the Amsterdam Internet Exchange (AMS-IX), the Hong Kong Internet Exchange (H-KIX), and the Frankfurt Internet Exchange (DE-CIX). 32These are all very critical worldwide hubs that transcend Sino and American interests, even when the two are combined.

As previously alluded, another game changer has been the evolution of international terrorism whereby war-fighting has migrated from the territorial to completely new frontiers. International terrorist organizations such as Hezbollah and the Islamic State have set up activities in the Americas and are heavily reliant on cyberspace and the anonymity it affords to promulgate their ideology, recruit new members, enlist jihadists and raise and transfer funds.

"Global Trends 2015 – A Dialogue About the Future with Non-Government Experts" identified the future "global drivers" over the next 15 years considered as the most likely conflicts as well as prospects that exist for cooperation.[33] The Report forewarned that future conflict would incorporate asymmetric threats in which state and non-state adversaries would avoid direct engagements with the U.S and instead devise strategies, tactics and weapons - some improved by "side-wise technology" – to minimize U.S. strengths and exploit perceived weaknesses. This observation is material to countries considered to be specially aligned to U.S. interests and more so that are co-combatants in the war on terror. ISIS has, as of June 2015, besides taking hostages executed numerous foreigners whose nationalities are reflective of the coalition of supporting countries engaged in counter-terrorist operations – journalists James Foley and Steven Sotlof; aid workers David Haines, Alan Hening and Peter Kassig; French citizen, Herve Gourdel and Japanese nationals. [34]

Despite stouthearted advances among Western coalition members, the Islamic State has prevailed over strategic parts of Iraq and Syria, simultaneously boring its way into Libya, Egypt and Nigeria, where ideologically affiliated groups have pledged allegiance. Furthermore, the movement now has an established presence in Latin America and the Caribbean, the U.S. third border. Financial and other Saudi support for Wahhabism continues to pour in unabated, extending across the Middle East, South Asia, North Africa and the Balkans. All the while, jihadist fighters are being recruited from across continents including the U.S. and its geographical approaches to the homeland in the Caribbean. A major aspect of the movement's expansion plan is attributed to the combined exploitation of the Dark Web to conduct psychological warfare capped by the strategic timing of video and other releases, an effective tactic credited to al-Furquan, its media wing. Added to the above are three often overlooked factors that give credence to the movement's ostensibly unstoppable trail: the decreasing quality and commercialization and consumerization of software and operating systems; the exponentially increasing demand for convenience and the desirability of cost reduction.

Threats to Network Connected Infrastructure

The Deep Web is teeming with illicit activities of every stripe primarily because it allows anonymous communication. The TOR network was conceived to enable users to surf the web privately and anonymously, particularly those living under oppressive regimes like China, North Korea and Myanmar and its method of payment for goods and services procured is typically anonymous. Lars Hilse, internationally reputed expert in cyber activity, observes that an ever-increasing number of infrastructure-hardware is connected to the internet for varying reasons and that notwithstanding hardware-controlling interfaces are set behind a firewall, their manufacturers individually password protect them to increase security. These security measures are invariably left unaltered meaning that the standard passwords set by manufacturers upon deployment are left in place by installing engineers. His research into TOR reveals that the high levels of proliferation of manufacturer passwords in relation to the build and make-up of such interfaces. This means that once the conventional IT barrier has been breached, the hardware-connected infrastructure could be readily exploited with the passwords. He concludes that in combination with Bitcoin, the TOR network could be exploited with relative ease by terrorists to conduct attacks since all necessaries are provided, the most compelling of which is, its anonymous design features.[35]

Terrorist Funding

The damage inflicted by cybercrime on the worldwide financial industry is estimated to exceed US$2 trillion. Bitcoin transactions is the most likely sought after medium of exchange over conventional currency and is typically used multiple times, turned into luxury high-priced commodities like gold and silver, and thereafter converted to conventional currency at which stage it becomes practically untraceable. The Deep Web facilitates the wholesale purchase of stolen credit cards, bank accounts, background information, national identification cards and passports often using the identification of existing individuals.[36]The prohibitive volume of illicit activity is reflected in the findings of analysts attached to Hold Security. This business concern announced in February 2014 that its search base managed to obtain as many as 360 million account credentials for web services from the black market after a mere three weeks of intense research.[37] Furthermore, the scale of terrorist linkages to surreptitious financing was openly acknowledged by Roger Wilkins, President of the Financial Action Task Force, which completed a comprehensive global intelligence report on ISIL funding during the first quarter of 2015. Wilkins remarked:

> "ISIL represents a new form of terrorist organization where funding is central and critical to its activities...Donors who provide

289

economic and material support through foreign terrorist fighters (FTFs) is a diverse and complicated area. Many of the FTFs come from a wide range of countries making this truly a global terrorist financing risk. The financing associated with FTFs is a cycle and support can take the form of self-funding for travel expenses, carrying money overseas for the benefit of ISIL, and providing funds to support these FTFs on the ground. As recent events have demonstrated returning FTFs and lone actors represent a significant terrorism threat to all countries.[38]

In so far as international drug trafficking goes, the most prominent recent example of cyber exploitation is "the Silk Road" in which its architect and founder, Ross Ulbricht, was convicted in the U.S. for drug distribution involving transactions exceeding US $1.2 billion.[39] Hilse's research unearthed the extent of exploitation of the Deep Web by transnational criminals intent on procuring an array illegal commodities and services, such as unauthorized software downloads, rocket-propelled grenades, military grade plastic explosives, access to child pornography sites carrying as much as 100 GBs and containing explicit material with instructions on successful propositioning, ranging from how to chloroform a minor to forced sodomy. Paid assassinations are reportedly also elicited through the Deep Web, in instances for as low as the equivalent of five thousand British pounds.[40]

Countervailing Responses

State-centric responses yield limited results within the setting of a 21st Century cyber-theater. Ergo, an essential constituent in the arsenal of any forward thinking government must include signals intelligence – infiltrating the adversary's communication flow electronically to make qualified decisions. In line with this, the data center in Bluffdale, Utah, an arm of the NSA, goes well beyond the world's billions of public web pages through an expanding array of theater airborne and other sensor networks to the deep net in order to retrieve data beyond the reach of the public. This includes password protected data, U.S. and foreign government communications, and non-commercial file sharing between trusted peers. Besides massive data storage acquired under the High Productivity Computing Systems Program, other capabilities deployed by the center include the codebreaking of heavily encrypted data through brute force computer attacks (a program that is projected to attain zettaflop to be followed by yottaflop speed) and accessing classified secrets of potential adversaries by employing "deep pocket" inspection of internet traffic as it passes through the 10 gigabit-per-second cables at the speed of light. This is processed with the utilization of highly sophisticated software attributed to superior technological capabilities and traded with unappeasable backers like the Israelis.[41]

To bolster all of this, the Pentagon is actively involved in expanding its worldwide communications network, the Global Information Grid, to handle yotabytes of data – the equivalent of septillion bytes – a volume so large that no one has as yet coined a term for the next higher magnitude. The justification for this capacity resides in the fact that, referencing a recent report by Cisco, global internet traffic will quadruple between 2010 to 2015, at which time it would have attained 960 exabytes per year. In 2011, more than 2 billion of the world's 6.9 billion people were reportedly connected to the internet and market research undertaken by IDC estimates that there will be 2.7 billion users by 2015. [42]

IV

Implications of the Energy Revolution for Cyber Security in the Great Power Play-off

Nonetheless the number one question remains just how vulnerable is the U.S. within its immediate approaches, particularly if China alongside crusaders of the like of Russia, North Korea and Iran are perceived as dangerous adversaries given to formidable technological capabilities, as substantiated?

A study entitled "Report on Cybersecurity and Infrastructure in the Americas," developed by Stephen Low, Professor of Computer Science and Electrical Engineering at California Institute of Technology, partially addresses the concern. The study takes note of the fact that the Americas is at the cusp of an historic transformation of its energy systems.[43] The power network from generation to transmission to distribution to consumption will undergo the same type of architectural transformation in the coming decades that computing and communications networks underwent in the preceding two decades. Dr. Low predicts that future energy systems will consist of hundreds of millions of distributed energy resources such as solar panels, wind turbines, electric vehicles, to name a few, and that these "intelligent" end points will not be merely passive loads as the end points of today, but will have the capability to generate sense, compute, communicate and activate.

291

Such quantum leaps court severe risks such as the motivations for cyber-attacks and produce inbuilt vulnerabilities. This highly respected regional expert anticipates that the transformed power network will be a materialization of the largest and most complex integration of cyber and physical networks in history. Intelligence will be embedded everywhere, from solar panels and electric vehicles to smart appliances and energy storage devices, from homes to micro-grids to sub-stations. More significant than all of this is the fact that such technological game-changers will usher new systemic predilections since despite the fact that their enhanced features are indispensable for the stability, efficiency and reliability of networks, they will create unlooked for fragility to cyber security threats. [44]

The majority of regions surveyed in the Report indicated that:

- Their ICD/SCADA equipment was being targeted by hackers, which indicated a broad amount of activity by threat actors
- Government and energy sectors are the top two industries that experience destructive attacks by threat, followed by communications, finance and banking
- Phishing was the primary threat used in targeted attacks and could be the true state of targeted-attack activities even though this was the lowest threat indicated
- Most countries feel prepared for a cyber-incident, although data in succeeding surveys was suggestive of unpreparedness for the number and sophistication of attacks and the need for improvement in detection, protection and response capabilities[45]

The Report, which analyzed the three most representative countries in the region – Argentina, Colombia and Brazil - noted that for the most part, Latin American countries were heavily committed to tracking the potential weaknesses and attacks carried out and developing countervailing responses. Each of these countries adopted different ways to deal with cybersecurity. Argentina for example, which is among the countries in the world with the highest levels of cybercrime activity, introduced a project called Open Industrial Computer. Argentina's goal is to provide computers that can work in real time to be used in industrial systems in small and medium-sized businesses that cannot afford international brands, which are also scarce. The country has created a National Program of Critical Information and Cybersecurity Infrastructures the goal of which is "driving the creation and adoption of a specific regulatory framework that promotes the identification and protection of strategic and critical infrastructures in the National Public Sector, inter-jurisdictional organizations, and civil and private organizations, and the collaboration of such sectors in order to develop appropriate strategies and structure to work together to implement a coordinated action by implementing the relevant technologies." [46]

Colombia has been embattled with the Revolutionary Armed Forces of Colombia (the FARC), an internationally listed terrorist organization for many decades, requiring the military forces and police to act in coordination with the private sector. Fortuitously, Colombia is currently in the final stages of developing a National Policy of Cybersecurity and Cyber Defense (CONPES 3701/2011) and in the process of establishing work groups comprising private organizations, the energy and communication sectors, and administrators of the co-domains to protect its critical infrastructures. The implementation of the plan will be steered by a designated Computer Emergency Response Team (colCERT) with the aid of the Spanish private sector. [47]

In Brazil, the number of industrial security incidents, particularly industrial cyber security incidents, has grown dramatically. Brazil is the largest and most digitized country of Latin America and fourth biggest internet user country in the world and approved its Internet Civil Framework in 2014. It is also one of the more heavily endowed Latin American nations in the sphere of Chinese investments, as discussed in Part I of this book. While the E.U. is the largest trade partner with Brazil with 20% of that total and China comes second with 17.2%, other Atlantic countries including the U.S. rank among Brazil's top ten trading partners – the U.S. (12.8%), Argentina (7.5%), and Mexico (2.1%). Brazil's cyber policy brief thoroughly enunciates the rights, rules and obligations for internet use and addresses data protection. [48]

In the Caribbean Community cybersecurity is an integral component in the regions "2013 Regional Crime and Security Strategy: Securing the Region" which was formally approved by the Conference of Heads of Government, the highest decision-making arm of that political and economic union. The implementation of the Strategy by Member States is proceeding at an uneven pace. The Report acknowledges that "daily functions of governments and citizens are becoming increasingly dependent on electronic networks and information systems" and that the region was "becoming more susceptible to cyber-attacks," while recognizing that regulatory systems are providing a permissive and fertile ground for damaging attacks. [49]

This critical geopolitical space is a segment of what defense planners commonly refer to as *the eastern corridor* - host to critical sea lanes that facilitate the transportation of high valued licit commodities including natural gas (emanating out of the Republic Trinidad and Tobago as a supplier to the United States) and is also renowned for a burgeoning cruise ship industry that is the commercial and economic mainstay of many island states that make up the Greater and Lesser Antillean chain. There is a corresponding need for more aggressive action beyond treaty ratification and national legislative enactments. Lending salience to this point and by its own iteration, the Report notes that "the greatest threat to the region's security and sustainable development are transnational organized crime activities involving illicit drugs and illegal guns; gangs and organized crime; cybercrime; financial crime and corruption." [50] Further to this, a nexus exists between transnational crime and terrorism in this part of the hemisphere, thereby escalating its vulnerability to cyber-attacks emanating from any one among a diverse array of subnational actors.[51]

Beyond doubt, increasing reliance on computer networks has made host nations in the Americas, including the United States, more attractive as targets for terrorists. Furthermore, the cyber networks that control and optimize the physical networks will greatly amplify the scale, speed and complexity of cyber-attacks as well as quicken and broaden failure propagation on the physical networks, making blackout mitigation much more difficult. Because China has invested heavily in the Western Hemisphere, particularly in nations of Europe, in the United States and across Latin America and the Caribbean, pragmatism should prevail. This implies that the issues should at best be hashed out from the standpoint of fostering each country's vested economic and political interests rather than unchecked rivalry in a zero sum game.

Conclusion

This chapter exposes the extent to which the rise of computer and information assets has precipitated a broad spectrum of threats and an equally broad range of capabilities and the fact that in the prevailing global landscape the motivation of adversaries in cyberspace can vary from the mere demonstration of technical prowess to scoring economic, political and diplomatic advantage. In combination, these issues transcend the U.S. – China contestation. The chapter also demonstrates the serious implications for the U.S., China and greater and lesser global players in the absence of regulatory and governance systems that are recognized and upheld by all nations as well as the fact that multilateralism is the most viable way ahead. No country can confront these issues better unilaterally and all countries should advisedly exploit opportunities made possible by international cooperation.

In sum, cyber-attacks may involve commodity capability by making use of tools and techniques that are openly available and simple to access. Alternatively, attacks may employ bespoke capabilities developed and deployed for specific purposes, including malicious codes (exploits) that take advantage of software vulnerabilities - bugs not known to vendors or anti-malware companies, otherwise referred to as "zero-day exploits." Attacks may be targeted or untargeted. Targeted attacks can range from phishing, water holing, ransomware and scanning; untargeted attacks could include spear phishing, deployment of botnet and subverting the supply chain. An unanticipated development with wide-ranging implications was the Ed Snowden incident of 2013, which raised the specter of insider threats. Insiders (anyone with access to systems, such as an employee or contractor) therefore ought to be considered as part of a holistic security regime since penetration of a host may be attained by social engineering i.e. persuading unwary or unguarded persons to breach security procedures or by employing technical skills. The chapter then calls attention to the unfolding stagecraft - ideas, ideologies, agents and instrumentalities - that define international terrorism and the simultaneous onset of fifth generation warfare that is tantamount to the colonization by brute force of inner space. This is the ultimate hallmark of omnipresence.

The trend towards greater diffusion of technology, the erosion of the nation state and the proliferation of dangerous substate actors, inimical in many instances to the U.S. and China alike, has contributed in no small measure to an already fragmented international system and shrinking world, rendering it increasingly vulnerable to attacks that defy all known frontiers. The phenomenon is one of growing concern not only for the future of state relations and direction of future diplomacy, but also for human survival. The inquiry recognizes that developed nations such as the U.S. and U.K. are pursuing cooperative multilateral solutions and multipronged, multi-tiered approaches to cyber threats and employing a whole-of-government approach, with directed focus on the roles of their respective defense, intelligence and enforcement communities. China should advisedly throw its gauntlet in the ring as a global, hemispheric and regional partner in combating this potentially universal menace, which in the view of this book calls for shared responsibility.

On a more optimistic tenor, the inquiry notes that the Inter-American system - which the PRC has successfully impregnated by virtue of its hefty investments in the diplomatic, economic, social and cultural spheres and more specifically in business, banking, telecommunications and critical infrastructure – provides a fine example of best practices, all worthy of emulation. Through relevant OAS organs there have been pro-active approaches on multiple fronts to manage and regulate the cyber domain.

Thus far, it is apparent that very many of cyber-attacks making news headlines and affecting the day-to-day lives of ordinary folk do not necessarily impact on State sovereignty but the imminence of mass casualties is nonetheless real. Compounding this, a precedent has been set for the use of cyber sabotage by one State or group of States against another and this raises the stakes in terms of long-term implications on political, jurisprudential and diplomatic considerations. Ipso facto, this inquiry calls urgent attention to the underlisted scenarios, all fact-based, that will shape 21ˢᵗ Century debates and command an exceptional menu of newfangled experimentations in yet-to-be-tested spheres of public diplomacy:

- The implications of forestalling impending news releases that are considered inimical to a nation's interests through the instrumentality of technical attacks on the IT infrastructure of private corporations or state institutions of the host country. Should nations take it upon themselves to censor content available to their own citizenry, as often obtains, it is conceivable that they will seek to censor their critics overseas as well.
- The need to prescribe minimum criteria for what constitutes a threat to a nation's national security and what can be deemed "an act of war" and serve as a possible basis for collective zero tolerance retaliation. Examples of such scenarios are: an attack on a government's infrastructure that could paralyze its functionality; or one that may be viewed as a threat to sovereignty; or one that can be construed as the erosion of a state's ability to maintain self-governance and protect its borders.
- The use of a cyber-attack against the backdrop of non-kinetic warfare in order to effect industrial sabotage on a subject (be it a government or non-state actor) deemed an adversary.
- The pernicious course of conduct – tantamount to "internationally wrongful acts" - among the growing body of internationally dispersed non-state actors, who subsequently claim attribution for facets of their activities that place civilian populations in harm's way and

whose actions are sanctioned, either purposefully or through complicity and surreptitiousness, by state actors.

- Possible ambiguities that can arise in the event that countries misattribute an attack, and in so doing, unduly retaliate or exacerbate a crisis; or alternatively are unable to attribute an attack, thereby preventing or delaying warranted reprisal or weakening their deterrence capability.

- Possible ambiguities that can arise in determining the rationale for an attack, thereby complicating a government's ability to decipher between outright espionage as distinct from precursory steps being taken for a cyber-attack.

CHAPTER TWELVE

AGGRANDIZEMENT UNMASKED

"The very multinational and exceptional nature of American society has made it easier for America to universalize its hegemony without letting it appear to be a strictly national one....To put it very simply, anyone can become an American, but only a Chinese can be Chinese---and that places an additional and significant barrier in the way of any essentially national global hegemony."

Zbigniew Brzezinski

he exponential changes undergone in the military in the realm of technology, lightweight and durability, miniaturized systems, precision-intelligent warfare, the proclivity currently displayed in irregular warfare for deploying unmanned weapons, increased lethality, and attempts to minimize collateral damage as we have seen in the previous chapter, are synonymous with the more sophisticated war-fighting modes that America has carved for herself on the global landscape. While China on the one hand has locked herself to a mindset that holds a steady gaze on numbers, size, and scale, the U.S. has migrated into efficiencies of scale that necessarily compel de-scaling to avoid mass casualties, while simultaneously exploiting the full advantages of stealth and inner space.

Amidst a trail of aggrandizement and seemingly obsessive pursuit, the Chinese have launched plans to build five aircraft carrier flotillas—three conventional and two nuclear powered by 2020[1]— and initial assembly work has commenced in Shanghai's Changxingdao Shipyard. Commensurate with this largesse, they have instituted a fleet-wide "flag upgrade" in anticipation of the much touted sea trials of her first aircraft carrier- reckoning that the size and configuration of the current naval ensign was regulated into use in the 1950s and is presently not proportional to the tonnage of new generation vessels and the Navy's increasing engagement with the foreign affairs of the country.[2]

Character of Western (European) Imperialism

Nowhere have the criteria of size, scale and proportionality defied conventional wisdom as in the historical narrative of European imperialism, more specifically Great Britain. Prior to industrialization in Western Europe major empire building initiatives had mushroomed out of Asia from among the Persians, Arabs, Chinese, Indians, and steppe-landers (such as the Mongol) which expanded by land into territories bordering on those of the conquerors. Chinese rulers, in sharp distinction, never sent their fleets beyond the Indian Ocean; neither did they deploy their land forces beyond Central Asia. Alongside these empires, smaller imperial ventures also set out to control trade rather than production and to dominate sea lanes and harbors rather than large expanses of land. This was the essential character of European imperialism in respect of which Britain had established an early lead. [3]

Central to Great Britain's primacy was its long-term vision of the world and the strategic maneuvers it would employ in the aggressive pursuit of this vision. To this we append the adroit combination of naval mastery, financial credit, commercial expertise and alliance diplomacy. Of further significance is the fact that unlike China and America, the country had been superbly successful in the pre-industrial mercantilist struggles of the eighteenth century and its pace of change was gradual rather than revolutionary.

Vision and Strategy

Following the defeat of Napoleon in 1815, the British government had already begun to think globally, locating colonies in strategic positions along the world's trade routes. This global impetus was, at times, taken to the extremes as demonstrated in the under-listed onslaughts:

- Launching an unsuccessful invasion of the River Plate region of South America
- Fighting the war of 1812 to check the ambitions of the United States
- Exploiting these wars to wrest colonies from France, Spain, and Holland intending to seize useful stations to control global communications by sea, including Malta and other Mediterranean Islands, South Africa, parts of the Dutch Indies, French islands in the Indian Ocean, islands and coastal positions in and around the Caribbean

No such vision of global projection was held at that time by any other government, not the least of which was China, which was by all accounts still very much self-absorbed and barely aware of events in the wider world. In support of this argument Mitchell et McGiffert (2007) affirm that while China "has historically had substantial and productive interactions with peoples and cultures beyond its borders, Imperial China's external relations through the centuries were infused more with alienation than with outreach. Its policy and perspective towards the outside world were closely hitched to its cultural heritage, its unique geopolitical situation and the imperative to attend to endemic internal challenges.[5]"

Moreover, the country's Confucian outlook, to which we alluded to in Chapter Two and its perennial concerns over the vulnerability of its periphery to external challenges, concerns over domestic turmoil—if not dissolution—and more, had all but fueled China's defensive approach to external relations.

According to Bairoch's "International Industrialization Levels" between 1760 and 1830 Great Britain was responsible for around two-thirds of Europe's industrial growth of output and its share of the world's manufacturing production leaped from 1.3 to 9.5 %[6]. In the next 30 years that followed British industrial expansion would push to a figure of 19.9% despite the spread of new technology to other countries in the west. By 1860, Britain had reached its zenith in relative terms, producing 52% of the world's iron and 50% of its coal and ignite, consuming just under half of the raw cotton output of the globe. Other endowments included 2% of the world's population and 10% of Europe's, with a capacity in modern industries equaling 40 to 45% of the world's potential and 50 to 60% of Europe's. Added to this, the energy consumption of Britain from coal, lignite and oil by 1860 was five times that of either the United States or Prussia/Germany, six times that of France, and one hundred and 55 times that of Russia. Furthermore, Britain boasted one- fifth of the world's commerce, two-fifths of the trade in manufactured goods, and in terms of dominion, over one-third of the world's merchant marine were flying under the British flag.[4]

This enterprising global projection was attained neither by weight of numbers nor by force of superior technology, but rather by the Crown's employment of direct and indirect rule. Britain's ascension to world power was to the credit of a clearly articulated long-term vision backed by a clever and flexible strategy. Filipe-Fernandez Arnesto in The World: A Global History illustrates that in the 1890s there were fewer than 1,000 British administrators in India, a country of 300 million people and British troops in India never numbered more than 90,000 men – 0.03 percent of the Indian population[7] The key to colonization was indirect rule "through the natives," and the most common device was harnessing cooperation.

Thus, the elicitation of consent tended to override the more formalized modes of control[8]

A second strategy employed by the British, and which further diminishes the significance of size and scale, is economic control. At a time when the world was becoming increasingly divided between primary producers and industrial manufacturers, interregional trade was vital. This mode of trade opened a wealth gap between primary and secondary producers, thereby permitting the rich of industrialized countries surplus capital with which to buy up the productive capacity of much of the rest of the world.

It is significant that Latin America registered the most obvious effects of this trend and by the second half of the nineteenth century foreign investors had become a powerful extra elite tier in Latin American society, the effects of which are still visible today. These investors were primarily Europeans from the major imperial powers: Britain, Germany, France, and the United States. Although the Monroe Doctrine of 1823 effectively placed a ban on European colonialism, a move that garnered support from the European powers, its restraints were circumvented through business imperialism, which turned out to be a collaborative project between the local elites and foreign capitalists. In the case of Latin America, British investments rose from $425 million in 1870 to $3,785 million by 1913, amounting to two-thirds of foreign investment in the region.[9] While the British were exerting power and influence in the coffee market, local authorities were demanding high levels of investment in addition to a high share of the yield for themselves. Another case in point was Chile where, by 1884, Europeans owned two-thirds of indigenous nitrates, the fertilizers of choice during that period. Costa Rica was also a preferred locale for imperial control through investment and profiteering. Arnesto expounds that the government of Costa Rica "contracted out its railway building program to an engineer from the United States following which his nephew used the railway to ship bananas to North America.[10]" Further to this, "his (the nephew's) firm eventually grew into the United Fruit Company—a conglomerate so rich and monopolistic that it became more powerful in the early twentieth century than any government in Central America.[11]"

This status quo was corroborated by Carroll Quigley, professor of history at the Foreign Service School of Georgetown University and former lecturer at Princeton and Harvard, who noted that four-fifths of the population of Latin America earned about $53 a year in the 1960s while a mere one hundred families held title for nine-tenths of the native-owned wealth of the whole area – the equilibrium being the most conspicuous in landholding.[12]

A third and final facet of global projection that subordinates the relevance of scalability is to stoke disillusionment and destabilize pockets of power. This is exemplified in the U.S. policy towards Venezuela which has taken a series of tactical turns within the preceding ten year period, with the clear intention being the dislodging of the administration, and reversing the Bolivarian revolution.

Washington has given backing to interests aimed at dislodging the regime, reputedly through lending patronage to the 2002 military coup; stoking forces behind the labor unrest in 2002-2003 thereby triggering a referendum, and egging on the local media and non-governmental organizations with the objective of abrading unpopular government policies. When efforts to co-opt collaborators failed, a medium to long-term outreach strategy got underway. This included the devising of a "cordon militaire," that is to say, surrounding Venezuela with a U.S. troop presence comprising bases and forward operating locations spanning Central America, the northern part of South America, and the Caribbean.

Notably, it is the very technology that has been developed in "the West" that China is currently deriving benefit from and at a pace that is clearly designed to outstrip the attainments of its unevenly matched competitor.

Fernandez-Arnesto notes with less than concealed temerity "...the allure of Western science proved irresistible...Western military technology won wars. Western industrial technology multiplied food and wealth. Information systems devised in the West revolutionized communications, business, leisure, education and methods of social and political control.[13] Furthermore, what Western science did was offer to the rest of the world, including the Chinese, a "promise of infallibility.[14] Along with this promise, however arguable, was a sense of certainty since "it matched observation, fulfilled predictions and withstood tests." In contradistinction, Chinese self-strengthening was infused with its lingering mistrust for foreigners, a fact that contributed somewhat to the restraining effects of delayed contact, and by extension, in the longer term to Western intellectual influence.

Imperial China was generally self-sufficient in natural resources, a condition that predisposed it to spur any attempt to compete with other nations to sustain its power or legitimacy. Seething discontent over western hegemony and over historical humiliations at the hands of the British during the Opium Wars propelled a redirection and kindled an irrepressible quest for grandeur of past empire. The appeal of modernization, more so, the desire to hobnob with the global inner circle of power have pricked China on to world leadership.

TABLE - 11 -1
CHRONOLOGY OF IMPERIAL DYNASTIES AND GOVERNMENTS OF CHINA
CULMINATING WITH THE PEOPLE'S REPUBLIC OF CHINA

Dynasty	Years
Xia Dynasty	2206-1766 BCE
Shang Dynasty	1766-1122 BCE
Zhou Dynasty	1122-770 BCE
Spring and Autumn Period	770-476 BCE
Warring States Period	476-221 BCE
Qin Dynasty	221-206 BCE
Han Dynasty	206 BCE-220 CE
Three Kingdoms Period	220-265 CE
Jin Dynasty	265-420 CE
Northern and Southern Dynasties	420-581 CE
Sui Dynasty	581-618 CE
Tang Dynasty	618-907 CE
Five Dynasties and Ten Kingdoms	907-960 CE
Song Dynasty	960-1279 CE
Northern Song	960-1127 CE
Southern Song	1127-1279 CE
Liao (Khitan) Dynasty	916-1125 CE
Jin (Jurchen) Dynasty	1115-1234 CE
Yuan (Mongol) Dynasty	1279-1368 CE
Ming Dynasty	1368-1644 CE
Qing (Manchu) Dynasty	1644-1911 CE
*Republic of China	1912-present
People's Republic of China	1949-present

*Relocated to Taiwan in 1949

SOURCE: Adopted from "China and the Developing World": Expanding the Strategic Periphery p.5 Mitchell and McGiffert 2007. [15]

PART IV

OVERVIEW

$\mathcal{T}$he Realist tradition examines relationships among men dating back to the beginnings of recorded history. Among its more distinguished adherents, was Hans Morgenthau, widely regarded as the precursor to classical Realism. Morgenthau's model of international affairs, as expounded in his work <u>Politics among Nations</u>, conflates two different processes. One associates the balance of power with the unintended outcome of great powers engaged in a mechanistic drive for hegemony; the other promotes a dynamic of ideational and material factors that ameliorate the effects of the first dynamic and assists the great powers in maintaining an equilibrium that promotes their collective security and common interests.

Of interest in Morgenthau's work is his conception of the balance of power matrix that evolved in the twentieth century in a bipolar world. He noted that when America and Russia dominated the world stage, each power was able to expand its territorial base rather unobtrusively while not taking a very active part in the balance of power. The long-term consequence of this trend was that late in the twentieth century both nations were continental in scale and from a territorial perspective, dwarfed other states of the world system. With the dissolution of the Soviet Union, a bipolar global system gave way to a unipolar one, with the U.S assuming premiership. Other centers of power have since emerged.

Morgenthau's analysis of multi-polar reconfigurations brings to light the following trends:

- Firstly, in a multi-polar system the defection of one state from an alliance can have alarming consequences on the distribution of power and accordingly in the given scheme small states now have a more significant role to play than previously
- Secondly, states are unwilling to operate without the support of allies despite the fact that they could never be certain that allies would stay on the same side
- Thirdly, because alliances tend to be fluid in a multi-polar system, so too is the distribution of power. The corollary to this is that multi-polarity is associated with a high degree of uncertainty, thereby encouraging states to exercise more caution in their estimations and policy formulations
- Finally, whereas in a bipolar system, a major shift in the distribution of power is highly unlikely, particularly when states are relatively small ones, a

move from one alliance to another is more likely to occur in an environment of multi-polarity with often dire consequences on the overall "balance"

A further conclusion drawn by Morganthau is based on the time-tested notion that "to be politically pertinent, power has to be defined in terms of the distribution of capabilities" and consequentially, that "an agent is powerful to the extent that he affects others more than they affect him." These precepts endure in the international setting, as presently configured.

What we are witnessing today in the international system where powers seek to ally in order to preserve their own interests is the emergence of a number of players that are not necessarily powers. Further to this and owing to the overriding interests of larger and more influential nations, such as the U.S. and China, these diverse players are exercising more flexibility to gain advantage and whatever political mileage they could accrue.

Justice is Only a Question of Equals in Power

Another view espoused by mainstream Realists is that survival and security are/should be the most important factors considered in the policies of and among states and that the primary consideration in accomplishing these goals is the relative power of nations in the international arena. In The History of the Peloponnesian War Thucydides depicts a dialogue between Athens (a democracy that operated a strong naval empire and dominated many of the cities along the Adriatic and Aegean seas) and the Melians (a colony from Sparta that had consistently refused to join the Athenian Empire). The Melians appealed to the Athenians for their right to neutrality and the latter, who are likened to the present day American Empire, promptly responded by educating their rivals on how righteousness is determined and dispensed in international affairs.

In the most derisive of tones the Athenians quipped:

> "...right, as the world goes, is only in question between equals in power... [and] of the gods we believe and of men we know, that by a necessary law of nature, they rule wherever they can..."

The underlying principle is that the standard of justice exercisable among the nations of the world depends on the quality of power to compel, and in fact the strong do what they have the power to do, and the weak accept what they have to accept. This irrepressible cannon propels the motivation and conduct of great powers of yesteryear and today.

More Globalized and Increasingly Segmented World

Thus far we have taken note of the forces that have disgorged the two foremost contenders - China and America - in their ultimate struggle for world domination. At this stage of the discourse a very important element that is defining and distinguishing the international global order is put forward - the thrust of global change and its impact on the world's political systems. In terms of change, although the world is becoming more globalized, it is simultaneously assuming an increasingly segmented and complex character. This fact is impacting upon on the relative sway held by the two major powers.

Who Holds the Reins of Power?

Another phenomenon worthy of attention is the fact that we are now witnessing the nascent stages of a global economic recovery (relative to banks and corporations) that trails the 2008 - 2009 downturn and this has prompted two very important questions. The first is - Who ultimately holds the reins of power? The second is closely akin to the former - How is this power being brokered and balanced in an international setting in which new and emerging contenders among which are both state and non-state actors, making calculable inroads into the global economic system? Confronted with this type of debate globalization and multi-polarity thus become important catalysts in the context of the Sino-America dynamic.

Historical Parallels and Divergences Unique to This Era

This section of our discourse therefore also concerns itself with historical parallels and divergences that make this epoch a distinct one. The post-World War II period saw the ushering in of a period in which global dominance was no longer shared primarily among European imperial powers. The American experience was also contradistinctive in that what followed after World War II, politically speaking, was noticeably divergent from past experiences in several ways elaborated on below:

Firstly, following the war, America had the capacity to shape a new world order and proceeded to do so in a manner that was far different in design from that of the "old Europe". The thinking was that if America had to lay the groundwork for everlasting world peace the nineteenth century conception that such a road to peace was best prescribed by a well-poised balance of power system, had to be discarded. (Graham, 1948. P.271). Thus the preservation of international peace became an enterprise that took root in the United Nations and Bretton Woods institutions that were set up specifically to maintain international peace, ensure financial and monetary stability, and foster the reconstruction of war-torn economies – all of this was against the backdrop of the U.S. dollar as the international exchange and reserve currency.

The second factor was the resolve of the Americans to establish a new global order. The idea was by no means exclusive to that country. Certainly the Soviets were of a similar mind although the order to which they committed was ideologically contra-distinctive to the model that the U.S. was prepared to promote. At the core of the U.S. doctrine was neo-liberalism, which was characterized by a move to open markets, low state intervention, free movement of capital and goods and the privatization of previously nationalized industries. These conditions permitted the flourishing of transnational and multinational corporations and precast the macro-economic template employed by the said Bretton Wood entities in which the U.S. enjoyed a disproportionately high stake, namely the International Monetary Fund, the World Bank, and the World Trade Organization. To date, neo-liberal values continue at the core of economic globalization and have been increasingly popular among western governments following World War II.

A third variable that sets the American experience apart from that of preceding global powers is that the U.S. has developed a weapons system with the potential for global destruction, a move that the USSR quickly sought to match through its technological capabilities in every sphere, including space exploration. The defeat of the National Socialists, coupled with the subsequent annexation of Germany in 1945 made such developments irreversible. Later on as rivalries clashed in the world's historical corridors during the 1950s, Nikita Khrushchev set the Soviet ideological footprint, while vaunting:

> *"The creative forces of the masses of people are pouring forth from thousands of springs throughout the whole country. The triumphant flights of Soviet men into outer space the first in human history, are like a crown of splendid victories, a banner of communist constitution raised high."*

Such radical distinctions had to be addressed within a balance of power framework that is today riddled with a fresh set of challenges posed by rapid globalization. This thrust has brought about fresh demands for a more effective global governance framework and indirectly bridles some of the ambitions of China and America in their wrestle for ultimate sway.

A fourth factor was the emergence of the European Union through the collaboration of nations in a bid to create a United States of Europe - a project that has been in the making since the end of the Second World War. This grand scheme was fueled by several factors, the primary being the desire to prevent another cataclysmic war from engulfing Europe. The second was equally pertinent - the fact that Europe was not content with being relegated to the status of a subordinate partner to the United States and that by the same token no single nation within Europe would be likely to emerge as a successful challenger to U.S primacy. A Union, conceptually at least, from the perspective of the Europeans (many of which were former powers in their own right), would serve to diffuse this shared concern.

American and European Banking and Financial Systems

The emergence of a European Parliament provided an ostensibly unified counterweight that could serve the interests of those countries who fathomed themselves as "the new Europe". The Parliament held its first Session as a Common Assembly on July 07, 1979. History is an unforgiving ally and recent events have seen a resurgence of long-held values embedded in old alliances, as national interests are ceded to established banks and multinational corporations.

Perhaps the most ambitious arrangement to have ensued from the Union was the creation of a single currency that would dominate a common market within Europe itself. The implications of this arrangement—which the British have steadfastly avoided—are that countries must trade in a common currency. Thus, the concept of a single currency makes it extremely difficult for any single member country to manipulate its local currency for monetary purposes without exacting adverse consequences on other members of the Union. The European Central Bank now controls the currency in Europe and in terms of powers and responsibilities, is assuredly the equivalent of the Federal Reserve in the United States. Prior to this arrangement each country in Europe was at liberty to manipulate its own currency against those of other members of the Union and the rest of the world.

Europe's Unification has sparked a new wave of intraregional rivalries.

The pact under the unified currency agreement stipulated that prices throughout the Union should be raised by the same amount, the target being 2%, and that furthermore, countries would pay their workers a rising wage roughly commensurate with productivity levels. It is therefore noteworthy that despite the fact that prices in Spain, Italy, Greece and Portugal rose in excess of 2%, the wages of workers were equivalently maintained consistent with the policy of the Union.

Germany, demurred, choosing instead a maverick-styled alacrity that saw it abrogating the agreement stipulated by the European Union. Firstly, the labor unions collaborated with both the Social Democratic Party and Christian Democratic Union (CDU) in the opposition to hold prices below what obtained in other parts of Europe. Secondly (and similar to what presently obtains in the United States), as productivity outstripped wages, workers were not paid corresponding wage increases. This meant that the cost of German goods and services was highly competitive when compared with the rest of Europe, and that it was more profitable to do business in Germany that in other part of the continent.

That being the case, there were other pertinent underlying factors that precipitated the Eurozone crisis. On the systemic level, the southern European countries were beset with higher taxes, a disproportionately large trove of regulations, higher wage levels and the shift of foreign direct investment funds away from Mediterranean jurisdictions to recently admitted Eastern European, former communist countries. Additionally, the northern economies were clearly ahead of the southerners economically speaking. For instance according to World Bank estimates all the northern economies of Europe rank among the top 15 countries of a total of 183 cited by the Bank as preferred venues for doing Business. Of these Sweden ranks the lowest at fourteenth.

Compounding this are identified systemic issues within the Union, the foremost of which were cited in a policy brief entitled The Euro Crisis and The New Impossible Trinity. Its author—Jean Pisani-Ferry—identified three irresolvable variables, which in his estimation lay at the root of the crisis, namely strict non-monetary financing; bank sovereign interdependence; and no co-responsibility for public debt. The other systemic issue of concerns, and which was pinpointed by the World Bank, was the notable slowdown in labor productivity with respect to southern Europe. Illustrative of this between 2002-2008, while Eastern Europe was accelerating to keep apace with the northerners, productivity actually plummeted among the countries in the south, specifically Spain, Portugal, Greece, and Italy. Last and by no means least is what is regarded as a distinctly European tradition. Whereas a substantial amount of investment in the United States is directed towards defense spending, a comparatively high social welfare program sustains European countries across the board, which is aimed at sustaining a minimum standard of living. Indebtedness and bankruptcy are therefore logical ramifications of excessive government spending, complicated by unwillingness on the part of governments to set up an efficient tax code.

The Aldrich Plan

Equally noteworthy is the fact that the Central Bank in Europe along with affiliated banking and the financial services industry are hooked up at the top tier to their U.S. counterpart, the U.S Federal Reserve. Spurred by his impressions of the European banking system, gathered while visiting Europe, Rhode Island Republican Senator Nelson Aldrich, along with a team of economists formulated proposals in 1912 to introduce a similar model in the United States. It was Aldrich's conviction that a central bank in America had to be contradictorily decentralized to avoid interference from politicians and bankers, as had the First and Second Banks of the United States.

The European Central Bank (ECB), as of today, remains completely independent, and by extension commandeered by parochial interests, as we shall demonstrate. Neither the national central banks of the Euro system nor any of the decision-making bodies (the Executive Board, Governing Council, General Council) can ask or accept instructions from any other body. This principle is assiduously upheld and adhered to by all European institutions and governments.

By all indications, the autonomy of the Federal Reserve in the United States has likewise endured. In a PBS News Hour Interview aired on September 18 2007, Jim Lehrer enquired of Al Greenspan, former Chairman of the U.S. Federal Reserve as to the nature of the relationship between the Fed and the U.S. government. His response is as follows:

"Well, first of all, the Federal Reserve is an independent agency, and that means basically that there is no other agency of government which can overrule actions that we take. So long as that is in place and there is no evidence that the administration or the Congress or anybody else is requesting that we do things other than what we think is the appropriate thing then what the relationships are don't, frankly matter. And I've had very good relationships with presidents."

Gauging from Greenspan's remarks, executive authority is not and cannot be exercised over the U.S. Federal Reserve. This historical exclusivity coupled with the interconnectivity with other Central Banks leaves much to speculation regarding (a) whose interests are ultimately promoted by this syndicate (b) what is in fact the role of these outfits as major creditors of the most powerful governments in the world and (c) to what extent is their influence being brought to bear on monetary policy.

Despite the apparent independence of private investment banks from mainstream politics and their ostensible detachment from the "nitty-gritty" of day-to-day decision-making, they exude the following characteristics:

- Their closeness to the center of political life and capacity to maintain the best possible relations with leading political figures
- Speed in receiving news of events on states ranging from a change in ministry to a revolution coupled with the uncanny ability to manipulate the transmission of news among the world's biggest investors
- The capacity to maintain a network of highly influential salaried agents whose job it is to ensure that their interests are best served through their appointments in strategic positions in the world's top corporate and political institutions

Their enduring and triumphal modus operandi and elevated style are captured in the words of Karl Ferdinand Graf von Buol-Schauenstein, diplomat and Foreign Minister of Austria from 1852 to 1859, during the Crimean War. In speaking about the House of Rothschild, arguably the world's wealthiest and most powerful investment bankers, Schauenstein makes the following claim:

"...The House has, through its enormous financial transactions and its banking and credit connections actually achieved the position of a real Power; it has to such an extent acquired control of the general money market that it is in a position, either to hinder or to promote, as it feels inclined, through its movements and operations of potentates, and even of the greatest European powers..."

Today N.M. Rothschild and Sons advises on some of the most high-profiled corporate restructurings in the world and is consistently ranked among the top 10 global investment banks for mergers and acquisitions. In 2011 Rothschild scored as the sixth biggest mergers and acquisitions advisor for completed deals worldwide. Equally noteworthy is the role played by the bankers in fixing the price of gold. Twice daily the price of gold was, until a few years ago, fixed at the Rothschild's New Court Headquarters in London by the world's top bullion houses – the Deutsche Bank, HSBC, Scotia Mocatta, and Societe Generale. Gold fixing has historically provided a recognized rate that is used as a benchmark for providing the majority of gold products and derivatives throughout the world's markets. The firm is particularly strong in Europe especially in the United Kingdom, France, Germany, Italy and the Benelux countries as well as throughout North and South America and the Caribbean. In each country where subsidiaries have been established Rothschild holds a top league position.

Most countries have some form of central bank that serves as the principal authority for the nation's financial matters. Besides implementing a monetary policy that provides consistent growth and employment and promoting the stability of the country's financial system, another major role of these institutions is to supply the operational capital to commercial banks by offering short-term loans.

Central banks are also there to ensure that the banking system has sufficient liquidity for businesses, for individual consumers desirous of borrowing money, and for the availability of credit, which in turn has a direct impact on business and consumer spending. By leveraging the relationship between short-term loans and the interest rates charged by the banks, Central Banks can influence the cost to the public of borrowing money. Additionally, if for some reason the central bank feels that more consumers spending is needed to stimulate the economy, it can lower short-term rates when providing loans to commercial banks. Conversely, the Bank can increase rates and thereby make loans more expensive to acquire with the aim of bringing about an overall reduction in spending.

Despite the fact that globalization has delivered more benefits than any other force in the recent past, the type of hyper-connectivity hitherto described is increasing in intensity and precipitating greater systemic risks. Interdependence implies constraints and one such constraint is that interests at national and local levels are not necessarily aligned with the decision-making process at global level. A major challenge therefore is how best states configure themselves to benefit from hyper-connectivity on so massive a scale.

CHAPTER THIRTEEN

UNBRIDLED FINANCIAL DEBAUCHERY
OR THE DEBT TRAP

"Power itself always exists in concentrated forms. In any organization it is inevitable for a small group to hold the strings. And often it is not those with the titles. In the game of power only the fool flails about without fixing his targets. You must find out who controls the operations, who is the real director behind the scenes."

Robert Greene

*D*ebt is deeply ingrained in human civilization. The language of debt is interwoven with matters of ethics, social contracts, community, familial, as well as other forms of social relations. However the problem arises when the day-to-day sociological application of the concept is usurped by a band of wily financiers who use debt as a perennial tool to subject people, governments, and nation states to interminable peonage. In effect, financiers use debt to capitalize on the commodification of human beings. Furthermore, the very flexibility of the concept is the basis for its power.

On the one hand, debt can be a victor's justice and on the other it can also be a way of punishing winners and on this basis has a long and checkered history in the sphere of geopolitics. Take for example, Haiti, which is well-known among the poorest countries in the world according to World Bank estimates, juxtaposed with the United States, which continues to hold premiership among the world's economies. Each in its own way is archetypical of the principle.

Having dared to rise up in rebellion amidst declarations of universal rights and freedoms and defeated the armies of Napoleon, France insisted that the new and liberated Haitian Republic of former plantation slaves owed it 150 million francs in damages for expropriated plantations and out-fittings for failed military exploitations. This sum was contrived and calculated in a manner that rendered it impossible to repay. Further to this, an embargo was imposed forthwith with the full support of other nations, including the U.S.

The narrative of the United States as a debtor, on the other hand, is compellingly different. Starting in the 1980s, the U.S had accrued debt that easily dwarfed that of the entire Third World, although America insisted on the strictest of terms for the repayment of Third World debt. America's foreign debt takes the form of treasury bonds held by institutional investors in countries like Germany, Japan, South Korea, Taiwan, Thailand and the Gulf States – jurisdictions that are effectively U.S. protectorates, adequately endowed U.S bases, and generously replenished with arms and ammunition paid for by funds derived from the very deficit spending.

There is a matter of opinion that the current debt crisis and credit crunch triggered within first world economies is a karmic effect of massive scale that trails the experiences of third world economies in places like Latin America and the Caribbean during the oil crisis of the 1970s. During that period, members of OPEC unleashed their freshly acquired monies onto Western banks that were at a loss as to how best to funnel these exorbitant cash flows.

Professor David Graeber, anthropologist, social and political activist, and author of Debt: The First 5000 Years analyses the function of debt in human history by tracing it from its early origins to modern economic crises.[1] He is severely critical of modern-day capitalism and questions many orthodox notions about the free market and the concept of money. He recalls how banks of the first world had sent their agents into third world countries with the intention of luring their political leaders (many of whom were dictators and politicians) to take out loans at highly competitive rates of interest. These rates skyrocketed shortly after the deals were made to figures in the vicinity of 20 percent as a result of stringent U.S. monetary policies introduced in the 1980s and 1990s. This course of action triggered what is historically referred to as 'the third world debt crisis.'

What defined that historical juncture was the insistence of the International Monetary Fund (the policies of which are strongly influenced by the U.S. government) that in order for affected countries to obtain refinancing they must be obligated to abandon price supports such as government subsidies on basic foodstuffs and suspend their state-funded social services such as education and health care. These harsh prerequisites for refinancing debt precipitated widespread social unrest, unemployment, poverty, endemic violence, malnutrition and a trail of 'broken lives' in relevant countries.

Contemporary thinkers such as Ivelaw Griffith, Hilbourne Watson, and Bernal, Lamar who noted that debt of itself was constraining structural adjustment within beleaguered Caribbean economies, provide a corroborative account of this economic debacle:

"The cumulative impact of all these structural reform measures is the increasing numbers of people joining the ranks of the poor, aggravating the competition for access to government scarce resources...Poverty in the Caribbean is now extensive, and presents a major challenge for countries in the region..."[2-4]

First and foremost, it must be recognized that bankers are responsible for the creation of crises for one reason. They make their money by creating debt and inducing others to become indebted.[5] One of the ploys adopted by banks to bring this about is the creation of asset price bubbles – an economic cycle characterized by a surge in equity prices, often more than warranted by the fundamentals, and usually in a particular sector, followed by a drastic drop in prices as massive sell-offs occur. This change in behavior that instigates a bubble is the defining feature of an economic cycle. Thus, when Japanese banks were deregulated in the 1980s and when the dotcom boom blasted off in the early 2000s, there was widespread speculation that stocks would surge in a particular area that could earn clients a higher price than what they originally purchased. Ultimately, confidence in these markets was lost causing a drastic drop in prices and as the free fall occurred, there were massive sell-offs.

Operations of Financial Services Industry Vis-à-vis Credit Crunch

The shadow banking system involves the facilitation of credit across the global financial system by entities that are not subject to regulatory oversight. Shadow banking has been able to escape regulatory requirements primarily because these operations do not accept bank deposits. Consequentially, many institutions and instruments were able to employ higher market credit and liquidity risks in the absence of any capital that was commensurate with those risks. The shadow banking system only became subjected to intense scrutiny following the sub-prime mortgage crisis in 2008.

The 2008-2009 economic downturn was rooted historically in three principal factors each of which took a severe toll on the global economy. The first is the fractional reserve banking system, which for purposes of this discourse may be referred to as the first cause. The second is a derivative of the former system and is referred to as re-hypothecation. These concepts will be expanded on in some detail later in our enquiry. The third is the coming on stream of financial innovations hand in hand with the derivatives markets in the US between 1973-2009 and the simultaneous deregulation of derivatives through legislative enactment.

ᅳ

Recent History of Financial Innovations

The shock of 2008-2009 and continuing aftershocks can be traced directly to the close succession of financial innovations that rolled out from as far back as the 1970s when mortgaged-backed securities were introduced for the first time. The 1972 Chicago Currency Futures Market and the 1973 Chicago Board Options Exchange closely followed. In 1975, trading in treasury bills and mortgage-backed bond futures were introduced followed by trading in Treasury bond futures in 1977. Within two years of these developments, the market saw the emergence of over-the-counter and unregulated trading, particularly in currency futures. However, the single and most distinct benchmark to have arisen during the 70s was the institutionalization of a credit economy.

By the 1980s, more sophisticated financial instruments set in. These included portfolio insurance, interest rate swaps, futures markets in euro dollars, certificates of deposit and treasury instruments. Further developments followed such as the ushering in of options markets on currency, equity values on treasury instruments, and collateralized mortgage obligations all of which were in vogue by 1983. Thus, when financial sparks blew as obtained in 2008-2009, corporations could quickly and surreptitiously retreat into conduits, in the form of an intricate web of instruments, in an attempt to "hedge" their accrued risks and losses to other places and parties.

1986 was another landmark year noted for the unification of global stock options and currency trading markets. By this time the existence of a fully blown "shadow banking system" of global proportion had become apparent. This new Frankenstein's monster, by the extent of the operations of a seemingly innocuous sector, seemed placed well beyond the reach of any government or stringent regulatory authority.

In 1987-1988 the collateralization of debt obligations got underway along with collateral bond obligations and collateralized mortgage obligations. Following this, futures on interest rate swaps came on stream in 1989. With amazing alacrity off-balance-sheet vehicles, more commonly referred to as "special purpose entities," kicked off in 1991 with the necessary sanctioning. Another major turning point, which proved to be the march towards the financial crisis of 2008-2009, and the Achilles heel of the resulting speculative market frenzy, was the deregulation of over-the-counter derivatives in 2000 with the enactment of the Commodity Futures Modernization Act. This initiative effectively eliminated government oversight of the over-the-counters derivative market.

Finally in 2009 when the downturn hit home and the international community was awakened in the manner of Rip Van Winkle to a cataclysmic reality, the unrestrained volume of trading, which though relatively insignificant throughout the 1990s, had escalated to an astronomic $600 trillion annually.

Re-hypothecation

The institutionalized practice by banks as well as brokers of using for their own purposes assets that have been posted as collateral by their clients is referred to as hypothecation and is an offshoot of the system of fractional reserve banking.

Fractional reserve banking occurs when bank deposits are backed by only a small fraction of the cash they promise to have in hand and redeem. Currently in the United States this minimum fraction is fixed at 10%. This practice became institutionalized subsequent to (a) the federal cartelization of the country's banks with the creation of the Federal Reserve System in 1913 and (b) the abolition of the gold standard by Franklin Roosevelt in 1913 hand in hand with the substitution of fiat paper tickets by the Federal Reserve as America's monetary standard.

A hypothecation contract is merely a contract between a debtor and a lender in which the debtor pledges some type of asset as collateral on a loan without actually delivering that collateral to the lender. Often the agreement provides for the establishment of a lien on the asset until the loan is paid in full. The agreement thus helps to reduce the risk taken by the lender and increases the chances that the lender will choose to do business with the debtor. One of the most common examples of such an agreement is a mortgage in which the purchased property is used as collateral.

Clients who permit re-hypothecation of their collateral may be compensated either through a lower cost of borrowing or a rebate on fees. In a typical example of re-hypothecation, as explained by Investopedia, securities that have been posted with a prime brokerage as collateral by a hedge fund are used by the brokerage to back its own transactions and trades. Until 2007, this form of re-hypothecation was commonplace. Following the collapse of Lehman Brothers in 2008-2009 and the subsequent credit crunch, hedge funds became more wary of it.

Matters get even worse when we consider what has for the last six years counted as collateral under re-hypothecation rules. Despite the fact that there may only be a quarter of the collateral in the world to back these transactions, successive U.S governments have softened the requirements for what can back a re-hypothecation transaction. Beginning with the Clinton-era of "liberalization" rules that had formerly limited the use of re-hypothecated funds to the Treasury state, and municipal corporations, were eased. The outcome was that between 2000-2009 as the restrictions gradually rolled back, customer money was applied to enter into re-purchase agreements or repos, foreign bonds, money market funds and other assorted securities. As a demonstration of this principle, when MF Global conceived of its Euro-zone repo plan, the firm resorted to the use of client funds for investment in AA rated European sovereign debt, despite the fact that many of its hedge fund clients may have well been against the performance of those said bonds. Later in this chapter we expand on the implications of these and other practices on the world's major economies.

In addition to being a collateral risk, re-hypothecation also creates significant counterparty risk and since as an off-balance sheet item, it is unrestricted by balance sheet controls. With collateral being re-hypothecated as much as four times, according to IMF estimations, the over-churning has created a tremendous amount of liquidity through leveraging, much of which has no real asset backing.

Derivatives

The part played by financial and over-the-counter derivatives in the context of the 2008-2009 financial debacles is worth recounting. The word "derivative" originates from mathematics and relates to a variable. Derivatives derive their value from the value of some other assets. In derivative contracts the parties enter into an agreement or option to buy or sell the underlying asset of the derivative up to a certain time in the future at a pre-determined price. By far the most highly utilized types of derivatives are "financial", "exchange traded" and "over-the-counter."[6]

The Bank for International Settlements, an intergovernmental organization of central banks which fosters international monetary and financial cooperation, noted the following in its appraisal of the scale and distribution of the derivatives market:

- The total global derivatives market is valued at $700 trillion
- A syndicate of five banks and their holding companies – JP Morgan Chase, Citibank, Bank of America, Goldman Sachs, and Morgan Stanley, monopolizes 95% of all U.S. derivatives. Together these banks hold $245 of the $248 trillion while their holding companies control $311 of the $326 trillion in derivatives held by holding companies

319

- These five banks and their holding companies combined hold $ 546 trillion in derivatives, a figure that converts to nearly 80% of the global market
- The total value of derivatives has increased by approximately 1000% since 1996 and 250% since 2006. This data has been corroborated by the U.S. government's Office of the Controller of the Currency

The value of derivatives in circulation in the global market exceeds by far the Gross Domestic Product of the entire world. [7] As a consequence, no single country, let alone a coalition of sovereign states have the capacity to stave of the collapse of this potentially fragile market. As a case in point, the Gross Domestic Product of the entire world is estimated at $60 trillion, a figure substantially less than the notional value of derivatives held by any of the five major U.S. banks. By all indicators, the market has exploded in recent years with investment banks selling billions of dollars' worth of these investments to clients as a way of offloading or managing market risks. Furthermore and more worrying is the fact that following the events of 2008-2009 and despite repeated calls for restraint, the number of instruments being issued has continued to climb rapidly.

It is widely known that the financial crisis that hit the U.S. approximately two years ago was triggered by over-the-counter derivatives the values of which were associated with the residential real estate market. These contracts were, of course, engineered by various assumptions tied to their values. To the extent that the selling price of an asset diminishes in value, the derivative to which it is linked would increase since the value of a derivative is tied to the value of the underlying. This assumes that the agreed price for re-purchase is higher than the selling price. Therefore, with the free fall in the housing market in 2008-2009, derivatives plunged in value and financial assets were similarly affected. The latter consisted of debt instruments, currency, share price indices, equity shares and the like which underlay financial derivatives.

Derivatives have enjoyed a long history despite their rather recent appearance in the wake of ongoing rhetoric over the bases of the recession. The first derivative, referred to as futures contracts, can be traced to the Yodoya rice markets in Japan around 1650. Derivatives have also had an enduring presence in India, where the commodity derivative market had been functioning since the 19th century in organized trading in cotton with the establishment of the Cotton Trade Association in 1875.

Thus, although these financial instruments may enjoy a legitimate place in hedging risks as risk management tools, the explosion in their growth within investment banking has created a huge potential for massive instability as a result of their large-scale abuse and the absence of appropriate restraints. The spiral that can lead to a corporate meltdown is therefore very real given the concentration of the facility within a closed syndicate of interests and its wide-scale application in critical areas of the market. Food speculation is illustrative of its potentially disastrous consequences. In the mid-2000s food prices across the globe surged as a result of artificially triggered factors, rooted in speculation and price controls. Within one year the price of wheat shot up by 80%, maize by 90%, and rice by 320%. Large-scale global hunger, malnutrition and starvation ensued. By 2008, prices without any identifiable reason regularized to previous levels. Today, there is every indication of a recurrence of this phenomenon in other targeted areas of speculative market activity such as the cost of oil, including alternative energies that would eventually replace oil. This is supported by one abiding premise: the primary objective of investors is to maximize returns and minimize risks.

Thus omnipresence, in terms of America's global reach, is an attribute enjoyed by syndicated interests that have a registered presence as firms and private corporations, investment banks and other financial institutions the interests of which are globally strewn. These interests maintain a stranglehold on the global financial system and are beyond the reach of the most powerful governments. It is this very same power that renders the United States vulnerable from within. The phenomenon has been widely acknowledged and disseminated by credible sources such as the Bank for International Settlements; federal departments such as the U.S. Office of the Controller of Currency, the Administrator of National Banks, online monitoring organs like Market Watch: The Wall Street Journal Digital Network, in an almost feverish quest for a resolution to the dilemma.[8]

Structure of Contemporary Banking

Banking as we have all come to know it is enigmatic of today's economic system. The word "bank" covers a range of commercial activities with very different types of implications. We shall therefore trace the evolution of the system that exists today from its earlier stages during the Renaissance when merchant bankers operated out of Europe. During that period merchants began to extend their credit to their customers and in the case of banking families, the credit aspect of their banking transactions soon evolved and overshadowed their normal mercantile activities. Eventually, firms began lending money out of their own profits and savings and were able to impose interest on these loans and consequently were able to realize productive investment on their savings.

Investment banking became popularized during the period of the 19th century and involved the application of capital by investment bankers or the capital invested or loaned by others to underwrite corporations that were accumulating capital by selling securities to stockholders and creditors. The inherent danger in these types of transactions lay in the fact that these bankers became quickly involved in the underwriting of government bonds and this exposed them to the rather questionable practice of manipulating governments so that taxes could be levied to pay off the bonds of the bankers as well as their clients.

Quiggley spells out this liaison in graphic detail in his classic, Tragedy and Hope, and provides a comprehensive chronology of the modus operandi of the dynasties of Rothschild of Western Europe and the House of Morgan in the United States. The House of Morgan anchored itself within the American system very early and took a lead in the cartelization of industries by investing heavily in railroads. Thereafter it utilized its power and influence to persuade the government to introduce policies aimed at restricting production and raising prices, in a manner that was favorable to the business interests of the company.

The Rothschilds, dispersed throughout every major capital in Europe, was a banking family that amassed gargantuan wealth through lending money and entrusted none of their business dealings to 'outsiders.' Their key to gaining wealth was to secure a foothold in the finances of Europe and they established themselves as the most powerful force in European finance and politics. Among their personal clients were members of European royal families.[9] One of their greatest contributions, institutionally speaking, emanated from the ceiling of the 1818 Prussian Loan. This transaction set in train for the first time in banking history the payment of foreign interest in the form of British sterling in London, the establishment of a British-styled sinking fund to ensure the amortization of the loan, and the establishment of a blueprint for an international bond issues market which swiftly became standardized. Once this system was put in place and investors became aware of it similar types of facilities were extended by Rothschilds throughout Frankfurt, Berlin, Amsterdam and Vienna to the reaches of Russia.

In the context of war-torn Europe, bonds held a significance that historians do not always spell out. They were very highly regarded among wealthy industrialists, bankers, speculators, and politicians - the latter grouping regarded the holding of bonds as a demonstration of confidence in the government, and by extension, a harbinger of short to medium-term market stability.

The internationalized hydra-headed character of the world's monetary system was thus firmly rooted during this nascent phase of central banking in the 1800s.

John Reeves, in his volume, <u>The Rothschilds: The Financial Rulers of Nations</u>, notes:

> *"The Rothschilds belong to no one nationality, they are cosmopolitan, and, while on the one hand they provided ships for the armies of Napoleon, on the other they raised loans for his foes who used the funds thus obtained in defraying the cost of their campaigns against him; they belong to no party, they were ready to grow rich at the expense of friends and foes alike."*

Prior to the institution of the Federal Reserve, banks were in operation in places like Amsterdam and Hamburg in seventeenth century Europe and served as the de facto warehouses for deposits. During that period, their receipts were fully backed with the assets that were deposited. Nowadays in deposit banking, banks lend out not only the deposits made by customers, but their own capital as well. Currently, in the United States the fraction of deposits the Federal Reserve System fixes that banks are permitted to hold is no more than 10 %. But even with the backing of the Reserve System, fractional reserve banking has proven to be fraught with its own inherent risks.

As will be explained below, the MF Global debacle in 2012 underscores the interconnectedness between the crisis in the U.S and the European Union, the danger of over-concentration of assets in the same repository, and the overall metastasizing nature of the crisis.

MF Global – A Microcosm of Wider Issues

The failure of MF Global is regarded as the eighth biggest bankruptcy in U.S history. Dating as far back as 1783, MF Global has had direct links with Europe. More recently it spun out of Man Group in 2007, which was a United Kingdom hedge fund. Reviews of what transpired immediately prior to the crash divulge that the firm moved $14.5 billion off its balance sheet into repos, many of which were tied to Euro-zone debt as their collateral. Under normal circumstances this move would have yielded enormous returns since yields on European bonds were soaring as a result of the perceived Euro-zone instability. Italian bonds for example had hit 7% and following this trend MF Global would have likely been in line to acquire huge profits.

According to review accounts of what ultimately transpired, the firm ploughed money into a balance sheet in a maneuver referred to as a repo or "sale-and-re-purchase agreement." This involves a firm borrowing money and putting up assets

323

as collateral - assets which it promises to re-purchase at a later stage.[10] By all accounts this type of transaction is a common technique used by firms to generate money but is not normally off-balance sheet and is treated instead as "financing" under accountancy rules. MF Global used a version of an off-balance sheet repo known as "repo-to-maturity" which involves borrowing billions of dollars backed by huge volumes of sovereign debt, all of which were due to expire at the same time as the loan itself. They reasoned that with the loan and the collateral becoming due simultaneously the firm would have been entitled to treat the transaction as a sale under U.S. GAPP. Moreover, the money that they would have received from the bonds' redemption would have been used to repay the loan, the difference being the profit. This interpretation of the transaction therefore enabled the movement of $16.5 billion by the firm off its balance sheet. Most of its debt involved was derived from Italy, Spain, Belgium, Portugal and Ireland.

It must be noted that despite the persisting Euro problem, the threat of default under the repo transaction would have been actually small – adding further credence to the decision by the firm to pursue this type of transaction. Another motivation for the transaction was very likely that measures had to be taken to prevent core sources on income from drying up since the business had been reportedly struggling financially for several years. In 2007, MF Global had booked revenues of $4 billion from interest it had earned on the billions of dollars on customer funds it held against outstanding trades. However with interest rates approaching near zero in parts of the world, this figure fell to under $517 million for the 2010 year. Appraisals of MF Global filings reveal that its sovereign debt exposure was likely due to this series of complex re-purchase agreements, and to the fact that the off-balance sheet risks that were of an unseen nature, proved too costly in the end.[11]

Several prognostications came too late to avert the crisis. For example, in March 2011 the Securities and Exchange Commission had sought clarification in relation to the firm's accounting treatment by way of letter. In response MF Global claimed justification in treating the repo-to-maturity transactions as sales on the basis that such agreements were different to other types of re-purchase agreements. They reiterated their line of reasoning that the re-purchase dates were the same as the date when the transferred assets matured and on that merit were being treated as sales.

It was in the face of these growing concerns expressed by the regulator that the firm moved to increase its net capital coverage of the repos. At that juncture a further request was made for a disclosure of the full extent of the firm's position in the Eurozone sovereign debt. The subsequent announcement by the firm that it entered bets on banks in as many of five different Eurozone countries (UBS,

ICAP, Tillet, Garban along with a string of others) had a rippling effect. It escalated margin calls causing the share price to collapse despite the fact that southern European countries had not defaulted. In the meantime it became increasingly difficult for the firm to meet its short-term liabilities as creditors instinctively moved to protect themselves, a development that ultimately careened the business into bankruptcy.

Under U.S Federal Reserve Board Regulations, T and SEC Rules 15C3-3, a prime broker may re-hypothecate assets to the value of 140% of the client's liability to the prime broker. In contrast in the U.K there is no statutory limit on the amount that can be re-hypothecated. Thus, some U.S prime brokers were making use of European subsidiaries since many of their brokerage agreements had provided for a U.S. client's assets to be transferred to the prime broker's U.K. subsidiary in order to circumvent U.S. re-hypothecation rules. Potentially, therefore having a U.K subsidiary entering into a prime brokerage agreement could allow a U.S based prime broker to take advantage of the U.K. unrestricted re-hypothecation rules.

Credit Default Swaps (CDS)

In order to stave off credit losses to holders of Greek, Portuguese, Irish, Spanish, and Italian debt and to boost the risk of payouts in the event of defaults, U.S. banks have resorted to increasing sales of insurance through instruments referred to as Credit Default swaps (CDS). According to the Bank for International Settlements, these insurance guarantees are provided by U.S. lenders on government, bank, and corporate debt and rose in these countries and rose by $80.7 billion to $518 billion.

According to the Office of the Comptroller of Currency, five banks - J.P. Morgan, Morgan Stanley, Goldman Sachs, Bank of America Corp (BAC), and Citigroup Inc. write as much as 97% of all credit default swaps in the U.S. Together, these firms had total exposure of $45 billion to the debt of the aforementioned countries.

What emerges from this part of our discussion is the symbiotic relationship between the financial systems of Europe and those of America. This interconnectedness, which is by no means a recent phenomenon, extends to the decision-making process at the highest politico-economic levels, which we elaborate on in Chapter Fourteen. Indeed, the intercontinental nature of business between the two continents spans hundreds of years and the main players –

wealthy merchants, bankers, brokers and financiers - have merely shifted their focus from the trade in goods to finance, more specifically the flow of money. A further danger lies in the concentration of assets, given the fact that a disproportionately small number of firms control most of the wealth.

Today the corridors of power are inhabited by a fusion of interests as various camps from within governments, corporations; the banking community and academia put their noses to the grindstone towards resolving common problems. This may not always be possible, given the fact that the underlying rationale of consensual decision-making is not necessarily grounded in political expedients. Further to this, money is peculiarly the province of private interests that have historically salvaged states from bankruptcy. This underlying dichotomy is one of the greatest challenges today and lies at the heart of corporatism, as an emerging new order that has the potential to challenge, alter and even circumvent the interests of governments.

This is all reminiscent of the investment banking houses that flourished in Europe in the nineteenth century. Investment bankers then would take their own capital, or capital invested or loaned by others, to underwrite corporations gathering capital by selling securities to stockholders and creditors. Fortuitously for them, their major fields of investment were in government bonds, which plunged them (in the words of Murray Rothbard), "hip deep into politics, giving them a powerful incentive for pressuring and manipulating governments."

Europe is evidently at the fulcrum of the global economic crisis. This implies that developments within Europe will inevitably affect America and beyond. Likewise, developments in America will impact on China. Similarly, as a major trade partner to China, Europe's woes will unavoidably resonate in Beijing. Key to all of this, are those players who decide in which direction the pendulum would swing.

CHAPTER FOURTEEN

POLITICAL REALIGNMENTS AND THE ECONOMIC OUTLOOK FOR AMERICA AND CHINA

"Power is essentially amoral and one of the most important skills is the ability to see circumstances rather than good or evil. Power is a game—this cannot be repeated too often—and in games you do not judge your opponents by their intentions but by the effect of their actions."

Robert Greene

he desirability of east-west political and economic unification has an enduring and rich legacy. One such plan towards the establishment of a Trans-Atlantic Economic Council in 2007 as a precursor to a Transatlantic Common Market, was hatched by the second Bush administration and went virtually unheralded. The establishment of this entity was intended to satisfy two criteria, the first: bringing the right players around the table representative of American and European interests in the spheres of politics, business, banking, the media, and economics;, the second: setting in motion a regulatory infrastructure to brace a common market thereby integrating and harmonizing the economies of participating western democracies.

These initiatives in a sense gave expression to the early designs of ideologue, Clarence Streit who almost 60 years ago conceived of a transatlantic common market that would effectively incorporate no less than the 15 western democracies, deemed at the time to be generating no less than 60 percent of the World's Gross Domestic Product.[1] The original grouping consisted of the United States, the United Kingdom, France, Australia, Belgium, Canada, Denmark, Finland, Netherlands, Ireland, New Zealand, Norway, Sweden, Switzerland and South Africa. Streit's grand scale idea was spurred by three main concerns: the demise of the League of Nations, the rise of authoritarian states within Europe, specifically Germany, and the emergence of a communist Soviet Union.

As a former New York Times correspondent assigned to matters related to the League of Nations prior to the whittling away of that institution, Streit quickly recognized that in a globalizing world the trend towards growing domestic pressure to external problems had led many countries to adopt a reactive posture. He observed that in certain parts of Europe, such as Germany, this translated into increasingly belligerent nationalism that sacrificed freedom for security. In the case

327

of the United States, it meant a form of isolationism that sought to defend against global conflicts. Streit therefore conceived of a Union along the lines of American federalism that would bring together the democracies of Europe, including their colonies, under a single government with the power to grant citizenship and wage war. He was also highly hopeful of expanded membership as more nations joined the Union.

In his estimation, a policy framework should exist that impels the U.S and European countries to forge economic integration, remove barriers to trade and investment, and ease regulatory burdens. The advancement of such a mechanism is taking place "in a very quiet way" in the words of Robert Bennet (R-Utah), member and advisor of a Congressional Group comprising at least 49 officials engaging with the Transatlantic Policy Network (TPN). This crisscross of notables which comprises an extraordinary brew of high-powered thinkers including politicians, corporatists, financiers and bureaucrats, is at work instituting the necessary regulatory changes and administrative rules incumbent on the U.S, under the arrangement. The end game emanating from these preparatory moves would be a full-fledged Trans-Atlantic Common Market by 2015.

Promotional linkages on either side of the Atlantic are evident. For instance, of the two Honorary Presidents of the TPN, either appears tactically placed to execute the "cosmopolitan" agenda. In particular, the Honorary President representing the European Union, Peter Sutherland, whose previous posts included Attorney General of Ireland, and E.U. Competition Commissioner, now serves as a non-executive Chairman of Goldman's U.K.-based broker-dealer arm, Goldman Sachs International.[2]

Given the metastatic nature of the global crises, this development represents another cog in the evolving global complex that will affect the balance of power. On the one hand, there will be a shoring in the common interests of certain countries, hand in hand with a diffusion of the interests of others. Developments of this nature influence state behavior and define and redefine loyalties and by extension, alignments.

The China-Russia League

Illustrative of the latter state of affairs China can now rely on Russia, an established nuclear power, as a strong proponent to effectively veto U.N Security Council voting and stymie the agendas and priorities of other Security Council members. Both countries are non-members of NATO and either has the capacity to invoke the veto power enjoyed by the five permanent members of the U.N. Security Council. This power enables permanent members to prevent the adoption of any substantial draft Council Resolution, irrespective of the level of international support that it may have mustered.

Both nations recently exercised a double veto in relation to the Security Council draft that condemned the violent repression being displayed by the Syrian government against armed demonstrations in that country. This maneuver has proven to be extremely injurious to Western solidarity, more specifically, to the motivations of a formidable coalition comprising NATO, Israel and the Sunni Muslim states, the latter strongly spurred by Saudi Arabia.

In a similar vein, Russia's assertiveness continues to be openly flaunted much to the chagrin of its challengers and is now re-energized by President Putin's popular and highly democratized 2012 re-election. Russia's re-legitimized standing was sufficiently baneful to the U.S to have featured on the agenda of a recent high-level meeting in March 2012 between U.S. President Obama and Prime Minister Cameron of Great Britain. The Russia-China alignment has temporarily derailed a formidable coalition of interests by scuttling a well-orchestrated Western agenda, aimed at dislodging the Syrian and Iranian regimes in close succession and short order.

Adopting as a referent Brzezinski's theory of the predisposition of states to shape their own objectives, and by this means, railroading the interests of others, China and Russia would appear to fit the traits of "active geostrategic powers" in relation to America's timetable.[3] China and Russia each possesses:

- The will and power to exercise influence beyond their borders
- A predisposition to be geographically volatile
- The resolve and resources to attain regional (and possibly global) dominance
- Motivation, by reason of their strong potential for aggrandizement; in the case of China its global standing as an economic power and in Russia's instance, its formidable and declared nuclear capability

A point of note is that the coalition of opposition groups in Syria in 2012 was comprised of Libyan and Syrian rebels, a hodgepodge of highly trained Salafi terrorists including al-Qaeda operatives, agents of the secret services of many NATO allies posturing as self-designated "Friends of Syria," all of whom were concertedly engaged in fomenting regional instability. The European Union is itself the most important weapons exporter to Saudi Arabia. Of all its members France is foremost in terms of the money value with 2168.6 Euro million of exports in 2010, followed by Italy which exported Euro 435.3 million, and Great Britain in third place, with exports valued at Euro 328.8. The Saudi government in concert with Qatar was particularly instrumental in providing financial support, weapons, covert fighters and strident diplomatic backing for the self-styled National Councils of Libya (2011) and Syria, respectively.

Of interest also in this milieu is the posture adopted by India amidst the political disarray. Credited as the largest democracy in the developing world with nuclear power status, and a recognized aspirant for regional preeminence, India broke ranks with "the West" and overtly defied a U.N. resolution aimed at imposing economic sanctions against Iran. Instead, the country opted to continue purchasing much-needed crude oil from its longstanding trading partner, using gold as the preferred medium of exchange in order to circumvent restraints imposed on international business dealings with Iranian banks.

India is by no means isolated in her single-minded convictions. Other "global south" members and contenders for political stature such as South Africa and Brazil have railed against any external intervention in affairs of neighboring Syria on grounds that a former U.N. resolution purporting to intervene in Libya to protect civilians was "misused" as a pretext for armed intervention, setting the stage for a war of aggression. Amidst the juggling and diplomatic gyrations, new coalitions of interests are being churned out and multi-polarity is playing a dramatic hand in how alignments are being reshaped in the context of regional pressures, such as Eurasia is experiencing.

The BRICS coalition, for example, comprising Brazil, Russia, India, China and South Africa, the five fastest growing economies in the world now serves as an effective counterweight to "the West". Together the economies of these nations, which account for 42% of the world's population and 25% of its landmass, will surpass that of the United States by 2015. On the occasion of the Fourth Annual BRICS Summit hosted by the Indian government in New Delhi in March 2012, these countries resolved to instigate a shift from the West by establishing a development bank among themselves with analogous lending powers to the World Bank Group and a capability to award loans to member countries in their local currency, in lieu of the U.S dollar as now obtains.[4] There is also agreement to adopt a common front on a range of political issues high on the agenda of the global inner circle (such as the management of the Syria/Iran impasse), based on their declared divergences with official Western positions. The contested race for global primacy undoubtedly rests with those nations that wield economic clout,

Impact of Iran-Syria Disturbances on U.S Economy in Relation to Oil

Another issue of relevance is the uneven footing of the U.S. due to its heavy reliance on crude oil imports and related petroleum products. Threats by Iran to block the Strait of Hormuz in response to economic sanctions being imposed on that country by "the West" have placed the U.S. on a war footing. Iran is yet another important player of geostrategic significance to the U.S. that cannot be ignored and is now well beyond peripheral status in the Sino-American face-off. Should Iran make good on its threats in blocking the Strait, as much as 20% of U.S. daily crude oil needs could be impeded. This would mean that the U.S. would be forced to rely on its Strategic Petroleum Reserve, which has the capacity of a mere six to eight weeks supply.

America currently imports 45% of its petroleum (down from 57% in 2008) whereas 51% is sourced from domestic supplies. Additionally, U.S. domestic gas prices fluctuate in direct response to increases and declines in the global oil prices which have in turn been driven up by the global economic recovery and market jitters over mounting tensions with Iran, one of the world' s largest producers.

More specifically, 49% of the U.S. crude oil was sourced from the Western Hemisphere in 2010. This speaks of North, South, and Central America along with the Caribbean inclusive of U.S territories. Additionally, roughly 18% of U.S. crude oil imports and petroleum products originate from the Persian Gulf countries of Bahrain, Iraq, Kuwait, Qatar, Saudi Arabia, and the United Arab Emirates, with the largest sources of net crude oil being Saudi Arabia and Canada. Admittedly, with the increased use of domestic bio-fuels (ethanol and bio-diesel), strong gains in domestic production of crude oil and natural gas plant liquids, following the financial crisis of 2008, there has been a reduced need for domestic imports. See Table 14 -1.

TABLE 14 - 1
TOP FIVE SOURCES OF CRUDE OIL AND PETROLEUM IMPORTS FOR THE
UNITED STATES IN 2011

Country	% Supply of Crude Oil and Petroleum Product Imports
1. Canada	25
2. Saudi Arabia	12
3. Nigeria	11
4. Venezuela	10
5. Mexico	9

SOURCE: United States Energy Information Administration
"Independent Statistics and Analysis" (Last updated - June 24 2011)

Saudi Arabia and Iran rank among the world's largest crude oil producers and are also the source countries for the largest volume of proven reserves with Saudi Arabia accounting for 259.96 barrels and Iran, 137.6 billion barrels of proven reserves.

So imminent is the likelihood of international turmoil of a scale never before witnessed in terms of a possible sudden and jolting impact of crude oil shortages, that an Executive Order, the National Defense Resources Preparedness, was hastily signed by President Obama on March 16, 2012. The executive order aims to secure federal control of food and strategic resources and ensure that all the authorities cited therein could be mobilized at short notice in war or peacetime to strengthen America's industrial and technical base for meeting national defense requirements.

For all practical purposes, the Order in question would appear to be a revival of the antecedent Defense Production Act of 1950, as amended (50 U.S.C. App. 2061 et seq.) and Section 301of Title 3 of the U.S. Code and is in effect a re-statement of executive order 12919 of 1994 brought under the then Clinton administration. The purport of the original instrument was to place the U.S on a war footing in the event of a nuclear attack that was highly likely during the years of the Cold War. With this most recent enactment, the President is vested with executive authority to take instantaneous control of all the country's civil energy supplies, including oil and natural gas, control and restrict all civil transportation which is almost 97% dependent upon oil, as well as enable an appropriate draft Order to be renewed.

Interconnectedness in the Face of Ideological Schisms

Apart from economically driven motivations, there are other points at issue determining the composition of new and emerging alignments. This was evident in the "Friends of Syria Meeting" which was dramatically choreographed by predominantly Sunni interests and promoted by Saudi Arabia. The crusade is wholly committed to averting the emergence of a Shiite hegemonic Iran with strong backing from its neighboring Syrian ally.

With this is view, there is a heavy accentuation among the Friends of Syria to co-opt Salafis into the opposition forces operating in Syria. This latter grouping is a special sect of Sunnis who employ the "Salaf" (the earliest Muslims) as a model for Islamic practices. Salafism has become associated with puritanical approaches to Islam and espouses radical jihad against civilians as a form of legitimate expression. It insists on a very narrow and confined brand of Sharia or religious law and in recent years has become associated with the jihad of al-Qaeda and related groups that advocate the killing of civilians. Hence, there are well founded concerns over strategies being employed by the West to oust the Assad regime, including financial backing to support the opposition forces in Syria. Such schemes are clearly at variance with the tenets of the U.N-backed Six Point Peace Initiative steered by Kofi Annan. Whereas the latter effort obliges all parties to cease fire with immediate effect, the former is a contributor to ongoing violence and mayhem, compounded by atrocities committed against civilians. Notably, members of the BRICS were similarly persuaded of the wisdom of adopting the peace plan.

The E.U. Fulcrum

The United States, the European Union, and China are the key supporting pillars of the world economy. This enquiry recognizes that the 2008-2009 economic crisis emanated from the housing market bubble that exploded in the U.S. and ultimately brought down key financial systems of the West. For this reason Europe buckled under crisis and there are now prevailing concerns as to whether this development presages the collapse of the Euro as a preferred medium of exchange. China experienced two decades of uninterrupted economic growth and appeared to be holding course, at least during the early to medium term. North Africa and Eurasia have also seen dramatic alterations.

Amidst all of this America persists as the world's largest economy and despite this China's alarming pace growth cannot be underscored; neither could the

333

escalated pace of economic expansion among other East Asian economies such as Malaysia, South Korea, and Singapore.

United States

The United States is presently more dependent than ever on two centers of power in terms of their impact on the wider global front, Europe and China, based on the symbiotic nature of trade relations between and among these nations and by virtue of China being a major exporter of cheap commodities. The U.S. is in its fifth year of continuing economic decline and the European economy is similarly disadvantaged not just economically but socially due to extreme workforce related challenges. These include weakening trade union representation and steadily declining levels of unemployment. In point of fact unemployment in the Euro-zone stood at 10.9% while the rate in the U.S. was 8.3%. Correspondingly, the Chinese domestic commercial sector has been hampered by developments within the U.S. and Euro-zone trade markets, both of which are its primary trade centers. This has resulted in the erosion of the purchasing power for Chinese exports in both jurisdictions.

America can by no means be expected to rely on a potentially folding Europe and a re-assertive PRC, to which it is beholden as a prime debtor. To compound this situation, the continuing failure of the Euro-zone to rebound from the current economic impasse severely constrains the ability of China to continue to trade and invest with countries that are substantially rich in raw materials. Brazil and certain other South American nations with which China trades would undoubtedly be adversely affected. Added to all of this Libya, Afghanistan, Iran and Syria, which until recently enjoyed viable trade relations with the Chinese, have been practically demobilized politically and economically as a result of assertive Western-led military campaigns.

Domestic Conditions in the U.S

In February 2012, the U.S. monthly budget deficit reached the $232 billion mark and government spending amounted to roughly $333 billion. The Obama administration estimates that by September 30 when the budget year ends, the deficit would have exceeded $1.3 trillion (the fourth consecutive year). The pace of economic recovery is proving to be extremely slow and this sluggishness in expanding has left the economy particularly vulnerable to aftershocks.[6] Analysts have traced the trend to disruptions in the supply chain emanating from the 2011 earthquake in Japan; the surge in oil prices; and spillovers from the European debt crisis. Thus, the pace of recovery continues to be uneven and is modest by historical standards.

There are five key determinants at work which were identified by the Chairman of the Board of Governors of the Federal Reserve, Ben S. Bernanke during his testimony to the Committee on the Budget in 2012, namely:

- Workers Who Remain Unemployed or Underemployed. The Chairman of the Federal Reserve noted that America still has a long way to go before the labor market can be said to be operating normally and that particularly disturbing was the long-term nature of unemployment, referring to the fact that more than 40% of the unemployed had been jobless for a period exceeding six months. This was roughly double the fraction of the preceding economic expansion of the previous decade.
- The Ability and Willingness of Households to Spend. Despite the fact that consumer spending rose in 2011, household income and wealth had stagnated during the course of that year and access to credit remained tight. Additionally, uncertain job prospects compounded by tight mortgage credit conditions have continued to hold back the demand for housing. Also, there was a persistent excess supply of vacant homes, largely stemming from foreclosures.
- Levels of Productivity in the Business Sector. The Chairman of the Federal Reserve reported that manufacturing production had increased by 15% since its decline, and that capital spending by businesses had expanded within the last two years, driven in part by the need to replace aging equipment and software.
- Consumer Price Inflation. This moderated considerably during 2012. During the first half of the year, a surge in the prices of food and gasoline, along with associated increases of other prices, on goods and services, pushed up consumer inflation higher. The cost of motor vehicles also surged following disruptions in relation to the earthquake in Japan.
- Financial Developments in Europe. High debt levels coupled with weak growth prospects in a number of European countries, particularly Greece, Spain and Portugal, have raised concerns about the health of European banks and associated reductions in confidence and availability of credit in the euro area. [7]

Bernanke forecasted in his dialogue with Congress that there are real risks that developments in Europe and elsewhere would unfold unfavorably and negatively impact on the U.S. financial system and economy. The endemic causes for this were averred to in the preceding chapter. Bernanke also forecasted that the U.S. employment rate will not return to pre-financial crisis levels "for several years," and further the current budget deficit of 9% of total economic output or GDP will fall to 5% in 2015 but rise again to 6.5% at the end of the decade.

Regarding the rate of inflation, consumer prices in the U.S. rose by 3% in 2011 while wages went up by 1.6% over the preceding twelve-month period. This means that the ability of the American worker to maintain a decent standard of living is being incrementally undermined. They are thus worse off than they were one year ago since to have maintained their former standard of living their wages ought to have increased by no less than 3%. This trend was corroborated by statistics released by the Bureau of Labor Statistics, which concluded that:

> *"Median weekly earnings of the nation's 101.5 trillion full-time wage and salary workers were $764 in the fourth quarter of 2011(not seasonally adjusted...This was 1.6% higher than a year earlier, compared with a gain of 3.3%in the Consumer's Price Index for all urban consumers(CPI-U) over the same period[8] In distinction to this data, productivity figures rose at a 2.3% annual rate during the third quarter of 2011, with output rates of 3.2% and 0.8% respectively.[9]*

Medium to Long-Term Impact of Deficit Spending

The federal budget deficit has widened considerably over the past three fiscal years, averaging around 9% of the country's Gross Domestic Product. The Federal Reserve Chairman pointed out that the structural fiscal imbalances did not occur overnight, but rather, were amassed over many years and exacerbated by the liabilities that accrued with having an aging population and fast-rising health care costs, a situation not too dissimilar to the one Europeans confront.

He warned of the severe consequences to the U.S. of having this large and continuing running fiscal debt, noting:

- Having a large and increasing level of government debt relative to the national income runs the risk that the trajectory of federal debt would crowd out capital formation and replace productivity growth
- To the extent that increasing debt is financed from abroad, a growing share of America's future income would be devoted to interest payments on foreign held federal debt

- High debt levels would also impair the ability of policy makers to respond effectively to future economic shocks and other adverse events
- Unsustainable deficits also have the capability to trigger sudden financial crises in instances of an unexpected surge in interest rates
- Overall loss of confidence among investors who become concerned over the inability of a government to manage its debts

Military Budgeting

Another point of note is the continuing cost of military engagements. China's policy, which was rolled out in earlier chapters, is directed at catching up and if at all possible, outstripping the U.S. America on the other hand, confronted with a widening fiscal deficit, has had no recourse but to make substantial adjustments in terms of decisive cuts in its military expenditure. As a consequence while China's budget reflected increases by 11% for the 2012 fiscal year, the U.S. defense budget was cut by a corresponding 11%. Notwithstanding strict austerity measures, the Chairman of the Federal Reserve noted that even if economic conditions return to normal in the short to medium term, America will still be confronted by a sizeable structural budget gap, given the present policies.

U.S. Economic Policy and Philosophy

The buzzword in use to describe the economic philosophy of the U.S. is purportedly 'Obamanomics.' This is a brand of economic management that demands lower tax rates for companies that meet certain criteria, such as maintaining a U.S. workforce and headquarters, and requiring higher taxes for high income families, investment in education, healthcare and the sciences. It generally stands in contrast to supply-side economics, which canvasses for the rich keeping more of what they earn, consistent with Keynesian economics, which advocates for active government intervention in the economy.

The existing deficit is compounded by a huge entitlement program amassed over successive administrations and the costly bailouts of banks and corporations facilitated by the Obama administration in 2009. These programs include –

- Social security entitlements and hospitals

- Medicare reimbursement to doctors program; and the Veterans Health Administration program
- Form subsidies
- Educational loans for middle class students; grants; scholarships
- Defense
- Food stamps
- Unemployment benefits (compensation)
- Federal employee and military retirement plans

Some of the highpoints in the FY 13 budget are in relation to defense spending which continues to tower over all other expenditure, the National Intelligence Program, Overseas Contingency Operations, the Department of State and other International Programs and the Department of Transportation – the latter includes critical infrastructure and border crossings.

The bulk figure of $525.4 billion goes to discretionary funding for the base Department of Defense budget, a decrease of roughly 1% of 2012. This will assist in achieving a $486.9 billion savings by 2015. A total of $52.6 billion has been appropriated to discretionary funding under the National Intelligence Program to support national security goals, focus on critical capabilities, curtail personnel growth, and invest in more efficient information technology solutions. Provision has also been made for $96.7 billion expenditure in Overseas Contingency Operations in Unified Defense, State, and U.S. Aid funding for Overseas Contingency Operations. This is a reduction of 24% below the 2012 level.

In contrast, modest figures featured in discretionary funding for: Agriculture ($23 billion); Commerce ($8 billion); Department of Education ($69.8 billion); Department of Energy ($27.2 billion); Department of Health and Human Services ($76.4 billion); Homeland Security ($39.5 billion); Department of Housing and Urban Development ($44.8 billion); Department of the Interior ($11.4 billion); Department of Justice (427.1 billion); Department of Labor ($12 billion); Department of State and other International Programs($51.6 billion). Total budgetary resources allocated to the Treasury amounted to $14 billion while historic levels of support continued in Veterans Affairs, which was generously and justifiably furnished with $64 billion – a 4.5% increase over the 2012 enacted level. The allocation discharges the Department to make good on its promise to take care of veterans and their families while working to improve on efficiency in a constrained fiscal environment.[10]

In the second edition of <u>Aftershock</u>, Weidemer et al predict that when the U.S government can no longer borrow and has a rapidly declining tax base, it will resort to massive spending cuts many of which will be unpopular. Simultaneous with this will be the imposition of larger tax increases on a diminishing work force. Another offshoot will be the inability of people to pay mortgages and other debts with no significant market for selling their properties.[11]

Two potentially explosive "bubbles" were identified. The first is retirement savings with the reductions of government contributions. Already pension fund investments in stocks, bonds and real estate are plunging in value even as government is seeking to cut the number of employees who are working. The second potential bubble is the massive increase in student loan debt. The impending bubble is being fueled by private credit. While acknowledging that the total student loan debt in the U.S. currently exceeds total credit card debt, the book notes that college fees and tuition have increased by over 400% since 1980, while the Consumer Price Index was up by a mere 100%.

The book advocates specific resolutions such as conversion from variable to fixed mortgage rates, migration from long-term into shorter term bonds, selling one's business sooner rather than later, buying gold, and demurring from paying off fixed mortgages faster than is necessary.

China – Over-investment and Overheating of Economy

Upheavals in North Africa, Eurasia, and the Persian Gulf /Arab world which are largely influenced by American foreign policy, have seriously challenged China's interests in these areas. Thus confronted in March 2011, the Chinese changed course politically speaking as a result of:

- The demand at home for prompt action to ensure the safety of approximately 35,000 nationals who were based in Libya on or around the period when the "No Fly Zone" was instituted in that country [12]
- Widespread support among Arab countries for tough action against former Libyan leader, Qaddafi
- The need to protect its economic interests; and
- The compulsion to take appropriate steps to avoid subsequent and likely penalization should the country be perceived as supporting the "wrong side." Indeed, the failure of China to take a decisive course of action would have been at odds with its economic interests in host countries

Based on the foregoing the government hastened to assuage domestic anxieties and preserve its own standing at home by facilitating the evacuation of roughly

35,000 stranded nationals who were employed in Libya in numerous large-scale projects in that country. These reputedly lucrative contracts amounted to $18.8 billion and involved private as well as state run corporations. The up-shoot of this was a plunge in the value of Chinese stocks by as much as 7% in Munich and Shanghai by the end of the first quarter of 2011.

It has been argued that the backwash from Europe and from the still tepid recovery of the U.S. will encourage China to rely more heavily on domestic demand as a source of growth and that this will mean allowing its currency, the Yuan, to float higher on the foreign exchanges. This in turn will encourage consumers to buy cheaper imports while making exports more costly. Following this line of reasoning it is further suggested that in the short run, such a move at home will help to diffuse protectionist sentiments in the U.S. and in the long-term will lead to a rebalancing of the global economy. However, given the fluidity now being displayed in the Chinese economy, which was for some time being masked by a steady double-digit growth rate, such projections will take some time to become recognizable.[13]

China is now wrestling with the typical aftermath that follows years of over-extension of credit. During the period of staggering economic growth the Communist leaders encouraged banks to keep the economy moving and at one stage the rate of the annualized credit had reached a staggering 170%. This overinvestment was channeled into industrial capacity as well as realty. The upshot is that China is currently awash with a glut of overpriced housing, reminiscent of what occurred in the United States leading to the sub-prime mortgage crisis. Based on recent history, this out of control surge in credit harbingers a possible financial crisis to which Beijing has responded. Credit constraints have now been relaxed in an attempt to curtail excess liquidity in the banking system. These are clear symptoms of an over-invested and overheated economy.

Power always exists in concentrated forms. Contenders for ultimate primacy should advisedly concentrate rather than dissipate their forces and energies at their strongest point. Intensity always defeats "extensity". In other words ill-judged outlays should be guarded against. A famous Chinese story is told of Wu as a paradigm of all empires. Wu became drunk with success and was driven by the insatiable impulse to overreach and encompass vast territories. In so doing the empire increased its vulnerabilities and eventually collapsed and fell into oblivion. This is an elemental lesson for the contenders of our time.

By the same token, the adoption of a position that affords the opportunity to retreat and disperse tactically, should circumstances become altered, is a wise move. Herein is the importance of cultivating friendships or becoming entwined along the way with other sources of power. It would be a mistake for a nation to regard opposing combinations of interests as cohesive and mutually exclusive leagues. Neither is amassing a stockpile of enemies is a good idea. It leaves behind a trail of shipwrecks that are like eternal phantoms in one's wake, phantoms that are not necessarily disposed to going away; and these ghosts of the past are somehow prone to manifest themselves at the most inopportune times.

Another important tenet in the power matrix is to retain ultimate control over the options placed on deck. If a country can permit only those options that are favorable to it to be placed on the negotiating table, it will invariably emerge with something in its favor. Consider the community of interests of states, both major and minor, and the fact that each point of intersection binds and serves to balance one set of interests against the other. The art of negotiation involves giving options to the other players that are aligned with your own interests while ensuring that the other players make the choice. This is also a sure way of taking the indirect route to what you want, by moving towards an object as rowers do, with one's back to it.

The international society has developed a general repugnance to the idea of dominance by any single power. Further to this, our enquiry discloses that the world system is currently evolving around centers of power that converge as satellites around the two major powers - China and the United States. Given the significance of economic power, this enquiry into the global power complex would be incomplete without referencing the three dominant ideologies of the world political economy – mercantilism, liberalism, and Marxism. [14]

Robert Gilpin examined each of these perspectives against the setting of domestic autonomy and international norms and concluded that the logic of a market economy as an inherently expanding global system collides with the logic of an inherently welfare state. He also noted that the welfare state and its survivability merely transferred the problem of the market economy to international level. The obvious analogies would be the socialist policies being promoted by the current U.S government and the migration of the Chinese economy from a closed to an open system.

This clash between domestic autonomy and international norms, which Gilpin recognizes as a basic international dilemma is today superseded in significance by the control that is jointly wielded; namely a syndicate of private international bankers and the emerging engines of world economic power from Asia and the global south. American omnipresence has thus far staved off the chances for political primacy being assumed by any other player. However, economic power looms large as a variable in the mantle of world premiership even as America continues to monopolize the grip of its presence on multiple fronts and in all known spheres.

SECTION II

PART V

OVERVIEW

"The true irony of socialism is that it creates conditions that is completely opposed to its stated goals – militarism instead of peace, poverty instead of plenty and the destruction of freedom instead of an increase of human growth and potential..."

F.A. Hayek

he picture overshadowing the global arena is this - decisions that affect the elementals of day-to-day social and economic life have been being plucked out of the hands of plebeians, usurped by corporate-financier interests, distilled and rubber- stamped by the mainstream media, and thereupon sold to voters by politicians. In the meantime as commoners become increasingly politically aware and awakened, movements of the like of Occupy Wall Street and in the case of China's legacy, the Tiananmen fiasco and smaller scale "look-alikes," mushroom. Authorities react from their respective enclaves, be it in Washington or Beijing, by deploying all forms of gadgetry, ranging from the enactment of legislative codes and crackdowns to drone missions to avoid risking the interests of the business elite and toppling the power machinery.

Part V of this disquisition confronts some inconvenient truths that shed light on the full range of perversions that now challenge Washington and Beijing. It scrutinizes the amazing interplay of the real power brokers and the hybrid character of the real behemoth that is keeping America propped up, and sustaining the status quo. The behemoth is comprised essentially of corporate-financier interests, the military-industrial complex, the intelligence machinery and the mainstream media. These enclaves and their dramatic impact on their respective host societies were crucial points of reference in the earlier chapters of this enquiry. However, what has become increasingly pronounced in recent times is the fact that the de facto *government* supersedes the more visible and familiar elected administrators, permeates every political party, and brings its influence to bear on the way of life of the average citizen through a less than discrete spread of social and political pivots that extend to on-line communities and "think tanks," all of which are engaged in the gainful business of stoking public sentiment and shaping opinion.

This book argues that the powers wielded by these seemingly unconstrained interests owe their genesis to policies and practices that erupted during periods of national crises, specifically between the two world wars. Those were periods during which emotive appeals were made by publics for various forms of governmental intervention in response to the array of social and economic challenges with which America was confronted, and gave occasion to breaking new ground.

Insofar as America stands, World War II afforded unmatched opportunities for technetronic advancements as described in the Introduction of this book; the adoption of ground-breaking scientific programs detailed in Chapters Ten and Eleven; improvised economic management schemes that led to large-scale deficit spending; wage and price controls; and the central allocation of raw materials through cartelization that typified the FDR era. More relevant to China, Chapter Two hashed out how the audacious interventions of the Mao administration of the late 1950s distinguished the era designated "The Great Leap Forward," leaving millions of Chinese reeling under throes of starvation of incalculable magnitude. It would take a further fifteen-year period and another revolution in the 1970s to catapult China into global prominence as a rising power of note. Significantly, in his capacity as the General Secretary of the Chinese Communist Party, Ju Hintao made a point in his November 08, 2012 Report to the Eighteenth CPC National Congress, "...the most important achievement in our endeavors in the last ten years is that we have founded the Scientific Outlook of development and put it into practice."

These developments demonstrate the extent to which periods of acute crises place tremendous strains on governments that often culminate in the adoption of extreme measures. Events such as these may be viewed retrospectively as mere throwbacks of an era of ideological schisms. During these ill-fated intervals, the voting public came to accept as normal government interventions that would otherwise be regarded as unconstitutional or beyond moral pale. The legendary McCarthy hearings of the sixties triggered by the "red menace" and legislative codes directly emanating from the intensification of mass surveillance in the aftermath of 9/11, typify the trend. What is noteworthy is that at the end of the day, the vested interests of the power elite remain firmly intact. At the core of this societal phenomenon is corporatism and its dramatic impact on the power structure, nationally and internationally.

This section of our enquiry examines the phenomenon through multiple lenses. The discussion commences with a retrospect on the cartelization of business interests as a policy device adopted by the state to eliminate competition and offset government deficits. This is a present practice that has its origins in the early years of the Industrial Revolution. The enquiry observes how Washington

346

and Beijing have together embraced central planning as the sine non qua for resolving economic woes and staving off imminent collapse. We assess the impact of statism as both governments move towards a prodigious enlargement of the state apparatus, while illustrating that consistent reliance on state-centered planning continues to be a key factor that has actually contributed to the collapse of fiscal and monetary systems. This explains why knee jerk reactions of governments promoted by technocrats in all-out frantic attempts to prop up failing structures, are to no avail.

Simultaneously, geo-political blocs are being rattled by economic and social disruption and continue to buckle in close succession under the shocks of the bedlam; statehoods are imploding, regimes heave in response to internal and external pressures ranging from sectarian clashes, to coups d'états to "humanitarian interventions." The apocalyptic frenzy appears at times to be spiraling out of control as the two major powers face-off in asymmetric warfare and lunge for the last spoils of essential resources that the planet could yield.

Chaos...Chaos... Chaos... the global systems are coming apart!

Centrality of Corporatism

Our argument is essentially that despite the ostensible political and ideological divide particularizing Washington and Beijing, the centrality of corporatism and the power wielded by big business is common to both powers. Inoffensively speaking, each is in a neck brace guilefully crafted and promoted by big business interests. This section of the discourse also demonstrates the likelihood that a major challenge to the status quo can well erupt internally. In point of fact, the very actions of the government, animated in its policy and law-making mandates risk spurring a scenario on home soil, homologous to the enigmatic "Trojan horse." This assertion holds equally true of China, with its perennial threat of large-scale uprisings that could topple the Chinese Communist Party at full tilt. In support of these conjectures, analogies are drawn in this section of the inquiry between the chain of events that occurred during the Roosevelt New Deal era and the current political and economic maneuvering, at the heart of which was both then and now, the interests of corporate and financial moguls, who are invariably hooked up with policy makers and their legislative counterparts.

The ubiquity of corporatism is discernible in every constituent of the national forum – from health and education to sport, the environment, energy, trade commerce, finance, transportation, the armed forces and lobbyists and "horse-traders" that inhabit the corridors of Congress. Chapter Fourteen is replete with insights into the leverage exerted by America's banking and financial cabals. The inexorable reality is that influential non-state actors now constitute an omnipresent limb of the national and international world stage. As the phenomenon pertains to China, Chapter Seven made mention of this trend in its examination of how the Industrial Commercial Bank of China and the China Construction Bank now figure among the world's largest banks, many of which have become acclimatized to privileges and concessions that largely outstrip their sphere of influence. Part V expounds on all of these themes.

The U.S. and Chinese governments have both audaciously opted to take on monumental, too big to fail type interests through bailouts and other forms of patronage and engage in balancing acts that test their grit for political survival. Of interest in the economic and political life of America's corporate world are the following notables:

- International Crisis Group which claims to be committed to preventing and resolving deadly conflict
- Foundations, the more eminent being the Ford, Bill and Melinda Gates and Rockefeller Foundations and the Carnegie Corporation of New York
- The Brookings Institution, a liberal think tank that conducts research on education, foreign policy, global economy and development; represented on its board are many executives of Goldman Sachs & Co.
- Oil companies, the more eminent being Exxon Mobil Corporation, Chevron and Shell Oil Company
- Military-industrial complex corporations, as for example Daimler, General Dynamics Corporation, Lockheed Martin Corporation, Northrop Grumman Corporation, Siemens Corporation, the Boeing Company, General Electric Company, Westinghouse Electric Corporation,
- Telecommunications and Technology entities such as AT & T, Google Corporation, Hewlett-Package, Microsoft Corporation, Panasonic Corporation, Verizon Communications, Xerox Corporation, Skype
- Media and perception management, among these McKinsey & Company Inc., News Corporation (Fox News)
- Pharmaceutical and Consumer Goods businesses such as GlaxoSmithKline, Target, Pepsi Co. Inc., Coca Cola Company

The situation in China is somewhat more nuanced since one of the critical challenges with which Beijing must now grapple is a highly diversified business elite circle as new enclaves control autonomous sources of power and occupy newly created political space. This emerging social class in China diminishes the historic

348

level of state control for which the Chinese society was reputed. Through this medium Chinese citizen had become heavily reliant on government spending for necessities and security in areas such as jobs, housing, and food.

A second anomaly that goes hand in hand with the corporate evolution that is evident in China is the phenomenon of "the contemporary technocrat." During the mid-1970s, as the Communist Party abandoned the class struggle in the interest of economic mobilization, the Chinese government co-opted technocrats to drive its agenda. These were not necessarily party loyalists, but rather, they possessed critical resources and expertise that were in high demand. With the passage of time, this camp became an influential game changer that is notoriously antipathetic to Communist Party conservatism. Nevertheless, the cooptation of non-politically aligned experts was a gamble made by the CCP in the interest of forging its new economic policy agenda. The evolving status quo has given birth to an emerging center of influence that is challenging the orthodoxy of the Chinese Communist Party.

Part V addresses these and other related components of the power coliseum in America and China and comments on:

- How the global economy is evolving
- How fiscal and monetary systems are buckling under misdirected policies which consistently fail to attain set goals
- The significance of the American and Chinese presence in Africa against the backdrop of competition for scarce resources, "land grabbing," increased militarization, while other centers of power such as Russia, India and Brazil, bulldoze along the flanks for a share of Africa's wealth
- The pivotal role of culture in arriving at an ultimate resolution in a multi-polar world

Principle of Complex Systems

We introduce the theory of "systems complexity" as another main pillar of the discussion thereby exposing the exponential nature of growth, the expansion of diverse and interconnected systemic parts and the imminent collapse of critical world systems. Systems complexity is the leading-edge approach to an understanding of how relationships between system parts give rise to the collective behavior of the whole, and how systems interact and form relationships with their environment on an ongoing basis. A basic tenet of this concept is that *order in market systems is spontaneous or emergent in that it is the inevitable result of its*

349

own momentum. In other words, the order displayed by systems is not materially what is produced by the execution of human design, since systems are inherently dynamic, self-regulatory, and self-correcting.

This concept is discussed at length by Gregory Bateson, who committed to extending systems theory into the wider sphere of the social sciences. Bateson views the world as a series of systems that are self-correcting.[1] Another theorist, Joseph Tainter, whose specialty is systems complexity vis-à-vis the collapse of civilizations, considered the range of factors that contributed to societal collapse within the framework of the relationship between people and society[2] Tainter's central hypothesis is that society of itself is a complex system, and that unlike earlier more autonomous civilizations, the twenty-first century society's inevitable collapse will occur initially as a trickle, which will be followed by an avalanche. He also pays close attention to the fact that authoritarian attempts to maintain cohesion, as exemplified in central planning, have placed greater strains on society, and these will ultimately hasten its collapse. Close heed should be paid to this equation in the U.S. – China contestation.

Complexity theory proponents share the view that in principle, whereas proto-global institutions that display high levels of centralization hasten the point of criticality, and will by extension escalate the collapse of global financial systems, their "de-scaling" (or alternatively maintaining their current size and making them more robust), is the only workable solution for reversing the precipitous course that the world has already embarked upon. However, in the given context this type of solution will demand ideological shifts that diverge from the neo-liberal way of thinking.

The impact of governmental intervention on economic systems is therefore crucial to our understanding of what is transpiring in world markets, since omnipresent agencies such as currencies, capital markets and derivatives, are by their very nature systems, and will follow the norms and processes of complexity theory.

Given their scale of interconnectedness, omnipresence becomes the critical attribute of protracted international economic and financial networks with their obscure asymmetries. Consider America is the center of gravity fueled by the indomitable Federal Reserve Bank, established institutional networks such as the World Bank Group, and a mind-boggling array of powerful trans-territorial corporations all yoked to Wall Street, and China compulsorily hitched to this unwieldy gargantuan.

Central Premise - Systems are Inherently Disposed to Self-Regulate

This aspect of the enquiry takes the form of an expository that provides a broad account of the extent of state activism in the U.S. and China and how this is adversely impacting on economic and social life, on the destabilization of their respective economic systems, and on the wars and conflicts taking toll on global peace and stability. This type of dynamic is dissected in F.A. Hayek's exegesis, <u>The Fatal Conceit: The Errors of Socialism,</u> wherein he argues that the essential conflict between advocates of the extended human order created by a competitive market and those who demand a deliberate arrangement of human interaction by central authority based on collective demand over available resources, is based on a *factual error* on the part of the latter group about how knowledge of resources is, and can be generated and utilized.[3] This suggests that the contemporary issues which are rooted in neoliberal ideology, are likely to be vigorously challenged in the process of resolving issues.

Pillars of Central Planning

The underpinning idea behind present day central planning is that power ought to rest in the hands of a designated "commander-in-chief," or at the very least a single staff of experts, whose actions must not be fettered by democratic procedure. What may not be immediately apparent is first and foremost that directed economies have been the driving force behind world economic systems for well over two hundred years, and beyond this, that the disposition of governments to manage and control economies and market behavior is not necessarily confined to societies with characteristically "closed" or "planned" economies. The practice was well in train in open market systems from as early as the mid-nineteenth century during the nascent phases of industrialization in Europe. Apart from the long-established nature of the practice, the tendency to "plan," alluded to by Lionel Robbins, was well dispersed among ideologically diverse political systems. In his words:

> *"Planning is the grand panacea of our age. But unfortunately its meaning is highly ambiguous. In popular discussion it stands for almost any policy which it is wished to be presented as desirable when the average citizen, be he Nazi or Communist or Summer School Liberal, warms to the statement that "What the world needs is planning," what he really feels is that the world needs that which is satisfactory."[4]*

The point was reinforced in the British Parliament at the height of World War II in February of 1947 when the Labor government under Prime Minister Clement

Attlee quoted from an article written in <u>The Economic Survey</u> (1947) which stated in part:

> *"There is an essential difference between totalitarian and democratic planning. The former subordinates all individual desires and preferences to the demands of the State. For this purpose it uses various methods of compulsion upon the individual, which deprive him of his freedom of choice. Such methods may be necessary even in a democratic country during the extreme emergency of Great War. Thus the British gave their wartime government the power to direct labor. But in normal times the people of a democratic country will not give up their freedom of choice to their Government"* [5]

Despite its enduring application, "central planning" boasts of an ignominious track record, the obvious reason being that it discards the logic of complexity theory. By extension, the Keynesian model of economics, popularly adopted among Western governments (which promotes state activism), is of itself inherently flawed. Chapter Fifteen elaborates on these ideas and questions the unflagging application of Keynesian principles by contemporary planners although their application has consistently worked to the detriment of the U.S economy. The government, as we shall demonstrate, is assuming greater and greater control over America's monetary and fiscal systems while a similar policy approach is being assumed by authorities in Beijing.

Indeed, ongoing moves in Washington towards enlarged government and appeals for more laws and regulations and intensified enforcement ignore the inevitable consequences of an impending "total government," a phenomenon very lucidly described in von Mises's classic, <u>"Omnipotent Government: The Rise of the Total State and Total War"</u> [6] The central idea behind Mises's inquisition is that such measures are responsible for catapulting economies towards increasing instability. This book argues that the more weakened the U.S. economy becomes as a consequence of an enlarged government and increasing attempts to centralize planning, the more enabled will the Chinese evolve, as a force with the capability of seriously destabilizing the U.S. economy. The Americans recognize this.

The Present Scenario

Concerning Beijing's ongoing approach to central planning, the World Bank Report, <u>China 2030</u> provided direction to the Chinese government drawing upon the experiences of emerging markets such as Japan, Korea, Hong Kong SAR, Singapore and Taiwan. [7] The Report made reference to the fact that in these societies the responsibility assumed by government as it pursued *the development path* was a straightforward one that entailed the provision of essential infrastructure such as roads, railways, and energy while simultaneously opening trade and investment policies. These facilities were geared towards the promotion of technological improvements that would enhance and complement private investment. The Report goes on to state: -

> *".... When a developing country reaches the technology frontier the correct development strategy ceases to be so straightforward. Direct government intervention may retard growth not help it. Instead the policy emphasis needs to shift even more towards private sector development, ensuring that markets are mature enough to allocate resources efficiently and that firms are innovative and strong enough to compete internationally in technologically advanced sectors.*[8]*"*

The thrust of the study is that Beijing should assume a supportive rather than an interventionist posture. Stated differently, the government's approach to planning should comprise mobilizing China's national resources in order to achieve improved living standards; granting rights to individuals, households, enterprises, communities, academia and non-governmental organizations to facilitate societal empowerment; and affording rights to civil society, that would be discharged through a system of clear rules that encourages the broadest levels of participation possible.

State interventionism in the U.S. is at play with the left wing promoting the view that the high unemployment rate is a serious drag on economic growth and for this reason raising taxes on the wealthy would be an acceptable way to balance the budget, reduce government deficits, and take some of the burden off the poor and middle classes. This grand scheme, in their thinking, would also bridge the widening gap between the rich and the poor which they recognize as yet another obstacle to growth and stability. A recent illustration of direct intervention was the government's management of the 2008-2009 industry bailouts. There is a school of thought that strongly admonishes the billions that were spent in filling the "air pockets" of deficit created by the big banks and influential financial institutions, and suggests that these same funds should have been better applied in the training and retooling of tens of thousands of workers who are incapable of producing revenue-generating products.

China now finds itself in a comparably detrimental quagmire amidst declining economic growth to an extent not experienced since the introduction of economic reforms in the late 1970s. The government has reacted by introducing a raft of policies all of which that are heavily state-underwritten and by initiating financial sector reforms.

CHAPTER FIFTEEN

THE MANAGED ECONOMY
AND WORLD ECONOMIC SYSTEM

"Direct government intervention may retard growth not help it..."

World Bank

he credibility of economic ratiocination is increasingly being undermined by day-to- day events as systems collapse under the worldwide slump. In terms of working towards resolutions, any new idea that goes beyond the parameters of present day thought is bound to have political implications. However, history is instructive. For an idea deemed "out of the box" to be accepted in the political process, it must first be rendered acceptable for public consumption by undergoing a transformational process that guarantees wide acceptance. A further prerequisite for its embrace must be the liberal free market ideology and the articles of faith of Keynesian economics.

This chapter affirms that as governments resort to large-scale planning in the form of macroeconomic management through fiscal and monetary manipulation instead of relying on the invisible hand of market forces as advocated in "complex systems" thinking, such approaches have left in their wake a string of negative repercussions. The consistency of the phenomenon compels a search for alternative approaches.

The reader should consider whether greater efficiency of large-scale production is really achieved with the disappearance of competition that ensues from state control or complete government takeovers. This proposition was officially considered in one of the more comprehensive studies on the topic titled "Final Report of the Temporary National Economic Committee of the Concentration of Economic Power.[1]" The study noted among other things, that:

> *"The superior efficiency of large establishments has not been demonstrated; the advantages that are supposed to destroy competition have failed to manifest themselves in many fields. Nor do the economies of size, where they exist, invariably necessitate monopoly....It should be noted moreover, that monopoly is frequently the product of factors other than the lower costs of greater size. It is attained through*

355

collusive agreement and promoted by public policies. When these agreements are invalidated and when these policies are reversed, competitive conditions can be restored[2]

Another point of note is that scientific planning, as commonly advocated, would appear to transcend political ideology. That parties on the right as well as on the left undertake central planning was the underpinning argument put forward by Professor Hayek in his book, The Road to Serfdom[3] in underscoring the point. Hayek noted that many intelligent and informed people of his day had been taken in by the claim that National Socialism was the next logical and historical phase of collapsing capitalism. Central to the claim was that fascism and communism both represented totalitarian systems that have much more in common with each other than either has with the governments and economic systems that exist under liberal free market democracies. Coming when it did in the 1930s, at a time when the Labor government in England was collapsing, the gold standard was being abandoned, and protectionist tariffs were being introduced, these ideas of state control and monopoly created a stir among conservative thinkers. In a later contribution to political philosophy, The Constitution of Liberty[4], Hayek would go further and spell out the philosophical foundations of liberal constitutionalism wherein he defined a sphere of authority that conferred on the state a monopoly of coercion and the application of coercive powers through the rule of law.

Few planners then and even now are willing to attest to the desirability of central planning as the panacea for resolving economic crises. They are even less disposed to acknowledging that planning is the raison d'etre of the bureaucracy. Many will nonetheless concede that planning becomes a necessity in times of emergency such as the declaration of war or impending economic collapse. Thereupon, it is invoked by the state via policy intervention and replaces open competition. This connection between planning and monopolization or the outright elimination of competition at its very source is referred to as cartelization or syndicalism and has been promoted by many governments as an economic strategy in times of national crisis and is an aspect of war-planning that governments have consistently exploited to this day. Once this economic policy becomes codified and firmly entrenched, as has been the case, it assumes a degree of institutional permanence.

Monopoly, on this scale and in such circumstances, necessitates full state backing, as obtained with the growth of cartels and syndicates in comparatively new industrial societies in the 1870s, such as the United States and Germany. To illustrate this, Chapter Thirteen averred to the extent to which competition was significantly reduced during the years of the New Deal when American industrialists were co-opted by the Roosevelt administration to assume control over

356

sizeable segments of the economy, such as agricultural farms and the railroad system. The removal of competition through monopolization was also manifested in other jurisdictions across Europe. Whether this aspect of state intervention was the outcome of technological developments, or whether it was prompted by political expediency on account of the war, or became necessary as capitalism evolved would explain the true motivation behind centralized planning.

What remains clear, however, is that the phenomenon was not restricted to advanced economic systems, but originated during early phases of Europe's industrial growth in the nascent economies of Germany, the Soviet Union, the United Kingdom and the United States. This section of the inquisition focuses on the impact of planning, and more specifically, the primary role that corporations have and continue to play in scientific planning orchestrated by government. The concluding paragraphs suggest that failed policies precipitated by ill-advised government intervention have now set the stage for economic and political chaos leading to war that is asymmetric in scope and global in outreach.

II

The Experiment of Scientific Planning

One of the earliest motivations to have spurred state intervention is budget deficit. During the nineteenth century, many countries occasionally ran into deficit spending when tax revenues were insufficient to meet expenditure. Niall Fergusson, author of The House of Rothschild: Money's Prophets 1798-1848,[5] observed that " ...all nineteenth century states occasionally ran budget deficits and some almost always did," and this state of continuing national deficit in government spending was the crux of what initially drove governments into the hands of bankers and corporatists, in a virtual neck brace that persists and is so visible today.

The expenditure imposed by war and war preparations accounted by far for the largest increases in expenditure, followed by expenditure occasioned by poor harvests and occasional trough cycles. Although the resulting fiscal deficits were relatively low, they could not be readily financed since at that period in time national capital markets had not as yet matured and the internationally integrated capital market, as we now know it, was yet at a stage of nascence. Budget deficits were therefore typically remedied in any of the following four ways: by borrowing at high interest rates since the state was perceived by investors as an unreliable creditor; in the case of Britain by sale of Royal Assets; by inducing inflation if the government were in a position to devalue the country's currency; or by raising taxes or introducing new ones. In any event any major changes in tax regimes would have required political consent.

Another ground for deficit spending was political expediency, as obtained during America's New Deal when prohibitive amounts of funds were allocated to welfare. In <u>The Political Economy of the New Deal</u>[6] authors Jim F. Couch, William E. Shughart II debated on the originations of America's welfare state and the extent to which a disproportionately large share of the federal government's relief funds was appropriated to states with healthier economies during the period of the Great Depression. The central argument in this study was that the motivation for largesse that typified the FDR administration's public choice policies was not founded upon genuine concerns for the unemployed, but rather was driven by the personal ambitions of Roosevelt himself.

Central Planning in Germany

In Germany, central planning became popularized amidst the scores of cartels and syndicates that bedecked the country's landscape from as early as the 1870s, when cartelization was a popular state-backed policy that was actively and systematically fostered by the government. The operation of such a policy entailed guaranteeing private entrepreneurs various forms of protection, providing direct inducements to business owners, and in instances using naked compulsion to foster monopolistic market behavior. This was all intended to ultimately regulate the price of goods and control sales. F.A. Hayek lauded the trend as one that was worthy of universal emulation, noting:

> "It is largely due to the influence of German socialist theoreticians, particularly Sombart, generalizing from the experience of their country, that the inevitable development of the competitive system of monopoly capitalism became widely accepted"."

He also noted that in the United States a highly protectionist policy made a somewhat similar development possible and seemed to confirm this generalization. He continued,

> "The development of Germany, however, more than that of the United States, came to be regarded as representative of a universal tendency; and it became commonplace to speak - of Germany " where all the

social and political forces of modern civilization have reached their most advanced form[8]. "

Russia's Reconstruction and Central Planning

Similarly, in the case of the Soviet Union, the motivation to escalate the pace of industrialization in 1928 spurred economic planning. Professor V. I. Grinevstsky suggested an elaborate plan for Russia entitled, "Postwar Perspective of Russian Industry[9]" Therein, he embarked on an overview of Russia's prewar industry, and based on his findings, created a blueprint for postwar reconstruction plans. Notably, the publication presupposed the continuance of the capitalist system. Notwithstanding this, Lenin did not falter in recognizing the true worth of Grinevstsky's propositions, and lost no time in applying it to the Soviet economy. Having consulted with a group of engineers, he commissioned a team of specialists with the task of planning the reconstruction of Russia's future based on the "Grenevetsky scheme". This auspicious team, whose first report was published in 1920, would be comprised of notables of the day including professors, engineers, and other types of specialists. Significantly, self-professed "communists" did not form part of this hand-picked corps and the offshoot of the endeavor was the establishment of a State Planning Commission (the "Gosplan"), the remit of which was the extension of Grenevstsky's planning concepts for all industry across Russia.

Lenin's original idea had been that Russia's postwar reconstruction would be based on electrification. Indeed, this was not lost to the Commission, which produced its first Piatiletka or Five-Year Plan committing to the restoration of the national economy. The Report proved to be all-encompassing and dealt with activities such as electrification; light and heavy industry; agriculture; transport; mail; telephones and telegraphs; consumers' cooperatives; labor; public instruction; scientific research; health protection and social life; housing and finance. The plan did not confine itself to the industrial sphere but also grappled with the educational and cultural aspects of Russian life. It presented proposals for health resorts, rest houses for workers, recreational tours, housing and other forms of welfare services. Considerable advances were proposed for each of these phases of activities some of which were from a practical standpoint, beyond human attainment.

At the end of the first five years, however, Russia had witnessed development in the electrical industry (Gordon, op, cit., p. 398), an increase in the mechanized production of coal, advances in the metal, chemical, and machine manufacturing industries and improvements in railroad plants These results were obtained at great cost since prohibitive sums were paid out by the government to import machines, engineers, and technicians. Between 1927-1928, industry contributed to the national budget 288 million rubles and received 783 million – for every ruble it gave it received in return three. By 1932 the entire revenue from the industry reached 943 million and in return the industry received from the government 15,357 million rubles, 16 rubles for every ruble it paid.[10]

The credit for Russia's take-off has been the topic of much controversy among academia.[11] Professor Antony C. Sutton, for example, makes some decidedly jolting assertions in his account, <u>Wall Street and The Bolshevik Revolution: The Remarkable True Story of the American Capitalists Who Financed The Russian Communists (1974).</u>[12] Sutton's theory is that U.S. corporations played a closeted role during the critical years of Russia's post-war planning. Dismissed and ostracized by many as "extreme," the central idea behind his findings is that the basics of the First and Second Five-Year Plans set up in Russia were in fact conceptualized in the United States with substantial inputs from U.S. corporations, specifically Aba Khan, among the foremost industrial architects in the U.S, whose contribution to Russia's first Five-Year Plan was impressively substantial. He credits American corporations for the establishment of industrial complexes in Russia, citing Du Pont, General Electric, Welti, Ford Motor assembler of the Goki trucks, Hercules Motor and Curtis Wright. Their allegedly U.S-designed plans and business success stories, in Sutton's estimation, were subsequently copied by the Soviets in a move, which based on his account, contributed to the tremendous industrial outputs of the Soviets.

A former research fellow at the Hoover Institution for War, Revolution, and Peace at Stanford California, Sutton lays further claim to historical linkages between "US capitalists" and "Russian communists." He charges that Morgan banking executives played a seminal role in "funneling" illegal Bolshevik gold into the United States, the co-option of the American Red Cross by powerful Wall Street forces, the "intervention" by Wall Street agents in freeing Leon Trotsky (the Marxist revolutionary whose well-known and affirmed aim was to topple the government of Russia), deals made by major U.S. corporations to capture the huge and largely untapped Russian market at least one decade and a half before the U.S. formally recognized the Russian regime, and last certainly by no means least, the "secret sponsoring" of communism by leading American businessmen who publicly championed free enterprise.

The end game of Sutton's anthology is a groundbreaking conspiratorial narrative suggestive of government interposition in the building of the post-war Russian economy and the fact that "the West" in fact played an integral role in this phase of Russia's past, with the direct effects felt until the 1970s. The latter point was spotlighted, to the utter consternation of mainstream conservatives, in a subsequent publication entitled <u>National Suicide: Military Aid To The Soviet Union (1973)</u>. [13]

Direct Government in America Today

Direct government has persisted in America's political history, ostensibly in an effort to stave off the impact of recessions and depressions. In the mythology assumed by the "welfare state," the New Deal in America exemplified government intervention at its height, as a triumph of public interest over selfishness. It represented a period of big government in which federal programs were advertised as the panacea for economic woes, insulated from the petty corruption and mundane rent. This was in fact not the case.

FDR and his advisors, under whose auspices the notion of big government was idealized, believed that the Depression was caused by low prices and assumed that high prices enforced by whatever means, be it threats, violence, coercion or intimidation by the State, would be the ultimate solution to chronic deficit and high unemployment. Indeed, the view that unemployment is caused by wage demands that are too high in relation to wages that employers are willing and able to pay, has been out of favor for more than 50 years. Keynesian and other macroeconomists have insisted that unemployment is caused by aggregate demand for goods in the economy being too low for all those looking for work to be hired at the given level of wages. It was on this merit that the Keynesians prescribed the introduction of government-led "demand stimulus" as a means of curbing unemployment.

The pre-Keynesian worldview has been staunchly defended by Vedda and Gallaway in their research (elaborated on in later paragraphs), which asserts that real wages – the cost of hiring workers after adjusting for changes in productivity and in the selling prices of goods in relation to the money wages paid to workers – increased during the early years of the Depression. They discovered that at the onset of the Great Depression in October1929, the unemployment rate in the United States was 2.5% and when the Depression ended the figure surged to 28% of the labor force. Despite the widely propagated belief that President Roosevelt lifted the U.S. out of the Depression, unemployment never fell below 12% after 1933 and was still in the range of 18-20% between 1938-1939. Typically, high unemployment and budget deficits have served as triggers for governmental intervention in the form of bloated programs funded by debt, now referred to, as "stimulus packages."

The U.S. government has embraced Keynesian principles but for these to be effective there must be certain preconditions:

- That economic "stimuli" are introduced as a short run measure where a liquidity crisis exists
- That the stimuli are not intended for application to chronic long-term economic conditions such deep insolvency
- That the economy enjoys low debt levels from the outset of stimulus injection

Reported successes of the New Deal based on the application of Keynesian principles are therefore arguable. Arrington (1969), for example, was among the first in a steady procession of analysts to engage in a comparison of New Deal spending with per capita across states. His research unearthed a string of anomalies including substantial variations in the distribution of New Deal funds per capita, misalignments in the allocation of benefits and inconsistencies in the assessed severity of the Great Depression. Reading (1973) came up with similar findings. Wright's work (1974) churned out data that confirmed the discrepancies and went further in noting that New Deal expenditures were systematically allocated to swing states to secure the re-election of FDR. Anderson and Tollison (1991) descried the clout that state congressional delegations seem to have held in the determination of New Deal transfers. This collection of highly rated research concluded that New Deal so-called "triumphs" cannot withstand statistical scrutiny and were largely driven by the political motivations of the executive.

The stockpile of evidence repudiating statist schemes was further cemented by Lowell E. Gallaway and Richard K. Veddler in their high-water erudition Out of Work: Unemployment and Government in 20th Century America.[14] Invoking a stockpile of empirical data, the authors delivered a strong rebuttal of reported benefits to the American people, which confirmed:

- That the Unemployment Act of 1946 made the eradication of unemployment a priority of the Federal Government. During the first 30 years of the twentieth century when government assumed absolutely no responsibility for unemployment, the mean unemployment rate was less than five percent and stable. In sharp distinction to this trend, throughout the years 1960-1989, the average unemployment rate was 20% higher and continued rising.
- That the massive unemployment of the Great Depression resulted from too much government intervention. The efforts of the Hoover administration to raise real wages generated an unemployment rate of 28% higher than it would have been if real wages had remained constant.

362

- That FDR New Deal plan prolonged rather than alleviated the Great Depression
- That following World War II an estimated 12 million Americans entered the job market at a time when government spending was considerably reduced. In a dramatic refutation of Keynesian theory, the market actually absorbed the workers and unemployment never rose over 4%.
- That there is a trove of statistical research demonstrating that during the 1970s the aggregate unemployment rate increased at a time when insurance benefits were being paid out
- When figures are compared, despite substantial differences in unemployment levels between states, the lowest unemployment figures are derived from locations with high agricultural employment, modest levels of unionization, and low rates of public assistance.
- Besides increased taxes levied on exports other aspects of governmental planning worsened the Depression - during the Hoover presidency, for example the government had resorted to binge spending on public works to the tune of 13% of the federal budget. For such a measure to succeed, it should have been accompanied by sizeable tax increases, but this was not the case.

The Gallaway and Veddler Study conceded the abnormally high levels of unemployment of the 1930s could have been avoided without New Deal policies. They estimated that by 1940 the unemployment rate was eight points higher than it would have been without the type of legislation that induced growth of unionism and government-mandated employment costs. Their conclusion was irrefutable - that the Great Depression was significantly prolonged both in terms of duration and magnitude as a result of the fiscal and monetary implications of New Deal programs.

The Directed Economy and Welfare in America

Augmenting the trove of notable literature undergirding concerns over interventionism, are:

- Against Leviathan,[15] in which Robert Higgs offers a self-styled epitaph of America's "much vaunted welfare state" while observing that "with its bewildering, incoherent mass of new expenditures, taxes, subsidies, regulations, and direct government participation in productive activities, the New Deal created so much confusion, fear, uncertainty and hostility among businessmen and investors that private investment and hence overall private economic activity never recovered enough to restore the high levels of production and employment enjoyed during the 1920s. "His study dissects the New Deal period into five segments: the Great Depression (1930-1940); transition to the War Economy (1940-1941); the War Command Economy (1942-1945); Demobilization, Reconversion, and Decontrol, also referred to as "The True Great Escape"(1945-1946); and Postwar Prosperity (1946 and beyond). He argues that the U.S. economy remained in depression because private investment never recovered sufficiently after the collapse during the Great Contraction

- Regime Uncertainty: Why The Great Depression Lasted So Long[16] in which the writer reinforces earlier findings while noting that there was a relative neutering of New Deal prices along with a reduction in absolute dollars of the Federal budget from $98.4 billion in 1945 to $33 billion in 1948. This brought about America's long awaited economic recovery. Private sector production increased by almost one-third of what it was in 1946 alone, and private capital investment increased for the first time in 18 years. In short, it was capitalism rather than New Deal policies that ended the Great Depression; by no means were wage increases, unionizing, and welfare and state expanding policies responsible for the let up in the Great Depression cycle.

- Thomas D. Lorenzo's article The New Deal Debunked (Again)[17] describing the first New Deal "(1933-1934) as *one giant cartel scheme* whereby the government attempted to enforce cartel pricing and output reductions on industries including agriculture.

- John Flynn's "The Roosevelt Myth"[18] first published in 1948, which reiterated Lorenzo's sentiments. The author noted that most American administrations typically dealt with economic issues either by doing nothing or by deregulating. Citing Martin Von Buren, the eighth president of the United States, in contrast to many other U.S. presidents, concluded that *all former attempts on the part of the government to assume the management of domestic foreign exchange have proven injurious.* Von Buren actually believed that meddling in interventionism as a response to recessions made things worse. Instead, his administration cut federal spending in absolute dollars by 21%, discontinued price control, and did all that was possible in the absence of direct control to move the market towards free trade. In Von Buren's thinking, *all that was needed was a system founded on private interests, enterprise and competition without the aid of legislative grants or regulation by law.*

New Deal principles were in actuality derived from policies of the Hoover administration that were reintroduced by FDR as expedients to resolve the issues relating to the Great Depression. These policies were strenuously promoted by Rexford Tugwell who was an acknowledged protégé of the Frankfurt School, [19] one of Hoover's principal advisors, an unabashed Soviet apologist, and ardent admirer of Josef Stalin. Tugwell had churned copious volumes of literature expounding on measures that should be adopted to revive America's deficient economy. He lauded Stalin's central planning approach and spurred Washington's policy makers to emulate the Soviet economic model.

The Smoot and Hawley legislative package provides a classic illustration of the potential for misdirected policies to trigger retaliatory governmental actions, create countervailing alignments and aggravate trade imbalances all at once. In anticipation of the enactment, countries including Canada, France and Great Britain hastened to root around for alternative markets for their exports [20] and data subsequently confirmed the extent of the free fall arising from tariff impositions on goods entering the U.S. market. From a policy-making perspective, what becomes demonstrably clear is that misdirected positions adopted by the government can lead to serious setbacks that reverse intended goals, render America more vulnerable, and equally important place strains on mutual relationships. This cannot be risked given prevailing volatilities in the global arena.

Spikes in food prices and food shortages are attributable to a range of factors including redistribution patterns of key food stock, increased demand in emerging economies, changes in monetary policy and financial speculation. But more than ever, it is primarily government-promoted export restrictions that drive the domino market closing effect.[21] This is what impelled the piloting of the legislation and is corroborated in Nadia et al findings that demonstrate that protectionist policies aimed at indemnifying the domestic economy from the vagaries of world markets have a direct correlation with food prices and export policies.

III

Government Intervention and Impact on the Global Food Prices

The nexus between government-imposed policy, food shortages and prices is irrefutable and continues to be a key concern, when one considers that the price of food escalated by more than 50% between the periods 2006-2007 and 2008-2010, precipitating extreme market volatility (Everett and Jenny, 2012). An often overlooked basis for the phenomenon is the surge in protectionist policies aimed at restricting food exports. Such increases could trigger artificial shortages and black marketeering, social divisions between the wealthy and the poor, and widespread violence and political instability. Ivanic and Martin's 2008 study concluded on "Implications of Higher Global Food Prices for Poverty in Low-Income Countries" that export restrictions destabilize global markets by increasing demand and lowering supply when price is already high, and furthermore, that the relaxation or removal of such policies can provide significant relief."

A study entitled, "Export Policy and Food Price Escalation,[22]" by Nadia Rocha et al examined the link between world food prices and protectionism and concluded that while a large number of factors may have contributed to the sudden and rapid spikes in food prices, in instances such as the reduction in food stocks, increased demand in emergency economies, financial speculation, changes in monetary policy in leading economies and government-sponsored trade policies actually aggravated the problem (Anderson 2002; Anderson et al 2010). Empirical studies involving a comparison of figures between 1990-2011 corroborate these findings and demonstrate that the normal value of food prices increased by 135% in 1996, to 215% in 2008, and 235% in 2011.[23]

Pascal Lamy, Director General of the World Trade Organization, commented in 2011 on the direct correlation between export policy and food prices. He noted, "...export restrictions were the single most important reason for the 2007-2008 price explosion in the rice market..." and to the blowback that ensued. He continued:

> "In response to the crises, some started looking further inwards and we saw a whole host of export restrictions flourish. These export restrictions had a domino market closing effect, with one restriction bringing about another[...24]"

This enquiry notes that the initial intent of government-sponsored adjustments to food export policy is invariably to stabilize domestic prices and shield the domestic economy from unfavorable developments in the wider international market. By the same token, a reciprocal co-relation should exist between international food prices and export policy. Failing this, the unilateral actions of exporting countries would trigger a harmful snowballing effect, via a principle that operates in macroeconomic theory. This implies that world food price changes should constructively inform export policy activism and vice versa. As the VOX Studies demonstrate, these correlations were clearly at work between January 2008 and

December 2010, when exporting countries, creating deleterious consequences that impacted on a world scale, imposed 85 new restrictions on food products. The restrictions were most noticeable in staple food products such as maize, wheat and rice. See Vox Study Table – 15 -1.

TABLE - 15-1
PRODUCTS COVERED BY TRADE RESTRICTIONS IN 2008-2010

Product	% Trade Covered by Export Restrictions
Staple food of which	19.01
Grain, sorghum	0.1
Wheat and meslin	30.6
Maize (corn)	23.1
Barley	7.1
Rice	39.1
Non-staple food	7.4

The Vox findings underscore the following trends:

- Export policy was an important contributing factor to the global food crisis in 2008-2010
- Global export restrictions on a product, that is to say the share of international trade covered by export restrictions, positively correlate with the probability of imposing a new export restriction on that product, especially for staple foods
- Large exporters are found generally to be more reactive to restrictive measures. This suggests that the "multiplier effect" is more likely than not driven by this group

All in all, export restriction modifications between 2008-2010 brought world food prices in heel, a fact that was proven with the application of a "back of an envelope calculation" on the coefficients of regression – a method that demonstrates that had exporters refrained from imposing restrictions, food prices would have been on an average 13% lower during the period under observation. The VOX study also illustrated that while the figures appeared sizeable, it represented "a conservative estimate" as it averages out across food products, such as staple products where the implications on restrictions are more crucial.

Fiscal Policy and Monetary Control in 2012

Interventionism has gained support not only in America but also in the E.U. As a case in point, François Hollande, socialist candidate who went on to win the 2011 French presidency election, had given forewarning during his campaign, of his intention to seek a renegotiation of the European Union fiscal treaty, in order to promote economic growth. Among Hollande's campaign promises was the creation of collective Euro bonds to be used for the financing of industrial infrastructure projects. This was in much the same vein as the interventions meted out by the Hoover, Roosevelt, and Obama administrations. Nonetheless, the idea was strongly resisted by Germany. In sharp distinction, the German Chancellor had propounded stringent austerity measures as a cure for Europe's sovereign debt crisis, an initiative that entailed requiring European Community Member States to limit their annual budget deficits to 3% of GDP by 2013. It is noteworthy that outgoing French President Sarkozy had strongly supported this scheme.

James Grant, founder and editor of Grant's Interest Rate Observer, who was featured on Russia Today, [25] made two specific observations in relation to intervention schemes that are currently being propagated by central planners. These were that governments and central banks are waging a war on supply and demand in order to affect the price mechanism; and that generally in America although the Federal Reserve may not overtly manipulate prices there is a mechanism facilitating a controlled financial market, whereby interest rates are manipulated and set by "our masters at the Federal Reserve system."

Expediency Through Interventionism

Federal Reserve Chairman Bernanke, at a Lecture Series hosted by the George Washington University, surprised many listeners in his audience at the George Washington University in 2012, when he asserted that manipulation of prices was in fact "a terrible idea." He explained that prices were the critical guiding mechanism in the market economy and that interest rates were the "traffic signals" that contributed to perceptions of the market value of stocks, shares, bonds and the like.[26] In the same breath, Bernanke iterated that the application of the gold standard prior to its abandonment in the 1930s did not permit the government to exercise the degree of flexibility that was then necessary to address economic issues such as controlling the volume of money in circulation, and this lack of flexibility had aggravated the Great Depression.

Grant favors a return to the gold standard despite the fact that central banks are likely to be opposed to the idea. He predicts the ultimate collapse of paper money to be followed by a free fall that would lead to one of two outcomes: either the denationalization of money via excision of the fiat system as advocated by libertarian Congressman Ron Paul and the coalition of the like-minded; alternatively, the replacement of the gold standard by the abrogation of legal tender laws. In his estimation, either option would harness the banality of bankers by supplanting the type of artificially supported prosperity that now obtains, whereby too big to fail banks in America are being "bailed out" via public funding.

IV

"Centralized" Planning in Twenty-First Century China

In China, the state sector has historically been the dominant driver of the economy and by extension economic reform. All areas that are considered key and strategic to China, such as banking, finance, petroleum, technology and telecommunications have remained firmly within the cusp of state-owned or controlled enterprises. Despite this the role of private initiative in economic activity has expanded incrementally first and foremost with the dismantling of collectives, followed by the provision of inducements to foreign investors, and the elevation of the private sector from being a mere augmentation of the state-controlled system to a sector that is of primary importance to sustained economic growth and development. Today, China boasts of more than 70 million small enterprises, which have a registered capital of more than $4.5 trillion and are capable of making estimated investments worth at least $9.6 trillion.

Among the more discernible measures taken by the government are firstly making all state-held shares of the country's 1,300 listed companies publicly traded[27] and secondly making an ideological shift which the government has gratifyingly showcased through private sector representation at the high-level CPC Congresses. Prior 2002, private sector representatives were excluded from attendance at the Congress of the Communist Party. However, the CCP extended invitations to 34 such delegates to attend the Eighteenth Congress in November 2012.[28] It is widely known in political circles that a CPC membership is a definitive boon to effective lobbying and being politically relevant. With this in view, many of the CEOs of prominent conglomerates represented at the 2011 Seventeenth

Congress lost no time shortly afterwards in applying and being endorsed for Central Committee membership.

In 1978 China's transition from a command economy to one that is open and free and driven by market incentives fueled by the government, was formally launched. This philosophy required the adoption of free market principles and the introduction of a line-up of schemes conducive to open competition. Ill-advisedly, the government went about setting quotas and purchasing manufactured goods at fixed prices and whatever basket of goods exceeded the quota was sold on the open market. The pitfalls of this push, which were foreseeable, were increased levels of inflation compounded by systemic corruption.

The second plank in PRC reforms evolved around the implementation of a "dual track" approach to the economic development plan. This entailed the continued "grand fathering" by the government of state-owned firms in established priority sectors in parallel with the promotion of private enterprise.[29]

A third important component of the reform was the ushering in of a gradualist strategy by "empowering" large state-owned firms via a "dual pricing" system that allowed them preferred benefits.[30] Although the economy exhibited rapid growth during this period, social inequalities widened unexpectedly amidst allegations of corruption leading to a loss of popularity for the programs.[31] By the mid-1980s, the government felt compelled to introduce remedial measures and this was in fact achieved by scrapping the ill-fated dual pricing model in favor of market pricing. This reversal of policy led to panic and increased volatility, which was yet another harsh lesson for state interventionism.

Against this setting Premier Wen Jiaboa presented a specially assembled Work Report to the National People's Congress at the Fifth Session of the Congress held during the first quarter of 2012.[32] The document expounded the measures the PRC would pursue to stabilize the market by narrowing the deficit. In 2011, this figure stood at 900 million *yuan* and was expected to fall to 800 billion by the end of 2012, resulting a decrease of an estimated 1.5 percent of the GDP. This data included 550 billion *yuan* in central government shortfalls and 250 billion *yuan* in bonds issued on behalf of local governments.[25]

The medium term resolutions explained in the report consisted of:

- Continuation of proactive fiscal, prudent, monetary policies
- Cutting GDP growth
- Deepening reform of financial systems
- Targeting 4% consumer price rise

370

- Increasing exports/imports by 10%
- Targeting 14% of M2 growth
- Creating 9 million new jobs in 2012

Added to these measures Beijing resolved to introduce a regime of social programs geared to resolve socio-economic and governance concerns that caught the attention of the World Bank, in a move that was bound to impose exorbitant demands on public expenditure. These consisted of:

- Reform of medical and health care services
- Increases in the volume of low-income housing to provide for 12 million
- Introduction of an old age pension scheme that would cover all residents
- Exertion of absolute leadership over the armed forces
- Strengthening innovative social administration
- Restraining moves that would violate farmers' rights to land

China has reshaped the global economy and will undoubtedly continue to affect the future trajectory of other major economies, including that of the United States, in very significant ways. This enquiry has noted that within an interval of three decades, the shift from a command to a market based economy proceeded with the Chinese Communist Party visibly at the helm throughout all phases of the historic transition.

A recently released Report entitled <u>China 2030: Building a Modern, Harmonious, Creative High Income Society</u>,[33] the product of a joint project of the World Bank and the Development Research Center of the PRC, projects the need for a further change on gear in the country's development path. In conceding that the reforms that pitched China into its current growth trajectory were inspired by Deng Xiapong, the document goes on to note that after more than 30 years of rapid economic growth, the country has now reached another turning point in its development path, and that an equally fundamental shift is needed to curtail centralized control even further.

Having acknowledged that savings was successfully mobilized and sizeable volumes of capital were poured into strategic sectors during the period of take-off in the 1970s, the World Bank Report recommended an approach that would address China's current circumstances:

- The disintermediation of the non-state sector, in particular micro, small and medium state enterprises that have substantially less access to formal financial institutions than state enterprises and large firms.

371

- Low lending rates, which would spur excessive investment and higher capital intensity
- Diminished credit allocation in central and provincial levels, which had previously resulted in the accumulation of contingent liabilities that were not easily quantifiable due to the absence of quantifiable data and reliable monitoring mechanisms

Beijing is presently being inspired by the World Bank to reduce its role in markets, resource allocation, production, and distribution and to step up support for the financing of public goods and services, protecting the environment, increasing equality of opportunity, ensuring an environment that was conducive to private sector development and enhancing the development of its human capital.

V

The Battlefield of Global Finance

We have thus far demonstrated that the imposition of controls by governments is highly prevalent and that ill-founded or poorly timed state interventions could prove to be both politically and economically calamitous to a country. This discourse has also demonstrated that the vitiation from government intervention goes beyond the parameters of domestic affairs and affects trade relations with international partners, at times compelling the latter to coalesce into countervailing alignments to the long-term detriment of the instigating country. This was certainly America's World War II experience.

Another aspect of central control, which is an even more definitive catalyst for intensified U.S. - Sino confrontation, is economic conflict arising from the manipulation of currency exchange rates. The principal accusation leveled by the U.S against the Chinese for several years is that Beijing persists in the manipulation of its currency to keep Chinese exports cheap, and by extension, more attractive to foreign buyers. A weak dollar is favorable to the United States in much the same way as China favors a weak *yuan;* either power's interest is in gaining a convincing edge in currency competition whereby cheap currency would bolster exports.

The motive behind the Chinese policy of undervaluing the *yuan* is to create much-needed jobs in China's coastal factories, assembly plants, and transportation hubs that are on the receiving end of massive migration flows of young person's originating from the country's central and southern rural provinces in search of jobs. The inability of the PRC to meet this gnawing demand could lead to widespread discontent, which could potentially explode into massive - scale demonstrations, reminiscent if the Tiananmen Square revolt, that could in turn catapult the country to internal chaos.

In a similar vein, America is in dire need of creating additional jobs as a means of revving up a distressed economy. It is worth recalling that in 1978 the U.S. government had passed the Full Employment and Balanced Growth Act, more commonly referred to as the Humphrey-Hawkins Full Employment Act, the intent of which was to address growing inflation and rising unemployment, to develop new monetary policies that would increase liquidity. All in all, the management of unemployment was added to the mandate of the Federal Reserve. Although the Act expired in 2000, it is still the official policy of the government that the Federal Reserve should focus on both the attainment of sound monetary policy as well as economic growth leading to full employment, which are often times contradictory mandates.

It was envisaged that following the enactment the numeric goal of 3% unemployment would be achieved by 1983.[34] However, the net result was that unemployment actually spiraled in the ensuing years, rising from 7.8% in 1992 to 10.1% in 2009 following the financial crisis. On May 04, 2012, U.S. Secretary of Labor Hilda Solis reported that unemployment in the U.S. had reached 8.4% in the preceding month.

Consumption levels in the homeland have stagnated, investment has slowed and government spending is severely constrained. The crux of the matter is that in America the government is now seeking to cut public spending, conserve on energy consumption, and rely on taxes and net exports to sustain the economy. These are serious constraints that spur the government towards the adoption of protectionist policies as for example competitive devaluation, tariffs or trade sanctions.

Non- Conventional Asymmetric Warfare

The central argument in Unrestricted Warfare: China's Master Plan to Destroy America, [35] co-authored by PLA Air Force political officers, Senior Colonel Qiao Liang and Senior Colonel Wang Xiangsui, is that the primary weakness of the U.S. in military affairs is its disproportionate focus and reliance on modern technologies and its effect on developing new capabilities. The publication went further in noting that the wider picture of strategy needed to be explored further in military thinking, taking other spheres into account. From the authors' perspective, reducing one's opponent can be accomplished in ways other than through direct military confrontation, and such methods could prove even more lethal to an opponent, without resort to offensive action.

While recognizing the need for more innovative thinking, the publication acknowledged China's capability and resolve to confront the U.S, and by extension its Western allies, by launching asymmetrical or multidimensional attacks in almost any aspect of social, economic, and political life. One such device is through currency wars, one of the most destructive and feared weapons in international economics.

James Rickards argues in his book <u>Currency Wars</u>, that the twentieth century is marked by two great currency wars and that the third is already in progress.[36] The first, which he designates Currency War I, stretched from 1921 to 1936, almost the entire period between World Wars I and II and throughout the Great Depression with which was closely associated. The second, designated Currency War II, persisted from 1967 to 1987 and was settled without resort to military conflict under two global agreements, the 1985 Plaza Accord and the 1987 Louvre Accord.[37] Rickard theorizes that Currency War III commenced in 2010 and is in progress spanning three critical theaters in global financing referred to as "the Atlantic theater," "the Eurasia theater" and "the Pacific theater." The economies of the U.S. and China are pivotal to all three.[38]

Rickards contends that "time and time again paper currencies have collapsed, assets have frozen, gold has been confiscated and capital controls imposed" and that presently the United States is facing serious threats to its national security ranging from "clandestine gold purchases by China to the hidden agendas of sovereign wealth funds." Game experts at the Applied Physics Laboratory have in fact concluded that sovereign wealth funds, which represent hard currency surpluses held by governments and which tend to be highly concentrated in one type of investment, could be used to exercise malign influence over target companies (and by extension governments), for the purpose of stealing technology, sabotaging new projects and stifling competition on a grand scale. Such malign attacks could be directed at critical choke points in financial systems but could nonetheless be staved off by timely market intelligence. [39] Rickards notes that at worst such wars can readily degenerate into bouts of inflation, recession, retaliation and actual violence as the scramble for resources leads to invasion and war, as obtained during World War I and II.

The Dollar, Euro and Yuan

Among the Atlantic communities the relationship of the U.S. dollar and the *euro* is one of co-dependence rather than confrontation due to the scale of interconnectedness between the U.S and European capital markets and banking systems when compared with other global financial linkages. This was brought into full glare when the disclosure mandate of the D-Frank legislation was invoked and the full extent of insolvency of the European banking system with its complex web of cross-holding between the E.U. and Wall Street, was finally unearthed.[40] At that time both the U.S. and China threw full support behind the European bailout purely on the basis of self-interest.

Accordingly, from the standpoint of the U.S, a strong euro would maintain a healthy demand for European machines, aircraft, pharmaceuticals, software, agricultural produce, education and a variety of goods and services that the U.S. has to offer. The consequences of a European sovereign debt default would be too great for the U.S. to sustain. For this reason Fannie Mae and Freddie Mac bondholders defrayed losses when the companies in the bail-out were facilitated by the U.S Treasury in 2008.

Conversely, although China's banks are not as intertwined and dependent with those of Europe as America's, the European Union surpasses the United States as China's largest trading partner. This affords China a higher degree of flexibility when compared with the U.S. given the timing and response options to the E.U. financial crisis. Added to this, Europe's crisis afforded a rare opportunity for China to diversify its reserve and investment portfolios away from dollars and towards the *euro,* acquire leading-edge technology systems that had been denied it by the U.S. and simultaneously develop platforms from which it could engage in large-scale technology transfer back to China.

Currency Wars on European Front

The second primary world venue for a major currency war cited is Eurasia and central to this is the relationship between the dollar and the *yuan.* The European Union is China's largest trading partner ahead of the United States and China's interest in supporting the *euro* is as great or for that matter greater than its interest in maintaining the *yuan* peg against the dollar. China assumed the role of "emerging savior" (an analogy drawn by Rickard), for certain peripheral European economies such as Greece, Portugal and Spain. By buying sovereign bonds from peripheral European societies, China helped Germany to bear the costs of the

European bailouts; and by propping up the European euro, China helped Germany avoid the losses it would have suffered, had the euro collapsed.

Likewise, in the Atlantic theaetr the U.S. support for the euro is self-serving. The collapse of the euro would harm the U.S. dollar and impact negatively on U.S. exports competing with markets in the Middle East, Latin America and South Asia. Conversely, the survival of the euro would help U.S exports as a whole.

Currency Wars on Pacific Front

At the height of the European crisis in 2011, Beijing and Washington continued sparring over China's currency at the G20 forum, with U.S. Treasury Secretary Timothy Geithner urging China to let the *yuan* rise more rapidly to benefit global growth, and with China reciprocating with a rebuff that its exchange rate would remain "basically stable" to protect its own interests. The creation of a China-U.S Strategic Economic Dialogue in 2006 on the initiative of the second Bush administration and the expansion of that forum under Barack Obama's presidency was a move that was clearly intended to resolve if not appease the disputation, and in deference to the interconnectedness of the geopolitical factors driving U.S. - Sino foreign policy. With this in view, the U.S Secretary of State and the Chinese State Councilor with responsibility for foreign policy are members of that forum. In addition to the Economic Dialogue, the annual G20 Meetings serves as another forum through which the U.S. hopes to reinforce moral suasion over Beijing.

Risk of Hyper-Inflation and Debt Deflation

Debt deflation is another very critical component in the financial impasse that has placed the U.S. and Sino economies in a virtual neck brace. Despite this, the issue remains conspicuously unaddressed in ongoing discourse among economic experts and financial analysts, and smothered behind the shroud cast by quantitative easing. [40]The latter is the mechanism of choice employed by the Federal Reserve to print notes in exorbitant amounts in order to spur growth, inflate asset prices, and offset the natural deflation that follows a crash, while simultaneously offering near zero long-term interest rates to banks and corporations. There appears instead to be a misplaced focus among analysts and investors on the risk of hyperinflation setting in. This enquiry posits that hyperinflation will not occur for some time to come because a phase of widespread deleveraging has now set in among private sector interests in the West, and to some extent, in China as well. [41]

It should be recalled that prior to the present global crisis, corporations and households were highly leveraged to the extent that that debt had become a pervasive feature of practically all businesses in America. However, with the peaking of the U.S housing market followed in close order by the collapse of Lehman Brothers, asset values plummeted but liabilities remained unchanged. The debt overhang born by the private sector was then partially offset by bailouts and this is one reason why despite the fact that the U.S monetary base has grown exponentially, the anticipated "kick starts" to the economy have not occurred, and the policies such as the Federal Reserve bailouts, have been ineffective. A similar experience has accompanied the monetary interventions in the Euro-zone.

Effective monetary policy is dependent on the function of what is referred to as the Monetary Transmission Mechanism. This is essentially where central bank policy-induced changes in the nominal money stock or the short-term nominal interest rate, impact on real economy variables, such as aggregate output and employment, through the effects this monetary policy has on interest rates, exchange rates, equity and real estate prices, bank lending and corporate balance sheets.

In America today, two monetary indicators may be regarded as markers to confirm the existence of serious discrepancies in the monetary transmission mechanisms. The first is the Money Multiplier and the other is the Money Velocity. The Money Multiplier refers to the measurement of the maximum amount of commercial bank money that can be created by a given unit of central bank money or the amount of total funds banks are required to keep on hand to provide for possible large-scale deposit withdrawals. In contrast, the Money Velocity is a measurement of the volume of economic activity associated with a given money supply.

In the case of the Money Multiplier, there has been a consistent decline in this index from the mid-1980s culminating in the 2008 financial debacle. Immediately after the collapse of Lehman Brothers, there was a surge of excess reserves climbing from roughly $1.5 billion to $1.6 trillion.[42] However, because money transfer mechanisms were overwhelmed, the monetary stimulus merely resulted in a huge build-up of bank reserves held at the central bank. It is theorized that if banks lend out close to the maximum allowed by their reserves, then the amount of commercial bank money will equate to the amount of central bank money available, times the money multiplier. However, should banks lend less than the maximum allowable in accordance with their reserve ratio, they will accumulate excess reserves, meaning that the amount of commercial bank money being created will be less than the central bank money being created. Such a situation arose during the 2000s and resulted in a continuous downtrend in the U.S. that turned into outright deflation in 2008.

In the instance of the Money Velocity, the digit has been consistently declining in the U.S. since the IT bubble burst in January 2000. Analysts have observed that velocity is somewhat of a behavioral phenomenon driven in large part by confidence levels in the economy. So that in a climate of intense deleveraging, when consumers are inclined to pay off debt, decrease spending and increase savings, velocity slows down. Thus, between 2008 and 2009 it dropped by roughly 7 %, from 1.80 to 1.67, and by 2010 it had leveled to 1.71[43] As a result of this, banks and corporations have been left with increasingly more excess, in the form of unused cash that was not being recycled back into the economy.

Quantitative easing is therefore very limited in terms of its impact in solving the financial crisis. It is logical to conclude that until the Money Multiplier and Money Velocity begin re-expanding, America will not experience the much-awaited sustainable growth of credit, job creation, sustained increases in consumption, and housing and other categorizations and signs of real economic activity. In the same vein, the speed of recovery would depend on how soon the private sector is able to extricate itself from a balance sheet of pernicious debt.

This flies against the grit of Chairman Bernanke's convictions. It would be recalled that in November 2002, he affirmed confidence "...that the Fed would take whatever means necessary to prevent significant deflation" by "...making use of a technology called the printing press that allows it (the government) to produce as many U.S. dollars as it wishes essentially at no cost..." in conjunction with "....cooperation between the monetary and fiscal authorities."[44] To date, the Reserve has been unable to eradicate the ongoing disinflation/deflation, despite consistent bids at balance sheet deployment.

Corporate sector deleveraging is also at an historical peak in China. Illustrative of this are the typical manifestations of debt deflation such as an extremely low demand for credit, a surge of intent on repaying debts, and shrinking bank deposits.[45] This is symptomatic of the overall slowing down of the economy. Preliminary data of monetary statistics released by the People's Bank of China in April 2012 reveals that money supply growth was 12.8% year-on-year in April 2012, down from 13.4% in March of the preceding year and below market expectations of 13.3%.[46] The largest decline by far was discernible in new loans figures. While the market was expecting RMB 780 billion in new loans, the Central Bank figures showed that new loans in fact amounted to RMB 681 billion. In addition, all bank deposits were down, with *yuan* deposits amounting to RMB

84.23 billion at the end of April, a decrease of RMB 465.6 billion. To compound the picture household deposits had fallen by RMB 637.9 billion.[47]

Private sector deleveraging may have a significant negative impact on aggregate demand, exposing the economy to notable downside risks. Despite the fact that leveraging of the household sector is not very high, leveraging of the corporate sector is at a peak as the latter continues to be under extreme pressure to reduce debt. This process is likely to necessitate the scaling back of industries that experienced overexpansion, thereby compelling the government to strike a delicate balance between maintaining economic growth while adjusting the country's economic structure.

VI

Trading with the Enemy

Of critical importance to "big business" interests is the operation of multinational corporations in times of war as they seek to exploit economic advantage behind enemy lines. In recent years the issue gained public attention in the aftermath of Libya's "democratization" in 2011 and the entry into that country of hordes of multinational corporations staking out oil investment opportunities.

Indeed, America's is a checkered past in this sphere of commerce and trade, particularly during wartime.

The list of institutions and industries that have been accused of "whitewashing their links to the Third Reich" is illustrative of the phenomenon. In point of fact, it was with this in view that the U.S. government had judiciously established a Board of Economic Warfare within the Department of Justice in 1942, with the specific intent of preventing "axis nations" from compromising the economic embargoes instituted by allied forces.

During this enigmatic period James Stewart Martin, an anti-trust lawyer, was tasked to lead a U.S. Army Economic Team that was hand-picked by Washington and dispatched to Germany to enquire into the methods of economic warfare that the Germans were employing against America. In his subsequent work, All Honorable Men: The Story of the Men on Both Sides of the Atlantic Who Successfully Thwarted Plans to Dismantle the Nazi Cartel System, [48] Martin describes a mire of collusive arrangements among multinational corporations, that were intent on benefitting from the war as a grand scale business, and which became entangled in business ploys that worked to America's detriment. The key findings unearthed by his team were, that:

- Germany began laying the groundwork for re-armament long before Hitler came to power (Ben Urwand's more recent Collaboration, elaborated on in later paragraphs, attributed partial funding for the rearmament of Germany to certain Jewish executives based in Hollywood during the years preceding and after the war, citing MGM movie studios as a key American business that actively participated in this aspect of subterfuge)

- German companies, following a plan worked out after WW I were using patents as a means of waging war

- American businessmen played a key role in gearing up Germany for war through a system more commonly referred to as "bottleneck deals"

- Hitler was being heavily influenced by Germany's business elite

- American bankers colluded with the Nazis to hide their loot when the collapse of the Third Reich was imminent

- After World War II, the German power structure remained virtually intact due to assistance rendered by American and British corporate interests

Production "bottlenecks," as Martin and his team would soon discover, were geared towards restricting the production of specific types of material in the U.S. that were critical to wartime production. One example was the restriction of plastic used in the manufacture of bomber noses under a special agreement involving I.G. Farben, Rohm and Haas of Germany and its subsidiary Rohm and Haas of Philadelphia. In another instance, there was a three-way agreement among the aircraft equipment firms of Bendix of the U.S, Siemens of Germany, and Zenith in England that blocked the British Air Ministry from expanding production of aircraft carburetors. Notably, a chain of Senate committees that were set up in Washington as the war progressed came upon a staggering number of similar arrangements in the course of their enquiries into "focal points" where it was possible to turn on and off main valves of economic pipelines, at the behest of big businesses.

Anthony C. Sutton's highly controversial expository Wall Street and the Rise of Hitler[49] provides an outspoken account of how several American multinational companies, such as I.G. Farben and German General Electric reportedly entered cartel arrangements with German-based companies. By this means these and similarly persuaded businesses were able to achieve improved capacity which enabled Germany to wage a relentless war and prevail for very prolonged periods. The state of affairs was confirmed by U.S. Ambassador to Germany William d, who in a diplomatic note addressed to FDR dated October 19, 1936, registered his concerns over the modus operandi of American corporations doing business in Germany, their alleged "cooperative understandings" with German companies, and the lucrative business opportunities that the war had manifestly presented them.

The relevant communiqué read in part:

> "...Much as I believe in peace as being our best policy, I cannot avoid the fears which Wilson emphasized more than once in conversations with me, on August 15, 1915 and later: the breakdown of democracy in all Europe will be a disaster to the people. But what can you do? At the present moment more than one hundred American corporations have subsidiaries here or cooperative understandings. The Du Ponts have three allies in Germany that are aiding in the armament business. Their chief ally is I.G. Farben Company, a part of the government, which gives 200,000 marks a year to one propaganda organization operating on American opinion. Standard Oil Company (New York sub-company) sent $2,000,000.00 in 1933 and had made $5,000,000.00 a year helping Germans make Erastz gas for war purposes; but Standard Oil cannot take any of its earnings out of the country except on goods. They do little of this, report their earnings at home, but do not explain the facts. The International Harvester Company president told me their business here rose 33% a year (arms manufacturer, I believe) but they could take nothing out. Even our airplane people have secret arrangements with Krupps. General Motor Company and Ford do enormous businesses here through their subsidiaries and take no profits out. I mention these facts because they complicate things and add to war dangers."[50]

In a 2013 publication, The Collaboration: Hollywood's Pact With Hitler,[51] Ben Urwand draws upon a wealth of previously un-cited documents to prove that Hollywood studios acquiesced to Nazi censorship in their attempt to preserve access to German audiences, and operated within the global propaganda effort of the Third Reich to maintain the German market for their movies. The phenomenon raises similar concerns to those raised in Ambassador d's diplomatic note, over the role big businesses continue to play in international politics, and highlights the extent to which war conditions are prone to exploitation by corporate interests and at worst weighted against the public interest.

In the face of widespread attestation, trade and financial wars and the political and corporate exploitation of war conditions have left their footprints between America and Europe. These said schemes are examples of among the non-kinetic attacks identified in the Liang and Xiangsui publication. Other tools of irregular warfare cited in the publication are cultural, ecological, media and facilitation warfare, resource-based war, smuggling, illegal drugs and mechanisms that are environmentally based. Given the interconnectedness of world systems, should the U.S. find itself a target of simultaneous or closely sequenced "hits" emanating from one or a combination of any of these originators, the fallout would undoubtedly be one of unimaginable devastation with far-reaching global implications.

By the same token, it can be argued that in light of the tremendous global reach of the U.S. Federal Reserve, which has been described as "the most powerful central bank in history" and "the dominant force in the U.S. economy today," omnipresence assumes wider implications in terms of monetary policy and how this impacts on the global economy. Rickards forecasts the ultimate collapse of the U.S. dollar due to the failure of the Federal Reserve to fulfill its core mandate - to preserve the purchasing power of the U.S dollar. In his view, unless debt expansion and money printing are discontinued in the near term, the outcome will be a greatly depressed dollar that would trigger a global consensus to have it finally replaced. He states in unequivocal terms:

> "...In the case of currency wars, the system is the international system based principally on the dollar. Every other market – stocks, bonds, and derivatives – is based on this system because it provides the dollar values of the assets themselves. So when the dollar finally collapses, all financial activity will collapse with it."

By the same token, China is a critical player in sustaining confidence in the U.S. dollar in the near term and ensuring its survival in the longer term. Beijing's responses have thus far assumed many versions of assault ranging from suggestions to trade partners to abandon trading in U.S currency, to engaging in "money swaps," as obtained with Argentina in 2009, pursuing the option of employing gold as an international reference point, or introducing the idea of a new global currency as broached among the BRIC membership during the 2009 and 2012 summits. Additionally, Beijing is actively diversifying its cash reserve position away from dollar denominated instruments of any kind, and investing in valuable commodity articles, as demonstrated in its scarcely concealed open-handedness in the purchase of gold.

In addition to these undercurrents, emerging regional pivots of influence such as the Bolivarian Alliance for the Peoples of Our America (ALBA), an international cooperation organization of nations within the Community of Latin American and Caribbean States (CELAC), whose socialist and social democratic governments are intent on the pursuit of political and economic integration based on the tenets of social welfare, bartering and mutual economic aid, is in the process of introducing the SUCRE as the regional currency. Initially this is envisaged to operate as a virtual currency among ALBA members, to be eventually succeeded by a hard currency that would replace the U.S. dollar. On July 06 2010, Venezuela and Ecuador conducted their first bilateral trade deal using the SUCRE. Other nations of the Americas that are members of this intraregional Alliance are Antigua and Barbuda, Bolivia, Cuba, Dominica, Nicaragua and St Vincent and the Grenadines.

Thus, the U.S. and China are both head-locked in monetary crises with all major world economies and economic blocs effectively enjoined to them. The omnipresence of the U.S. dollar as the internationally accepted leading reserve currency and its criticality to international monetary stability, are undeniable. Despite the dollar's steady decline and impending debasement, a fact admitted to by the IMF, it has thus far survived and prevailed as the dominant instrument of exchange. Any alteration to the present status quo, be it in the form of multiple reserve currencies, the IMF - created special drawing rights (SDR) as the global currency, or a return to the gold standard would lead to a diminution of omnipresent power, prestige and influence on America's part.

It was with these risks in view that the CIA launched Project Prophecy shortly after the events of 9/11. Shepherded by Jame Rickards in his capacity as Financial Threat and Asymmetric War Advisor to the Pentagon and CIA, the long-term program is intended to identify and closely monitor the flashpoints in the U.S. financial market that could precipitate the collapse of the American economy. These include foreign ownership of the U.S. debt held primarily by China and Russia; the strategically-timed dumping of U.S treasuries in advance of U.S. sanctions against its rivals as occurred with Russia in 2013-2014; and the rise of a shadow banking system in China whereby the PRC is ploughing, or rather dumping, billions of dollars (held as treasuries) into ghost mega-cities and white elephants strewn across the Chinese landscape. Other indices of note that Rickards describes in his book The Death of Money are the rate of stock market capitalization to GDP which is currently twice that of the period of the Great Depression; the dangerous slowdown in the velocity of money due to the fact that consumers are not borrowing and spending; and the gross notional value of derivatives in the world which is estimated at $700 trillion, exceeding the world GDP ten-fold.

Meanwhile, the Chinese government's recent roll out of alternative energy programs is a demonstration of its intent to continue to dominate world supplies of rare earth elements (REEs). These developments are precursory to a resource showdown among the world's major players. Indeed, the unapologetic assertiveness being displayed by the Chinese shows beyond doubt that they are assiduously planning ahead for a global scenario in which supplies of hydrocarbon and other important minerals will be acutely deficient. Resource wars are merely a subset of economic warfare on a grander scale, the full dimensions of which are already evident as the contest reinvents itself each day.

The global impact of corporatism and the imminence of economic war have underpinned this discussion. The next chapter addresses the implications of America's disproportional reliance on China for rare earth mineral supplies, the likelihood of escalated international tensions over this vital commodity, and the extent to which America's affiliations in the wider global setting would provide political capital to its economic and geopolitical standing in relation to this critical commodity.

CHAPTER SIXTEEN

WAR ON MANY FRONTS AND PROGRAM 863

"The enlightened ruler lays his plans well ahead; the good general cultivates his resources."

Sun Tzu

he functionality of twenty-first century civilization, with its orientation to sustainability, clean energy and long-term solutions to climate change hinges on the ability to harness rare earth metals. Consumer use of cell phones, solar cells, hybrid cars, wind turbines, and solar cells are illustrative of the types of ingredients that would be needed to sustain a twenty-first century way of life. None of these end user products could function without rare earth metal inputs.

Neodymium, terbium, and dysprosium are essential ingredients for magnets, wind turbines, and computer hard drives; likewise neuropium is a component of compact fluorescent bulbs and television and iPhone screens; other special minerals are needed for nickel-metal-hydride rechargeable batteries that power electric vehicles; cerium and lanthanum are required for catalytic converters; and the platinum group of metals are used as catalysts in fuel cell technology. Other categories of elements are needed for solar cells, cell phones, computer chips, medical imaging, jet engines, defense technology, and much more.

A U.S. Congressional Report (June, 2012) noted that world demand for REEs was estimated at 136,000 metric tons annually in 2010, that production levels were 133,6000 annually and the shortfall was then covered by above ground stocks and inventories. The report went on to forecast that these figures would increase and that the demand by 2015 would be roughly 210,000 tons per year. The figures presented were based on data collated by the Secretary General of the Chinese Rare Earth's Industry Association. The International Minerals Company of Australia registered a substantially lower estimate in demand by 2015, amounting to 185,000 metric tons per year. Given the patterns of market manipulation being orchestrated by China, non-Chinese output will have to amount to approximately 45,000 - 70,000 metric tons, to satisfy the global demand. Furthermore, although new mine production may compensate for some of the lighter elements, there would still be a shortfall in supplies of other light rare earth elements and several categories of the heavier ones. While America, Australia and other countries are attempting to gain ground in the production of viable amounts of light rare earth elements, a measure of difficulty is being experienced in mining heavier metals such as dysprosium, terbium, europrium, and ytterbium, which are the most important.

China is undisputedly the dominant supplier of the world rare earth complex, yielding 97 percent of the global demand and enjoying a complete monopoly of metals at the heavier end of the spectrum. This lion's share dropped to 70 percent by 2014. This is made possible by virtue of the concentration of rare earth production in that country, its role in market manipulation via the imposition of trade embargoes and highly restrictive quotas, and the impact of these maneuvers on price spikes. Taken in combination, these actions have triggered mutations in the market behavior of other nations that is tantamount to hysteria. As a case in point, countries, such as Japan, are now mulling on the possibility of seabed exploration while others are considering tapping into asteroids in space, either of which is prohibitively costly and environmentally hazardous.

China's Baotou industrial zone is reputedly the locus of the world's highest concentration of rare earth reserves. Located in the central part of Inner Mongolia and occupying 27,691 square kilometers, Baotou is regarded by the Chinese as a principal strategic area linking the economic zone to northwest Baotou where prolific rare earth mines are located, yielding high grade ores. Also noteworthy is the fact that the world famous Shenfu-Dongsheng coal deposits are co-located in the Baotou region. Furthermore, North Korea, with its rugged mountains covering 85% of the country, presently sits on the world second largest supply of rare earth metals, along with deposits of coal, iron, gold and copper. Undoubtedly, this may well be one of the many factors fueling the continuing the U.S. – North Korea standoff.

The Chinese government's rapid rollout of alternative energy programs signals that Beijing is preparing for a world in which supplies of hydrocarbon and other important minerals will be decisively phased out. In outward contrast to China's break neck economic growth, America's pace of development amidst the present Great Recession, does not suggest a willingness to sufficiently address an immediate need for dealing with resource scarcity, particularly in the field of rare earth minerals.

From the mid-1960s to the mid-1990s, Molycorp's Mountain Pass Rare Earth Mine in California was the largest supplier in the world and the sole rare earth mineral mine in the U.S. The U.S. share of production gradually declined due to stringent anti-pollutant stipulations, negative environmental impact, increased costs of production and undercutting of production costs by the Chinese. These setbacks in the domestic market served as catalysts for the foothold gained by China in production by 2002.[2] Additionally, Chinese mining companies benefitted from other opportunities such as government support, research and development, and training programs to boost the supply chain, all of which pushed the country's share of production from 27 percent of the global market in 1970 to 97 percent in 2011.

Molycorps U.S. was re-commissioned in 2012 at which time it was envisaged that the facility would produce 3,000 metric tons of rare earth annually, to be increased to 20,000 metric tons by the year's end. Cerium, lanthanum, praestymium, and neodymium would be mined and supplemented by smaller amounts of the heavier samarium, europium, gadolinium, terlium, dysprosium, and erbium. However, in 2010 the U.S. General Accountability Office, citing country estimates, forecasted that rebuilding a rare earth supply chain may take up to 15 years and is dependent on several factors, among which are securing capital investments for infrastructure, developing new technologies, and acquiring patents which are currently held by international companies.

For necessary clarification, a rare earth mineral is scientifically defined as one that contains one or more rare earth elements as a major metal constituent. These are usually found in associated alkaline to peralkaline complexes, in pegmatite's associated with alkaline magmas, and in or associated with carbonalite intrusives.[3] The US Geological Survey defines rare earth elements as elements that comprise part of the family of lanthanides on the periodic table with the numbers 57-71. The survey distinguishes between the light and heavy rare earth elements. Among the former are lanthanum, cerium, praseodymium, neodymium, and samarium, identified by their atomic numbers, 57- 62. Heavy rare earth elements, in contrast, are to be found in less abundance than those categorized as "light."

A total of 17 minerals comprise the rare earth category, and despite the fact that they are fairly widely dispersed within the crust of the earth, it is only in select areas that these are to be found in concentrated nodes sufficient to make mining economically viable.[3] A second important factor to be taken into account is that the mining of such minerals generates extremely high levels of pollution.

The Chinese Society of Rare Earth noted that for every ton of rare earth produced, 18.7 pounds of fluorine and 28.7 pounds of dust are generated and that with the use of concentrated sulphuric acid at high temperature calcination techniques, one ton of calcinid rare earth produces 9,600 -12,000 cubic meters (339,021 - 423,776 cubic feet) of waste gas containing dust concentrate, hydrofluoric acid, sulphur dioxide and sulphuric acid and approximately 75 cubic meters of acidic wastewater and 1 ton of radioactive waste residue. The Society has also observed that in the Bantou area alone, no less than 10 million tons of all varieties of wastewater are produced on a daily basis and that most of this waste discharged is not effectively treated. In fact, the contaminants affect potable water supplies and other aspects of the environment including irrigated farmlands. Bantou is but one of the many affected areas. Others are Inner Mongolia, Shangdong, Guandong, Jiangxi, Sichuan, Hunan, Guanxi and Fujian[4]

Rare earth elements are China's most important strategic resource and although there are substitutes for some of the elements essential for use in emerging technologies many cannot be substituted. Neodymium and europium are cases in point. The former is a necessary ingredient in high intensity magnets which have a variety of important uses, one example being the operation of motors in wind turbines. Europium on the other hand is used in the manufacture of fiber optics, lasers, and LED lights which are energy-efficient replacements for incandescent and compact fluorescent bulbs. According to the US Geological Survey, bastnaesite deposits in the U.S. and China make up the largest percentage of economic rare earth resources in the world; while monazite deposits which are found in Australia, Brazil, China, India, Malaysia, South Africa, Sri Lanka, Thailand and the U.S. make up the second largest segment.

Another compelling factor in relation to the importance of rare earth minerals to the Chinese is that such elements are essential in transitioning to alternative energies, because of their integral part in the production of wind turbines and solar panels. REEs are also required for the manufacture of hybrid cars, computers, cell phones, energy-efficient EEG light bulbs, and other applications of significance in the defense industry such as night vision gear, range finders, precision guided munitions, targeting lasers radar systems, and satellites. These elements are also indispensable in specific high-tech applications including iPods, liquid crystal displays, catalytic converters, fiber optic cable, and magnetic resonance imaging systems.

Magnetic technology is by far the most important usage to which REEs are employed due to their employment in energy and military applications. Permanent magnets therefore dominate the rare earth market since unlike electrical magnets they produce their own magnetic fields. In this regard, the two primary rare earth magnets, somarium cobalt (SnCo) magnet and the neodymium-iron-boron (Nd FeB) magnet, fall under this category. Somarium cobalt's distinctiveness lies in the fact that it is able to retain its magnetic strength at elevated temperatures and because of this feature, its thermo-stability is ideal for special military technologies such as missiles and smart bombs. Rare earth elements are therefore central and indispensable to America's electronics and defense industries.

America's Immediate Concerns

The designation of REEs by the U.S. National Research Council Report 2012 as "critical minerals" that are vital to the U.S. economy was accordingly an inexorable conclusion. Critical minerals are so deemed because of their susceptibility to supply restrictions and high impact outcomes, when one takes into account the effect of restrictions in situations of supply reduction from a geological, technological, social, political, or environmental perspective.

Insofar as U.S. military priorities are concerned, less than 5% of rare earth minerals used in the U.S. are required for defense purposes. An interim document titled "Report to Congress: Rare Earth Materials in Defense Applications" and published under the authorization of Section 843 of the PL 111-383, advised that that seven of the 17 earth elements were found to meet the criteria set in that provision in relation to military applications, and that by FY/2012, with the exception of yytrium, U.S. production of those seven would be adequate to meet defense needs. Notwithstanding this assurance, the potential shortfall in supply remains a concern to the government.

"Trickling Down Economics"

According to the 2013 Energy Policy unveiled by the Executive Office of the President, titled "The President's Climate Action Plan" (June 2013), biofuels have an important role to play in increasing energy security. On this basis, and having regard to prevailing consumption trends, the establishment resolved to deploy three gigawatts of renewable energy on military installations including solar, wind, biomass, and geothermal by 2025. With this target in view, the U.S. Navy and the Departments of Energy and Agriculture are collaborating with the private sector to accelerate the development of cost competitive advance biofuels for use by the military and commercial sectors. The current biofuel initiative has partially assuaged domestic concerns to access non-fossil-based energy supplies, despite the fact that the endeavor is manifestly among the most costly and controversial to be undertaken by the Navy in recent years. The Navy has further committed $510,000,000.00 U.S over a three-year period (2012-2015) to develop alternatives to fossil fuels with the objective that by 2020 at least half of the unit's energy would be derived from non-fossil fuels. In a similar vein, the Air Force has set in motion a biofuel initiative with the ambitious aim of cost-competitively acquiring 50% of its domestic aviation fuel from alternative fuel blends. All this is being promoted on the premise that the innovation and advances of the Department would somehow "trickle down" on the rest of society, but is there necessarily pragmatism in this thinking?

China's Rare Earth Policy and Program 863

Technological advances, control of export supplies, and attempts to invest in or control overseas business interests in rare earth elements are among the stockpile of schemes embarked upon by Chinese authorities with the aim of maintaining world dominance in supplies, production, and related technologies.

That the Chinese are long-term thinkers is beyond cliché. From as far back as March 1985, a team of three scientists proposed a series of programs and targets aimed at accelerating the country's advancements in high-tech investment. One such plan, Program 863, was intended "...to gain a foothold in the world arena; to strive to achieve breakthroughs in key technical fields that concern the national economic lifeline and national security; and to achieve leapfrog development in key high-tech fields in which China enjoys relative advantages or should take strategic positions in order to improve high-tech support to fulfill strategic objectives in the implementation of the third steps of China's modernization process..."[5]

Step-by -Step Tactical Moves

In the government's estimation, once this high-end mandate was set in train, it would narrow the gap in technology between the developed world and China. This initial step would then be followed by other measures that would be strategically introduced and state-managed. Accordingly, from the inception of the plan resources were open-handedly channeled by the government into biotechnology, space exploration, and information technology with emphasis placed on cyberspace, laser technology in medical and other sciences, automation, energy, and new materials. This necessitated the involvement of specialized institutions and laboratories working collaboratively, engaging in keystone research projects that complemented each other and simultaneously pursuing enterprises that would guarantee China's lead over the rest of the world in rare earth science. The institutions most favored by the government were:

- The CAS Key Laboratory of Rare Earth Resource Utilization (est. 1987) [6]
- The State Key Laboratory of Rare Earth Materials Chemistry and Applications, University of Peking (est. 1991) [7]
- The Baotou Research Institute of Rare Earth (est. 1963) [8]
- The General Research Institute for Non-Ferrous Metals (est. 1952) [9]

Monopoly and Market Manipulation

The second major tactical leg that the government embarked upon was gaining outright control of global supplies. This was ensured by two prerequisites - ensuring that prices remained high and competitive and maintaining a world market monopoly. Currently a few state-owned, private, and centrally owned firms dominate the rare earth industry in China. Mongolia Baetou Steel Rare Earth High-Tech Company is the industry leader in Northern China while China Minmetals Corporation is the main player in the south. Aluminum Corporation of China Limited and China Non-Ferrous Metal Mining are also highly regarded.

In 2011, China used up a mere 62% of its export quota of REEs and by July 12, 2012 only 25% of the year's initial quota had been applied. The government permitted companies to export no more than 21, 226 tons for the current year and there were plans to maintain the 2012 quota basically flat, compared to 30,184 tons in 2011. These actions have prompted protests and legal complaints from primary trade partners including the United States, the European Union and Japan.

Take-Over Bids

Penetrating foreign markets was the third major plank in China's road map. With this in view, at least two landmark moves were attempted to acquire controlling interests in rare earth mineral mining enterprises, and in each instance the PRC's bid was foiled as a result of the imposition of domestic restrictions to Chinese ownership by host country governments.

The first PRC gambit occurred in 2005 when China National Offshore Oil Corp (CNOOC) submitted an $18.5 billion cash bid for Unocal in the U.S,

391

outbidding Chevron by one-half of a billion dollars in the process. This overture came at a time when Mountain Pass had begun to process samarium oxide and neodymium oxide, both of which are critical components for two specific types of permanent magnets. Had the bid been successful, China would have gained control of Molycorp through CNOOC's purchase of Unocal, and thereafter progressed towards acquiring a complete monopoly over rare earth elements globally.

A more recent attempt at acquiring controlling interests from the very source of supply was made in Australia in 2009 when Lynas Corp, a local mining company, was in the initial stages of plans to construct a large rare earth mine at Mount Weld in South-Western Australia. At that time, operations had been temporarily halted as a result of cash-flow issues and in May of that year the China Non-Ferrous Mining Co. lost no time in positioning itself to invest $252 million (an amount that would have been adequate to offset the debt owed), in return for a 51.6 percent stake in the company. However, Australia's Foreign Investment Board judiciously insisted on several revisions to the Chinese proposal. Had Beijing conceded to these requests China's intended stake in the venture would have been reduced to less than 50 percent. However, after having considered the proposed amendments, the Company balked and withdrew its interest.

Control of Domestic Mining

In 2008, the Institute for the Analysis of Global Security noted that bootlegging had become so rampant across the provinces that as much as one-third of the total volume of rare earth material mined in China was being smuggled out of the country. These types of actions within the market were an attempt by perpetrators to circumvent the high prices of the legal export market. China is therefore taking decisive measures to control local mining domestically through direct government intervention at the very source of supply. To this end a White Paper was drafted in 2012 requiring minimum output levels. Such a move would undoubtedly result in the closure of smaller scale mixed production rare earth mines, which would be severely challenged to maintain the proposed quota of 2,000 tons per year. This is the rationale employed by the government in its acknowledgement of the general disorderly development of the industry at home. The immediate concerns of the authorities are managing the large number of unmonitored business outfits that are mushrooming within the mining sector, moving against large-scale smuggling, putting a stop to poor management practices and mitigating extensive environmental damage as previously described.

Fall-Out in the International Arena - Trade Wars Rage

Based on the forgoing issues, the key drivers of the ongoing resource war may be summarized as:

- Monopoly of the global market
- Manipulation of prices
- Abrogation of World Trade Organization trade principles
- Laxity and/or lack of enforcement of environmental regulations.

The curtailment of rare earth exports at the behest of Beijing has led to contentions in the international arena in relation to fair trade ground rules determined by the WTO. On this account, the U.S, E.U. and Japan lodged a formal complaint against China with the WTO in March 2012 in a move that was widely anticipated and Vietnam, Norway, Oman, Taiwan, South Korea, Saudi Arabia, Brazil, India, Canada, and Colombia lost no time in hinting their intention to exercise third party rights with a view to positioning themselves to monitor and influence the proceedings. The bone of contention was China's dominance of the production of all 17 metallic minerals that are essential for a range of sensitive cutting edge technologies including missile defense systems, wind turbines and smart phones. Not unexpectedly, Beijing responded with a vigorous defense of its policy as a responsible promoter in controlling an environmentally polluting industry.

II

China's public environmentalist stance gives credence to the view that this is a mere sham intended to mask the underlying reasons for its energetic pursuit of a renewable energy policy and its quest to be viewed by the developed world in a positive light. One of the ramifications of this grand standing is that by frustrating the meaningful actions of other nations, the PRC is positioning itself to maximize the use of alternative energy within its own borders. This is the central argument advanced in Stephen Leeb's book <u>Red Alert: How China's Growing Prosperity Threatens the American Way of Life.</u>[10]

Leeb explains what he interprets as a ruse being perpetrated by the PRC, in these words:

"... The logic behind the apparent contradictions between China's actions in Copenhagen and its grand plans to adopt alternative energy technology now should be much clearer. The People's Republic is not building alternative energy because it has suddenly gotten religion on climate change - if that were the case it would have wanted Copenhagen to result in a treaty binding on all participants. Rather it's moving forward as quickly as it can to obtain essential materials before the developed world mobilizes with the same goal. It is rushing forward before the developed world mobilizes with the same goal. It is rushing forward before large quantities of these indispensable commodities run out. The United States, in contrast, is doing nothing to prepare for the trouble that lies ahead.[17]"

The obvious implication of failure among participating nations, including the world's largest energy consumers, to reach a common accord at the Copenhagen Summit, means that there is presently no universally binding treaty to reduce carbon emissions; neither are there incentives among developing nations to act unilaterally to reduce carbon emissions, with the latter option being left largely to the free market. Correspondingly, countries such as China are at liberty to continue to emit carbon to enhance development, while earning undeserved plaudits for the pursuit of renewable energy policies. Crucial to all of this is the fact is that of all the world powers China alone possesses the full range of scarce elements required to build a viable and lasting alternative energy infrastructure, a status now potentially rivaled by North Korea.

Notwithstanding its environmentally motivated stance, the amount of energy that had to be harnessed within the last decade to buttress the country's industrialization drive resulted in a doubling of total energy consumption from 1.6 billion tons of standard coal equivalent in 2002 to 3.5 billion tons in 2011. This is corroborated by the International Energy Administration, which also reported that the energy consumption of the PRC surpassed that of the U.S. in 2009. Moreover, the bulk of consumption continues to be derived from coal whose dominance in China's energy mix has remained fairly constant, despite substantial increases in the use of natural gas and renewables. This appears to be a squander of opportunity on China's part, and a cause of concern.

In contrast, the U.S. Energy Information Administration Annual Report (2012) Analysis and Projections released on June 25, 2012 provided an optimistic medium-term outlook, noting specifically:

- Domestic energy consumption growth at an average annual rate of 0.3% from 2010 to 2015
- Modest growth in demand for energy over the next 25 years
- Reduced U.S. reliance on imported oil
- Increased domestic crude oil and natural gas production largely driven by rising production from tight oil and shale resources
- Increased domestic production of natural gas that would exceed consumption
- A growing share of electric power generation that would be met with natural gas and renewables
- Energy-related carbon monoxides remaining low below 2005 level from 2010 to 2035, even in the absence of federal policies geared towards mitigating greenhouse gas emissions

Consequences for Climate Change

Stephen Leeb anticipated that following the Copenhagen convocation, countries would very likely have proceeded with a rapid build-up of alternative energy infrastructure and that this would generate a corresponding demand for rare mineral.[12] His surmises proved true to life in the face of retaliatory actions adopted by many concerned nations in response to China's unfair market share advantage. Furthermore, the curtailment of rare earth mineral supplies by the Chinese ostensibly in the interest of being environmentally friendly, has led to sharp spikes in the price of REEs on the international market and artificial shortages that have worked to the detriment of would-be purchasers. Added to this is the deterioration of diplomatic relations with countries whose economies stand to be the most seriously affected.[13]

Spats and Trade Wars

One of the regional players to be substantially injured economically by this state of affairs is Japan. It is widely known that REE supplies buttress the Japanese industrial base and that in recent years the stable procurement of rare minerals has grown increasingly difficult, at China's behest. Overdependence on any single country in world trade, as obtains, invariably leads to chaotic shortages and high prices. As a case in point between January 2010 and July 2011, the price of dysprosium was increased no less than 23 times. This element in particular is considered "the rarest" of all rare earth elements and Japan relies on China for 100% of its supplies, which are channeled into the manufacture of electrical vehicles, hybrid vehicles and related electronic products in the automotive industry. Following tensions with China that reignited afresh in 2010 when a Chinese fishing boat was involved in a highly publicized collision with a Japanese Coast Guard craft, China purposefully disrupted exports to Japan. To compound the situation, long-standing tensions between the countries over the disputed Senkaku Islands have not ebbed. [14]

Leading Japanese industry giants such as TDK Corp., Panasonic Corp., and Honda Motor Company were adversely affected by the trade impasse to the extent that some companies explored alternative sources. As a consequence of this, Toyota Tsusko Corporation is scheduled to commence rare earth imports from India by the end of 2012 and Sumitomo Corporation will be importing dysprosium from Kazakhstan in 2013. [15]

An emerging trend against the setting of China's stranglehold on the REE market is that its customary trading partners have devised a range of schemes aimed at diminishing their reliance on any single supplier. As a case in point, Japan launched a major project in 2007 entitled "The New Energy and Industrial Technology Development Organization Rare Metal Substitute Materials Development Project." The initiative entails two limbs: firstly, monitoring specific materials that are required in the Japanese economy and which are likely to be in short supply and secondly, conducting research and development geared towards developing substitute rare minerals. [16] By capitalizing on these types of state-driven initiatives, Toshiba has been able to develop a high-rim concentration samarium cobalt magnet that is free of dysprosium, a key material in the creation of heat resistant neodymium magnets. Such magnets are also widely used in the traction motors for hybrid and electrical automobiles, railroad vehicles, and the motors for industrial equipment that operate at relatively high temperatures. Toshiba has been able to use this heat resistant technology to improve the magnetic force of the samarium cobalt magnet while boosting its performance to a level that surpasses that of the heat resistant neodymium magnet. Further to this, the company has plans to launch mass production at the end of the 2012 fiscal year and to promote its use for all applicable equipment.

III

Pursuit of Renewable Energies

Stephen Leeb is careful to delineate two schools of thought among the cohort of highly-touted "global environmentalists" and a grasp of the implications of these distinctions sheds considerable light on China's posture and long-term goals. The first, which is identified by Jared Diamond in his title <u>Collapse: How Societies Choose to Fail or Succeed</u> [18] proposes that environmental damage is responsible for the destruction of civilizations, and provides an expository on the relationship between pollution and global warming, while de-emphasizing the significance of resource depletion. The second line of thinking, propagated by Joseph Tainter and discussed at length in his book, <u>The Collapse of Complex Societies,</u> [19] challenges the argument that environmental degradation is responsible for the disintegration of civilizations, and attributes it instead to energy scarcity. [19] Under the first model the development of renewable energies will necessitate the use of fossil fuels; this contrasts with the second model, which suggests that fossil fuel use would actually worsen pollution and deplete present energy supplies. The common strand of either argument is the imperative to develop alternative energy.

China has gravitated towards marketing its claim to "global environmentalism" while sidestepping the arguments surrounding resource scarcity. While on the one hand the development of renewable energies will necessitate the use of fossil fuels, this contrasts with the second model that suggests that fossil fuel use would worsen pollution and deplete present energy supplies. This explains the PRC's preoccupation with accessing primary resources and controlling supplies from their very source. Since REEs are critical to the installation of renewable energy infrastructure, China has taken a head start in the race by transitioning to renewable energy derived from wind, solar and hydroelectricity sources, well ahead of other countries that may be similarly persuaded. [20] Its success in diminishing dependency on coal however remains arguable.

How Realistic Is Beijing's Intent to
Migrate from Greenhouse Pollution?

In 2013 China was still producing 70% of its energy from coal, emitting more carbon dioxide than the next two largest countries combined (USA and India), while its emissions were increasing by as much as 10% per annum. Based on this non-plus track record it is widely believed that coal will continue to be China's main energy source (50% or more) until 2050 and possibly beyond. Chinese experts are estimating that by 2050 the percentage of China's energy requirements will have declined to 30-50% of total energy consumption and the remaining 50-70% will be provided by a combination of oil, natural gas, hydropower, nuclear power, biomass and other renewable sources. Understandably, from an energy and environmental standpoint, clean coal technology will be the most important issue engaging local authorities for some time to come.[21]

China has become the world's largest producer of solar energy as well as solar hot water heating capacity, while solar PV production is in rapid development. Further to this, its wind power capacity reached 44.7 GW in 2010, making it the world leader in installed wind power generation capacity, and the center of the international wind industry.[22] Currently, the United States ranks second to China among the top ten countries in accordance with wind turbine capacity followed by Germany, Spain, India, Italy, France, the United Kingdom and Canada in that order.

Regarding the future outlook, through its five-year Plan Beijing has forecasted that wind, solar, bio-gas and hydro power derived renewable energy would account for approximately 10% of the country's energy consumption by 2010 and 15% by 2020, with the aim of reducing its dependence on coal and escaping the effects of coal pollution.[23]

Other Vital Minerals

Copper, silver and zinc are among a very limited number of vital resources that are indispensable in the wholesale transition to renewable energies. Thus the Sino capitalization of Africa's wealth is a trump card in China's foreign policy agenda and is strongly motivated no doubt by the existence in Africa of prodigious reserves of every mineral that is crucial to twenty-first century living, and by extension, the survivability of the world's major economies. Oil, coal, iron, zinc, lead, tungsten, cobalt, coltan, copper, molybdenum, manganese, chromium, antimony, niobium, industrial diamonds, uranium, platinum group metals, silver and gold are among the array of minerals to be found in Africa in unrivalled amounts.

Chinese Demand for Copper

The PRC has already launched plans to install high voltage power lines for its national electronic grid and to become one of the largest players in the global automotive industry as part of its grand scale aim of transitioning from internal combustion engines to hybrid cars. Hybrid cars demand twice as much copper as standard cars because of their battery requirements and these enterprises will exact substantial supplies of copper, the extraction of which demands huge supplies of energy. In Stephen Leeb's estimation, the global electric grid project alone would demand over 10% of the world supply of copper now left in the ground. In fact, so compelling is the need for this primary resource that its impending scarcity was sufficient to spur the Chinese government into purchasing the rights to copper deposits located in a former al-Qaeda stronghold south of Kabul in Afghanistan at a cost of $1 billion, above bids submitted by U.S, Canadian, Russian, and Kazakh companies. This historic deal was formalized by China Metallurgical Group Corporation, a state-owned conglomerate, during the last quarter of 2009 and it is projected that when full-scale operations commence in 2014, the Aynak copper field would be one of the biggest foreign investment projects in the history of Afghanistan.

As a thermal and electrical conductor silver is also in extremely high demand. Added to this, it is of critical importance in solar energy production, which has been a growing enterprise in China since the early 2000s. With dwindling supplies of silver on the world market, China may opt to restrain future supplies of solar modules in much the same way as it has done with rare earth elements. Such a move would adversely impact on the U.S. as one of China's principal buyers and with its increasing demand for solar power capacity. These are merely two instances in which the stakes are being raised in transitioning to alternative energy.

To date, China is one of the world's top producers of renewable energies and has the potential of producing as much as 50% of domestic needs. Greenpeace has projected that 37% of this figure could be derived from solar power alone. Compared to China, the U.S gets roughly 7% of its energy from renewable resources, of which wind makes up 5%. Within the framework of the government's 12th. Five-Year Plan for Renewable Energy[2] Beijing forecasted that wind, solar, bio-gas and hydro power- derived renewable energy would account for approximately 10% of the country's energy consumption by 2010 and 15% by 2020, as part of the dependency reduction on coal and coal pollution.[24]

U.S. Blueprint for a Clean and Secure Energy Future

Compared to China, the United States is the world's second largest energy consumer in terms of total usage, and ranks seventh in energy consumption per capita after Canada and a number of small nations. The majority of this energy is derived from fossil fuels. 2010 data shows that 25% of America's energy was derived from petroleum, 22% from coal, 22% from natural gas, 8.4% from nuclear power, and 8% from renewable energy - the latter primarily from hydroelectric dams in addition to wind power, geothermal and solar energy.[25] Until the 1950s, coal had been the country's dominant source of energy followed by petroleum, and subsequent to that, natural gas and the primary demand sectors were transportation (28%), industry (20%), residential and commercial (11%), and electric power (41%).

Because energy consumption in the U.S. has outstripped the pace of production, the resulting deficit must be offset and this has typically been addressed via imports and by the employment of unorthodox methods to source natural gas within the homeland. In this connection, the policy of the Obama administration now rests on three primary pillars:

- Creating new clean energy jobs and technologies
- Making America more energy independent
- Reducing carbon emissions

Pursuant to this philosophy, the administration's clean energy policy would be driven by the under-listed actions [25]:

- Challenging Americans to double renewable electricity generation
- Directing the Interior Department to establish an energy project to permit 10,000 megawatts of renewables on public lands
- Supporting responsible nuclear waste strategy
- Cutting oil imports by half in less than a decade
- Achieving sustained investment in technologies that promotes maximum energy production and reduces waste
- Committing to public- private sector partnerships

The Status of Nuclear Power in the U.S. – China Face Off

Nuclear power plants are thus increasingly becoming an important source of electrical power due to the fact that they are considered the most efficient low carbon energy source and enjoy the additional bonus of scalability. For this reason this source of energy is integral to the Obama clean energy policy. Nevertheless, America's political will to make advances in this area is arguable. There are currently 441 nuclear operating power plants (NPPs) dispersed globally among 30 countries, with a further 60 plants under construction. The share of nuclear generated electrical power supplied by these plants ranges from a miniscule percentage in certain countries to as high as 75% in others such as France, and 40% in the Kirsko Nuclear Power Plant in Slovenia.

In the 1950s the U.S. Navy was at the forefront of the industry and developed a light water reactor in 1954 intended for use in submarines. Engineers of that era were preoccupied with designing reactors driven by a range of agents such as gas, mercury and water. However, China currently enjoys a clear lead over the rest of the world in terms of its nuclear power infrastructure and conventional reactors designed for commercial use, with 14 NPPs operating commercially, 27 under construction, a further 51 planned, while 120 are at varying stages of proposal. In contrast, there are now 154 reactors in the U.S.

Four categories of plants are in operation at various world sites: the pressurized water receptor (PWR); the boiling water receptor (BWR); the gas cooled reactor and advanced gas cooled reactor (AGR); the light water cooled graphite (LWGR); and the pressurized heavy water moderated reactor (PHWR). A recent study by Natural Hazards, prompted by damage caused to the Fukushima I nuclear plant in Japan following the tsunami of March 2011, noted:

- In total, 23 nuclear plants housing a total of 74 active nuclear reactors are located in high-risk areas in the east and south-east of Asia, including Fukushima I
- Of the 23 plants, 13 with 29 reactors are active; other plants (containing 20 reactors) are being expanded to house nine additional reactors
- 7 new plants with 16 reactors are under construction
- 27 of the 74 reactors in the world that are currently under construction, are in China and 19 of the 27 are being built in areas deemed high-risk and dangerous

What these findings demonstrate is twofold – firstly, that China enjoys a clear lead in civil nuclear power infrastructural development; and secondly, that nuclear reactors are disproportionately dispersed in high-risk areas of the Asian peninsular and more specifically, within China. This status quo underscores two areas of global concern that have been iterated by Dr. Richard Lester, head of department of Nuclear Science at MIT:

- The need for greatly strengthened global governance or the "soft side" of policy that deals with people, processes, institutions, and the bureaucracy in general
- The requirement for innovation that is safer, less expensive, more resistant to proliferation and terrorism, and compatible with organizations that must build and operate them. Innovation would necessarily include devising safe and efficient methods of disposing of approximately 2,000 metric tons of high-level waste in the U.S. and 9,000 metric tons produced by reactors throughout the rest of the world.

Recently, an MIT-affiliated company announced the development of a system that is immune to the melt down that destroyed the Fukushima reactors following the 2011 tsunami and with the capability to circumvent the disadvantages of light water reactors used in America.[26] WAMSR takes the nuclear waste fuel pellets, dissolves them into molten salt, and the resulting fluid is then pumped into graphite core to generate heat, which in turn drives the steam turbines and produces the power. With 270,000 tons of nuclear waste produced worldwide, WAMSR would be potentially capable of absorbing this waste and supplying all the world's projected electric power needs for the next 72 years, while simultaneously consuming 98% of the potential energy contained in the uranium pellets. The success of such an ambitious venture undoubtedly rests on political will.

IV

Unconventional Gas Extraction Techniques and Their Environmental Impact

No discussion on energy sources would be complete without an examination of the unorthodox measures being taken by the governments of developed Western societies including the U.S. In order to make good on its commitment under the clean energy policy to reduce carbon emissions, the Obama administration is intent on pressing ahead with programs and methodologies that have raised alarm among environmentalists. This present state of affairs emanated from the publicized studies that were conducted into the consequences of unorthodox inshore natural gas extraction methods that involve directional drilling and hydraulic fractioning. Notably, the governments of the United Kingdom and Australia are also sanctioning similar schemes.

Unconventional gas extraction may take several forms. One such method, referred to as fracking, is a technique by which deep wells are drilled into underground shale deposits and pumped with water laced with sand and chemical agents. This process results in the fracturing of rocks and the release of natural gas along with contaminant H2O, often in the form of residual sludge. Another approach, dubbed coalbed methane extraction, involves the drilling of wells into coal seams, followed by the pumping out of water, which results in gas being released from the coal and brought to the surface. A third scheme, termed underground coal gasification, which is being mulled over in the U.K, involves the partial burning of subterranean deposits.[27]

One of the perils of the fracking method common in the United States resides is the leaking of un-combusted methane into wells, pipelines and storage facilities and its short-term potency as a greenhouse gas with implications for global climate change. The U.S. Environmental Protection Agency estimated that 2.3 percent of production of this lethal gas is lost to leakage but this estimate is based on dated studies that go back to the 1990s. On the other hand, the industry is now claiming a leakage of 1.6 percent while Cornell University professor Robert Howarth has estimated total fugitive emissions of as much as 3.6 to 7.9 percent over the lifetime of a well.

Presented below is a sample of recent findings: [28]

- In February 2012, a Denver-Julesburg Co: Tower Study by NOAA/UC suggested that up to 4 percent of the methane produced at that field near Denver was escaping into the atmosphere

- In December 2012, at an American Geophysical Union meeting in San Francisco, the NOAA/UC team described the unpublished results of a study on the Uinta Basin, Utah, and suggested even higher rates of methane leakage to an amount of 9 percent of total production

The National Academy of Sciences in the United States has noted that in aquifers overlying the Marcellios and Utica formations of north-eastern

Pennsylvania and upstate New York, there is systemic evidence of methane contamination of drinking water and this has been directly associated with shale gas extraction.[29] Furthermore, in active gas extraction areas (one or more gas wells within 1 km), average and maximum methane concentrations in drinking water wells have increased substantially.

The British government is also promoting new inshore gas exploration methodologies. In March 2013 the Cameron administration set up an Office of Unconventional Oil and Gas for the purpose of promoting new methods of gas exploration in locales such as the Bowland Basin in Lancashire, the commuter belt village of Lancombe and Warrington in Cheshire. What these venues have in common are medium term schemes that would usher in the hydraulic fracturing of shale deposits via coalbed methane extraction or possibly the fracking of local shale. In April-May, 2011, two earth tremors in Blackpool linked to local test fracking operations led to the discontinuation of operations at that site amidst wide-scale public protestations. Likewise, the Australian government is moving ahead with medium to long-term plans to institute the expansion of coal seam gas drilling promoted in the government's Energy White Paper (Nov.2012). The findings of a study conducted by researchers at the Southern Cross University on the Tare Gas Field near Condamine, disclosing that greenhouse gas levels were over three times higher in that location than in surrounding districts ignited public debate over the environmental and social impact of hydraulic fracturing technologies.[31]

Admittedly, the systemic measurement of the impact of emissions across geographies and over extended time periods is now required to scope the dimensions of the issue with specific attention paid to fugitive methane emissions at the stages of production, gathering, processing, long distance transmission and local distribution. The U.S. Environment Protection Agency is bound to work alongside industry partners and scientists to properly assess the impact of these emissions and devise timely correctional and mitigation measures to stave off their adverse consequences. In this vein, data gathered through studies ought to inform future policies and be matched with the overall public good.

Another important consideration in the debate is that while big business interests (at least 22 investment firms worth $240 billion in assets), would prefer to see the government tackle energy and climate change as top economic priorities, the present U.S. administration regards these items as a third ranking priority on its second term political agenda, trailing behind the fiscal cliff, immigration and economic growth.[32] It may well be that the ongoing debate is a more nuanced one than is readily being admitted.

A Consumption Crisis

To qualify this point, Ozzie Zehner, author of <u>Green Illusions,</u>[33] offers alternative perspectives on the causes of the present energy crisis and possibilities that lie ahead for clean energy sources and the future of environmentalism. His central idea is that the world is experiencing a consumption crisis, as distinct from an energy crisis, and that changes in consumption patterns are integral to resolving greenhouse issues. He notes that despite the fact that governments have advanced variations in their approach such as the use of solar cells, wind tunnels, and bio-fuels, alternative technologies come with their own side effects and limitations. In this connection, he stirs interest in making a paradigm shift from dwelling on issues associated with alternative energy to improving political and social elementals such as managing consumption patterns and introducing a more enlightened governance regime.

Professor Robert B. Laughlin, Nobel Laureate in Physics, in his publication <u>Powering the Future,</u>[34] ruminates on his vision of a world in which nuclear power, algae bio-fuels, and gas made from animal waste will keep civilization running. He foresees a transformational future in which there would be "...billions of robots on the ocean floor tending to tanks of compressed air that power turbines, the south-west is known as algae country and energy traders make their fortunes speculating on the price of chicken manure gas." Laughlin's mirage may not necessarily be an unlikely scenario.

The challenges entailed in making quantum leaps away from fossil are clearly recognizable. Firstly, cost constraints will be especially severe in struggling to re-task the earth's resources in new ways; and secondly, the ever-increasing human demands on the earth's resources would be considerably worsened. Either of these is politically consequential and America's biggest challenge lies in reconciling technological realities with *real politic*. Laughlin recapitulates the dichotomy in these terms:

> *"Transporting ourselves mentally beyond any living person's self-interest has the great advantage of separating technical matters from political ones. Modern energy concerns are inherently political, of course, so divorcing the two completely makes no sense. But we save ourselves much time and vexation if we deal with the much simpler technical issue first. Think of it this way: To build a power plant we need both enough votes and enough concrete, but if there isn't any concrete we're simply not going to build the plant.*[35]"

The arguments put forward in this chapter are replete with contradictions and ambiguities that give no assurance that the planet's eco-systems would not continue to be jeopardized. Additionally, recent finds of rare earth elements in other jurisdictions have raised hopes that the Chinese monopoly will not endure. In this regard four points are worthy of iteration: first, other countries as previously mentioned, with Brazil and India included, have developed their own rare earth supplies; second, companies have found ways of using less dysprosium in order to make a key magnet for use inside electric cars; third, China's export curbs were not effective because producers found a way around the ban so that the rare earth shortage resolved itself; the fourth, while back in 2010 members of the U.S. Congress were sounding alarm bells to pass measures aimed at subsidizing U.S. rare earth production, the market adjusted relatively quickly rendering this push unnecessary.

China's pre-eminence in ownership and supply of REEs provides no guaranties that energy derived from fossil fuel and associated greenhouse gas emissions will diminish to any substantial degree in the near future. In point of fact, according to the International Energy Agency, cumulative worldwide investment in fossil fuel extraction and processing will surge to an estimated $22.87 trillion between 2012-2035 while investment in renewables will amount to only $7.32 trillion. Investment in oil alone at an estimated $10.32 trillion is expected to exceed spending on wind, solar, biofuel, hydro, nuclear and every other form of renewable energy combined.[36]

Burgeoning investments will be devoted to non-conventional forms of oil and gas, such as fracking rather than in transitioning from fossil fuels. This implies that the vision offered by President Obama and his counterparts in China, the United Kingdom, Australia, Canada and even Venezuela, is inconsistent with the direction in which the energy industry is headed which is plainly to amass historically unheard of profits.

What is also certain is the growth of the superconductor industry, which is being driven by the increasing role in diverse end-use application areas such as industrial, commercial and health care. This looming windfall, which is driven by Asian power houses particularly China, is forecasted to increase at a compound annual growth rate of 12.6% over the next five years, rising from a valuation of $1.8 billion in 2012, to be worth a market value of $3.3 billion in 2017.[37]

Reciprocally, the U.S. should promote an energy policy that is not only environmentally friendly, but compatible with its diverse and politically sensitive interests. Such interests are expected to include the employment of geo-engineering techniques to promote *solar radiation management* which entails launching material into the earth's atmosphere to block the Sun's rays; *carbon dioxide removal* which involves taking carbon emissions out of the climate through a variety of means from structures that eat air pollution to capturing carbon emissions as they come out of smoke-stocks; and finally by no means least using *weather as a* force *multiplier* via techniques such as cloud seeding to gain combat advantage, as obtained during the Vietnam War.[38]

The National Academy of Sciences has already commenced a 21 month study, which is intended to provide a carefully mapped scientific foundation that will inform the ethical, legal and political issues surrounding geo-engineering.[39] The findings of the study, scheduled for release in the fall of 2014, will inform future colloquy within the CIA and concerning the more long-term strategic interests of the U.S. homeland.

In the meantime regulatory regimes such as the WTO may well assume the role of the third force in the Sino - U.S. REE faceoff, should an intervention in the global supply chain become essential amidst a groundswell of overarching concerns, in order to serve the wider global interest.

CHAPTER SEVENTEEN

AFRICA UNDER SIEGE

"We kind of gave Africa to the Europeans first and to the Chinese later, but today it's wide open to us."

General Electric Chief Executive, Jeffrey Immelt

Europe Emerges from Slumbers

On the threshold of modernity stood the hunger for commerce and the lunge of empire spurred by the legends of Prester John and Marco Polo's travels; Moorish domination of maritime trade in the Mediterranean; the Crusades that plunged Europe into an economic lethargy and whispers of unimaginable wealth in Africa and Asia. Society in Europe was enmeshed in turmoil coupled with fanaticism amidst the throes of change in relation to the emergence of the nation state. Assuming supreme authority in sacred and secular matters, the Catholic Church instigated the Inquisition resulting in the expulsion of Spanish Jews and the Moors from the body politic in 1492. Marginalized and persecuted, they both departed for Northwestern Africa. Later on, Columbus's voyages financed by Marranos—Luis de Santangel, Gabriel Sanchez and Isaac Abrabonel—would pave the way for Jewish entry into the Americas. History is not without a sense of irony. Talk of colonization took root among monarchs and intellectuals until it materialized into small-scale experiments on Africa's doorsteps. Herein lies the beginnings of Africa's troubles.

The process of colonization began off the Northwestern coast of Africa on the Canary Islands early in the fourteenth century. It entailed cutting timber or gathering wild honey, subsequently evolving into wheat and sugar plantations whose profitability were anticipated and realized. According to historian John Thornton, the actual motivation for European expansion and for navigational breakthroughs was spurred by the incentive to accrue profits. It had two objectives:- (a) to obtain slaves and precious metals (gold) – if feasible establish trade with locals along commercial routes or raid them (b) to capture arable land. Thus, the Canaries provided a convenient base for the Europeans who thereafter bored their way farther southwards along the Atlantic Coast. This advantage was contingent to the willingness of financiers who were not averse to risks and uncertainty and had the confidence that these voyages would be worth the risks they entailed. Such expansion was not achieved overnight, but by piecemeal initiatives.[2]

Africa's Current Woes Adjudged by Historical Antecedents

The socio-political and economic conditions that burden Africa can be explained by the following factors.

Firstly, the demographic drain precipitated by the trans-Atlantic slave trade. There is broad agreement that the trade which spanned a period well beyond 500 years was demographically damaging from a fairly early period, especially when examined from a local and regional perspective. The loss of large numbers of adult males was particularly injurious to the sex ratios, dependent rates and perhaps the sexual division of labor.

Secondly, the depletion of indigenous skills and industries. Notably, the particular skills that African slaves possessed favored African, as opposed to Native American slavery. For instance, African slaves possessed the necessary skills for raising cattle and riding horses that were noticeably absent among Native Americans. On this account, slaves from the Mbundu group were consigned in prohibitive numbers during the seventeenth century to cattle farms in Venezuela. Likewise Africans from the Gold Coast who were strong divers participated in the prolific pearl trade in the area known as the Pearl Coast. West Africa bestowed the Americas with highly skilled slaves: the Igbo were seasoned metal workers, textile manufacturers, copper and bronze miners and craftsmen; the Yoruba were experienced farmers, ironsmiths, glass workers, and textile manufacturers. As recently as the 1850s, Benin boasted the manufacture and trade of soap so exquisite that the Portuguese were compelled to impose an outright ban on soap from West Africa during the seventeenth century to protect their local enterprise. Slaves from the Kongo came from a culture that nurtured ironsmiths creating an array of utensils from forged knives, weaponry to jewelry while Ghana yielded metal and goldsmiths, even leather dealers.

A third factor is the political naiveté of the ruling elite both past and present. "Global Trends 2025"[3] notes that as this circle of wealthy notables continues to amass greater income and wealth, poverty will persist or worsen in the continent's rural areas and sprawling urban centers and the divide between the elite and non-elite populations would continue.

A fourth factor is the invalidated concept of the nation state vis-à-vis Africa. The West tends to define continental polities along the narrow, predetermined lines of nation state, thereby imposing alien political and cultural systems on African societies. Africa was once blessed with a rich mosaic of complex kingdoms, federations, and empires prior to its precipitous decline into vassalages of Europe. At their zenith, African societies thrived on early forms of secular, democratic governments ruled by an executive monarchy.[4] Much like today's voting system, monarchs were chosen by election. Europe's malign decision to reconfigure, demarcate and redraw the continental geography ruptured Africa's historical continuum, placing it under the heels of diverse powers vying for primacy.

Alas, the Berlin Conference of 1884 set the stage for Africa's subordination. Fourteen countries participated in the inaugural meeting held on November 15, 1884: Austria-Hungary, Belgium, Denmark, France, Germany, Great Britain, Italy, the Netherlands, Portugal, Russia, Spain, Sweden-Norway, Turkey and the United States of America. Of this group France, Germany, the United Kingdom and Portugal, which collectively controlled most of colonial Africa at that time, dominated the meeting. Edwin Torrel and Henry Casson represented the United States. By 1914, all countries that were in attendance at the original meeting arrived at a consensus among themselves on the superimposition of their domains on the African land mass.[5]

According to Matt Rosenberg's account in "Berlin Conference 1884-1885 To Divide Africa: The Colonization of the Continent by European Powers," the new configuration reflected "...geography of disparate new countries that lacked rhyme, coherence, and reason." This cartogram of politically, socially and culturally incompatible parts could neither be eliminated nor made to operate satisfactorily—a status quo that persists until this day[6] European powers through such schemes eventually succeeded in entrenching their culture, language, political, and economic systems on their colonies. As a result, when African nations ultimately attained their independence and breathed a long sigh of relief, they were all the while constrained in assuming the mantle of nationhood. In short, they achieved nominal independence, while their former European masters glanced jealously over at the sumptuous prize.[6]

Africa's wealth much spoken about is bound to its ancient history, ethnographic character, eco-systems, diverse wild life, topsoil, and plentiful sources of water derived from rivers, lakes, and aquifers. The wealth of the West on the other hand is a totally different matter, engineered to service a virtual slot machine driven by exuberant risk-taking and wedded to institutionalized oligarchy, whose life blood is political chaos, deprivation, bankruptcy, and indebtedness. Blythe Masters 'enculturated' in a winners-take-it-all environment fostered the creation of complex credit derivatives (i.e. credit default swaps), opening a Pandora's box to reckless manipulations of the international financial market enacted on a daily basis by investment banks in partnership with hedge funds-a grand scheme of global dimension captured in gruel detail in Gillian <u>Tuitt's Fools's Gold: How the Bold Dream of a Small Tribe at J.P. Morgan Was Corrupted by Wall Street Greed</u> (2009) and in Pierre Jovanic 's subsequent biographical rendition titled "<u>Blythe Masters</u>" (2014).

And of course, there is Francophone Africa. La Francophonie exists as an overarching composite. It is a network of institutions and projects aimed at fostering and consolidating the political, economic, and cultural links between France and her former overseas dependencies. This organization is designed to ensure the continued dominance of the ruler over the ruled and is effected through student exchanges, the promotion of the French language, the hosting of exhibitions, and the management of foreign policy, particularly economics and state security. (Renou, 2002). France mandated its former colonies to put roughly 80% of their foreign currency reserves into the French treasury in addition to a further percentile for financial liabilities. The upshot of this is that France's former colonies are now relegated to the indignity of borrowing their own money from the French bank at high rates. Added to the scheme, France reserves the right to buy or reject any natural resources found in the land of Francophonie countries. Perhaps the most burdensome issue is the legacy of the commissar system detailed in Appendix A.

Today's geopolitical reality has the world in the grips of a fierce tussle over natural resources involving the viability of oil and alternatives, rare earth minerals, as well as precious metals. In the absence of essential raw materials—the building blocks of a functional economy typified by WEIRD countries—twenty-first century civilization premised on renewable energy, exponential growth, sustainability, nanotechnology, and the promises of artificial intelligence will all become but ragged futurist dreams bereft of substance, leaving then swathes of the human population to fend for themselves in a primeval struggle for survival.

Therefore the presence of China and America in Africa comes as no surprise. Beyond the shadow of a doubt, Africa is the most fortuitously endowed apportionment of real estate on the global landscape. Illustrative of its scale of wealth held in trust, despite occupying a mere 1% of the earth's land surface, southern Africa alone boasts of being the world's largest producer of gold, chromium, diamonds, vanadium, manganese and platinum. Africa is also a world-class producer of iron, titanium, zinc, coal, fluorspar, refractory minerals, phosphorous and lead. By all accounts the transformation of the subcontinent from an agrarian to an increasingly industrialized economy was catalyzed by the discovery of diamonds along the Orange River in 1860. In the decades that followed the initial discovery, gold was discovered in Limpopo, Mpumalanga and Zimbabwe and in subsequent years, the largest deposits of platinum, chrome, manganese, iron ore, uranium, coal, and titanium to name a few, would be unearthed at that said location.[7] Table 17.1.

Caricatures of Africa, while based on some kernel of truth pertaining to social underdevelopment are nevertheless overplayed via the mass media highlighting deprivation, endemic starvation, genocide, and disease across the continent, effectively masking miraculous growth that is predicted to outstrip China's economic boom. The International Monetary Fund estimates that sub-Saharan economies will grow 5.4 percent in 2014 and 5.8 percent in 2015, compared with 1.7 percent and 3 percent in the U.S. for the same two years respectively. China's growth is expected to hover around at 7.4 percent in 2014 and decrease by 7.1 percent in 2015. The crown in the anticipated renaissance is expected to go to none other than Nigeria, whose economy, rated as Africa's largest, has the potential to expand about 7.1 percent a year through 2030, according to the Mc Kinsey & Co. Nigeria could easily find itself among the world's top 20 economic heavyweights.[8] The two major reasons for Africa's economic growth are direct foreign investment and state infrastructural investment spending.

Increasingly across the region governments have stepped up investment spending in most countries geared towards power generation and the construction of roads and port facilities as is the case with Ethiopia, Ghana, Namibia, Niger, Nigeria, South Africa, Tanzania, Uganda and Zambia.

The data reveals two significant details: America's growth will drag into the near future with no spectacular performance waiting in the wings. Furthermore, China's economic miracle, though it has not come to a dead standstill at the moment, is slowing down considerably.

Table 17.1

Manganese	80	4bt	1	20	3.6mt	1	3b
Chrome	76	5.5bt	1	45	6.6 t	1	7b
PGM	56	63,000t	1	46	207t	1	25b
Gold	52	40,000t	1	17	428t	1	30b
Vanadium	44	12mt	1	57	18,000t	1	780m

Vermiculite	40	80mt	1	45	210,000t	1	132m
Refractories				36	183,000t	1	118m
Zirconium	22	14mt	2	28	0.25mt	2	7m
Titanium	20	146mt	2	23	213,000t	2	1,000m
Fluorspar	10	36mt	3	5	11mc	3	
Diamonds	11mc				11mc	5	
Uranium	9	0.2 bt	4	2	860 t	9	
Nickel	8	12 mt	6	3	37.000 t	9	
Antimony	6	8 mt	4	3	3,700 mt	4	
Phosphate	7	2.5 bt	3	2	2.8 mt	9	
Copper	2	13 mt	14	1	0.14 t	13	
Zinc	3	15 mt	5	1	63,000 t	18	
Lead	2	3 mt	5	2	75,000 mt	9	
Iron	1	1.5 bt	9	4	34 mt	8	
Coal	11	55 bt	5	6	224 mt	6	

SOURCE: The Story of Earth and Life. Struick Publishers Cape Town 2005 p 12

II

Caught Up Betwixt Rivals
- How China Gained Its Foothold on the Continent -

At the height of the Cold War China began in earnest to assert itself as a third world leader by aggressively courting Sino-African relationships. Many African conflicts that raged during the Cold War were reflective of the global contest between the United States and the Soviet Union, a fact that is underscored in Elizabeth Schmidt's insightful text, Foreign Intervention in Africa: From the Cold War to the War on Terror (2013)[9]. With the waning of the colonial era in the late 1950s, the PRC lost no time establishing diplomatic ties among newly independent African states, to be followed by the signing of bilateral trade agreements and offers of aid in infrastructural projects.

Between 1968-1976, as the liberation struggle against white minorities in apartheid South Africa intensified, China built a 1,100 mile railway linking the port of Dar-es-Salaam in Tanzania to Zambia. To this day the enterprise is considered a high point in terms of the technical support it demanded and the strategic advantage it earned. Thousands of Chinese nationals were directly involved in this project, which assured the two affected front line states a measure of independence from Rhodesia. A notable aspect of this development that ought not to be overlooked was China's self-perception as a world leader and its continuing disputation with Taiwan—a territory that is until day considered by mainland China as a renegade province to be reined in at all costs.

The fallout that ensued from China's ongoing tensions with the USSR, which did not subside until the official dissolution of the Soviet empire in 1991, was also noteworthy. Its strategic relevance rested largely on the alterations in state relations between African societies in the aftermath of the Soviet collapse and the subsequent de-scaling of Russia's presence, paving the way for the inevitable entry of emerging power centers on the continent. Among the line-up: India and Japan, the latter on an impressive upward economic trajectory. (Winters and Yusuf, 2007).

Cold War discontinuance brought temporary respite among Western nations from their ongoing wrangling for the favors of local governments. During this historical juncture, many African countries became heavily indebted, dependent on foreign aid, and began competing among themselves for economic advantage. Western Europe in the meantime reoriented its focus towards Eastern Europe drawn no doubt to the latter's capital-starved markets and well-educated work force, while the U.S. proceeded to invest in energy security and engaged in a series of costly, inconclusive wars in the Islamic world. Issues affecting Africa were largely defined on the basis of humanitarianism, which were typically relegated to the lowest rung of foreign policy priorities of the developed world.

Extra-regional shifts in state relations with China migrated from an ideological and political stance to a more pragmatic posture and became increasingly so following China's admission to the World Trade Organization in December 2001 (Winters and Yusuf, 2007). In the meantime, Beijing maintained a firm hold on trade and investment opportunities on the continent, a move that paid off handsomely so that by 1995 China was able to secure trade and investment ties with the oil sectors of Angola, Nigeria, and the Sudan; and the copper, cobalt, and platinum mining enterprises of the Congo and Zimbabwe. The story does not end there. China without reluctance seized the opportunity to negotiate cheap supplies of food to satisfy its domestic needs and land acquisition programs. The latter initiative called for hefty investments by Chinese state farms in the agricultural sectors of Senegal, Zambia, and other nations.

414

Much to the consternation of the West, the PRC by 2008 became an affirmed major player in sub-Saharan Africa (Jacoby: 234) and went on to outstrip Europe and America as Africa's number one trading partner. How did this occur?

In The New Presence of China in Africa[10] Meine Pieter van Dijk explains the extent to which the combined use of aid, investment, and trade requires a unique political coordination, which the Chinese have ingeniously deployed to muster policies reinforced by feasible strategies. A certainly unlooked for development is that despite the fact that its pragmatic economic power projection has paid off, the PRC has recently been compelled to become involved in targeted multilateral interventions in support of peace and security initiatives in the oilfields in South Sudan and similarly affected localities, with the objective of protect its commercial interests and that of host governments.

Furthermore, under China's Peaceful Development Road, an official policy brief created in 2005, the PRC undertook the following:

- To provide a zero tariff treatment for all products of the 39 Least Developed Countries (LDCs) having diplomatic relations with China
- To expand aid to Heavily Indebted Poor Countries (HIPC) and Least Developed Countries through bilateral channels
- To exempt or rescind all outstanding interest-free and low-interest government loans due at the end of 2004 and owed by all Heavily Indebted Poor Countries having diplomatic relations with China, within a two-year time frame
- To finance US $10 billion in preferential loans and preferential export buyers credit to developing countries to help them upgrade their infrastructure within three years
- To endorse industrialization at bilateral level and carry out joint venture cooperation
- To increase aid to developing states in general, but more specifically to African states, by supplying them with medicines such as preventive drugs for malaria; and by building medical facilities and training medical personnel within three years

China presently enjoys infrastructure-for-resource deals with no less than 35 sub-Saharan nations. Under such programs, countries are awarded concessional and low-interest loans in exchange for permitting Chinese state companies access to resources. In addition to government guarantees for bank loans, Chinese firms also receive export credits for financing the operational cost of African projects as well as credits for capital goods and machinery. The largest of such projects has gained ground in the Democratic Republic of the Congo—a fiercely contested territory. Among the more lucrative Sino-Africa deals are oil from Sudan, Angola, Nigeria and Ghana; iron ore from Sierra Leone; manganese from Gabon; copper from Zambia and the Democratic Republic of the Congo; and timber from Madagascar. In addition to trade and direct foreign investment (DFI), development aid increased at a rapid pace. To the credit of PRC business aplomb, FDI and aid were so intertwined as to mutually reinforce each other. China's strategic lead has compelled the U.S. to seriously reassess its standing and take decisive measures to neutralize its key competitor on the continent and secure its primacy.

III

The U.S. Vision

Lelitia Lawson, writing for the Center for Contemporary Conflict in 2007 noted that the U.S. policy towards Africa in the medium term appeared to be largely defined by international terrorism, the increasing importance of African oil to American energy demands and the dramatic expansion of Sino-African relations since the turn of the century. Both terms of the Obama administration have reinforced this perception epitomized in the build-up of Cooperative Security Locations and Forward Operating Sites across the continent under the overall mission plan of security cooperation.

But does this necessarily insinuate a lack of appreciation on America's part of the full scope of potentialities in a strengthened relationship with Africa? Is there a grand design, and if so, how is this being pursued?

America's first President, General George Washington reminded his countrymen of the centrality of their country's national interest:

> *"... It is a maxim founded on the universal experience of mankind that no nation is to be trusted further than it is bound by its interests, and no prudent statesman or politician will venture to depart from it."* [11]

Somewhat refreshing in light of Washington's obstinacy towards change is President Obama's frank admission that the global ecosystem belongs to everyone.[12] His acknowledgement that the world of 2014 marks the end of unipolarity is not to be taken lightly. Spelled out in this statement is recognition of an array of systems, polities, and interests in co-existence vying for space to maneuver, along with America's difficult task of promoting a policy for Africa that coalesces around its homegrown needs without negating American priorities. Hope is thus roused for Africa's further integration into the global economy, penetration of overseas capital markets and more importantly, access to U.S. direct foreign investment. This by no means signals an abandonment of the fundamentals of transparency and democracy; neither does it demand de-scaling the principles of stability and good governance both of which are necessary prerequisites for economic and social advancement. What it does entail is a comprehensive and sustained multi-track endeavor combining soft power with America's ideologically motivated global economic footprint.

The President's second point: Africa presents "fascinating opportunities to leapfrog certain technologies and skip certain phases of development."[13] In short, he hints at the underlying goal, which is to make the continent more investor friendly for American corporations. This is already materializing in nascent projects such as Power Africa launched in 2013 with the objective of installing 10,000 megawatts of new generation capacity and connecting 20 million new customers across Africa by 2018.

Moreover, President Obama has noted that despite the discursiveness of the global ecosystem, the United States sees itself 'central' to the process of moving Africa to the next stage of growth. Given Africa's gargantuan size; its daunting political, economic and cultural complexities, as described, the task exacting large-scale and continuing inter-continental engagement backed by heavy investments across the board can only be beholden to a nation with unrivalled worldwide capacity and an established legacy in spawning equally formidable offshoots of itself, mirroring an ideology and way of life that is uniquely American.

Cognizant of Africa's exploding youth demographic dividend, the Young African Leadership Initiative (YALI) commissioned in 2010 wherewith the U.S. has committed significant resources to enhance leadership skills, bolster entrepreneurship, and connect young African leaders to one another, is a major long-term investment program that imparts the requisite skills to aspiring African leaders who would one day assume the helm of Africa's governments. The post-World War II era saw the United States investing heavily in rebuilding and serving as a mid-wife to many economies and democracies in Europe and Asia often with creditable results. It is noteworthy that of the 15 largest U.S. trading partners today, 11 are former recipients of U.S. aid. America's humanitarianism however, is informed by its economic interests, which supersede all other considerations. The White House strategy for Africa must therefore carefully balance the financing of humanitarianism geared towards furthering social development and alleviating under development with America's desire to make African markets more efficient for American businesses, while concurrently use its economic footprint to hedge itself against China's encroachment. Promoting democracy, political stability and good governance, securing safe and reliable energy sources and advancing military aims will attain this.

Infrastructure projects are in fact subsumed under the mandate of the Department of Defense, which supports anti-malaria programs in Ethiopia, funds research for a viable Ebola vaccine, and provides vaccination for goats in Uganda to name just a few. U.S. policy makers and members of the business community are anxious to lend support to developmental projects across Africa insofar that such aid programs open up trade corridors; enable faster more efficient regional exchange; connect urban centers to the hinterland and economize on transport or logistical costs.

The 2014 U.S.-Africa Leaders Summit was hosted in Washington from August 4th-6th. The event represented a groundbreaking shift from bilateral to continental-wide engagement, bringing together over 40 heads of state to deliberate over trade and economic development. Aid dependency at this point has taken to the crumpled pages of a by-gone era. Less evident to the public is the U.S. master stroke, co-opting Pan-Africanism in the light of day from its historical socialist, anti-imperialist leanings envisioned by Trinidadians Henry Sylvester-Williams, George Padmore and C.L.R. James in the early twentieth century to an openly corporatist agenda specifically crafted to align African priorities with those of the Anglo-American ruling class. Johann Wolfgang von Goethe, the German novelist once solemnly remarked, "None are more hopelessly enslaved than those who falsely believe they are free."

The highpoints on the opening day were America's commitment to renew and enhance the African Growth and Opportunity Act (AGOA); commit an additional $7 billion to financing and promoting America's exports to the continent; build infrastructure' assist African nations in forging trade among themselves by removing prevailing barriers; and empowering the next generation of African leaders and entrepreneurs.[14] That aside, aid projects at the summit were a high priority with an estimated $498 million in public funds being allocated to power projects in Ghana, a country hailed by the U.S. as a model for democracy. An entire day was devoted to a business forum in which American chief executives advised African leaders on which reforms they thought were needed to trigger an investment surge in their respective countries.

However, key to all of this is the re-authorization and refinement of the AGOA of 2000. Set up under the Clinton administration, the AGOA authorizes the president of the U.S. to determine on an annual basis which sub-Saharan countries are eligible for trade preferences and duty free benefits. Its primary goal is to assist African economies and improve economic relations with the U.S. and the region.

As would be expected, countries' inclusion has fluctuated with changes in the local political environment. In December 2009, Guinea, Madagascar and Niger were removed; by October 2011 eligibility was restored to Guinea and Niger and by June 2014 to Madagascar. Currently, Nigeria and Angola are the largest exporters and South Africa is the most diverse in terms of its export products.

On the Ground in Africa: Oil, Drugs and Terrorists

Of immediate concern to the U.S. are al-Qaeda in the Islamic Maghreb which is active in northern and western Africa; Boko Haram in Nigeria and al–Shabaab in Somalia; and even more so, China's economic and diplomatic influence. In this vein, Washington has been maintaining a concise account of Africa's growing significance as a repository of all the world's vital resources. Since the discovery of untapped oil reserves in November 2000, attention zooms in on Africa's oil and mineral deposits as well as its trading networks. Following the discovery of oil, the National Intelligence Council predicted sub-Saharan Africa would before long play a larger role in global energy markets. The prediction would prove accurate since almost one-third of the world's new oil discoveries were made in Africa and the continent remains among the world's few relatively unexplored regions.

By no means of lesser importance is the U.S.—led continental antidrug initiative which has become a primary pillar in bi-regional cooperation. Within a two-year period 2009-2010, American counternarcotics assistance alone in West Africa totaled $50 million with the introduction of the West Africa Cooperative Security Initiative. This project has been sustained on a year on year basis. Its 15 beneficiaries are nations that are estimated to be primary channels along the continent's renowned drug shipment routes. Additionally, the U.S. as a key player in the ongoing Cocaine Route Program, a major trans-Atlantic initiative facilitated by the European Union Latin America Caribbean Coordination and Cooperation Mechanism Against Drugs, the objective of which is to disrupt the sizeable portion of cocaine flows emanating out of source countries in the Andean community, transiting the Caribbean Sea and on to West Africa, bound for Western Europe.

Notwithstanding its good intentions, U.S. inculpation in African affairs has not gone unchallenged. Washington is repeatedly taken to task for being too militarily involved in the continent's affairs by a cross-section of critics at home and abroad.[15] The commissioning of AFRICOM in 2007 followed by a steady stream of deployments has undoubtedly fueled this perception. AFRICOM initially fell under European Command and transitioned to independent unified command in October 2008. At its inception, all efforts were directed towards synchronizing the

419

scores of activities that were inherited from the three regional commands that previously coordinated and provided support to engagements on the continent. The force presence in Africa has since expanded well beyond the level of activities prevalent during the Bush era. Demonstrative of this, of the 54 countries that now make up the landmass, there is a U.S. military presence in no less than 49. Engagements range from base construction, security cooperation arrangements, training exercises, advisory deployments, and special operations missions to more elaborate infrastructural investments and delivering humanitarian assistance programs such as the construction of schools, orphanages and medical facilities.

The justification for military expansion and force rebalancing however lies in the details, as spelled out by Colonel Tom Davis Director of U.S. Africa Command Office Public Affairs:

- At the end of October 2008, there were roughly 2,600 U.S. military personnel and civilians on the African continent or on ships within the command's area of responsibility. That number has since increased to about 5,000, more than half of who are service members committed to tours at Camp Lemmonier in Djibouti with the remainder serving on a temporary basis ranging from a few days to several weeks.

- Besides the above "base" the U.S. maintains temporary facilities elsewhere in Africa where personnel serve as guests within the host nation and work alongside or coordinate their activities with host nation personnel

- Military advisors have been deployed to four nations in Central and East Africa. Advisory teams working alongside national militaries in Obo and Djema in the Democratic Republic of the Congo. Personnel are also based in Nzara in South Sudan and Entebbe in Uganda.

- There are humanitarian work sites in the Ethiopian towns of Humble, Hula and Dube assisting in the drilling of wells, administering veterinary/medical assistance and constructing schools and clinics. Teams are also providing base/life support services to U.S. military personnel collaborating with Kenyan armed forces.

- The U.S. conducts exercise programs through bilateral and multilateral exercises

- Counterterrorism training takes place in Algeria, Burkina Faso, Chad, Mauritania, Niger and Tunisia. Joint training exercises are also facilitated in Morocco, Cameroon, Gabon, Botswana, South Africa, Lesotho, Senegal, and Nigeria.

- Special Operations Forces have been deployed to assist and enable local forces to crush the threat of the Lord's Resistance Army (LRA) in Uganda, the Democratic Republic of the Congo, the Central African Republic (CAR) and South Sudan.[16]

Army Major General Carter F. Ham's testimony to the House Armed Services Committee on February 29, 2012 underscored even further the need for an escalated force presence. He explained, *"given the vast geographic space and diversity in threats, the command requires increased ISR assets to adequately address the security challenges on the continent."* In his estimation "external actors" were posing a threat to many African nations, driving up the demand for building capacity to prepare local leaders for the surge of challenges.[17] Additionally, the public formalization of the long-standing merger between al-Shabaab and al-Qaida in the Horn of Africa, violent attacks by Boko Haram against Western interests in Nigeria compelled the need to strengthen regional capabilities. In his view, despite overall resolve, meeting intelligence, surveillance and reconnaissance requirements continued to pose challenges for the troops.

IV

America's Blueprint

America's 'manifest destiny' is to propagate its ideological footprint worldwide central to which is the promotion of democracy. This imposes an obligation under successive U.S. administrations to cultivate abiding relationships with countries around the world by forging dialogue and diplomatic ties. The basic tenet beneath all of this is that in order for prosperity to be achieved there must be effective governance.

The most striking phenomena on the African socio-political landscape are: increased urbanization; the dramatic shifts in demographic patterns; the mushrooming and spread of extremism; proliferation of and wider access to lethal weapons especially those with precision strike munitions; the challenge to governance presented by non-state actors; the imperative to secure sources of energy and energy flows; and the impact of emerging power centers like China that have implanted their interests across the continent. Inter-continental dialogue, summitry, military engagement including technical or logistical support and promotion of trade and economic networks contribute to America's policy in relation to Africa.

The 2014 U.S.-Africa Leaders Summit was therefore ground-breaking in many respects, but primarily from the point of view that it was the first time that the U.S.

engaged with Africa at intercontinental level; added to which the breadth of America's trade with Africa going into the summit was remarkably insubstantial. This was reflected in President Obama's opening remarks when he stated that "of all the goods we export to the world only about 1% goes to sub-Saharan Africa." On that account, the Summit provided a platform for an overdue overhaul of U.S. policy and enlarged the playing field for the government and private corporations to pursue intercontinental trade and investment through public-private sector partnerships that surpasses already existing arrangements under the AGOA forum. The forum is currently hosted once every two years in Washington, and every other year in an AGOA eligible country.

THE THREAT SCENARIO

America is resolute that the danger presented by the spread of Islamic extremism demands an aggressive national security apparatus that is homegrown and bolstered by a worldwide surveillance network shared among partners and allies. For this reason anti-terrorist initiatives are a main pillar of its continental strategy. The 2014 Quadrennial Defense Review underscores the point that Africa is an area of strategic concern in light of its potential for rapidly developing threats, particularly in fragile states, for violent public protests, and related terrorist attacks place U.S. interests at risk.

North Africa is a breeding ground for radical Islam and the systemic havoc sweeping through the region finds a definite starting point: the 2011 NATO intervention in Libya catalyzed by the United States, Britain and France who sought regime change and invoked the right to protect civilians. One of the most highly regarded politico-academic institutions, the Belfer Center for Science and International Affairs at the Kennedy School of Government at Harvard University, released a report authored by Dr. Alan Kuperman that challenges the rationale for the war. Gaddafi was singled out and blamed by the mainstream for murdering his own people, a fabricated pretext exploited to justify a 'humanitarian' intervention. The Report highlights the disastrous effects of the mass campaign of disinformation including the massacre of civilians and the "cleansing" carried out against many innocent black Libyans.[18]

NATO's Libya campaign would later hemorrhage into a civil war in Mali, where Tuaregs that fought alongside Gaddafi seized Libyan weapons and attempted to create an independent state, until Al-Qaida in the Islamic Maghreb (AQIM) muscled in on the vacuum left after the toppling of President Amadou Toure.[19] Three years after the intervention Libya, a country once credited as the most wealthy and developed African nation, spiraled into fresh turmoil. Wracked by lawlessness, the escalation of extremism, sporadic outbreaks of violence between militias driven by factionalism, gang skirmishes and the absence of a robust central government, the reignited violence in Tripoli n July 2014 forced the special evacuation of embassy personnel and closure of the U.S. mission office.

Of what import are these upheavals to countries in North and sub-Saharan Africa, and more importantly, in the face of Chinese diplomatic, political and economic investments?

Libya is a key geostrategic pivot on the African continent. The country sits atop a natural resource that is arguably more valuable than oil – the Nubian Sandstone Aquifer - a vast underground reserve of fresh water estimated to be the largest in the world with the potential to turn Libya, a country that is 95% desert, into an arable oasis. Currently, France's megaworks components –Suez, Ondeo, Saur - control the world's $400 billion water market.

In the case of Somalia, beyond doubt almost every nation represented in the Horn of Africa is militarily engaged in that country, which is home to the Islamist group, Al-Shabab. In 2006 the U.S. instigated the invasion of Somalia by co-opting the Ethiopians into an incursion of that country resulting in total collapse from which it is yet to emerge. Then in 2011 the U.S. enlisted Kenyan support in Somalia's occupation - a move that incurred the irascibility of Al-Shabab. Subsequent offensives aimed at overwhelming Al Shabab have fanned the flames of strong nationalist sentiment sparking a series of proxy wars: thus, Ethiopia's regional leadership is currently challenged by the rise of Kenya a favored U.S. proxy, since both countries share borders with Somalia.[20] To compound the situation, based on historically preceding demarcations, Kenya and Ethiopia are both laying claim to adjacent Somali boundaries. All the while, Al Shabab is intent on annexing a large swathe of Somalia's southern territory historically known as Azania; while Ethiopia targets the central area and Kenya is gunning for the south.[21]

The situation in Mali, a nation of strategic importance to France, is no less protracted. And the crown jewel of all is of course Nigeria, Africa's wealthiest nation, foremost oil producer, and sixth supplier of U.S. crude imports. Nigeria, to the envy of many, is slated to become one of the most economically vibrant countries in the world on to 2030. This makes the operation of groups like Boko Haram, a Salafist organization seeking to overthrow the country's elected secular administration, politically and economically consequential from both a local and international standpoint. Underpinning all of this is the influence of al-Qaeda which maintains a stranglehold in the region by successfully mounting spectacular operations throughout the Maghreb and Sahel that have attracted worldwide media coverage, while providing advanced training and financing to other groups like the Movement for the Unity and the Jihad in West Africa. Despite a severely weakened with the annihilation of key leaders, al-Qaeda has been able to bore its way beyond its reputed Algerian base deeper into Central and West Africa.

The Ominous Peril is oblique

Whereas these threats represent the visible and more tangible justification for American interposition, the greater menace by far is of a less direct nature – China's demand for land, water and natural resources and its booming economy. This verdict was plainly reflected in " Ensuring a Strong Defense for the Future" a Congressionally mandated report drafted by the National Defense Panel, co-chaired by Dr. William Perry and General John P. Abizad. The Report provided an appraisal of the 2014 Quadrennial Defense Review, called for radical change, and warned of the dangers confronting the U.S. by specific countries deemed "growing powers"[22] which, in the view of panel members were to be regarded as potential targets for military action. Heading the list was China, followed by North Korea, Iran, Iraq, Syria, the Middle East and Africa.

The appraisal found that there is a growing gap between the strategic objectives that the U.S. military is expected to achieve and the resources required to do so and suggested a more expansive sizing construct for the military. Additionally, there was a dire need tor the military to build a capacity and capability to deter or fight in several regions possibly in overlapping timeframes. The panel foresaw a strong likelihood of imminent confrontation between the U.S. and its nuclear adversaries even while pinning down counter-terrorism operations worldwide.

This book notes that more often than not fiscal policy outweighs defense requirements. Furthermore, with intensified demands placed on deployments, responding to Africa's realities would require a multi-tiered scheme with innate flexibility; the capability to respond on multiple fronts to evolving threat pictures and mutating scenarios occurring in rapid succession; commandeering access to relevant air and sea lanes and specific targets and the technological wherewithal for persistent and integrated surveillance of persons or locations of interest.

Strategic Pillars

In a sense, the war on terror providentially oils the wheels for access to the continent since it provides a justification for America to – (a) set up shop in virtually any part of the region either permanently or on a rotational basis (b) adopt countervailing measures against state and non-state actors that are inimical to U.S. interests (c) disrupt and nullify China's economic and diplomatic progress (d) consolidate mutually reinforcing relationships with host governments and local militaries (d) co-opt NATO allies with which the U.S has shared interests (f) stoke conflict to the extent that it is strategically advantageous to the U.S. (g) establish permanent ideological, military and economic footprints consistent with a broader foreign policy agenda (h) elicit the required backing from international bodies, businesses, multinational corporations, financiers and civil society; and (h) continuously assess the threat picture from an on the ground perspective. Such leverage is certainly not behooved to the Chinese.

Assessing the Terrain

Apart from the phenomenon of extremism, the destabilizing effects of environmental, energy, and economic shocks and more recent pandemics — a classic case being the spread of the deadly Ebola virus — have spurred defense planners into a heightened response mode. Blending creativity with paradigmatic resourcefulness, the Department has rolled out a line-up of programs, worthy of special mention.

Firstly, the multi-million dollar Minerva Research Initiative which was established in 2008 to improve the Department's appreciation of the social, cultural, behavioral and political forces that shape regions of the world so that decision-makers are better equipped to develop medium and long-term war-fighting insights. Many top universities have been co-opted into this enterprise, which is coordinated by military agencies such as the U.S. Army Research Office and the U.S Air Force Office of Scientific Research.

Secondly, the development of an empirical model of social movement mobilization trends under the Human Terrain Systems Program. The scheme is geared towards determining well ahead of time, the tipping point of social contagions by studying their digital traces, and "feeding" the results into application tolls that could be taken directly into military field operations.

Thirdly, drawing from lessons learned in other regions of the world for input into simulation training. The 2011 Egyptian revolution, the 2012 Nigerian fuel subsidy crisis, the 2011 Russian Duma elections and the 2013 Gaza park protests in Turkey provide realistic "test cases" for forecasting and making appropriate reconfigurations for changing theaters. Taking note of this, Richard Reeve, lead author of the Oxford Report, "From New Frontier to New Normal: Counter-terrorism Operations in New Sahel-Africa" (2014) observed:

> *"The remote Sahel-Sahara is the laboratory for experiments in 21*. *century counter-terrorism operations. These are defined by their open-ended length, "light-touch" approach – with limited boots on the ground, and a reliance on special forces, drones and private military companies and an increased capacity and willingness to intervene militarily to protect U.S. interests.*"[23]

Concomitant with the 2008 commissioning of AFRICOM, the U.S. Army War College in Carlisle Pennsylvania included for the first time in its history Africa-centered war games. Consistent with the DOD's impressive war-planning perspicacity, one of the four scenarios was responding to a crisis in Nigeria in which the government was in a state of near collapse and rival factions and rebels were fighting for control of oilfields in the Niger Delta.[24]Another scenario was a response to a crisis in Somalia spurred by escalating insurgency and piracy. Insofar as this fictional representation converges with policy, it has been theorized that a shattered Nigeria would ultimately create conditions where China's growing cooperation with Abuja can be challenged or ultimately disrupted and, as this enquiry will demonstrate, serve U.S. interests.

Geopolitical Areas of Interests

For reasons that are now manifestly clear, the U.S. medium to long-term strategy narrows in on specific geo-political areas of operation in Africa's northern and eastern tiers reputed for rampant violence and extremism:

- The Sahara-Sahel region, branded as "the new frontier" in global counter-terrorism operations in the Oxford Research Group study "From New Frontier to New Normal: Counter-terrorism Operations in the New Sahel-Africa."
- Djibouti in the Horn of Africa where, in combination with Joint Task Force-Horn of Africa, is overseeing Open Ending Freedom in order to promote stability
- The Central African Republic, gripped in an unbroken struggle between the Seleka (a coalition of dissident extremists, grossly lacking a clearly conceptualized political base) and deposed President François Bozize ; the

issue was compounded by the award of lucrative oil and uranium contracts to China and South Africa respectively, sparking the irascibility of France and the United States.

- Somalia, which is now a crucible for military engagement of every country in the Horn of Africa, that shares borders with that country

Rebalancing and Expansion

As a combatant command, AFRICOM has created a distribution network that links military posts scattered across Keyna, Uganda, Ethiopia, Djibouti, Ghana and Senegal. The Defense Logistics Agency has disclosed that the U.S. operates ten gas and oil bunker locations in as many as eight countries, in addition to its presence in Cameroon, Cape Verde, Cote D'Ivoire, Gabon, Ghana, Keyna, Mauritius, Namibia, Nigeria, Seychelles, South Africa and Tanzania. Furthermore, America maintains a Naval Medical Research Unit, which is part of its medical investigation unit, operating in Kisumu and Kencho.

Not all U.S. Africa bases are operating on the continent. AFRICOM's headquarters is in Stuttgat-Moehringer, Germany whereas the U.S. Air Force Air Operating Center is in Ramstein. There are logistics support hubs in Spain, Aruba and Greece and a forward operating site on Britain's Ascension Island off the coast of Africa. A special purpose Marine Air Ground Task Force is based at Naval Air Station Sigonella, Italy. What's more by 2018, U.S. Army Africa would have established a base of operation at Caserma Del Din in northern Italy at an overall cost of $310 million.

America leaves no stone un-turned. The Oxford Research Group Report noted "with the drawdown of foreign forces in Afghanistan 2014 would become a critical year for militarization of the Sahel-Africa and for the entrenchment of foreign powers" there. It also projected that bases were to be established under a crisis response concept referred to as "new normal," wherein U.S. Marines will be tactically assigned to locations across the continent and equipped to respond within hours to locations where U.S. citizens and interests were deemed to be under threat. As well too, Nick Turse reports that AFRICOM's $7.1 million construction projects in 2014 entail the construction of schools, orphanages, and medical facilities in 19 countries.[25]

Threat Picture

To what extent is the ongoing turbulence impacting upon with China's relations with governments in the region with which it has built strong ties? And just as importantly, how is this impacting on other major players with similar interests?

Chinese demonstrated profligacy in the continent's extractive, manufacturing, trade and commercial sectors has no doubt served as a catalyst in prodding Washington into taking actions geared towards diminishing its economic and political leverage. The exodus of Chinese businesses from Libya during the 2011 "humanitarian intervention" by NATO forces was a clear demonstration of the disruptive effects that continuing instability was having on overseas investors and more broadly, on China's economic interests.

Brzezinski, who has in the past been a highly influential figure in shaping a U.S. foreign policy that thrives on fomenting instability and fragmentation of existing nation states that sees the emergence of "micro-states" based on localized cultural, ethnic and religious peculiarities as obtained in Afghanistan many years previously, introduces the concept of "micro-nationalities" in the African setting. He theorized the removal of national borders established in the nineteenth century in favor of a quilt of weak tribal entities. The corollary to this is that a balkanized Nigeria (a country that has received considerable economic, military and political support from Beijing and which is reciprocally an important source of oil and petroleum), would create conditions in which China's growing cooperation with Abuja can be easily challenged, and possibly disrupted.[26]This mode of fragmentation is likely to have a similar impact in strife-ridden Mali, Ethiopia and Somalia which like Nigeria, are endowed with valuable natural resources, concomitantly plagued by sectarian strife and of comparable strategic importance to China, America and Europe.

1. Dislodging the Chinese – Aerial Command and Ground Control

Seeing that the Chinese already enjoys ground base advantage on the continent, a major pillar in America's arsenal to loosen the grip of its rival lies in asserting aerial command of Northern Africa at a time when many governments are sliding into pandemonium from internal pressures. America's official base in Africa is Camp Lemonnier, a former French foreign legion post in Djibouti. However, a close look shows that force build-up is well underway, incorporating intelligence-driven, surveillance and reconnaissance missions; operating drone bases out of Diori Hamani International Airport in Niger; managing a mini-base as a first step towards constructing MILCON aircraft parking aprons at a future venue; operating another airbase in Ouagadougou, the capital of Burkina Faso, which provides the hub for the Joint Services Operations Detachment; commissioning the Trans-Saharan Short Take-off and the Landing Airlift Support Initiative. Additionally, the U.S. shares multiple military bases and an airport in Mali that was previously taken over by extremists during the 2012 upheavals, but has since been re-taken by French and Malian troops.

While admitting that the true nature and extent of counter-terrorism operations in the Sahel-Sahara can only be guessed at, the Oxford Research Report "From New Frontier to New Normal" notes that Air Mobile U.S. Marine task forces are increasingly deploying to Africa from bases as far off as Spain and Italy and are known to be seeking at least one Intermediate Staging base in coastal West Africa, with the most potent UAVs perhaps based in Sigonella in Sicily.[27] It is even speculated that given the current gaps in UAV coverage from Niamaj, Sigonella and Djibouti the U.S. is likely to seek out new basing facilities in Senegal and Chad.

2. Promotion of Trade and Economic Networks

Brazil, China, the European Union, India, Japan, South Korea, Turkey are major players on the continent, with long-running and formalized political dialogue among African leaders geared towards productive, harmonious relationships. Other notable forums are: Japan's Tokyo International Conference for African Development inaugurated in 1993 and which convenes at five-year intervals; China's Forum on China-Africa Corporation which convokes every three years, having taken off in 2000 at the height of trade and investment schemes during the much-acclaimed Sino-African nativity; so too is the E.U.-Africa Summit which was launched in 2000 and has since convened on no less than three occasions. Geostrategic blocs have also assumed a unique pride of place in Africa inter-continental forums, with the Africa-South America Summit and the Arab-Africa Summit standing out. On this merit, the Brookings Institution was of the view that insofar as framing a strategy for Africa goes "the United States is playing catch up."

The 2014 Leaders' Summit in Washington opened the door for an overhaul of U.S. policy towards Africa. This is premised on an appreciation on America's part that people are Africa's greatest resource. Without people opportunities to interact, cooperate, build partnerships and engage in profitable commerce would not be possible. Business leaders value the potentialities in "the new Africa that is emerging," a continent endowed with some of the fastest growing economies in the world, a rapidly mushrooming middle class and a thriving telecommunications market. A modern, telecommunications system thus translates into more efficient trade and business transactions that can be accomplished in real time and enable rapid response to market shocks as well as social crises. Modest government reforms in Africa are currently attracting a record level of foreign investment. Last but not least, the continent boasts the fastest growing cohort of youth ready to advance their education, so that their dreams get fulfilled. Not surprisingly the theme of the summit was "Investing in the Future."

"An Analysis of Issues Shaping Africa's Economic Future," produced by the Office of the Chief Economist for the World Bank noted that economic activity remains strong in much of sub-Saharan Africa and is driven by robust domestic demand; that after an increase on 4.2 percent in 2012 GDP growth was expected to strengthen to 4.9 percent in 2013; and that the region's growth is underpinned by strong private and public investment which in combination account for the region's largest source of capital flows Furthermore while investment has increasingly flowed to the natural resources sector the non-resources sector is similarly lucrative, attracting increasing flows of investment driven by the buoyancy of telecommunications, finance, retail, real estate and transportation sub-sectors.[28]

American businesses seek stable markets where they can diversify their corporate portfolios and lessen their exposure to financial risks in the developed world currently burdened by sluggish growth, private debt, and the possibility of deflationary contraction. Underdeveloped but growing markets with a guaranteed consumer base as obtains in Africa provide opportunities for this to be realized.

Marriott's strategic acquisition of Protea Hotels of Capetown testifies to the achievement American multinationals wish to attain.[29] Marriott owns hotels in Egypt and Algeria, with others under construction in Rwanda, Tunisia, Nigeria, Ghana, Morocco, Ethiopia, Gabon and Benin. Several Protea branches were, until the time of buy-out, operating in secondary and tertiary markets. Nothing short of a continental presence is Marriott's objective. In effect, Marriott will be the largest hotel in Africa and based on The World Travel and Tourism Commission Reports—which stated that travel in Africa increased by 34% since 2006—Marriott is now positioned to respond to market trends. [29]

South Africa, according to its deputy Foreign Minister Marius Fransman, "presents a gateway for investment on the continent." His observation is justified since in 2010, 17 out of 20 leading African companies were based in South Africa. [30] The sectoral trend in relation to mergers and acquisitions is underscored in the same Report, which noted that of all the mergers and acquisitions that had occurred; the services and manufacturing sectors attracted an average of 53.4 and

33.5 percent in 2011-12, respectively; while the primary sector accounted for only 13.2 percent.

The U.S.-Africa Leaders Summit, co-sponsored by the U.S. Department of Commerce and former New York Mayor Michael Bloomberg's foundation, and attended by chief executives of top U.S. conglomerates such as General Electric Coca Cola, Wal-Mart, IBM presented a golden opportunity for President Obama to articulate his administration's policy.[31]

A comprehensive portfolio of investment opportunities included:

- Investment in energy projects
- Promotion of hydro-projects that will ensure the availability of clean water to communities
- Development of infrastructure, including telecommunications
- Expansion of other sectors while injecting state-of-the-art technology – clean energy, aviation, banking, construction

Special appropriations were dedicated to promote U.S. exports to and investments in Africa - $14 billion in new investments by U.S. corporations; $15 billion from Coca Cola for manufacturing equipment; $15 billion in new commitments for Power Africa to open the door for multinational corporations to engage in energy deals and thereby double the number of people with access to power in the sub-Saharan region. The Doing Business in Africa Project promises the requisite institutional support to be achieved through:

- Continued bipartisan efforts in updating and refining the AGOA
- Inauguration and strengthening of trade missions
- Signing of an Executive Order establishing a Presidential Advisory Council of Business Leaders to help do business in Africa
- Forging partnerships with African entrepreneurs to build infrastructure so that economies can flourish on both sides
- Promoting shared commitments between the African Development Bank (ADB), governments and the private sector
- Catalyzing intraregional trade among African countries by building local capacity to enable them to transact efficiently across borders

How America supplants China in Africa economically while winning friends and building confidence remains crucial.

V

CHINA'S BLUEPRINT

While on the one hand America's focus has been dominated by security, heavy energy investments, and interventions in the Greater Middle East that have led to a series of costly and inconclusive wars, China on the other hand sees itself as the global economic superpower of the twenty-first century. By employing a strategy of gradualism, the PRC is using Africa as a spatiotemporal launching pad to secure its long-term ambition. In order to sustain a booming economy, China must accelerate its supply of consumers to buy its manufactures, utilize huge supplies of raw material, and develop arable land on which to plant and repatriate food to sustain a burgeoning population at home. This underscores Africa's importance.

China dreams of a continent on which Chinese goods, services and brands would be sold to every man, woman and child on the continent which is slated to become the largest reserve of consumers on the globe for multinational exploitation. For this reason China is at a greater advantage to realize its vision. The PRC's grand strategy evolves around this vision. It is noteworthy that although raw materials are widely regarded as the mainstay of Chinese economic interests, extractive enterprises serve merely as a means to an end. China's major springboard rests on business investments that have the potential to transform its homegrown corporations into highly competitive global players, rivaling their Western counterparts. [32]

With this long-term goal, Chinese companies have been consolidating and diversifying their portfolios in order to prepare themselves to penetrate bigger and more formidable international markets in the future, while accumulating wealth and business acumen along the way. This strategy is highly visible in the telecommunications and infrastructure sectors, where firms such as Tecno, which produces cellular phones, and ZTE which is engaged in the development of telephone infrastructure, have made inroads in preparation for a larger –scale worldwide take-off. Familiarizing consumers with Chinese products and building brand equity in the markets of the West are integral to the strategy. [33]

China is already host country to the worlds' largest body of Internet users with more than 500,000,000 and is home to the world's largest high-tech industry. Alibaba Group Holding Ltd took Wall Street by storm in 2014 with $25 billion in public shares. The firm controls 80% of China's e-commerce and globally 10% of its shares are outside China; it is set on investing heavily in India and the U.S. Huawei is a telecommunications giant in 140 countries, specializing in high-end smart phones at highly competitive prices and is widely regarded as the "Apple of the East," after overtaking Erikson three years previously. Likewise, Lenovo is another record breaker. After releasing its first computer in 1988, the company went on to become the largest PC vendor in the world by the end of the nineties and in 2004 and bought over IBM's PC division. By 2013, Lenovo was not only the world's largest PC manufacturer, selling one in every five PC brands, but by the first quarter of 2014 was gunning for the $3 billion acquisition of Motorolla to further strengthen its position in developed markets.

A third pillar of the Sino strategy is capitalizing on the opportunity presented by Africa's favorable demographic dividend which places most of the increasingly urban and highly globalized population in the most productive, youthful and consuming phase of their lives. China wants to take advantage of this game-changing transition so that it will be at greater advantage in realizing its vision. Africa's population is set to double by 2050 and most of this population will be comprised of productive, youthful persons at a heavily consuming phase of their lives - China's vision is to be able to sell Chinese goods, services and brands to every man, woman and child on the continent which is slated to become the world's largest reserve of consumers for multinational exploitation.

To boot, African investment in the field of education is among the highest in the world in terms of percentage of GDP and could barely keep apace with the demand for learning. As a fillip to this, African investment in education is among the highest in the world in terms of percentage of GDP and can barely keep apace with the demand for learning. [34] This thirst for education is corroborated by U.N. data, which shows that enrollment in secondary schools jumped to 48 percent in sub-Saharan Africa between 2000 and 2008, and higher education rates grew by 80 percent. The trend signals the emergence across the board of a vibrant, high-consuming middle class with further opportunities ahead to develop human capital. With this demographic end run Africa offers a handsome alternative to the debt-saturated markets of the West.

A fourth point of note relates to the inroads that have already been made in the sphere of infrastructural development and extractive industries both of which provide the backbone for access to raw materials that support industry on the continent and at home in China.

A fifth and equally important feature is China's ideological stance. Unlike the American policy towards to peacekeeping, China has maintained a non-doctrinaire stance in seeking entry into African markets, and until recently, has upheld a "no boots on the ground" policy, insofar as it has opted out of direct military engagements on the continent. Since it assumed a U.N. Security Council seat in 1971 at a point in time when it rejected the entire concept of peacekeeping,

China's approach to peacekeeping has evolved. China's motivations towards peacekeeping have led it to adopt a case-by-case approach that balances its motivations against its adherence to non-intervention.[35] This is shaped by three factors: first, participation in peacekeeping reflects an overall effort on China's part to become responsive to international expectations and position itself as a responsible power; second, participation is a means of putting into action former President Jintao's undertaking that the PRC would perform new historic missions in the twenty-first century; and finally, the gesture carries important practical and military application since the continued deployment and redeployment of Chinese military units throughout Africa means that over time they will accrue operational knowledge and a better understanding of the political and societal dynamics and complexities on the ground as they interact with other militaries. From the perspective of Chinese leaders themselves, participation in peacekeeping missions serves to dampen regional concerns over Beijing's pursuit of a hegemonic path.[36] This book adds that Chinese peacekeeping missions serve to solidify and consolidate the nation's Great Power status and balance it against Western influence in the world's key hot spots.

The recent change by deploying Chinese troops to the continent is impelled by the need to protect the PRC economic interests and ostensibly that of respective host governments. Lastly it may be argued that the tangible support meted out by the Chinese in "rehabilitating" Africa's infrastructure and its contributions to U.N. Peacekeeping initiatives ensures the type of groundwork that is critically needed now more than ever to pave the way for regional stability and development. This should augur well even among its competitors. Of all the countries of the developing world, China is currently among the most forthcoming in terms of U.N. Peacekeeping contributions. As of December 2012, a total of 1,842 PLA officers and men were implementing peacekeeping tasks in nine U.N. mission areas, including the Democratic Republic of the Congo, Darfur, Sudan and Liberia[37] Matching this challenge, President Obama publicly committed on the final day of the U.S. - Africa Leaders' Conference to deepening security cooperation by supporting peacekeeping missions of the U.N. and African Union by co-opting Ethiopia, Ghana, Rwanda, Senegal Tanzania, Ethiopia and Uganda – countries, which in his estimation, have a demonstrated track record of peace keeping.[38]

VI

Africa's Dilemma - Water Scarcity and Land Title

Challenges to nationhood posed by large-scale systemic corruption, the deplorable lack of effective governance, lack of transparency and inclusive civil society participation are all ingredients exploited by foreigners time and time again who are narrowly committed to their own sustenance. Historians and anthropologists have noted African societies' absence of private land ownership, a peculiar cultural character that makes it easy prey to outsiders attuned to private, revenue-producing property. It is within this milieu that highly contested resource wars among western powers, oil-rich Gulf States and more recently BRICS member countries, take place. Land has now emerged as a strategic commodity market for governments and this has presented new challenges.

Further to this, a special issue of "Water Alternatives" entitled "Water Grabbing: Focus on the Re (appropriation) of Finite Water Resources" stated that water is now one of the prime drivers of the global rush to acquire land. A distinctive aspect of the land grabbing frenzy is that (Barras et al, 2012) it is inextricably interwoven in the dynamics of reactionary capital accumulation strategies in the face of multiple crises.[39] These were identified as:

- Food, energy/fuel, climate change, and the financial crisis (where financial capital started to look for new and safer investment opportunities Mc Michael, 2012)
- Emerging needs for resources by newer hubs of global capital, especially the BRICS and powerful middle income economies
- Demands for flex crops with multiple uses that can easily and flexibly interchange e.g. soya(food, fuel, industrial; corn (food furl, ethanol); and sugar cane (biodiesel, food)

The United States, Canada, Australia and Argentina constitute the primary lead grain exporting countries that are actively seeking to access suitable land for use in growing food and generating bio-fuel. Simultaneously, China is in dire need of extensive tracts of arable land for producing critically needed food to sustain its booming population. For this reason, the PRC has incorporated overseas land acquisitions into its foreign policy.

This section examines the nature of competing interests over land and water on the continent and the wider issue of social and environmental impact, which, as disturbing as it may seem, appears to be of lesser concern to host governments. What emerges is a picture in which China finds itself in direct competition with the

435

U.S. Western allies such as Canada, Europe and the oil-rich Gulf States as well as with populous capital strong Asian neighbors such as Japan, South Korea and India all of which are avowed friends of the West.

Millions of hectares of land around Africa have been acquired by foreign interests in the last decade taking advantage of windfall gains. A key consideration in all of this is the fact that 60% of the world's remaining arable land is in Africa and that when land is acquired and earmarked for development, this invariably holds far-reaching implications for the region's water supply, the water rights of occupants, title, rights of occupancy, use and access as well as environmental sustainability.

The GLP International Project Office of the University of Copenhagen[40] undertook a study of the pace of land acquisition on the continent and found that the extent of land deals in Africa was extremely substantial and near crisis point. Of the top 13 recipient countries that were assessed on the basis of estimates of the magnitude of all land deals as a percentage of the total land area and the agricultural area plus the forest-covered area, the following patters were visible:

- Land deals were generally very large in scope and took up fairly high percentages of existing land resources in host countries

- For 10-13 of the recipient countries, the land deals amounted to 5% of the agricultural land and for 5 countries over 8%. In Mozambique the potential land deal represents 13.1% of the total land area and over 21% of agricultural lands. A very large land deal with Agriculture SA plays a major role there.

- Land deals in Uganda also represented a significant part of the country's agricultural area

- For the three countries with the largest land deals, Ethiopia was proportionately the largest in terms of agricultural area and forest

- The figures in the DRC were particularly interesting because they show up potential environmental issues – if the deals are to be signed on existing farmland, they will cover up to 48.8% of the acreage, but if the forested acreage is considered the figure will fall to 7.1%

- Investors, principally in the Sudan, are primarily from the Gulf States of Saudi Arabia, Qatar, Oman, Bahrain, Kuwait and Jordan [41]

With substantial tracts of Africa's agricultural and forested land increasingly falling under the control of private foreign interests, the U.S. and China will inevitably find themselves in direct competition with each other as well as with external contenders for scarce resources.

Land Use, Agriculture and the Impact on Food Prices

The 2007-2008 spikes in global food prices triggered two reactions - the spontaneous rush for land and the panic within the developed world to secure future supplies. Not surprisingly, although much of the global capital that is appropriated to land deals is being injected into large-scale agriculture employing a range of instruments including investment subsidies and guarantees and the establishment of sovereign funds, a mere handful of investors with different and self-serving agendas and motivations, is actually spearheading the rush. This is clearly not happening in isolation, but is part of a process of expansion and restructuring of agri-business involving corporate integration, the emergence of new actors, rising South-South capital flows, the deepening financialization of agriculture, and in the displacement and destruction of peasantries and rural peoples as private interests assume control over natural resources, and in instances destabilize ecological balances.

The food crisis concomitant with the 2012 Arab Spring catapulted the food security concerns among wealthy the Gulf States. Having lost confidence in normal food supply chains, governments lost no time in introducing land acquisition as an institutionalized strategy. Devlin Kuyek, a researcher at GRAIN noted, "Between 2008-2009, rises in food prices caused protest movements in Egypt and Morocco. This has become an important concern for countries in the Arab region which want to meet the growing demands of their populations." [42] Under the newly introduced state-promoted policy, the private sector and international bodies are being co-opted into long-term food security schemes and investment sometimes takes the form of long-term leases, as opposed to outright purchases of land with many leases running for periods ranging between 25 to 99 years. [43] In the Gulf States alone there were no less than 100 "food security deals" shadowing the 2008-2009 financial crisis. See Table 17.2.

Table 17.2.
Gulf States Alone – 100 Food Deals

Target Countries	No. Land Grabs	% Population Officially Hungry
Sudan	20	26%
Pakistan	15	24%
Philippines	9	18%
Egypt	8	4%
Turkey	6	<5%
Ethiopia	5	46%
Kazakstan	5	<5%
Australia	5	<5%
Ukraine	4	<5%
Vietnam	4	14%
Thailand	4	7%
Cambodia	3	33%
Indonesia	3	6%
Burma	2	5%
India	2	20%
Morocco	2	5%
Kenya	1	31%
Tanzania	1	44%
Senegal	1	20%
Laos	1	19%
Mali	1	29%
Total	102	18%
Average		

SOURCE: Land Grabs and the Global Food Crisis GRAIN 11/2011

Having scrutinized Word Bank figures, the Inter-Press News Service Agency noted that in 2011 land deals amounted to roughly 80 million hectares and the main countries targeted for land acquisition by area were Brazil (11 percent); Sudan (ten percent); Madagascar, the Philippines and Ethiopia (eight percent); Mozambique (seven percent); and Indonesia (six percent). Australia, New Zealand, Poland, Russia, Ukraine and Romania had also fallen prey, albeit to a far lesser extent to unscrupulous bids.[43]

In striking contrast Africa has borne the brunt of the gulled deals, mirrored in the under-listed examples:

- Ethiopia has made deals with investors from Saudi Arabia, as well as India and China, giving foreigners control over half the arable land in the Gambela region.
- Powerful Saudi businessmen are pursuing deals in Senegal, Mali and other countries that are giving them control over several hundred thousand hectares of their country's most productive farmland
- A Saudi Arabian company, al-Amoudi has acquired 10,000 hectares in South-West Ethiopia to produce rice. Saudi Arabia, which until recently was the world's sixth largest wheat produce, has decided to phase out wheat production by 2016 because of the significant depletion of its fresh water supplies (Schuffer, 201 1b)
- Some governments of the member states of the Gulf Cooperation Council – Bahrain, Kuwait, Oman, Qatar, Saudi Arabia and the United Arab Emirates have adopted policies to encourage their citizens to invest in food production overseas as part of their long-term food security strategies
- In Liberia alone as much as 67% of local farmland is in the hand of foreigners; in Sierra Leone 15%; in Ethiopia 10%; in Guinea 11% .[44]

Three categories of Investors

Broadly speaking there are three distinct groups of land investors jostling for the choicest deals – the first: populous, capital-strong Arab and Asian powers (including India, Japan and South Korea) that are investing in agricultural land in Africa to secure their domestic supplies of food and energy (Smaller and Mann, 2009). These countries are motivated by the dire need to attain food self-sufficiency in the face of high population growth rates and domestic pressures on their land and water resources at home. Next in the line-up are the Gulf States, many, affirmed allies of the U.S., seeking to secure cultivable land to sustain their populations and growing masses of migrant workers. The third cohort is also closely affiliated with Western interests and comprises large multinational private companies, primarily from the United States, Europe, Israel and Australia (Daniel and Mittal, 2009; Gorgen et al, 2009; Smaller and Mann, 2009). These business concerns are bent on the production of food and bio-fuels. The United States and other grain exporting states such as Canada, Australia and Argentina are rooting around for swaths of cropland and greater volumes of irrigation water, notwithstanding the fact that bio-fuel technologies are becoming more efficient, mindful of official long-term projections that in light of the highly competitive fuel-farming trade and associated export controls on grain, there are likely to be sharp fluctuations in grain prices at levels well above today's highs in approaching years. Additionally, there is a line-up of investment companies and development banks are queuing for land that could serve as a negotiable instrument as for example investment and diversification. Included in this line-up are better-known names such as Goldman Sachs, the Deutsche Bank and competitive spoken for Arab players such as Citadel Capital, an Egyptian private equity fund.

Implications of Water Scarcity for Africa, U.S. and China

Water is one of the primary reasons in the global rush for land and in most countries land deals are necessarily connected to access to water supplies. Nowhere in the world is water stress as profound as in sub-Saharan Africa. In all 66% of Africa is arid or semi-arid with more than 300 million in sub-Saharan Africa living on less than 1,000 cubic meters of water resources daily. In contrast, North America and Europe are endowed with ample renewable water resources. Demographic pressures, increased urbanization, overconsumption and climate change compound the situation on the African continent. A global survey titled "World Water Resources – A New Appraisal and Assessment for the Twenty-First Century," commissioned by the United Nations Educational, Scientific and Cultural Organization, to assess the extent of available resources, availability, protection and management of the world supply by region, revealed that between 1970-1994 the water availability for the world's population from 12.9 down to 7.6 thousand cubic meters per year per person. The greatest reduction was observed to have occurred in Africa (by 2.8 times), in Asia (by two times), and in South America (by 1.7 times). In contrast water supplies for Europe's population declined by 16% for the same period.[45] The precariousness of the demand-supply imbalance is further amplified when account is taken of the fact that the U.N. Food and Agricultural Organization and U.N. Water observed that within the last century global water use has been growing at more than twice the rate of population increases.

Asian Domestic Water Scarcity

Studies have shown that three specific trends have raised the stakes among serious contenders for primacy in Africa. The first is that large swathes of China, India and Pakistan are buckling under physical and economic water scarcity while North

America and Europe are amply supported with renewable water resources. Secondly, all Arab countries are considered water scarce with consumption of water significantly exceeding total resource supplies. Finally, that most of the global retrievable water is currently being utilized in large-scale farming. China's situation at home is particularly critical with the exploitation of groundwater and resources and the depletion of natural flows in major places such as the Yellow River where water crowding and severe shortages are now prevalent. Most of China is unproductive desert and inaccessible mountains and most of the population lives in the eastern provinces. The most water-stressed parts of the country are the Hai-Luan basin hosting the cities of Beijing and Tientsin and the Huai basin source of the Yellow River. The Yellow River is currently in a state of "chronic scarcity interval" with 1400 p/flow and the use-to-availability ratio in these rivers is already dangerously high, between 50-98.[46] With most of the country's grain production coming from irrigated agriculture, water plays a major role for food security and poverty alleviation.

Based on these pressing considerations China will remain a powerful and influential player on the African continent; and reciprocally African countries will continue to be put under increased pressure due to a combination of factors, primarily dubious land acquisition policies, untenable demands on water resources by extractive industries owned and operated by Chinese corporations, industrial-scale agriculture operated by multinational companies and the continent's own growing population.

The looming worldwide crisis is confirmed in Global Trends 2025, which cautions:

> *"Lack of access to stable supplies of water is reaching unprecedented proportions in many areas of the world and is likely to grow worse owing the rapid urbanization and population growth. Demand for water for agricultural purposes and hydro-electrical power generation will also expand – use of water for irrigation is far greater than for personal consumption. In developing countries agriculture consumes more than 70% of the world's water..."[47]*

A Social Dilemma

Ruthless land grabbers have consistently exploited legal lacunas surrounding land rights and access to water supplies. This is due primarily to the fact that in many parts of rural Africa indigenous populations still occupy large belts of land under customary law, whereby land is held in trust by the state or a tribal leader, on behalf of occupants. This informal system of land holding is well suited to traditional systems of agriculture that are characterized by shifting cultivation. However, with the formation of the modern nation state, several statutory laws based on civil and common law are superseding local custom. And this also explains why at political level proponents of land deals are able to successfully deploy powerful and persuasive narratives that suggest that underutilized land and water resources need to be invested by governments as a means of unlocking their full potential. This popularized line of argument is invoked to justify the displacement small-holder populations, whose contribution to community level food production and maintaining the ecological balance often goes unacknowledged.[48]

Most of the lands currently being earmarked for deals are covered by tropical rain forest, located in protected natural areas, or are already being used for shifting cultivation or the grazing of animals (Ramkutty et al.). An added inducement to land deals is attributed to the fact that the commercial value of the land is relatively low and this raises the expectation of large returns in the future when amidst the predicted struggle for scarce resources land value would skyrocket (Cotula et al.). Conversely the host countries are invariably extremely poor and intent on luring investors. Albeit shortsightedly, many African governments see land deals as an opportunity to get funds for the development of agriculture or infrastructure, unmindful of the more long-term deleterious social consequences.

A second major issue surrounds the local impact of a projected global water scarcity crisis. A 2013 study entitled "The Looming Threat of Water Scarcity," established that almost one-fifth of the world (or 1.2 billion people) live in areas of water scarcity, another 1.6 billion face economic water shortages and by 2025, 1.8 billion people will be living in countries with absolute water scarcity of two types, either physical or economic. Whereas, physical water scarcity occurs when there is not enough water to meet demand and is a by-product of degradation, declining ground water, and unequal water distribution, economic scarcity results from the lack of investment and proper management to meet the demands of persons who do not have the financial means to use existing supplies.[49] Economic scarcity of water results from poor infrastructure - a phenomenon afflicting large swathes of Africa and providing a trigger for governments to enter permissive land deals, oft-times unscrupulous investment in extractive industries intemperately buttressed by infrastructural projects that ensure the requisite supplies of water, electricity and roadway access, as a composite business deal. The overt profligacy is further compounded by the fact that across the continent water used in agriculture tends to be inefficiently appropriated and this leads to over-exploitation of ground water and continuous depletions in natural flows - a phenomenon replicated in the Ganges River in India and the Yellow River in China.

The jostle for access to water is by no means confined to the U.S. and China. Most Arab countries are considered water scarce along with large sweeps of India and Pakistan each beset by physical and economic scarcity, hence the Gulf State governments have been proactively engaging with African leaders. Canada and the U.S. however are in a less precarious position, being endowed with an estimated 85,310 and 9,888 cubic meters of resources per person, respectively compared to Africa, which has less than 1,000 cubic meters per person. This comes as no surprise since 66 percent of Africa is arid and semi-arid. [50]

A third factor appears to be working against the U.S. and its Western allies – intercontinental programmatic responses to issues surrounding food security, poverty reduction and land use, and the future prospects of the New Alliance Security Initiative inaugurated at the G8 Summit in the U.S. in 2012. The goal of the latter program is to lift African people out of poverty by "unleashing the power of the private sector" and the plan is especially designed to pair markets and producers with private investors – an arrangement that has triggered growing criticism among many vocal civil society organizations and international advocacy groups that have pointed out the adverse impact of large-scale agri-business on vulnerable local populations. Four concerns are now at the center of intense debate across continents.

The first is recognition that land is the most important factor of production in agribusiness projects; that these projects disproportionately target areas where land is abundant; and that large-scale grabbing challenges access to both land and water particularly among the low-income rural poor. The second is that agriculture is the dominant source of livelihood in Africa with about 70% of people employed directly in the sector, which accounts for 30% of the region's GDP. The dismantling of small-scale agriculture is particularly detrimental to local communities where women as small-holder farmers are the primary producers who have sustained localized -economies for many generations. [51] The third point is a corollary to the second - the substantial depletion of available arable land on the continent, a feature corroborated by the World Bank. Areas of arable land in Africa dropped from 450 million hectares in 1990 to 405 in 2011. While on the one hand the agricultural land is more or less even-handedly distributed across regions (26% Eastern; 24% western; 21% Northern; 15% southern; 14% central), arable land (land suitable for cultivation) on the other hand constitutes a mere 20% of this area. However there is a countervailing narrative that is being strongly promoted by international corporate interests - that the promotion of small-scale agriculture in Africa is receiving the active attention of private interests and international bodies as a means of improving self-sufficiency and the fight against rural poverty and hunger. The Rockefeller Foundation, the World Bank, the New Partnership for Africa's Development and individuals like Bill Gates and Jeffrey

Sachs have been proactively campaigning in favor of the role of small-scale agriculture, while employing the concept of a "New Green Revolution" that highlights the role of new technologies in maximizing the productive capacity of African agriculture.[52]

The fourth and equally salient point pertains to the ecological sustainability of land and water resources allocated to foreign investors The introduction of intensive agricultural production for export and commercial purposes can seriously threaten biodiversity, carbon stocks and land and water resources. The conversion of forests and rangelands to monocropping under large-scale acquisition projects will, in the longer term, reduce diversity in flora and fauna, agro diversity, as well as above ground and sub-surface carbon stocks. As far back as 1990, soil degradation was estimated to have affected 500 million ha or 17% of Africa's land. Susceptible dry lands are the worst affected - covering 43% of Africa, with the worst affected areas impacting on 485 million people; while 65% of agricultural land, 31% of permanent pasture, and 19% of forest and woodland were estimated to be affected by some form of degradation. (Jama and Pizzaro, 2008).

So that while on the one hand the Chinese are being upbraided for their profligacy in resource-for-infrastructure swaps with high-ranking African bureaucrats within the extractive sectors and for the tens of thousands of migratory workers who have made the continent their home after their contracts have ended[53]at the other end of the spectrum Western players are to be held no less accountable. Success has to be construed in the wider context of human cost and the success of the New Alliance and similarly disposed programs that rely on land acquisition and the large scale commercialization of the agricultural sector is contingent to the following: effective collaboration between investors, host governments and key stakeholders; ensuring that a judicious balance is maintained between the interests of agro-industry entrepreneurs who are undoubtedly driven by the need to maximize profits; adopting people-oriented approaches aimed at increasing productivity; alleviating poverty by creating jobs; recognizing the rights of each individual, community and nation to maintain and develop its own capacity to produce basic foods; while respecting cultural norms and traditions, productive diversity and the harmony of the environment (Patel, 2003).

VII

Is a Second Cold War Looming?

What members of the Western coalition all share as they jockey for space in Africa, is bankruptcy. With this diversity of players pursuing an array of agendas amidst internecine conflict and externally instigated interventions, the logical question arises: is a second Cold War looming? And more importantly to what extent is Africa's "subordination" as presaged in Brzezinski's <u>Grand Chessboard,</u> affording the tactical leverage that is needed to accommodate America's widening orbit on the continent? This is best appreciated within the framework of alliance formation that took root during World War II, present day emerging multipolarity and alliances of convenience, in an obvious all-out lunge for resources.

The China-Russia Unwritten Compact

The first Cold War was an ideological crusade fought out between America as the primary beneficiary of the collapse of Japanese and western colonial powers. During that era, American culture replaced European models in Canada, Australia and Latin America and we observed the U.S. shifting from the status of an Atlantic state with a continental hinterland to a de facto continental power, commandeering two oceans in a mode of empire that passed from Britain. Furthermore, the relative strength of the West was enervated by schisms within the Communist bloc between China and the Soviet Union and this afforded the U.S much sought after geopolitical advantage.

First, one may question of what relevance is increasing the Sino-Russian connection in a post-Cold War order? This issue was catapulted as a front burner concern in the U.N. Security Council voting deadlock over NATO's planned invasion of Syria in 2013, and subsequently, in the face of the impasse[8] surrounding American analyst Ed Snowden. Either way, Russia and China jointly succeeded in trumping American, and indeed Western, resolve. The Russia-China affinity is discernibly no more than a marriage of convenience since both countries are competing over political supremacy and economic advantage in Central Asia, so that the U.S thus becomes the common obstacle. Furthermore, although the prospects of direct military confrontation between the U.S. and Russia may have declined dramatically with Cold War discontinuance, the risk of trade wars is steadily materializing, and beyond this Russia remains the United States' only peer in terms of nuclear weapons capabilities. Moscow's inventory is stocked with a triad of land-based intercontinental ballistic missiles, ballistic missile submarines, and long-range cruise missiles delivered by strategic bombers in addition to a large non-strategic nuclear force. Most notable, the National Defense Panel co-chaired by Dr. William Perry and General John Abizad in its Report to the U.S. Congress entitled "Ensuring a Strong U.S. Defense for the Future" noted inter alia that "China, Russia, North Korea and Iran each pose different but real challenges to regional stability that require DOD to plan for plausible contingencies."[54]

Coalition Support is Vital

A second significant factor that gives the U.S a decisive strategic edge is the fact that in the years following World War II America was assured of coalition support from Western allies, that resulted in remarkable success in its policy of containment, economic warfare, intervention in secondary theaters in Europe, Africa and Latin America, and the careful avoidance of full-scale main-force conflict through the effective use of proxies. Through its strategically adopted alliances, the U.S. was able to prevail in struggles in the Congo and Angola during the seventies; in South Asia where it relied on Iran to support the Kurds against Iraq; and in Honduras and Brazil where it backed military coups in the eighties and nineties against leftist regimes. America was then very much cognizant of the revolutionary winds of change and its transmogrification on the African continent. By the mid-1960s it became clear to Moscow and Washington that the focus of the Cold War competition in Africa was shifting from north to central and southern Africa, due to the Marxist orientation of many of the region's liberation movements.

It is therefore urgent now more than ever that America capitalizes on its worldwide footprints while remaining closely affiliated with former colonial powers - Britain, France, Spain, Portugal, Holland and Germany with which it shares a common identity in the form of Germanic stock. Added to this, its bond with the Breton Woods institutions - international central banks and the central world monetary system - provides worldwide economic and political clout. In contradistinction, besides being fundamentally antipathetic to the existing global monetary regime and its fundamental tenets, China lacks similar collective backing.

A third salient point is the reality of a vibrant South-South coalition. Sino-U.S. relations and competition for the control of resources lies at the heart of twenty-first century international relations and the U.S is boring its way through new coalitions to neutralize regional power pivots such as China and Russia. Thus, in the context of BRICS membership, South Africa serves as the gateway to the African continent and has been co-opted as a key player in Washington's trans-continental agenda; while Russia and China are being ostracized and kept at bay as a result of ongoing tensions in Kiev amidst revived pro-Russian sentiments. More dramatically, Russia's expulsion from the G8 and the imposition of sanctions following the BRICS summit in Brazil in 2014 the catastrophic downing of the aircraft and Russia's continuing aggression in its own neighborhood have merely stoked already strained relations in what can only be regarded as a U.S-China-Russia mare's nest. In sum, NATO members are being co-opted to execute America's overseas policies and advance its interests insofar as these relate to suppressing Arab nationalism to the extent that it forestalls the rise of the Shiite minority; cordoning off Israel's adversaries; containing Russia; enervating China's foothold in Africa; and restraining China and Russia's joint ambitions within the BRICS.

Fourth and by no means least is NATO's role vis-à-vis Africa as a strategic front. Essentially a military coalition, NATO was originally founded following the Second World War since Europe was devastated and needed to be rebuilt from bottom up. Individual European countries were losing their grip on overseas dependencies strewn across both hemispheres upon which they derived raw materials for industrialism. Added to this was the rise of independence movements, pre-staged by the Pan-African conferences held in London and the concomitant challenge of African nationalism. European powers were desirous of regaining their pre-eminence. Finally, with the international aspirations of the Soviets there was a dire need to put the spread of Communism permanently in check. A mechanism therefore had to be devised to maintain Western dominance and NATO provided that vehicle. With the collapse of the Soviets in the nineties, its core mission was partially trounced... for the time being at least. However, the urgency of access to secure energy supplies and other vital resources in Africa and Middle and Far East is reigniting Cold War tactics, and stoking the re-emergence of long-standing Anglo-European alliances. To illustrate the point, NATO Response Force's (NRF) Steadfast Jazz, reputedly the largest exercise within the last seven years combines land, air, naval and special forces. Sweden, building upon participation in the Euro-Atlantic Partnership Council and the Partnership for Peace and previous involvement in E.U.-led crisis management operations, has offered substantial forces in NRF's annual rotations. The Ukraine and Finland, who have committed forces in 2014 and Georgia, which will contribute to formations in 2015, will complement these.

NATO Alliance Strategically Critical to Securing Regions

For NATO, this reassertion entails shoring in all of Europe and its eastern flanks – to this end, Finland and Sweden which remained neutral during the Cold War, are being induced strategically while interoperability is being bolstered among Asian "peace-keeping nations" some of which were part of the former Soviet bloc. A second tactic in NATO's assertion is exploiting territorial, religious and ethnic disputes among countries antithetical to U.S. interests by befriending their neighbors and/or facilitating military support. A third stratagem entails staking claims to oil sites through investment accords and diplomatic negotiation. On these grounds, Africa's become a prime target.

Against this setting, it may be argued that a more evolved and sophisticated Cold War is in fact evolving in respect of which Africa is integral. The engagement is taking the form of a trans-continental interplay that is metastasizing into regions as far off as Central and South Asia, and making its way downward to the South China Sea. With this in view the Benghazi face-off and the role played by U.S. deployments in the city is instructive. Unlike World War II, which was rooted in ideological hostilities, the second Cold War has taken the form of a full-scale military campaign that is non-conventional and being waged on multiple fronts with Africa center-stage. Labeled in Oxford Research Group's New Remote Control Report as "the pivot to Africa," the campaign has morphed into a sweeping Middle East – Central Asian conflict zone. Africa is at the heart of this inexorable contest. Geography in international affairs is euphemistically regarded as destiny. If anything, this underscores the continent's distinct stature key to which is its geographical location astride the world's major oceans, seas, and strategic sea lanes and its unchallenged ranking as absolute trustee of the planet's vital minerals, oil, water and arable land.

Conclusion

Disparate Approaches, Converging Interests on the Great Continent

This chapter makes one point clear. What is at stake here is an intense and sustained lunge for primacy on the world's most highly valued swathes of territory. The engagement is mutating as a full-scale, non-conventional military campaign waged on multiple fronts and metamorphosing with America's corralling of its most strategically important partners. The chapter has also demonstrated how the 2011 Libyan "humanitarian intervention" served as a major catalyst in the aggressions; that conflict is being choreographed along strategically dispersed basing footprints aided by friendly forces; that the sea and air are commandeering sites for force projection and zones for confrontation; and that the arrant quest for ownership and control of territory among contenders and their backers in business syndicates...with often competing goals is even finding expression in proxy wars. All of this is buttressed by coalition support from NATO, with the French and British playing the most influential roles, and the Saudis on close heel. At the heart of this inexorable contest is poised the central continent.

Notwithstanding the disparate approaches in the vision and strategies employed by China and the U.S, there is a convergence of interests with the underlying driving force being the internal logic of capitalism - to expand outward in a quest to maximize profit margins. Either way, their respective strategies are clearly reflective of self-serving political and economic objectives.

Against this setting, there remain more ominous challenges ahead. Consider this. Given the interdependent nature of the global "ecosystem" to which President Obama alluded, what transpires in Africa would have implications for the rest of the world, even the planet's very survival. This central concern supersedes all ongoing contestations. Accordingly, it is crucial that dialogue at every level be grounded in transparency and mutual respect, with even greater importance attached to the quality of life and life chances of the continent's people as its most treasured resource.

CHAPTER EIGHTEEN

LEADERSHIP, DIPLOMACY, AND THE EMERGING NEW ORDER

"If political, military and economic power could not be expressed in terms of precise measurement, the successful use of this power was dependent on skill – more specifically the interacting role of personalities, structures, and international circumstances."

Jeremy Black

he notion of superpower was the creation of 20th Century nuclear weapons technology despite the fact that the term, as originally conceived in 1944, did not envisage the nuclear threat that would quickly unfold in ensuing decades.[1] As the Cold War advanced however, what distinguished a nuclear superpower from a 19th century great power was the capability of ultimate destruction of its foes and the incorporation of the strategic doctrine of nuclear deterrence as part of its defensive regime.[2] Some have argued that in today's global arena with increasing interdependency and multipolarity among nations, the concept of superpower may well be an anachronism.

Robert Cox adopted an alternative outlook, opting instead to define and interpret the world order in terms of phases of evolving hegemony, distinguishable by four periods, 1884-1875, 1875-1945, 1945-1965 and 1965 to the present.[3] Against the backdrop of the final phase of metamorphosis, he identified three possibilities for structural transformation in a "U.S - based world order," namely:

- A reconstruction of hegemony with a broadening of political management along the lines envisaged by the Trilateral Commission
- Increased fragmentation of the world economy around "big-power centered" economic spheres
- The possible assertion of a Third World-based counter hegemony, with a concerted demand for the New International Economic Order as a forerunner

This enquiry has demonstrated that Cox's prognosis has run full course and that the concept of omnipresence represents the ushering in of a new index on the global calculus of state capacity that cannot be readily outrivaled. Moreover, the concept of great power has now assumed a more evolved and complex index of criteria. Certainly, in terms of the social and economic cost, the affordability of greatness now lies within the grasp of few.

Hedley Bull's treatise, The Anarchical Society,[4] conceives of a great power as one that belongs to a society of states that maintains the balance of power to prevent the emergence of a global dictatorship through imperial conquest. Within this system, great powers engage in preserving the mechanisms of international law and diplomacy and jointly managing the system through restraints, and war as necessary, as a means of preserving the system and not destroying it. In the present technetronic era, the realms of inner and outer space present frontiers that any nation vying for great or superpower status must be prepared to set foot in and prevail. In this regard, omnipresence becomes an imperative for superpower status.

In contrast, Kennedy's[5] epic argument as to the constituents of great power status which has endured, proposes a correlation between economic capability, productivity and the given international balance, the capacity to generate revenues which are key ingredients to military power. However, Kennedy took account of other factors such as national morale, geography, military organization and individual action. This enquiry contends that great power also encompasses the adequacy of a nation's reserve of diplomatic, economic and military resources which are critical for the preservation of the very international order that such power presumes itself to be part of, as a preeminent actor. The concept of great power is also founded upon the capacity of a nation to engage productively in mega-programs of transnational or global dimension and significance, while effectively tackling new and emerging transnational threats. In this respect, the U.S. and China occupy a global space that is sui generis. Their test now is to prevail on all fronts and in all realms.

The ability to supersede competing cultures and ideologies were additional features of great power status that Black[6] has registered, in addition to the imperial ethos, based on the notion that *power in its material conception is designed to seize resources*. Thus, the acquisition of land and labor as key inputs of production become especially important in this aspect of rivalry. These non-systemic types of criteria on the global calculus assume greater significance when new and emerging patterns of migration and recent ecological considerations are taken into account.

China of itself presents the classic example of a paradigm power in the sense that it serves both as a source of example for contemporaries and a point of study for scholars. More explicitly, China has illustrated that it is possible for a great power to rise, fall and rise again. This is very unique and must not be overlooked.

It must be recalled that commencing from 1680 to the close of the 18th century, China presented the perfect anomaly of the Western-centric bias whereby non-Western states were rarely accorded great power status amidst the interplay within the global power balance. Having been conquered by the Manchus, China not only made major territorial gains at the expense of non-Western states, especially Tibet and Xinjiang-based Zunghar Confederation, but succeeded in driving the Dutch out of Taiwan and the Russians from the Amur Valley.[7] Another demonstration of Chinese formidability as a power with an economically defined global ambit was the voluminous consignments of silver brought by Western traders to Canton to purchase Chinese goods. Unrivalled in porcelain ceramics and with few rivals in silk, China once also enjoyed world economic preeminence in production as well as export. This feat afforded China a pivotal space in a Sino-centric international order that not only extended far beyond its Asian tributary network but was decidedly ahead of rivals in Europe and the Americas.[8]

China has restored its global legitimacy among sovereign nations. This has been achieved firstly through its expansion of diplomatic representation within the developed and developing world and accruing the prestige and authority that comes with Permanent Membership of the U.N. Security Council, a privilege not beholden to other aspirants to primacy, such as India and Japan. Secondly, mindful of this unique status the PRC projects a "status quo oriented" approach to business in the sense that when adopting positions, it seeks out mutually supportive strategic relationships and avoids placing itself in a setting of isolation. Thirdly, and from a military standpoint, the PRC's defense posture is one of deterrence – China's nuclear warheads are designed for ostensibly deterring missions consistent with its international standing, while its conventional forces can be effectively deployed in defensive mode in the event of hostilities.

A fourth and very significant aspect of China's acclaim is that the PRC is capitalizing on the thin line of legitimacy being straddled by the U.S. in its unlimited course of aggression, despite a significant draw-downs of force presence in Afghanistan and Iraq.[9] Banking on the overseas expeditions of its primary rival and a chain of possible miscalculations on America's part in North Africa and the Asian ambit, China has stoked strategic gains by allying with key state actors (the most notable thus far being Russia), that have been tactfully circumventing what may be construed among international observers as a proclivity for lethal force as the emerging universal remedy for conflict resolution.[9]

Finally, having closely studied the machinations of Western powers in dealing with his country, former President Hu Jintao's reaction underscored the importance attached to Chinese cultural cohesion at home and its flexibility abroad, when he voiced the following concerns :

> "...We must clearly see that international hostile forces are intensifying the strategic plot of Westernizing and dividing China and ideological cultural fields are the focal areas of their long-term infiltration...we should deeply understand the seriousness of the ideological struggle, always sound the alarms and remain vigilant and take forceful measures to be on guard and respond...[10]"

Chinese cultural distinctiveness is therefore central to its public diplomacy agenda. To this end China has developed a keen eye for grand scale public events that project on a world stage positive images of itself and its achievements and takes full advantage of country-to-country exchanges through competitive sport to bolster patriotism at home and to woo admiration abroad.

As for America's part, the emergence of a military-industrial complex following World War II signaled a new dawn in the country's international power projection. As an emerging paradigm, the superstructure encompassed relationships brought about by the conjuncture of the armed forces, domestic weapons contractors, and elected representatives in Congress, while incorporating an array of other factors such as political patronage, decisions surrounding defense spending, and associated lobbying and oversight arrangements that are exclusive to the defense industry.

The magnitude and influence of this complex is beyond dispute. William Hartung, director of the Arms and Security Initiative at the New America Forum, noted in his book <u>Prophets of War: Lockheed Martin and the Making of the Military-Industrial Complex</u>,[11] that Lockheed Martin, Pentagon's largest contractor, is involved in a full hoard of weapons programs and was awarded roughly $29 billion in defense contracts comfortably outstripping its strongest competitors. Lockheed, in his view, has become in all practicality an indispensable component of America's defense hardware industry due to the Company's exceptional capacity to research, create, design, develop, produce and test state-of-the-art-technology. Its robust supply chain transformed the Company into a hefty contributor to the financing of think tanks, the shaping of public opinion on pertinent defense related themes such as regime change and the development of nuclear arsenal. In essence, Lockheed is archetypical of American corporatism, a synthesis of big business, congressional sway and the premier status accorded to the military as an appendage of executive power.

This emerging paradigm has made tremendous impact in American society from the outset. As a precursor of the future landscape it would form the linchpin of Dwight Eisenhower's Farewell Address to the Nation on January 17, 1961 when he cautioned:

> "...This conjunction of an immense military establishment and a large arms industry is new in the American experience. The total influence on the economic, political and even spiritual is felt in every city, every Statehouse, every office of the Federal government. We recognize the important need for this development. Yet, we must not fail to comprehend its grave implications... In the councils of government, we must guard against the acquisition of unwarranted... influence, whether sought or unsought by the military-industrial complex...[12.]

Was Eisenhower's intention to highlight what he discerned as the society's predisposition to neo-militarism that was becoming increasingly perceptible in light of the authoritative role increasingly assumed by the armed forces in domestic and foreign policy? Did he foresee an emerging political temperament with possible inherent dangers? He cautioned that despite pride of preeminence, power should be responsibly discharged and his concern brings into focus two important criteria and their interconnectedness - leadership style and state conduct.

Decades later Richard Kohn would remark that the American military has grown in influence to the point of being able to impose its own perspective on many policies and decisions and questions, "...do officials charged with developing and executing foreign policy in the U.S. and abroad see teamwork and deference to civilian authority from the regional commanders or do they sense an improper loss of power to the military?" The question certainly beckons a closer scrutiny of the nuances in leadership style and how this impacts on executive authority, defense policy, the exercise of diplomacy vis-à-vis the prevailing national culture, all of which ultimately play into America's projection of itself. Jeremy Black eclipses the issue in his summation that:

> "...America has a political culture that is hostile to compromise with foreign states...the notion of American exceptionalism does not encourage the exigencies of compromise nor the idea that the response of others can or should play a major role in ensuring legitimacy for American policies. Indeed, the history of American foreign policy is that of American leadership and thus, does not lead to an interpretation of alliances based on mutual needs.[13]

Public Diplomacy and Political Leadership

State relations are influenced and reinforced by the ideological orientations of their leaders, their mutual perceptions of each other, their character and motivations, the policies they adopt in response or reaction to each other's style of rule, and ultimately the effect of this combination of factors on the interests and security of the nations they lead. Relations between leaders are recognizable in the contrastive approaches of the U.S. and Chinese incumbencies, and attested to in various media such as speeches, public reports, parliamentary debates, social banter and the anecdotal accounts of personal aides and advisors.

A classic example of leadership style and posture and its impact on policy and politics is to be found in President Carter's 1980 declaration which iterated the American political culture and foreign policy in the sense of securing a region that was considered then and even today as one of strategic significance to the U.S. In what later became popularly known as "the Carter doctrine," the president's clarion call would echo resoundingly in subsequent military campaigns as the beacon of American idealism:

> *"...an attempt from any outside force to gain control of the Persian Gulf region would be regarded as an assault on the vital interests of the United States to be repelled by any means necessary"*

Presidential successors would thereafter invoke the dictum even to the point of applying its implication beyond its originally intended parameters with the objective of fulfilling their larger ambitions. We see the ethic, and indeed practice, continuously iterated in a succession of future engagements that were by no means exclusive to:

- The Afghanistan War I (1979-1989)
- The Beirut Bombing – President Reagan's intervention in Lebanon (1983)
- The War Against Khadaffi comprising a series of non-conclusive skirmishes against Libya (1981-1988)
- The Tanher War in the Strait of Hormuz (1984-1988)
- The Iraq War culminating in an armed confrontation with Saddam Hussein (1990-1991)
- The Somalia Intervention which culminated in the Mogadishu firefight (1990-1993)
- The Afghanistan War, launched in the wake of 9/11 (2001-2003)
- Iraq War II, the resumption of large scale hostilities against Saddam Hussein

- Iraq War III, held to pacify Iraq against insurgents and Islamic radicals raised up in Iraq War II (2004-2010)
- Afghanistan War III that was expanded, given the deepening US involvement in Afpaq, Pakistan (2009)
- The Libyan War, that took the form of "humanitarian intervention" to facilitate the toppling of the Gadaffi regime (2011)
- The Egypt War, that took the form of violent civil disturbances, supported by the U.S. and which preceded the resignation under duress of Muhammad Hosni Sayed Mubarak, leader and military commander (2011)
- Ongoing hostilities in Syria, foisted by opposition support from the Western Alliance, and intended to ultimately depose Bashar Hafez al-Assad, President of Syria (2011 to date)

Several decades previously, on the verge of the declaration of World War II, the response of leaders of the major powers to Roosevelt's overture for a global meeting of minds spotlighted the contradictions that often propel the conduct of the world's most consequential officials. When World War II was initially declared in 1938 Roosevelt, it is reported, had no definitive strategy for opposing Hitler, and suggested to Britain's Neville Chamberlain in January that a White House Conference of world leaders should be called for the purpose of defining and establishing rules of international behavior.[14] Perceiving the overture as nothing more than a disruption to his own private plans to drive a wedge between Hitler and Mussolini, he declined.[15] In April 1939 Roosevelt would send a dispatch to Hitler to which was appended a list of names of 31 countries which he exhorted the Germans not to attack.[16] Despite this last minute appeal, America's ultimate influence in the events preceding the war up until that point in time, was negligible.

On the occasion of the 2012 U.N. General Assembly in New York, which coincided with the build-up to U.S. presidential elections, President Obama appeared, in the estimation of many, to have squandered a golden opportunity to engage with very influential world leaders on pressing issues in which the U.S played a pivotal part. One point of view at that time was that such an auspicious event would have afforded the president a rare and momentous opening for crucial bi-lateral talks to:

- Engage in person-to-person dialogue with Benjamin Netanyahu, leader of the nation most affected by Iran's perceived atomic aspirations
- Convene with key leaders regarding the bloody impasse in Libya which resulted in the loss of more than 20,000 lives since its commencement in 2011

- Consult with China and Japan amidst heightened diplomatic tensions in the east and south China Sea, emanating from ongoing territorial disputations
- Confer with his Libyan counterpart, whose country was the venue of the untimely demise of U.S. Ambassador Stevens and at least three other members of his contingent

Another more recent exemplification of highly consequential decision-making implications was the cancellation of a meeting in Moscow scheduled to be held in September 2013 between the U.S. President with his Soviet counterpart, following Russia's decision to grant temporary asylum to former intelligence analyst, Ed Snowden. This resolve may well have derailed a long awaited U.S. - Russia détente. Officials in Washington and Moscow had hoped that policies surrounding arms control, missile defense, Syria, trade and human rights would have been hammered out between their respective leaders, and decisively registered President Obama's signature effort to transform U.S. - Russia relations.

These scripts typecast the divergence in perceptions between elected officials and wider publics as well as in relationships between leaders and accentuate the perception that public diplomacy would forever remain enmeshed not only in the business of public affairs, but more so, in the personal choices of those sworn to lead. As developments in the public arena bring to the fore the changing landscape of international actors and the variations in their motivations and impel the need for innovations in diplomatic systems that will ultimately achieve the public good, the issue remains how would diplomacy continue to feature in a sharply reshaped world order and what form would it take?

Diplomacy Now Open to New Global Players with Sharply Competing Ideologies and Interests

In its current application, and more specifically in the context of the U.S. - China relationship, the concept embraces many aspects of international state conduct beyond the direct interaction among national governments. Diplomacy consists of a combination of public attitudes on the formation and execution of foreign policies; the diplomatic process carried out between a government and foreign publics through information transmission and intercultural affairs; as well as the formal and informal interactions of private groups. As to the direction to which the craft is headed, its application will very likely extend to alternative approaches to issues. A new brand of diplomacy is bound to go strikingly beyond conventions

457

and normative codes particularly in light of the diversity and complexity of issues commanding attention. The flexibility that is now afforded in state-to-state conduct opens a range of new media for global discourse.

Without doubt, diplomacy will continue to provide the mechanism for formalized dialogue to the extent that its relevance and applicability remain intact. That its relevance has endured is underscored by Gordon A. Craig, world-renowned diplomatic historian, whose evocative works continue to provide a reliable guide to academia and practitioners alike in the field of international politics.[17]

Craig has carefully mapped the extent to which the small Eurocentric diplomatic community that had dominated world affairs for many centuries was forced to open its doors to new members.[18] This was obvious from as far back as the Paris Peace Conference in 1919 and was demonstrated more dramatically one year later at the First General Assembly of the League of Nations. On that occasion almost 50 nations, the majority of which were non-European, made their case to be heard on important matters affecting world affairs.

Following World War II, U.N. membership grew from strength to strength and in the ensuing decades more than one hundred nations maintained permanent missions with that body. This remarkable assertion of diplomatic visibility proceeded hand in hand with the diminishing homogeneous make-up of the original diplomatic community. Not surprisingly, the time had arrived well within the sixties when the collective membership was no longer in a position to draw upon a common history. Instead, what obtained was a situation in which ideological differences (which were virtually unheard of in the diplomatic system until then), tended to snarl communication as totalitarian governments, to adopt Craig's reference, *made a fine art of defying the rules.*[19]

In reinforcing these phenomenal changes the disposition of new Member States, many of which had recently acquired their independence was to exhibit a studied disregard of standards and procedures set by their forerunners. This situation accounted in part for the high degree of incoherence in international discourse that typified that phase of the organization's evolution. Today, the U.N. is a mosaic of ideological orientations diffused among a cross-section of political groupings including the Group of 77, the G8, the G20, the Non-aligned Movement and the Organization of Islamic Conference, to name a few. Given the influence of these confederations, amidst nations now regarded as centers of gravity such as Iran, Russia and Venezuela, various groupings can muster solidarity within their bases and prevail by virtue of numerical advantage.

458

What does this portend for America's future influence? This book has demonstrated that as the pivot of the Western Alliance, America is able to bring its weight to bear through the global dispersed network of central banks, the international monetary system, multinational corporations, foundations and think tanks, the mass media, the intelligence machinery, and basing footprints which in combination guarantee an absolute diffusion, an omnipresence, even amidst China's affairs.

Effective Governance as a Foreign Policy Plank

To what extent does political popularity and support in Washington and Beijing impact on the discharge of their respective foreign policy agendas? Morgenthau concedes that the best conceived and most expertly executed foreign policy will inevitably come to naught if it fails to draw upon a foundation of good government. Good government as a requirement to national power requires three criteria. The first is a balance between a country's material and human resources that go into the making of national power and those appropriated to overseas policies; the second is the balance between both sets of resources which in turn gives credence to social and economic stability; and the third, the political popularity of policies.[20]

A corollary to the above is that elected leaders are obligated to ensure that the objectives and methods being employed in the execution of their foreign policy plans are assigned the power that is actually available, as distinct from what is being projected, since foreign policy is ultimately a function of national power. It is therefore paramount for leaders to be vigilant and exercise extreme care in the outcropping of their political, economic and military capabilities, while mindful of the repercussions that lie ahead, should their calculations ultimately prove ill-founded.

CHAPTER NINETEEN

DOES A RESOLUTION LIE AHEAD?

"To the statesman of the day the essential purpose of the eighteenth century balance of power was the perpetuation of the European status quo. This balance did not require peace; quite the contrary. The balance of power relied on an assumption that any state might align itself with any other - if, by making such an arrangement, the overall European political equilibrium and individual interests of states might be enhanced. Alliances shifted and numerous wars were fought, usually with the result of restoring the status quo ante bellum."

James A. Nathan

his enquiry has established that over the long-haul power and the frequently brutal way of power politics are conceived in the bowels of entrenched interests that invariably defy the supporting pillars of statehood including sovereignty as the single and supreme locus of political authority. Furthermore, such interests are employing their transformational capacity to bring influence to bear on domestic political discourse, global issues, and the present and future international order. The United States and China are central figures in this interchange.

China's self-assertion, not to mention its proneness to make common cause with players that are decidedly antithetical to Western tradition - institutions, values, customs, beliefs, the concept of the free market and democratic norms – has precipitated partisanships that are many a time divergent to U.S. interests. It may even be argued that the U.S. - China interplay is reminiscent of the U.S. - Soviet rivalry at the height of the Cold War when the Sino-Soviet bloc at once dominated most of Eurasia. Significantly, that stand-off was finally resolved not by military might but by a flexible amalgam on America's part of political machinations, economic dynamism, technological sophistication, and its role as prime mover in the creation and control of an array of global institutions. By no means least as a deciding factor was American culture that basked in a unique and unrivalled universal allure.

Confronted with a fated erosion of its global ranking and overwhelmed with the reignited ambitions of influential players, primary among which is China (with ample stocks of support to draw upon from within the G 20 nexus, Russia's truculence and an equally motivated Global South), the U.S. now finds itself in a tussle to sustain premiership. Overcoming this challenge will entail prevailing over domestic economic challenges and simultaneously addressing the diminishing role of the dollar in international trade and reserve balances; maintaining political leverage in key regions of the world; giving substance to the legitimacy of its actions in the wider global international society as well as within the western international community; and triumphing in all critical forms of combat. What's more, this phase of the end game is making its way beyond the tellurian realm into boundless exoplanetary spheres... and embracing the fathomless frontiers of inner space. On this account, the concept of omnipresence, as distinct from Empire, commodiously befits the framework of reference of both contenders in the Great Game.

Even so, military might continues to be America's ace in the hole. Any rapid or ill-conceived contraction of U.S. foreign interests at this stage, however, is likely to unsettle the power balance of the entire global political system. Therefore the strategy it must now prosecute will entail bolstering its capacity to prove superior in those areas most important to its continued global dominance - the Middle East, the Americas, the Western Pacific, Africa, and the European bridgehead. Embracing this grand vision and maintaining its omnipresence will exact a redefining of all existing frontiers, as we know them as of now.

Amidst these antithetical currents is the larger picture of the steady deterioration of all the global systems. If the ongoing struggle among the major powers is maintained, what does this portend for civilization? This is by far the more important aspect of our enquiry. The U.S. - China debate, while of germane imperative, dissolves in the face of their power structure and common ambitions. Consequentially, what are the implications of such parallelism for human civilization on a finite planet if it is to be believed that the future of the human species rests on exoplanetary colonization?

And further to this, what of America's obsession with material excess and its predisposition to project itself in absolute terms whether that be politically, economically, socially, militarily and culturally? And in what ways do these relate to its culture, and more specifically, to the idea of American exceptionalism?

Culture, according to Wade Nobles, is "a process which gives people a general design for living and patterns for interpreting their reality." Its aspects, in his view, consist of "ideology," "ethos," and a "world view," and its factors are "ontology," "cosmology," and "axiomology."[1]It is through culture that a society develops awareness, identifies as a collective and is disposed to a world view on the basis of which people interpret the world, relate to it, and interact with it.

Dr. Marimba Ani's rendition of the concept of culture is expressed as the *asili,* a Kiswahili word construed to mean beginning, origin, nature (in the sense of the nature of a person or thing), essence or fundamental principle. It can also be taken to mean the "seed" or "germ" that serves as an organizing principle or logic for development. This rendition aids in an understanding of the defining characteristics of the thought process and behavior of a collective that comprises a society, the cultural DNA as it were.[2]

In this regard, the *asili* of a culture is formulative and ideological in that it gives direction to development. It also accounts for the direction and consistency of the collective and by extension, for tenacity of purpose, for behavior, as well as self-realization.

America was from the very outset a business civilization sworn to economic liberalism which has endured as the society's defining feature, meaning "...you contribute to the public good by means of your own individual economic activity which was actually aimed at private gain." [3] Overcoming the frontier is an elemental aspect of this impetus, beginning with what William Appleman Williams, in Contours of American History describes as "a Manifest Destiny." This entailed "swallowing up half of Mexico," "reconciling the scramble for private property with the ideal of Christian commonwealth," and continuing to this day along the lines of "Empire," which in the present scheme of things is being vindicated as "the only way to honor (both) avarice and morality." So too were the nation's sense of "aggressive individualism," "optimistic materialism," and "pragmatic interest group politics" referred to by Joyce Appleby in attempts to vindicate the ideological fervor of the revolution. Morris Berman's incisive dissection, Why America Failed: The Roots of Imperial Decline, argues that at the end of the day "virtue was probably the crux of it" since the classical definition of republicanism meant subordination of private interest to the public good.[4]

Nonetheless, as a neoliberal archetype, America has now found itself plagued with a welter of crises that cannot be readily resolved with the deployment of neoliberal economic principles and at risk of steadily deteriorating instability. Any serious intellectual undertaking to critique American industrial society and its dominant culture would likely be meted with retort and dismissed as an alarmist or uninformed and irrational persuasion, or at worst, the resultant of some "nut job."

However, in order to understand the American culture it is necessary to delve into European culture and to fathom its unique ability to self-sustain and self-perpetuate. The mind is trained to think in terms of dichotomy and antagonistic opposites, rather than in terms of holism. This was discernible in the north-south upheaval, the impulse to conquer the western frontier, the Cold War, the War on

Terror and ongoing ideologically based hostilities in the Middle East and North Africa. It is a deeply ingrained behavior code, the history of which can be traced to the early Greek philosophers.

Marimba Ani's exhaustive elucidation of the phenomenon explains:-

> "But what Plato seems to have done is to have laid a vigorously constructed foundation for the repudiation of the symbolic sense – the denial of cosmic intuitive knowledge. It is this process that we need to trace, this development in the formative European thought which was eventually to have had such a devastating effect on the non-technical aspects of culture. It led to the materialization of the universe as conceived by the European mind – a materialization that complemented and supported the intense psycho cultural need for the control of the self and others"[5]

Her narration continues,

> "Contrary to our image of the philosopher as being otherworldly and remote, even irrelevant (Aristophanes, The Cloud), Plato appears to have been very much aware of himself as a social and ideological architect. His success was eventually overwhelming. The power of his ideas was evidenced by the way in which they have contributed to the growth and persistence of a new order. This is precisely the power of the Euro- Caucasian order: Its ability to sustain and perpetuate itself."[6]

The notion of dichotomy, opposition, and absence of harmony and disparity within the pair that defines the greater at the expense of the lesser in the realm of evolved thinking was affirmed by Robert Armstrong in his work <u>The Wellspring: On the Myth and Source of Culture</u>, wherein he observes,

> "...(we) see the world as delicately constituted of both terms in an infinite system of contrasting pairs and bound together by the tension that exists between them. To be sure one term in each case is, by definition, of greater value than its opposite. ...In large measure then, the myth of the consciousness of Western Europe is the myth of bipolar oppositions"[7]

It is against this backdrop that American culture has a predilection to identify itself through the alienation and marginalization of societies and groups that do not subscribe to the American way, and for this reason constantly finds itself at loggerheads with the Savage Other. This is attributed to cultural animation and reinforced by historical experiences as the society evolved within the framework of

modernity. Morris Berman espies Walter Hixson's <u>The Myth of American Diplomacy</u>, in which the author observes:

> "...in the sixteenth and seventeenth centuries, Euro-American history developed within the framework of modernity. That is to say these nations defined themselves as modern, in contrast to those they labeled "backward," and colonization and imperialism followed from a world view that apotheocized the new mode of existence. On this scheme, these peoples who lived in accordance with different realities were viewed as unenlightened and thus fair game for Western (Occidental) control. [8]

This inherent proneness to seek out and create and re-create enemies was noticeably beholden to totalitarian regimes typifying the epoch of Nazi Germany and Stalinist Russia.[9] Mass denunciation of the Other amidst mounting moods of hysteria was vindicated by Lenin in the following terms: "The inalienable quality of every Bolshevik under present conditions should be the ability to recognize an enemy of the Party no matter how well he may be masked." Hitler was even subjective in his categorizations of the Other as he made the dubious distinction between "objective enemies" who knew that they were "criminals without a crime" and the "true foes of the regime." [10]

Thus, it was the desire to expand westward and conquer the frontier – the meeting point between savagery and civilization – that triggered the civil war since there was no room for conciliation between two economic systems: the north capitalist, and the south neo-feudal. In the context of bipolarity, the elimination of the Savage Other was the only recourse and so republicanism was overcome by liberalism, which persists today as the dominant ideology. In point of fact, against the backdrop of the frontier mindset, anything or anyone that stood in the way of expansion would be hitherto regarded as "unalloyed evil beyond redemption."

Culture is thus ideological and ideology is premised on a myth that expresses the conscious and preconscious expressions of culture, their inter-relatedness, and how society is able to perceive itself and the world around it. Armstrong imports into his disquisition the concept of "primal consciousness" which he defines as a code of awareness that instills each person causing him to inherit and to help constitute his culture and dictating the terms under which the world is to be perceived. This "consciousness," he notes, acts as a "generative germ" and consequentially becomes the "causative factor of culture." The factor is by nature "pre-conceptual," "pre-affirmative," "pre-spatial and pre-temporal" and maintains within itself the integrity and homogeneity of the culture. Armstrong labels this feature the "mychoform."[11]

Armstrong's approach to what he adopts as "humanistic anthropology" is far in advance of typical Euro-centric social science, and in Ani's view, the concept of the "mychoform" opens up more liberating possibilities than the traditional European anthropological paradigm.[12] Thus, in linking the "conscious" to the "unconscious" expressions of culture, the cultural process can be better appreciated as migrating from "mychoform" to "myth" to "ideology." Ani resolves the cross-over, so to speak, in pronouncing that, "...Mythological systems present synthesizing symbols that help to collectivize the consciousness of persons, within the culture, at the same time stating pre-conscious hidden experience in a more outward modality."

She explains that whereas mychology creates ikons out of collective unconscious experience, ideology is an intensely self-conscious extension of the process which began with the preconscious "mychoform," based on the term ascribed by Armstrong. So that ideology involves the more intentional use of the sacred ikons of the culture for political purposes, more explicitly put, "for the survival, defense and projection of the culture." Ideology thus becomes "the political interpretation of the myth" and this would explain for example the Nazi's invention and relentless pursuit of the myth of the Aryan race.[13]

To put it simply, the American mythical model is laced with a pseudo-religious impulse that translates into the triumph of good over evil.[14] The myth was distinguishable among the revolutionaries in Europe where a religious dimension was inextricably wielded into the fabric of its adherents. It is this mythological model that gives coherence and meaning to the imperial adventure. To underscore the point, in books such as The Puritan Origins of the American Self [15] and The American Jeremiad,[16] historian Savcan Bercovitch demonstrates that it was more the rhetoric of the Puritans than the specific content of their ideas that created the American ideology. This amounted to a single comprehensive vision – a mychology, as he called it, homologous to Armstrong's "michoform." Moreover, the language that was used in the punctilious narrations associated with that era, invested America with a sacred history in which the land was analogous to Canaan, and the Puritan settlers to the Hebrews who crossed the river Jordan. America thus became the heir apparent to this legacy, which historian David Harian likens to "a theocratic prophecy."

James Billington, in his classic Fire in the Minds of Men,[17] shed further light on the phenomenon of the mythical model and its religious undertones in recounting that,

"The recurrent mythical model for revolutionaries – early romanticists, the young Marx, the Russians of Lenin's time, was Prometheus, who stole fire from the gods for the use of mankind. The Promethean faith *of the revolutionaries resembled in many respects the general modern belief that science would lead man out of darkness into light. But there was also the more pointed millennial assumption that, on the new day that was dawning, the sun would not set. Early during the French upheaval was born a "solar myth of the revolution," suggesting that the sun was rising on a new era in which darkness would vanish forever. This image became implanted at a level of consciousness that simultaneously interpreted something real and produced a new reality."*

Thus, the mychoform bequeaths the myth and the myth gives rise to ideology out of which a new reality comes forth, taking form and shape. Ipso facto, the belief that science would ultimately redeem mankind from his imperfect condition, as for example by infusing the universe with artificial intelligence through singularitarianism is but a materialization of the Promethean myth, that gives impetus and more so justification, to America's unceasing imperial enterprise.

The irony in all of this is that in the case of America, the revolutionaries themselves quickly became akin to the very system against which they so vehemently fought in Europe – hereditary rule, a landed gentry, and continued political dominance of the feudal aristocracy. Indeed, the enduring nature of this disposition was inescapable being inexorably rooted in the culture of the society. Berman points out:

"In a word, once the dust settled on the revolution, it began to look as though the Founding Fathers had had one type of society in mind, and the general citizenry another. The latter was interested in profit, competition and new consumer goods, whereas the former believed that these things were important, but by themselves could not constitute the stuff of commonwealth.[18]*"*

This insatiable quest for profit and commerce, reminiscent of the Europe that was left behind, drew remonstration even among the revolution's vanguards in the persons of John Adams and James Madison who, in Berman's words, "...even began to wonder if the monarchy was all that bad, for at least it organized a nation around a higher purpose than getting and spending, as Wordsworth would put it just a few years later."

George Washington, himself, during the war years spoke out against the "insatiable thirst for riches" that had seized the American society," adding that there was an absence of public spirit and want of virtue." [19] The primary concerns being ventilated within the closed circuit of the leadership were deciphered by Berman in the following words:

> *"...Adams claimed that the United States had proven to be "more avaricious than any other nation that ever existed. "Bedevilled," Benjamin Rush called the place, adding that without a curbing influence, this not-so-enlightened citizenry would start devouring each other like beasts of prey." (One wonders what these men, if they were alive today, would think of Goldman Sachs and the AIG). Forrest Mac Donald, in Novus Ordo Seciorum, says of the passing of this generation, "...After that the Populares took over, a race of pygmies came to infect the public councils.*[20]*"*

For all its ideological fervor, the conspicuous materialism consuming the moral fabric of society permeated the very constitution that was meticulously scripted both in terms of spirit and substance, influenced the form of government that was taking shape, and persists today as a theology of progress mediated by modern technology. This antithetical component of the Revolution in relation to its enunciated ideals, philosophy, and ideology vis-à-vis the jolting consequences that ensued thereto once it became consummated, is registered by Berman. He unveils what he perceives as a historical aberration in these terms:

> *"...As for conflicts of interests, these were philosophical as well as material. Diggins argues that republicanism was in large part a symbol for the Founding Fathers, and that while Madison, Hamilton and Adams did believe in the classical ideal, they nevertheless created a government with no need for men committed to civic humanism. The constitution they created represented the eclipse of political and moral authority and the legitimation of pluralism, individualism, and materialism, the very forces the humanist tradition identified with corruption and loss of virtue. The Founders created a weak government whose center had no compelling moral ballast*[21]*"*

That absence of "moral ballast," to adopt Berman's reference, denoted a lack of pith and contributed to the already existing void within the society that needed to be suffused. This was evident in the populace's unending compulsion to project itself through violence in a relentless pursuit for a clearly defined identity. Any semblance of such identity that existed was by nature fragile: having defected from Europe and established itself as a free standing society, America could do no more than seek to redefine itself in relation to what it was opposed to, what it had rejected outright, what it did not want, and to what it did not wish to return. This absence of a kernel fueled the impulse to cast itself in a timeless crusade to save the rest of the world, albeit through force and might.

Walter Hixson analyzed how a decidedly militant identity came to be ingrained in the myth of America. The cultural process, in his view, is laced with bloody national narratives, a pathologically violent foreign policy, and driven by a form of cultural hegemony that arrogated to Christian European settlers a morality which in their thinking was higher than that of the Savage Other. In mapping the historical continuum he observes, "...the frontier encounter unleashed violence unparalleled (proportionately) by even the Spanish conquistadores" and is "sustained into the twentieth century by a rhetoric of holy war against everything un-American." He concludes that in the American thinking, "...victory in war merely affirmed the guiding hand of providence." [22] In sum, the Puritan War pursued by Euro Americans affirmed the myth of American identity.

Hixson's summation is that America's violent disposition is a direct response and proportional to the society's collective internal anxieties and this expression of the collective self is pathological by nature. Furthermore, in diagnosing the cultural processes that account for the interconnectedness between what he designates as "psychic crisis," "aggression," "national identity" and "foreign policy," he found that choosing war in affirmation of a national identity betrays profound "psychic anxieties" inherent in the human and by extension America condition. This trait he explains in terms of "...trauma, anxiety, and fear of the unknown inherited in the frontier encounter with the indigenous first enemy, producing an especially violent form of identification." [23]

Ben Kierman undertook a comprehensive study of the social, political and intellectual history of genocidal violence in his title <u>Blood and Soil: A World History of Genocide and Extermination from Sparta to Darfur</u>.[24] Keeping in sight through history the extermination of anything new that stood in the way of descending throngs of Germanic tribes sweeping southward, and subsequently gobbling up Eurasia, the African continent, the Pacific Islands and the Americas, simultaneously decimating indigenous populations en masse in the process, he notes that this cult of antiquity (which found expression in a genocidal ideology), was a bearing that became more frequent and pronounced after European expansion in 1492 and on the brink of modernity "...even as they took up technological innovations, including some that facilitated mass murder..."

Is there a resolution? The answer is embedded in the very nature and purposes of culture as well as in the fact that cultural mychology, as propounded by Bercovitch, operates at a subliminal level – below the threshold of sensation and consciousness. This infers a form of collective oblivion of its effects on its subjects, who Bercovitch refers to as "a secular modern nation living in a dream" and an example of a "collective fantasy" in its finest form.

The collective oblivion would explain the fervency and fanaticism of the crusade. James Webb underscores this very point, almost apologetically, in noting that "...it is no exaggeration to say that despite its obsession with race and ethnicity, today's America has a hole in its understanding of its own origins." This perceived lacuna he attributes to a "lack of cultural awareness." [25] In his view, "even the complexities of its mixed heritage eludes the national mind...the Scots-Irish had nothing in common with either the English aristocracy in Virginia, or the New England WASP settlers. Nor for that matter the typical English who made their way into the mountains to join them."[26]

As a stabilizing and unifying force, culture orders the experiences of the members of a society and provides them with a world view that offers up orienting conceptions of reality. Regarding a society's identity, it is culture that provides the medium for shared historical experiences and creates a sense of collective. It tells its members what to do and consequently serves as a voice of prescriptive authority. Culture also facilitates the creation of shared symbols and is in this sense a primary creative force of collective consciousness, which inevitably translates into national consciousness.

More importantly, culture provides a basis for commitment, priority and choice thereby imparting direction to group development and behavior. Thus, the central function of culture is creation of group cohesion and its primary purpose is to unify society and limit change. Limiting change is crucial because this protects unity and guarantees cohesion; and these are elementals of stability since they guarantee the survival of the collective. On this premise it can be argued that America is inherently incapable of changing itself...unless as Bercovitch suggests, "counter forces" become sufficiently forceful as to smash the myth. And because culture is immaterial and the society as a collective is unavoidably and inextricably linked to it, unveiling the allegorical *Matrix* as portrayed through the medium of film by directors Lana (born Lawrence) and Andrew Wacowski, may well have been among the more heuristic attempts in the recent past to aid the society in a comprehension of itself, in other words the True America.

Bercovitch sees no hope of recovery from the cultural mychology bequeathed by the Puritans and which continues to operate on a subliminal level because in his estimation, American history possesses no counter forces sufficiently potent to shatter that mythology. "The myth is simply too powerful, too all-encompassing in its scope..." he remonstrates.

Berman foresees continuing decline, denial of such decline and the absence of a resolution and reckons:

> *"...The functioning of the accumulation element in this system depends on a dysfunctional element. As a result neoliberal regimes are plagued*

by crises. These crises cannot be managed temporarily or even for a long while; but ultimately cannot be resolved within the context of neoliberal economics. Over time they multiply and deepen so that the regime is condemned to a condition of permanent instability. The upshot is that a nation such as the United States has only two options: replace the neoliberal regime with something else (which I personally don't believe is going to happen), or watch it get worse overtime. For America this can only mean a steady disintegration of its institutions, its culture, its infrastructure and so on. This process will occasionally be punctuated by violent events represented by 9/11 or the crash of 2008, for example and there are certainly additional, and more catastrophic events waiting for us down the road; of that we can be sure. But for the most part daily deterioration will be the norm."

This inquiry could all but concede that the very nature of culture itself curtails the chance of change and renders the possibility of resolution the more elusive.

REFERENCES AND NOTES

PROLOGUE

1. International News Services Associated Press. November 14, 1990.

2. **Moyers, Bill.** "*The Secret Government: The Constitution in Crisis.*" Washington D.C.: Seven Locks Press, 1988.

3. "The NS WC/WOL Wind Tunnels" NSWC Pamphlet, August 1979, ONH

4. Carl Zeiss to USFET Headquarters "Report on Evacuated Scientists Jena." July 17, 1946, G-2 Paperclip. "Top Secret." Files, R G 319, WNRC.

5. **Lasby, Clarence.** "*Project Paperclip.*" New York: Athenican, 1971.

6. Herbert Wagner. JIAO Dossier. RG 330, NARS.

7. Address. Video. "Remarks on American Leadership." Speaker: Hillary Rodham Clinton, Secretary US Department of State. Presenter: Richard Haass, Council on Foreign Relations. Washington. January 31, 2013.

8. **Eichholtz, Dietrich.** "*War for Oil: The Nazi Quest for an Oil Empire.*" Virginia: Potomac Books, 2012.

9. **Hayward, Joel S.A.** "*Stopped at Stalingrad: The Luftwaffe and Hitler's Defeat in the East 1942-1943.*" Kansas: University Press of Kansas, 1998.

10. Brzezinski, Zbigniew. "*The Grand Chessboard: American Primacy and Its Geostrategic Imperatives.*" New York: Basic Books, 1997.

PART I

CHAPTER ONE

The American Political Identity

1. **U.S Secretary of State Hillary Rodham Clinton** Foreign Policy Address at Council on Foreign Relations July 15 2009. On that occasion Secretary Clinton outlined the Obama administration's foreign policy, which was widely touted as a sharp break from that of his predecessor. Early in her speech she established a framework of three ideals – liberty, democracy, and justice. Secretary Clinton demitted office on February 01 2013.

2. Transcript of "Remarks by the President on Osama Bin Laden" 11.35 East Room PM EDT May 01 2011 Also see:

   coalitiontechnologies.com/livestream.Osama_announcement1208/

   The relentless war to ensure the dislodging of Taliban influence remains unabated. As recently as January 11 2012, the American Forces Press Service reported that an Afghan-led and coalition supported force captured "a top Taliban facilitator" in the Ghazni province; that the detainee was actively involved in the planning of roadside bomb attacks and in the distribution of heavy weaponry throughout the province. Afghan-led forces trained by the US military also interdicted caches of rocket-propelled grenades, small arms ammunition and multiple improvised explosive device materials and bomb components.

3. A Congressionally mandated Report of the strategy and posture that sets the long-term course to assess threats and challenges that the nation faces and the re-balancing of its strategy and forces.

4. The inauguration of a Quadrennial Diplomacy and Development Review (analogous to the Pentagon's Quadrennial), was first announced by Secretary of State, Hillary Clinton at a town meeting on July 10 2009.The first review meeting was held in October 2009 at the Willard Intercontinental and hosted by the Global Leadership Coalition. The final Report, which concluded in December 2010, recommends a bureaucratic overhaul of those state

institutions engaged in foreign policy and international affairs and proposes structural and role revisions within the State Department. The venture has been met with mixed reaction among high-ranking officials and think tanks. The Heritage Foundation and the Cato Institute, for example, displayed pessimism regarding the initiative and its possible merits.

5. **Zbigniew Brezezinski,** prominent geostrategist and political scientist and author of the Grand Chessboard (1997), served as National Security Advisor under the Carter administration between 1977 and 1981. Central to his thinking is that the "chief geopolitical prize for America is Eurasia" since any power that dominates Eurasia would control "two of the world's two most advanced and economically productive regions." Eurasia accounts for 75% of the world's people; most of the world's physical wealth both in enterprises and underneath its soil; 60% of the world's GDP; and about three-fourths of the world's energy resources. Additionally, Eurasia is the location of most of the world's politically assertive and dynamic states and the world's two most populous aspirants to world hegemony and global influence- "The Grand Chessboard" p.231. Among America's major policy events under Brzezinski's previous tour were the Signing of the second Strategic Arms Limitation Treaty (SALT III); the financing of the mujahideen in Afghanistan in response to the deployment of forces there by the Soviet Union to deter an all-out Russian invasion; the brokering of Camp David Accords; and the relinquishing of US control of the Panama Canal under the terms of the Torrijos-Carter Treaties.

6. **Arnas N.** *"Fighting Chance: Global Trends and Shocks in the National Security Environment."* Potomac Books Inc. National Defense University Press 2009. Print.

7. **Hart, Michael and Negri, Antonio.** Empire, Havard University Press 2001, Cambridge University Press, London 2000. Print.

This title co-authored by Marxists philosophers, Michael Hardt and Antonio Negri theorizes on an ongoing transition from a modern phenomenon of imperialism centered around individual nation states to an emergent post-modern construct created among ruling powers. This construct is labeled "Empire" and is constituted by (1) a monarchy consisting of the US, G8, and international organizations such as NATO and the IMF; and (2) an oligarchy consisting of multinational corporations and other non-states

8. Ibid, **Hardt and Negri,** 2001.

9. Barber Benjamin R. Jihad vs. McWorld: How Globalism and Tribalism Are Re-shaping the World Ballantine Books New York 1995, 1996

    Barber's thesis is that consumerist capitalism and religious tribal fundamentalism constitute the central conflict of our times. These diametrically opposed forces are tearing apart and bringing together the world and undermining democracy. The latter is dissolving the social and economic barriers between nations and transforming the world's diverse populations into a blindly uniform market.

10. **Wolin, Sheldon.** Democracy Inc: Managed Democracy and the Specter of Inverted Totalitarianism Princeton University Press. USA 2008. Print.

    Wolin, political philosopher and professor emeritus of Princeton University, introduces a theory of government wherein "managed democracy" has been instrumental in the creation of a totalitarian form. He presents a picture of an America of today in which capitalist forces have merged to create an environment reflective of dictatorial styles of leadership. Furthermore, ordinary citizens are discouraged from actively participating in government through various forms including (1) the role played by the media as the promoter or non-promoter of their interests (2) the culture of elitism whereby elected officials have few or no ties with those whom they represent and (3) the seeming similarity between the policies of the two main parties

11. Gries et al. The Chinese Quarterly March 11 2011 No. 205. "Patriotism, Nationalism and China's U.S Policy: Structures and Consequences of China's National Identity, "also referred to as "The Kosterman and Feshbach Study"

    The premise of this research paper (conducted in the US and China in 2009) was that the nature of the Chinese past encounters with the outside world may affect the nature of Chinese identity as well as perceptions of an external threat in the present. To support the study four items were introduced which, in the view of the analysts, tapped Chinese beliefs about two distinct historical encounters viz. that a growing American military is bad for China; that the recent increase in U.S defense spending undermines Chinese society; that American criticisms of Chinese human rights are really just attempts to humiliate China; and that American support for Taiwan and Tibet is really about insulting Chinese people.

CHAPTER TWO

Power Components

1. **Lewis Snider's** Article provides useful reading on this theme; it represents a departure from the measurements of state power based on material capabilities as well as capacities to convert material resources into political power. Snider's approach differs from other empirical definitions of power in that it taps at the strength of government with regard to its own society as well as to the international environment. Other useful reading is *"War and the Three Faces of Power: War Making and State Making in Europe and the Americas."* Comparative Political Studies April 01, 1992 25:26-62. This Article examines the war/state building relationship and the issue of resource mobilization.

2. **Martin *Jacques*** *"When China Rules the World: the Rise of the Middle Kingdom and the End of the Western World"* Penguin Books Ltd. London, England 2009 pp. 149-56

3. The Great Leap forward was an economic and social campaign conceived of by the Chinese Communist Party under Mao Zedong in which the population was used to transform China from an agrarian economy into a communist society by means of rapid industrialization and collectivization. This proved to be a period of economic regression for China, especially between 1958-1961. Historian Frank Dikotter asserts that, "coercion, terror, and systemic violence were the very foundations of the Great Leap Forward."

    Also see **Larely R. Nicholas, K John *Fairbank*** *"The Chinese Economy under Stress" 1958-1965.* (1987). **Roderick Mac Farquahar** (ed.) *"The People's Republic Part I: The Emergence of Revolutionary China" 1949-1965.* Cambridge: Cambridge University Press p.367.

4. **Dikkoter, Frank.** *"Mao's Great Famine: The History of China's Most Devastating Catastrophe."*1959-1962" Walker & Co., 2010 p.33

5. The Economic Journal *"*Food Availability Entitlements and the Chinese Famine *1959-1961"* **Justin Yifi Lin and Dennis Tao Yang** Volume 110 Issue 460 pp. 136-158 January 2000. This Paper examines the Chinese famine 1959-1961 and the decline in food availability as its causes. The

Paper found that both factors contributed significantly to the increase in death rates during the famine.

6. Post. See chapter seven for elaboration of the impact of land ownership and land use reform on rural population.

7. **Martin Jacques.** "*When China Rules the World*" In Chapter 6 "China as an Economic Superpower" the author engages in an insightful discussion on the "scale effects" of China's burgeoning economic growth, namely its total population size, the size of its labor force, the impact of its economic scale on the rest of the world; and the impact on world trade. Each of these "scale effects" has made a major impact on the rest of the world, stimulating overall global growth

8. **Susan L. Shirk**. "*China Fragile Superpower How China's Internal Politics Could Derail Its Peaceful Rise.*" Oxford University Press Inc. 2007. New York USA pp.136-8. Shirk, a former Deputy Assistant Secretary of State, responsible for China and present Director of the University of California's Institute on Global Conflict and Cooperation observes that, "American and European economic pressures to force Iran to abandon its nuclear programs and Sudan to stop its tragic genocide are complicated by China's ties with these countries."

CHAPTER THREE

A New Game of Balance

1. **Kennedy Paul** "*The Rise and Fall of Great Powers: Economic Change and Military Conflict From 1500 to 2000.*" Random House Inc. New York. 1987 p.514-15

2. **Jacques, Martin** "*When China Rules The World: The Rise of the Middle Kingdom and the End of the Western World.*" 2009 Penguin Books Ltd., London p.7 Print.

Jacques notes in his title that deployments have got steadily longer and redeployments more frequent and surmises that the United States will find it increasingly difficult to maintain a huge distant global presence "with over 800 American military bases dotted around the world."

3. Ek Carl Congressional Research Service. "NATO Common Funds Burden-sharing: Background and Current Issues" April 22, 2010. Also see Congressional Budget Office brief "NATO Burden-sharing After Enlargement" August 2001. For full text of "NATO Strategic Concept" See www.nato.int/docu/pr/1999/p99-065e.htm

4. "Defense Budget U.S 2010 Fiscal Year"
   http://en.wikipedia.org/wiki/Militarybudget_of_the_United_States
   Also see Defense Industry Daily May 11, 2009.

5. U.S Department of Defense Quadrennial Defense Review 2010"
   http://www.defense.gov/qdr/

6. Ibid.

7. "U.S Department of Defense Nuclear Posture Review 2010"
   http://www.defense.gov/

8. http://www.nytimes.com/2010/04/09prexy.html
   "Nuclear Arms Reduction Pact" **(Peter Baker and Dan Bilefsky)** New York Times April 08, 2010. Also CNBC Video Live in Prague "Obama in Arms Control Treaty"

9. The 1913-14 *Simla Accord*, resulting from a conference between Britain, India, and China drafted. Under the pact, Britain recognized China's suzerainty but not sovereignty over Tibet. All parties but China signed the agreement; China demurred with the Sino-Tibetan boundary. In 2009, a statement made in the British House of Commons by Foreign Minister David Milibrand appeared to have abandoned the Pact. It is believed that the concession extended to China by the U.K may now weaken India's case in its territorial dispute with China, thereby re-igniting old tensions. Also see:
   http://articles.timesofindia.indiatimes.com/2001-01-09/india/28139275_1_david-milibrand

10. This region now falls within the ambit of the "southern geographic approaches" to the US Homeland. The Cold War has been succeeded by

the war on drugs and counter-terrorist responses being waged by the U.S. with the support of its OAS allies under various legally and politically binding Inter-American Conventions and other instruments a la United Nations Resolutions.

11. New York Times *"U.S Approval of Taiwan Arms Sales Angers China"* Helene Cooper. January 29, 2010.

12. www.nytimes.com/2010/01/30/world/asia/30arms.html
    "China Fumes at U.S Arms Sales to Taiwan" The Observer. January 30, 2010(Tania Brinigan and Paul Harris)
    www.guardian.co.uk/world/2010/jan/30/china-reaction-us-arms-sale-taiwan
    "Arms Sales Causes Severe Damage to Overall China U.S Cooperation"
    Xinhua English News. January 30 2010, Xninhuanet.com**Hu Duang Ph. D, Tim Se PhD.** Asia Sentinel Consultancy October 2010.

13. Ibid., **Fisher R.** *"China's Military Modernization"* pp.10-11

14. **R E Ellis and Associates** Boos Allen Hamilton Center for Hemispheric Policy University of Miami. China-Latin America Task Force March – June 2006 "The Military Strategic Dimensions of Chinese Initiatives in Latin America." February 16, 2007.

15. A comprehensive exposition of China's bilateral and multilateral trade links with Latin American nations is to be found in "China and The Developing World" by **Joshua Einseman** et al Chapter 6 "Hegemony or Partnership: China's Strategy and Diplomacy Toward Latin America" pp.84-112. Chung-chian Teng tackles the divergent views concerning China's rise.

16. Ibid., **Kennedy P**. *"The Rise and Fall of Great Powers"* pp. 514-35

17. **Lutze, Catherine**. "The Bases of Empire: The Global struggle against U.S Military posts "New: New York University press 2009;
    Also see Center for World Dialogue web site
    http://worlddialogue.org/content.php?id=450
    Also see Article
    Grossman, Zolton. *"Imperial Footprint: America's Foreign Military Bases"* Winter /Spring 2009;
    Also see Geopolitical Monitor

ww.geopoliticalmonitor.com/us/us-military-bases-a-global-footprint-1;
Also see Base Structure Reports FY 2009 Baseline.
Also www.defense.gov/pubs/pdfs/2009baseline.pdf "Department of Defense Base Structure Report Fiscal year 2009 Baseline" A Summary of 's Property Inventory.
18. Missile Defense Agency U.S Department of Defense web site http://www.mda.mil/
    Also http://www.mda.mil/system/c2bmc.html
    Also http://www.mda.mil/system/sensors.html

19. These itemized exigencies have been the preoccupation of successive US administrations that have continuously wrestled with options geared towards the attainment of diminished bureaucracy and realizing economies of scale. The expediency of such measures is driven by present cutbacks in spending being advocated across the board. See Addendum.

20. **Ganser Daniel.** *"Nato's Secret Armies: Operation Gladio and Terrorism in Western Europe."* Frank Cass New. USA 2005. Print.
    For the first time in this book, Dr. Daniel Ganser, Senior Researcher at the Center for Research Studies at the Federal Institute of Technology has collated the full account of the "stay behind" secret networks that were established after World War II and the signing of the NATO pact. Dr. Ganser gives an illuminating account of what these networks actually did, utilizing their Cold War capabilities and taking directives from premier U.S and British intelligence agencies. He concedes that many of their accomplishments, which resulted in "a spiral of manipulation, fear, and violence" were in fact antidemocratic, undermining the fabric of the societies they were meant to protect. In his conclusion, more far-reaching questions are posed that cast a new light on the question of sovereignty in Western Europe and the unyielding and subterfuge manipulation of its democracies.

21. Quoted in Jan devWillems, Gladio Brussels: Editions EPO, 1991, p.13

22. The Secretary -General Manfred Worner made this statement at the re-union with the NATO ambassadors of the 16 allied nations. NATO's official position at that time was that the Organization would not comment on official secrets

23. **Allen Dulles,** who replaced Bedell Smith as head of the CIA in 1953, was convinced that covert action was a formidable instrument with which

communism could be combated and closely monitored the work of the CIA's OPC, collaborating closely with Gerry Miller, chief of CIA Western Europe, in the setting up of some "stay behind" outfits. By this means, should the Russians succeed in taking over any or all of the countries in the continent, their secret soldiers could activate well-armed and highly organized partisan uprisings. According to their understanding, the war had never ended. Further, next to the Pentagon, the U.S Special Forces worked alongside the British SAS and trained members of the "stay behind" units. After the wartime secret service OSS was de-commissioned, the Special Forces was re-incarnated in 1952 (as the Psychological Warfare Center) under General McClure, with headquarters in Fort Bragg, Virginia. The "10th Special Forces Group" in particular, was trained in sabotage missions and to recruit, train, and equip guerillas for clandestine Gladio networks and other activities. European language capability was an essential pre-requisite for enlistment. Germany was the location of their first base, which was set up in November 1953 in the former Nazi SS building. At all times the U.S Special Forces collaborated with the CIA.

24. In July 1995, the London-based Imperial War Museum disclosed for the first time evidence of MI6 involvement in Gladio operations. The revelation took the form of an exhibit – an inconspicuous commentary in one of the windows, which read "Among MI6 preparations for a Third World War were the creation of "stay behind" parties ready to operate behind enemy lines in the event of a Soviet advance into Western Europe."

25. In his conclusions Dr. Ganser notes: (a) regarding democracy, "the manipulation of democracies in Western Europe by Washington and London on a level many in the European Union still today find difficult to believe violated the rule of law and will require further debate and investigation."(b) on the issue of accountability that, "international legal experts and analysts of dysfunctions of democracies will find data on the breakdown of checks and balances within each nation," and (c) on transparency, that "the clash between mandatory secrecy and mandatory transparency, which lies at the heart of "the Gladio phenomenon," directly points to the more general question of how much secrecy should be granted to the executive branch of a democracy."

CHAPTER FOUR

Institutional Configurations in the Inter-American Framework

1. The OAS currently comprises 35 Member States guided by the organization's overarching Charter. Its primary institutions include the Secretariat, the Inter-American Drug Abuse Control Commission, the Inter-American Committee against Terrorism, and the Secretariat for Multidimensional Security.

2. This obtained in the political, economic, and cultural spheres

3. The "good neighbor" policy is embodied as the central tenet of the Inter-American Treaty for Reciprocal Assistance, which came into force on December 03, 1948 – namely that an attack against any one country within the Americas is deemed as an attack against all. The catalyst for this instrument was the recognition by the U.S that the Axis powers had been making overtures to several Latin American governments for military cooperation; in principle signatories committed to assuring each other of their good intentions.

4. This self-assertion on the part of the U.S led to political fragmentation, particularly among the Latin OAS membership

5. **Lynch, Edward** (Policy Analyst, Pentagon) *"Moscow Eyes the Caribbean"* Report No. 284 August 07, 1987.

6. **Joseph-Harris**, Serena. *"The Alpha Barrier of North-South Dialogue"* Fortis Publishing. USA 2010

7. **Griffith, Ivelaw** *"Caribbean Security: Retrospect and Prospect"* Latin American Research Review Volume 30 No. 2 (1995) 3-32.

8. See (1) United Nations Office on Crime and Drugs 2010 Annual Report (2) United Office on Drugs and Crime Transnational Organized Crime Threat Assessment 2010 (3) Joseph-Harris, Serena *"The Alpha Barrier of North-South Dialogue"* Fortis Publishing USA 2010

9. The Joint Report on "The Energy Forum of the James A Baker III Institute for Public Policy Rice University Houston Texas and The Stanford Program on Energy Sustainability" May 26, 27 2004 – expands on the geopolitical consequences of a major shift to natural gas in world

energy markets; includes an Innovative World Gas Trade Model (IWGTM) and details historical political case studies of major gas infrastructure projects.

Reference: www.bakerinstitute.org/events/the-geopoliticsof-natural-gas. Further useful reading in (a) Case Studies Presentation entitled "Gas as LNG for Trinidad and Tobago to the U.S" by James Ball, President and Chief Mentor Gas Strategies Consulting Ltd. and Economatters Ltd; and (b) Report entitled "Natural Gas in Mexico – Current Trends and Alternate Scenarios" by Congressman Francis Xavier Salazar Diez de Sollano, Chairman Energy Commission Mexico May 10, 2004.

Regarding copper, more than half of the copper entering the U.S comes from Chile. Between January-July 2010, the U.S imported $1.38 billion in copper of the world's $2.7 billion of copper imports. Two-thirds of the U.S imported copper enters through the Florida panhandle, 25% through the Port of New Orleans, and 9% through the Port of Houston. See: www.worldcityweb.com/trade-connections/717-chile-provides-half-ofus-copper-1.

The largest standing armies in Latin America/ Caribbean nations in the 1980s were disproportionately weighted in favor of countries that served as proxy states for the Soviet Union. For example, in 1988 Nicaragua's military spending as a proportion of the country's Gross National Product was 17.2% and the highest in the region. Guyana's was 14.6%. Under a 1982 bilateral Agreement with the Soviet Union, Grenada received $58,000 worth in military supplies. A similar 1982 Agreement provided, inter alia, for 30 anti-tank guns, potable missile launchers, 30-76m.m. guns, and 2000 AK 47 rifles.

10. A succession of attempted coups and internal rebellions threatened governance structures in the region throughout the 1980s – Dominica (1981), Grenada (1979-1982), St. Vincent and the Grenadines (1979). This period was immediately followed by calls for a regional standing army to serve the Eastern Caribbean (Black 1985; Griffith 1993)

11. In 1996, the Panama Ports Company (PPC) granted concessions to the Hong Kong-based Hutchinson Port Holdings Group, the world's largest independent port operation, for the use of the Canal. The concession covered the ports at Balboa on the Pacific and Cristobal on the Caribbean, with payments to the Panamanian government totaling $22.2 million per

year. These developments ignited concerns over key choke points being used and controlled by "unfriendly forces."

12. 1999 WorldNetDaily.comHowardPhillips. Note: The concerns expressed by Admiral Moorer were corroborated by William Ratcliff of the Hoover Institution at Stanford University (December 1999) and John T. Tierney of the Institute of World Politics in Washington D.C

13. **Veillette, C** Coordinating Analyst in Latin American Affairs; **Ricardo C; Sullivan M**. (Defense and Trade Division) U.S Dept. of State "CRS Report for Congress – U.S Foreign Assistance to Latin America and the Caribbean " Order Code RL 32487 Dated January 03, 2006

14. CRS Report for Congress – "Article 98 Agreements and sanctions on U.S Foreign Aid to Latin America April 10 2006" Order Code RC 33337

15. **Joseph-Harris, Serena** *The Alpha Barrier of North-South Dialogue* Fortis Publishing 2010 pp. X-XVI. Print.

16. A "multinational exercise" involves the armed force of more than two countries; a "multinational exercise" becomes a joint multinational exercise if more than one service participates.

17. See
    https://secureweb2.hq.da.pentagon.mil/UDAS_ArmyPostureStatement /2011/information_paper

18. Ibid., 2011 Army Posture Statement.

CHAPTER FIVE

America's Policy of Expansionism in Eurasia

1. Ibid., **Brzezinski.** "*The Grand Chessboard.*"

2. **Jacques Martin**: When *China Rules The World – The Rise of the Middle Kingdom and the End of the Western World.*" Penguin Books Ltd. London, England 2009 pp. 4-8

3. **Nye, Joseph**, author of "*Soft Power: The Means to Success in World Politics,*" Perseus Books Group Cambridge MA 2004, is Dean of the Kennedy School of Government at Harvard University and a former Chairman of the National Intelligence Council and Assistant Secretary of Defense under the Clinton administration. Nye coined the concept, "soft power" and this has since transformed the analysis of global affairs. He observes that the U.S is the strongest nation, not only as a military and economic power, but also in a third dimension labeled "soft power." He examines the sources of American soft power, its domestic values and policies, and the substance and style of U.S foreign policy while drawing comparisons with the soft power of other countries and non-state actors. Also see Nye's prequel entitled "*The Paradox of American Power*" 2002.

4. The Multi-track system originated due to the inefficiency of the pure government approach compounded by increases in inter-state conflict in the 1990s. This led to a shift in approach from state-centric types of outreach to a more interpersonal mode. Joseph Montville, a former diplomat conceived of the Two Track Diplomacy in order to incorporate citizens with a diversity of skills into the mediation process. Lumping all two track activities, however, failed to capture the complexity and breadth of unofficial diplomacy. Thus the migration to a multi-track system arose to incorporate all levels of society. For further useful reading on the tenets of this new discipline, see "*Multi-track Diplomacy: A Systems Approach to Peace*" by **Dr. Louise Diamond** and **Ambassador John McDonald**. Kumerian Press, 1996.

5. Ibid., **Brzezinski** "*The Grand Chessboard.*"

6. Web
   http://mepi.state.gov/about-us.http
   http://www.medregion.mepi.state.gov/mepi/about-us.html;
   http://www.abudhabi.mepi.state.gov/
   http://mepi.stste.gov/about-faq.html.

7. **Dunn, John** "*Modern Revolutions: An Introduction to the Analysis of a Political Phenomenon*" Cambridge: Cambridge University Press (Toronto MacMillan), 1972. Also see Canadian Review of Political Science (1973) 6:164-165 Volume 6 Issue No. 1- Reviews.

8. **Dunn, John** *"Modern Revolutions: An Introduction to the Analysis of a Political Phenomenon."* Cambridge: Cambridge University Press. Introduction to Second edition p. xxi

9. Web Article (Infographics) *Digital marketing Trends in the Middle East 5:5 Million Twitter Users in Arab World* by **Gaith Saiger** Founder and editor of Arab Crunch Date: March 30, 2011. Also Web: http://arabcrunch.com/2011/03/infographics-digital-marketing-trend-in-the-middle-east-5-5-million-twitter-users-in-the-arab-world.html; http://arabcrunch.com/2010/08/facebook-population-arabic-the-fastest-growing-english-falls-from-the-majority-leadership.html

10. Statement by **Professor Noam Chomsky** to the U.N General Assembly Thematic Dialogue on The Responsibility to Protect (R2P) Project U.N New York July 23, 2009.

PART II

CHAPTER SIX

China's Shift from Centralized Planning to Free Market Enterprise

1. *"Making Sense of China's Economic Transformation"* by **Dic Lo** Department of Economics School of oriental and African Studies University of London and Yu Zheng School of Economics Renmin University China and department of Economics School of oriental and African Studies London in collaboration with Project entitled "Technological Innovation and China's Economic Growth with Support from "The 9-8-5 Research Funding Program." Also see Journal School of Oriental and African Studies University of London Department of Economics Working Paper No. 148 "Making Sense of China's Economic Transformation" by **Dic Lo** March 2006

2. China's Statistical Yearbook. Although Naughton (2007 Chapter 6) notes that official data remain the most reliable, Xu Xianchun (2001), a leading researcher with the National Bureau of Statistics, contends that his office has devised a verification system that makes the necessary adjustments to incoming data. Dr. Dic Lo asserts that although the quality of China's statistical data has invited suspicion, among scholastic literature the

foremost sceptics accept that accelerated growth performance over the long-term is not significantly different to official data provided.

3. In 2004 the United States of America, Japan and the European Union rejected the classification of the Chinese economy as a market model.

4. Ibid., **Dic Lo** and **Lu Zhung**

5. **Kennedy, Paul**. "*The Rise and Fall of Great Powers: Economic Change and Military Conflict From 1500 to 2000.*" Random House Inc. New York 1987 p.458

6. Ibid., pp. 458-68

7. **Pollack, Jonathan** "*China and the Global Strategic Balance,*" in Harding (ed), China's foreign relations in the 1980s, pp. -173-74

8. World Economics Volume #7 No. 2 April/June 2006 "Understanding China's Economic Transformation" **David Bromley** and **Yang Yao**

9. Useful reading on the impact of economic liberalization policies in Latin American countries adopting the Washington consensus can be found in Andy Baker's "The Market and The Masses in Latin America." The author marshals public opinion from 18 Latin American countries to show the effect of free market reforms on prices of consumer goods and services, the replacement of the new political economy of consumption by the dominant politics of labor, and the moderation and nuanced approach of left wing parties to policy-making, while embracing globalization and stalling or reversing privatization.

10. **Naim, Moses**; Telchin, Joseph L. "*Competition, Deregulation, and Modernization in Latin America: Policy Perspectives*" Lynne Reinner Publishers Inc. 1999.

11. **Bilgaiser, Glen** Texas Technical University and **Brown David S.** University of Colorado. Political Research Quarterly December 2005 Vol. 58 No.4 pp. 671-680

12. Universia Business Review Fourth Quarter 2010 ISBN 1698-5117.

13. **Jacques Martin** "*When China Rules The World: The Rise of the Middle Kingdom and the End of the Western World,*" Penguin Group. London England 2009 p.186

CHAPTER SEVEN

Challenges From Within

1. WTO News Press/243 17 September 2001 "The WTO today (17 September) successfully concluded negotiations on China's terms of membership of the WTO, paving the way for the text of the agreement to be adopted formally at the WTO Ministerial Conference in Doha, Qatar, in November."

   Under the Chairmanship of Ambassador Pierre-Louis Girard of Switzerland, the Working Party concluded almost 15 years of negotiations with China and agreed to almost 900 pages of legal text by 142 Member countries of the WTO. During the 12 year period commencing with the date of accession, it was understood that there would be a Special Transitional Safeguard Mechanism in cases where the import of Chinese products cause market disruption among other WTO members.

2. Economic Development and Cultural Change Volume IX No. 01 October 1960 University of Chicago Press 1960. "*Economic Change in Early Modern China: An Analytical Framework*" by **John K. Fairbank** Harvard University; **Alexander Eckstein** University of Rochester; **L.S. Yang** Harvard University This foundation paper alludes to the process of China's economic change to gain perspective on the current century of economic transformation and places in wider context world economic development.

   Further reading "Stages of Urbanization: Is China's Urbanization Poised to Take Off?" by **Junsin Feng** Tsinghua University School of Economics Management; David D. Li Tsinghua University Hong Kong University of Science and Technology. September 24 2006. Writer's Note: The analysts argue, using a panel data set of 38 country and 50 years covering1975-2004, that when China's level of per capita income increases, the elasticity should be low and then high and low again. They find that (1) China's urbanization process followed this path during the first take-off stage, commencing 1978 and (2) China was in 2000 deemed to be at the second stage of take-off.

An extended perspective is offered by **Ken Ohasi**, World Bank Country Director for Nepal, in his Article "Economic Take-Off Stages, Barriers and Conditions" Himalayan Times August 09, 2004. He identifies seven conditions typically important to get low-income countries on a path of sustained economic growth, namely (1) Switch focus from political to economic (2) Maintain national unity (3) Openness to the world (4) Giving economic freedom to individuals (4) Giving economic freedom to individuals (5) Rewarding entrepreneurship (6) Avoiding extreme income inequality (7) Transparency in government policies and bureaucratic decisions.

3. 2010 Report to Congress of the U.S.- China Economic Review Commission November 2010 p. 59.

4. BBC News April 09 2009 "China to Retain Relaxed Monetary Policy (Tags - Bank of China; monetary policy); Caijing Magazine May 06 2009 "China's Loan Binge: Stimulus or Insanity" (Tags – bank lending, banking); Wall Street Journal June 13 2009" China Urges Action in Toxic Debt (Tags - bank lending and banking); BBC News August 06 2009 "China Faces Delicate Task Reining in Bank Lending" (Tags- bank lending, economic recovery); New York Times April 16 2010 "China's Recovery Keeps Focus on Interest Rates and Currency" (Tags – currency evaluation, economic recovery, inflation);Washington Post January 02 2010 "Chinese Banks Found Their Credit in High Demand" (Tags – bank lending); Journal - Big Government. Editor in Chief - Mike Flynn. Chris S.W. Street April 18 2011 "China is About to Suffer a Banking Crisis" The central thesis of Street's Paper is that the economic growth of China is driven by two factors, namely currency manipulation and an exponential growth of risky bank lending.

5. The China Quarterly. "Foreign Trade and Investment in China's Economic Transformation." No.114 pp. 1065-1082 Doi 101017/5030574; 1000004732.

6. In his disquisition "Economic Globalization and the Internationalization of Authority" (Geo Forum Volume 23 Issue 3 1992 pp.269-283), Gill notes as the central thesis that the post-war internationalization and global production, finance and exchange has not been matched by corresponding internationalization of political authority, especially with regard to economic matters. He argues further that the central contradiction in the development in the post-war economy lies in the *territorialization* of the

political economy and identity, usually identified with the nation state and the *universalization* of economic forces increasingly associated with the deepening and spread of commoditization and *marketization* of social life. Thus globalization as he sees it proceeds along three primary and interconnected streams – political, economic, and cultural.

7. **Nicholas R. Randy** (1995); "*The Role of Foreign Trade and Investment in China's Economic Transformation*". The China Quarterly, 114 pp1065 - 1082 Doi 101017/5030574; 1000004732]

8. **Navarro, Peter W. and Autry Greg W.** "*Death by China: A Global Call to Action.*" Pearson Inc. NY USA 2011. Review by Chriss Street. Also "China is About to Suffer the Mother of all Banking Crisis". April 2010.

9. "Libya Crisis: Britain, France and US Prepare for Air srikes against Gaddafi: U.N. security Council Expected to Pass Resolution calling for States to Protect Libyan Civilians..." The Guardian. March, 17, 2011.
    "French Foreign Minister to U.N. or Libya Vote" March 17, 2011. Expatica.com.

    Speaking before the U.N. vote, **Alain Juppe** Minister of Foreign Affairs of France claimed that the world was experiencing "a wave of great revolutions that would change the course of history" as people through North Africa and the Middle East were calling for a breath of fresh air for freedom of expression and democracy. On that premise, it could be argued that the economic interests of any member of the voting Council members, including China, were readily superseded by the imperative to "take all necessary measures, notwithstanding paragraph 9 of Resolution 1970 (2011) to protect civilians and the civilian populated areas under attack in the Libyan Arab Jamahiriya, while excluding a foreign occupation force of any form on any part of Libyan territory..." Subsequent hostilities in other parts of Africa would disclose that there is in effect a scheme among NATO members to impair the PRC's advancements on the continent. Part IV elaborates on this point.

10. **Naim, Moses.** "*Fads and Fashion in Economic Reforms*" Foreign Policy. October 26, 1999.

11. **Ampratwum, Edward Fakuoh.** *Journal of Money Laundering.* ISSN: 1368-5201. Volume II Number I. "The Fight Against Corruption and its implications for Development in Developing and Transition Economies." University of Cambridge United Kingdom. 2008.

12. "The Socio-Economic Impact of HIV/AIDS in China." Presented by NCAIDS, Chinese Center of Disease Control and Prevention, Health Economics Institute, Futures Group International. March, 2002; August 2002.

13. **Sorman, Guy.** "*The Empire of Lies: The Truth About China in the Twenty First Century.*" Encounter Books, USA, 2008. Print.

14. Ibid., **Sorman, Guy.**2008.

15. Ibid.**, Brezezinski.** pp 162-164.

16. Ibid. **Shirk.**

PART III

Overview

1. Wolin, Sheldon. "***Democracy Incorporated: Managed Democracy and the Specter of Inverted Totalitarianism***" Princeton University Press. NJ. USA. 2010. **Print**

2. Wolf, Naomi. "*The End of America: Letter of Warning to a Young Patriot.*" Chelsea Green Publishing Co., Canada

3. **Shirk, Susan L.** Shirk is a respected and long-standing expert on Chinese affairs. In 1997-2000, she served as the U.S. Deputy Assistant Secretary of State in the Bureau of East Asia and Pacific Affairs, with responsibility for China, Taiwan, Hong Kong and Mongolia. In 1993, she founded and continues to lead the North-East Asia Cooperation Dialogue (NEACD), an unofficial "track-two forum" for discussions on security issues among defense and foreign military personnel, and academics from the U.S. China, Japan, Russia, and the Korea. Her publications on China are as prolific as they are insightful. Among her selections are "How China Opens Its Door: The Political Success of the PRC's Foreign Trade and Investment Reforms;" "The Political Logic of Economic Reform in China;" "Competitive Comrades: Career Incentives and Student Strategies

in China;" "China Fragile Super Power;" and more recently, "Changing Media Changing China," which was released in 2011.

4. **Shirk, Susan.** "*China: Fragile Superpower: How China's Internal"* Politics Could Derail Its Peaceful Rise. Oxford University Press.UK. 2008.

CHAPTER EIGHT

Defining America

1. The apparatus of the PRC's internal repression is considered more extensive and advanced than that of any other country in the world. In September 2000, the Chinese State Council Order created the first content restrictions for Internet content procedures. As a rule, China-based websites cannot link to overseas websites or distribute news from overseas media without separate approval from local authorities. Article 14 permits Chinese authorities full access to any kind of sensitive information they may wish.

2. Amnesty International notes that China has the largest number of imprisoned journalists and cyber dissidents in the world and that the extension of the government's efforts to neutralize online opinion came after a series of large anti-Japanese, anti-pollution, anti-corruption protests, and ethnic riots many of which were instigated or pushed via instant messaging services, chat rooms and text messages. http://enwikopedia.org/wiki/internet_censorship-in-the-People's-Republic-of-China.

3. More U.N. entities and specialized agencies. Website: United Nations Rule of Law. URL>http://unroll.org/article.aspx?article-id=19IMF Quotas. Website: International Monetary Fund. Published March 25, 2014. URL>https://www.imf.org/external/np/exr/facts/quotas.htm **Foot, Rosemary St.** Anthony's College Oxford University; **MacFarlane S. Neil** St. Anne's College Oxford University; **Mastanduno, Michael** Dickey Center for International Understanding Dartmouth College. Oxford Scholarship "U.S. hegemony and International Organizations" Online Monographs February 2003 pp. 92-115

4. **Friedman,** "*New York Times Week in Review"* June 02 1992. Huntington, "International Security *"* 17:4 1993

5.	"The dinner that cost Bill Gates, Warren Buffet and other celebrities billions" *"The Telegraph"* Friday 08 April, 2011. Useful reading is provided in Frank, Robert *"Richistan - A Journey through the American Wealth Boom and the Lives of the New Rich"* Three Rivers Press USA 2007. The paper notes that in 2004, the richest 1% of Americans earned more than $1.35 billion a year, greater than the national incomes of France, Italy, and Canada and that notwithstanding the events of 9/11, the number of millionaire households in America has more than doubled since 1995. For an update on further contributions to the Bill and Melinda Gates Foundation, see *"Buffett gives $1.78 billion to Gates, family charities"* The Economic Times. July 08 2011.

6.	**Dr. Andrew Cooper**, CIGI Distinguished Fellow, is a prolific writer and authoritative voice in the study of global governance. His recent projects focus on national perspectives on G 8 and G 20 and unconventional diplomacy in areas such as celebrity activism. See "Celebrity Diplomacy" Boulder, CO Paradigm Publishing 2007.

7.	Cooper explores the shift from traditional diplomacy by professionally trained civil servants to a new form of advocacy by famous entertainers and entrepreneurs. He suggests that these new actors have a significant role to play in the world of diplomacy. Also see (1) April 06, 2009 Interview by Fox News about G 20 meeting (2) March 26, 2009 Quoted in Politico piece on "the evolution of celebrity diplomacy"(3) March 13, 2009 Interviewed in Al Jazeera English about celebrities and their popular support for Buddhism and the Tibet cause.

8.	Cooper

9.	"Thriller" is a viral video featuring the dancing inmates of Cebu Provincial and Rehabilitation Detention Center. Byron F. Garcia, official security advisor of the center who was assigned as head of the prison by the governor of Cebu, is credited for starting this series of choreographed exercise routines for inmates. Criticism of the program has emanated from certain camps – rehabilitation experts and human rights campaigners allege that the institution is enforcing routines that are exploitative and inconsistent with proper rehabilitation. Amnesty International has stated its overall concerns in relation to the existence of overcrowding, insufficient production, poor ventilation, and sanitation. Nonetheless the overwhelming footage of the viral video reported over 45 million views by October 25 2010. For further reading,

10. http://www.enwikipedia.org/wiki/Thriller_Cebu,_Phillipines_Inmates%27_Video
11. **Meghan Keanneally**, "CIA's Top Lawyer John Rizzo tells all in new book," Mail Online 9th October, 2014. http//www.dailymail.co,uk/news/article-2536830/From-Hollywood-stars-demanding-cocaine-waterboarding-terror-suspects-The –CIAs-lawyers-tells-new-book-three-decades-intelligence-agency.html.

12. *Diop, Cheikh, Anta*. *"Civilization or Barbarism: An Authentic Anthropology. New York: Lawrence Hill Books, 1991. Pp133-155."*

13. *"Val Hill, "Postmodernism and Cinema." In Routeledge Companion to Postmodernism, ed. Stuart Sim. London, Great Britain:Routeledge, 2011.pp143-155."*

14. **Rosendorf Neal, Moses**.PhD. *Social-Cultural Globalization: Concepts, History, and America's Role.* (chapter in Joseph S. Nye and John Donahue, eds., Globalization and Governance in the Twenty First Century , Brookings Institution Press, 2000); Propaganda: What Hollywood Can Do for (And To) China. The American Interest March/April 2009.

CHAPTER NINE

Democracy and Mass Manipulation

1. Eldon Taylor is a practicing criminologist who has made a life-long study of the human mind and earned doctoral degrees in Psychology and Metaphysics. He is a fellow of the American Psychotherapy Association and a non-denominational minister and president and director of Progressive awareness Research Inc. His central theses evolve around how choices have been programmed and how our thinking is often programmed.

493

2. Bernays sought to evolve a form of communication by advancing the theories of his uncle, Sigmund Freud. According to Freud, there was in existence a decision-making unconscious mind. Although this model was rejected by notable American philosopher/psychologist, William James in principles of psychology who argued that the mind was limited to conscious processes alone, subsequent research proved Bernays correct – the work of Benjamin Libet (1967) and more recently, John Dylan-Haynes of the Bernstein Center for Computational Neuro Science in Berlin.

3. Declassified documents from the joint hearing before the Select Committee of Intelligence and the Sub-Committee on Health and Scientific Research of the Committee on human resources, 95th Congress, First Session August 03 1977, disclosed that over the 10 year life of the CIA-administered project code named "the MK Ultra Program", the Agency was actively pursuing additional avenues to the control of human behavior. These included "radiation, electric shock, various forms of psychology, psychiatry, sociology and anthropology, graphology, harassment substances, and paramilitary devices and materials. See Norton, PJ 2008 *"Bush and the CIA" Freedom of thought, Public Journal March 12*
   http://journals.aol.com/pomansings/freedom-of-thought/entries/2008/03/12/clinton-george-h.w-bush-and-the-cia/1032

4. Source: www.comicsalliance.com/2011/04/27sperman-renounces-us-citizenship/

5. See: http://www.reuters.com/article/2011/05/13/us-bobdylan-idUSTRE74864A20110513?feedType=RSS.
   http://www.guardian.co.uk/music/2011/april/10/bob-dylan-china-censorship/print

6. **Chomsky, Noam**. (1989) *Chapter 1 & Appendix 1 in Necessary illusions: Thought Control in Democratic Societies.* Concord, Ontario: House of Anansi Press, pp. 1-20, 137-180.

7. Ibid

8. Al Jazeera – English. Listening Post – *general McChrystal: Taken Down by the Media.* www.youtube.com/watch?v=SQesdDxjqZw
   Larry Logan, Chief Foreign Correspondent of CBS News on Early Show, enquired of a shocked public, "How did this reporter get inside the

inner circle of trust and did he violate the trust?" The overriding concern was endorsed by CNN in its Developing Story on June 22 2010 under caption "Runaway General Recalled to DC." The news anchor sounded alarm, in posing the question, "Does Rolling Stone Magazine usually get that kind of access?" No less livid was the Fox News Channel in its Talking Points Commentary, voicing incredulity and seeking answers as to, "Why would the government allow a guy like that access to him and his staff?"

9. Film producers have approached the relevant offices for assistance in film shoots. The duly authorized offices exercise utmost discretion in agreeing or refusing to provide support. Typically, film scripts are closely scrutinized. A first or peripheral reading is undertaken by analysts for main points; a second more critical reading examines the script to ensure that there is nothing in the storyline or proposed imaging that is offensive or repugnant to Departmental standards and practice. Notably, the film "Top Gun" to which was rendered some measure of logistical support, was subsequently adopted in enlistment marketing schemes because of the positive images conveyed about U.S military life. A surge in enlistment reportedly occurred after the film's release, attesting to its favorable impact on the wider public audience.

10. **Alford M. Reel**, *"Power Hollywood Cinema and American Supremacy,"* Pluto Press New York; 2010 pp. 4-5

11. Ibid.,p 5

12. Ibid.,p 5

13. Ibid., p 39

14. Ibid.,p39

15. Ibid., p 51 Also see **James H** (2003) K230 Hollywood, tec *"A rose is a Rose for Now"*, Coplet News Service March, 17

16. **Chomsky N.** *"Necessary Illusions thought Control in Democratic Societies,"* Concord, Ontario: House of Anansi Press, p.1-20, 137-80.

17. **Lippman, Walter. Public Opinion.** Greenbook Publications. USA. 2010. Print

18. "The Garrison State" **Laswell, Harold**. The American Journal of Sociology. Volume 46, No.4 Jan., 1941, pp 445-468. Chicago Journals. University of Chicago Press. Laswell argues that specialists in violence are the most powerful group in society, hence the supremacy of the soldier. Another and equally important central idea is that in the "garrison state" the ruling elite will acquire most of the skills that we have come to accept as part of civilian management.

19. **Bailey, Thomas, Andrew**. "*The Man in The Street: The Impact of Public Opinion on Foreign Policy.*" Macmillan, New York. USA 1948. Print.

CHAPTER TEN

The Threshold of Infinite

1. The dropping of the atomic bomb in Hiroshima was the first of two strikes intended to demobilize the Japanese industrial war-fighting capacity and break the will of the Japanese. The second bomb was launched 3 days later in Nagasaki. On August 14 1945 the Japanese eventually surrendered to the Allies.

2. The first man-made object to reach the surface of the moon was the Soviet Union's Luna 2 Mission on September 13 1959; in distinction to the first manned-mission to land on the Moon, achieved by the U.S on July 20 1969.

3. The intense and expensive effort devoted in the 1960s to achieving firstly, an unmanned and ultimately, a manned moon landing, can best be understood in the political context of its historic era, viz. (a) World War I with its 60 million dead (2) the introduction of deadly innovations including deadly "Blitzkrieg attacks" (c) the V2 Rocket which killed thousands in London and Antwerp(d) the atomic bombings of Hiroshima and Nagasaki and (e)the development of the hydrogen bomb by the USSR and USA which emerged victors in the ideological face-off during the 1960s.

4. **Kurzweil R.** "*Singularity is near When Humans Transcend Biology.*" New York: Penguin Group; 2005 p. 9

5. Ibid., p. 331

6. Ibid., p.13

7. Ibid., p. 331 Also see **Parmentola John A**, "Paradigm Shifting Capabilities for Army Transformation" invited Paper presented at the SPIE European Symposium on Optics photonics in security and defense, October 26-28, 2004; available electronically at Bridge 34.5 (Fall 2004), http://www.nae.edu/NAE/bridgecom.nsf/weblinks/MKEZ-65RLTA?OpenDocument

8. Ibid., p.332

9. Ibid., p.332 Also see **Bayles F**, "High-tech Project Aims To Make Super-soldiers," USA Today, may 23, 2003,
http://www.usatoday.com/news/nation/2003-05-22-nanotech-usat_x.htm
See the Institute for soldier Nanotechnologies Web site,
http://web.mit.edu/isn
Putnam S. "Researchers Tout Opportunities in Nanotech," MIT News Office, October 09, 2002, http://web.mit.edu/newsoffice/2002/cdc-nanotech-1009.html, Ibid

10. **Kennedy Paul.** "_The Rise and Fall of Great Powers: Economic Change and Military Conflict from 1500-2000_" p.521-25

11. Ibid., p.521

12. **Kurzweil R.** p.333. Also see Sandhana L, "_The Drone Armies are Coming_" Wired News, August 30, 2002,
http://www.wired.com/news/technology/0,1282,54728,00.html
See also: Gela M., et al, "Minute Man: Forward Projection of Unmanned Agents Using the Airborne Internet." IEEE Aerospace Conference 2002, Bid Sky, Mont. March 2002:
http://www.cs.ucla.edu/NLR/wireless/uploads/mgerla_aerosopace02.pdf

13. **Arnas N.** "_Fighting Chance: Global Trends and Shocks in the National Security Environment_" Potomac Books, Inc. National Defense University Press 2009 p.110

14. **Kurzweil R.** p.335

The potential applications of Nanotechnology span virtually all areas of defense, including sensors, armor, weapons, ground transport, avionics, computing, energy, medicine, the environment, and emergency management.

15. Ibid., p.356

16. Ibid., p. 357

17. **Magueijo J, Barrow J D, Sandvik H B**, *"Is it e or is it c? Experimental Tests of Varying Alpha."* Physical Letters B549 (2002): 284-89

18. Moore, Max. "The Principles of Extropy." Version 3.1. 2003. A proponent of transhumanism, Moore believes in the discarding by man of constraints to progress by the removal of totalistic dogma typified by political, cultural, biological and psychological limits and in its place promoting secular, unconventional responses.

19. **Brzezinski, Zbigniew.** *"Between Two Ages: America's Role in the Tectonic Era."* The Viking Press New York, USA 1970. Print. p 12.

20. **Mc Donald, Gordon**, J.F. PhD. Served on NSF Panel for Weather Modification 1964-1967. Concluded that weather modification was possible. The opinion was repudiated by Journal of American Statisticians Association June 1967edition.

21. **Donald Michael M**. in *"Some Speculations on the Social Impact of Technology"* – Mimeograph text (p.6) – Address to the Columbia University Seminar on "Technology and Social Change" – Among his more eminent related publications: "Cybernetics and Human Behaviour." Proceedings of the Military Medicine and Allied Sciences Course, Army Medical Service Graduate School, Washington, D.C, April 1954; "Psychological Effects on Ground Force Troops in Combat of Exposure to Atomic Attack" Weapons System Education Group. Joint Chiefs of staff 1954 (Confidential); "Civilian Behaviour Under Atomic Bombardment," Hearings before the Subcommittee on Civil Defense of the Senate Committee of the Armed Forces pp 901-907; and *"Psychological Effect of Thermonuclear Attack on the U.S."* Washington, D.C Industrial College of the Armed Forces. March, 1956.

22. Note: The ADS is a non-lethal direct-energy weapon that was developed by the U.S. military under the sponsorship of the Non-Lethal Weapons Program, with the Air Force Research Laboratory serving as lead agency. The originally intended use of the weapon was area denial, perimeter security, and crowd control. It is activated by firing a high-powered beam of high frequency millimeter waves at 95 GHz (a wavelength of 3.2 mm) and its waves are able to penetrate the top layers of skin with most of the energy absorbed within 0.44mm. The beam irradiates all matter in its targeted areas including everything behind and beyond it that is not shaded, without discriminating objects, people, or material. Persons subjected to ADS, including volunteers from the armed forces report that it causes immense pain but no lasting physical damage. The heating of water and fat molecules beneath the skin's surface causes the pain. Despite the affirmed safety record of ADSs, attested to by Dr. Stephanie Miller of the A/RDHR, Laboratory, a conclusion drawn from a Penn State University Human Effects Advisory Panel - that ADS is a non-lethal weapon with a high probability of effect and a low probability of injury (roughly 0.1% chance of injury from a System I or System II experience), the device has raised sufficiently lingering concerns as to deter its deployment to war theaters overseas, specifically in Iraq (2004) and Afghanistan (2012). In making a case that favors the non-lethality of ADSs, the authorities argue that other crowd control methods, such as sound cannons acoustic hailing device, tear gas, water cannons, rubber bullets and slippery foam "carry implicit dangers of temporal or permanent injury..." in contradistinction to ADSs.

CHAPTER ELEVEN

At War in Cyberspace

1. **Rattray Gregory J** Cyber Space "_Fighting Chance Global Trends and Shocks in the National Security Environment_" Potomac Books Inc. Virginia 2009 p. 115

2. Ibid., p.15

3. **Tzu, Sun.** "_The Art of War: the Oldest Military Treatise in the World._" Theophamia Publishing. 1910. Print.

4. **Liang Q. Col and Xiangsui Wang Col.** "*Unrestricted Warfare: China's Master Plan to Destroy America.*" Pan American Publishing Company. Panama. City. 2002. Print.

5. **Fisher Richard D Jr.** "*China's Military Modernization: Building for Regional and Global Reach.*" Stanford University Press. California 2010

6. **Chang Yao-Chung, Lennon.** "*Cybercrime in the Greater China Region: Regulatory Responses to Crime Prevention across Taiwan Strait*" Edward Elgar Publishers Limited. U.K. 2012. Print.

7. "China and Cybersecurity: Political, Economic and Strategic Dimensions." Report from Workshop - ICGG Project. University of California, San Diego. April 2012.

8. Council of Europe ETS No. 185. Also known as the Budapest convention is the first international treaty to address computer crimes and Internet crimes by harmonizing national laws. The U.S. Senate ratified the instrument by unanimous consent in August 2006 after which the Convention came into force on January 01, 2007.

9. The August 2000 Stanford Draft International Convention to Enhance Protection for Cybercrime and Terrorism proposed the establishment of an International Agency for Information Infrastructure Protection (AIIP) to serve as a formal forum in which interested groups would cooperate through experts in developing standards and practices.

10. United Nations General Assembly Resolution 55/63 and 56/121 regarding combating of the misuse of information technologies; resolution 57/239 concerning the creation of a global culture of cyber security; and resolution 58/199 on the creation of a global culture of cyber security and protection of critical infrastructure systems.

11. In February 2009, President Obama gave his National Security and Homeland Security advisors 60 days to conduct a Cyber Security Policy Review. The review discussions in DC were attended by the author and its stated purpose was to provide a comprehensive assessment of U.S. policies. Prior to this mandate being given, in January 2008, President Bush had established a Cyber Security Initiative which represented a "combination of efforts...to secure government networks, protect against constant intrusion attempts, address vulnerabilities, and anticipate future

threats," according to then White House spokesperson, Scott Stanzel. The details of the preceding Plan remain classified. Nonetheless, its main elements were to deploy trusted Internet connections, passive sensors across Federal Systems, and intrusion prevention devices in Federal Systems,

12. "U.S. Initiatives to Promote Global Internet Freedom: Issues, Policy and Technology." Congressional Research Service. 7-5700. R41120. September, 2010. Submitted by: Patricia Moloney Figliola Coordinator Specialist in Internet and Telecommunications Policy et al. The Report provides, inter alia, information regarding the role of the U.S. and other foreign companies in facilitating Internet censorship by repressive regimes overseas. It was supportive of previous legislation, to wit the Global Online Freedom Act of 2009 (GOFA) (H.R. 2271) introduced by Rep. Christopher Smith, which "...mandated that U.S. companies selling Internet technologies and services to repressive countries take actions to combat censorship and protect personally identifiable information..."

This does not preclude proactive measures taken by the government aimed at monitoring and censoring websites such as keyword list blocking; domain name system poisoning; IP blocking; band width throttling; traffick classification; shallow packet inspection; deep packet inspection; and packet fingerprinting.

13. AG/RES 2004(XXXIV-0/04) entitled "Adoption of a Comprehensive Inter-American Strategy to Combat Threats to Cyber-security: A Multidimensional and Multidisciplinary Approach to creating a Culture of Cybersecurity."Adopted at Fourth Plenary session held on June 08 2004.

14. China's National Medium to Long-Term Plan for Development of Science and Technology

15. **Sega A.** Senior Fellow for Counter-Terrorism and National Security. Council on Foreign Relations. Testimony on Oversight and Investigations about Chinese Cyber Espionage April 15, 2011. Also see www.most.gov.cn/eng/pressroom/200507/t20050706_22978.htm.

16. Ibid., Sega A.

17. Ibid., Sega A.

18. Deveese et al 2009 Report Prepared for U.S China Economic and Security Review Commission

http://www.uscc.gov/researchpapers/209/NorthopGrunman_PRC_cyber_Paper_FINAL_Appr

19. Ibid., **Fisher R.** "*China's Military Modernization*" pp .249-55

20. "Who should lead U.S. Cyber Security Efforts." New, Kevin. National Defense University Press. Prism 3 No. 2.

21. "America's Cyber Future: Security and Prosperity in the Information Age" Volume I. June 2011. Contributors Robert Kahn, Gregory J. Rattray et al. Center for New America Security.

22. FOCAL. The Caribbean – The Third U.S. Border. Source: Hilton Mc David. Adjunct Professor, National Defense University.

23. www.focal.ca/.../focalpoint/394-february-2011-hilton-a-msdavid.

24. Economic blocs and political unions to have emerged along the U.S. third border include: CARICOM est.**; the Bolivarian Alliance for the Peoples of Our America (ALBA) launched in 2004; the Union of South American Nations (UNASUR) set up in 2008; and the Union of South American and Caribbean Nations (CELAC) commissioned in 2010.

25. Joseph-Harris Serena. "On the Throes of Transition: Countering the Stereotype of a Tropical Paradise." Essay Series ISBN 978-976-95599-2- 9. Pp 21-48. Sirius International (Caribbean) Defense Contractors Ltd. Port 2015. http:sirius-defense-joseph.com.

26. Nick Hopkins, Julian Borger, Luke Harding. "GCHQ: Inside the Top Secret World of Britain's Biggest Spy Agency." The Guardian. 01 August, 2013.

27. Ibid.

28. Ibid.

29. https://www.gov.uk/.../CommonCyber_Attacks_headingtheImpact.pdf.

30. http://rt.com/news/176268-chinese-hackers-israel-iron-dome.

31. GCHQ was originally established after the First World War as the government Code and Cypher School and set up in Admiralty Room 40 (NID 25) and War Office MI 16 and was known under that name (GC&SC) until 1946 at which time it was relocated and famed for breaking the German cyphers. A warrant was issued under David Miliband's Labor Government conferring power on the GCHQ to gather intelligence about the political intentions of foreign powers, terrorists, proliferators, private military companies etc. GCHQ is able to tap into data from underwater fiber optic cables passing through all regions of the world and give "early warning signals" which it shares with NSA. Also see: "Britain Has Secret Listening Station in the Middle East." The Telegraph. 23rd August 2013. www.telegraph.co.uk/Britain-has-secret-listeing-station-in-Middle-East.html.

31. "Cyber Attack War Games to be Staged by U.K and U.S" BBC News. 16th January 2015. http://www.bbc.com/news/uk-politics-30842669.

32. The (2015) "Report on Cybersecurity and Critical Infrastructure in the Americas."www.trendmicro.com/.../security.../reports/critical-infrastructures-west-hemisphere.pdf.

33. Lars Hilse. "Advanced Cybercrime/-terrorism Report: Threats to Network Critical Infrastructure and Drug Trafficking Through Anonymously Flying Drones." May 2014. Globalsecurity.com.

34. "Global Trends 2015: A Dialogue About the Future With Non-Government Experts." NIC 2000-02. National Intelligence Council. December 2000.
http://www.dni.gov/files/documents/Global%20Trends_2015%20Report.pdf.
34. Frank Camp. "ISIS Executes Japanese Hostage and Issues Frightening Ultimatum." IJReview.
www.ijreview.com/2015/238681-isis-executes-japanese-hostage-gives-japan-fighters-ultimatum-release-second-hostage. Accessed 01 June, 2015.

35. Lars Hisle. "Advanced Cybercrime/- terrorism Report: Threats to Network Interconnected Infrastructure and Drug Trafficking through Anonymously Flying Drones." May 2014.Global Security.com. Accessed 01 June 2015.

36. Ibid.

37. Jay Mc Gregor. "*The Top Five Most Brutal Cyber Attacks of 2014.*" 28th July 2014. http://www.forbes.com. Accessed 01 June 2015.

38. Andre Bagoo. "Worry Over Terror $$ in TT." Newsday Headline News, Section A p3. 31st May 2015.

39. Pimenidis L, Renner J. "Performance Analysis of Anonymous Communication Channels Provided by TOR." Inf IV RWTH. Pages 221-228. Department of Computer Science, Aachen University, Aachen.

40. Ibid.

41. James Bamford. "The NSA Is Building the Country's Biggest Spy Center (Watch What You Say)." 15 March 2012. http://www.wired.com/threatlevel/2012/03/ff_nsadatacenter/all/1.

42. Ibid.

43. Report on Cybersecurity and Critical Infrastructure in the Americas." www.trendmicro.com/.../critical-infrastructures-west-hemisphere.pdf.

44. Ibid.

45. Ibid.

46. Ibid.

47. Ibid.

48. Ibid.

49. "CARICOM Crime and Security Strategy 2013: Securing the Region." Adopted at the Twenty-Fourth Inter-Sessional Meeting of the Conference of Heads of Government of CARICOM, 18-19 February 2013, Port-Au-Prince, Republic of Haiti. http://www.state.gov/documets/organization/210884.pd.

50. Ibid.

51. Joseph-Harris, Serena. "Countering the Stereotype of a Tropical Paradise." Sirius International (Caribbean Defense Contractors Ltd.) Essay Series. 2015. http://sirius-defense-joseph.com

CHAPTER TWELVE

Aggrandizement Unmasked

1. **Brzezinski, Zbigniew."***The Grand Chessboard: American Primacy and Its Geostrategic Imperatives."* New York: Basic Books, 1997, p 210.

2. **Peter Foster**, "China's navy to assert might with bigger flags." Date: 20 May 2011. Website: The Telegraph. (http://www.telegraph.co.uk/news/worldnews/asia/china/8523609/Chinas-navy-to-assert-might-with-bigger-flags.html).

3. Foster,China's navy.

4. **Black, Jeremy.** *"Great Powers and the Quest for Hegemony: The world order since 1500."* New York:Routeledge, 2008. pp71-88.

5. *"China and the Developing World: Beijing's Strategy for the Twenty-First Century."* Ed. Joshua Eisenman, Eric Heginbotham and Derek Mitchell. New York: M.E. Sharpe, 2007, pp3-28.

6. **Kennedy, Paul.** *"The Rise and Fall of Great Powers: Economic Change and Military Conflict from 1500 to 2000New York: Random House."* 1987.

7. **Armesto,** Filipe-Fernandez *"The World A Global History."* USA: Prentice Hall, 2010.

8. **Armesto.**

9. **Armesto.**

10. **Armesto.**

11. **Armesto.**

12. Quigley, Carroll, Tragedy and Hope: A History of the World in Our Time. Vol i-8.New York: The Macmillan Company, 1966.

13. **Armesto.**

14. Armesto.

15. Armesto.

PART IV

CHAPTER THIRTEEN

Unbridled Financial Debauchery or the Debt Trap

1. Graeber, David. "*Debt: The First 5000 Years*." Brooklyn, New York: Melville House, 2011. Print.

2. Griffith, Ivelaw L. "Drugs and Political Economy in a Global Village." "*The Political Economy of Drugs in the Caribbean*." Ed. Ivelaw L. Griffith. New York: Palgrave, 2000. Print.

3. Bernal, Winsome J. Leslie, and Stephen E. Lamar. "Drugs, Debt and Structural Adjustment in the Caribbean." "*The Political Economy of Drugs in the Caribbean*." Ed. Ivelaw L. Griffith. New York: Palgrave, 2000. Print.

4. Watson, Hilbourne A. "*The Globalization of Finance: Role and Status of the Caribbean*." New York: Macmillan Press, 2000. Print.

5. Schicht, Hans. "*The Death of Banking and Macro Politics*." Gold-Eagle. 4 Feb. 2005. Web. 1 April 2012.

6. Hetamsaria, N., and Vivek Kaul. "*All you wanted to know about derivatives!*" rediff.com. 19 April 2005. Web. 1 April 2012.

7. Steinhauser, Gabriele. "*OECD Pushes for $1.3 Trillion Eurozone Crisis Fund*." Huffington Post. Web. Mar.27 2012

8. Ferguson, Niall. "*The House of Rothschild: The Money Prophets*." YouTube. n.d. Web. 27 Mar. 2012.

9. MF Global Wikipedia. Web. Mar. 14 2012. Online.

10. **Elias, Christopher.** "MF Global and the Great Wall Street Re-hypothecation Scandal. "Thomson Reuters News & Insight. 12 July 2011. Web. 13 March 2012.

CHAPTER FOURTEEN

Political Realignments and the Economic Outlook for America and China

1. **Streit, Clarence.** *"Union Now."* London: Harper and Brothers Publishers. 1939. Print.

2. Note: Transatlantic Policy Network – Of the two Honorary Presidents of the TPN, Honorable Robert Bennet is a U.S. Congressman. Three of the eight members of the Steering Committee are also U.S. Congressmen, namely Jim Costa, Ron Kind, and Devin Nunes.

3. **Ibid, Brzezinski, Zbigniew.** *"The Grand Chessboard."* pp. 40-43

4. "Brave New Bank? BRICS Moot Dropping Dollar, IMF." Russia Today. You Tube. 29 March 2012. Web. 29 March 2012.

5. **U.S. Energy Information Administration.** *"How Dependent Are We On Foreign Oil?"* EIA. 24 Jun. 2011. Web. 1 April 2012.

6. **Goldfarb, Zachary A.** *"Bernanke: Economy, job creation likely to stay sluggish for several years."* The Washington Post Company. 29 Feb. 2012. Web. 13 Mar. 2012.

7. **Bernanke, Ben S.** *"The Economic Outlook and The Federal Budget Situation:* Before the Committee on the Budget, U.S. House of Representatives, Washington, *D.C."* Board of Governors of the Federal Reserve System. 2 Feb. 2012. Web. 13 March 2012.

8. "Usual Weekly Earnings of Wage and Salary Workers Fourth Quarter 2011. "Bureau of Labor Statistics Economic News Release. 24 Jan. 2012. Web. 26 Jan. 2012.

9. *"Consumer Price Index Summary."* Bureau of Labor Statistics. 19 Jan. 2012. Web. 26 Jan. 2012.

10. **Stegon, David.** "FY 13 Budget: Agency Breakdown." *Fedscoop.* 13 Feb. 2012 Web.13 Mar. 2012.

11. **Weidemer, David, Weidemer, Robert, and Cindy S. Spitzer.** "*Aftershock: Protect Yourself and Profit in the Next Global Financial Meltdown.*" 2nd ed. New Jersey: John Wiley & Sons Inc. Print.

12. *"35,860 Chinese evacuated from unrest-torn Libya."* Xinhua News Agency. 3 Mar. 2011. Web. 8 Mar. 2012.

13. **Elliot, Larry.** "Cannes shows how power has shifted to Beijing: The G20 summit proved that China had overtaken the west—and acquired some of its problems on the way." The Guardian. 6 Nov. 2011. Web. 7 Nov. 2011.

14. **Gilpin, Robert.** "*Three Ideologies of Political Economy. Understanding International Relations: The Value of Alternative Lenses.*" 5th ed. Ed. Daniel J. Kaufman, Jay M. Parker, Patrick V. Howell. Grant R. Doty. Boston: Mc Graw Hill. 2004. Print

PART V

CHAPTER FIFTEEN

The Managed Economy and World Economic Systems

1. Final Report and Recommendations of the Temporary National Executive Committee, the United States of America, 77th. Congress, 1st Session, Senate Document No. 35, 1941, p 89. [President Roosevelt's Speech, an excerpt from which provides the quotation at the beginning of chapter I, was the impetus for the formation of the Temporary National Committee.]

2. "Competition and Monopoly in American Industry." **Wilcox, Claire.** Temporary National Economic Committee (Monograph No. 21) Washington DC; U.S. Government Printing Office, 1941 p341.

3. **Hayek, F.A.** "*The Road to Serfdom.*" Text and Documents. The Definitive Edition. The University of Chicago Press Rutledge (Original Text) 1944 Published 2007. Print p.341.

4. Hayek, F.A. The Constitution of Liberty. Chicago. University of Chicago Press 1960. Hayek bemoaned the fact that western democracies were increasingly circumventing the spirit of liberal constitutionalism by passing coercive legislation, typically under the guise of achieving social justice, but in reality serving well-organized coalitions of special interests; Also see Road to Serfdom p24.

5. **Fergusson, Niall** "*The House of Rothschild: Money's prophets 1798 - 1848.*" Penguin Books. New York, USA Published 1999. Print.

6. **Couch Jim F. and Shughart, William E. II.** "*The Political Economy of the New Deal.*" Edward Elgar Pub. USA. Published 1998. Print.

7. Ibid. Hayek p93.

8. **Reinheld, Niebur.** "*Moral Man and Immoral Society: A Study in Ethics and Politics.*" New York Charles Soubner's Sons, 1932, p.182. Print.

9. **Laidler, Harry W.** "*History of Socialism: A Comparative Survey of Socialism, Communism, Trade Unionism, Cooperation, Utopianism, and Other Systems of Reform and Reconstruction.*" New York. Thomas Cromwell and Co. 1961 p.397. Print.

10. **Ibid**; Laidler p400.

11. There has been considerable controversy surrounding the pace and nature of Imperial Russia's economic growth during the years 1895 - 1914. For a more thorough appreciation of the topic the following readings are suggested (a) "*Russia's Age of Silver" Precious Metal Production and Economic Growth in the Eighteenth Century*" (London, New York, 1989), chapter 5 and appendix 2, revised in Ian Blenchard, "*Le developpement e'conomique en perspective historique: l'avenir de la Russie a la luminiere de son evolution a l'epoque moderne (1700 - 1914)*"

in Michele Merger and Dominique Bargot (eds) (b) Economic Backwardness in Historic Perspective (Cambridge Mass., 1962), particularly essays 1-3, 6 which have been subjected to methodological attacks prior to the more definitive studies of Paul Gregory in "*Russian National Income 1885 -1913* "(Cambridge, 1984), and "*Before Command: An Economic History of Russia from Emancipation to the First Five Year Plan*"(Princeton, NJ.,1994) chapters 2-4.

12. **Sutton, Antony C**. "*Wall Street and The Bolshevik Revolution: The Remarkable True Story of American Capitalists Who Financed the Russian Communists.*" Clairview Books. New York. Published 2011. Print.

13. **Sutton, Antony, C**. "*National Suicide: Military Aid to the Soviet Union.*" Arlington House. USA 1973. Print.

14. **Vedder Richard K. and Lovell E**. "*Unemployment and Government in Twentieth Century America.*" NYU Press. Updated Edition 1997. Print.

15. **Higgs, Robert**. "*Against Leviathan: Government Power and A Free Society.*"The Independent Institute, California US 2004. Print.

16. **Higgs, Robert**. "*Regime Uncertainty: Why the Great Depression Lasted So Long and Why Prosperity Resumed After the War.*"

17. "*The New Deal Debunked (Again)*" **Lorenzo, Thomas D. Mises** Daily September, 17 2004.

18. **Flynn, John**. "*The Roosevelt Myth: A Critical of the New deal and Its Creator*"Ludwig von Mises Institute U.S. 2007. Print.

19. Note: Frankfurt School - In 1923 a group of German intellectual Marxists founded the Institute of Social Research modeled after the Marx-Engels Institute in Moscow. When the Nazis came to power in Germany, this intellectual grouping fled to the US and found job opportunities in many of the major universities such as Columbia, Princeton and Berkley, California. There, they proceeded to introduce a wave of "faddish" multicultural subjects such as radical feminism, deconstructed relativism etc. These are now serving (their) collective purpose of undermining the perpetuation of Western civilization, as we have come to know it. Tugwell, a protégé of that school, adopted an experimentalist approach to planning

and viewed the industrial planning of World War I as a successful experiment. He advocated agricultural planning led by industry to stop rural poverty that had become prevalent due to the postwar crop surplus and went on to become Director of the New York City Planning Commission, a forum that set the framework for socio-economic planning, land use, and long-term development.

20. Having introduced the *"Smoot Hawley Tariff Act 1930"* in the middle of a recession by increases in 900 separate American import duties, an all-out trade war ensued. The legislation was intended to curtail trade in order to promote domestic economic activity and revitalize the agricultural sector. However, the 60% duty imposition prompted retaliatory tariffs among many important trading partners. The free fall resulted in diminished volumes of trade among America's 70 top trading companies. In some instances volumes decreased by as much as by 80% within three years. Added to this, there was an overall plummet in American exports by 53% between 1929 and 1932. Even while the Bill was being piloted in 1929 in the House of Representatives there were riots and boycotts and foreign governments swiftly moved to increase rates against American products. By May of the following year, Canada retaliated by imposing new tariffs on 16 products that accounted for 3% of U.S. exports to that country, simultaneously redirecting trade links with other members of the British Commonwealth. Likewise, France and Britain renegotiated bilateral agreements and the Germans resorted to their own system of autarky.

21. Since the bursting of the "tech bubble" in 2000, there has been a fifty-fold increase in dollars invested in commodity index funds. During the first 55 days of the food crisis in 2008, speculators paid in $55 billion to commodity markets and by July of that year roughly $318 billion was reportedly "roiling in the market." Beyond this period the market appears to have rebalanced.

22. **Rocha, Nadia, Giodani, Paolo and Ruta, Michele**. *"Export Policy and Food Price Escalation"*. May 09 2012. Also see Anderson, **Kim; Nelgen, Signe** Center for Economic Policy Research - Discussion Paper# 9086. August 12 2012; Also see *"Agricultural Trade Distortions during the Global Financial Crisis."*

23. **Anderson, K** ed. (2009), *"Distortions to Agricultural Incentives:* A Global perspective 1955-2007, Palgrave Mc Millan & the World Bank;" **Chaffour, J.P** (2008), "Global Food Price Crisis: Trade Policy Origins and Options"

trade Note 34, World Bank; **Evenson, R.** (2001), "Economic Impacts of Agricultural Research and Extension" Chapter 11 in **Evenson R. & Pengali, P** eds. Handbook of Agricultural Economics, 1(1) 533-626, North Holland Amsterdam; **Ivanic M. & Morton, W.** (2008) "Implications of Higher Global Food Prices for Poverty in Low-Income Countries." Agricultural Economics.

24. **Lamy, Pascal,** General Director World Trade Organization. WTO News - Speeches. "Opening Address to Berlin Agricultural Ministers Summit, January 22, 2011.

25. Opening Statement for James Grant, Monetary Policy Hearing March, 17 2011. Hearing of the Domestic Monetary Policy and Technology sub-Committee chaired by Congressman Ron Paul (R).

26. Federal Reserve Chairman Ben Bernanke's Lecture Series hosted by the George Washington University (GWU) School of Business, Washington D.C. consisted of four consecutive Modules that focused on (a) the origins and missions of central banks (b) the role and actions of the Federal Reserve after World War II(c) the causes and responses to the current financial crisis and (d) a review of recent cases of government's policy responses. References – "Bernanke – Federal was helpless in Lehman Failure." Annalyn Censky. CNN Money. Dated March 27, 2012; "Bernanke Defends Bailouts in Third GWU Lecture." March 27, 2012 CNN Money; Live Video: http://www.ustream.tv/federalreserve; huffington post.com/2012/03/19/ ben-bernanke-lectures-at_n_.

27. "China Eases Restrictions on Listed Firms: New Capital Raising Activity Likely in Coming Weeks as firms Complete Reforms." Market Watch April 17, 2006; "Overview of Governance of State-Owned Listed Companies in China." DRC/ERI-OECD. Policy Dialogue on Corporate Governance in China. May 19, 2005. Beijing, China.

28. "CCP Delegates from Private Sector Doubled." **Zeng Yangpeng.** Chinadaily.com.cn/china/2012cpc/2012-11/07/content_158889.

29. "Reform Without Losers: An Interpretation of China's Dual Track Approach to Transition." **Lawrence J. Lau** et al Stanford University; "Modernizing China's Growth Paradigm." **Eswar Prasad and Raghuram G. Rajan.** IMF Policy Discussion Paper. PDP/06/3. March 2006.

30. "The Effects of Reform of the Chinese Dual Track Price System." John Bennett et al. February 26, 2008; "The Dual Pricing System in China's Industry." **Wi Jinghian & Zhao Renwei.** Journal of Comparative Economics, 1987, vol. 11, issue 3, pp 309-318. 1987.

31. "Corruption and Resource Allocation under China's Dual Track System." **Wei Li.** The Fuqua School of Business, Duke University October 1999.

32. "Work Report Delivered on the Work of the Government." March 05, 2012. Presented by the Premier of the State Council at the Fifth Session of the Eleventh National Congress, the report provides statistically supported government-led strategies intended to sustain China's continued economic growth.

33. "China 2030: Building a Modern, Harmonious, and Creative High Income Earning Society." The World Bank Development Research Center of the State Council, the People's Republic of China. Conference Edition 2012.

34. "Twenty Year After Humphrey-Hawkins." Independent Review Lipford Jody. June 22, 1999; "Revisiting Humphrey Hawkins." John Feheerey; [Reference:U.S. Dept of Labor Statistics issued by Secretary of Labor.]

35. **Liang Qiao, Colonel; Xiangsui, Wang Colonel.** "*Unrestricted Warfare: China's Master Plan to Destroy America. Pan American Publishing Co, 2002 Panama City, Panama. Print.*"

36. **Rickards, James.** "*Currency Wars: The Making of the Next Global Crisis*" Penguin Books, London, England pp. 56-97.Print 2011.

37. The "Financial War Game" hosted by the Applied Physics Laboratory (APL) was the Pentagon's first effort (March 17-18, 2009) through its Warfare Analysis Lab to gain an appreciation of how an actual financial war can evolve and what lessons could be learned. This exercise was premised on an earlier paper that Rickards had presented in 2006 to STRATCOM on MARKINT, which involved analyzing capital markets to find actionable intelligence on the intention of market participants. The September and October 2008 sessions focused on financial war games in which other leveraged instruments such as futures and derivatives could be used to manipulate underlying physical markets, including those in strategic commodities such as oil, uranium, copper and gold.

38. Ibid., Rickards pp. 56-124.

39. Ibid., Rickards p. 113.

40. A court ruling that hung on provisions of the Freedom of Information Act led to public disclosures relating to the allocation of bailout loans in government's $2 trillion bailout program. The Federal Reserve had initially refused to disclose which financial firms it lent money to and the amount or assets put up as collateral, on grounds of the "competitive harm" that would result as against the substantial public interest such disclosure would serve. See: "News Organizations Support Bloomberg's Bailout Suit." Reporters Committee for Freedom of the Press December 15, 2009; "Court Orders Fed to Disclose Emergency Bailout Loans" Bloomberg August 25, 2009; and Court Ruling: "*Bloomberg LP v. Board of Governors of the Federal Reserve System. 08-CV-9595. U.S. District Court South District of New York (Manhattan)."*

41. "U.S. Hyperinflation is a Myth."
    http://theautomaticearth.com/Finance/us-hyperinflation-is-a-myth.html

42. Ibid.

43. Ibid.

44. Ibid.

45. "Debt and Deleveraging: Uneven Progress on the Path to Growth." January 2012, McKinsey Global Institute.

46. "CICC: Corporate Sector Deleveraging is Happening in China" May 28, 2012. Sprach Analyst.

47. "China Monetary Statistics."
    http://www.alsosprachanalyst.com/economy/china-monetary-statistics-for-april-2012.html

48. **James Stewart Martin**. "*All Honorable Men on Both Sides of the Atlantic Who Successfully Thwarted Plans to Dismantle The Nazi Cartel System.*" Little Brown & Co. 1950. U.S. Print.

49. **Sutton, Anthony C**. "*Wall Street and the Rise of Hitler.*" Buccaneer Books. New York, USA 1976. Print

50. Ibid.

51. **Urwand, Ben**. "*The Collaboration: Hollywood's Pact with Hitler.*" Harvard University Press. USA. 2013. Print.

CHAPTER SIXTEEN

War on Many Fronts and Program 863

1. The central thesis of Stephen Leeb's book, "*Red Alert: How China's Growing Prosperity Threatens the American Way of Life,*"*(2011)*, is that "key commodities that are essential to our daily lives ...are running critically short." Leeb argues that "while America has been fighting wars in Iraq and Afghanistan, China has focused its substantial muscle on securing vital commodities from these and other lands.... " For further references, see: "*The Race for What's Left: the Global Scramble for the World's last Resources*" by **Michael Klare,** Professor of Peace and World Security, Hampshire College, Massachussettes. Published by Yale Environment 360. May 28, 2012; and B.P. Statistical Review of World Energy; U.S. Geological Survey.

2. "China's Rare Earth Elements Industry: What Can the West Learn." **Cindy Hurst,** Analyst U.S. Army Foreign Military Studies Office, Fort Leavenworth. March 2010.

3. It is acknowledged that the term "rare earth" is a misnomer since these minerals are fairly abundantly dispersed throughout the earth's crust, but not necessarily in sufficient quantities as to make their mining commercially viable. Ref. Hurst Appendix "B" p. 41 for Classification of the Seventeen Rare Earth Elements by Date of Discovery and Atomic Number.

515

4. The Society was established in 1980 and publishes two Journals: "*The Journal of the Chinese Rare Earth Society and Chinese Rare Earths.*"

5. Established in 1986, the program which was personally approved of by Deng Xiapong for implementation by the Ministry of Science and Technology and was the brainchild of four top Chinese experts: Deheng Wang, Jiachi Yang, Gangchang Chen and Fangyan Chen. Its overall objective was to boost China's innovation in high-tech strategic fields.

6. Professor Xi Guangxian, who is widely considered the father of Chinese rare earth chemistry, established the State Key Laboratory of Rare Earth Materials Chemistry and Applications (affiliated with Peking University, Beijing). During his illustrious career Professor Guangxian pioneered research in many ground-breaking areas including metal extraction, radiation chemistry, extraction of nuclear fluids and extraction of praseodymium from rare earth as laser material.

7. The State Key Laboratory of Rare Earth Resource Utilization is affiliated with the Changchun Institute of Applied Chemistry. This facility, which was renamed the CAS Key Laboratory of Rare Earth Chemistry and Physics, focuses on rare earth separation techniques, exploration of new rare earth functional materials and optical, material and magnetic properties. Its laboratory is equipped with a spectrofluorometer, FED-PDP spectrophometer, UV-Visible-NIR spectrophometer, and thermal expansionmeters. Its main research fields are: rare earth luminescent materials; research and application of Mg-RE Alloys; thermal barrier coating material for gas turbine; low temperature battery cathode; and the bioinorganic chemistry and chemical biology of rare earth elements.

8. Located in the Baotou industrial zone, Bautou Research Institute of Rare Earth Elements falls under China's Ministry of Military Industry, and is reputedly the largest of its kind in the world for some 30 years.

9. Established in November 1952, the Beijing General Research Institute for Non-Ferrous Metals is the largest R & D Institute in the field of non-ferrous metals in China. It was officially transformed into a large-scale high-tech enterprise in January 26, 2000 when it obtained a business license as a central enterprise. Headquartered in downtown Beijing in an area of 250,000 square meters, with a production quarter of 300,000 square meters, its research covers: micro-electric and photoelectric areas,

rare and precious metals, rare earth materials, energy technology and materials, light metal structural materials, special alloy powder, infrared optical materials, non-ferrous metals processing industry, advanced mineral processing, and metallurgy materials analysis and testing. The Institute is currently headed by an Honorary President- Profesor Dianzou Wang and President- Dr. Hailing Tu, expert in semi-conductor materials.

10. **Leeb, Stephen**. *"Red Alert: How China's Growing Prosperity Threatens the American Way of Life."* Business Plus Hatchet Group Book. New York, USA 2001. Print.

11. Ibid., p.11

12. Ibid., p 4.

13. "Rare Earth Prices Soar as China Stocks Up." **Leslie Hook.** Financial Times. June 19, 2011; "The Significance of China's Recent Increase in Rare Earth Metal Export Quotas." **Allison Withers.** Submityourarticles.com. August, 30, 2012; "Little Change to Rare Earth Export Quotas." **Wang Zhouqiong**. China Daily. August 23, 2012.

14. "Traders: China Halts Rare Earth Exports to Japan" Boston.com. September 23, 2010; "China Has halted Rare Earth Exports to Japan Reports the Times" Popsci. **Clay Dillon.** September 23, 2012; "Japan's Mineral Rare Earth Discovery Cold Fix Pad Supply Shortages" Huff Post Tech. May 07, 2011.

15. "Japan's Rare Earth Mineral Discovery Cold Fx ipad Supply Shortages." Huff Post tec. 2011.May 07, 2011; "Traders: China Halts Rare Earth Exports to Japan." Boston.com. September, 23, 2010; "China Has Halted Rare Earth Exports to Japan Reports the Times." Popsci. Clay Dillov. September, 23, 2010.

16. "US, EU, Japan Challenge China on Rare Earth Export Restrictions" The Vancouver Sun March 13, 2012. **Jennifer Freedman and Jurgen Van Del Pol**, Bloomberg.

17. Ibid., p.22

18. **Diamond, Jared**. *"How Societies Choose to Fail or Succeed."* New York U.S.A. Penguin. 2005. Print. The writer theorizes that the collapse of

many past societies was triggered by environmental problems, a proposition that is strongly corroborated by archaeologists, climatologists, paleontologists, historians and palyndogists. Diamond identifies eight specific categories of environmental damage that have occurred in support of his argument: deforestation, habitat destruction, soil problems, water management problems, overhunting, overfishing, effects of introduced species on natural species, human population growth and its impact on per capita of people.

19. Tainter, Joseph A. "*The Collapse of Complex Societies.*" Cambridge University Press. New USA. 1988. Print.

20. Scientific America, 2009 – Mark.

21. "Energy and Advanced Coal Utilization in China." **Professor Ni Weidou,** Tsinghua University, Chairman of Steering Committee of Tsinghua University – BP Clean Energy Research and Education Center, Member of the Chinese Academy of Engineering.

22. http://www.businessweek.com/ap/financialwars/D9DKN
    http://wwindea.org/home/images/stories/pdfs
    "World Wind Energy Report 2010" – World Wind Energy Conference and Renewable Energy Exhibition. Greening Energy: Converting Deserts into Powerhouses." Cairo, Egypt. 31 October & 02 November, 2011.

23. "China's Big Rush for Renewable Energy." **David Biello.** Scientific America. August 04, 2008.

24. "China Releases 12th. Five Year Plan for Renewable Energy." Platts News Article and Story.
    http://www.platts.com/latest-news/electric-power/Singapore/China-releases-12th-five-year-plan-for-renewable-energy

25. "President Obama's Blueprint for a Clean and Secure Energy Future." White House Office of the Press Secretary. Fact Sheet.

26. "MIT Develops Meltdown Proof, Nuclear Waste-Eating Reactor." Oil Price. Brian Westinhaus. March 17, 2013; "MIT Kids think They've Solved How to Get Rid of Nuclear Waste." **Rob Wile.** June 07, 2012.

27. "Fracking the Nation: the Dash for Gas Beneath Rural Britain." The Guardian. **John Harris**. June 28, 2013.
www.guardian.co.uk/.../28/fracking-dash-gas-rural-englan

28. "Measuring Fugitive Methane Emissions." Environmental Defense Fund. Stephen Hamburg. January 04, 2013.

29. "Methane Leaking from Coal Seam Gas." The Sydney Morning Herald. Ben Cubby, Environmental Editor. November 14, 2012.
www.smh.com.au/.../methane-leaking-from-coal-seam-gas
30. Ibid., "Fracking the Nation: The Dash for Gas Beneath Rural Britain."
31. Ibid., "Methane Leaking from Coal Seam Gas." The Sydney Morning Herald. **Ben Cubby**. Environmental Editor. November 14, 2012.

32. "Obama's Second Term Priorities." CNN White House Correspondent by Don Lothian. January 22, 2013   cnn.com/2013/01/21/politics/obama-four-more

33. *Zehner, Ozzie. "Green Illusions: The Dirty Secrets of Clean Energy and the Future of Environmentalism (Our Sustainable Future)."*

34. *Laughlin, Robert B. "Powering the Future: How We Will (Eventually) Solve The Energy Crisis and Fuel the Civilization of Tomorrow."* Basic Books New York 2011 Print.

35. Ibid., Laughlin

36. "The Third Carbon Age: Don't for a Second Imagine We're heading for An Era of Renewable Energy." **Klare, Michael**. Truth.com. TomDespatch. August 08, 2013.

37. "Global Superconductor Markets Driven by Asian Power Houses Such as China and India." Companies Markets – Energy and Utilities.

38. "Weather as a Force Multiplier. Owning the Weather in 2025" Report Research Paper. Col. Tamzy J. House. August 1996; "Weather Modification" – Document Title. Hearings before The Sub-Committee on Oceans and International Environment of the Committee on Foreign Relations of the United States Senate. Jan.01, 1974. Note: Project Popeye (March 20, 1967 to July 05, 1962) was a U.S. - devised military operation, executed by the 54th Weather Reconnaissance Squadron during the Vietnam War. The objective of the mission was to create muddy tracks

with the objective of slowing down local truck traffic in designated zones. This entailed a scheme, referred to as cloud seeding, involving the employment of silver iodide to induce unusually heavy rainfall and artificially extend the monsoon period. The operation was deemed successful since the monsoon period actually increased to an average of 30-45 days in critical locations such as the Ho Chi Minh Trail in Laos.

39. "The CIA Wants to Know How to Control the Climate." The Verge. **Carl Franzen.** July 17, 2013.

CHAPTER SEVENTEEN

AFRICA UNDER SIEGE

1. **John Thornton.** "*Africa and Africans in the Making of the Atlantic World.*"

1400-1800. (New York: Cambridge University Press, 1998), 23.

2. Ibid., 27-32.

3. "Global Trends 2025: A Transformed World." *U.S. National Intelligence Agency.* (US Government Printing Office, 2008), 56.

http://www.aic.pa.org/research/cpahorizons2025/globalforces/downloadeabledo cuments/globaltrends.pdf.

4. **John Thornton,** "*Africa and Africans in the Making of the Atlantic World,* 83.*"

5. Matt Rosenberg. "The Berlin Conference of 1884-1885: The Colonization of the Continent by European Powers."

http://geography.about.com/cs/politicalgeog/a/berlinconference.htm.

6. Ibid.

7. **Terrence McCarthy, and Bruce Rubridge**. "*The Story of Earth and Life: A South African Perspective on a 4.6 Billion Year Journey.*" (Cape Town: New Holland Publishing, 2005), 4-6.

8. Mike Cohen, Rene Vollgraaff, and Yinka Ibukun. " Booming African Lion Econmies Gear Up to Emulate Asians." *Bloomberg.* 4 August 2014.

http://www.bloomberg.com/news/2014-08-03/booming-african-lion-economies-gear-up-to-emulate-asians.html

9. **Elizabeth Schmidt.** "*Foreign Intervention in Africa: From the Cold War to the War on Terror.*" (New York: Cambridge University Press, 2013), xiii.

10. **Meine Pieter** van Dijk, ed., "*New Presence of China in Africa. (Amsterdam)*"

Amsterdam University Press, 2009), 10.

11. "George Washington: [I]t is a maxim." *We Still Hold These Truths.* 2012.

http://westillholdthesetruths.org/quotes/1766/it-is-a-maxim

12. Air Force One and Washington, D.C. " America and Africa: The Next Great Disruption." "*The Economist.*" 2 August 2014.

http://www.economist.com/news/united-states/21610323-barack-obamas-ambitions-africa-will-be-measure-american-engagement

13. Ibid.

14. Garrett Brinker. " President Obama Speaks at the U.S.-Africa Business Forum."

"*The White House.*" 5 August 2014.
http://www.whitehouse.gov/blog/2014/08/05/president-obama-speaks-us-africa-business-forum

15. Howard D. Belote. " Proconsuls, Pretenders, or Professionals? The Political Role of Regional Combatant Commanders." *Mercury.ethz.ch.* n.d. Web.

16. Nick Ture. "Tomgram: U.S. Africa Command Debates TomDispatch." *TomDispatch.* 26 July 2012.
http://www.tomdispatch.com/post/175574/tomgram%3A_u.s._africa_command_debates_tomdispatch/

17. US AFRICOM Public Affairs. " Transcript: General Ham, Admiral Stavridis Testify Before House Armed Services Committee." *United States Africa*

Command. 29 February 2012. http://www.africom.mil/newsroom/transcript/8834/transcript-general-ham-admiral-stavridis-testify-b

18. Alan Kuperman. " Lessons from Libya: How Not to Intervene." *Belfer Center for Science and International Affairs.* September 2013." http://belfercenter.ksg.harvard.edu/publication/23387/lessons_from_libya.html

19. Pascal Fletcher. " Mali's Soldier of Democracy Toppled by Own Army." *Reuters.* 22 March 2012. http://www.reuters.com/article/2012/03/22/us-mali-army-toure-idUSBRE82L0RL20120322

20. Margaret Kimberley. " Al-Shabaab, Death and Somlia." *Global Research.* 2 October 2013. http://www.globalresearch.ca/al-shabaab-death-and-somalia/5352865

21. Ibid.

22. Patrick Martin. " Washington Plans for World War." *World Socialist Web Site.* 6 August 2014. https://www.wsws.org/en/articles/2014/08/06/pers-a06.html

23. Richard Reeve and Zoe Pelter. " From New Frontier to New Normal: Counter-Terrorism Operations in the Sahel-Sahara." *Oxford Research Group.* August 2014. http://oxfordresearchgroup.org.uk/sites/default/files/From%20New%20Frontier%20to%20New%20Normal%20-%20Counter-terrorism%20operations%20in%20the%20Sahel-Sahara.pdf

24. Daniel Volman. " Africa; U.S. Military Holds War Games on Nigeria, Somalia." *AllAfrica.* 14 August 2009. http://allafrica.com/stories/200908140153.html

25. Nick Turse. "Tomgram: Nick Turse, AFRICOM's Gigantic "Small Footprint." *TomDispatch.* 5 September 2013. http://www.tomdispatch.com/post/175743

26. Nile Bowie. "Nigeria: Fertile Ground for Balkanization." *NileBowie.blogspot.*

ca. 10 April 2012. http://nilebowie.blogspot.ca/2012/04/nigeria-fertile-ground-for.html

27. Richard Reeve and Zoe Pelter, From New Frontier to New Normal, 2.

28. Punam Chuhan-Pole et al., Africa's Pulse: An Analysis of Issues Shaping Africa's Economic Future. *The World Bank*. August 2013. https://latest-taxnews.rhcloud.com/preview/an-analysis-of-issues-shaping-africas-economic-future/

29. Bill Marriott. " *Into Africa: Expanding in a Growing Market." Marriott on the Move*. 22 January 2014. http://www.blogs.marriott.com/marriott-on-the-move/2014/01/africa.html

30. Marius Fransman. " Roundtable Discussion by Deputy Minister Marius Fransman at the University of Stellenbosch on the theme " South Africa: A strong African Brick in BRICS." "*Department of Foreign Affairs, Republic of South Africa.*" 21 November 2012. http://www.dfa.gov.za/docs/speeches/2012/frans1121.html

31. Jessica Pugliese, Andrew Westbury and Amadou Sy. " The U.S. Africa Leaders Summit: Building a Strategy Together with Africa." "*Brookings Institution.*" 18 June 2014. http://www.brookings.edu/blogs/africa-in-focus/posts/2014/06/17-us-africa-leaders-summit-pugliese-westbury-sy

32. Howard French. " *High Stakes in Africa: Can the U.S. Catch China?* " *Bloomberg Businessweek*. 31 July 2014. http://www.businessweek.com/articles/2014-07-31/how-the-u-dot-s-dot-can-rival-china-in-africa

33. Ibid.

34. Ibid.

35. International Crisis Group." China's Growing Role in U.N. Peacekeeping." CrisisGroup.org. 17 April 2009. http://www.crisisgroup.org/en/regions/asia/north-east-asia/china/166-chinas-growing-role-in-un-peacekeeping.aspx

36. Ibid.

37. "Safeguarding World Peace and Regional Stability." White Paper.
http://www.china.org.cn/government/whitepaper/2013-04/16-content_28556977.htm.

38. "Obama Announces Rapid Response Peacekeeping Plan." "*Voice of*

America." 7th August, 2014.

http://www.voanews.com/content/obama-announces-rapid-response-peacekeeping-plan/1973380.html.

39. Mehta, Lyle; Veldwich, Gert Jan; Franco, Jenifer. "Introduction to the Special Issue: Water Grabbing? Focus on the (Re) appropriation of Finite Water Resources." *"Institute of Development Studies"* 1st June, 2012. Copenhagen.

http://www.wateralternatives.org/index.php/alldoc/articles/vol5/vol5issue2//165-a5-2-1file.

40. Cecilie Friis & Anette Reemberg "Land Grab in Arica: Emerging Land System Drivers in a Teleconnected World ." A Joint Research Agenda of IGBP & IHDP, the Global Land Project International Project Office. GLP International Project Office. Copenhagen, Denmark. 2010.

http://www.ihd.unu.edu/docs/Publications/GLP/GLP_report_01.pdf.

41. Mona Alami. *"Land Grabbing – A New Political strategy for Arab Countries."* Inter-Press Service for News Agency. 30th July, 2014.

http://www.ipsnews.net/2014/07/land-grabbing-a-new-political-strategy-for-arab-countries/

42. Ibid.

43. Ibid.

44. "Liberia Among Top Five Countries Giving Farmland to Foreigners." Liberian Observer. *Actmedia News Agency.* 12th January, 2012. Liberia. http://farmlandgrab.org/19871.

45. Igor A. Shiklomanov. "World Water Resources – A New Appraisal and Assessment for the Twenty-First Century." United nations Educational, Scientific and Cultural Organization. 1998.

http://www.caee.utexas.edu/prof/mckinney/ce385d/Papers/Shiklomanov.pdf.

46. "Yellow River Shows Signs of Life – The Future of North China as a Region of Extreme Water Scarcity." *"Stockholm Waterfront – A Forum for Global Water Issues."* No. 2 June, 2003 pp 10-11. June. 2003. Sweden.

http://waterfootprint.org/media/downloads/Water_front_June2003.pdf.

47. "Global Trends 2015 – A Transformed World. U.S. Government Printing Office/ November, 2008. http://www.aic.org/research/cpahorizons2025/globalforces/downloadableddocuments/globaltrends.pdf.

48. "Land Grab in Africa." IHDB Global Land Project. International Project Office, University of Copenhagen, Denmark.

http://www.ihdp.unu.edu/docs/Publications/GLP/GLP_report_01.pdf.

49. Supriyah Kumar. "The Looming Threat of Water Scarcity." Vital Signs Global Trends. *WorldWatch Institute.* 2013.

50. Ibid.

51. "Africa's Changing Landscape – Securing land Access for The Rural Poor." *"FAO Regional Office for Africa.* Accra, Ghana." April, 2010.

FAO%20LAND%20Access20for%20the%20Rural%20Poor%20n%.

52. "Bill and Melinder Gates, Rockefeller Foundations Form Alliance to Help Spur Green Revolution in Africa."

www.gatesfoundation.org/.../Foundations-Form-Alliance-to-Help-Spur-Green-Revolution-in-Africa.

53. Note: Howard French's China's Second Continent: How a Million Chinese are Building a New Empire in Africa, notes the phenomenal volume of Chinese migrants who reside permanently in Africa. The migratory pattern was spurred by a range of factors the most notable being wider economic opportunities, improved quality of life, comparatively less corruption, availability of arable land and natural resources and land acquisition opportunities added to which for many years the continent appeared to have been ignored by the West.

54. The National Defense Panel co-chaired by Dr. William Perry and General John Abizad in its Report entitled "Ensuring a Strong U.S. Defense for the Future" noted , "China, Russia, North Korea and Iran each pose different but real challenges to regional stability that require DOD to plan for plausible contingencies."

CHAPTER EIGHTEEN

Leadership and Diplomacy

1. The concept of "superpower" was first applied to the British Empire, the Soviet Union and the United States of America. "Second superpower" has been more recently ascribed to China by scholars who view the country's emergence to great power status as a real and present challenge to U.S. primacy.

2. "Lonely Superpower or Unapologetic Hyperpower? Analyzing American Power in the Post-Cold War Era." **Nossal, Kim Richard**. Dept. Of Political Science Mc Master University, Canada. Biennial Meeting, South African Political Studies Association. June 29 - July 02, 1999.

3. **Cox, Robert W**. "*Gramsci, Hegemony and International Relations.*" pp. 59-66.

4. **Bull, Hedley**. "*The Anarchical Society: A Study of Order in World Politics.*" Palgrave, New York, USA 1977. Print.

5. Ibid., **Kennedy, P.**

6. Ibid., **Black, J.**

7. Ibid., **Black, J.**

8. **Gunder Frank, Andre**. "*Re Orient: Global Economy in the Asian Age.*" University of California Press, Ltd. 1988 pp. 108-117. Print.

9. "Lawfulness of a Lethal Weapon Directed Against a U.S. Citizen Who is a senior Operational Leader of Al-Qa'ida or An Associated Force." Department of Justice White Paper.

10. "China's President Lashes Out at Western Culture." **Wong, Edward**. New York Times. January 13, 2012; "Pushing China's Limits on the Web if Not on Paper." **Wong, Edward**. New York Times. November 06, 2011.

11. **Hartung, William**. Prophets of War: "*Lockheed Martin and the Making of the Military-Industrial Complex.* Nation Books USA 2011. Print.

12. "Eisenhower's Farewell Speech." Television Broadcast. January 16, 1961.

13. **I. H. Dadler and J. M. Lindsay.** *"America Unbound: The Bush Revolution in Foreign Policy" (Washington D.C., 2003); Prestowitz, C. "Rogue Nation: American Unilateralism and the Failure of Good Intentions"* (New York, 2003).

14. For the origins of the plan, see RFA, vol. VII, pp. 29ff., and Dallek, Foreign Policy, pp. 149, 155-157.

15. RFA, vol. VIII, p.122.

16. RFA, vol. XIV, p. 315ff.

17. Gordon Alexander Craig (1913-2005). Fmr. Member of the Academy of Arts and Sciences, American Philosophical Society, the Orden Pour le Merite fur Wiisenschaften und Kunste, President of the American Historical Association, President of the Conference Group of Central European History, and Vice president of the Comite International des Sciences Historique

18. **Craig, Gordon A.** *"Tact and Intelligence: Essays on Diplomatic History and International Relations."* The Society for the promotion of Science and Scholarship Inc., USA 2008.p. 18.

19. Ibid. p.18.

20. **Kaufman, Daniel et al.** *"Understanding International Relations: The Value of Alternative Lens."* "Elements of National Power." Morgenthau, Hans J. United States Military Academy 2004. p.231.

CHAPTER NINETEEN

Does a Resolution Lie Ahead?

1. **Ani, Marimba. Yurugu.** "*An African-Centered Critique of European Cultural Thought and Behavior.*" Washington D.C. Kkonimfo Publications, 1994. p. xxxiii

2. Ibid., p. 4.

3. **Berman, Morris.** "*Why America Failed: The Roots of Imperial Decline.* New Jersey, USS John Wiley & Sons, Inc. 2012 Print. p.5.

4. Ibid., 5.

5. Ibid., 30.

6. Ibid., 30.

7. **Armstrong, Robert.** "*The Wellspring: On the Myth and Source of Culture.*" Berkley, California. USA U of California Press, 1997. Print. p 116.

8. **Hixson, Walter M.** The Myth of American Diplomacy: National Identity and U.S. Foreign Policy. Yale University Press. 2008.

9. In the "Origins of Totalitarianism" (xxiii), Arendt asserts that one of the peculiarities of totalitarian regimes, as displayed under the Nazi and Bolshevik types of rule, was the propensity to create new classes of enemy. In the case of the Nazis, the "objective enemy" was defined in terms of who you are rather than what you do. This cohort reacted with complete passivity to Nazi terror. Stalin's pronouncements, unlike Hitler's, prescribed "thou shalt bear false witness," and was a general rule that facilitated "dekulakization." Likewise, Hixson noted that as Euro-American settlement evolved in America, so did the cultural process of enemy categorization of the inferior Other, manifested in references such as "dark," "evil," and "uncivilized." See: Hixson's "Myth of America" p.19.

10. Ibid., p xxiii-xxxiv.

11. Ibid., Armstrong. p 10-11.

12. Ibid., Ani. pp. 9 -10.

13. Ibid., Ani. pp. 9 -10.

14. "Myth" in this literal context connotes "an invented story used allegorically to explain some natural event or phenomenon or some aspect of the human condition or psyche." Fritze, Ronald "*Invented Knowledge: Fake History, Fake Science and Pseudo-Religions.*" London, U.K. Reakton Books. 2009. Print.

15. **Bercivitch, Sacvon.** "*The Puritan Origins of the American Self.*" Yale University Press. 1975. Print.

16. **Bercovitch, Sacvon.** "*The American Jeremiad: Studies in American Thought and Culture.*" Anniversary Edition with a New Preface. University of Wisconsin Press. 1978. Print.

17. **Billington, James H.** "*Fire in the Minds of Men: Origins of the Revolutionary Faith.*" New York, USA, Basic Books. 1980. p 6. Print.

18. Ibid., Berman. p 9.

19. Ibid., Berman. p 9.

20. Ibid., Berman. p 9.
21. Ibid., Berman.

22. Ibid., Hixson, Walter L. pp.17-20.

23. Ibid., Hixson, Walter L. pp.14-15.

24. **Kierman, Ben.** "*Blood and Soil: A World History of Genocide and Extermination from Sparta to Darfur.*" University of Yale USA 2004 Print.

25. **Webb, James.** "*Born Fighting: How The Scotts Irish Shaped America: Reeters and Rednecks.*" Broadway Books 2004. USA 2009 Print.

26. **Ibid.**

APPENDIX A

The Economic Relationship between France and Its Former Colonies

France, unlike other former colonial powers, had installed the *commissars* at the heart of the economic and monetary framework of its former colonies in West Africa, and to date, maintains almost unchallenged control over them. The system was originally conceived and implemented by Germany during the 1930s and 1940s, with the sole objective of usurping France and other German-occupied nations.

On May 09 1941, amidst the height of World War II, the German ambassador to France declared that he had signed a treaty with French Admiral Darlen, the upshot of which was to effectively place German *commissars* within the French National Bank's department of foreign currencies and international commerce. Essentially, commissars are agents of the colonial or occupying power, whose sole responsibility it was, to exercised ultimate control inclusive of veto power, over the monetary and economic systems of the host territory and ensure that whatever appointments were made and policies enforced, were at the sole discretion of the commissars and ensure that the policies of the French government were fulfilled. By this means control of the economies by host governments has been effectively usurped.

The veto right of the French commissars that sit on the boards of the National Central Banks extends to the nomination of the governor of BEAC whose election must be unanimous by way of vote of the Board of directors. Thus, despite the acknowledged reserve of human and capital resources with which the continent is endowed, France is indebting and enslaving Africans buy using their own wealth.

Additionally, the French National Bank also reserves the power to grant credits to national treasuries at its discount rates and to hold a sizeable quota (as much as 85 %) of all foreign currency reserves of the 15 nations of the union generated outside of the union's territory. In 2010 the former French Minister of Finance asserted, "...*The Bank of the States of Central Africa, for instance places 90 percent of their reserves in the French National Bank...*"The system is further compounded by the fact that the gold reserves of the 15 nations are held in France, supposedly to guarantee the value of the CFR-Franc. The latter was a currency that was specially created for African states, as distinct from their own national currencies, by the late President Charles de Gaulle with the setting up of the Monetary Union. In 2001, the estimated value of gold reserves held by France was 206,528 billion CFR-Francs.

Thus, despite the existence of the central banks in member countries of the Western African Monetary Economic Unions - the BEAC, the B.C.C and the BCEAO – the French government exercises near absolute control over these economies. This includes the granting of credits for the current accounts of national treasuries, making determinations about the total amount that is granted for financing the economies of each of the member states, and influencing appointments to the board of directors of national central banks. As cases in point, three of the 13 directors of the BEAC are French and four of the eight directors of the B.C.C. are French. Sixteen directors, two from each country and two additional directors from France constitute the BCEAO.

Further to this, the foreign currency reserves of member states are deposited in a shared reserve fund and these shared reserves are subject to depositions in an operations account of the French National Bank. Regarding the East African states of Kenya, Tanzania and Uganda, the early stages of monetary evolution in these countries occurred during British rule when trade with India was extremely lucrative. The arrangement led to the use of the Indian rupee as the preferred medium of exchange to British sterling. Thereafter in 1919, the East African Currency Board was established following the acquisition of Tanganyika as a form of booty from the Germans. It was not until the three colonies dissolved in 1965, that the East African Currency Board was wound up and the territory finally attained notional monetary sovereignty.

France currently has the right to invest in the Paris bourse as it sees fit and enjoys the privilege of not being obligated disclose to African governments how much these investments earn. Logically this state of affairs is extremely demoralizing for African leaders. Added to which CFA zones are inherently politically unstable and economically vulnerable. Of the 107 banks that were operating in 1990, 42 were deemed bankrupt.

Suggested Further Reading:

Articles: "French Africa Policy Damages African and European Economies Our World Commentary: The Colonial Pact: How France Sucks the Life Out of Africa." January, 25 2013; "Jeune Afrique." **Lagorde, Christine**. May 03, 2010.

APPENDIX B

The Sino-Russian Threat and U.S Strategic Interests in Africa in the 1960s

"African socialism" as a post-independence era ideology in the sense of egalitarian distribution through planned development, was popularized at a time when Africa had become a battleground between the United States, the Soviet Union and China, for predominance over the newly independent states. The vanguard leadership of newly independent African states that ushered the region through its post-colonial phase consisted of Julius Nyerere,[1] Jomo Kenyatta, Kenneth Kaunda, and Kwame Nkrumah.[1] Nyerere was himself inspired by Fabian socialist ideas, and completed sold out to the notion that rural Africans and their traditions and *ujamaa* (a system of collectivization) were present in Africa well before European imperialism. Significantly, in South Africa the African National Congress (ANC) abandoned its partial socialist allegiances after taking power and followed a standard neoliberal rule".[3]

Perceiving the currents of change sweeping the continent during the early sixties at the height of the Cold War, and distrustful of popular Third World Nationalist movements which were viewed as likely to be crypto-Communist, the U.S. launched an assertive agenda that took the form of countervailing responses to the Chinese and Soviet influence on the continent. As a case in point and based on closed source accounts, at the All-Africa Peoples Conference (AAPC) held in 1961, the conservatism of Tom Mboya and Taleb Slim of Tunisia was closely monitored by U.S. agencies and contrasted with policies emanating from the strain of Nkruma and other African heads. Additionally, the "pro – Communists" who were elected to the AAPC's Steering Committee at the March 01 Cairo Conference (which was also attended by Mboya), were identified in staff reports as: Addoulaye Diallo, AAPC Secretary General of Senegal; Ahmed Bourmendjel of Algeria; Mario de Andrade of Angola; Ntau Mokhele of Basutoland; Kingue Abel of Cameroun; Antoine Kiwewa of Congo(Leopoldville); Kojo Botsio of Ghana; Ismali Toure of Guinea; T.O. Dosomu Johnson of Liberia; Modibo Diallo of Mali; Mahjoub Ben Seddik of Morocco; Dijbo Bakari of Niger; Tunji Otegbeya of Nigeria; Kanyama Chiume of Nyasaland; Ali Abdullahi of Somalia; Tennyson Makiwani of South Africa, and Mohamed Fouad Galal of the United Arab Republic. The only attendees in Cairo who were given a *clean bill of health* by the Americans were Tom Mboya, the Kenyan nationalist labor leader and politician, and Joshua Nkomo of Southern Rhodesia.

Mboya would subsequently become a credible and important agent of influence for the U.S. government, displaying irrefutable first-hand awareness of day-to-day politics and the extent of pro-Communist activity that was sweeping the region.[4] Through his instrumentality, an Airlift Project would be successfully activated in collaboration with the African-American Students' Foundation, to provide opportunities for African youth to attend American universities on scholarship arrangements and advance their higher education, while affording them the opportunity to assimilate Western culture.

The project was partly aided by the Joseph P. Kennedy Foundation and backed by the CIA. By 1959, the first of a group of 230 students would touch U.S. soil and be followed by hundreds more between 1961-1963. Most of the candidates were sourced from Kenya, Uganda, Tanzanyika, Northern and Southern Rhodesia, and Nyyasaland, countries that were reputed hotbeds for communist ferment. Similar types of campaigns were being pursued at that time by the Soviet Union and China so that the airlift scheme provided a critical counterweight to U.S. adversaries.

The East-West Center of the University of Hawaii would later assume greater significance. This was the locale where Ann Durham would meet and wed Barack Obama Sr. in 1960 while they were colleagues attending the same Russian classes, and beyond this in March 1965, Lolo Soetoro during Dunham's re-enrollment at the said institution. During the early period of her second marriage, Seotoro, who was an army colonel, would be recalled to Indonesia immediately prior to a CIA-backed coup that resulted in the ousting of President Sukarno.

Following Mboya's assassination, many theories surfaced, one being that his demise was instigated by Chinese agents working in concert with "anti-Mboya factions" within Jomo Kenyatta's administration, with the intent of eliminating the emergence of any avowed pro -U.S. leader in Africa.[5]

Today, the U.S. presence and influence in Africa continues to exert far-reaching implications not only from the standpoint of U.S. - Africa relations but also from the perspective of relations between Africa and other competing world powers, the most recent being Russia, insofar as they tie back to U.S. interests.

Suggested further reading:

1. **Nyerere, Julius** *"Ujamaa - Essays on Socialism."* Oxford University Press 1968; Pratt, Cranford. *"Julius Nyerere: Reflections on the Legacy of His Socialism"* Canadian Journal of African Studies. Volume: 33, No. 1(1999), pp.137-152. Published by the Canadian Association of African Studies;

Fatton, Robert (Jr.). University of Virginia; "*The Political Ideology of Julius Nyerere: The Structural Limitations of African Socialism.*"

2. In October 1945, Jomo Kenyatta a member of the Kikuyu, Kenya's most dominant tribe, was one of the organizers of the landmark Pan-African Congress that met in Manchester, England. Years later he would be involved in organizing a leftist underground movement, the Mau Mau, when representations for Kenya's independence were initially turned down by the British. Kenyatta would become the country's first President in 1963. Kenneth Kaunda, his contemporary, led Zambia into independence in 1964. He had previously served as interpreter and advisor to Sir Stewart Gore-Browne, a liberal white settler and member of the Northern Rhodesian legislative Council. Kaunda became the Chief Organizing Officer and Secretary General of the ANC, the first major anti-colonial organization. Differences within ANC leadership pertaining to strategy between 1959 -1960 compelled him in taking its main operating structure with him into the Zambia African National Congress. Thereupon he was able to obtain agreement from the British on (a) the squashing of proposals to form a federation of Northern and Southern Rhodesia and Nyasaland; and (b) the employment of Zambia's Congress as an instrument for executing positive non-violent action towards ultimate independence.

3. ANC was established on January 06, 1912 with the aim of fighting for the rights of black South Africans. ANC became South Africa's elected governing party in 1994 and until 2011, enjoyed over 60% electoral support. Prior to the dissolution of the apartheid system, a military arm of the ANC (MK-Umkhhonto we Sizwe) was formed. This was in 1961 and was in reaction to the institutionalization of white minority rule and the atrocities of repression that became associated with that form of administration. Nelson Mandela was a member of this unit, a fact that catapulted his prolonged prison term. The ANC is still a member of Socialist International and has a historic alliance with the South African Communist Party and the Congress of South African Trade Unions.

4. WMR Special Report. Intelligence Weekly Summary - November 19, 1959. Files indicate his importance to the U.S. as an agent of influence.

5. CIA Staff Notes on the Middle East, Asia, and South Asia (Declassified). UNRA, handle via COMINT Channels. Dated, July 24, 1975; harvested from intercepts in Kenya. Closed source reports stated that upon subject's death, with the notable exception of the People's Republic of China, embassies in Nairobi flew their flags at half-mast.